THE FOOTBALL GROUNDS
OF ENGLAND AND WALES

THE FOOTBALL GROUNDS OF ENGLAND AND WALES

SIMON INGLIS

Published in association with
The Football League
and The National Dairy Council

WILLOW BOOKS
Collins
8 Grafton Street, London
1985

THE AUTHOR

Simon Inglis is a freelance writer based in London. He reports soccer regularly for *The Guardian*, and his first book, *The Usborne Guide to Soccer*, is now in its second edition. *The Football Grounds of England and Wales* reflects two of the author's lifelong interests, soccer and architecture. In researching the book he visited over 100 grounds and despite the 7000 miles of travel that this entailed, his enthusiasm for football grounds – their individual character, their architectural merits and their ability to stage great events – remains undiminished.

COLOUR ACKNOWLEDGEMENTS

Front Jacket Liverpool, Aerofilms; Sunderland, Sporting Pictures; Tottenham Hotspur, Colour Library International; Exeter, Aerofilms; Aston Villa, Colorsport
Back Jacket Burnden Park in 1952, BBC Hulton Picture Library

Colour section *page i* Adrian Gibson; *page ii* top Odhams Press bottom Syndication International; *page iii* top Sporting Pictures bottom Sport & General; *page iv* top Sport & General bottom Colorsport; *page v* top Colorsport bottom Sporting Pictures; *page vi* Colorsport; *page vii* top left Sport & General top right and middle Syndication International bottom Sporting Pictures; *page viii* top Aerofilms bottom Peebles Publications

Willow Books
William Collins Sons & Co. Ltd
London · Glasgow · Sydney · Auckland
Toronto · Johannesburg

Inglis, Simon
The football grounds of England and Wales
1. Soccer grounds – England
I. Title
796.334′06′80942   GV943.9.S6/

ISBN 0-00-218189-4

Designer: Caroline Hill
Illustrations: Dave Eaton

Set in Linotron Century
by Rowland Phototypesetting Ltd,
Bury St Edmunds, Suffolk
Printed and bound in Great Britain by
Wm Collins Sons & Co. Ltd, Glasgow

CONTENTS

ACKNOWLEDGEMENTS

Without the help and encouragement of so many individuals this book would have been an impossible task. I would like to thank specifically the many members of the Association of Football Statisticians, and in particular Keith Warsop, for many hints, facts and references; for advice on architectural matters, Ernest Atherden, Harry Faulkner-Brown and John Rich; for advice on administrative and technical matters, Thorn EMI, Bertie Mee, Dr Peter Hayes and his staff at the Sports Turf Research Institute; and the staff at RIBA, Sheffield, Liverpool, Cardiff and especially Manchester Public Libraries.

Having visited every one of the 92 League grounds plus several more in England and Scotland, my thanks go also to the many club secretaries and groundsmen who tolerated my questioning, especially those at Bristol Rovers, Glasgow Rangers, Grimbsy Town, Huddersfield Town, Ipswich Town, Luton Town, Nottingham Forest, Preston North End and Southampton. Their knowledge and care of their grounds gave me vital reassurance and confidence in this project.

I am additionally grateful to friends and relatives who put up with me during this difficult year, and those who also put me up on my travels; to Lorraine Raja for typing the manuscript; and most of all to Jackie, who was a constant source of support, encouragement and affection.

Additional information was supplied by: Arthur Appleton, Geoff Allman, William Bancroft, Ted Brammer, Randall Butt, Derek Buxton, R. A. Clarke, Vic Couling, Trevor Denton, David Downs, H. Ellis Tomlinson, Keith Farnsworth, Maurice Golesworthy, Ted Griffith, Alf Hall, Stan Hall, Brian Horsnall, Malcolm Huntingdon, Paul Joannou, Tom Lane, Desmond Loughrey, John Lovis, Bill Miles, J. C. Morris, Simon Myers, Geoffrey Needler, Paul Plowman, Sam Rendell, David Roberts, Dave Russell, Revd Nigel Sands, Stan Searl, Richard Shepherd, Tony Thwaites, Howard Walker, Harry Warden, R. J. Wash, Eric White, Ted Wilding, Alex Wilson, Mike Wilson, Harold Wolfe, John Woodcock and Ted Woodriff.

The Football League, The Football Association, Football Grounds Improvement Trust, Institute of Structural Engineers.

Birkenhead News, *Bolton Evening News*, *Bury Times*, *Chester Chronicle*, *Crewe Chronicle*, *Cumbrian Newspapers*, *Manchester Evening News*, *Oxford Mail*, *Portsmouth Evening News*, *Sheffield Morning Telegraph* and *Star*, *Stoke Evening Sentinel* and *The Architects' Journal*.

FOREWORD

The National Dairy Council were responsible for a milestone in the history of British football when, in 1982, they sponsored the Milk Cup which replaced The Football League Cup. The sponsorship, worth more than £2 million over four years, created a British sports' sponsorship record.

Like football itself, the football grounds of England and Wales are part of our heritage. Many of Britain's sporting dramas have been played on their turf. The players are household names. Fans have been enthralled by their skills – but the grounds remain largely unhonoured.

This book by Simon Inglis will set the record straight. The National Dairy Council are pleased to be associated with the book and the fans to whom it will give great pleasure.

PREFACE

Britain's football grounds can be all things to all men, and to an increasing number of women too. The mention of a famous name can make a youngster's eyes sparkle with eager anticipation or an old man's eyes mist with nostalgia.

I enjoy the best of both worlds. I still remember the youthful glow which preceded a visit to a big ground and I have a job that has taken me to most of the Football League's grounds.

Every ground has its own character. When I visit them on non-match days, the ghosts are always present. Stan Matthews is still weaving his way down the touchline at Blackpool, a sorcerer in soccer boots. Tom Finney still flashes past non-existent full-backs at Preston. On match days a transformation; 'the beautiful game' as Pele calls it, which entertains and thrills millions of fans a year.

But what is so special about a football ground, bricks and concrete with a piece of turf in the middle? Far more, perhaps, than you might imagine before reading this book. I congratulate Simon Inglis on both his industry and his ability to breathe life and light into that same brick and concrete. I congratulate him, too, on filling a gap in soccer's literature. This is the definitive work on football grounds.

It has brought back more than a few memories for me. The grandeur of Villa Park on first sight with Blackpool gaining a meritorious draw and goalkeeper Gordon West, later to play for Everton and England, defying the Villa forwards. Back again to Villa Park in 1963–64 to see Preston beat Swansea 2–1 in an all-Second Division FA Cup semi-final when Preston half-back Tony Singleton smashed in a spectacular long-range goal.

I was sitting on the running track at a packed Ewood Park when Blackburn scored a late equaliser to get an FA Cup replay against Blackpool. Those were the days when Rovers, who were beaten 3–0 by Wolves in the Final, fielded England stars Ronnie Clayton and Bryan Douglas and Welsh international Roy Vernon.

Blackpool, of course, recalls Matthews, Stan Mortensen, Ernie Taylor, Bill Perry and Allan Brown who always used to look back over his shoulder towards the goal after making a scoring attempt, as if warning the goalkeeper that he would be back. And how many right wingers must I have seen who were being groomed to succeed the great Matthews? About 50 I should think. An appropriate number because Stan was 50 when he played his last League game.

The Preston–Blackpool derbies with the pre-motorway 17 miles between the two towns choc-a-bloc with traffic. And how embarrassing, now, to have to recall that in the big Matthews v Finney debate the great Tom Finney was always rated 'useless' by young Kelly!

Upton Park, West Ham, means to me the brilliant team of the mid-1960s, which included Bobby Moore, Martin Peters, Geoff Hurst and Johnny Byrne.

Everton evokes memories of a match against Poland as England began their run up to the World Cup triumph in 1966. Manchester United summons up the Busby Babes and the European Cup. I recall seeing Burnley at Manchester City and catching a glimpse of the young Denis Law before he went to Italy. I remember Chelsea's Peter Osgood at Burnley scoring one of the most memorable of goals by walking the ball round the goalkeeper after having beaten four players in a run from the half-way line, and other visits to Turf Moor to enjoy the rich skills of Irish mid-field player Jimmy McIlroy.

Liverpool? No, not the European triumphs but the début of Alan Ball for Blackpool, then a right winger. Matthews was about to be seen off at last.

So many memories. So many football grounds, each with a character all its own and each maligned by the frequently repeated allegation that many of them are relics of the Victorian era.

Some grounds, notably Port Vale, Hull City and Southend United, have been built since the Second World War. Others have been considerably modernized. Generally, facilities are much improved. The Football League clubs spent something in the region of £53 million on their grounds in the six years between 1976 and 1983. That is a great deal of money.

I am delighted that the National Dairy Council, the backers of the Milk Cup, have seen fit to sponsor this volume. It is yet another example of how sponsorship associations can work for the good of the game.

I am pleased to give this book an official Football League endorsement. There has never been one quite like it published before. But I must warn that it is a trap. Once picked up, it is very difficult to put down. From now on, I am sure football fans will see their favourite clubs' grounds in a somewhat different light.

Graham Kelly
Secretary
The Football League

INTRODUCTION

Anyone who has been to a football match will know that rush of excitement when first catching sight of the floodlights and stands. Once inside there is an almost exultant feeling as you emerge onto the terrace or into the stand, and see the arena for the first time.

The experience of visiting a football ground is inseparable from the game itself, for every ground provides a different backdrop and a different atmosphere colouring your entire appreciation of a football match.

This book is a celebration of such variety; an attempt to define the differences by describing each ground, its history and development. So many football spectators spend at least two hours a week at a ground, often waiting an hour or so before the game has even started. It is my hope that this book will enable them to look around and appreciate more fully their surroundings.

Inevitably, there are statistics, but they are not the essence of this study. More important is the spirit. Even when a football ground is empty it retains a special aura. Max Hodgson, writing in the *Brighton and Hove Gazette* in 1959, expressed it well:

> 'Every morning my bus takes me to work by way of the Goldstone, and I advise those who live on the other side of town just to ride past and see for themselves the general air of purpose behind the high fence. Kept fresh by constant watering, the grass has a brilliance which contrasts beautifully with the new yellow paint on the crush barriers; there is a clean look about the stands . . .'

We have all, however subconsciously, reacted in this way to a football ground's apparent sense of purpose, to its clean, orderly appearance. We have been excited by the knowledge that although empty, a ground has the ability to stage great events and great moments.

The lover of football grounds will pass through a town, by train or car, and strain to see floodlights on the horizon. The merest glimpse of a stand or a pitch is tantalizing.

Thousands of people attend matches every Saturday, and though numbers are dropping alarmingly, more people still go to some local grounds than all the local churches put together. And yet the architectural books are full of studies of even the dullest church. For example, Nikolaus Pevsner has compiled the most comprehensive guide to *The Buildings of England*, and yet only two football grounds are mentioned, Wembley and Hillsborough, and those only in passing. He will describe a perambulation of the suburb of Everton, mentioning churches, parks and public buildings, but walks past the solid mass of Goodison Park as if it did not exist. Similarly in Highbury, there is no indication that he even recognizes the presence of Arsenal.

Whether this is elitism or the fact that in the majority of cases football grounds boast no architectural merit is hard to judge. I hope to show that grounds like Goodison Park and Highbury *do* possess certain architectural qualities and are of interest not merely to followers of football. I would go so far as to suggest that certain football grandstands are worthy of study and preservation.

However no one would deny that while we rejoice in so much variety and individual character, we also suffer poor design, outdated facilities and extremes of discomfort. Those clubs therefore who take exception to what follows must accept that all was written in a spirit of constructive criticism, together with an appreciation of the economic realities.

Furthermore, in describing over 100 grounds, all of which I visited in person, some contentious points are bound to be made. To those who feel slighted, and to those statisticians who find errors, I can add only that this book is the first on the subject, with all the difficulties that entails.

There are many stories still untold or unsubstantiated – of the Third Division manager who, as the main stand burnt to the ground, delayed the arrival of fire engines in the hope that the insurance would help keep his club in business; of how an aggrieved groundsman who had been dismissed did not tell the new incumbent where the underground taps were situated, resulting in the need to dig up parts of the pitch in a treasure hunt.

There has not been room to explore the tax structures which dictate that clubs often find it more beneficial to buy players than to spend money on ground improvements. Nor is there space to explore the legal wranglings some clubs have experienced with local authorities, in their attempts to relocate their grounds.

Part of my purpose has been to show that smaller, less developed grounds have as much importance and charm as the bigger, wealthier stadiums; that Aldershot has as much intrinsic value as Anfield.

And to show this before it is too late. For even in the two years since the first edition of this book appeared, in November 1983, there have been several changes. Some of them have been forced upon clubs. For example, a fire destroyed much of Brentford's main stand in 1983, and Stoke's 'antiquated bird cage' which formed the original end of the Butler Street stand has had to be taken down.

Other changes have been made to modernise certain grounds. Rochdale's old-style timber and cinder terracing, pictured on page 63, has now been covered over with concrete, while at the opposite end of the League but not so far from improved Spotland, one of Old Trafford's original corner rooves has been replaced by a cantilever construction, thus bringing nearer to completion the remodelling which began in 1964. Also in the past two years Queens Park Rangers have modified their artificial surface to reduce its original, unpopular high bounce. But League clubs will not have to contend with another plastic pitch in the foreseeable future unless Luton Town, as is threatened, actually move to a new stadium at Milton Keynes.

Another experiment, the creation of an all-seated stadium at Coventry, has had to be modified under pressure from the fans. Part of Highfield Road's Spion Kop has been reopened to standing spectators, and in 1984 a study undertaken by Leicester University's Department of Sociology revealed serious defects in the theory of all-seated grounds, especially as a means of reducing hooliganism.

As I write, there are warning bells at several grounds whose owners are only too aware of the profits to be gained from property development. Stamford Bridge and Craven Cottage in West London are particularly coveted sites.

But the saddest loss since 1983 has undoubtedly been that of the White City, also in West London (see page 267), demolished in 1984 with hardly a murmur from the press, public or sporting authorities. Thus one of Britain's greatest stadiums has gone, without even being replaced.

Percy Young wrote in 1960, 'there are some who collect theatres . . . or it may be railway stations . . . some day some scholar will arrive at the conclusion that there remains one definitive work still to be written: on the architecture of football grounds.'

I hope at least to have satisfied that brief.

London
March 1985

THE AUTHOR

Simon Inglis is a freelance writer. Born in Birmingham, he studied and taught modern history in London before spending six months in Latin America. He then concentrated on journalism in Manchester and wrote *The Usborne Guide to Soccer* and, in 1983, *The Football Grounds of England and Wales*. In researching the book he visited over 100 grounds and despite the 7000 miles of travel that this entailed, his enthusiasm for football grounds – their individual character, their architectual merits and their ability to stage great events – remains undiminished.

A contributor to the *Observer*, the *Guardian* and the *Radio Times*, Simon Inglis has recently completed his second book for Collins Willow, *Soccer in the Dock*, a history of football scandals from 1900 to 1965 due to be published in September 1985.

Now living in London, the author still watches out for the Aston Villa result every week.

·1·
HISTORY

Early Stadiums

Apart from the ancient Greeks and Romans very few civilizations have built stadiums. In fact, between the fall of Rome and the rise of Roker (which falls somewhere between the fall of Athens and the rise of Aldershot) not one stadium was constructed in Britain.

No permanent sports arenas were built in Europe during the Middle Ages; the only spectator sports being belligerent activities like jousting, or cock-fighting, neither of which inspired any lasting architecture. The only major examples of purpose-built arenas for open air events are found in Latin countries, where the bull ring developed, more as a theatre of ritual than a sports stadium.

So when the likes of Everton and Celtic wanted to build football grounds in the 1890s their only historical models were Greek hippodromes – U-shaped and primarily designed as race-tracks, and Roman examples such as the Circus Maximus – an arena built in Rome and reputed to have held 255 000 in three tiers. Initially these ancient arenas were for the performing of religious rites and worship only. Competitions and races came later as an accompaniment to the celebrations. The most famous arena however was the Colosseum in Rome, completed in 80 AD, which could hold about 50 000 spectators, and even had a canvas cover which could be drawn across the stadium as a roof. The Colosseum was very adaptable, for it could be flooded in order to stage mock naval battles. The word 'arena' is Latin for sand which was used to absorb all the blood left behind by gladiators, man-eating lions and other sadistic displays. From Latin we also get the word 'vomitory', referring to the access points within a grandstand.

The Mexican Aztecs built stadiums of sorts. There is one at Chichen-Itsa in the Yucatan peninsular, where a strange kind of ball game was played in a long court with high stone walls, with protruding rings acting as goals.

The nearest our English ancestors came to a fully enclosed football ground was the university quadrangle, where undergraduates sometimes used to have a kick around between tutorials. Not until the nineteenth century do we find anything remotely akin to a football ground.

Development

Cricket clubs were the first to establish properly enclosed grounds, and inevitably some of them decided to form their own football teams, or rent the facilities to an outside club. Cricket grounds were not in use during winter, often had a pavilion of sorts, and certainly had the best pitches, so they were perfect for staging football. Grounds like Bramall Lane, the Oval, Trent Bridge and the Racecourse Ground, Derby, were among the first multi-purpose grounds in this country. Other early football clubs played on fields near a public house (although at Gainsborough, Trinity players had to walk 150 yards along busy streets in order to reach the pitch!). The public house provided changing rooms, a place for an after-match meal and also for the committee to meet in during the week. In return for their generosity the public houses enjoyed increased custom from among the club's followers.

Certain clubs soon found that people were turning up in such numbers that it was worth hiring a separate field and even passing a collecting box around to help pay expenses.

More spectators meant more thirsts to quench, votes to attract, loyalties to win, and sixpences to be earned, and within two decades of the FA being formed, football was already on the way to becoming a business.

The first step was to fence in the field, with gates where spectators could be charged. The fence also established a club identity. Before long the fence began to carry advertisements, an additional source of revenue. In order for more people to have a better view, the next stage was to build sloping banks around the pitch. Local coal-mines were able to supply ash and cinders, and several clubs invited the public to come and dump their rubbish at the ground. Fulham used street-sweepings for their viewing slopes. Once the rubble and muck had settled, the club could cut steps, or terraces, into the compacted material.

The original Goodison Road Stand at the turn of the century (*Book of Football*)

Meanwhile, the owners of the breweries and businesses which had invested in the clubs wanted somewhere for themselves and their visiting committee members to sit under cover, so small wooden grandstands were built on the half-way lines. The players were usually kept separate in a dressing tent or hut in a corner of the ground. But not all stands were covered. Wooden constructions for standing spectators were also put up, and were especially useful as temporary accommodation at cricket grounds.

But real progress did not begin until after 1888, when the Football League was formed and crowds increased. Of the 12 original member clubs, only three still use the same grounds they occupied then – Stoke (since 1878), Preston (since 1881) and Burnley (since 1883). The plan of Deepdale shows that it was perhaps one of the most developed at this time (although it had been used as a sports ground since 1875).

Of the nine other clubs, three played at rented cricket grounds (Accrington, Derby and Notts County) while six were using grounds they would vacate within 12 years. Everton were based at Anfield which, like most of the grounds, was barely developed.

The first major developments took place during the 1890s, not only in Britain but in Greece, where an almost exact copy of an ancient hippodrome was built in Athens for the first modern revival of the Olympic Games in 1896.

In Britain Goodison Park and Celtic Park were built in 1892 (for a detailed description of these grounds see both club entries). These were followed by redevelopments at Ewood Park (opened 1890), Molineux (where Wolves had played since 1889), and the opening of several major grounds: Burnden Park (1895), Villa Park (1897), Roker Park and The Dell (both 1898), Hillsborough (then called Owlerton) and Fratton Park (both 1899).

Between 1889–1910 58 clubs belonging to the current League moved into the grounds they now occupy. Eight were already in occupation before then, and the remaining 26 moved to their present grounds between 1912–55.

At least 35 of the current League grounds were recreational or sporting grounds in some form before the clubs moved in. Villa Park and Molineux were, for example, well-established amusement areas in regular use for major sporting events, while several clubs simply took over the grounds of failing clubs.

In Yorkshire, Valley Parade and Elland Road were rugby grounds, Bootham Crescent a cricket ground. In London, Loftus Road and Brisbane Road belonged to struggling amateur soccer clubs, while Stamford Bridge was an athletics ground.

Other sporting venues taken over were Derby's Baseball Ground (baseball was a popular sport in the late Victorian era) and Wrexham's Racecourse Ground. Venues like Gay Meadow and the Old Show Ground were also popular open areas used for a variety of events, until football clubs took them over.

In short, so powerful and popular was the game of football in the first three decades of the League that in many towns and cities it was able to monopolize some of the prime open land which might otherwise have remained or become public property. In several cases, if the clubs themselves could not afford to purchase, breweries or businessmen were willing to help in return for control of the clubs. In other cases favourable rental arrangements were agreed.

But the majority of clubs took on sites that were far from ready for immediate use. For example, St Andrew's, Ninian Park, Maine Road, Burnden Park and The Valley were originally rubbish dumps, disused quarries or pits. Craven Cottage and White Hart Lane were overgrown wildernesses, and Owlerton (Hillsborough) an outlying rural region far from the city centre.

Whatever their beginnings, there is no doubt that

Stamford Bridge in 1945; the beginning of the attendance boom which was to test the capacity of every ground in the country (Syndication International)

the existence of a football ground was considered to be highly prestigious, not merely for clubs but for the local municipality. These lines are from the *Chatham and Rochester News* in 1893:

> 'The "colony" of New Brompton is laudably ambitious and kingly desirous to at least keep abreast of its neighbours ... it possesses a Technical Institute which 'ere long will be open to students: it has a safe dock ... the foundation work for a new pier goes on slowly, but surely to crown it all a football ground has been purchased and laid out ...'

The ground in question was Gordon Road (now the 'Priestfield Stadium').

The openings of grounds were often occasions of ceremonial pomp and splendour. Roker Park enjoyed a particularly spectacular opening, with pipe bands marching through the town, two steamboats on the river, and Lord Londonderry officially opening the pitch's entrance gate with a golden key.

A football ground was in many ways as much part of a burgeoning corporation as a public library, town hall or law courts, and was certainly used by more people. Furthermore, a football ground was often the only place in a town outsiders would visit.

In order that away spectators would have easy access to the new grounds, proximity to railway stations was vital. This is one of the reasons why so many grounds are now in hemmed-in locations, too near town centres. But the grounds also had to be convenient for local inhabitants, which meant they had to be within easy access of public transport.

Inevitably there were many mistakes in choices of location. For example, Newton Heath found their Clayton ground too distant from the major centres of population, while Woolwich Arsenal saw their only salvation as being a long-distance move to another part of the city altogether. York City's ground was too far from the supporters' homes and the railway station, so the club canvassed supporters for their views and moved to Bootham Crescent. In 1910 Torquay moved from a central ground by the railway station out to the suburbs, in the hope of winning more support. Arguably this was not a good move. Nevertheless, very few clubs have moved very far from their original sites. Moving too far away carries the risk of losing loyalties and perhaps, as Arsenal discovered, of trespassing on other clubs' territory.

Two grounds that did have great potential but for various reasons were abandoned were West Ham's Memorial Recreation Ground and Queen's Park Rangers' Park Royal. The former was reputed to have a capacity of 120000, the latter 60000. Had either survived until each club reached the League they might well have become major football and sporting venues.

Charlton's directors made the apparently ridiculous decision to forsake The Valley, having invested large sums on it a year before, for another ground which needed yet more money spent on it to make it only half-usable. They were back at The Valley within a few months. QPR tried leaving Loftus Road twice, each time for the wide open spaces of neighbouring White City. Each time the club lost a great deal of money and games.

Becoming a Business

Every League club is a limited liability company. In the majority of cases the change from being a committee-run club to a joint stock company, issuing shares and being run by a board of directors, was the result of the rise of professionalism and the desire to purchase or rent and develop better football grounds. The second factor was often the more important.

For example, Everton turned professional in 1885, but did not become a limited company until 1892, when they were forced by a greedy landlord to seek another ground. In order to raise the £8000 necessary to buy and develop Goodison Park they had to issue shares to the public. A year later Woolwich Arsenal, who became professional in 1891, did the same so that they could purchase the Manor Ground.

This also occurred with Aston Villa, Reading and Bolton in 1895, Luton Town in 1897, Tottenham in 1898 and The Wednesday and QPR in 1899.

In several other cases clubs were formed, turned professional, became limited companies and adopted their new grounds all in one move. Liverpool were the first such 'instant' club, moving into Anfield a short time after Everton departed.

Two clubs came into being because there existed a ground for them to occupy – amateurs Plymouth

The second Goodison Road Stand, the first double-decker to be built (Popperfoto)

Argyle turning professional and becoming a limited company when they moved into Home Park in 1903, and Chelsea, whose birth in 1905 was due only to the fact that no existing club wanted to use Stamford Bridge.

In the beginning, many of these limited companies were not only interested in staging football. Their homes were called 'Athletic Grounds' and were used for exactly that purpose, for although attendances were rising rapidly, they were still well below the peak averages reached in the 1930s and 1940s. By the turn of the century crowds of 20000 were still considered high. In addition, the idea of mass spectator sports was still relatively new, and the public thirsted for almost any kind of spectacle – sporting or otherwise. Floodlit games were just one example of early attempts by promoters to find money-spinning attractions (see Floodlights). Goodison, Burnden, Villa Park and Molineux each had cycling and running tracks. They staged parades, pageants, and even rugby games until just before the First World War. There was also a thriving but short-lived baseball league involving several League clubs.

Elland Road's unfinished redevelopment, victim of recession (Adrian Gibson)

Saturday afternoon: an idealised view of the typical, small-town ground, cramped but cosy (Frederick Joseph Yates, *Football & the Fine Arts*)

But football crowds continued to grow, and by 1914 most of the cycle and athletic tracks had gone, swallowed up by the need for extra terracing. Multipurpose stadiums had come and gone in the space of only 25 years, and from then on, a football ground was a football ground, and nothing more.

Those grounds which retained their elliptical shape were able to stage either or both of the new popular sports, speedway and greyhound racing. Wembley and White City helped start the ball rolling, followed by Eastville and Somerton Park in 1931, Stamford Bridge in 1933 and Vicarage Road a year later. Field Mill and The Shay also staged racing. At the same time, there were League clubs renting facilities at greyhound stadiums, including Southend (from 1934–55), Clapton Orient (1930–37) and the short-lived East London club, Thames (1930–32).

After the First World War attendances reached unprecedented levels, and it is interesting to note

that only one club's attendance record dates back to before 1914 – that of Bradford City in 1911. The 1920s and 1930s saw 36 grounds enjoy their largest ever attendances, most of them the older, established First Division clubs.

A direct result of these larger attendances was that football grounds changed dramatically in order to cope (see Design and Safety). With greater size came greater prestige. Goodison Park was again at the forefront of these developments, followed by such grounds as Villa Park, Highbury, White Hart Lane and Hillsborough. Grounds became symbols of grandeur; outward expressions of power and success.

Stadiums also reflected national pride, such as Wembley, or the Olympic Stadium in Berlin. Indeed, every Olympic games seemed to give birth to yet another bigger and better stadium, as each country tried to outdo the previous hosts.

But whereas in several countries the existence of such magnificent new stadiums prompted a number of neighbouring football clubs to share the facilities, in Britain the growing prestige of clubs and the expanding football industry had the effect of entrenching 'ground identity' even further. Directors and supporters alike saw no reason to share grounds while the going was good.

By 1939 the establishment of football grounds was complete, both physically and in terms of tradition, and once the latter had set in, it became even harder to contemplate radical change.

In fact football grounds spent the next 30 years blissfully content with their pre-war designs, ideals and standards. If not for the disaster at Bolton in 1946 (see Safety) there might have been even fewer changes than there were before the 1960s. Most of those that did occur were quantitive rather than qualititive, except at grounds recovering from war damage, or those of smaller clubs on their way up, such as Peterborough and Ipswich.

Three other exceptions were Hull, Port Vale and Southend, where completely new grounds were built between 1945–55. Also, the 1950s did witness one major innovation, the development of floodlighting (see Floodlights).

In fairness to the clubs, two additional obstacles were placed in the way of further developments: the introduction of entertainment tax and the restrictions on building materials after the War. The former was particularly burdensome. Entertainment tax (revived now in the form of Value Added Tax) took one penny in 1s 6d and 3½d in 1s 9d. Crystal Palace, for example, paid £3000 tax in the 1952–53 season.

The greatest single boon to development occurred in the late 1950s, with legislation allowing clubs to run their own pools. All over the country, supporters began raising vital extra funds by this means and thus were able to contribute to new building projects, especially the provision of floodlights. Pools revenue alone has been the biggest single factor in ground development since the War. Ibrox Park is the best example (see Rangers).

The 1960s were boom years, with a succession of large stands being built and grounds being improved. But, as discussed in the chapter on Design, not all the work was successful or well thought out. There was too much piece-meal patching up and not enough long-term planning.

Today, crowds are back to their pre-First World War level (and falling), and clubs are gradually realizing the need to use their grounds for more than just football.

The football grounds of today are uncomfortably situated in the locations of yesterday, in a world in which motorways are more important than railways and luxury boxes attract a new class of spectator.

Today's football grounds are seldom packed to capacity and are expensive in rates and maintenance, when they could be sold off as prime land for development and resited elsewhere as multi-sports stadiums. Yesterday's prestige has become today's

Kenilworth Road; gardens lie behind the Oak Road End (Simon Inglis)

burden.

This book is a catalogue of individual club's problems arising from the changing requirements for football grounds. Some extremes include: cramped Luton who want to move but cannot get backing or a new site; Watford, who want to redevelop but cannot get planning permission, or permission to relocate; Sheffield United, who have redeveloped but at such crippling cost that they can hardly survive; and Chelsea who were almost ruined by building for prestige.

The history of football grounds has not been a long one and after 1960 many themes intrude. These are dealt with in more detail in subsequent chapters. But however permanent and secure we think our current grounds to be, in the history of architecture and ideas they are but one element of a passing age, with no more right to survival than any other structure within our midst.

As the experiences of Accrington Stanley and Gateshead have shown, what football clubs build, soon lays waste, unless the developers nip in first (see Lost but Not Forgotten Grounds). It could happen at Old Trafford or anywhere else quite easily. Football could become as much a curiosity of the past as those gladiators in the Colosseum.

If future generations do study our contemporary sporting foibles, let us hope they will at least have a few surviving relics of football grounds to study at first hand.

·2·
DESIGN

The First Steps

The history of football ground design in Britain is not notable for great names or achievements recognized outside the narrow circles of football. There is, however, one man whose name appears time and time again and to whom in many ways we are indebted for the shape and form of all our major grounds. Thousands have sat in his grandstands and stood on his terraces without ever knowing his name – Archibald Leitch. He was a Scottish engineer and architect and very little is known about his life.

Here, in rough chronological order, are the grounds which Leitch certainly either designed, improved and/or built grandstands for: Parkhead, Ibrox Park, Hampden Park, Goodison Park, Ewood Park, Stamford Bridge, White Hart Lane, Craven Cottage, Leeds Road, Hillsborough, Highbury, Tynecastle Park, Douglas Park (Hamilton), Cardiff Arms Park, Roker Park, Fratton Park and Selhurst Park. Several more grounds bear his stamp, even in work completed after his death in 1939.

Archibald Leitch was born in Glasgow in 1866 and attended Hutcheson's Grammar School and Andersonian College, before being apprenticed to the engineering works of Messrs Duncan Stewart and Company Limited, Glasgow, at the age of 16. After five years there, plus six months as a draughtsman, Leitch spent three years at sea as an engineer. In 1890 he obtained a Board of Trade certificate and returned to Duncan Stewart, where he became superintendent draughtsman in its Marine Department. Eight months later he resigned, and in 1897 set up his own company.

In 1902, his business reasonably established, Leitch was elected a full member of the Institute of Mechanical Engineers, and was appointed consulting mechanical engineer to a number of county councils and public bodies in Scotland. He was also known for his activities as a lecturer. But this emphasis on his engineering capabilities is important, for he was principally a technician.

It was around the beginning of this century that Leitch's association with football grounds began, probably at Ibrox and Parkhead and then for the construction of Hampden Park in 1903. At these

Archibald Leitch c.1930 (Sport & General)

grounds the Leitch formula was laid down – a formula that he was to repeat at every other ground he worked on. This was simply the provision of a full-length, two-tier grandstand on one side of the pitch and three open sides of terracing.

Possibly his first contact with clubs south of the border was between 1904–05, when Gus Mears and Frederick Parker of Stamford Bridge travelled to Glasgow specifically to meet Leitch and see his work (see Chelsea).

In 1905 Leitch was responsible for the design of Stamford Bridge, Ewood Park, Craven Cottage and the beginnings of White Hart Lane's redevelopment.

The East Stand, White Hart Lane, under construction (BBC Hulton Picture Library)

Soon after he began work at Huddersfield and Goodison Park.

Many of his two-tier stands were identical, his trademark being a pedimented centre gable on the roof, as at Chelsea, Fulham, Spurs and Huddersfield. The only known survivor is at Craven Cottage, where the gable is still prominent. At Fulham and Blackburn he designed ornamented brick frontages, each still in existence.

During the first decade of this century Leitch moved to offices at 66 Victoria Street, London, SW1, although he retained his office at 30 Buchanan Street, Glasgow. Certainly the biggest concentration of his work was in London, culminating just before the First World War in the lay-out of Arsenal's new ground in Highbury.

After the War his style changed, and it may be significant that in 1925 he was admitted to the Incorporated Association of Architects and Surveyors, to which he applied by citing his work as designer of all the Scottish tube works around Glasgow, and various (but unnamed) football grounds. He did not, however, join the senior body of architects, the Royal Institute of British Architects, which suggests that he remained essentially a technician.

His post-war stands differed from his earlier work in two respects. Firstly, they were not all main stands. He designed both end stands at White Hart Lane and Goodison Park for example. Secondly, his major works were double-decker stands. All of these were unmistakably Leitch, with the now familiar white balcony, criss-crossed with steel framing. There are surviving examples of this at Ibrox, Goodison Park, Roker Park and Fratton Park. Only once did he return to his pre-war style, and that at Selhurst Park was probably because the club had less money to spend.

Leitch's career reached its peak on 1 January 1929, when his largest stand, seating 10 000, was opened at Ibrox Park. The criss-cross balcony was there, and also a castellated press-box high up on the roof, such as he had designed at Hampden. This stand survives today, and is still the club's proud centre-piece, despite their £10 million redevelopment of the rest of the ground. A few months later he designed a smaller version of the same stand for Sunderland, and another at Celtic Park.

His final work for football grounds was at Roker Park and White Hart Lane in the summer of 1936, by which time he was 70 years old. The East Stand at Tottenham will perhaps always be his most dramatic work; certainly it was his most expensive – Everton's

Bullens Road Stand, built by Leitch in 1926, had cost £30 000 whereas ten years later Spurs paid £60 000 for their East Stand.

There was nothing new about the design, although the criss-cross balcony wall had become simpler and lighter, but the stand was built on a shelf of terracing which made it much higher and more imposing, with the press-box towering above his West Stand, built opposite before the First World War. The East Stand was the last of the truly great inter-war stands. Significantly only a few miles away at Highbury, an acclaimed architect was already surpassing Leitch's work. Artistry and contemporary design had easily eclipsed Leitch's more mechanical approach.

He died on 25 April 1939 virtually unrecognized by the press and the world of architecture. However his designs did not die with him. For example, when Plymouth Argyle rebuilt their bombstruck ground in the 1950s, the new main stand was virtually a carbon copy of one of Leitch's double-deckers.

Demands and Restrictions

Designing a football ground in Leitch's time was basically a question of filling the space left available once the pitch had been marked out. With the money available one had to try and fit in as many spectators as possible.

Open terracing was the cheapest and most spacious solution but those who wanted and could afford to sit also had to be provided for. Seats took up a lot of space, as did changing rooms, tearooms, board rooms and such like, so putting all these facilities under one roof was the wisest plan.

The grandstand was in fact an enlarged version of the pavilion, beginning as a wooden and iron structure on the half-way line until it gradually stretched along the length of the pitch.

In England the first major grandstands were at Goodison (1892, replaced in 1909), Anfield (1895, replaced 1973) and Villa Park (1897, redeveloped 1964). There then followed a spurt of building activity between 1904–14, in which major stands at at least 19 grounds were completed. It is significant that building costs during this period were no higher than they had been 30 years previously, but were to shoot up by over 50 per cent in the 1920s.

Having spent most of the money on the main stand, the rest was open to adaptation. Terracing could be built in two ways: either in three rectangular blocks or in an unbroken U-shape with the main stand forming the fourth side. An elliptically-shaped ground allowed more terracing, and the installation of a track, which could be used for staging other events such as cycling and athletics.

Once the basic shape was established, how could the grounds then expand? In Scotland, where an elliptical shape was favoured at Hampden, Ibrox and Celtic, the answer was to raise the terracing. Rangers tried to do this by erecting a massive wooden structure, with disastrous consequences in 1902 (see

Safety). Earth banking was obviously a much safer method, although just before the First World War Sunderland showed at the Roker End how concrete could be used to construct a solid platform for tall terracing. (In practice however concrete was rarely used until after the 1940s because it was more expensive. Wembley was an exception.)

But in England stadium design took a different turn. Grounds were changed from elliptical to rectangular shapes, with terracing coming within yards of each goal-line. Examples of this transformation were at Burnden Park, Goodison Park and Villa Park. In each case the running and cycle tracks were removed to allow for the expansion.

Leitch's plans at Goodison and Hillsborough show that the most efficient use of the rectangular space was to have four curved corner sections linking each side. Though each site placed different demands, from 1900 onwards it is true to say that most clubs wanted this shape of ground, with only a few exceptions. Southampton for example did not have enough space at The Dell for high banking, so they built two grandstands on either side and small open terraces at each end. The Dell was, in 1898, possibly unique in having seats on both sides of the pitch.

Visitors to Leitch's grounds before the First World War would have noticed very few differences between them apart from the relative heights of the terracing. One suspects that he hardly changed his plans at all.

The next stage in design was to improve the lot of the standing spectators, firstly by providing a roof and secondly by concreting the terracing. A correspondent signed A.H.M., summed up the necessity for this in a letter to the *Birmingham Mail* in 1905: 'Why not covered accommodation for spectators, dry ground to stand on, and a reduced admission if possible,' he wrote. 'The profits will stand it. Many a wreath has been purchased by standing on wet grounds on Saturday afternoons.'

Events on the pitch suggest that this was by no means an over-dramatic statement. One example will suffice: when Villa played Sheffield United in November 1894, it is reported that the weather was so cold that several players collapsed during the interval (which was always spent on the pitch) and that some wore great-coats in the second half. One Villa man was even said to have used an umbrella! It was quite common for players to have to retire early because of cold and exhaustion, so imagine how much more uncomfortable it must have been for the standing spectators.

But the covering and concreting of terraces took some while. Indeed some of Leitch's grounds had no standing cover for years. Stamford Bridge had a token cover (The Shed) in the 1930s, but Craven Cottage had none until 1961 and Selhurst Park none until 1969. Probably the first ground to have some cover on all four sides was Goodison Park in 1909.

The principle of two-tier stands – a stand with seats at the back, and a small standing enclosure in front –

was already well established by that time. But in 1909 Leitch designed the country's first double-decker, in which the seating tier was actually above part of the terrace. This was a major advance because it enabled more spectators to be accommodated in less space.

The most characteristic elements of a grandstand were its size, its facings (balcony wall, gable, fencing) and its roof. There were three different styles of roof used for grandstands built before the Second World War. The most popular, as used by Leitch, was a pitched roof. Cheaper than this was the barrel roof, as at Villa Park, St James' Park and Middlesbrough. To provide extra cover it could be doubled with two barrels, as at Anfield and Elland road. The third type, found only at five grounds, was the multi-span roof – which from the front resembled a series of pedimented gables. Old Trafford's original main stand had such a roof, as did Highbury, before 1936. There were other examples at Molineux, Clapton's Homerton Ground and The Valley. None survive.

If Leitch's work at the beginning of the century was one landmark in ground design, the next came in the 1930s at Highbury, with the building of the West, then East Stands in 1932 and 1936.

It was not the first time a recognized architect (as opposed to an engineer) had been commissioned to design a grandstand. At the Boleyn Ground, Sir E. O. Williams had designed West Ham's East Stand (repeated at Filbert Street) and Wembley was the work of architects John Simpson and Maxwell Ayrton.

But the Highbury stands by Claude Waterlow Ferrier and Major W. B. Binnie were in many ways the first attempts to translate contemporary forms and style into football ground design. They were, in that case, outside the main stream of such design, for until the 'cantilever era' began in 1958 football grounds were always some way behind trends in architecture.

Arsenal were able to make this break because they had the funds. But perhaps more importantly, they had imagination also. Until then stadium design had been largely concerned with technical, rather than aesthetic requirements. For example, Edward Bill, writing on the design of football grounds in *Architects Journal* (24 February 1926) considered it purely functional. 'The entrances to the higher priced seats should be kept away from the entrance to the open stands and if possible, on a different side of the ground.'

With this kind of progressive thinking it was no wonder British grounds were even then well below the standard of many foreign contemporaries. For example, cantilevered roofs were already in existence in Rio de Janeiro, while the Municipal Stadium, Cleveland and the Los Angeles Colosseum, among several in the United States, were far in advance of even Wembley and Hampden Park.

Most British football clubs lacked both imagination and money. If a new stand was to be built, directors invariably opted for the familiar, asking for

Maxwell Ayrton's futuristic 1945 scheme for Derby (*Building*, 1948)

something similar to one belonging to another club. Had the grounds been municipally owned and community based there is no doubt that progress in design would have been much quicker – albeit not necessarily the right sort of developments – but two pilot schemes at Derby and Wolverhampton after the Second World War showed just what could be done.

For Derby in 1945, Maxwell Ayrton designed a 78 604 capacity stadium which could be used as a health centre during the week (see illustration). Reviewing the plan in *Art and Industry*, August 1945, the editor commented: 'Without enlarging his stands, or increasing the cost of the football ground as such, he [Ayrton] has converted mere platforms for sightseers, used on comparatively few occasions, into a composite building for many activities, functioning every day of the year, for the benefit of each section of the community, and continuously earning revenue to make it self-supporting.'

The scheme was never carried out. Clubs buried their heads in the sand and maintained their grounds as outdated temples of under-use.

As the editor concluded in his appreciation of Ayrton's plan: '. . . it is a new conception of the development of the social usefulness of a football stand that has never before been attempted.' and was not going to be attempted for another three decades at least.

A rare architectural indulgence: Filbert Street's classical players' entrance (Simon Inglis)

Hillsborough's pride, the cantilever (SWFC)

Post-War Design

After the War no-one had the money to emulate Highbury (see History) and few had the will even though attendances were at their highest.

Stand design did at least take a major step forward in the 1950s. At St Andrew's and Elland Road the first of a new generation of stands were built – propped cantilevers, in which the number of supporting uprights was reduced dramatically and all-round vision improved. Then in 1958 came a breakthrough, at a most unexpected venue.

Jack Arlidge of the *Brighton Evening News* wrote: 'It was at Scunthorpe that I saw a new cantilever stand, a very modern looking affair and the sort we can expect to see more of in the future.' This was the country's first cantilever stand at a football ground; quick to build, perfect for viewing, and attractive in appearance. The next cantilever was built at Dundee United's Tannadice Park, this one an L-shaped stand covering one corner.

But the new era really caught the nation's imagination at Hillsborough in 1961, with the completion of Wednesday's full-length cantilever North Stand. Not since the redevelopment of Highbury

between 1932–36 had such an exciting and bold initiative been taken. The architectural press took notice, and even Pevsner saw fit to mention it in passing – the only time a League ground is mentioned in his guides to the *Buildings of England*.

The Hillsborough stand was revolutionary in three ways. It utilized new building techniques and materials, especially aluminium roof sheeting. It was an all-seater with no standing paddock in front. It also looked modern; even today it retains a streamlined quality rarely matched by recent stands.

From 1961 the trend, at top grounds at least, was to increase seating capacities, and to make those seated areas more comfortable. Elsewhere, the design of stands carried on apparently oblivious to change, as smaller clubs did what they could to improve their grounds on the slimmest of budgets. Yet new building methods were available to help them build more quickly and cheaply. For example, in 1957 Portsmouth redeveloped the Fratton End of their ground with prefabricated concrete units for only £10 000. Coventry also used prefabrication to build the Sky Blue Stand in stages during 1963–64. Blackburn covered one end of Ewood Park with a massive concrete cantilever cover in 1960–61.

Manchester United took the cantilever theme one step further in 1964. Like Wednesday's new stand, the United Road Stand sat 10 000, but also had a paddock in front. But its most significant feature was the addition of private boxes, the first to be installed at any football ground in Europe. This was indeed an indication of how football audiences were changing. The executive customer was asked to invest large sums in the club over the space of two or three seasons, in return for luxury accommodation. Chelsea followed suit, and by 1983 21 clubs had private boxes in one form or another. With 80 boxes Old Trafford has the most.

Still at Manchester United, another important feature of the new cantilever stand was that it was designed as part of an overall development scheme. Until then every stand had been seen as a separate entity, with no particular long-term plans in mind. So that where United were able to add to the new stand by continuing it along the Scoreboard End, clubs like Aston Villa and Liverpool built stands which fitted into no overall plan. Lack of planning, allied to a lack of money and an impatience to build, meant that in later years clubs would regret their earlier investment and be unable to add the kind of structures they would have wished.

For this reason, only a few British grounds have any structural unity; Old Trafford (since 1964), Goodison Park (since 1938), Loftus Road (since 1982) and Elland Road (since the 1970s). Apart from Highbury, which will always be a special case, the vast majority have at least one stand which was built to solve only short-term demands. Between 1958–68 it is estimated that League clubs spent £11 million on ground improvements, £6 million of which was by

First Division clubs. But during that period building costs had risen by nearly 30 per cent. Examples of higher costs were £2000 spent by Aldershot just to build two refreshment huts; £25 000 spent by Bolton to concrete their car-park, and £2000 spent by Bradford City for new seats. In other words, building new stands was becoming the prerogative of the rich and for the rest it was mostly a case of maintaining what they already possessed.

The new generation of stands began, as mentioned above, at Hillsborough in 1961 where completion costs amounted to £150 000 (compare this with the £130 000 Arsenal spent on their East Stand in 1936). Old Trafford's United Road Stand cost £350 000 in 1964, but could yield a higher income. In 1970 Bristol City found a cheaper method of building a column-free stand by suspending the roof from a huge goal-post structure, in which the vertical supports were outside the stand. This cost £235 000, but it did include a lucrative indoor bowling club underneath, worth around £20 000 a year in rental today. Villa Park, Celtic Park, Ibrox and Carrow Road all have stands built on the goal-post principle.

In 1971 Everton built the then largest stand in Britain – a triple-decker main stand – which cost £1 million, and just as transfer fees were rising to equally dizzy proportions, Chelsea spent twice as much on only a slightly bigger stand in 1974. The 1970s and early 1980s saw major stand construction at no fewer than 27 League grounds, with smaller stands being built at another 13 grounds at least. Prices never ceased to rise. For example, Chester's new stand cost £556 000 in 1979. Three years later the same stand was quoted to another club at £1 million. Three stands represented another landmark in ground design, beginning at Molineux in 1978–79 and followed at the City Ground and White Hart Lane.

For Wolves and Spurs the architects were Mather and Nutter, who had also designed Old Trafford's cantilever stands. At Nottingham, the Sheffield company of Husbands (designers of Wednesday's cantilever) built an almost identical stand for Forest.

These three are advanced in two ways. Firstly, they are just one phase of an overall development (though it seems unlikely that further work will be carried out for some time yet), and secondly, they set a standard for future generations. For example, the private boxes (42 at Molineux and 72 at White Hart Lane) were placed between two tiers of seats, unlike Manchester United's which are at the back of the stands.

But perhaps more importantly, they catered for the need to earn additional income other than on match days. Molineux's stand has office accommodation, White Hart Lane's has two large reception areas. The ideas of Maxwell Ayrton for Derby in 1945 were at last beginning to take effect. The trend continued with the total redevelopment of Ibrox Park, to include two stands with office and exhibition space (see club sections).

At the other end of the scale there were few developments. Many grounds gathered dust and weeds, while only a handful had facelifts. As gates declined from 1976 onwards it became apparent that pre-war design had become obsolete and was sometimes not even worth keeping in repair. For example, after the Safety of Sports Grounds Act 1975 (see Safety) Orient found it cheaper to install seats than restore the terracing. It hardly mattered that the seats did not yield much more revenue than standing spectators – demand for the terraces was not high anyway. Other clubs simply fenced off terracing rather than spend large sums on repair. This raises the question of all-seater stadiums. What do the spectators feel about them?

This is an incident told by an official of Coventry City, the first English club to make its ground all-seated. He was discussing the development with an extremely disgruntled Sky Blue supporter who had stood on the terraces all his life but would never consider sitting at Highfield Road, not even to see Manchester United.

'That's a shame,' the official replied, 'because I was going to offer you a free seat ticket for the match against United next week.'

'Ah well, that's different,' said the man, taking the ticket, 'Thanks very much.' And of course he did carry on watching his favourite team. Coventry have suffered from their decision, in that the conversion of the ground coincided with the recession, which hit Coventry harder than most cities. Despite the team's encouraging performances, gates were among the lowest in Division One. There are two other all-seater stadiums in Britain. Pittodrie was the first, converted in 1978. Clydebank's ground followed. In England, QPR made a move towards all-seating, but in 1982 took out some seats under pressure from their followers, who still wanted some standing space.

There is no doubt that all-seated stadiums do help to curb hooliganism (cited as the main reason for converting Highfield Road), if only because they make it easier for the police to see trouble brewing and stop it at the outset. They are safer for crowd control, easier for segregation, and potentially higher in revenue. Conversely seats are expensive to maintain (they need replacement every eight to ten years), reduce capacities, and demand cover of some sort. It is less uncomfortable to stand than sit in the rain.

The best solution, one which QPR and Coventry seem to have realized, is to offer a mixture. Old Trafford and Goodison Park are the only examples of grounds with both seated and standing provision on all four sides (White Hart Lane and the Baseball Ground were until recently). In order to increase their seating capacities however, some clubs have made rather too hasty attempts to convert terracing to seated areas, by simply bolting seats onto old steps which do not have the correct rake for adequate viewing. Examples of such conversions which are not conducive to easy viewing are Maine Road and Burn-

Clashing styles and unconventional angles at Anfield (Simon Inglis)

den Park (where the seats are comfortable but the sight lines are very poor). There are excellent conversions at The Valley and the Goldstone Ground.

Seating is one way of improving an outdated ground. But it is only one way, and depending on the club's circumstances and support may not always be the means of salvation. As Watford have demonstrated, the relationship between the club and its followers is just as vital as the improvement of facilitites. Several clubs have consciously decided against installing private boxes, preferring instead to update their general accommodation. As the experience of Spurs has proved, installing boxes can have the effect of vastly increasing building costs and reducing the number of other seats available.

Perhaps the best example of a ground rescued from pre-war decay is Loftus Road. In 14 years, QPR have rebuilt all four sides, quickly, cheaply and efficiently and with the minimum of fuss and disruption. They have three double-decker stands, 17 500 seats out of a total capacity of 23 000, and above all, have retained the ground's famed and cherished intimate atmosphere. This is no small achievement on a budget of around £1 million, because development can either ruin or enhance a ground's atmosphere. In all too

many cases, the former has resulted.

Since the introduction of the Safety of Sports Grounds Act in 1975 (see Safety) and the rise in building costs, the need for careful planning has become more important than ever. Football creates its own requirements for spectators. A cricket ground, for example, needs space for crowds to circulate behind the stands. Football grounds are for viewing only. The majority of spectators go straight to their positions, and apart from brief sorties to toilets and refreshment stalls, stay there. Once the game is over they leave as soon as possible, many before the final whistle.

Viewing requirements are also different. Spectators at rugby and athletics matches prefer to watch from the side. But in football the tradition of 'ends' is still strong. Very few grounds see the younger, more vocal elements congregate on the sides, unless absolutely necessary, as at Maine Road for example, where both ends are seated, or if the ends are uncovered. The notion of being on the side is still regarded by many as being somehow non-commital. An 'end' stands for identity, and generally the further one is to the back of the terrace, the more vocal and partisan the crowd seems to become.

Harry Faulkner-Brown, who leads the team of architects in the north east who were responsible for the redevelopment of St James' Park, has made a study of spectator accommodation at football grounds. He emphasized that football grounds, like theatres, need to bring the crowd reasonably close to the players. Spectators want to be able to see their heroes' faces, expressions and movements.

Taking his calculations from a number of stadiums, Faulkner-Brown has determined that the ideal limit for viewing football is roughly 90 metres from the centre circle, or 150 metres to the furthest corner flag. The maximum distance should be 190 metres. The plans below (taken from *The Architects' Journal*, January 1979) show how these calculations relate to some contemporary football grounds.

(Dark circle line is 90 metres radius from centre spot, or 150 metres from furthest corner – the optimum viewing distance. Broken line is 190 metres from furthest corner – maximum viewing distance.)

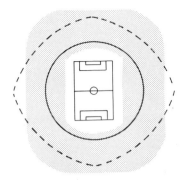

The Aztec Stadium was built especially for football, yet still suffers from too many spectators too far from the action. It is built in the quadric plan, whereby each side is not parallel to the touchline, but curved slightly to allow better sight-lines. The Greeks curved the seats of the arena with a chord of 3 metres in a 200-metre arc, a calculation also used at the Aztec Stadium.

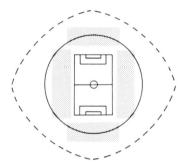

The traditional football ground with four rectangular stands, parallel to the touchlines, but without using the corners for viewing. Although most of the ground comes within the optimum viewing circle, the number of columns and barriers obstructing the view has to be taken into account.

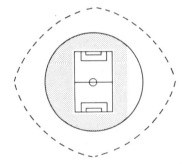

The ideal football ground follows the quadric plan but keeps all the stands within the optimum viewing circle. If space is limited the West Side should be larger, so that more view the game with the sun behind them.

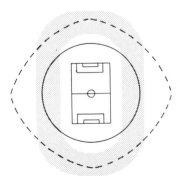

Elliptical grounds such as Wembley show that the majority of spectators are outside the optimum viewing circle, and maybe one-fifth (20 000) are beyond the maximum viewing circle. Wembley also suffers from being a one-deck stadium (ie not double-deck) and having a wide perimeter track.

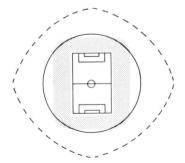

To fit a rectangular shaped piece of land the stands can be made parallel to the touchlines and outer limits (roads, houses etc) but with curved corners. This plan is followed at Old Trafford, and is the basis for St James' Park's redevelopment.

In order to fit more people into a ground, but at the same time bring them closer to the play, added tiers are the best solution, though costly. The diagrams below show how four different stands distance the spectators from the pitch.

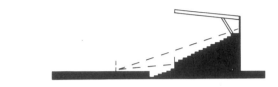

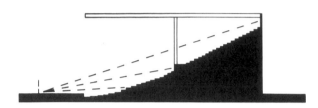

At Coventry, two tiers are sufficient to hold a moderate number of spectators near to the pitch.

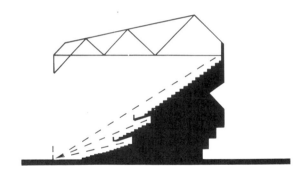

At Wembley, where the numbers are greater two tiers are too shallow and make the back rows too far from the pitch, a situation exaggerated by the extra width of the perimeter track.

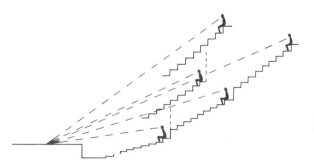

At Chelsea the distances are relatively small, but the three decks are very expensive to build and make the top, back rows very high up.

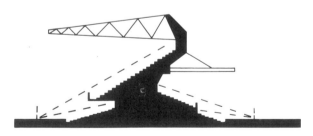

Cardiff Arms Park (designed by Osborne, V. Webb and Partners) has a unique set-up, in which overlapping decks are used, the upper with a steep rake, but behind the stand is built another stand for the Cardiff Rugby Club. If some major cities were to have football stands like this, the top clubs could use the main stand, and lesser clubs the rear stand.

Three straight tiers of seating are cheaper to build but take up more room. By separating and overlapping the tiers the spectators are closer to the pitch with better sight lines. The angle of rake should not be steeper than 35 degrees, for safety reasons.

If this is not complicated enough already, there are still several more design and building problems to be considered.

There is a danger that new and bigger stands have the effect of alienating support. I was told, for example, at Tranmere and Chester that the most ardent supporters complained for years how cramped and inadequate the old main stands were, but once these were replaced by efficient, but soulless concrete and steel structures fans pined for the old wooden stand. The success of Loftus Road's redevelopment was that it kept the new stands within the size and shape of the ground. Similarly, West Bromwich Albion's new main stand crept into The Hawthorns almost imperceptibly, without affecting the atmosphere at all.

Another problem is that some clubs have tended to build big on their way up, and then suffered as a result. The history of ground design is full of clubs who declined rapidly after building a major stand. To name just a few: Sheffield United, who completed a £750 000 cantilever stand in 1975, but seven years later were in Division Four for the first time in their history; Bristol City, who built a stand in 1970 when they were doing well and then found they had the best ground ever to grace the bottom of the Fourth Division; Burnley, who also redeveloped their ground to the possible detriment of the team. The most extreme example in another respect is Chelsea, who began building their enormous East Stand in 1972. Soom after it was finished two years later the club was relegated and in deep financial trouble. Large stands have caused similar financial problems for Wolves and Spurs.

The lengthy redevelopment at Chelsea also affected the atmosphere of the ground. Their decline coincided exactly with the building of the East Stand, when one side of Stamford Bridge was completely out of use, with an inevitable loss of revenue (from seats) and atmosphere. On the other hand, while the same occurred at White Hart Lane for one year, the club still managed to win one major trophy.

An admirable compromise has been reached by several clubs, among them Ipswich and WBA, whereby stand redevelopment during the season is done in such a way to allow a certain section of seating along that side to be used continually. Similarly, Peterborough, Swindon and Chester built their main stands behind the existing stands, with the minimum of disruption to atmosphere. And once again I must cite the case of Loftus Road, where virtually all the work on three sides took place during successive close seasons, thereby allowing both players and supporters to adjust to the changed circumstances gradually.

A further point, as several experts both in design and administration have stressed for some years, is the crucial need to design stadiums as a means of regaining support. Few extra spectators are going to be lured to a ground to sit in a more expensive seat if they are already tired of the product on view. They have to become accustomed to going to the ground for other purposes. In other words, a football ground has to be more than a football ground. By turning the football ground into a community area in daily use, for whatever purposes, the public would establish a closer relationship to the club, and in that way attendances might rise.

Already several clubs have training pitches, artificial and all-weather, which they share with the community as part of a Sports Council scheme. But there are still grounds with excellent facilities that lie dormant for most of the week.

Reading is one example of a club who did not take the opportunity to share in a community scheme, despite the fact that it had received grants to build a sports centre at Elm Park. The choice is there and for some clubs it could mean the balance between survival and extinction.

Finally, a brief look at some of the long term requirements of football ground design.

The axis of a ground is important, in terms of wind and sun. The best orientation is a long axis of north to south (that is, the ends are north and south), with the main stand on the west, so that the afternoon sun is behind the stand.

In order that the pitch is exposed to natural ventilation, for drying, it is also important to have one end open, or at least with a low roof. Those grounds which have all-round cover, such as Old Trafford and the Baseball Ground, certainly suffer from more pitch problems (see Pitches), especially if the sun is unable to penetrate. Lack of sun means slower drying and slower growth.

Car-parking is a further bugbear. In the United States several stadiums are completely surrounded by open parking areas, as at the Houston Astrodome. At Cincinnati a stadium has been built over a huge underground car-park. The West Germans plan their new stadiums on the basis of one parking space per four spectators. Hardly a ground in Britain enjoys such an advantage, although Plymouth's Home Park and Doncaster's Belle Vue ground are well blessed for parking space in proportion to their number of spectators.

The ideal ground would satisfy the following requirements: safety, compactness (a good pitch/stands relationship), variety (seats/standing), comfort, flexibility (for ground sharing with other sports), economy (to maintain), continuity (minimum disruption of existing facilities if extra development undertaken), identity, attractiveness, and finally sympathy with its surrounding environment (no huge stands in low rise areas, sensitive landscaping and so on).

If it were possible, the ideal ground would be quadric in plan and with three sides covered, two of them double-decker stands, and be surrounded by parking space for at least a few thousand vehicles, preferably with easy access to the main routes. There is, after all, little point in building a wonderful new 50 000 stadium in the midst of small streets.

Those large-scale redevelopment plans which do exist, such as at Molineux, White Hart Lane, Old Trafford and Stamford Bridge, even if completed would still suffer with access problems. If the sites were sold however, would the profits be sufficient to rebuild adequately? Southampton considered this possibility and stayed at The Dell.

But in defence of the bad old British ground, it is true to say that the traditional atmosphere is still highly regarded. Would we really want to see our local teams perform in soulless concrete bowls that look much like any other concrete bowl?

Isn't the essence of British football grounds the tremendous variety and idiosyncratic qualities of each – however uncomfortable and ramshackle some of them may be?

I believe that the present generation of football enthusiasts may feel this deeply and this book is in many ways a celebration of our eccentricities. But what about the future footballing generation, if indeed there is to be one?

Wherever possible, clubs should always seek to improve grounds along the lines that men like Harry Faulkner-Brown have suggested, and in that way preserve the closeness always demanded between the spectators, and the players, who, like actors, need a good audience at every performance. Maybe Wembley does provide the best atmosphere for a football match we could ever aspire to in this country. But modern football ground design can do a lot better than they even knew was possible in 1923. New grounds will bring new traditions, however much traditionalists will claim otherwise. Every ground has to start somewhere.

Over the Top

Before leaving the subject of design, a quick look at what is happening to stadium design elsewhere in the world and what might happen in the future.

If you do not relish the idea of multi-purpose stadiums this may be because the British are not used to watching football across an athletics track. But instead of giving up the idea of multi-purpose grounds, the stands could be moved to fit the event. This is not as ridiculous as it sounds. The Houston Astrodome can change the seats around within hours for soccer, baseball or whatever. In Denver, the Mile High Stadium has grandstands which move on water. In Hawaii, the Aloha Stadium needs one man to move each of the four grandstands, in 25 minutes. They change positions by using air cushion lift pads.

We can put a roof over our ground of the future. A sliding roof even, so that during the week the pitch is protected, but on Saturday afternoon it opens. Or we can have a permanent roof, such as QPR are considering, and air-condition the entire ground. Light plastic covers, supported by air, make such roofs a very real possibility.

If we can move stands and cover pitches, we can

theoretically combine our three most beloved spectator sports – football, rugby and cricket, just as in the late Victorian era.

For decades football clubs have been notoriously inexperienced clients for architects, lacking foresight, imagination and often good business sense. Thankfully that is now changing.

One day there will be no trace of Archibald Leitch's work – of his fine pedimented gables, his sweeping banks of open terracing and his towering, precarious press boxes high up on pitched roofs, and however exciting the challenges and possibilities of modern design outlined in this chapter, when that day comes we will have lost one of the most important, though barely recognized parts of our footballing heritage.

·3·
SAFETY

History and Background

One of the remarkable features of the history of British football grounds is how few tragic incidents are recorded. Since 1945 League attendances in England alone have totalled about 1 100 000 000 and yet there have been less than 50 fatalities from accidents throughout that period. Although not a bad record, millions of pounds have been spent during the last decade in making sure the number of injuries will be even smaller.

A century ago clubs did virtually nothing to protect spectators. Thousands were packed onto badly constructed slopes with hardly a wooden barrier in sight. About the best that can be said of the early grounds is that with only ropes around the pitches there was little to stop a build up of pressure sending hundreds pouring onto the pitch. On the other hand, as incidents at Fallowfield showed in 1893, there was also little to stop many non-paying customers from gate crashing (see Cup Final venues).

Yet apart from regular problems of overcrowding, accidents were rare until clubs started developing their grounds; then one starts reading of collapsing terracing and broken fences. At Blackburn in 1896 part of a stand caved in and five people were injured. Rovers were found to have been negligent and had to pay one spectator £25 compensation. At Newcastle shortly afterwards a railing collapsed and one boy lost his foot in the crush.

Pitch invasions and unruliness were far more commonplace than today, as fans assaulted players, referees and even their own club's property. Nevertheless there were still surprisingly few casualties.

The first major tragedy was at Ibrox Park, Glasgow on 5 April 1902, when Scotland were playing England. Rangers were so proud that Ibrox rather than Celtic or Hampden Park had been selected as the venue that they spent large sums on improving the ground. A huge, wooden stand was erected behind the west goal, and it was the top rear section of this which collapsed, apparently when the crowd strained to follow a Scottish move down the wing. The wooden planks gave way under the strain causing 26 people to fall some 40 feet to their deaths below, while another 500 were injured. And yet the game went on

1902 disaster at Ibrox, as portrayed in the *Graphic* (BBC Hulton Picture Library)

and the surviving 68 000 crowd saw a one-all draw. Thereafter such high wooden terracing was banned. As one observer wrote: 'Not even the cries of dying sufferers nor the sight of broken limbs could attract this football maddened crowd from gazing upon their beloved sport.'

Less serious accidents continued however – the collapse of a wall at the Penistone Road End of Hillsborough, causing injuries to 80 people, a man's death in a crush at Burnley.

It is interesting to note, however, that at the first

29

Wembley Cup Final, when 200 000 were said to have packed into the new stadium, there was not one recorded incident of violent behaviour. People were crushed, shunted about, by one another and the police, and yet by all accounts the afternoon passed off peacefully. After these chaotic scenes, a report on the problem of: 'abnormally large attendances on special occasions' was ordered by the country's first Labour Government.

A Departmental Committee on Crowds was set up, with representatives from Wembley Stadium, the Rugby Football Union, Aston Villa, Manchester United and Queen's Park, together with the Chief Constables of Doncaster, Liverpool, Birmingham, Glasgow and the Metropolitan Police, and the chiefs of various transport companies. (The FA in its infinite wisdom refused to comply with a request for information, while Chelsea also declined to give evidence, even though they had staged three Cup Finals at Stamford Bridge only a few years previously.)

The committee undertook tours of Roker Park, Hampden and Ibrox, Villa Park and St Andrews, and attended an RAF pageant at Hendon and a race meeting at Doncaster, before delivering the report to the Home Secretary, Arthur Henderson, on 13 March 1924 (Command Paper 2088).

This was the first serious attempt at understanding the nature of safety at large grounds, and however unscientific many of the methods, some of the conclusions were very similar to those reached by studies conducted 50 years later.

The committee stressed the desirability of using mounted police where possible, no doubt in reaction to the efficacy of horses at Wembley, and these became a common sight at most major grounds thereafter. Not only are horses a daunting and persuasive form of crowd control but from the higher vantage point officers have a clearer view of crowd flow and possible areas of difficulty.

Another suggestion was that Chief Officers, rather than ground officials, should determine how many policemen are necessary, and that the clubs would have to pay for that number, or incur a heavy responsibility in the event of trouble or accidents. This rule is still in force.

To co-ordinate policing and stewarding the report also recommended that telephone links be placed around the ground (this was before the days of personal two-way radios).

Advanced booking was to be encouraged wherever possible and certainly for Wembley Cup Finals. (Wembley, said the report, was a special case not only because of the large crowds but because the majority of spectators were unfamiliar with the stadium and its locality.) This suggestion was adopted immediately, so that the events of 1923 were never repeated.

On the construction and design of grounds, the 1924 report made several proposals. Smaller sections, or pens, on the terracing were suggested as a means of dividing crowds and lessening movement.

This was one far-sighted idea not fully implemented until the 1970s, since when most large grounds have fenced off larger areas of terracing.

The approaches to grounds were also to be divided by barriers, to channel spectators towards clearly designated turnstiles, of which there should be at least one per 1250 people. Groups of turnstiles were to be under the supervision of one man who could open and shut gates as and when necessary. This supervisor, said the report rather optimistically, should: 'keep an approximate count of the numbers who have come through the turnstiles'. But until the introduction of electric automatic counters on each turnstile, the task of counting was far beyond the capacity of one individual.

On the evidence of Hector McKenzie of Queen's Park, the committee recommended the use of crush barriers with a wire rope slung between the verticals, as at Hampden Park. These, he believed, were safer because they yielded to pressure. Rigid barriers were nevertheless installed almost universally, and wire ropes soon passed out of use.

Perhaps one of the most telling points made by the 1924 report concerned the placing of barriers. They should be staggered, it advised, to prevent the existence of vertical gangways on the terracing, and where terracing was curved or angled, the barriers should be continuous. Again, these findings were exactly those enforced 50 years later, and the failure to apply them contributed a great deal to the Bolton disaster in 1946.

One practice the report disfavoured was having lines of seats inside the perimeter fence. This was quite common at many grounds, the seats being offered on a first come, first served basis at the same price as a place on the terracing. But the occupants could easily mount a pitch invasion, as at White Hart Lane in 1904. So the only people allowed to sit inside the perimeter fence were to be officials and first-aid personnel. The report added that it did not wish to stop the practice of allowing disabled men to be wheeled into favourable positions near the touchline.

The actual stability of stands was not the committee's problem. That was taken care of by the Public Health Act of 1890 Part 4, and was apparently quite adequate, for apart from Ibrox in 1902, there are few recorded cases of stands actually collapsing with people in them, although people were often injured when falling off roofs.

The committee was also unable to cast judgement on the usually inadequate sanitary arrangements at sports grounds. An Act of 1907 already enforced the provision of toilets, but did not mention improvement where they already existed.

The report concluded that licensing of grounds might be a good idea, although it added that without licensing there had actually been very little trouble. But if licences were to be introduced, the authorizing body should be the local authority, in conjunction with the police. There might be three categories of

Burnden Park 1946. The shoeless body of a woman attending only her second football match lies near her dead brother. Most of the crowd thought the victims had fainted and roared for the game to restart (Popperfoto)

grounds; those with a capacity of under 3000, under 10000 and over 10000. This last point is the essence of the 1975 legislation on ground safety, and it took two major accidents for its value to be recognized.

The first of these occurred at Burnden Park on 9 March 1946, but it might have happened almost anywhere else. Bolton were in many ways unlucky to have been caught out by a series of unfortunate circumstances on the day, and were no more to blame than dozens of other clubs who had not fully implemented the 1924 recommendations.

The fault arose in the north west corner of the ground, where a section of turnstiles was overrun by part of an unexpectedly large crowd of 85000. Inside the ground, the corner terracing became so overcrowded that 33 people died and 400 were injured in a quite horrific crush. (For a full account of the disaster, see Appendix.)

Immediately after the event, the Labour Home Secretary, Chuter Ede, appointed R. Moelwyn Hughes KC to set up an enquiry, and yet again another set of conclusions and recommendations was preferred to the authorities.

'How easy it is for a dangerous situation to arise in a crowded enclosure,' wrote Hughes. 'It happens again and again without fatal, or even injurious consequences. But its danger is that it requires so little influence – an involuntary sway, an exciting moment, a comparatively small addition to the crowd, the failure of one part of one barrier – to translate the danger in terms of death and injuries.'

It was reckoned that a total of 28137 people had paid to enter the section of terracing in question, the Railway End. This was not the largest number ever recorded. There had, for example, been 28435 at that end in 1929. Since then extra terracing had added 300 places. But on 9 March between 1000 and 1500 people had gained unauthorized entry, mainly by climbing over gates and through an emergency gate, so that at the time of the disaster there were probably 29000 to 30000 people in the Railway End.

How could it be known what the true capacity of such a terrace really was? And how could the club know when that capacity was reached, especially since the counters on the turnstiles were not looked at until the end of the game? The report embarked on some calculations of its own:

If each person filled a space of 1½ square feet, the Railway End's capacity would be 28600. Alternatively, if each person had a width of 15 inches and there

Safety officers test crush barriers at Highfield Road (Syndication International)

were two people per step of terracing, by measuring the total length of terracing, plus a few areas not terraced but with a view of the pitch, the capacity came to 26 530.

The situation of the Railway End at Bolton is complicated, however, by the existence of turnstiles on one side of the terrace only. In view of this the 1946 report considered a maximum capacity of 25 000 to 26 000 to be safe.

Therefore, if there were 28 137 paying customers, plus 1500 gatecrashers, but 2500 to 3000 of them were removed from the Railway End to the Burnden Stand, the final total was probably about 26 500; more or less a reasonably safe number.

So if numbers were not the problem, how did the accident occur? The report blames three factors. Firstly, it took too long, about 15 minutes, to close all the turnstiles, by which time it was too late. Secondly, there had been a large scale illegal entry over the turnstiles and fences and through one door. Thirdly, there was evidence that one of the barriers which collapsed had a rusty upright.

Surprisingly, especially in view of the 1924 report's findings, the lack of continuous barriers in the corner section of curved terracing, where the fatalities occurred, was not blamed. Even though there was a barrier-free pathway down to the front, the 1946 report claimed that downward pressure was filtered 'round the ends of the barrier'.

Finally, Hughes concluded that Bolton were not to blame. There were sufficient police – 103 for this game, compared with 60 for a previous game attended by 43 000 – but the ground officials had placed too great a burden on them. Co-operation between the police inside and outside the ground had also been defective, and the reserve call-up had been haphazard.

So Hughes made his recommendations. Some of them had been made before and some would be made again. He called for closer examinations of grounds, for licences to be issued and for a more scientific

method of calculating a ground's capacity. The only work on the subject Hughes was able to find came from what he described as, 'crowd-fond Germany'.

Knowing the true capacity is only worthwhile however, if it is known when that point is reached, so Hughes suggested an electrical means of counting be found, adding up at a central point. This last idea was adopted once the technology became affordable, and by the mid-1960s all large grounds had some centralized method. Now of course computers have made the task very simple.

As a result of Hughes' enquiry, in 1948 the FA began a system of voluntary licensing for all grounds holding 10 000 or more. But the system was still inadequate, because all it depended on was proof that an inspection had taken place. It did not lay down specific standards, gave no guidelines, and the FA accepted each report without question. Furthermore, the FA did not specify what it meant by 'qualified personnel' to carry out the inspections. It could have even been the club chairman.

Clearly there had to be more than general advice, for although many clubs did their utmost to improve ground safety factors, in the absence of any real standards it was too easy for the FA to be lenient towards those clubs it knew could not afford to make improvements.

But as the 1950s wore on it became apparent that the post-war boom in attendances had been a flash in the pan, and that in future crowds would not be so great. People were still packed in, but clubs at least knew when to close the gates.

Nevertheless, there were still accidents. At Ibrox Park in 1961 two people died when a wooden barrier on a stairway collapsed. Eighty people were injured in a crush at Roker Park three years later. In 1968 a fire in the main stand at the City Ground, during a match, highlighted the need for quick evacuation procedures.

The 1969 report by Sir John Laing was not so much the result of these events as the rise of football hooliganism. This was the era of 'bovver boys'. After 16 months of investigation, Laing came up with yet more recommendations, some of them affecting football grounds.

He considered the existing system of voluntary licensing to be sufficient, but thought that if more seats were installed, less hooliganism would occur. The police said that having seating behind standing areas was a significant aid to their own abilities. It enabled officers to look down on the terraces from the seats, and reduced the potential areas of trouble, although they recognized that many standing spectators did not want to see their favourite end chopped in two.

Countering Laing's theory was a report by the Sports Council and the Social Sciences Research Council which stated that: 'it should not be assumed that seating will necessarily limit unruly behaviour'.

In view of subsequent events it would seem that

both reports contained a measure of truth. Extra seats do not stop violence breaking out, but they do make it easier to stop. Laing also found that the majority of arrests and ejections took place in the hour before kick-off and in the first 15 minutes of the game, when, as any terrace regular will confirm, bad tempers often arise from cramped conditions and boredom. Once the match gets going attention is diverted. If more people were seated, or at least in their seats only shortly before kick-off, much of the frustration would be relieved.

Laing's report was an interesting document but it had little effect. It needed another major accident to bring about definitive recommendations, and eventually legislation.

The second Ibrox disaster, on 2 January 1971 was, the most serious ever to occur in Britain, and also perhaps the least avoidable. Celtic were beating Rangers 1-0 in the annual New Year derby match when, with only two minutes left, Colin Stein equalized for the home team. At that moment thousands were already leaving the ground on stairway 13 and, as many of them heard the cheers, they tried to get back up the stairs to find out what had happened. On their way they met those still trying to exit, and in the resultant crush 66 people were suffocated or trampled on and more than 140 others injured. In many ways therefore Stein's was quite the costliest goal ever scored.

The inevitable report on the Ibrox incident was delivered in May 1972 to the Conservative Home Secretary, Reginald Maudling, and the Secretary of State for Scotland, Gordon Campbell. Called the Wheatley Report (Command Paper 4952) it was the first stage in the process which led to the Safety of Sports Grounds Act of 1975.

Wheatley referred to previous guides on safety and also the Laing Report on crowd behaviour and the Chester Report on the state of football, completed in 1968. It began by stating that the system of voluntary licensing was inadequate, that it was not sufficient for a qualified person to make an annual inspection of grounds holding 10000 or more, be he architect, consulting engineer, the chairman or secretary of the club. Instead, the report considered other methods of inspection.

The first was a regional panel of experts to cover all the grounds in its area under the jurisdiction of the FA. This, it was concluded, would involve the football authorities in too much work and expense in bringing members of the panel together.

A second suggestion was that grounds be brought within existing legislation, and therefore not issued with insurance certificates if found to be unsafe. Insurance inspectors would at least have the qualifications to pass judgement. This too was deemed unsuitable, because it exposed clubs to possible commercial exploitation. The best solution seemed to be a licensing system operated by local authorities, an idea mooted in the 1924 report.

Behind bars (Syndication International)

The reasoning behind this recommendation was that a sports ground depended on the paying public, so its owners had a duty to make it safe, as did proprietors of other public buildings. A local authority could call on a variety of sources: building inspectors, engineers, sanitary inspectors, surveyors, architects, the police and the fire brigades, all accustomed to this type of inspection work in their other duties for the authority. A football ground would be treated in the same way as a cinema, a library or a restaurant. There was, however, a danger that the inspectors would be too zealous, led perhaps by personal or local considerations and that there might be inequality of application throughout the country.

Despite this danger, it was felt that any form of governmental supervision would be too expensive and that local authorities were best equipped to deal with licensing.

But it was no use delaying any further, stated Wheatley. The idea of licensing had been around a long time, and as the Ibrox disaster showed, a club could have spent, as Rangers did, a great deal on ground improvements but still have faulty or inadequate design and construction. There was a need for standard guidelines and legislation to enforce their implementation.

The Wheatley Report was the first stage. The second was the setting up of a working party by the Minister of Sport, Denis Howell, to produce a set of guidelines, called the *Guide to Safety At Sports Grounds*, published in 1973. It is otherwise known as the Green Code. Then in August 1975, 51 years after the first investigation into safety, the Safety of Sports Grounds Act was passed. This was at a time when clubs were being caught in the whirlwind of falling attendances and rising costs. Suddenly they were confronted with yet another burden on their dwindling resources.

The Safety of Sports Grounds Act 1975
When the *Guide to Safety at Sports Grounds* was published shortly after the Wheatley Report, many

clubs voluntarily acted on its recommendations. The 1975 Act introduced the system of compulsory licensing and thereby made adherence to the guidelines a matter of priority. Either a club conformed or it would not get its licence.

Briefly, the Act specifies:

Grounds which, in the opinion of the Secretary of State, hold more than 10 000 spectators may be 'designated'. A designated ground must have a safety certificate issued by the local authority, specifying the ground's capacity, the activities for which the ground is used, and for how long the certificate applies. (A special safety certificate may also be granted for specific events – perhaps concerts, prayer meetings or other sporting events not mentioned on the general safety certificate.)

The safety certificate not only specifies the ground's total capacity, but how many each section might hold, and the number, size and situation of all the entrances and exits (including emergency and fire exits). These should all be maintained and kept free of obstruction.

The certificate also states how many crush barriers are necessary, and their strength and situation.

If a ground has been designated but a safety certificate not applied for, and that ground is then used, an offence has been committed. Similarly if a ground is used for an activity not covered by the safety certificate, if spectators are allowed into sections prohibited from use by the certificate, or simply too many spectators admitted, the person guilty for allowing this will be fined not more than £400 or sent to prison for not more than two years, or both. To date this has never happened. The adverse publicity would be a great deal costlier than the punishment.

The Act does not state what improvements should be made, simply that local authorities have the power to issue safety certificates. The Green Code exists to help determine what work is necessary before a certificate is issued. The legislation was enforced in stages, to give clubs time to liaise with their local authorities and carry out the improvements. In 1976 all First Division and international grounds were designated. Second Division clubs followed in 1979. Apart from the international rugby grounds (Twickenham, Cardiff Arms Park and Murrayfield) no other sports grounds have so far been designated.

Once a ground is designated, it remains so no matter what the club's rank, so that clubs like Bristol City do not lose designated status once they drop from the Second Division, unless they decide to reduce their capacity to below 10 000.

In 1982–83, a total of 50 League grounds were designated: all 44 in Divisions One and Two, plus both Bristol Clubs, Orient, Cardiff, Wrexham and Preston. Yet the best ground in the lower divisions was Bramall Lane, which eluded designation status when Sheffield United were relegated to Division Three in 1979.

Once a club is promoted to Division Two, if its ground has not previously been designated, it will receive notification from the Home Office and must apply for a safety certificate. The procedure from then on varies according to local authority.

Broadly speaking the authorities send building inspectors, fire and police officers to visit the ground to determine what, if anything, needs to be done, and what the ground's capacity should be until the work is completed. Some authorities, like South Yorkshire for example, have enough designated grounds within their jurisdiction to justify the setting up of a working committee specifically concerned with the issuing of safety certificates. In most cases the clubs are well acquainted with their local officials, especially in the police and fire departments, so there is constant interchange.

But how strict each authority is varies. To take a hypothetical example: Borchester United are promoted to Division Two. The local authority draws up a list of improvements to be made if a capacity of 20 000 is to be maintained. The authorities refuse to issue the certificate until this work is finished, so the club works feverishly in the summer, but by the opening day of the season have not completed it. The authority issues a certificate for a capacity of 15 000. As well as carrying out the remaining work, to amend the certificate might cost Borchester £500 alone. But their season goes badly, attendances are nowhere near 15 000, so they decide to stay as they are. At the end of the season they are relegated back to Division Three, but must stay designated. Their brief encounter with the Second Division has cost them dearly in terms of building work, and however badly the team fare thereafter, their ground will still be subject to all the necessary inspections and maintenance, unless its capacity is reduced to below 10 000.

Another club might have quite a different experience. Casterbridge City, for another example, who were promoted with Borchester to the Second Division, find that their local authority gives them a safety certificate before the improvements are undertaken, but advises the club that certain work must be carried out in the near future. Casterbridge then spend the money they might have had to use on all the safety improvements to buy a few star players, and they then do very well the following season. The necessary works are done gradually and as the club can afford them.

These two extreme examples show how differently the Act can be applied. But it should be stressed that in the majority of cases there are few problems between clubs and the authorities. Generally a club will always do as it is told, and if it dislikes some of the recommendations there is usually room for negotiation.

If the club still feels a local authority has been too demanding, they can appeal to the Secretary of State. St Mirren did this and the Scottish Secretary of State overruled the local authority's decisions.

Yet even after a certificate has been granted, there can still be problems. A newly appointed fire officer may be stricter than his predecessor, or may have different theories. To aid this, the Government has, since 1975, asked local authorities to be 'reasonable' in their interpretation of the Green Code.

Here are some fairly typical problems raised by the Act. One designated club found that all its crush barriers were 2 centimetres lower than the minimum height recommended by the Green Code. The authority did not order replacement. Barnsley discovered that it would cost £80 000 to add a further 2000 to their capacity which was hardly worthwhile. Preston ran out of steel for new barriers so accepted a lower capacity. Several clubs, such as Chelsea, Brentford, Bury and York fenced off sections of their terracing, rather than have to pay large sums to maintain their capacities. Falling attendances have meant that capacities have not had to remain so large.

The Green Code
The advisory document is not light reading. For example, the Code advises on terraces and viewing slopes:

15.4.1 The capacity of a terrace or viewing slope should be assessed from the area available for standing (that area of the terrace or viewing slope from which the whole of the playing area can be seen, excluding gangways) by allowing a packing density of between 54 and 27 persons per 10 square metres, depending on the condition of the terrace or slope. For this purpose the extreme allowances are:
a. 54 persons per 10 square metres when the terrace or viewing slope is in good condition (as defined in paragraph 7); and
b. 27 persons per 10 square metres when it materially deviates from the recommended guidelines, so as to constitute a possible hazard to individuals closely packed.
  It may be necessary to interpolate between these figures where conditions fall between the two extremes. When the positioning and width of gangways do not meet with the recommendations of paragraph 7.5.1, an appropriate reduction should be made in the area available for standing.

15.4.2 When crush barriers conform to the recommended guidelines on spacing (see paragraph 12) the capacity of the terrace is calculated by multiplying the area available for standing by the appropriate packing density. The following formula may be used:

$$\text{Capacity (no. of persons)} = \frac{A}{10} \times 27 \text{ or } 54$$

Where A is the area available for standing in square metres.

Putting across the message at Eastville . . . (Adrian Gibson)

. . . at The Den (Adrian Gibson)

. . . at Home Park (Adrian Gibson)

Compare this with the calculation made in the 1947 Report on the Burnden Park disaster. Ground safety nowadays is no longer a matter of simple arithmetic.

The Green Code outlines three basic problems: firstly, hazards to individuals which might cause tripping, slipping and falling are to be avoided by the general construction of the ground. For example, there must be sufficient lighting, strong walls, well maintained gangways and railings, and precautions to stop people climbing structures like floodlight pylons.

Secondly, crowd pressures must be controlled, especially on the terraces and exit routes, by the provision of adequate crush barriers, gates, and stairways.

Thirdly, the ground must be able to handle quick evacuations arising from fires, hooliganism, or any emergency situation. One very obvious recommendation is that all exit doors must be capable of opening outwards. If a stand is made of non-combustible material it should have sufficient gangways and exits to allow for a complete evacuation within eight minutes. If the stand is wooden or otherwise a greater fire risk, that limit is two and a half minutes.

And the best place to evacuate everyone to is the pitch, so there should be no security fences in front of seats.

In addition to some very technical points concerning terracing, gangways, seats, fencing, lighting, flow rates and such like, the Green Code has some advice on crowd control.

Terraces, it recommends, should ideally be divided into self-contained sections, home and away fans should be segregated, as now happens everywhere, and it should no longer be possible to transfer within the ground.

Security fencing should divide standing spectators from the pitch, but allow for the police or first-aid personnel to enter and leave the terracing at certain points.

The cost of all these changes is astronomical, which raises the question of who pays.

Football Grounds Improvement Trust (FGIT)

Had there been no outside help given to football clubs after the passing of the Safety of Sports Grounds Act most would not have coped, so in 1975 the Football Grounds Improvement Trust was set up.

Its role is to give financial aid to clubs who have to carry out safety improvements, but certain conditions were introduced in June 1982 to avoid abuse.

Firstly, the club must notify the FGIT what work is to be carried out. FGIT then sends its own appointed surveyors to assess these plans and decide whether they are necessary for 'spectator safety'. Anything beyond the players' tunnel is not eligible – that is improvements to dressing rooms, directors' lounges, or anything merely concerned with comfort or cosmetic appearance, though naturally a club will often try to convince the surveyors that their plans are of course essential to safety.

If approved by FGIT the work must then be put out to commercial tender. Once completed the work is then inspected by the surveyors, and if in order, FGIT pays the grant. Each designated ground is allowed a total of 60 per cent of the cost, up to a maximum expenditure of £600 000. So that if a club has spent £600 000 it will receive back £360 000. If it has to spend above that amount FGIT will not provide further assistance.

In 1975 the limit was £200 000, since when it has risen progressively to the present amount, so that for example, Blackburn Rovers reached their limit in 1981, but the amount was raised and they were able to spend more thereafter. By mid-1983 only one club had reached the total, Southampton, with Blackburn Rovers just a few thousand pounds below. In Scotland St Mirren had reached their limit, with Celtic just behind.

Some clubs have spent very little. Bristol Rovers, for instance, do not own Eastville and have an uncertain future there, so increased expenditure would not therefore benefit them in the long run.

In addition to helping designated grounds, FGIT also gives aid to Third and Fourth Division grounds, as well as those in the Scottish First and Second Divisions and some in Northern Ireland. The spending limit for non-designated grounds is £400 000, that is, a grant of £240 000. By 1983 all 92 Football League clubs had received some aid, and all but one in Scotland (Airdrie).

FGIT's money comes from the Pools Promoters Association (PPA), which gives 60 per cent of the weekly turnover from its Spot the Ball takings to the Football Trust, which in turn gives FGIT 60 per cent. (The Football Trust was set up to help football at a community level, and has also funded projects like the new railway line to Wembley and an external security system at Villa Park. Littlewoods, the pools company has an influential voice on the Trust.)

Future Problems

While attendances continue to fall the need for further safety improvements will not be so acute. The majority of grounds are now much improved but fewer people are reaping the benefits. Nevertheless, the work of FGIT is by no means over, for there is the distinct possibility that by the mid- to late-1980s the 1975 Act will assume broader control by taking in Third and Fourth Division grounds, plus all other Scottish League grounds and those of Rugby League clubs. If that happens, and there is considerable lobbying to make sure it does not, FGIT's resources are going to be stretched to the limit. As it is, the PPA has no legal obligation to continue giving aid.

Modernizing certain lowly grounds is by no means undesirable, but the costs will again be enormous, and FGIT can only provide grants where the club can supply at least 40 per cent of the outlay. The prospect for smaller clubs is awesome.

Promotion to Division Two can mean financial disaster for clubs with poor grounds, and as the hypothetical example of Borchester United showed, it can have a significant effect on their playing fortunes.

In short, the Act may have made grounds safer, but it made the already precarious task of keeping a football club afloat even more difficult. On the other hand, it is doubtful whether events such as those at Burnden Park and Ibrox Park will ever occur again.

·4·
FLOODLIGHTS

An early floodlit game at the Oval, November 1878. Clapham Rovers v. the Wanderers (BBC Hulton Picture Library)

Two of the most significant developments affecting modern football have been the growth of international air transport and the use of floodlights. Without the former there would be no European Championships, no European club competitions, and considerably smaller World Cup competitions. With floodlights all these extra games have been made possible, and in England and Wales they have allowed the creation of a host of new competitions, notably the League Cup, now the Milk Cup.

Floodlights have brought to an end the long practice of staging mid-week replays in the afternoon, causing thousands of fans to leave their workplaces, officially or on false pretences and whole towns and factories to grind to a halt.

Floodlights meant that Saturday afternoon fixtures could all have the uniform kick-off time of three o'clock, instead of some time between one and two o'clock, depending on when it became dark. No longer would games have to finish in the evening gloom; the ball barely visible against the darkening background.

To the present generation, which knows no other way, it is hard to believe how anyone could possibly object to the introduction of floodlighting. Like goal-nets, the idea seems so obvious and simple. But the idea was vehemently opposed for years, and while some parts of the world became quite accustomed to watching floodlit sport, Britain lagged behind. For instance, Wembley was built at the same time as the Los Angeles Coliseum in 1923 and yet the Coliseum had floodlighting from the very beginning and Wembley not until 1955.

Yet England was probably the first country in the world to have used floodlights for a sporting event. The venue was Bramall Lane, Sheffield, on Monday 14 October 1878. Here is how the *Sheffield Independent*'s reporter described the scene:

'Those who have seen the enclosure under a blaze of a sun, with thousands of excited spectators witnessing the performances of Yorkshire's favourite cricketers, can hardly possess a complete idea of the black wilder-ness it presents by night when there is no moon or the heavens are overcast. To walk there is literally like wandering about a bleak moor, for look which way you will scarcely a light can be seen except it may be from the bedroom windows of an adjoining row of houses.'

Two Sheffield representative teams were billed to play, but the public came to see the spectacle rather than the game. Altogether around 20 000 packed into Bramall Lane for the scheduled 7.00 p.m. kick-off but although the organizers, Messrs Tasker, had lit the pitch, the gates and fences were not illuminated, and only 12 000 people paid to enter, the rest sneaking in under cover of darkness!

Mounted on four wooden towers, one at each cor-ner, the electric floodlights were powered by Siemens dynamos; driven by two 8-horsepower engines be-hind each goal. By 7.30 p.m. they were working, and with their reflectors the lights were hauled up the towers to a height of 30 feet above the ground (the average floodlight pylon nowadays is 100 feet), where they were described as giving out 'a soft blue light . . . under which players could not only play the game but the points were distinctly visible.' It was, said the *Sheffield Independent*, 'a scene of great animation'.

The lights, according to *The Guardian* correspon-dent, were equal to 8000 standard candles, and cost under 4d an hour to operate. Another correspondent from Manchester noted how 'additional fun was now and then caused when a charge was made in the face of the lights and they (the players) became dazzled.' The only real criticisms were that at first the lights were too bright (Mr Tasker solved this before kick-off) and that perhaps the towers were too close to the pitch. Otherwise the experiment was a great success. The crowd had been four times larger than that of the 1878 Cup Final (attendance 4500) and was the first gate higher than 10 000 recorded for a match outside of Glasgow.

Eleven days later there were two more attempts. At Chorley, Lancashire, 8000 people waited two hours in torrential rain before the electrician gave up trying to switch on the lights, while up in Glasgow at Cathkin Park, the lights did work with great success.

But the next game, at the Aston Lower Grounds, Birmingham (now Villa Park) was another flop. This time there were 12 lights spaced evenly around the pitch, but wind and rain led to several of them failing and the game took some time to complete. Two more attempts took place a week later on 4 November, at Accrington and at the Oval where Clapham Rovers played the Wanderers. As in Birmingham the event was not a great success, and significantly there were the first recorded signs of an attitude which the FA was to assume towards floodlighting for the next 80 years. For example, one observer wrote in *Illustrated Sporting and Dramatic News*:

'. . . remembering that the attempt was of necessity an experiment, its comparative failure is no very important matter. Besides who wants to play football by artificial light? As a novelty now and then, or to attract wandering shillings after dark, it may be all very well, but for the real purpose of the game daylight is quite good enough and long enough.'

In the weeks after this, a whole series of floodlit exhibitions was held up and down the country at Crewe, Nottingham, Chorley and Glasgow.

Meanwhile on 25 and 26 November Messrs Moo-tham and Barnes held bicycle races and football under lights in Dean Park, Bournemouth (next to the present ground). On 27 November the show moved to Southampton's Antelope Ground, but heavy rain forced postponement until the following night, when a rugby match was played.

After this series of matches either the novelty wore off or promoters felt they were not reaping sufficient profits to carry on. Certainly we read very little of floodlit games until 1887 when the FA gave permis-sion for two floodlit games to be held in Sheffield. Note that the FA by then deemed this a matter for its control. Then on 26 February 1889, the two leading Manchester clubs, Newton Heath and Ardwick (later Manchester United and City respectively) played a floodlit match at Belle Vue, thereby raising £140 for the Hyde Colliery Explosion Fund.

What is interesting about this match was that instead of using electric light, illumination was pro-vided by Wells' lights, a system which was to prove popular over the next decade of floodlit football. For example, eight Wells' lights were used at Clee Park in April 1889 for exhibition matches between Grimsby and Boston. As one advertisement for a match in Glasgow said: 'This light has the reputation of being possessed of the finest illuminating properties,' and is 'excellently adapted . . . for the purposes of out-door recreation.'

Light was produced by pumping inflammable oil under high air pressure to a burner, creating a flare. But it needed a great deal of attention and much oil. One match at Turf Moor in 1891 was lit by 16 Wells' lights, which used up 140 gallons of creosote oil, and one can readily imagine the acrid smells that must have drifted across the pitch. The barrels of oil were also a fire risk.

Celtic tried another form of floodlighting in 1892. Their idea was to string a series of lamps on ropes hung 50 feet above the pitch, but inevitably the ball kept hitting them. Another idea was to follow the ball with a spotlight!

Spotting the ball was in fact a major problem, for although the players could wear bright colours, leather in those days was leather, dark and brown, especially in wet weather. One way to solve this was to have a number of balls on hand and keep dipping them in whitewash. As the white wore off, another ball would be thrown on! This was the method used at a testimonial match played under Wells' lights for Blackburn's forward Jack Southworth, at Ewood Park on 31 October 1892, watched by 8000.

Floodlights continued to be something of a curiosity in this country until after the First World War, with the FA definitely opposed to clubs using them for anything but friendlies or charity games. But abroad, and especially in the Americas floodlighting was becoming a regular feature at stadiums, for baseball, grid-iron football, and in South America for soccer. Advances in technology made powerful and more reliable electric lighting possible, and of course in hot climates it was preferable to play matches at night when the air was cooler. So while in Britain the only floodlit games were exhibition events, for example a ladies' match at Turf Moor in 1924, elsewhere they were being taken very seriously indeed.

The FA's response to the growing demand for action was quite simple – in August 1930 it placed a complete ban on any member clubs taking part in a floodlit match. (It was not just floodlights of which they disapproved. Other innovations such as the numbering of players or entering the World Cup were equally scorned.) Not everyone was happy to let the matter rest however. Herbert Chapman, the Arsenal manager argued (among several of his progressive ideas) for the introduction of modern floodlighting to Britain.

After visiting Belgium in 1930 he wrote:

'The field was illuminated by lights fixed to five standards running down one side behind the spectators. From each standard the rays of 20 powerful lamps were thrown

Going through the roof at Burnden Park (Ged Murray)

across the pitch at different angles, and as they intersected and spread they did not leave a dark or even a dull patch . . . I wished that the public at home could always have such a good view.'

In Austria Chapman saw another floodlit game, played under the lights of car headlamps, and decided on his return to install some lights on Arsenal's training pitch behind Highbury. A railway company provided the equipment, and Chapman was so sure that the idea would catch on that he invited the press to come and see his 'lanterns'. The reporters were cool about the idea, saying it was too cold at night to expect the public to attend. But Chapman believed that night matches would attract more people away from the growing popularity of greyhound racing, which swept London in the late 1920s and early 1930s. He even went as far as putting lights on the stands for training purposes, but again the FA banned its use for official matches. (I am indebted for this information to Stephen Studd, author of Chapman's biography.)

Tottenham were also pressing for the FA to lift its ban. They called a meeting of every London club, with the result that the FA permitted a floodlit match to take place at White City, by then, the top greyhound stadium in London and also being used by

QPR. The match was played on 4 January 1933 between two representative teams from London clubs, in front of a very disappointing crowd of 12 000. The old bucket of whitewash trick was still in use even then (strangely enough Chapman had tried white balls and dismissed them as a gimmick!).

After this relatively unsuccessful trial the idea lay dormant once more. Chapman died in 1934, and as Britain was hit by the Depression it was felt that most clubs would not be able to afford lights anyway. Typical of the official view was the opinion of Sir Frederick Wall of the FA. He wrote in 1935:

'Clubs cannot do just as they like – even if they desire floodlight football. That may be in the future. I cannot easily predict an era when the sorcerers of science may easily turn night into day as they now talk to a man on the other side of the world.'

Immediately after the Second World War however, the argument for floodlights began to gather momentum. Attendances were reaching an all time high, and industry could ill afford to have its workforce taking afternoons off to watch football. But even if the FA had given its approval it is doubtful whether many clubs could have obtained the necessary material until rationing and austerity measures eased.

One advocate of floodlights was Liverpool, who went on a summer tour of the United States in 1946 and on their return suggested setting up a mid-week floodlit league. A few years later Southampton and Arsenal also undertook foreign tours and reached similar conclusions. Eventually the FA withdrew the ban in December 1950.

Small semi-professional teams led the way. In 1949 South Liverpool played a floodlit friendly v. a Nigerian XI in front of 13 000 spectators at their Holly Park ground. Of the present Football League clubs, the first was Headington United, who played Banbury Spencer under floodlights on 18 December 1950, in aid of a local children's charity. Mounted on individual wooden poles around the pitch were 36 lamps, borrowed from various buildings in Oxford which had their walls lit up at night for effect. Only 2603 attended the game, but other clubs soon heard about Headington's trial installation and there started a steady stream of League clubs, large and small, asking to play matches at the Manor Ground and ask advice from the Headington directors.

Among the visitors were Brentford, Cardiff, Tottenham, Charlton, Fulham, Northampton, QPR, Millwall, Colchester, Leyton Orient, Watford and Wolves. But the first club to act on what they had seen at Oxford was Swindon Town, then in Division Three South. Town were the first League club to install lights, eight behind each goal, first used on 2 April 1951 for an exhibition match v. Bristol City.

In January 1951 the FA had added a qualifying clause to its original lifting of the ban. This stated that no competitive matches were to be played under floodlights without permission from the FA or the County FA and the organizers of the competition concerned.

Not surprisingly Arsenal was the next club to install lights, and at Highbury, with two stands of the same design and height on either side of the pitch, installation was relatively simple. The first game was a friendly v. Hapoel Tel Aviv in September 1951.

But the first test of the new FA ruling came weeks later when Southampton asked the Football Combination for permission to stage a reserve match at The Dell under their £600 lights, installed a few months before but used only for training. The Combination gave their approval, and on Monday, 1 October 1951 the first competitive football match under floodlights was played in Britain. An enthusiastic crowd of 13 654 attended the match, and as the Southampton manager, Sid Cann remarked the following day, 'Floodlit soccer has come to stay'.

On 17 October Highbury staged their second exhibition match, this time the annual challenge match v. Glasgow Rangers, watched by a huge crowd of 62 500.

At the end of the month The Dell staged another competitive game, a Hampshire Combination Cup tie between Southampton and Portsmouth, watched by 22 697. Then in Scotland, in the apparently unlikely surroundings of Ochilview Park, Stenhousemuir staged the first Scottish floodlit match in modern times, a friendly v. Hibernian on 7 November 1951.

Floodlit matches still took time to spread. Indeed the last Football League club to install lights was Chesterfield, in 1967, and in Scotland Stranraer was the last, in August 1981.

After 1951, the next major development was the staging of floodlit games against European opposition, an important factor in the subsequent organization of the European Cup in 1955. Wolves were the best known of the floodlight pioneers. After switching on their lights in September 1953, they played famous games against Honved of Hungary (December 1954), Moscow Spartak and Moscow Dynamo. Tottenham Hotspur switched on their lights with a friendly v. Racing Club de Paris, also in September 1953. And significantly in Scotland, Hibernian were the first British team to enter the European Cup, having switched on their lights in October 1954.

Not only had the floodlit era begun, but so had a whole new era of international club football.

The next stage was for the FA to allow FA Cup matches to be held under lights. Permission had already been refused Headington, who wanted to stage their replay v. Millwall in 1953–54 under lights, a decision which drew national attention (see Oxford), but eventually in February 1955 it was decided that the following season floodlights could be used for replays up to and including the Second Round. The first was Kidderminster Harriers v.

Brierley Hill Alliance in a Preliminary Round on 14 September 1955.

The first such match to involve two League clubs was Carlisle v. Darlington, a First Round replay played at St James' Park, Newcastle on 28 November 1955. Two days later Wembley had its first taste of international floodlit action when the lights were switched on for the last 15 minutes of the England v. Spain match, because of fog (although England had already played one complete game under lights, v. USA in New York on 8 June 1953).

Then in December 1955 the FA relaxed its rules even further by stating that Third Round ties played on 7 January could be played all or in part under lights, which is what happened at Highbury, Fratton Park, Hillsborough, White Hart Lane and the Boleyn Ground.

Meanwhile, the Football League had been having its own discussions on the matter. At the annual meeting in June 1955 Sunderland proposed that post-poned League matches be played under floodlights if both clubs agreed. This was adopted, although at the time only 36 League clubs actually had lights.

The Football League's big night came on Wednes-day, 22 February 1956, at Fratton Park, with Ports-mouth scheduled to play their postponed Division One match v. Newcastle. The whole country had been submerged in snow, Fratton Park's pitch was rock hard, and it was a bitterly cold night. Nevertheless, the evening represented a significant breakthrough, and was greeted enthusiastically by almost every-one. *The Times* correspondent, for example, seemed particularly inspired:

Old and new lights at Spotland (Ged Murray)

'. . . there arose a vision of the future. In 20, even 10 years time, will all football be play-ed under the stars and moon? There is much to recommend it. There is a dramatic, the-atrical quality about it. The pace of the game seems accentuated, flowering patterns of approach play take on sharper, more colour-ful outlines. In the background of the night the dark, surrounding crowd, half shadow, yet flesh and blood, can produce the effect of a thousand fire-flies as cigarette lights spurt forth.'

And it was true. Floodlit football did have a different edge to it.

But the players themselves were not so keen, or at least that was the impression they gave. For them, floodlit football meant working nights, travelling at more unsociable hours, and adjusting to a new set of conditions. They were earning little enough as it was, in their view if not their employers', so after the Fratton Park game the Players Union banned its members from playing in floodlit games from 13 March onwards. Just two days before that date, however, the League agreed to consider their extra wage demands, and in June the players were told

that an extra £2 to £3 would be paid for every player taking part in a floodlit game.

At the same time the Football League relaxed its rules by allowing any League match to be played under lights, as long as both clubs agreed. Yet still only 38 of the 92 clubs had floodlights.

Two years later, at the annual meeting in June 1958, the final restriction on League games was lifted – that is, it would no longer be necessary to obtain the agreement of the other club for staging a floodlit game – but the League did state that clubs' lights would have to be of a sufficiently high standard for League fixtures, and several installations were obviously not.

Indeed the standards varied enormously. Some clubs still had individual lights on wooden poles around the ground, while more were replacing their original systems with four corner pylons. Costs were naturally rising all the time. Sunderland's four 75-feet pylons with a total power of 72 kilowatts cost £7000 in 1952, but by 1956 Stockport were paying £17 000 for only a slightly more powerful set of lights.

Not everyone was convinced about floodlights, and there were still several teething problems to over-come. Many club chairmen saw lights as a passing fad and would not invest funds to buy them, leaving in most cases the supporters' clubs to raise the money. The view of Gillingham's Vice-Chairman was quite typical. 'I don't think there is any future in it at all,' he said, 'the novelty will wear off soon.' In one sense he was right, the public soon became accustomed to floodlit games, and attendances gradually reduced to a level more in keeping with afternoon games.

The difficulty of spotting the ball was less acute by this time, because developments in the treating of leather soon made orange and white balls quite commonplace. But floodlights did present a problem concerning kit. Clubs found they had to use lighter shirts to be visible, not only to the crowd but to their own players. Glossy, new, synthetic shirts appeared as a result.

But what about the match officials, still in their all-black strips? They were the least visible against dark backgrounds. For one match, Tommy Lawton's testimonial at Goodison Park, the referee and linesmen wore specially made fluorescent shirts, and although the experiment was favourably received, the idea was never taken further.

Another problem was reliability and design. All kinds of technical problems arose during the first decade of floodlit football. Lights failed, or were misdirected by the wind. Some lights were too low and dazzled the crowd and the players. Doncaster's for example, had to be low in order to avoid glare for pilots landing at the adjacent airfield. Clubs found that as technology advanced they were having to replace their installations every few years to maintain standards.

And finally, floodlit football created one difficulty for journalists. Afternoon games presented no deadline problems, but a game finishing at 9.00 p.m. or later, demanded a whole new school of reporting, concentrating on the first half's action with a hastily added final score at the end. Never had there been such a scramble for the telephones.

As the 1950s wore on and more clubs had lights, there were suggestions for new competitions to be played solely on mid-week evenings, for example, a Southern Floodlit Cup and an Anglo-Scottish Floodlight League, neither of which materialized. One suggestion did find root however. The proposed Football League Floodlight Cup was adopted in 1960, but under the name of the Football League Cup. All its games were played mid-week, and most therefore under floodlights, and it was only from 1966 onwards that the Final was played on a Saturday afternoon when the venue was switched to Wembley.

When the League Cup began, 68 League cups had floodlights and only two in the First Division were without – Forest and Fulham.

But the existence of this potential money spinner inspired a rush of clubs to get lights installed. Seven clubs had them put in by October 1960, and by the end of 1961 only a handful of clubs were still without. The last two clubs in the League to install lights were

Hartlepool in 1965 and Chesterfield in October 1967.

Floodlighting involves several factors which may seem surprising to the average spectator. For example, the way the pitch has been rolled can actually affect the illumination as can the turf's moisture content, colour and condition. The placement of stands is important, explaining why some clubs have light pylons tucked into the corner of the pitch while others have them high up on roofs or embankments. Luton Town wanted to have corner pylons but had so little room that each pylon would have had to be ridiculously tall, so they had to opt for shorter ones along each side. Some grounds now have lights along the eaves of the stands, or hung underneath them, as at Goodison Park, The Dell, Anfield, Arsenal and Ibrox. This is cheaper to install and easier to maintain, but can cause glare to spectators opposite, and to television cameras. But worst of all they make it very hard to find the grounds! There is no better homing guide for any traveller than the sight of distant floodlight pylons.

The demands of colour television, accompanied by significant advances in lighting technology have meant that several top grounds now have lights up to four times more powerful than before. Measurement is now in lux, a term for lumens per square foot. This indicates how much light is available on the working plain, but because we look at the players and the ball, the measurement usually taken is one or one and a half metres above pitch level. Television needs a level of about 800 lux for adequate colour coverage, though for long lens close-ups they prefer up to 1400 lux. The minimum UEFA requirement for their matches is 750 lux. Modern lamps last much longer than the older types (about 1000 hours compared with 200 hours), cost less to run, but are very expensive to replace. A Thorn CSI sealed beam lamp, as used at Old Trafford and other large grounds for example, costs about £106 to replace.

Despite the advances, there is still a wide disparity between some League grounds, from the tallest pylons at Elland Road to the simple poles at Exeter. Several top clubs have threatened not to play Cup replays at smaller grounds because of the lower level of lighting. This should become less of a problem as the lamps themselves become more powerful and therefore fewer are needed.

It has taken almost a century to get this far, but despite the earlier misgivings there is no doubt that floodlighting has contributed a great deal to football in Britain and world-wide. It remains to be seen whether other ideas such as artificial turf and covered stadiums will take another hundred years to gain acceptance. The experience of floodlighting suggests that sooner rather than later would be to everyone's advantage.

·5·
PITCHES AND POSTS

Groundstaff at Tottenham laying down 3000 bales of straw to combat frost in 1925 (BBC Hulton Picture Library)

The development of grounds' fixtures and fittings has been mainly a matter of experimentation and luck, shaped along the way by a series of random decisions.

Today, over a century after the birth of the FA, it is hard to see how the basic concept of pitch, goals and nets might be changed. Technological advance may allow the use of new materials, but the shape and form seem almost sacrosanct. For this reason, while all around, grandstands, players' kit, spectators, tactics and customs change with every season, the fixtures and fittings needed for a game of football are the most dependable constant we have.

Pitches

In common with cricket, rugby and hockey, football pitches can vary greatly in size, as long as the so called 'appurtenances' are of the required dimen-

sions; that is the penalty area, goal area and centre circle.

When the first sets of laws were drawn up, each group of rule-makers deliberated according to the facilities they had available, so that Harrow School stipulated a maximum length of 150 yards and a maximum width of 110 yards, while Winchester's rules stated a pitch measurement of 80 × 27 yards. They also required that 'the ground is to be of good level turf'. Eton's early footballers had no such luxuries. Their eighteenth-century wall game was played on a patch 120 yards long but only 6 yards wide.

The first set of FA rules, drawn up in December 1863, stated that the playing surface should be a maximum of 200 × 100 yards, to be marked off with flag-poles (rather than pitch markings).

As the game became more organized and the

crowds bigger, pitch markings were introduced in 1882, but only to mark the four boundaries. A half-way line was then added, not only for kick-offs but also to mark the extent to which a goalkeeper could handle the ball! Incredibly the goalkeeper was confined to handling the ball only within the penalty area as late as 1912.

By 1887 there was a centre circle, and two 6-yard semi-circles in front of each goal from which goal-kicks could be taken. A line 12 yards from the goal-line was added for penalty kicks, introduced after a suggestion from the Irish FA in 1890, and behind this was a shorter 18-yard line behind which players had to stand when the kicks were taken. Originally the penalty kick was taken from any point on the 12-yard line and the goalkeeper could advance 6 yards from the goal-line. The minimum distance an opponent could stand from a free-kick was 6 yards.

Finally in 1902 the more familiar markings of today were adopted, and have remained the same with just one addition – the penalty arc, brought to this country from the continent in 1937, when the minimum distance from free-kicks was raised to 10 yards.

At this stage of the pitch's evolution, only one feature had survived from the earliest laws, the corner flag, and only one change to the present pitch markings has been seriously suggested since. This was the addition of offside lines 35 yards from each goal-line. The idea originated in the United States, where soccer often had to take place on the narrower grid-iron pitches, and it was felt that by reducing the area in which a player could be offside would improve tactics and create more goals. It does have some advantages, in that play is less concentrated in the middle third of the pitch, but Britain and the FIFA have essentially been unimpressed by the US innovation.

The current rules concerning pitch dimensions date back to 1887 and apply to all League clubs. They state that the length of the pitch should be a minimum of 100 yards (90 metres), a maximum of 130 yards (120 metres) in length, and a minimum of 50 yards (45 metres), a maximum of 100 yards (90 metres) in width, as long as the pitch is rectangular (that is, not 100×100 yards (90×90 metres)).

For international matches however, a slightly narrower margin is required: between 110 and 120 yards (100 and 110 metres) length and 70 and 80 yards (64 and 75 metres) width. In fact, every one of the 92 Football League grounds and all but ten in Scotland come within those narrower margins, albeit some only just.

The exact half-way points of both national and international sets of measurements represent a pitch 115×75 yards (105×69.5 metres), and it is no surprise to find that this is the most popular dimension found at top-class football grounds. Apart from Wembley and Hampden Park, 13 grounds are this size, including all three Birmingham clubs, Ibrox and

Celtic Parks, St James' Park and Hillsborough.

The League's biggest pitch used to be at Belle Vue, Doncaster, until the manager decided to lop off 8 yards, so now Maine Road is the largest, measuring 119×79 yards, or 9401 square yards in area. But Maine Road is neither the longest nor the widest pitch. The County Ground, Northampton is the longest, 120 yards, while Edgar Street, Hereford is the widest, 80 yards. Generally, pitches are now much smaller than they were before the First World War, when, for example, the City Ground and the Priestfield Stadium had playing surfaces measuring 120×80 yards. The extra yards were used for expanding terraces and also the increasing number of running tracks laid down for training. But some grounds were big enough for large pitches and tracks. The Hawthorns originally had a pitch 127×87 yards, with a 9-foot wide cinder track.

The smallest pitches in the Football League are at Eastville, the Vetch Field and The Shay, each measuring 110×70 yards, or 7700 square yards in area. Imagine therefore the physical and psychological differences between playing on these grounds and at Maine Road, which is 1701 square yards larger, or the equivalent of a stretch of turf 120 feet square. When you are fighting for breath it is an appreciable amount.

It might be concluded therefore that the proportions of a pitch have a marked effect on the style a team might adopt, but this does not seem to be the case. For example, the flying wingers of the Wolves in the 1950s had a field only 72 yards wide, exactly the same as that of the Boleyn Ground, and yet West Ham's ground is generally thought to be narrow and cramped. And neither Manchester City nor Hereford United have been renowned for consistently producing first-class wingers.

The design of the ground is far more important to one's perception of pitch size than its dimensions. One would never have thought Highbury's pitch to be small – it is such an uncluttered, grand stadium – and yet the pitch is actually a fraction smaller than those at West Ham, Luton and Southampton, and is the smallest League pitch in London! Similarly we talk of the wide open spaces of Wembley, but never of Cambridge, even though the playing surfaces are of equal size.

In Scotland pitches are generally much smaller. Indeed the largest, at Hampden, Ibrox and Celtic Parks are equal to the average English size of 115×75 yards, or 8625 square yards. The smallest Scottish pitches are very much smaller than the smallest in England. For example, Brechin City's pitch, the smallest in Scotland, is 110×67 yards, or 7370 square yards, which is 2031 square yards smaller than Maine Road. But Montrose have an even narrower pitch – just 66 yards wide, and Hamilton's is shorter, at 104 yards long. There is, therefore, a considerable variety of shapes and sizes. However, there are very few instances of clubs who have failed

Waterlogged pitch at Tottenham in 1937 (BBC Hulton Picture Library)

to meet the requirements set down by the FA concerning pitches, the prime examples being Exeter between 1908–11 and Clapton Orient in 1930, when their pitches were either too short or too narrow.

The most important factor is quality rather than quantity; I mention the statistics in this section mainly to emphasize the importance of architecture and design to one's image of a football ground. The numbers game can otherwise be a misleading diversion.

Turf Technology

Having decided the dimensions of the pitch, how can the actual playing surface be improved? In the early years teams were quite happy to find a reasonable patch of grass in a public park, but once they asked spectators to pay to watch, it was only right that they should provide the best possible surface on which to display their talents.

Yet even today some top clubs are guilty of concentrating a disproportionate amount of funds on transfer fees and executive boxes, to the detriment of the turf, and to the ridiculous extent that one leading First Division club, having spent a few million pounds to assemble a team, would not spend £3500 on a new lawnmower. In other cases clubs have spent large sums on sophisticated new pitches but then only the bare minimum on vital maintenance. Much depends on the circumstances of the club and the ground. To sustain a good playing surface needs

money, but more than that it needs expertise and dedication.

The location of a ground is also crucial. A groundsman in an area of high rainfall has a much harder job than his counterpart in a drier region with a milder climate: so between Lancashire and Suffolk there is a significant difference. The height of the ground and its proximity to rivers can also have a marked effect on the quality of the pitch and the level of maintenance needed.

Stadium design is important. Every pitch needs natural ventilation and sunlight, but tall stands and completely enclosed grounds hinder both. The shadows from a stand can make one side of the pitch hard and threadbare while the other side is perfect.

But perhaps the most significant feature of a pitch lies underground, in the sub-structure and drainage, and when the Sports Turf Research Institute in Bingley, Yorkshire, conducted a survey of League grounds in 1982, 50 per cent only of the clubs replying could give any details of their drainage system. And yet the most common cause of postponed matches is a waterlogged pitch.

In the early days of League football, conditions were quite different. There are reports of steeply sloping pitches, as at WBA, surfaces as hard as pavements, as at Newton Heath, and methods of maintenance which seem positively ridiculous by today's standards. A favourite remedy for waterlogged pitches was to smother the surface with straw. In 1893 Gillingham bought 2 tons of coconut fibre to solve their watery problems, while Newcastle once tried to melt frost by laying down straw and setting fire to it. Once the fires got going, rain started falling and left the pitch a glutinous morass. United therefore covered the whole lot in sand!

To make matters worse, in many cases football pitches were used for a variety of other events – fêtes, parades, athletics, and most common of all, for grazing animals. A player launching himself into a sliding tackle had no guarantee of what he might land in! Grazing was allowed because it brought in much needed revenue, and it saved on cutting the grass.

There was also much greater access to the pitch from the terracing, so that before and after matches it was quite easy for hundreds of people to wander across the turf. Then during the week the pitch became the team's training ground. (Nowadays even the humblest clubs can find somewhere else to train for at least a couple of days a week, while those with their own training grounds need never set foot on the pitch at all between home games.) In the early years therefore, the standard of playing surfaces was well below that to which we are accustomed now.

So many clubs had had to construct pitches on what had been waste grounds or refuse tips that it was often a mammoth task just to level the surface. The most effective sub-layer for drainage was clinker – the burnt ash residue from coal. Tons of this dirty, black substance were dumped on grounds all over the country, not only on the pitch but on the running tracks and to cover the terracing. In only a very few cases was the natural soil suitable for drainage, and even when it was the ground had still to be levelled, so that no pitch is truly 'natural'.

The value of a cambered surface was also realized, one of the first being at Burnden Park in 1895. Gibson and Pickford commented that the pitch had: 'a curious whale-back surface so that those sitting at one side of the ground only have the upper half of the players on the opposite wing in their vision.' They go on to state rather dubiously that this must be something to do with the drainage.

In fact Burnden Park's camber is still very pronounced, but the usual crown is about a foot higher in the centre circle than on the wings, and is often most noticeable along the bye-line where the turf rises up towards each goal post.

Installing proper drains underneath the pitch was another new idea, although the drains themselves were useless if the sub-soil was impervious or the top surface compacted. Often the drains would collapse or crack in extreme winter conditions, leaving puddles and damp patches. Very few clubs enjoyed the services of a full-time, trained groundsman. It was often left up to the trainer or a few unemployed labourers on a Saturday morning to give the pitch a quick forking over. In return, the men would be given free admission in the afternoon. During the Second

World War it was quite common for prisoners of war to be commandeered in the event of snow. Just before the Second World War the Wolves' manager Major Buckley tried to gain an advantage for his players by watering the Molineux pitch during the winter, because he felt they were at their best on heavy grounds, and that the ball was too lively on hard pitches. The FA did not approve of this, and allowed watering between March and October only.

Another short-lived idea in the 1930s was a spray developed at the Baseball Ground which melted frost. Herbert Chapman went especially to Derby during the hard winter of 1933 to see the spray in use, but found that the frost soon returned within an hour or so.

In the 1950s Arsenal tried undersoil heating using electric wires, while both Liverpool clubs abandoned early attempts at heating and had to reconstruct their pitches. Nowadays most undersoil systems are oil powered, with hot-water pipes to melt the frost and drain pipes to carry off the excess water, and there is absolutely no doubt that the system works very effectively. In the winter of 1982 it was noticeable that Maine Road's pitch was in regular use, while Old Trafford suffered postponements. City had undersoil heating, United did not.

But the system is expensive. In 1982 the undersoil heating at Maine Road cost £4500 to operate during the season. Oldham Athletic paid £8000 (although Boundary Park is on high ground and suffers more from the cold). Everton's bill was £5500. Yet there is no point in heating a pitch if the terraces and approaches to the ground are still ice-bound and too dangerous to use, and the public is unlikely to want to spend an afternoon or evening in the freezing cold.

Another idea was to protect pitches from above, by enormous plastic sheets draped over the turf. Leicester City installed a 'tent' which covered 90 000 square feet and was raised by means of blowers. These not only melted the frost but also allowed the players to train underneath, albeit in rather claustrophobic circumstances. Nottingham Forest and Aston Villa also installed plastic pitch covers. But none of these systems achieved what was hoped of them. The plastic tears easily and if the covers stay on too long there is a danger of fungus growing on the actual turf. They are mainly useful for protecting the pitch against rain for a few hours before kick-off, and after a heavy snowfall are quicker to clear than grass. But the cold air can still penetrate and allow frost to set in, so they are only about 40 per cent effective.

The pitch of today gets very little use. In the First Division typical usage is four hours a week, and even in the lower divisions the average is only five to seven hours. If it was not for bad weather therefore, all the grounds would have almost perfect playing surfaces.

So how has turf technology developed to cope with the British climate? The Sports Turf Research Institute (STRI) is the main centre of research in this country, and was set up in 1929 to help not only

Polythene balloon, supported by a cushion of hot air, hovers above Filbert Street's pitch – a miracle cure which did not catch on (Syndication International)

football but much tougher customers like crown green bowling, cricket, lawn tennis and golf. It is a non-profit making body funded by a grant from the Sports Council, with research commissioned by the Department of the Environment. It gives advice to local parks and professional clubs, from Hackney Marshes to Wembley Stadium.

In May 1982 the FA and the Football Trust helped the STRI set up a laboratory to research the particular needs of football, the results of which will have a significant effect on football grounds in the future. The Institute studies types of grass, methods of irrigation, fertilization and drainage. It even tests turf for ball bounce. (There is as yet no standard factor of 'ball bounce', but the usual is about 30 to 35 per cent, meaning that a ball dropped from a height of 10 metres will bounce to a height of 3 to 3.5 metres.)

The researchers also have a machine to test wear and tear with different types of stud. It measures the vertical forces which produce compaction of the turf, and horizontal forces which tear the surface as, for example, would a sliding tackle.

There are three different types of pitch. The simplest, which has the minimum amount of drainage, would cost about £8500 to install, and is sufficient for perhaps local authority usage of up to three hours play a week. A better pitch with sand-slitted drain-

Ground sharing at Elland Road. Notice the fine old stand of the greyhound stadium in the distance, sadly now demolished (Adrian Gibson)

age could cost £17000, but could withstand up to nine hours a week. Sand-slitting is a system whereby every 2 feet a slit 2 inches wide is cut into the turf, filled with sand which carries the excess water down through a gravel channel to the sub-layer of slightly coarser gravel underneath. The advantages of the system are that it is cheaper and involves less reconstruction, but it can if badly installed create small dips in the surface. Also, if the turf is torn, or sheared, the sand-slit will be covered, or capped, and therefore make the drainage inoperative.

The Rolls Royce of pitches is a sand-ameliorated construction, which has an 80 per cent base of sand on a gravel carpet. This costs about £50000 to install, but can be used up to 20 hours a week. Portman Road and Ewood Park both have such a pitch, and it is no coincidence that both are highly commended by players. There is one at the FA coaching centre in Lilleshall which supports 40 hours a week.

But no matter how well the pitch is constructed, if it is not tended properly it will spoil rapidly. An example of this is at Elland Road, where in 1970 the new pitch was probably the best in the country. A variety of factors since then have combined to lower its standard, the main one being lack of money.

For instance the best way to cure a waterlogged pitch is to apply sand to the surface. Sand helps to break up a clogged top surface and thereby allows the water to filter down into the drains. But sand now costs up to £7 a ton, and if 100 tons are needed it might be cheaper to postpone, especially if a low attendance is forecast. But Leeds' problems go further.

To ease its financial problems, the club hired out Elland Road for a rock concert in the summer of 1982. Groundsmen never like this sort of event, because sound equipment is very heavy and the pitch is usually filled by thousands of people. As other clubs discovered, the effect of this is to compact the turf so much that water cannot be absorbed. Wembley Stadium suffered in a similar way after the Pope's visit.

The next season Elland Road became one of the football grounds being shared with Rugby League clubs. Rugby League itself does not spoil the turf. In fact groundsmen at Fulham, Cardiff and Carlisle have found that soccer causes much more damage, especially in concentrated areas in the centre and goalmouths. Rugby is more evenly spread and despite the tackling does not shear the grass as badly. Nevertheless, Elland Road's pitch was being used twice as much, but receiving far less care and attention. And so the recession had set up a vicious circle.

Leeds are by no means the only club to have suffered in this way. The trend suggests that more and more clubs are cutting back on turf maintenance as one of their first economizing measures.

Which is why artificial turf is so tempting a prospect. Consider the facts: the maximum reasonable usage of a high quality natural surface is perhaps 20 hours a week. A synthetic surface has unlimited use, not merely for sport but for exhibitions, concerts, and even markets. It allows a football ground to be used every day of the week, and therefore offers a hard-pressed club (and every club is hard-pressed) a chance to make some money.

If only it was that simple.

Artificial surfaces are not new. In 1906 a man called E. Cleary drew up a scheme to play indoor football matches at Olympia in London, under electric light and on a synthetic grass mat, reputed to have cost £5000. The FA naturally disapproved most strongly, but it need not have worried because the scheme was a complete flop. Indoor football itself was not uncommon; for example the two Nottingham clubs played each other annually in a large indoor hall for many years before the First World War. But unnatural surfaces were anathema.

The modern generation of synthetic turfs began with an embarrassing mistake in Houston, Texas. The Houston Astrodome, which likes to call itself the eighth wonder of the world, was the first and largest indoor stadium built for major sport. It was opened in 1965, with a natural grass surface. Unfortunately, the glass skylight panels in the domed roof had to be painted in order to reduce the glare of sunlight on the field, and as a result the grass could not prosper, and the pitch soon became a dusty, dry and hard surface.

Fortunately for the owners, the Chemstrand Company was able to develop a new artificial grass, which on installation in March 1966 became known as 'Astroturf'. So was launched 'a new and wondrous era in recreational engineering', in the words of Houston Judge Roy Hofheinz, whose idea the Astrodome was. A year later Astroturf was developed for use outdoors, and all over the United States stadium authorities began to rip up their turf and lay down the revolutionary plastic grass. By 1970 there were 27 Astroturf pitches, and by 1975 it was widespread for baseball, grid iron football and soccer.

Other chemical companies took up the idea, and a decade later Astroturf was already obsolete. It had a reputation for causing burns, for putting players' joints at risk, and above all for taking the element of unpredictability out of the game – whatever the game. Also after ten years' use it needed replacement, by which time the newer types of synthetic surface had ironed out some of the problems.

But not all, which leads us to Loftus Road, the first League ground to have installed an artificial surface. QPR chose a £350000 system called Omniturf, already popular around the world and even used for a tennis court at Wimbledon. Omniturf is a sand-filled surface with grass made out of polypropylene fibre. Rangers wanted it to be strong enough to withstand not just regular sporting activity but also rock concerts and even performing circus elephants. But with the technology advancing so rapidly, it was in many ways a calculated risk, because Omniturf had not been tested in this country for football. Its main success had been in the United States.

Firstly, although the Football League gave its approval for an initial three-year period (1981–84), the FA was far from happy (shades of 1906), and there was a possibility that it would not permit Cup matches to be played on the new surface. Eventually permission was granted, although UEFA has yet to be confronted.

At first Loftus Road buzzed with activity. On one day alone three football games were held: a youth match, and two senior non-League fixtures. There was a four-nation hockey festival (artificial grass is particularly well suited to hockey), a London rugby Sevens' competition, and plans galore for pop concerts, US football and baseball matches. But the dream did not come true. Loftus Road was not in use every day of the week, and the rest of the footballing fraternity did not seem particularly amused by the thought of Rangers bringing their Omniturf with them into the First Division in 1983–84.

But QPR's experience has demonstrated several interesting points. Firstly, although expensive to install, artificial surfaces can be used in all weathers and need virtually no maintenance. The Loftus Road pitch needs irrigation to stop the sand blowing away and to keep the drains in working order, but apart from clearing away litter, no groundsman is needed.

Secondly, an artificial surface is no more of a hazard to players than is natural turf. Indeed the QPR's club doctor considers Omniturf to have a slight superiority to grass. Although there is a risk of burns these clear up very quickly, and the major problem seems to be sore feet. Some players attribute poor performances to Omniturf, while others think it marvellous. What evidence there is of long term physical damage to players comes from the United States, is hardly scientific, and certainly inadequate to draw any conclusions. QPR's club doctor reckoned that tennis players have to endure very similar physical demands throughout their careers and there have been no proven ill effects of their playing on harder surfaces.

Thirdly, it is not wholly true to suggest that Omniturf or any artificial surface distorts the nature of football. Certainly they require a different approach, but many people, such as Malcolm Allison and Lawrie McMenemy, believe that the pitch can have a beneficial effect. It encourages skill, gives a truer reflection of a player's ability to control the ball, and reduces the purely physical elements of the game. And as David Miller of *The Times* wrote: 'The variations of conditions is one of the fascinations of sport. Wimbledon is Wimbledon precisely because it differs from the wood, plastic, shale and above all the slow clay of Paris . . .' He adds that if Rangers have a slight advantage in playing regularly on the pitch, should we also say the same of Arsenal and Manchester City because they enjoy undersoil heating? 'Vive la difference!' writes Miller. And after all, clubs have to play on it only once a season.

At £350000 a go it is unlikely that many League

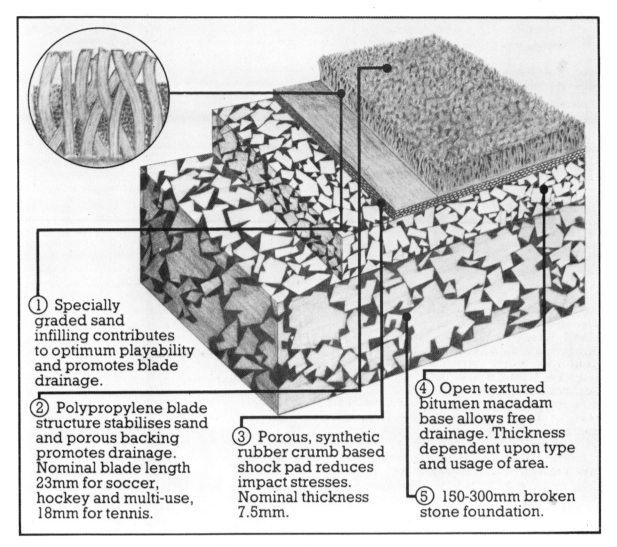

1. Specially graded sand infilling contributes to optimum playability and promotes blade drainage.

2. Polypropylene blade structure stabilises sand and porous backing promotes drainage. Nominal blade length 23mm for soccer, hockey and multi-use, 18mm for tennis.

3. Porous, synthetic rubber crumb based shock pad reduces impact stresses. Nominal thickness 7.5mm.

4. Open textured bitumen macadam base allows free drainage. Thickness dependent upon type and usage of area.

5. 150-300mm broken stone foundation.

En-tout-cas, one of several types of artificial pitch construction

clubs would install artificial turf even if they wanted to, but if they did, they might well learn from a few of QPR's less encouraging experiences.

The idea of using a ground all week is attractive, but if it is to be for spectator events one has to take into account the feelings of local residents. Loftus Road is in a built-up residential area, and there is a limit to how much activity residents will tolerate. Manchester United suffered a slightly different problem when they wanted to stage a rock concert at Old Trafford. The local authorities would not give them planning permission. So it does not necessarily follow that once a ground has artificial turf it may put on any event at any time.

In addition, a club must consider how many extra bookings it could get, and whether its spectator facilities would be adequate to cope with the expectations of non-football audiences.

QPR wanted their surface to withstand the heaviest use, but in providing for this they had to alter the base recommended by the manufacturers. Hence the pitch was harder and bouncier than is generally acceptable for football. So a club must decide which comes first, football or circuses.

Throughout this book there are examples of clubs and the authorities being afraid of innovation and new developments, so it would be rather unfair to criticize QPR. True, they might have waited for further developments and more research but someone had to do it sooner or later, and Loftus Road was one of the most suitably designed stadiums to cope with the events made possible, having a large proportion of seats and almost total cover on four sides.

QPR, I believe, are to be saluted, in exactly the same way that Herbert Chapman deserved praise for trying to get approval for floodlighting.

The FA did not like that idea either, but 30 years later almost every club in the League had floodlights.

And now almost exactly the same process is happening with artificial turf. Tranmere Rovers, a club narrowly saved from extinction in the 1982–83 season, applied to the Football League for permission to install a synthetic surface, a request which the League put to a postal vote among member clubs. As Tranmere saw it, clubs like QPR saw the new turf as a means of raising vital extra cash, whereas their need was to have a pitch which could turn Prenton Park into a community sports centre financed by the local authorities and various other bodies. For them it was almost a last chance to survive. If the League clubs voted against Tranmere, they would have nothing to offer the council but a poor pitch, which even they could use only for first team games, while the reserves played elsewhere. And if Rovers could not get permission, how much more would this deter other councils and private investors from helping out other struggling clubs?

In the end the League clubs did vote against, and Tranmere were bitterly disappointed. They did not have the money to build a new natural surface, and no outside bodies were interested in anything but an all-purpose synthetic pitch. Back to square one.

But even if attitudes do soften – and it may take the extinction of one or two clubs like Tranmere to change attitudes – there is still little doubt that only a few clubs would install artificial pitches. Not because the experiment has been a total failure, which it has not, but because new technology suggests that the pitch of the future will actually be a subtle mixture of natural *and* synthetic elements.

Perhaps the most promising idea comes from Switzerland – the Cell System – chosen by Fulham in 1983 to replace their overused and once diseased pitch at Craven Cottage.

This is a natural surface built on a sand-based sub-layer which is lined underneath by polythene, therefore creating a controllable environment for growth and maintenance. The pipe system can hold or release water as required, and has the capacity to drain up to an inch of water an hour. In comparison a sand-ameliorated pitch can cope with 2 to 4 inches a day. But because the Cell System pitch drains so well, it also means that the vital nutrients wash through the sub-layer much quicker, so extra fertilization is necessary – up to twice as much as a conventional pitch.

So the pitch needs more attention, though maintenance is comparatively simple, and also costs more to install – about £160 000. In return, however, it will theoretically be playable for more hours and in worse conditions.

It has certainly been a success in places like the Greek National Stadium in Athens, in Vancouver and various stadiums in the Middle East, but in the British climate? Results at a trial pitch in Southwark, London, indicate that the Cell System has an excellent chance of success in League football.

For roughly the same cost as this system a club could also install an artificial surface with a natural base. The system employs a similar top surface to the Omniturf variety, but rests on a nylon filament mat on top of the existing surface (if the drainage is sufficient). This provides extra 'give', absorbing shock and allowing a ball bounce equivalent to that of a normal turf pitch – about 30 to 35 per cent. Because it can be laid without extensive excavations it costs around £180 000 to £200 000.

Other developments include the possibility of natural grass grown on a plastic mesh, a combination of real and artificial turf able to withstand harder wear and last longer through a process of regeneration.

Although Omniturf and its sisters will not necessarily catch on in League football, it will undoubtedly become the accepted surface for local authority sports centres, where 60 to 80 hours a week is the normal playing requirement. Indoor football has also benefited from the new surfaces. Arsenal have one which is already in advance of the one at Loftus Road, and six-a-side indoor football has been a success since its introduction from the United States.

Inevitably, the last word must concern cost. A synthetic pitch will last approximately 10 to 12 years and costs about £35 a square metre just to replace the carpet and shock pad. If used for 50 hours a week, allowing for depreciation and interest charges it will cost about £25.40 an hour. A sand-ameliorated natural surface will last up to 30 years and costs about £11.50 an hour of its maximum use.

You could argue either way – a small club cannot possibly afford to install artificial turf, or, a small club cannot possibly afford *not* to install it.

This one will run and run for sure, and the outcome is impossible to predict accurately, given the speed with which new developments are being made. With the state of affairs as it exists in the mid-1980s, it seems probable that League grounds will not turn to wholly synthetic surfaces but will lean more towards the Cell System and other improved types of natural pitch construction. Artificial turf will be found more on training pitches, which the clubs will share with their local communities, and in indoor arenas for six-a-side soccer, hockey and tennis.

If every surface was perfect, football would become soft and too clinical. And surely, no amount of technological advance would be able to reproduce the smell, the lush swath of a freshly mown pitch. No plastic could change with the season, or remind you that this is Burnley on a wet, winter's evening, or Blackburn on a sunny afternoon. There has to be variety.

A hundred years ago players were lumbering about sodden, bumpy pitches, kicking a ball so heavy with water that some actually died from heading it. Matches finished with greatly reduced teams because players had had to go off from exhaustion. The standard of football pitches has to continue to improve, and if artificial turf stimulates that process it is decidedly a good thing.

Goals

It has taken a long time for the present style of goals to evolve, through a process of trial and error combined with a large measure of arbitrary judgement. Early forms of the game did not always require goals; the 'goal' was often simply to get the ball across a distant line, or hit a certain wall. For example the Eton wall game, dating from 1717, used a garden door for a goal at one end, and an elm tree marked in white at the other. At Winchester there were no specific goals, although it is recorded that on one occasion a boy acted as a goal by standing with his legs apart, potentially a very painful role for anyone to play. Westminster School used two trees, 20 yards apart as their goal.

In 1720 Matthew Concanen described the goals at a match in Ireland as being, 'form'd by sticking two willow twigs in the ground, at a small distance, and twisting the tops, so that they seem like a gate'. Joseph Strutt's account of football in 1801 refers to the goals as 'two sticks driven into the ground about two or three feet apart'.

The poles rather than the Irish arch caught on during the nineteenth century, and Eton's rules between 1800–63 stated that goals should be formed by two 7-feet poles placed 11 feet apart. Harrow School had a quite extraordinary rule: if the first day's play should result in a draw, the space between the poles was to be doubled from 12 to 24 feet. How different the game would have been had this rule been adopted more widely. Harrow called their goals 'bases'.

A most influential set of rules came from Cambridge in 1863, and these allowed for two poles of indeterminate height to be placed 15 feet apart. A goal was scored if the ball passed between them, but at any height, so it was as well that most of the participants were sporting gentlemen who would not see fit to dispute an umpire's decision. The FA, formed in October 1863, stated in its rules that goals were to consist of poles set 8 yards apart, and this apparently random choice has persisted ever since.

About three years later the Sheffield Association started using crossbars, although this was possible because their goals were 9 feet high but only 4 feet wide. The expertise for having longer crossbars did not exist. But the FA did decide to place a tape across their goals on the suggestion of the Chairman, who had seen a goal scored at Reigate from a kick which sent the ball between the posts but 'quite 90 feet in the air'. There was also pressure from Sheffield to adopt the use of a crossbar, but the FA would not permit this until 1875. Finally the crossbar became obligatory after a conference in Manchester in 1882. The 8-foot high, 8-yard wide goal had arrived to stay.

From then on, it was a question of what shape and size the actual posts and bar should be, and in 1895 the final ruling was that the width and depth of posts should not exceed 5 inches (12 centimetres). One club, Turton FC near Bolton, had used telegraph poles for their goals, sunk half their length into the ground. But even the much thinner posts, now obligatory, had to be sunk into the earth and supported from behind either with guy ropes or stanchions. It was nevertheless quite common for goalposts to collapse in the course of a game. The shape could be round, half-round or rectangular, but was usually square.

Then in 1920 a new company in Nottingham called Standard Goals developed an entirely different type of goalpost and crossbar, shaped elliptically. A set of these goals was presented to Nottingham Forest in 1922, and although the FA did not give its official approval until just after the Second World War, every League club in England adopted the elliptical posts. This led to one legalistic problem. Should the 8 yards be measured from the innermost plane of the posts, or the front edge? The FA ruled in 1938 that it should be the inside measurement, and for several years the City Ground's goals were about 2 inches narrower than all other clubs'.

The elliptical posts were different in two ways. Firstly the shape made a rebound more unpredictable than the square posts, and secondly they were stronger. The modern crossbar is reinforced with a metal rod to give it greater suppleness without breaking, and can be deflected up to a foot up or down. Previously crossbars were prone to sagging, so the new reinforced bars are actually manufactured in a banana shape, so that when hung between posts the curve is straightened up by the force of gravity.

Most goals are made out of hardwearing Douglas Fir, and if looked after by a conscientious groundsman can last up to 15 years of League football. But it needs only one pitch invasion to permanently damage a set, or as used to occur but is now banned, for a goalkeeper to swing on the bar. This happened once at Prenton Park when Rochdale's keeper managed to snap the bar.

A set of wooden elliptical posts, with ground sockets, costs about £300, or a crossbar alone about £91, and even though they are supposed to last a while, many clubs choose to replace them at the end of each season.

Instead of wooden goals, several clubs have started to use aluminium sets, imported from Sweden, which cost almost twice as much but are lighter and need less maintenance. On the other hand they are more brittle in collision. Wembley has a set of aluminium goals, and they are round rather than elliptical in shape.

The shape can make a difference to a game, if one compares the rebound of shots against a square post and an elliptical post. The majority of Scottish grounds have the square post, largely for traditional reasons.

There have been many suggestions made over

Portman Road's clever aid to grass cutting (Simon Inglis)

recent decades to enlarge goals in order to increase the chances of scoring, but there has never been any attempt to change the colour of the posts. White may seem the most obvious choice, but with new developments in luminous paints and plastics there is no reason why bright green or orange goals could not be used. Outside Britain it is quite common to see black and white striped posts, so there is no hard and fast rule.

One day perhaps we may even see electrically lit goals, the posts and bars having fluorescent tubes inside. These would look marvellous at night matches. Another development might be electric eyes to determine whether a ball has gone over the line.

Traditionalists may scoff, but without innovation or evolution we would still be playing with two poles and a tape.

Nets

Anyone who has played football without nets will know how difficult it can be to assess whether or not a goal has been scored. Yet it was not until 1892 that the idea was finally approved by the FA. Until then a shot on target could quite happily sail into the crowd, or even bounce back off spectators behind the goal.

The apparently obvious, but simple idea of nets is attributed to J. A. Brodie, the City Engineer of Liverpool, although there is a suggestion that they may have been tried in Birmingham as early as 1885. It apparently took Brodie 20 minutes to work out his design in 1889, but he then put it away and forgot the plans until reminded a year later by a letter in the press, suggesting the introduction of nets. Brodie had his design made up and tried out at a game on the Old Etonians' ground in Liverpool, situated almost exactly where the present entrance to Anfield now stands.

A further trial took place in January 1891 at a North v. South game at Forest's Town Ground, and also for a League match between Bolton Wanderers and Forest, when nets were used in only one goal.

The FA gave its final approval in February 1892, when it was agreed with the patentee what price clubs should pay for the nets. Brodie then went on to engineer the country's first dual carriageway, the Queen's Drive in Liverpool, and later assisted in the designs for New Delhi, India. Yet it is for his nets that he became famous; such is the power of football.

In March 1892 goal nets made their first appearance at the Cup Final, between WBA and Aston Villa at the Oval, and have been a compulsory feature at grounds ever since – although the FA rules still say that nets 'may' be attached. But as Raith discovered to their cost in 1894, it was even then generally accepted that all clubs should have nets. Rovers had to replay a Scottish Cup tie v. 5th Kings Rifle Volunteers because they failed to supply any nets for the original tie.

Having established the principle, it then became necessary to perfect the arrangement. For example, in 1908–09 WBA scored a goal v. Blackpool, but the nets were so tightly drawn that the ball bounced back into play. Although it came straight to the feet of an Albion forward who could have simply tapped it back in, the players all trotted back for the restart. But the referee waved play on, thinking the ball had hit the bar.

Albion scored another two goals, both rebounding out, but both allowed. The cancellation of the first goal proved to be very costly, since Albion missed promotion to Division One by 0.0196 of a goal. Who said goal nets were uncontroversial?

In more recent years at Filbert Street, in 1970, Aston Villa scored, but the ball hit the back stanchion and rebounded out. Even though Leicester's goalkeeper said it was a goal, the referee waved play on. That disallowed effort eventually meant Villa were relegated to Division Three. As a result of this and similar incidents, goal nets have been adjusted to hang in front of stanchions, at least where the stanchions are very close to the posts.

The introduction of modern materials has meant that goal nets can be any colour, even striped as at Blundell Park, and will last much longer. Most clubs change the nets every season, but they should have a total life-span of up to ten years. There are two types; the conventional 5-inch square mesh, usually made of polythylene, which cost about £90 for a pair, and a new type of anti-vandal nylon nets, with a closer mesh, more expensive at about £220 a set.

Even though the new generation of nets are weather resistant, they still have to be taken down for pitch maintenance, except at Portman Road, where the groundsman has devised a simple system for lifting the nets clear off the pitch without unhooking them (see Ipswich Town). Another apparently obvious, but remarkably simple idea.

NORTH WEST

MANCHESTER
•UNITED•

Previous Grounds

Manchester United's first home was at North Road, Monsall, just north east of the city centre. The club formed as the L & Y Railway FC and in 1878 became Newton Heath, named after the company's main Manchester depot. Described as 'a mud-heap' at one end and 'hard as flint' at the other, North Road was often submerged in smoke from nearby locomotives and chimneys.

Newton Heath joined the League in 1892 and in 1893 moved a short distance to Bank Street, Clayton. Gibson and Pickford were highly complimentary in 1906 when they noted that, 'today at Clayton one sees palatial stands, 20th Century appointments everywhere'. In fact the ground stood in the shadows of a chemical works and was little better than North Road, as *The Guardian* correspondent wrote of a match against Portsmouth in 1907: 'All the time the struggle was waging the 30 Clayton chimneys smoked and gave forth their pungent odours, and the boilers behind goal poured mists of steam over the ground.' A further disincentive to the fans was the ground's distance from the road. So badly off were the club that for offices they borrowed a wooden hut erected by the *Manchester Evening News* for their football correspondent's telephone. On one occasion bailiffs waited at the turnstiles to impound the gate money, and the gas supply was cut off. The club went into liquidation in 1902 after the team finished near the foot of Division Two. But they were rescued, and transformed into Manchester United by a local brewer, J. H. Davies, who invested £500 and paid for a small stand. Bank Street was even the venue for an inter-League game between Scotland and England.

After Cup Final victory in 1909 Mr Davies gave the colossal sum of £60 000 to purchase a site several miles away to the south west of the city centre, adjacent to the headquarters of Lancashire County

Cricket Club. United played their last game at Clayton on 22 January 1910, beating Spurs 5-0. Shortly after one of the stands collapsed in a storm. Both North Road and Bank Street still exist, but of the grounds there is no trace.

Old Trafford

Bobby Charlton called Old Trafford 'a theatre of dreams'. It is the best attended stadium in Britain and one of the most popular among visiting players.

When the Stretford End roars the noise is equivalent to a modern jet airliner taking off. United fanatics from all over the world come to tour Old Trafford with all the reverence and awe normally reserved for stately homes or cathedrals.

An early sketch of the ground shows Old Trafford was the identical shape it is today, but in 1909 there was only one stand with a multi-span roof on the railway side where the main stand is now. The official opening was on 19 February 1910 when a 50 000 crowd saw Liverpool win 4-3.

It was at this time that the FA held an enquiry into the club's affairs and found it 'extravagantly run'. Davies was receiving £740 rent for 14 acres of land which the club did not even use. United were called 'moneybags United' and stigmatized for being a 'private monopoly'. Much of the criticism was justified, but the element of jealousy was equally strong, for Old Trafford was, in one writer's words, 'a wonder to behold'. It had a billiard room, massage room, a gymnasium, a plunge-bath, a capacity of 80 000 and attendants to lead patrons to their five shilling tip-up seats from the tea-rooms.

Soon after the War, Old Trafford witnessed two very different record attendances. On 27 December 1920 United's largest ever League attendance, 70 504, watched a League match v. Aston Villa. In May the following year, only 13 people bothered to pay for a Second Division fixture between Stockport County and Leicester City. Edgeley Park had been closed following crowd disturbances, County were also doomed to relegation, so the fans decided to boycott proceedings. In fact there were about 2000 at Old Trafford to see the game, but the majority had stayed on after United's afternoon match v. Derby

Old Trafford between the wars. Notice the multi-span Main Stand roof (Aerofilms)

County to see two games for the price of one!

By the late 1920s Old Trafford had become rather outdated as other clubs developed their own grounds along modern lines, and by 1939 was indeed rather ordinary.

Old Trafford is very close to the Manchester Ship Canal and the important Trafford Park industrial estate. During the War German bombers spent many nights trying to cripple key installations, but they also dropped two bombs on United's home on the night of 11 March 1941, one virtually destroying the Main Stand, another hitting the United Road terracing and cover. The pitch was also scorched.

To rebuild the stadium required determination enough, but to develop a comprehensive rather than piecemeal restructuring demanded admirable foresight and confidence. Indeed it was United's ability to survive and conquer after 1941, just as much as after Munich in 1958, which has won the club its magical aura. When Jimmy Murphy joined United in 1946, the task of rebuilding was formidable. He recalled: 'The ground was a bombed out shell; we had no money; there was some sort of pokey little dive of an office where Walter Crickmer as Club Secretary operated; then Matt (Busby) got hold of a nissen hut which the lads used for changing. The practice pitch was a mile or so away, while the business of the directors was carried on largely at Mr Gibson's, the Chairman's office at his storage firm in Cornbrook.'

United were by no means the only club to suffer war damage, but they were certainly the worst hit. In August 1945 the War Damage Commission granted the club £4800 to clear the debris, with a further £17478 to rebuild the stands. A keen United supporter at this time was the Stoke MP, Ellis-Smith, who lived in nearby Eccles. He tried hard on the club's behalf to increase the Ministry of Work's aid, especially after the Chancellor of the Exchequer said in the House of Commons in February 1948 that his Labour Government 'desired to encourage all forms of entertainment'. United planned a stadium to hold 120000, but in the end settled for a simple stand to replace the old one, built of tubular steel and scrap metal. United were then £15000 in debt, and were paying out large sums to Manchester City to use Maine Road until Old Trafford was rebuilt. City fared well from their neighbour's inconvenience since United were having a good Cup run and attracted huge attendances. For the 1947–48 season alone United paid City £5000 plus a share of the gate receipts. Eventually, after eight years at Maine Road, City asked United to leave, so the Ministry of Works stepped up the repairs and on 24 August 1949 the Reds went home to beat Bolton 3-0.

At that stage the Main Stand was seated but not roofed, and the two corner sections which had survived the War provided the only cover. The United Road terracing opposite and both the Stretford and Scoreboard Ends were open. In 1951, as materials became available, the Main Stand roof was completed.

Although their training ground at The Cliff had been floodlit a few years before, Old Trafford's lights were not switched on until 1957, first used for a League game on 20 March, v. Bolton Wanderers. Until then United had played their mid-week European games under Maine Road's floodlights.

After Munich, and as United built the famous team of the 1960s, Old Trafford began to assume the form it takes today. The Stretford End was covered in 1959, then in 1962 the club were asked to prepare for the 1966 World Cup. With a grant of £40 000 the United Road cover came down in 1964 to make way for a magnificent cantilever.

Taking responsibility for this was a Manchester firm of architects called Mather and Nutter which later went on to design stands at Molineux and White Hart Lane. If the Hillsborough cantilevered stand can be regarded as the first large-scale modern stand of the post-war period, the United Road Stand at Old Trafford must be seen as the actual trendsetter.

Firstly, it allowed for expansion at either end. Secondly, it recognized the spectators' preference for both standing and seated accommodation, but thirdly, and most important of all, it incorporated the first private boxes ever seen at a British football ground. To persuade the United directors, Mather and Nutter took them to see private boxes installed in their new grandstand at the Manchester racecourse, but with little effect. Who would want to watch football behind glass? Soccer fans were surely a breed apart from the racing fraternity. But the architects persisted, and as the new stand progressed they sat the directors in seats placed at the back of the stand and asked them to visualize the possible lay-out. Immediately their clients saw the advantages, and the boxes were installed.

When completed the United Road Stand had accommodation for 10 000, with a covered paddock in front. Its total cost was £350 000, and it quite transformed the ground. Old Trafford had built a team for the 1960s, and now they had the beginnings of a super stadium to match. The sleek cantilever reflected well the popular image created by the likes of George Best and Denis Law, so that Old Trafford was in many ways as much part of the period as were the Beatles and swinging London. All over the world people wanted to support Manchester United, to an extent which even more successful clubs, like Liverpool, have never quite enjoyed.

After the United Road Stand, a further £76 000 was spent on ground improvements for the 1966 World Cup, in which Old Trafford hosted three games in Group Three. Two years later United reached their

Old Trafford in 1983 looking towards the Stretford End (Ged Murray)

peak, winning the European Cup.

The last section of the ground to be covered was the Scoreboard End, a name retained after the cantilever stand was carried round to that end to meet up with the Main Stand roof in 1973. An additional 5500 seats were installed, and the number of private boxes totalled 80. Even now this is more than any other ground. In place of the old manual scoreboard, an electronic system was introduced in the corner.

The next development was the removal of the Main Stand roof and its replacement with a cantilever section.

The next stages, as and when money becomes available, are quite obvious. The cantilever roof will be carried around the entire ground so that Old Trafford will be the first British club ground completely enclosed on four corners with a continuous roof. But stadium redevelopment is not just a question of money. Other clubs have spent as much as United but achieved far less. The crucial factor at Old Trafford has been adherence to a sensible plan over 20 years. With two-thirds of that plan now complete, the ground has a capacity of 58 500, of which 20 000 are seated. But there is still standing on all four sides.

Ground Description

Old Trafford is on the border between Manchester and Salford, which to visitors seem like one entity, but to locals are definitely separate. If taken on its own, Salford is the largest town in England without a League club. Behind the ground runs the country's oldest canal, the Bridgewater Canal, and a few hundred yards north are Manchester's docks, connected to the sea by the Manchester Ship Canal – hence the apparently incongruous sight of dockside cranes on the skyline around inland Old Trafford. To the east is the massive industrial estate, Trafford Park, and to the south the more famous Old Trafford Cricket Ground. Also nearby is the now disused White City Greyhound track.

The ground is best approached from Warwick Road North, past numerous fast-food take-aways, over the railway bridge, to the forecourt where in 1958 Manchester United fans gathered in reverent silence to pay tribute to the dead after the Munich aircrash. A clock over the offices is dedicated to their memory, and further along on the back of the Scoreboard End Stand is a plaque recalling those players and officials who died.

Inside, the ground is like a huge red cavern, with two sides of modern cantilever stands and two sides of older constructions.

The Main Stand is caught between the two. On either wing is an old corner, covered in curved pitched roofs. The centre has a new roof, but traditional wooden seats and red wooden fencing. In the middle, by the entrance to the press-box is another plaque, this one to commemorate the names of the eight journalists who also lost their lives in 1958.

From here, to the left is the Stretford End, named after the district. Most popular ends are all standing but there is a small section of 1500 seats at the back of the stand, barely visible from the front. You can see quite clearly from the colour of the roof where the 1959 Stretford End roof was built onto the pre-war corner section of the Main Stand.

Opposite is the United Road Stand, running the length of the pitch and curving round the corner along the Scoreboard End. The roof seems quite small from here, but it does in fact span some 100 feet. The fascia is plain, and the paddock rear wall is bare concrete, but to compensate all the seats are red.

The boxes at the back barely intrude at all, unlike the black fronted boxes in more modern stands. These boxes were used for a scene in Albert Finney's film, *Charlie Bubbles* (1968), which showed the disappointment of a child taken to Old Trafford but separated from his heroes by the sheet of glass, a poignant indication of how removed the supporter could be from the essential experience of live football.

Peeping over the stand roof is the top of an electricity generating station.

An all-enclosed stadium is all very well in a hot country, but in rainy Manchester it has presented problems for the Old Trafford pitch, which does not get enough natural ventilation.

Old Trafford is not as apparently impregnable as Anfield, or as grand as Villa Park or Highbury, yet its more uniform design and three covered corners make it a sound trap of red and white aggression. Since United are so well supported, consistently, I would add that for sheer partisan noise and atmosphere, there is not a ground in England to match Old Trafford.

Given time and money, both of which they seem to have, United will make it into the best club ground in England. But it will never be the most interesting.

◆ MANCHESTER CITY ◆

Previous Grounds

Manchester City were originally called Ardwick FC, a club formed in 1887 by the amalgamation of two teams, West Gorton St Mark's and Gorton Athletic. The former had begun playing in 1880 at a rough cricket ground on Clowes Street, just off Hyde Road. A season later they moved to Kirkmanshulme Cricket Club, on the corner of Kirkmanshulme Lane and Pink Bank Lane. But the cricketers objected to the damage to the turf so Gorton switched to a field on Queens Road, called 'Donkey Common'. This ground was next to a very noticeable spice mill. From 1884–87 the club played on another field off Pink Bank Lane, until one day when taking a short cut to his work in a timber yard, the Gorton captain, K. McKenzie, climbed over some hoardings in Bennett Street and discovered a perfect patch of waste ground. It turned out to be the property of the Manchester, Sheffield and Lincolnshire Railway Company, which agreed to let the land at £10 for seven months from August 1887. This was the club's first properly enclosed ground, and became known as Hyde Road, the nearby main road running from Manchester to Hyde, Glossop and Sheffield.

It was here that the name Ardwick FC was adopted, and in 1892 the club joined local rivals Newton Heath as members of the Football League, although Ardwick were elected to the Second Division, and Newton Heath went straight into the First. Some would say it has been a bit like that ever since (although Newton Heath soon joined Ardwick in the lower division after two disastrous seasons in the First Division).

Hyde Road was a fairly large ground, but hemmed in by the railway to the west and sidings to the north, and railway drivers would often slow down as they went past for a quick view of the game, as happened at Burnden Park and The Den. According to one observer Hyde Road was characterized as being surrounded by subterranean passages and railway arches. There were two stands, and an estimated capacity of about 40 000.

Hyde Road was visited by King Edward VII, an occasion very nearly ruined when a small fire broke out in the Main Stand, and also by the Prime Minister, A. J. Balfour.

By the beginning of the First World War, when Hyde Road was taken over as stabling for 300 horses, it was becoming apparent that the ground was no longer adequate for the growing number of supporters. The decision to move was given greater urgency when, on the night of 6 November 1920, the Main Stand burnt down. The cause was not, as might be thought, a stray firework but a cigarette end carelessly discarded during the afternoon's reserve match.

All the club's records perished in the fire, as did

their faithful watchdog 'Nell', an Airedale terrier. The stand was all wooden and held 4000 people, but the ground had another stand opposite and this had to suffice until other arrangements were made. Meanwhile, 50 men were hired to clear up Hyde Road, and it was reported that they must have been City devotees because they finished the work at a speed which would have shocked other contractors!

For a time it had been planned for City to move to nearby Belle Vue, a large pleasure park where they had played before in an early floodlit game v. Newton Heath, and where the existing speedway and greyhound stadiums still stand. But the site available was only eight acres, and City wanted somewhere larger.

The club soldiered on at Hyde Road until the summer of 1923, by which time their new stadium at Moss Side was ready. The last game at the ground, whose lease was up in any case, was a public practice match on 18 August 1923. City left straight after, taking with them just a few turnstiles and the goalposts. The remaining stand was sold to Halifax Town for just under £1000, and is still the largest building at The Shay.

Hyde Road today is the site of a bus depot, the actual pitch being covered with a skid pad for training in Bennett Street. All the previous grounds have been built over, except Queens Road, which now forms part of Gorton Park, on Hyde Road and Belle Vue Street.

Maine Road

In moving to Moss Side, City were moving closer to Manchester United. The new site at Maine Road was two miles west of Hyde Road, and about three miles east of Old Trafford. There seemed to be two advantages. Firstly, Moss Side was a densely populated suburb close to a vast new council housing development, with easy access from all South Manchester and the city centre, but secondly and more important the site offered the chance to build the biggest stadium in England apart from Wembley, which had just been completed.

An architect called C. Swain was assigned the task of designing the new stadium, and the first job was to drain and level the site, until then used as a claypit for brick making. Only one stand was built, but it was huge, seating just under 10 000 on a single tier, even though it did not run the complete length of the touchline. The rest of the ground was open terracing, a total of 20 miles of concrete steps. In plan it was identical to Old Trafford, a rectangle with slightly rounded corners, but it was bigger. Estimates of its capacity ranged from 80 000 to 100 000, and the total cost of building came to nearly £200 000, a vast sum in those days.

One week after City's last game at Hyde Road on 25 August 1923, a crowd of 60 000 saw Lord Mayor W. Cundiff pronounce Maine Road open, before City's opening First Division fixture v. Sheffield United, the

Maine Road's all-white new Main Stand roof (Press Association)

visitors rather spoiling the occasion by winning 2-1.

The ground soon proved its capabilities. For example, a crowd of 76 000 saw City v. Cardiff in the FA Cup quarter final later that season. On route to their second FA Cup triumph City played Stoke City in the 6th Round, on 3 March 1934. The attendance of 84 569 was not only the highest at Maine Road but also the highest for any English club match apart from a Cup Final, and the first of several attendance records Maine Road was to notch up in the coming years.

But before these, there was another development at the ground. Just before the War the Main Stand roof was carried round the corner and extended over the Platt Lane End.

After the War Maine Road became the busiest ground in the country, for Old Trafford was unusable after extensive bomb damage (see Manchester United) and City played host to their neighbours. They could not have picked a better time to share the ground, because United were in top form in both League and Cup. This, allied to the spectacular rise in attendances following the War meant that Maine Road was regularly packed to capacity.

The attendance of 80 407, for a Cup semi-final replay between Derby and Birmingham in 1946, was the highest ever recorded for a mid-week game, at a time when these were played in the afternoons. The following season City won the Second Division Championship, United were runners-up in the First Division, two representative matches were held at Maine Road, plus the Cup semi-final between Burnley and Liverpool, and finally the ground also staged the Northern Rugby League Final. Altogether some 2 250 000 spectators had attended Maine Road in just one season, a record for any League ground.

The following season saw United runners-up again in the League and winners of the Cup. By now attendances of over 70 000 were commonplace at Maine Road, and in a short space of time in 1948 United attracted 82 950 for a match v. Arsenal – the highest ever League match attendance – then 81 000 for their Fifth Round Cup tie v. non-League Yeovil (won 8-0).

Maine Road therefore held the record attendances

for both League and Cup matches. But even though City were charging United up to £5000 a season (as in 1947–48) plus a share of gate receipts, in 1949 they asked United to leave. Old Trafford was restored for the beginning of the 1949–50 season, and City now had their ground all to themselves again. It did them no good however, for in 1950 they were relegated.

Those post-war years brought in large profits, and part of these were spent on an unusual development, the installation of seats on the Platt Lane terracing. Nowadays this is a common occurrence, but it was quite novel then. It took Maine Road's seating capacity to about 18500, more than any other club ground in Britain.

City were once more back in Division One, and on 14 October 1953 they switched on their floodlights for a friendly v. Hearts. This innovation brought Manchester United back to Maine Road for a series of vital mid-week matches in various competitions, until Old Trafford had its own lights in 1957.

In 1956 City won their third FA Cup, and a huge roof was built over the Kippax Street banking opposite the Main Stand. This left only the North or Scoreboard End uncovered, and meant that Maine Road was almost identical to Old Trafford for a spell during the 1960s. But there were small changes. The Main Stand had a very slight semi-circular gable in the centre of the roof, with decorative moulded fascia. In the 1960s this was replaced with a new roof which had a raised section in the centre, allowing an unhindered view for at least the two middle blocks of seating, but at the same time robbing the stand of any dignity. It now looked larger but very plain.

In 1963–64 the floodlighting system was sold to non-League Leamington, and replaced with four very tall pylons visible from miles around, plus another smaller gantry on the Kippax Street roof. During a run of successes in the 1960s the Scoreboard End was rebuilt and covered by an impressive cantilever stand. Unlike Old Trafford's Scoreboard End cantilever, this one was all-seated and could not link up with its neighbours. The Main Stand rear wall was too high and it would have been too costly to adjust the two structures to fit each other. Called the North Stand, it holds 8100 seats.

The most recent development has been the replacement yet again of the Main Stand roof in the summer of 1982. Ostensibly the first phase of a £6 million redevelopment scheme – at a time when the club was heavily in debt – the new roof cost £1 million to erect and was paid for by the Supporters' Development Association. Work began on the last day of the previous season, and the builders promised City £50000 compensation for every home game played with the roof incomplete. After a difficult summer's work, the stand was finished on time, and both parties were happy.

Maine Road's capacity was not affected by the work however, and now stands at 52500: no longer the largest club ground in England, but with more seats,

26150, than any other. In view of this, why is Maine Road not used more for major games, such as Cup semi-finals? As described below, 'quality not quantity' is the crucial factor.

Ground Description

Maine Road is approached from any of the several back alleys or small streets, some of them named after famous City players, like Frank Swift (who died at Munich) and Sam Cowan.

The main entrance on Maine Road is very simple; the facade is large, but without distinction.

Inside the ground the most immediate focal point is the new roof, a huge white canopy resting rather awkwardly above the old stand. This canopy is composed of 16 barrel-vaulted sections of glass-reinforced plastic panels, joined together to resemble a huge piece of corrugated iron. Each panel can bear the weight of 7½ feet of snow and also had to be tested to withstand the heat given off by the floodlights above.

Supporting this structure is a huge steel cross-beam, itself supported at each end by 3 feet thick steel uprights. The roof is therefore not a cantilever.

From other parts of the ground the roof looks totally out of place, and even rather awkward, especially at the North End where it overhangs the original stand but does not quite link up with the North Stand cantilever roof, several feet lower. But the Main Stand's old roof made it quite the gloomiest, most miserable stand imaginable, whereas now it is transformed into a light and pleasant seated area. The white panels and steel work contrast well with the new blue seating, but make the old wooden bench seats with their curled iron armrests seem wholly incongruous. It is an uneasy marriage of old and new. Along the cross beam, high over the seats, new executive boxes are planned, though the position seems uncomfortably high over the near touchline.

From here, to the right is the Platt Lane Stand, curving round from the Main Stand to the far open corner, in a style similar to that of the old corners at Old Trafford. The roof is wooden, with advertisements painted onto the wooden fascia. One of them seems like a relic from a bygone era: 'Coughing?' it asks, 'Covonia kills coughs. Mentholated bronchial balsam'. Just the sort of encouraging thought one needs on a drizzly Manchester afternoon.

The stand has bench seats bolted onto the old terracing, and has been built up at the back on wooden terracing. The rake is therefore unchanged, and with a line of uprights along the front, viewing is not always ideal. Compared with the North Stand opposite the arrangement is positively archaic, and is no doubt part of the reason for Maine Road not being able to attract semi-finals. But possibly the most telling weakness of the ground is on the east or Kippax Street Side, now the only part of the ground left for standing spectators. Controlling rival supporters, who must stand on either half of the Kippax Street bank, demands considerable effort. Once inside the ground they are barely separated by a thin gangway.

The Kippax roof is vast, dark and low, so that when standing under it, even the sunniest day seems quite cold and gloomy. In the centre of the roof is a faded sign welcoming you to Maine Road.

The North Stand is the neatest and most complete part of Maine Road, and until the erection of the new Main Stand roof it would have seemed logical to continue the cantilever roof round that side of the ground. This was technically impossible, but the cantilever might still be extended towards Kippax Street (it is one of Maine Road's peculiarities that Kippax Street is actually behind the North Stand, while Platt Lane is several streets away from the Platt Lane Stand).

The North Stand lacks colour, being essentially grey and light blue, but offers a quite superb view. At the back is an electronic scoreboard, just like Old Trafford.

If this account of Maine Road's development seemed taken up with statistics, I fear I must now introduce one more, for here is the largest pitch of any British football ground. This size is most evident by the Kippax Street touchline, where instead of high security fencing, there is room for an additional fence a few yards beyond the perimeter wall, and even then there is a wide running track and spare turf along the touchline. City have installed undersoil heating.

Nowadays size is not the most crucial factor at a modern football ground. Villa Park is several thousands smaller in capacity than Maine Road but can still attract big games, even though Maine Road has more seats. The ground is a frustrating mixture of the very best and the very worst, from the spacious North Stand to the confined Kippax Street enclosure. It lacks stylistic unity and identifiable character because it has not had a feasible development plan. For this reason Maine Road will always seem second best to Old Trafford. On the other hand, bricks and mortar are not everything, and sheltered within Maine Road is one of the friendliest clubs in the League.

STOCKPORT ·COUNTY·

Previous Grounds

County started life in 1883 as Heaton Norris Rovers, playing at the Heaton Norris Recreation Ground. The following season they moved to the Heaton Norris Wanderers Cricket Ground on Brinksway, not far from Edgeley Park. In 1885 Rovers moved to Chorlton's Farm, off Didsbury Road, then amalgamated with local rivals Heaton Norris and played at the Ash Inn Grounds on Manchester Road. 1887 saw them at Wilkes Field, Belmont Street, until 1889 when they found their first enclosed ground at the Nursery Inn, Green Lane, Heaton Norris. They changed their name to Stockport County, and the players built a wooden stand which held 4000 but had no roof. After 12 years they moved to their seventh ground, Edgeley Park. Since it was at the time also the home of Stockport Rugby Club, County continued to play some first team and most reserve games at Green Lane whenever fixtures at Edgeley Park clashed. Only a bowling green remains on the built-up area of County's first proper ground.

Edgeley Park

When County joined the rugby club at Edgeley Park they had been in Division Two for two years. In 1921 they suffered a disastrous year in which they were relegated to Division Three (North) and the ground was closed following crowd disturbances.

The 1930s saw a revival. County scored a record number of goals, including a 13-0 win over Halifax, but were plunged into despondency on 22 July 1936 when the first wooden stand was burned down. In the blaze the club records were lost, though one player, Billy Bocking, heroically managed at least to save his beloved boots. The present main stand was built soon after.

Edgeley Park (Ged Murray)

Whereas the Army had used the ground during the First World War, the Second World War saw the return of rugby with Broughton Park RFC, whose own ground was used for military purposes.

The post-war boom in attendances brought Edgeley Park's largest crowd on 11 February 1950, for the visit of Liverpool in the FA Cup 5th Round. A crowd of 27 833 saw County lose 2-1.

Floodlights were installed with £17 000 raised by the Supporters' Association, and were first used on 16 October 1956 for a friendly game versus the Dutch team Fortuna '54 Geleen. Edgeley Park's present capacity is 16 000.

Ground Description

From the Main Stand on Hardcastle Road you can see the Railway End to the left, behind which runs the main line to London.

Opposite the Main Stand is the Popular Side which originally held 16 000 standing but was cut in half in 1979 to provide space for an all-weather five-a-side pitch behind. This explains why the roof appears awkwardly high over the terracing.

To the right is the Cheadle End, named after a nearby suburb, with 1000 seats under cover. Behind stands a tall chimney belonging to a bleach works.

The Main Stand seats 1850 and once accommodated Queen Elizabeth when she visited Edgeley Park for a display by schoolchildren during her Jubilee Year; 9000 people attended, which suggests County might be wise to offer Her Majesty a season ticket. The ground also staged the World Lacrosse Championship of 1978, held between England, Canada, Australia and the USA.

◆BURY◆

Gigg Lane

Bury have played at Gigg Lane since their formation in April 1885. The club immediately secured a tenancy of the land, which formed part of the Earl of Derby's estate. If the ground seems larger and more imposing than one might expect of a club in the lower divisions, remember that Bury have spent most of their existence in Divisions One and Two, and were twice winners of the FA Cup in 1900 and 1903.

But in June 1885, in order to attract the public's attention, Gigg Lane's first match was an exhibition game between Accrington and Church. Bury's first home game was v. Wigan. A stand was built for £50 11s 8d, and it is said that before the First World War a valuable source of income was from a 'smoking cafe' at the ground. During this period the existing South Stand was built. The adjacent Boys Stand was a later addition.

Bury had just returned to the First Division after a 12-year absence when the present Main Stand was built in 1924. The Manchester Road End Stand was opened in August 1938, when the club were back in the Second Division, and held 5000 standing spectators. The ground's capacity was then 40 000. Gigg Lane was the first ground in the north west to have floodlights, when on 6 October 1953, 17 272 saw Bury beat the pioneers of floodlit football, Wolves. It was also the first ground to stage floodlit cricket, long before the Stamford Bridge experiment in 1981. The match was England v. Commonwealth XI and was played on two successive nights in October 1954, to raise money for the floodlights. Unfortunately the experiment was a financial disaster. A total of only 1782 spectators attended on both nights.

A gale in the late 1950s tore down a cover at the Cemetery End, but was replaced with the existing cover at the turn of the decade. This period also saw the highest crowd at Gigg Lane, 35 000, for a Cup-tie

Gigg Lane's South Stand (Ged Murray)

v. neighbours Bolton in January 1960.

The ground's present capacity is still a healthy 35 000, including 7500 seats, but since this has not been tested since that Bolton match it may be therefore a slightly misleading figure.

Ground Description

Bury's ground is the most attractive in the north west. Tucked away off the Manchester Road, with squat floodlights making it hard to spot behind the tall trees, the approach to Gigg Lane is along narrow streets lined with low, stone terraced houses. Entrance to the ground is through a long fence which runs along Gigg Lane, past a car-park large enough to lay another football pitch, with the massive blue wall of the Main Stand ahead, gaunt with small windows.

Inside one feels touched by the remnants of an era of confidence and ambition. The Main Stand is distinguished by glass screen ends chequered with blue squares, and the high, blue, terrace rear wall which juts in and out along the front of the seats. The old blue and white vertical stripes would look well here. Seating 5500 (more than Bolton's Main Stand) it is one of the largest of the old stands still in use.

To the left is the Cemetery End terrace, with a modern, plain corrugated roof. Next to it, in the far south east corner is the small wooden Boys Stand, rather like the old Motor or North West Stand at Bloomfield Road. It is really just a covered series of wooden steps, used for seating, and can be entered only from the terrace at the front. It makes an agreeable adjunct to the South Stand.

The South Stand, with trees along the back, is low and rather uneven, with louvred windows at the rear, a low beamed roof and wavering wooden benches. Notice the iron pillars, which despite their regularity are narrow enough not to impede the excellent view from here. However basic, the stand is nicely faced with a high, blue, terrace rear wall which mirrors that of the Main Stand.

To the right is the Manchester End covered terrace. Manchester's northern suburbs are only three miles south of the ground. Half of the covered section is now fenced off as unsafe. There are traces of old wooden sleepers at this end.

But undoubtedly the pride of Gigg Lane is the pitch. One observer at the turn of the century noted: 'its turf is reputedly unsurpassed'. There is no running track and the pitch extends to the perimeter walls. It still is in good condition, mainly owing to the fact that since 1919 there have been only three groundsmen. Jim Savery served from 1919 until 1938, when his assistant since 1924, Tommy Marshall took over. Tommy died in August 1981 after 56 years in charge. If the new young incumbent serves as long, the three men will have tended Gigg Lane for a century.

So much green, so much blue paint; Gigg Lane is compact, homely but with an appealing residue of stateliness. A most satisfying ground to visit.

◆OLDHAM ATHLETIC◆

Previous Grounds

Although Lancashire is regarded as the birthplace of the Football League and of those teams who prospered in it during the early years, not all Lancashire clubs predate 1888. Oldham Athletic's history, as told by Stewart Beckett in *The Team from a Town of Chimneys*, began in 1897 in the form of Pine Villa, a pub team playing on a pitch near Pine Mill. When the town's professional soccer team, Oldham County, went into liquidation two years later, Pine Villa moved to their home at the Athletic Grounds, on Sheepfoot Lane. Now called Oldham Athletic they turned professional, but after only a few months had a rent dispute with the landlord and had to move to a pitch by Westhulme Hospital, at Hudson Fold. During the summer of 1906 they moved back to Sheepfoot Lane, to their present ground.

Boundary Park

Boundary Park was the property of J. W. Lees Brewery, a family firm which has had close dealings with the club since. Athletic's first game at the new ground was on 1 September 1906 v. Colne, attended by 3454.

Boundary Park had two stands. On the North Side, where the present Main Stand is situated, was an odd-looking construction: an ordinary low, wooden stand with seats at the back, an uncovered terrace in front, but over the centre was a viewing balcony for important persons, like a log-cabin on stilts.

On the lower roof, and on that of the opposite Flat or Broadway Stand, additional spectators used to perch for an uninterrupted view. One of them was Oldham's manager, who would follow play by running up and down the Flat Stand roof in his bowler hat.

The present Main Stand was completed by 1920, although it was intended to add wings as finances allowed. One of the highest attendances at the ground was not for football but for the Prince of Wales's visit in 1921.

Oldham were already an average Second Division team when in October 1927 the Chadderton Road Stand, a covered terrace, was opened. But not for long. A winter's gale blew it down again soon after. When reconstructed, openings were put along the back wall to let the wind blow through the stand, and the roof has been secure since.

Boundary Park's highest ever attendance, 47 671, came to watch Athletic's 4th Round FA Cup tie v. Sheffield Wednesday, the First Division Champions on 25 January 1930.

Three decades later the club had to seek re-election and was near to closing down completely, but a year later Oldham installed new floodlights, first switched on for a friendly v. Burnley on 3 October 1961. Athle-

Boundary Park's Rochdale Road End and neighbouring mill (Ged Murray)

tic were the last League club in Lancashire to have lights.

Years of optimism followed, with the club in Division Three and plans were prepared to transform Boundary Park into a super stadium. By the end of the decade the plans were forgotten as Athletic slipped back into the Fourth Division. But when they made a quick recovery in 1971, a new stand was indeed built, for Oldham had not only won promotion, but also a short-lived competition known as the Ford Sporting League.

Held for one season only, Ford gave points for goals, but deducted them for bad behaviour on the pitch, and they stipulated that Oldham had to spend their £70 000 prize money on ground improvements, even though at the time the club were receiving aid from the local council just to stay in business. The result was a quickly-built new stand named after the sponsor, in place of the old Broadway Stand. This brought the seating total to 2939, but after the introduction of the Safety of Sports Grounds Act, as a Second Division club Oldham had to spend £250 000 to keep all those seats in use. The overall capacity was nevertheless reduced by some 8000, and now numbers 26 324.

Ground Description

The name is apt. From the new roads linking Oldham with the motorway, Boundary Park appears to stand quite on its own, unchallenged on the skyline except by the large Monarch Mill to the north west.

The Main Stand is a short, blue-painted stand, oddly angled to the west as if it were meant to continue to the goal-line but could not quite reach. The roof appears to have bowed with the effort. In front of the high paddock rear wall is now a line of modest private boxes.

From here, to the left, is the covered Chadderton Road End, a simple pitched roof over a dark interior. The blue barriers cease where there are wooden terraces at the rear. It is said the stand is haunted by the ghost of 'Fred', a man who stood at the same spot

on these terraces for many a year, until his death during a match in the early 1960s.

Opposite is the Ford Stand, also not running the full length of the pitch. The stand is a very simple modern version of the traditional post and beam construction, a necessary choice because in 1971 £70 000 did not go far. In fact, it seems hardly different from the previous Broadway Stand. It seats only 1406, with an uncovered paddock in front.

To the right is the open Rochdale Road End. Spotland is six miles to the north. The banking is characterized by new concrete terracing at the bottom, but the predominant image is that of the Monarch Mill, looming up behind the bank, a chimney pointing up between the floodlight pylons.

Finally, notice how sharply the pitch slopes, by almost 6 feet from the Rochdale Road End down to the Chadderton Road End, following the gradient of Sheepfoot Lane. Under the pitch is 16 miles of piping for undersoil heating, installed in 1980 at a cost of £60 000. Boundary Park is one of the highest grounds in England, and was therefore prone to freezing more than most. Since then, the pitch has been usable when others have been frostbound, as for example when Boundary Park staged a Rugby League match for their neighbours Oldham RLFC, and on Boxing Day 1981, when for the first time in League history, the venue of Athletic's away game at Ewood Park was switched to Oldham in order to play the match. So as earthy and undeveloped though Boundary Park may seem, with the mill, surrounding scrubland, humble stands and sloping pitch, like a true Lancastrian, underneath the surface lies a good deal of sophistication.

·ROCHDALE·

Spotland

Spotland was originally called St Clements playing field. The first football club to play there was Rochdale AFC in 1900, followed in 1903 by another team, Rochdale Town. Both clubs disbanded after only one season at the ground, which was then used for rugby. In 1907 the present Rochdale club was formed and has played at Spotland ever since.

Rochdale bought the ground for £1700 in 1914, and joined the League in 1921. In their first season occurred the first of three mishaps to befall the Main Stand, which has survived until the present day. In December 1921 a gale blew down the roof, causing £500 damage. The club also finished bottom of the League, a position it has occupied four times since.

The Pearl Street roof dates from this period, and in 1927 the Willbutts Lane Side was also covered.

The Spotland pitch had a notorious 5-foot slope from west to east, until the summer of 1948 when the excess earth was dumped onto a corner of terracing, forming a miniature Spion Kop. Crush barriers were put up on this new mound for the visit of Notts County in the FA Cup in December 1949, which attracted Spotland's record crowd of 24 231.

Floodlights were first used in February 1954 for a friendly v. St Mirren, but although Rochdale was only the third club in the north west to have lights, in his history of the club Brian Clough reports that manager Harry Catterick described the 7000 gate as 'the lowest so far for the opening of any floodlight installation in the country'.

Fate dealt the Main Stand a second blow in August of that year, when a fire caused £350 damage. From that figure one can guess the size and structure of the stand in question.

A new cover over the Sandy Lane End was built in 1961, with £6000 raised by the supporters. Five years later, as if it had not suffered enough, the roof of the Main Stand collapsed once more, this time under the weight of a heavy snow fall.

Spotland was in the news again for the wrong reasons in 1970, when Coventry City refused to play a postponed FA Cup match under Rochdale's by now outdated floodlights.

To add insult to injury, their manager Noel Cantwell added the gamesman's retort, 'Where's Rochdale?' He soon found out, for 13 011 people turned out on a Monday afternoon to see Rochdale beat the First Division team 2-1.

However, in August 1971, the lights were replaced with the present set for the cost of £18 000, and were officially switched on by Sir Matt Busby.

The present capacity is about 20 000, but there are only 730 seats, the lowest at any League ground. In 1983 Rochdale bought Spotland back from the coun-

Remnants of old-style timber and cinder terracing at Spotland; the goalposts newly painted (Ged Murray)

cil, to whom they had sold it in times of trouble, for £83 000.

Ground Description

The Main Stand is situated well back from the touchline, behind a wide track and a flat path that runs round three sides of the ground. This distance, and low terracing and seating, makes viewing far from ideal. The stand's front wall shows the effects of the 1954 fire, for it is wood on one side, concrete on the other. Behind the stand is the very heart of Rochdale, the supporters' social club, without which survival would be even more difficult than it is.

From the seats you can see Knowl Hill straight ahead on the left, and Rooley Moor on the right, both over 1300 feet high.

To the left is the Sandy Lane End, a covered terrace, ahead is the Willbutts Lane cover, much improved in 1982, and to the right is the Pearl Street End. Still in front of its set-back roof are poles carrying the old floodlights. The terracing, which is very shallow all round the ground, stops under the roof and gives way to an ash bank with sleepers, jammed into the ground with wooden pegs, a rare surviving example of early terracing. Behind the Sandy Lane roof, with its battered advertising hoardings, you can see the steeple of St Clements church.

The highest ground is the south east corner, the Kop, or 'the hill'. Otherwise even the neighbouring terraced houses are as tall as the stands.

The overall combination of a wide pitch, a wide perimeter track, low stands and distant hills give Spotland a distinctly dated appearance – too open to be cosy, too underdeveloped to have much distinction. This is of course exactly what the condescending 'Where's Rochdale?' brigade would expect: stone walls, open moors and cobbled streets. And yes, they are all there around Spotland, but those who know this part of Lancashire appreciate that the scale and spirit of Rochdale will long survive, even though three miles away a motorway entices people to Old Trafford and other more glamorous neighbours.

· BOLTON · WANDERERS

Previous Grounds

Bolton adopted the title 'Wanderers' for the obvious reason, that they had no particular home to call their own. The club formed in 1874 as Christ Church FC but disagreement with the vicar forced it to break away three years later. Among many early grounds used were the Park Recreation Ground and Cockle's Field, until Wanderers finally struck roots at Pikes Lane in March 1881. Dr P. M. Young's history of the club tells us much about Bolton's grounds, beginning with how notoriously muddy was the Pikes Lane pitch.

Pikes Lane also suffered from being situated at the foot of a hill, from where an excellent free view was to be had. *Athletic News* reported in February 1884 that between 4000 and 5000 spectators had assembled on the slopes during Bolton's Cup replay v. Notts County, and an enterprising farmer charged them half the Pikes Lane entrance fee.

Annual rent for the ground was £35 in 1881, but by 1893, with Bolton now in the Football League and enjoying higher gates, this rose to £175. All around, building speculators were closing in, so the club began to look for a more suitable site. Bolton Corporation owned some land on the Manchester Road, bought with the intention of expanding the gasworks, but when these plans fell through Wanderers made enquiries to the local Gas Committee, in August 1893. Soon after losing in their first FA Cup Final, at Goodison Park in 1894, Bolton were told they could have a 14-year lease on the 5-acre plot, at an annual rent of £130. Two small roads would have to be closed, which meant seeking permission from the Tar Distillery Company and Bleachworks, and in order to gain more influence, Wanderers became a limited company. Pikes Lane was last used at the end of the 1894–95 season.

Burnden Park

In 1895 the site of Burnden Park was miserable; one end bound by a railway, and the land a stagnant mess of dumped refuse and chemicals from nearby works. This was a frequent sight in Victorian industrial cities, yet time and again football clubs were able to transform such wilful neglect into order.

It was said that the pitch was built up on old barrels and cotton bales, but whatever its foundation, this was the most cambered surface ever seen in the League (see Pitches).

A Scarborough contractor was called in to lay out the new ground, under instructions from John Norris, who specifically requested a cycling track round the pitch, just like the one laid for the King of Italy. A firm called Coopers of Bolton built the Darcy Lever Grand Stand, opposite where the present Main Stand is situated. Apart from an old house abutting on the north west corner, the front courtyard was entirely clear up to the Manchester Road. (This house survived until 1946.)

As at Goodison Park three years earlier, Burnden Park was opened on 17 August 1895 with an athletics meeting, the town's 9th Annual Athletics Festival, attended by an impressive crowd of 15 000. Bolton played their first game at Burnden Park on 11 September, a benefit match v. Preston North End.

However fluctuating the team's performance in the next few years, Burnden Park was a successful stadium, and in 1901 was chosen as the venue for the Cup Final replay between Tottenham and Sheffield United. In eager anticipation of a bumper crowd – the first game was watched by 114 815 at Crystal Palace, England's first six-figure attendance – the town's tradesmen brought in massive stocks of pies and souvenirs. But the day turned into a disaster, for Bolton Railway Station was in the process of being rebuilt and the railway company refused to offer cheap-day excursion tickets. A lot of merchandise went to waste that day, known for years afterwards in Bolton as 'Pie Saturday'. There were undoubtedly more than the official gate of 20 740 present, perhaps up to 30 000, but still this represents the lowest crowd at an FA Cup Final in this century.

But it was a mystery why the FA chose Burnden Park in the first place. Goodison Park was objected to as a venue by neighbours Liverpool, who had a home game on the same day, but what was wrong with Villa Park, or The Victoria Ground, Stoke?

Poor Bolton were never honoured again. While neighbours Blackburn, Burnley and the two Manchester clubs were all chosen to host England international matches up until the Second World War, Burnden Park was overlooked.

If 1901 was disappointing, the club won back much of its pride in 1904 by reaching its second Final, this time at Crystal Palace. Although they lost, the extra revenue enabled Bolton to start building the first section of the existing Main Stand, on Manchester Road, for a cost of about £3500. That season Wanderers returned to Division One, and Bolton Corporation extended their lease by ten years and still on the original terms. Also that year, in order to accommodate the growing crowds, Burnden Park's cycle track was taken out.

During the following season, with Bolton back in Division One, the Great Lever End was terraced and covered. In 1915 the Main Stand had an extra wing added at the Southern End, so that the stand rather resembled Ewood Park's Main Stand, with a cranked end section. (Both grounds in fact developed in a similar pattern, though Rovers were slightly more lavish.)

After a period of considerable success, Bolton began in 1928 to build a new structure seating 2750 in

The players' view from the tunnel, facing the Burnden Stand at Bolton (Ged Murray)

place of the original Darcy Lever Stand. But just before its completion controversy struck. The Burnden Stand cost £20 000 to erect, not a vast amount when compared with the £30 000 Everton had spent on their new Bullens Road Stand two years earlier, and surely not beyond the means of a successful club with two packed Wembley finals recently under its belt. So imagine the uproar in Bolton when their Cup-winning hero David Jack was transferred to Arsenal in October 1928 for the then record fee of £10 340. As *Athletic News*' correspondent remarked, 'Bolton's choice: new stand but no new players'.

Burnden Park's official highest crowd was 69 912, for the visit of Manchester City in the FA Cup in February 1933. During the Second World War the ground was taken over, the pitch for use by the Education Authorities, the stands by the Ministry of Supply. The Burnden Stand was still full of food supplies when the event which was to stand out in the history of all football grounds occurred on 9 March 1946. (For a full description of the disaster, in which 33 spectators died and 400 were injured, see the appendix.)

The match was unusual in itself, for that season immediately after the War it had been decided that every Cup tie up to the semi-finals should be two-legged. These extra games would help to compensate for the fact that League Football did not resume on a proper basis until September 1946. Bolton had won the first leg of this quarter-final tie at Stoke 2-0, and an estimated 85 000 squeezed into Burnden Park in the afternoon, most of whom knew little about the tragic events at the Railway End.

In the depressing aftermath, questions were raised which were to bring about lower capacities at every ground. Bolton felt a great deal of remorse although the report did not blame the club specifically. After the government report, in 1947 the club spent £5500 modernizing the Railway End, improving the turn-stiles and gates, adding barriers and fencing off the railway line (see Safety).

Since then, only a few changes have been effected. On 14 October 1957, Bolton's new floodlights were switched on for a friendly v. Hearts. It was claimed that they possessed sufficient power to light the streets from Burnden to Blackpool.

During the summer of 1979 the entire pitch, a poor drainer despite the camber, was dug up and all manner of compressed, rotting matter was found underneath. Undersoil heating and sprinklers were installed and the pitch has looked fine ever since. Also at this time 4342 seats were put on the terracing at the Great Lever End, making a total of 11 446 seats in an overall capacity of 41 646.

Ground Description

Approaching the ground from Bolton station, Burnden Park is on the left of Manchester Road, just beyond a railway bridge once bearing the Bolton to Yorkshire line behind the terracing. The line is now disused.

The Manchester Road Stand is almost hidden behind a complex of offices, social clubs and executive facilities. The car-park and back of the Main Stand was the backdrop for L. S. Lowry's painting *Going to the Match*. Inside the stand is the predictable, creaky, wooden stand of the early 1900s. The later right wing is angled towards the pitch. There are 4644 seats, surprisingly many considering the low roof makes the stand seem small. Unfortunately, the seats are all red, while the woodwork (and most of the stand is wooden) is in dark blue; a jarring combination. On the roof is a prominent television gantry, which does not enhance the stand's appearance either. Yet jumbled though it seems, Burnden Park's age gives it a definite sense of tradition.

To the right is the covered Great Lever Stand, named after the district nearby. Apart from the huge, bright advertisement on the black roof its most prominent feature is the floodlight pylon on the far side. All the terraces have now been covered with seats, a rather careless conversion it has to be said, effected when the club were briefly back in Division One. Plastic bucket seats have been bolted onto the original terraces, and therefore the rake is too shallow to provide a good all-round view, especially as the high security fences still line the front. The same firm which put up this cover, John Booth of Bolton, also built the Manchester Road Stand and erected much of the steelwork at Wembley Stadium in 1923. A luminescent sign with their name adorns the top of the Great Lever Stand.

Opposite the Manchester Road Stand is the Burnden Stand, a simple 1920s' design with a large paddock in front of a covered seating area accommodating 2460. White roof fascia and terrace facings emphasize its simplicity. Notice how the uprights seem to branch out at the tops and how the entire back row is well lit by a line of windows.

To the left is the Railway End, still slightly curved around the pitch. The north west gangway where the disaster brewed is exactly in the corner between the Manchester Road Stand and the end terracing, just behind the corner flag. Above there is a huge bunker-like set of toilets, backing onto the fence which now separates the ground from the railway line. It was from this line that Burnden Park played a small part in Arthur Askey's film, *Love Match* (1954), in which a train-driver pulled up on the tracks behind the Railway End to watch a stirring match played in front of a packed crowd, all wearing cloth caps and smoking Woodbines. Now the Railway End is lined with barriers and fences, crowned by a fading half-time scoreboard.

Finally, Burnden Park's pitch deserves attention. The camber, as noticeable as in 1906, is all the more pronounced because in places the turf is actually 3 feet higher than the perimeter track. Behind the goals, where the pitch is slightly rounded, are large patches of turf also rising from the track up to pitch level, but undulating like a miniature golf course.

Burnden Park shares many similarities with its neighbours Ewood and Boundary Parks, but somehow does not quite achieve the spruceness which distinguishes the former, or the open, hardiness of the latter. More than a new coat of paint, for it is already quite neat, the ground needs more focus. There are too many bit parts, not enough upstaging. A new Main Stand could achieve wonders in this direction, though if Bolton had the capital, would they again choose a new stand in favour of new players?

BLACKBURN ·ROVERS·

Previous Grounds

Blackburn spent much of their first season without a home but still managed to win every 'away' game. When in 1875 they did find a pitch, on a farm by Preston New Road, it was barely adequate, for in the middle was the farm's drainage pool or 'cow-pit'. The father of Duckworth, one of the Rovers team, was a timber merchant and so the club was able to cover the pool with planks and disguise it with turf. In 1876 they moved to Alexandra Meadows, the East Lancashire cricket ground, where they attracted a record gate of 5000 for a game v. Partick Thistle. In 1881 the club switched to Leamington Road where a grandstand seating 700 was built. The move obviously suited Rovers, who immediately enjoyed a run of 35 successive games unbeaten. Having just won the FA Cup for the fourth time the club moved to their present ground, Ewood Park in 1890.

Ewood Park

In common with much urban development in industrial Lancashire, Ewood Park was built in the late Victorian period, and has suffered from being outdated ever since. The first match there was v. Accrington in September 1890, but the following Christmas brought crowd trouble. Darwen were the visitors, and so incensed were their supporters when Rovers saw fit to field only three first team players they pulled up and broke the goalposts, smashed dressing room windows and tore up carpets in the reserved seating section.

An early attempt at floodlit football was made at Ewood Park in October 1892, also for a game v. Darwen (see Floodlights), then in 1895 Rovers bought the ground for £2500. At the same time the club's headquarters were moved from the Bay Horse Hotel to Ewood Park.

Further crowd problems during Everton's visit in January 1896 arose when part of a stand collapsed among a 20 000 crowd. Five people were injured and one of them won £25 compensation for his injuries, the club being found negligent. Possibly in reaction to this court case Rovers became a limited liability company soon after.

A photograph of Ewood Park taken before 1906 shows a small hut in one corner, presumably the changing rooms, a wooden railing round the pitch, which had no track, and wooden barriers dug into grass banking. The Darwen End of the ground had been covered in 1905 at a cost of £1680 and held 12 000 spectators.

1906 was a year of major improvements, all still visible. The main Nuttall Street Stand, designed by

Ewood Park in 1905 looking towards the recently-built Darwen End (*Book of Football*)

Archibald Leitch, was built at a cost of £24 000, a considerable outlay even then, and opened on New Year's Day 1907 for a match v. Preston. Though only mildly impressive from without, the Nuttall Street Stand was very good within and has, in part, been lovingly preserved by the club. In between two Championship wins in 1912 and 1914 the club built another stand, the double-decker Riverside Stand, and in 1915 reported the capacity of Ewood Park to be a massive 70 886, including 7000 seats. In 1928 the wooden perimeter railing was replaced by the present concrete wall, the Blackburn End was terraced and the Riverside Stand reroofed for a total outlay of £1550. A year later Ewood Park saw its largest crowd, 61 783, for a Cup tie v. Bolton on 2 March.

In 1958 the club installed floodlights, first used on 10 November during a friendly v. Werder Bremen of West Germany. A Cup Final appearance in 1960 provided funds for erecting a concrete cantilever roof over the Blackburn End terrace, an early example of cantilever construction and its first use for an end terrace.

Ewood Park has had to adapt more than most grounds to the requirements of the 1975 Safety of Sports Grounds Act, having spent nearly all their grant from FGIT (see Safety). Even with this enormous outlay the capacity is only 23 400, a substantial reduction from the original capacity of 70 886, although the ground is still basically the same size.

Ground Description

As you leave the main road and walk past rows of terraced houses to Ewood Park, you can see how the club has actually grown into its surroundings. There is, for example, a programme seller's window in one house's backyard wall. The club's offices are in a small block on one street corner and one terraced house, 112 Nuttall Street, belongs to Rovers.

The redbrick Nuttall Street frontage reminds one of the stand's exact contemporary at Craven Cottage, also the work of Leitch (see Design). Having already passed down either Tweed Street or Velvet Street it should come as no surprise to find at the Darwen End of Nuttall Street, the cobbled entrance to Fernhurst Mill.

To the Blackburn End of Nuttall Street is Kidder Street, also cobbled and with a line of particularly well kept houses. And just in case any southerner is still not convinced of Ewood Park's solidly northern credentials, he should also notice the old tramlines in the street.

The turnstiles in this corner of the ground were used in a television commercial for a type of bread, with the predictable accompaniment of brass band music.

Before we enter the ground proper, two further points are worth noting. Firstly, the graphics which adorn every part of Ewood Park, inside and out, are a commendable feature of the club's policy of both informing the public and maintaining a high standard of appearance at the ground. Watford have used a similarly uniform system of lettering and colours to create such a corporate image, which other clubs might do well to imitate. Secondly, although few visitors can gain access, the oak-panelled boardroom in the Nuttall Street Stand is quite magnificent, and by no means a dusty inner sanctum.

The Nuttall Street Stand is cranked and some distance from the touchline. Like the rest of the ground it is brightly painted in blue and white. Red fences and barriers, a cream-coloured perimeter wall and a neat terracotta track add to the ground's spruce appearance. The players' tunnel is covered by a clear

Ewood Park's Blackburn End turnstiles, familiar to television viewers in different guise (Simon Inglis)

perspex barrelled canopy, with the club's crest on a sign above the entrance. White moulded fibre-glass dug-out covers flank the tunnel and give it prominence. Because the stand is basically wooden throughout, stringent fire precautions have been taken, especially underneath where there is often a chaotic bottleneck at half-times. My advice is to stay in your seat if you can hold out!

To the right is the Darwen End. Darwen is a small town four miles from Blackburn and had its own League club for eight years in the 1890s. This covered terrace is slightly cranked, with a line of 13 pillars along the front and many signs warning against the fragile roof.

To the left is the more modern Blackburn End, its cantilever roof angled at several points. The slabs of grey concrete of this bus shelter-like roof are in dull contrast with their freshly coloured surrounds. Opposite is the Riverside Stand, tall and narrow with red concrete facings and a steep uncovered terrace in front. It is less impressive from the back where it is clad in weathered sheets of corrugated iron. The stand is so-called because behind runs the narrow River Darwen. There is a grass-covered pathway between the riverbank and the foot of the stand. But for the litter strewn across the water, this would be a pleasant little brook. As it is, limited access to the stand from Kidder Street only, is a major safety consideration for the club.

Note especially two gateways in the perimeter wall in front of Blackburn's Riverside Stand, with stone ornamental spheres on top of each gate-post, picked out in blue to contrast with the cream wall. Such attention to detail, in what is an undeniably dated ground, prevents Ewood Park from appearing dowdy and the pitch, laid down by the Sports Turf Institute, is one of the best in the country. Ewood Park is proof of how conscientious maintenance and a touch of elbow grease and imagination can bring back life to the worn and weary.

·BURNLEY·

Turf Moor

Burnley Rovers played rugby at Calder Vale, and their players had to bathe in the river after each game. In May 1882 they formed a soccer club and dropped the name Rovers soon after. The club made their first appearance at nearby Turf Moor on 17 February 1883, for a local match v. Rawtenstall. Only Preston and Stoke have been in longer continuous residence than Burnley at their grounds.

Turf Moor is as it sounds, a patch of turf amid moors, but it is also a well-developed ground, suitably modified to the needs of a small town. Burnley is the smallest town to have sustained a First Division club for any length of time, with a population of about 75000. (In League history Glossop, in Derbyshire, was the smallest town to have a First Division club. More recently, Carlisle, slightly smaller than Burnley, enjoyed just one season at the top.)

The ground's early history is recorded in David Wiseman's history of the club (*Up the Clarets*, 1973) which begins with a description of Turf Moor from the magazine *Football Field*, in September 1884. Burnley had built a grandstand seating 800 and 'added to and rearranged a natural earth work making standing room for 2000 more'. An uncovered stand, along two sides of the field and accommodating over 5000 was also in the process of being erected. We presume the work was completed, for in March 1884 12000 people came for a match v. local rivals Padiham, in those early days an enormous crowd indeed. Only 4000 attended that same year's Cup Final.

Turf Moor is believed to be the first football ground ever visited by a member of the Royal family, when in October 1886, having just opened the nearby Victoria hospital, the Queen's son Prince Albert watched Burnley v. Bolton in the company of 9000 others, some of them paying a guinea just to sit near the Royal party. Afterwards Burnley were nicknamed the Royalites, and appropriately it was Burnley who played in the first FA Cup final to be watched by a reigning monarch, at Crystal Palace in 1914.

By 1908 the two sides were covered; the Main Stand on Brunshaw Road and opposite, the stand known as the Star Stand. When more room was needed for an FA Cup match v. Manchester United this stand was moved backwards to make an enclosure in front, and £600 was spent on extra banking and barriers. Considerable improvements were necessary in the summer of 1913 because gates were rising every year, up to 49734 for one match in 1914, roughly as many as lived in the town itself! The record gate was in February 1924 when Huddersfield Town were the visitors in the FA Cup; 54775 attended, but one man died in the crush. Three months later a First Division game at the ground attracted only 3685.

In 1954 a new roof costing £20 000 was built over the terracing on the Long Side, opposite the main stand, and the floodlights were switched on in December 1957 for a friendly v. Blackburn Rovers.

In 1967 work began on a new stand at the Cricket Field End. Finished in 1969 at a cost of £180 000 it housed all the players' facilities, and was the first stand in Britain to incorporate underfloor heating for the 4500 seated spectators. The system was powered by an oil-fired air heater, but was used only for two seasons before being pronounced uneconomical. The stand was given official blessing by the Prime Minister Edward Heath, a personal friend of Burnley's Chairman Bob Lord, on 23 November 1973.

For a while the Cricket Field Stand became the Main Stand, while the original Main Stand was taken down and replaced by the new Bob Lord Stand. Some locals called it the Martin Dobson Stand, after the Burnley player whose £300 000 transfer to Everton in August 1974 was said to have paid for the construction.

Edward Heath also opened this stand, on 14 September 1974. It seats 2500 people. Unfortunately the club slipped out of the First Division two years later and by 1980 were in Division Three, having two smart new stands but having sold most of their valued players.

The capacity of Turf Moor is now 21 000 including 6800 seats; less than half the club's record gate.

Ground Description

Turf Moor is one of several grounds to use a combination of cream and green to good effect, and the green particularly stands out. This may be to reflect the image of 'turf', or could be a throwback from the days when the team played in green.

The Bob Lord Stand stretches along Brunshaw Road, next to the club offices. The design is very simple; a plain flat roof, steeply raked seating leading down to the front cream-coloured wall. Notice in the centre a wooden gate with steps and the club crest. There is a large proportion of executive seating in the centre, and you can see rolled up covers at the front, used to protect the carpets.

To its left is the Cricket Field Stand, named after the sponsors, 'Burnley's Building Society Stand' in 1982. Behind it is the cricket field belonging to Burnley Cricket Club. The stand is quite unusual for an end stand, firstly because it houses the players' tunnel, to the right of the goal – as found only at Bloomfield Road, The Den and Meadow Lane – but is a long way from the offices, and secondly because it looks like a box made out of children's building bricks. The screen ends have distinctive square panels of glass, the stone walls are cream and the seats green. Though it has aged, its size commands attention.

The rest of the ground is standing only. Opposite the Bob Lord Stand is the Long Side cover, a large structure of exactly the same design as at Leeds

Turf Moor in the early 1920s before the Long Side was terraced. Notice the centre spot (Aerofilms)

Road. From here you can see the moors rising up beyond the stand opposite. Along the front perimeter wall notice the old dug-outs, used when the Main Stand was being rebuilt. The size of the rather drab roof is another dominant feature of Turf Moor, and needs more than the present dull advertisement hoarding (which ironically advertises paint and varnish). To the right is the open bank called the Bee Hole End, after a colliery which once stood nearby. The bank is a maze of barriers running in every direction. The floodlight pylons, one of which stands outside the ground behind this end, are of the same design and manufacture as those at Burnden Park. From the top of this terrace one gains the best view of Turf Moor. It seems from here as if the ground has been denied any bright colours, and even the club colours, claret and blue are absent. The pitch once sloped quite badly, as one can see from the height it has been raised above the cinder track behind the Bee Hole End goal.

For a small town, Turf Moor is indeed a finely equipped ground, much of which is due to the effort and energy of the late Bob Lord. But it has to be repeated that the improvements cost Burnley nearly £1·5 million, and coincided with the team's decline. Had the club waited a few years, no doubt the rise in prices would have made such developments less likely, though they might have received aid from the Football Grounds Improvement Trust. Modern stands or not, the ground even now barely stands out from the East Lancashire landscape of rolling hills and decaying mills. Turf Moor is in name and appearance a down-to-earth venue, a compromise between the demands of the new generation and the traditions of the old.

· PRESTON · NORTH END

Deepdale

Preston began playing Association football in 1881, but had existed for many years before as a cricket, rugby and athletics club. When they moved to Deepdale in 1875, as Preston Nelson, the ground was part of Deepdale Farm, owned by a Mr Noble. Opposite was the recently opened Moor Park, where the club had played in their early days.

Preston North End, as they became, soon found soccer to be their forte, and crowds gathered in increasing numbers as the club took on older, more famous teams such as Queens Park, and Old Carthusians. Banking and fences were gradually constructed around the pitch, though sheep were still allowed to graze there, and the club even had to abandon their policy of allowing in ladies free of charge, so many turned up to see this new local attraction.

In Berry and Allman's *Centenary History* of the club is a sketch map of Deepdale, drawn in November 1890, showing two stands, 'Large' and 'Small' on the west side, with a press-box in between, and uncovered stands on the north and east sides. Along the east touchline were to be 3 feet 6 inch high railings (just under the present recommended height of 1.1 metres for crush barriers) and a new stand, not roofed, was proposed for the South End. A covered stand was also planned alongside the 'Small Stand' on the west. In the north west corner, at an angle, was the Dress Tent, a hut containing changing rooms. The club's Chairman, William Sudell, a pioneer in the fight to establish professional football, was said to have had his own entrance to the ground. Reports from *Athletics News* suggest the Large Stand dated from 1883 and held 600, and that the uncovered stands were 'staging' which gave the place 'the appearance of a huge amphitheatre'.

In 1893 a magnificent new stadium was planned for Preston's all-conquering 'Invincibles', next door to Deepdale. It was to have a large Main Stand and a cycle-track, as grand as Molineux (opened 1889) and Goodison Park (1892), if not quite so big. But nothing ever came of the plan, and Deepdale changed little until the turn of the century, by which time it was quite primitive compared with the likes of Villa Park, Burnden Park and Ewood Park.

But Preston fought their way back into Division One in 1904 and in January 1906 a new stand was built to replace the three older buildings on the west side. The Grand Stand housed dressing rooms and offices, and although modest in comparison with contemporary designs such as those of Leitch at nearby Ewood Park, it did provide Deepdale with a memorable feature that still survives today and remains one of the finest relics at any British football ground.

In January 1921 the club extended and covered the North End of Deepdale at a cost of £19 000. Preston were back in Division Two four years later, but definitely on the way up when the next major development was undertaken in 1934. This was the construction of the Pavilion, opposite the Grand Stand. In order to raise the necessary capital, the club's chairman, J. R. Taylor, set up a separate Preston North End Pavilion Company with 9999 shares issued at £1 each. The actual building cost a little over £9000 and when completed in February 1934 added another distinctive piece of architecture.

It was only 50 yards long, built on the half-way line, and had new offices, dressing rooms, an elegant boardroom and guest rooms on three floors, with an electric lift to the top storey. At the same time, a new stand was built on the Town End for standing spectators, as modern as the Pavilion was sumptuous, and the Grand Stand quaint.

In 1936 another stand was completed, called the South Pavilion (although on the east side it was south of the original Pavilion). It was in effect an extension of the Pavilion, though a little less luxurious. Also in 1936 the firm of Abbotts in Lancaster installed specially-designed stained glass windows in the boardroom, and not even Highbury had those. Deepdale's highest crowd of 42 684 saw Preston v. Arsenal, a clash between two Championship contenders.

The ground was taken over by the Army in May 1941, in return for £250 a year compensation; then in March 1943, they commandeered the club's car-park for a mere £5 a year.

Since the War, Deepdale has changed little in outward appearance, but substantially in other ways. In October 1953 the floodlights were first switched on, for a Lancashire Senior Cup match v. Bolton. On their promotion from the Third Division in 1978, the club found Deepdale far below the standards required by the new Safety of Sports Grounds Act. A total of £500 000 has since been spent on the ground, much of it on new barriers, fencing and access points. At one point the club ran out of steel for new barriers, and being unable to afford a further £50 000 outlay, elected instead to have the capacity of one section reduced. The total capacity is now 25 000, reduced from 37 000, and there are 4200 seats.

Preston do not own Deepdale. Most of the land belongs to the council. But in 1926, the club purchased the northern section of the car-park. In the 1970s, Preston and the council swapped this bit of land with an equivalent portion where the Pavilion stands, so now at least the club own some of the ground.

Ground Description

That Deepdale has not seen much glory in recent years is plain to see. Not because the ground is in a state of disrepair. On the contrary, it is spick and

Deepdale's pride, the immaculate Grand Stand dating from 1906 (Simon Inglis)

span throughout. Not because the stands are aged. The Baseball Ground, even Highbury, are no more modern. There is a peaceful, untroubled air at Deepdale and one could no more imagine a club winning the European Cup there than one could think of Anfield hosting a Fourth Division match.

The sense of composure begins on Lowthorpe Road, where the back of the Pavilion is clothed in ivy, and the top windows are stained glass. Inside the stand, across the Korkroyd floors, up in the lift to the Directors' Box, it is like Highbury built in miniature and on a lower budget.

The original Pavilion, that is the section over the half-way line, seems like any ordinary stand but its seats are spaciously arranged, gangways wide, and best of all, the roof is concealed by a low, white wooden ceiling, creating a most exclusive environment. J. R. Taylor obviously knew how to obtain the maximum luxury with the minimum outlay.

To the left is the less commodious South Pavilion. Looking at both stands from the ground, the join is in the middle, where Preston's crest appears on the blue roof fascia. This long blue board along the gutter is the only modern addition, and ties the two pavilions together neatly. But then everything at Deepdale is neat. In front of the stand is a line of private boxes, a rare reminder of modern times.

Again from the Pavilion, the remaining 20 yards of this touchline towards the North End, are open terracing, which bends round the north east corner to the North End. This is covered only at the very back, by a plain, gently sloping roof.

On the west side, its roof touching part of the North End roof, is the quite exquisite West or Grand Stand, probably the best preserved stand of its age. Gillingham's Gordon Road Stand is older, but much smaller. In design it could not be more basic: a barrel 'Belfast' roof made of wood is supported at the front by a line of very thin, round iron poles, spaced only 10 or 12 feet apart. The seating tier is composed entirely of benches, brightly painted in a shadowy interior. The facings are blue, the ironwork white. (Notice the mouldings along the guttering, at the top of each column.) All is in perfect harmony and proportion, and Preston have tended it with care and sensitivity.

To the left is the Town End, at first glance a modern construction like a propped cantilever, with a flat roof pitching steeply upwards. Deepdale's floodlights are unusual also; mounted on low, box-like pylons of the same width from top to bottom. The south east pylon has additional lights on the back, to illuminate the club's training pitch behind the Town End Stand.

Finally, Deepdale's turf seems very wide, partly because the stands lie well back from the perimeter. In fact the pitch is 78 yards in width, with an extra few yards to spare on either side, perfect for the likes of Finney. One of the club's directors, Ted Griffith, recalls one match in 1973 when Preston needed a point to stay in Division Two while their visitors, Burnley, needed the same to win the Championship. In order to cramp Burnley's successful wing-playing style, the North End manager ordered the touchlines to be brought in by 6 yards. A one-all draw resulted, and Lancashire breathed a huge sigh of relief.

◆ WIGAN ATHLETIC ◆

Springfield Park

Football is only one of an unusual variety of sports played at Springfield Park since at least 1897. In the 1920s, for example, horse-trotting was very popular at the ground. There was a half-mile track for the horse-and-traps to negotiate, and stables on the town side of the ground. There was also a cement cycle track around the pitch, some of which is still evident. In addition, Springfield Park was used for rugby and by the local police for their athletics meetings.

The ground has been the home of no less than five clubs bearing the title Wigan. From 1912–21 teams called Wigan County, Wigan Town and Wigan United had brief spells here, followed by Wigan Borough, a club that joined the newly formed League Division Three North in 1921, but had to resign because of insolvency on 26 October 1931. The following year Wigan Athletic formed and bought Springfield Park from the liquidators. During the Borough years, the existing standing covers were erected, the first in the early 1920s at the Shevington End, the second on the Popular Side in the late 1920s. The original Main Stand dated back to this era also, but was gutted by fire in May 1953. The present Main Stand was built the following year.

Wigan Athletic established themselves as one of the top non-League clubs in the country, and despite having to contend with their famous Rugby League neighbours at Central Park, Wigan regularly commanded gates envied by many League clubs. When the Springfield Park capacity stood at 35 000, a non-League encounter v. Hereford United (then in the Southern League) attracted their highest attendance, 27 500, in December 1953. The present capacity is reduced to 20 000, including 1069 seats.

The floodlights were first switched on in October 1965, for a Northern Floodlit League match v. Crewe Alexandra (Central Park did not have their lights until 1978).

Athletic joined Division Four in 1978, in place of Southport, and have since spent about £40 000 on ground improvements at Springfield Park.

Ground Description

Visitors to Wigan beware! The most prominent set of floodlights in the town belong to the rugby club, Wigan Athletic's ground is further from the centre and has smaller lights.

Once you find Springfield Park, through a network of narrow streets, the first sensation is of breezy openness as you emerge onto the ground's large exposed car-park.

Because this side of the ground stands high above the town, the Main Stand seems particularly tall and vulnerable to the elements. It is about 50 yards long and sits behind a terraced enclosure on the half-way

Springfield Park (Simon Inglis)

line; a solid, box-like post and beam construction with a gently sloping roof. Wigan is one of the very few clubs in the lower divisions to have installed private boxes, despite the fact that only Rochdale's Spotland ground has fewer seats. The rest of the ground is relatively undeveloped.

At either end the terraces are shaped around the compressed oval-shape of the pitch, a reminder that it was once surrounded by a track. Indeed the actual terrace steps at the Shevington End, to the left of the Main Stand, were visibly constructed on the old track. They rise up in shallow fashion a couple of yards, behind which a grass slope leads to a very basic and hardly used cover at the back. The club did try to erect a proper roof over the actual terracing in 1972, but this was taken down four years later, because it was too close to the pitch and reduced the numbers who could see from that end. The story had a happy ending though. Wigan sold the steelwork to an engineering firm for more than it cost them to build the cover in the first place. You can still see the foundations in the concrete.

Opposite the Main Stand is the Popular Side, on St Andrew's Drive, half covered along its length. The roof was built in two sections and is slightly angled at one end.

To the right is the open Town End, also curved round the pitch, with a mixture of blue and white barriers. Behind it is an all-weather floodlit pitch which the club shares with the community. The best overall view of the ground is from here and also of the flat landscape of housing, fields and industry, beyond the Main Stand.

If the club could afford it, or the local council were willing, Springfield Park would make a perfect site for a modern multi-sports stadium. The ground occupies a 14-acre site, much of it flat and unused except for parking. Alternatively, Wigan Rugby League Club have a large and much better stadium of their own in the very centre of town. Since soccer and rugby league have been shown to be happy 'ground-mates' elsewhere, it seems only logical for the two clubs to share either of their grounds.

·BLACKPOOL·

Previous Grounds

Blackpool formed in 1887 and first played at Raikes Hall Gardens, a venue made famous since by its Crown Green bowling tournaments. In 1897 the club moved to the Athletics Grounds, next to the cricket ground in Stanley Park, but had to move back to Raikes Hall in January 1899. After three seasons in the League, Blackpool amalgamated with another local team, South Shore, whose ground in Bloomfield Road became the new club's headquarters in December 1899.

Bloomfield Road

There is always an irresistible urge to associate Blackpool with the great days of Matthews, Mortensen *et al* in the early 1950s, but Bloomfield Road itself, though improved during this period of success nowadays appears much as it did before the Second World War.

Before explaining this, we must go back to the beginning of the century, when the all-wooden West Stand was built. It is a miracle that it has survived until now, for directly behind used to run a railway line, so close that passing locomotives would shower the back wall with sparks. Apart from structural repairs, the West Stand is unchanged. In 1925, as part of a general scheme of improvement, the existing South Stand was built behind the goal, with new offices and players' facilities, for the cost of £13 146, a good price even then. Between the South and West Stands a tiny corner stand was built at an angle to the pitch.

The North End at this time housed a small wooden seated stand, called the Motor Stand, as behind it was a small car-park. On promotion to Division One in 1930 this structure was moved to the north west corner where it linked up with the end of the West Stand, and the Kop banking was hurriedly raised. When the club returned to the First Division in the late 1930s the present East Paddock roof was erected. When War broke out the RAF immediately requisitioned the ground and used it as a training centre.

The club's golden era came soon after 1945 and the Kop was covered at the turn of the decade. Bloomfield Road was therefore covered on all four sides, and though somewhat unusually balanced, with two tall ends and two low sides, it was a happy home that would no doubt adapt to modern demands.

As a further sign of success, a record gate of 39 118 attended a League fixture v. Manchester United in April 1952, then in October 1958 the first floodlit game was staged, v. Hearts.

There have been two alterations to the ground since then, both regrettable. Seats which had been installed in the East Paddock – a forward thinking move – were removed after a short period to compen-sate for the results of the second change, the removal of the Kop roof in the late 1970s.

The supporters are still bitter about this measure, which it is thought was effected in a state of panic, when following the introduction of the Safety of Sports Grounds Act surveyors deemed the roof to be unsafe, despite the fact that it was barely 30 years old. It cost £40 000 to demolish, but a new one would have cost at least five times that amount. If, as has been said, it could have been easily strengthened, the hasty decision to remove it was even more unfortunate. The standing spectators sought cover thereafter in the East Paddock, hence the withdrawal of the seats.

The present capacity is now a much reduced 18 000, including 6500 seats.

Ground Description

Thousands of holiday-makers see the ground without visiting it, from the observation platform of nearby Blackpool Tower. At street level you cannot miss Bloomfield Road (though beware of confusing its floodlights with those of the neighbouring rugby league and greyhound stadium), for the back of the South Stand is a garish wall of bright orange, lined with advertisements.

Though behind the goal, this stand is the administrative centre of club and also houses the players' tunnel, an arrangement found elsewhere only at Turf Moor, The Den and Meadow Lane.

The South Stand has been completely refurbished inside, but still looks remarkably young for its age, with the minimum of pillars and a tall roof. Unfortunately its new red seats clash painfully with the green woodwork and orange uprights. The small box to the left is the South West Stand, now accommodating the directors (who were formerly, and apparently quite happily seated in the West Stand). It closes off the corner quite neatly, and provides an excellent view.

From this end you can see the Blackpool Tower behind the Kop. The Kop still keeps the back wall and the remains of the roof supports, and although not an eyesore, for those who knew it when covered it now seems somehow naked and inadequate. The two side stands needed the end roof to disguise their lowliness.

To the right of the South Stand is the covered East Paddock, known more familiarly as the Scratching Shed. Along its low black roof is a marvellous fading advertisement which recalls Blackpool not only as the home of stylish football but as a popular resort with exotic fantasies: Ismail and Company, Tea and Coffee Merchants.

One observer described Bloomfield Road as the most uncomfortable ground in the League. He probably had the West Stand in mind. What the Roker End at Sunderland was to labyrinthine concrete, the West Stand is to wood. Behind and underneath it resembles a timber merchant's yard, made more hos-

73

Bloomfield Road in the mid-1930s (Aerofilms)

pitable but more cramped by a line of small offices, refreshment huts and all the paraphanalia of ground maintenance equipment.

The stand has a seating tier with narrow terraces in front, covered by a low sloping roof adorned with more large advertisements. Roof advertising is something of a mania all over Blackpool, and when you are at the top of the Tower you can understand why.

At the northern end of the West Stand is the also wooden but very short North West Stand, with a few more wooden seats overlooking that corner of the pitch.

It has needed considerable attention to keep the West Stand safe after 80 years of use, but since every

attempt by the club and developers to rebuild on that side and on the disused railway line behind have all failed at the planning stage, this effort has been worthwhile.

The ideal replacement West Stand would, if funds were available, incorporate catering and hotel facilities for use by holiday-makers. Behind the Kop there is an enormous car-park and plenty of space for access. Redevelopment is surely imminent.

There ought to be tours from the Promenade taking visitors to Bloomfield Road, if only to see the West Stand before it is pulled down or falls down. It is the quintessential English football grandstand and impossible to recreate in concrete and steel.

⬥CARLISLE UNITED⬥

Previous Grounds

Carlisle had two grounds before Brunton Park. Their first was at Milholme Bank, used for two years after the club formed in 1903. The site is now built over, but their second home at Devonshire Park is now playing fields for Trinity School. Carlisle played there until 1909.

Brunton Park

There have been three League clubs in the Cumbria area, but only Carlisle remain, since both Barrow and Workington failed re-election in 1972 and 1977 respectively. A local derby for Carlisle now means a 58-mile trip to Newcastle, although Berwick or Stranraer are not much further away. This distance has always marked Carlisle apart from other League clubs. Norwich are also some distance from their nearest club Ipswich but have a neighbourly affinity with them, 43 miles away. Carlisle, however, is separated from the pack by long stretches of mountainous, open countryside.

Sometimes unfair words have been written about Brunton Park. When Bill Shankly joined the club in 1949 he called the ground, 'a hencoop, a glorified hencoop. The stand and terraces and everything about the ground were in terrible condition, except for the pitch, and that was always a good one.' It has never been an easy life at the outpost of the League.

Carlisle played their first game at Brunton Park on 2 September 1909, a friendly v. 'nearby' Newcastle. But it was not until the club joined the League in 1928 in place of Durham City that the ground was properly developed. First the small wooden stand was extended and turnstiles built. The club bought the site for £2000, and in 1929 relaid the pitch with Solway turf, the type favoured for bowling greens (Solway Firth is about ten miles west of Carlisle). As Shankly commented, the pitch was indeed one of the finest in the country. In the early 1930s United sold their promising young winger Jackie Cape to Newcastle for £1500, and were thus able to build the 'Scratching Pen', a cover over part of the terracing opposite the Main Stand.

Soon after the Second World War, Ivor Broadis joined Carlisle from Tottenham Hotspur. Now a local journalist, he wrote that it 'was like stepping down from the Savoy Hotel into the Jungle Cafe. The Spurs cockerel with its dazzling plumage, or a worn-out, tired looking Cumberland fox . . . conditions were a bit primitive, the old wooden stand looked to be reeling drunkenly under the weight of its years, the sleepers providing the terraces where ashes weren't banked, resembled a switchback, and I imagine that fans leaned on the post and rail fence surrounding the pitch at their own peril.'

When Pat Waters came to Brunton Park from Deepdale in 1950 he called the Main Stand, a 'big wooden rabbit hutch'. Nevertheless, Carlisle were the first English League club north of London to install floodlights. These were switched on first for a friendly v. Blackburn Rovers on 25 February 1952.

It was after another floodlit game, in March 1953 v. East Fife that the 'rabbit hutch' burned to the ground. For a while the club was in difficulties, having to borrow kit from Newcastle and using James' Street swimming baths as changing rooms for the players. A temporary stand was erected at the Warwick Road End. But the following year, helped by the transfer of Geoff Twentyman to Liverpool in December 1953 and the formation of a supporters' club, a new Main Stand was built. Ronald Cowing wrote in his history of the club, from which much of this information derives, that the fire formed a turning point in the club's history.

In 1957, a full house of 27 500 was recorded for the first time, for a Cup tie v. Birmingham on 5 January. On promotion to Division Two in 1965 the present Warwick Road End was covered.

The 1970s were an eventful decade for Carlisle, beginning with another full house in February 1970 for a 5th Round Cup match v. Middlesbrough. But the greatest event came in 1974, when Carlisle finished third in Division Two, and so won promotion to the First Division. The summer was spent building extra wings onto the Main Stand, erecting impressive new pylons, and of course constructing a television camera gantry onto the Main Stand roof.

But though their success was short-lived, that season had the all-important effect of giving the club and its supporters expectations. Several developments occurred during those five years which were to make Brunton Park a much more viable ground. One of the greatest problems over the years had been flooding from the nearby River Petteril, so badly that once in the 1970s one of the crossbars was just under water, but the other stayed above. From this the groundsman, in a boat of course, was able to determine that the pitch sloped 3 feet! He had also to rescue several wooden floating sleepers that had become dislodged from the terracing. After this flood the club concreted over part of the terraces. The Water Board has since built a bank to prevent the worst of the flooding, but water can still rise up from under the pitch.

In order to reduce the effects of flooding, the club spent £36 000 on new drains, but even these proved inadequate, and as a result the pitch is no longer the fine Solway turf it once was.

In 1981 Brunton Park's other sporting facilities were opened, comprising squash and tennis courts, an all-weather floodlit pitch and an indoor gym. The club even own their own guest house at the ground, Brunton House. Executive boxes were built at the back of the Main Stand, and a Rugby League team formed at the ground. The aim has been to make Brunton Park in use all-year round, every day of the week. Carlisle were lucky to have space to develop

Brunton Park in the late 1970s (Aerofilms)

– they own 18 acres in total – but there is no doubt that their self-confidence arose largely from the realization that even though they might not be able to sustain a First Division club, sound planning and sensible management would ensure that never again would Brunton Park be spoken of with derision, least of all among the community in which they are now playing such a part.

The current capacity is 25 000, of which 2600 are seated.

Ground Description

Approaching from the M6 Motorway, Brunton Park stands out as almost the first set of buildings in an otherwise rural landscape, with the extremely tall and thin floodlights especially prominent.

Whenever television cameras come to Brunton Park they usually open with a wide angle shot of the fields beyond the Popular Side. Such a setting invites such an angle.

The main gate is adorned with the metal silhouette of a player kicking a ball, rather akin to those pictures so often seen on club programmes in the 1950s. There is a sizeable car-park with room for 1500 vehicles – an asset many clubs would envy. At the back of the Main Stand is an excellent new entrance hall, tastefully designed in almost high-tec decor, with rubberized floors, tinted glass and potted plants; a welcome and encouraging relief from all those football ground entrances decked in formica, garish carpets and simulated wood.

Unfortunately, inside the ground the Main Stand is somewhat less appealing. You can see clearly where the wings have been added to the original 1954 central section, which resembles in many ways a section of Birmingham's Main Stand – plain brick, blue steel, utilitarian and uninspiring. There is a paddock in front with room for 7500. As the rest of the ground is comparatively low this Main Stand seems

tall. From the back seats can be seen the view already described, of unbound countryside stretching beyond the opposite stand.

To the right is the Warwick Road End covered terrace, with a multi-span roof similar to one at Prenton Park, but slightly larger. The crush barriers at this end are of curious design, similar to walking frames used by the aged and infirm, but sturdy no doubt.

To the left is the open Petteril or Waterworks End, an exposed bank behind which runs the River Petteril, on its way to link up with the River Eden and so into the sea at Solway Firth. Also behind the terracing is the new sports centre, such a vital element of the ground's new role. At the back of the bank stands a scoreboard and flagpoles, constantly buffeted in the stiff breezes which add to your sense of being out in the wilds. Notice how large the playing surface is at Carlisle. Since the introduction of Rugby League, extra turf behind the touchlines has been added, and the overall length and width makes this pitch second only to Maine Road in area.

Opposite the Main Stand is the Popular Side, the central section covered by the old roof affectionately known as the Scratching Pen, which for once I am bound to say is a name thoroughly deserved. The terracing on either side of the cover is of wood and concrete, and at each end near the pitch are crush barriers apparently made of sawn-up telegraph poles.

No doubt it was the view from the Main Stand which prompted the lyrical words of the *Daily Mail*'s football writer Brian James in *Journey to Wembley*, (Marshall Cavendish, 1977). He called Brunton Park, quite rightly, 'a frontier post of football indeed, guarded only by sheep. Nothing moves out there. And the notion that a ball kicked over the wall would go bouncing until it dropped off the end of the world is hard to shake off.' One comment among many about a ground that despite many failings is actually better prepared for the needs of its patrons than some of the grander stadiums which seem so splendid on Saturdays but lie idle the rest of the week. Carlisle, population 70 000, cannot expect much better, and at least the Cumberland Fox looks a lot more spritely.

·7·
NORTH EAST

·MIDDLESBROUGH·

Previous Grounds

The club was formed in February 1876 but did not apparently play its first proper game until a year later, at the Old Archery Ground, Albert Park. As attendances grew the Parks Committee decided the turf had suffered enough, and in March 1879 Middlesbrough moved to Breckon Hill Road, where they rented a field from a Mr Kemp. The following summer they moved again, to Linthorpe Road, the home of Middlesbrough Cricket Club, conveniently placed next to the Empire Hotel, which belonged to the club chairman. In 1885 some members of the club decided they would like to turn professional. They left Linthorpe Road, rented the nearby Paradise Ground on Milton Street (Paradise Found?) and as Middlesbrough Ironopolis joined the Football League in 1893. Amateurs Middlesbrough were in danger of being completely upstaged as Ironopolis attracted better gates. But football plays some funny tricks on public expectations, and despite finishing their first season in eleventh place Ironopolis slipped out of the League.

The last game at Linthorpe Road was in April 1903. Since then the site has been covered by buildings, between Princess Street and Clifton Street, although the Empire Hotel still stands. Breckon Hill Road Ground is part of Longlands College, and the Old Archery Ground is still in Albert Park, behind the groundsman's cottage. The Paradise Ground has been lost to developers.

Ayresome Park

Middlesbrough was already a First Division club when Ayresome Park was officially opened on 9 September 1903, for a League match v. local rivals Sunderland. Performing the ceremony was James Clifton Robinson, the Managing Director of the local Tram Company, who, according to Arthur Appleton's book, *Hotbed of Soccer*, not only devoted his life to tramcars but died in one in New York seven years later.

The new ground was quite magnificent for its time, having cost £11 000 to buy, with a capacity of 40 000 and two stands. The one on the South Side was about 50 yards long and had come from Linthorpe Road. The North Stand, which still exists, was an impressive full-length structure built at a cost of £1250 (the highest transfer fee of this period was £1000, paid by Middlesbrough for Alf Common from Sunderland). It had a barrel roof with a small, semi-circular gable, topped by an ornate wrought-iron flourish.

To honour Middlesbrough the FA chose to stage an international v. Ireland at Ayresome Park on 25 February 1905, the first of three full internationals played at the ground. But it is really as a venue for amateur games that Ayresome Park was most favoured, staging three amateur internationals and nine Amateur Cup Finals.

The next development followed during the club's spell in Division One between 1929–54. The South Stand was demolished and the existing construction built in 1936. The terraced banks at either end were also rebuilt, the rear sections being on concrete frames similar, though far less intricate, to those at Roker Park. The West End cover was also erected.

These improvements gave Ayresome Park a capacity of 54 000, a total almost reached in December 1949 when 53 596 saw Middlesbrough play Newcastle United in the First Division. This is the ground's record gate, but it was only one of several occasions when the ground's gates were locked.

It was reported that for one 6th Round FA Cup game v. Burnley in 1947 the thousands locked outside were given a running commentary of the action by the Chief Constable of Middlesbrough, A. E. Edwards, himself once an officer in Burnley, who stood on a wall surrounding the ground.

The ground's floodlights were first switched on for a friendly v. Sunderland on 16 October 1957, when Middlesbrough were in the Second Division, and ironically the ground's greatest honour came when the club was at its lowest ebb in the Third Division. Ayresome Park staged three World Cup matches in 1966, having been chosen as a venue relatively late, in April 1964, in place of St James' Park.

To prepare hurriedly for the tournament a new

Ayresome Park's North Stand. The 'dashboard' gable was once crowned with ornate ironwork (Simon Inglis)

East Stand roof was built and 4000 seats installed on the terracing. An extra 3600 seats were put on the North and South Stand paddocks, reducing the ground's overall capacity to 40 000.

Middlesbrough hosted three games in Group Four, including the unforgettable heroics of North Korea, but the total attendances at the games amounted only to a disappointing 57 200.

Since then a television gantry has been added to the South Stand, and all round improvements made to the ground's safety, but the capacity has been retained at 42 000, including 9500 seats.

Outside the ground there have been substantial developments, including the building of a £1·2 million sports hall in 1981. The hall has been shrouded in controversy ever since building began, according to the local council, without planning permission. Additions were made in later months, again allegedly without planning permission, and even though the club received a total of £325 000 in grants for the sports hall, it was still not open, or completed in April 1983. In despair the club tried to sell the building to the council, which refused the offer. A great asset to both club and community therefore lay unused for two years.

Ground Description

The usual trick for finding previously unvisited football grounds is to look for floodlight pylons. At Middlesbrough this is like looking for a needle in a haystack, for there appear to be floodlight pylons strewn across the Teeside horizon, and Ayresome Park's are not easily distinguished.

The North Stand is of considerable interest to the connoisseur of football ground architecture. It has a large barrel roof whose supports have been adapted from their original form to having a pillar at each end, plus two extra pillars halfway back in the middle. The most prominent feature is the central gable, its round clock flanked by two roundels, part of an advertisement on the gable front.

On the upper tier are red- and ochre-coloured seats,

on the front tier white seats. A splash of colourful advertisements and two early-style electric scoreboards make this a very busy interior. It is one of the oldest stands still in use as a main stand in the League, yet still looks fresh.

To the left is the East End with ochre seats at the back and a standing enclosure at the front, under what appears to be a typical pitched roof, such as is found over many a terraced bank. The seating is flanked on both sides by two open corners of terracing curving round to meet each side stand, with barriers, but no screens, dividing the seats from the terraces.

The South Stand would be a fairly straightforward design were it not for its deep overhanging pitched roof. Two white poles in front of this support not the roof but the extra weight of the television camera gantry. The platform itself has two covered pigeon loft covers on either side, as if it were an army gunpost.

To the right is the West Stand, almost identical to the East but for standing only, and with two uncovered corners. The chimney behind is part of a hospital complex.

In plan Ayresome Park resembles Maine Road or Old Trafford – a rectangle with neatly curved corners, and plenty of space between touchline and perimeter fence, especially on the sides, where there are wide cinder tracks.

Here are old fashioned stands and old fashioned proportions, all looked after with pride. Due to licensing difficulties, no alcohol may be sold on the premises. With a sports hall lying unfinished and crowds dwindling, this enforced dryness is yet another loss of potential income. Ayresome Park will therefore remain unchanged a good while longer; one of the last of the really big grounds to have eluded the modern era of stadium design.

·DARLINGTON·

Feethams

Football has been played at Feethams since at least 1866, when a group of enthusiasts hired the land next to the cricket pitch from John Beaumont Pease, and laid it with turf taken from another cricket pitch in Old Park Street. A football club was formed in 1883, but by the beginning of the First World War it was in dire financial straits. An up and coming local team, Darlington Forge Albion offered to amalgamate in 1917, and immediately fortunes rose. In 1919 the club finished building the East Stand, begun in 1914, joined the League in 1921 and there followed a spell of success which saw Darlington into the Second Division and the building of the West Stand.

Feethams was also host to several amateur semi-finals and finals, in a period when north eastern clubs dominated the competition. A crowd of 20 000 attended a Final replay at Feethams in 1933.

The ground changed little until 1960. In the summer a simple cantilever cover was put over the shallow Cricket Field End terrace. Then on 19 September, Darlington's floodlights were first used for a 4th Division game v. Millwall. Later that night the West Stand burned down, though there was apparently no connection between the events. Shortly after, in November 1960, Feethams had its highest attendance of 21 023 for the visit of Bolton in the League Cup.

Of course the supporters expected to see a bright new stand in place of the West Stand, and were amazed to see an exact replica of the old one being built instead in 1961.

Feethams holds the unfortunate record of the lowest crowd ever to watch an FA Cup tie between two League teams, when only 1763 saw Darlington v. Wrexham in November 1972. The present capacity is 15 000, including 1200 seats.

Ground Description

The ground and its environs are unashamedly charming and belong to a middle-class Edwardian world.

You must approach the ground from Victoria Road, where you see first a solid redbrick wall with an ornamental gateway, and the words Darlington Cricket and Football Club written between two decorative towers. As Frank Tweddle, the club historian remarks wryly, they are the only twin towers Darlington are ever likely to see!

Through these gates you come to the cricket pitch, around whose boundaries you must pass to reach the football ground on the furthest side of the pitch, a reminder of how these English sports once coexisted so closely. The cricket club own all the land, charging the football club a nominal rent.

The East Stand adds to this nostalgia. It runs two-thirds of the length of the pitch, with six flood-light gantries on a barrel roof – a sort of Newcastle in half-scale. Along the front is a line of white steel pillars, formed into distinctive arches under the eaves. Frank Tweddle observes that, coincidentally, there are the same number of arches as there are letters in the name Darlington. Behind the stand is the River Skerne, across which is a tree-lined avenue of Victorian villas. You can see at the back how steel supports have been bolted to the stand's wooden frame to strengthen it.

To the left is Polam Lane running behind the Polam End open bank. There is a small brick cottage next to the terracing, and more football pitches beyond. From here the handsome town clock tower is visible straight ahead.

Opposite is the West Stand, in fading blue, looking every bit a 1920s' wooden box stand, sitting on the half-way line. Only a plaque on the side confirms that it was built in 1961. To its left is a fenced-off terrace where a sports hall has been built with grants from the Playing Fields Association. Behind the stand is the tall shell of a wooden barn, through which spectators must walk on entering that side of the ground. There can be few more rural entrance ways. On the right, on a rise behind the ground are the huge northern works of the National Bus Company.

Finally, to the north is the cricket pitch, blocked from view by the cantilevered covered terrace, which hardly protects anyone from the weather but does stop wilder shots going onto the cricket field.

Feethams is the sort of ground where one sees the odd squirrel scooting across the terraces; evoking memories of how football and football grounds once were – not an imposition upon the landscape, but a place where sporting young men turned out for the love of the game.

Feethams: football and cricket living side by side

HARTLEPOOL ·UNITED·

The Victoria Ground

A rubbish tip opposite the Hartlepool docks was made into a sports ground in 1886, and named after the Queen, who celebrated her Golden Jubilee in the following year. In those early days, the Victoria Ground and the adjacent Hartlepool Stadium were linked, and used mainly by the West Hartlepool Rugby Club. Association football was played there from 1890, and in 1908 it became the home of the newly formed professional club, Hartlepools United. The rugby and soccer pitches were divided and the one ground became two separate entities.

The Victoria Ground does not occupy much space in the annals of great soccer, but it did witness an unusual event during the First World War. On the night of 27 November 1916 two German Zeppelins were attempting to raid the town when they were caught in the searchlights, and hit by guns of the Royal Flying Corps. The airships jettisoned their load of 100 bombs, then burst into flames and crashed into the North Sea. The *Daily Mirror* described the raid as 'a complete fiasco' in which the only casualty was a woman who died of shock, but they did not mention that two of the German bombs had fallen on the wooden grandstand at the Victoria Ground.

For several years after the War United conducted a lengthy correspondence with the German Government, demanding compensation of £2500. (Their pleas went unanswered, and during the Second World War German bombers returned over Hartlepool, but just missed the football ground.)

Although they joined the League in 1921, United decided to build only a temporary replacement to the Main Stand. This was especially sensible because the council had plans to widen Clarence Road, behind the stand, which would mean shifting the pitch several yards to the west. But the club was not the only body short of funds, and as the years went by although the traffic grew heavier the road stayed as it was.

So to 1957, and the visit of the Busby Babes, Manchester United, in the 3rd Round of the FA Cup, on 5 January 1957. A record gate of 17 426 squeezed into the Victoria Ground as Hartlepools were squeezed out of the competition. Manchester United went onto the Final, but Hartlepools United had earned sufficient to extend their north and south terracing and prepare for the eventual moving of the pitch. And the years went by but the road stayed as it was.

In 1965 a young Brian Clough became manager of the club and noticed immediately that the Victoria Ground had no floodlights. By the end of that year lights had been installed and first switched on for a

The Victoria Ground's all-wooden Main Stand, Hartlepool (Martin Parr)

game v. Southend. For the first time in their history, United won promotion in 1968. Down came the old cover over the terracing opposite the Main Stand, and up went a splendid new full-length cantilever stand, at a cost of £40 000.

Quite sensibly, this new stand was erected some distance from the touchline, to allow room for when the pitch was inevitably moved. Also in 1968 the club changed its name to plain Hartlepool, but in 1977 changed again to Hartlepool United. Despite all these disruptions, the road remained as it was. By 1982 the capacity of the Victoria Ground was 18 000, including 2320 seats, but the road . . .

Ground Description

United's ground is in location similar to Blundell Park, Grimsby, a short distance from the sea with a railway line in between. But the Victoria Ground is more open and windswept and therefore more a part of the seaboard landscape.

The Victoria Ground presents a miserable, long blue wooden fence to the outside world, with a small sign saying 'Official Entrance'. The crumbling planks at the back of the small stand, clad in plastic sheeting, just a pavement's width from *the* road, present an unlikely entrance to a Football League club.

Once inside there is a dark alley with wooden doors and patched-up walls, supported by cross-beams at all angles, leading to narrow corridors under the stand. Are those old telegraph poles holding up the stand at the front? Isn't that a roof strut flapping loosely in the sea-breeze?

Although it covers only a third of the touchline and is barely 20 feet deep, the stand accommodates 620 people, plus dressing rooms, a tiny office and club-room. Another office in the town centre serves as the club's real administrative centre. The council has still not decided on a plan to widen Clarence Road, and perhaps it never will. But the authorities are not to blame for this stand. It may be bigger than the one at Halifax, it may be marginally more comfortable, but it is certainly the most precarious of any Main Stand in the League. When the wind is high the roof sways, so shutters at the back have to be lifted. But when bits have blown off, games have had to be postponed.

To the left is the Town End terrace, behind which is the Hartlepool Stadium, used for greyhound racing. To the right, or north, is the Rink End terrace, named because there was once a popular roller skating rink behind. Both terraces are covered at the back with narrow, flat roofs on stilts, like bicycle sheds.

Across the pitch, one of the widest in the country and with yards of turf to spare because of the road plan, is one of the finest stands in the lower divisions. The Mill House Stand, named after a nearby pub, seats 1700 quite comfortably and is a copy-book pre-fabricated structure, built behind a line of terracing.

From here one has an excellent view, over Clarence Road to the railway line which runs from Sunderland to Newcastle, beyond which are the docks. The fresh sea-air is more noticeable up in the stand, blustering across the ground into the spectators' faces. To the right, over the Town End, you can also see the stands of the Hartlepool Stadium. It is typical of the haphazard development of English sport that two such grounds should be so separate, but United could not play there anyway because the pitch is not large enough and the rent would be too high.

Underneath the Mill House Stand, between the already rusting steel supports, is a great deal of room; surely enough to house all the facilities now crammed into the stand opposite. This could happen if the club owned the ground, but the council now owns it and have asked for £64 000 to sell it back. If United ever do repurchase, the Sports Council has offered to help build a sports centre, based at the back of the Mill House Stand. Years of inaction and inflexibility have always threatened the club, but the tragedy is that if this procrastination continues the Victoria Ground will never develop and Hartlepool will remain the largest town in England without a community sports centre.

◆ SUNDERLAND ◆

Previous Grounds

No other Football League club has had the history of its grounds better chronicled than Sunderland, thanks to the research of Arthur Appleton. His *Centenary History of Sunderland*, written in 1979, leaves hardly a question unanswered. Sunderland's first home in 1879 was the Blue House Field, Hendon, not far from the Board School where the idea for a club originated with one of the teachers, James Allan. The ground lay next to the original Blue House public house. But Sunderland and District Teachers AFC found the annual rent of £10 too high, so in 1882 after trying various pitches they moved to Groves Field, Ashbrooke, probably on the site of the Ashbrooke Ground, formally laid out in 1887. Sunderland moved to Horatio Street, Roker in 1883. This was their first ground north of the River Wear, the others being on the south side close to the seafront and docks.

Horatio Street itself was then built up, but on the other side of the pitch was a claypit and brickworks. The pitch had a heavy surface and was sometimes called 'a clay-dolly field'. The ground is now covered by Givens Street and Appley Terrace. After only one season there, Sunderland moved to Abbs Field, Fulwell Road, their first properly enclosed ground. Rent was a paltry £2 10s to begin with, but as the club attracted more support and a better reputation, it rose to £15 in the second season. The ground was near where the Central Laundry now stands, opposite Cliff Road.

Sunderland had already played some games at the neighbourhood's best ground on Newcastle Road, owned by two sisters called Thompson, and in early 1886 the club succeeded in procuring a year's lease for the ground, at a rent of £15. The ground already had walls round three sides, so Sunderland had only to board up the Newcastle Road Side, at the east end of the pitch. Two players were each paid five shillings for tarring the new fence, and a clubhouse was bought for £2 10s.

On the north side was built a small wooden grandstand on the half-way line, seating 1000 spectators, the work carried out mainly by supporters from Thompsons North Sands shipyard.

Sunderland's first game at Newcastle Road was on 3 April 1886 v. Darlington, and the ground obviously met with approval for attendances rose rapidly. But the club was still technically amateur, and although turnover was high, it still felt the need to rent the ground for grazing in return for 30 shillings a year – cheaper than a lawnmower. The Thompsons also helped out by handing back the first season's rent to Sunderland.

The issue of professionalism was almost the ruin of Sunderland, beginning with their expulsion from the

Roker Park from the Roker End in 1966 (Syndication International)

FA Cup after a tie v. Middlesbrough at Linthorpe Road. A disgruntled Jimmy Allan, the club's founder, decided to break away and form a proper professional outfit called Sunderland Albion. Taking seven of Sunderland's Scottish players with him, he set up on Sunderland's original ground, the Blue House Field. Money was poured into Albion, who would have comfortably surpassed Sunderland and become the town's premier club had intense local rivalry and bitterness about Allan's actions made Sunderland determined not to play second fiddle.

In the summer of 1889 Newcastle Road was downcast, overshadowed by events across the Wear, until the shrewd appointment of Tom Watson. Backed by shipbuilding money, he rejuvenated the club and ensured its ascendancy. Newcastle Road was improved with a new clubhouse and an enlarged stand. Capacity rose to 15 000, making it the biggest and best ground in the north east (St James' Park was not improved until 1898). A cabin for reporters was placed in the stand.

Also in 1889, Watson assembled the famous 'Team of All Talents' at Newcastle Road, whose highest attendance, 21 000, saw a Cup tie v. Everton in January 1891. Two months later the ground was chosen for an international v. Wales.

Despite having laid the only cinder cycling track in Sunderland and built 'substantial' stands at the Blue House Field, interest in Sunderland Albion waned so drastically once Sunderland became a major national force, that Albion went into voluntary liquidation in August 1892.

Meanwhile to cope with Sunderland's growing support, Newcastle Road was again extended, to a capacity of 18 000, although not everyone had a good view and the stand roof was often covered with spectators. Rent in 1896 was up to £100 a year and a limited liability company was formed in July of that year, because although the previous seasons were remarkably successful, very little capital had been amassed. Issue of shares helped of course, but the club could not really develop Newcastle Road as long as it had an annual lease. If Sunderland could have bought the freehold, a cycle and athletics track might

have been laid, new stands built and the capacity enlarged. But gates were down to a few thousand, Watson had been lured to Anfield, and they probably could not have afforded to buy the ground anyway.

There then appears to have been a disagreement with the Thompson sisters; perhaps over rent, perhaps because the ladies wished to sell the site for development. Whatever the reason, chairman Henderson and his brother started looking for an alternative site in 1897, and found Roker Park. Sunderland played their last game at Newcastle Road on 23 April 1898 v. Nottingham Forest.

There is one famous picture of Newcastle Road still in existence, on view in the main foyer at Roker Park. It is an oil painting by Thomas M. Henry, depicting an extremely crowded goal-mouth incident during a match v. Aston Villa in the 1894–95 season. The North Stand is just visible on the left of the canvas. Behind the goal is a steep, probably exaggerated representation of the sloping terraces.

The actual pitch was built over by Netherburn Road and Newington Court. Ellerslie Terrace, where the club's headquarters were, was demolished in the mid-1960s and became a car lot.

Roker Park

Since moving north of the Wear, all Sunderland's grounds had been within a couple of hundred yards of each other. The site picked by chairman Henderson was farmland belonging to a Mr Tennant, who leased the site only on the condition that the football club's activities would not prevent the building of houses on the remainder of the site up to Fulwell Road. Henderson had to agree to pay the ground rents until the sites were sold.

The grandstand was a single-deck having 3000 seats with a small paddock in front. Opposite was the original Clock Stand, for standing only, with 32 wooden steps each rising 9 inches (228 millimetres, compared with the current recommended height of between 75 mm and 180 mm). The open ends of the ground were called North and South, as they were for at least 30 years until the present names, Roker End and Fulwell End were adopted. Finally, fine quality

Irish turf was imported, a perfect camber created, and drainage installed.

Roker Park was opened with much pomp on 10 September 1898, in front of 30 000 spectators, when Liverpool were the visitors. Sunderland's President, Lord Londonderry, opened the small gate leading from the dressing rooms onto the field with a golden key, photographs were posed for, and Lord Londonderry praised the Henderson brothers for their efforts in delivering Sunderland 'from the misfortune of being without a football ground'.

Events at St James' Park on Good Friday 1901 (see Newcastle) had shown quite vividly how fanatical north east football followers could be, and how a minority of Sunderland's supporters proved themselves to be especially unruly, committing offences which make the present day hooliganism seem almost tame.

One referee had to escape from Roker Park disguised as a policeman, as angry men waited for him outside after the match. In 1903, The Wednesday team were stoned by Sunderland fans as they drove away from the ground along Roker Baths Road, and in punishment Roker Park was closed for one match, which Sunderland played at Linthorpe Road, Middlesbrough.

There were more pitch invasions during games v. Newcastle – often owing to overcrowding rather than malice – but in September 1909, a police horse was stabbed as police cleared the pitch at the Fulwell End. There was another invasion when West Bromwich were the visitors in February 1912, hardly surprising since the attendance of 43 383 was some 13 000 above the ground's capacity. Later that year, as more people struggled to see Sunderland v. Manchester City in the Cup (the match had been switched to Roker Park after a pitch invasion at Hyde Road in the first meeting), a crowd watched from the roof of the nearby Roker Coal Depot. This gave way under the weight and 20 people were hospitalized.

Naturally, success brought security and improvements at Roker Park. The ground was bought in 1905, for £10 000, and in 1912 the Roker End was enlarged at a cost of £20 000. Instead of being built up on earth banking, as was common practice, the terracing was built on a huge, labyrinthine base of concrete supports, like a complex M. C. Escher fantasy framework. It was an early example of the art of on site concrete building, which was to develop to the level of sophistication seen at Wembley Stadium in 1923. The structure also provided the players with a covered, if rather gloomy area under which to train during wet weather. Roker Park's capacity was now 50 000.

By 1929–30, the ground had grown to hold 60 000, after extensive improvements in the summer. Most important was the erection of the present Grand Stand, in place of the original wooden stand. Archibald Leitch was the designer, and although built on a slightly less grand scale than contemporary Leitch

stands at Goodison and Ibrox Parks, it has stood the test of time as well as any other. At Roker, Leitch's criss-cross steelwork balcony – his trademark – was painted red, whereas the other clubs he designed for used blue, so this one was unique at least for that.

Opened on 7 September 1929, the new stand cost £25 000 (compared with Everton's expenditure of £30 000 in 1926 for their Bullens Road Stand) and at the same time the Clock Stand was extended.

Attendances still grew, reaching a climax on 8 March 1933, when on a Wednesday afternoon 75 118 saw Sunderland lose in extra time to Derby County in a Cup 6th Round replay. Arthur Appleton was in the packed crowd, unable to raise his arms in the crush or prevent himself being carried from the back to the front of the Roker End. The rest of the town seemed to shut down just for that afternoon.

Yet just one month later only 4000 turned up to see Sunderland's final home game v. Portsmouth, because most people were pressed up against a wireless set listening to the live broadcast of the FA Cup Final at Wembley. Armchair football was then a novelty, and not until after the Second World War were Finals played after the last Saturday of League football.

In the midst of a successful run in Division One, the Clock Stand was rebuilt in the summer of 1936. Archibald Leitch was again the designer, and it was one of his last major works at a football ground before his death in 1939 (see Design). The new Clock Stand ran the full length of the pitch and held 15 500, in two sections of terracing; the rear half being wooden terracing, the front paddock having ash and concrete terracing. Lady Reine opened the stand in September 1936.

Roker Park was unaffected by the War until March 1943, when bombs fell on the pitch and just outside the ground, killing a policeman. In May, more bombs damaged the car-park and the clubhouse, then at the corner of Roker Baths Road.

After the War, the upper section of the Grand Stand paddock was converted into a seating tier in 1950, making a total of 5400 seats at the ground (Everton did the same to their Bullens Road Stand).

In December 1952 Roker Park became the second First Division ground to have floodlights (Highbury was the first), switched on for a friendly v. Dundee, that year's Scottish Cup runners-up. The lights were updated in 1973 for £22 000.

The next major developments came with the World Cup in 1966. Roker Park and Ayresome Park were chosen to stage matches in Group Four, with Sunderland also hosting the quarter-final between the USSR and Hungary. The Roker pitch had to be extended by 3 yards, permanent seats installed at the rear of the Clock Stand, and temporary seats added to both paddocks and the Fulwell End. This end was also covered for the first time. Altogether there were an extra 9000 seats. A television camera gantry was built on the Clock Stand roof. But perhaps the most substantial improvement was behind the Grand

Stand, where new offices and executive facilities were built on stilts. Much of the outlay was provided by a government grant and a loan from the FA.

During the 1970s, less noticeable but no less important innovations were private boxes in 1973, an underground sprinkler system for the pitch in 1974, and then to conform to the Safety of Sports Grounds Act, over £250000 had to be spent on new barriers, access points, lighting and refreshment bars.

Sadly, in the summer of 1982, safety requirements dictated the demolition of most of the Roker End's maze of concrete supports, so that the capacity of the terrace was reduced from 17150 to 7000. This left Roker Park with a total capacity of 36000, of which 9000 are seated.

Ground Description

Once you have become immersed in the built-up streets of Roker, having crossed the big red bridge across the Wear, it is almost impossible to know how close Roker Park is to the sea.

Before 1983 it would have been worth taking a walk around the back of the Roker End before gaining admission, just to see the concrete struts holding up the terracing. It is hardly surprising they had to come down; they were like a concrete version of Ibrox's wooden terracing in 1902, like grey logs bolted together. And yet they withstood so many huge crowds for so long. Rising 50 feet above the street, the Roker End was like an unfinished tower block, its guts exposed to the passer-by, who could see deep into a dark cavernous web of beams. Truly there was never terracing like it, nor ever will be again.

But all that is no more, and we must return to the Grand Stand, to the dark passages underneath the executive suites and social clubs. Inside the foyer is Henry's painting of Newcastle Road.

The Grand Stand is typical Leitch, but with a distinctive character of its own. Some of the balcony wall has been obscured by advertising, but enough remains to mark it clearly as Leitch's work. Underneath the balcony is a line of private boxes, more like commentary boxes than executive ones, but no doubt much warmer than the very exposed seats in the rear paddock. Every seat on this side is scarlet, which adds neatness and shows how uniform colours can create style, even in the oldest stand. The roof and sides have also been refurbished, and the screen ends are chequered with glass and red panels, another pleasing touch; quite a contrast to the predominantly blue and white examples of Leitch's other stands in this mould.

From here the open Roker End is to the left, now in its truncated form, half the original size. The floodlight pylons are almost on the lower corners, and thus parts of the terrace have an obscured view, especially the corner meeting up with the Grand Stand.

Opposite is the Clock Stand, with of course a clock on the centre of the roof. But such a small clock, dwarfed on either side by the cumbersome camera gantries! Presumably this clock predates the other one placed above the players' tunnel. The stand is low, with a pitched roof, and half-time scoreboards at each end, one of them tucked inside the screen wall so that it is barely legible from beyond the shadows. There is a paddock in front of the seating tier, but it was once all standing and therefore a very unusual sort of standing cover for the side of a ground. Perhaps Leitch had always intended it to be converted into seating.

To the right is the covered North, or Fulwell End, named after the nearby district. This holds 12500 standing, and has a high roof, almost higher than would appear necessary, in gun metal grey. Next to such a modern, plain roof, the presence of a wooden fence around the back of the terracing seems wholly anachronistic. In fact the fence was there to stop people falling over the side of the tall banking before the roof was put up, and has never been removed simply because if hooligans wish to bang their fists and feet against something they can do less damage to a solid wooden fence than to thin metal sheeting.

Despite the modernization of both ends, Roker Park is still an essentially pre-war ground with new trimmings, as for example the Baseball Ground or Burnden Park. It falls between the major stadiums and those archetypal Second Division grounds. But the feature which elevates Roker Park to the ranks of 'special' is the people who fill it and the Roker Roar which when caught in the sea breeze, is sent swirling across the ground and over the rooftops.

NEWCASTLE ·UNITED·

St James' Park

United began life as Newcastle East End in 1882, playing on a ground at Chillingham Road, Heaton. To the west on Town Moor, played their greatest rivals, Newcastle West End. West End had taken over the ground from a team called Newcastle Rangers, and had a 14-year lease. The pitch had the slight disadvantage of an 18-foot slope from north to south, but was perfectly located for the city centre and public transport. The club allowed butchers to graze their sheep on the pitch to fatten them up before slaughter.

In 1892 Newcastle West End amalgamated with East End, changed their name to Newcastle United and moved into the Town Moor ground, which became known as St James' Park. Facilities were negligible, the home players having to change at the Lord Hill pub on Barrack Road, the visitors at other local hostelries. West End had put down wooden boards in 1889 to prevent spectators getting wet feet on the rough banks, and a press box stood on the Leazes Terrace Side. Leazes Terrace, still partly visible from the ground today, was part of a larger Georgian development for the gentry built in 1829, on the pattern of Eldon Square, Newcastle, or Regents Park, London. Leazes Park, to the north of the ground was laid out on part of the Town Moor.

United negotiated a lease for St James' Park in 1892, but could not purchase the freehold because all the land occupied originally by Town Moor had been granted by Newcastle to the Freemen of the city. This is how the situation remains today, the club having two landlords, the city council and the Freemen, who are entitled by law to all the 'eatage and herbage' of St James' Park.

United joined the League in 1893 but it was not until 1898 when they were promoted to Division One, that a dressing room was erected, and this was for the home team only. The visitors changed in the County Hotel and were ferried to the ground in landaus. As more and more people packed into the ground, its capacity was stretched to the limit, once with terrible consequences. In a First Division match v. Blackburn Rovers some railings collapsed, one youth had his foot torn off, another suffered a broken leg and there were many minor injuries.

A complete restructuring was imperative. During the following summer of 1899, an extra 4 acres of land were leased, and by moving the pitch and shifting tons of soil, United were able to reduce the slope to about 4 feet from north to south. Terracing was cut into the banks on the Leazes Park End and the Leazes Terrace Side, increasing the ground's capacity to

St James' Park; the West Stand entrance (Syndication International)

28 000. 'Immense structures of corrugated iron' surrounded the ground, giving it the enclosed impression of a hippodrome, wrote Gibson and Pickford in 1906.

Still the ground was not large enough to cope, nor the pitch quite up to standard requirements. A report in February 1901 tells how in an attempt to melt the frost-bound pitch, straw was laid down on the turf and then set alight. But rain started to fall, the straw stuck in the mud, and sand had to be laid over the whole glutinous mess!

But worse was to follow on Good Friday, 5 April 1901. Sunderland were the visitors, and they were a few points above their north east rivals in strong contention for the Championship. An estimated 35 000 crowd tried to squeeze into St James' Park, with as many more outside desperate to gain admission. Fences were trampled down, and before long the pitch became a battleground between rival supporters. *Athletic News*'s correspondent reported that the: 'club flag was torn from its staff and riven into shreds; the goal nets at one end shared a like fate'. He went on to note, 'we are delighted to hear that the cross-bar in falling fetched one or two of the rioters a reverberating "sock" on the headache department.' It took until 5 o'clock for the police to clear the ground, using truncheons in a less than restrained fashion, and the match had to be abandoned.

Incredibly only nine people were sent to hospital, including one reported to have fallen out of the grandstand, which nearly collapsed. One Sunderland supporter sued Newcastle for his money back, lost his case and had to pay expenses of around £70 (it was not until a riot occurred at Goodison Park a few years later that League clubs began posting up signs warning that in no circumstances would money be refunded).

Although they lost for the second successive year, in the Cup Final of 1906, United undertook further improvements at St James' Park using their profits. The club built a new West Stand seating 4680 and costing £8082 14s 11d, and at the same time increased the banking on all three open sides, to double the ground's capacity to 60 000.

The new stand was similar to one at Anfield, built a few years earlier, in that it had a distinctive curved gable in the centre of the roof. Underneath the stand was a small swimming pool for the players. The West Stand still exists, although the pool has since been covered over and is now used as a reservoir for the pitch's sprinkler system.

The ground remained unaltered until the summer of 1930 when the Leazes Park End was covered. The roof carried some 20 yards round the north east corner along the Leazes Terrace Side, and remained in its truncated L-shape form until 1978. No sooner had the roof gone up, than St James' Park saw its highest ever gate of 68 386, for the visit of newly promoted Chelsea on 3 September 1930.

In 1948, the open Leazes Terrace Side and the Gallowgate End were laid with concrete terracing, and in 1953 St James' Park became only the third First Division ground to have floodlights, switched on for a friendly v. Celtic on 25 February. These first lights were mounted on telegraph poles and were used for the first ever floodlit FA Cup match between two League clubs, Carlisle and Darlington, in a 1st Round replay on 28 November 1955. An improved system on four pylons was installed in 1958, and were switched on for a Football League v. Scottish League representative game in March.

The 1950s were prosperous years at St James' Park, United winning three Wembley Cup Finals between 1951–55. Reflecting this success was the West Stand's new Director's Suite, added in 1957, and giving the club a grander entrance and foyer in typically 1950s' style; ivory terrazzo floors and mahogany clad walls, the polished utilitarian style.

In 1967 the city council asked a firm of architects to investigate ways of making St James' Park the centre of a multi-pupose sports complex. A plan was drawn up showing the ground as an elliptical-shaped stadium with a sports centre under a new West Stand for use by the community and Newcastle University. The East Stand would be solely for United's purposes. Overall there were to be 31 000 seats and room for 32 000 standing (at a time when St James' Park still only had 4680 seats) and the ground would have a practice pitch and car-parks, also for sharing with the University. To tempt United with the proposals, the council offered the club the security of a long lease (for a detailed study of the plan, see *Architectural Review*, May 1968).

United's willingness to enter such a scheme was not the major barrier. Money was. The scheme never left the drawing board, and so United have had to pay for the redevelopment of St James' Park without the council's aid. But they did negotiate a 99-year lease with their landlords before commencing work.

The club's plans centred on the Leazes Terrace Side, where for years they had considered building a double-decker stand, but had never had sufficient capital or security to go further. The long lease helped, but as important was the revenue earned during three consecutive seasons competing in the European Fairs Cup from 1968–71, the first of which saw United winning the trophy.

Building began in 1972 and finished in March 1973, later than planned because of a building workers' strike. Thanks to the keen interest in stand design by the architects, there is a detailed account of which factors they considered important (see Design). The factors which related specifically to St James' Park were that the stand had to offer standing room, for traditional reasons, had to be part of an overall development plan, and most importantly, had to respect the architectural integrity of the Georgian Leazes Terrace. How this was accomplished is described below, but such constraints added to the cost,

St James' Park; the West Stand (Simon Inglis)

finally agreed at £420 000. The East Stand had seats for 3400.

The capacity of St James' Park was then set at 55 000, but when the Safety of Sports Grounds Act was introduced, United suddenly faced a bill of £150 000, to comply with its recommendations. Again the ground's consultant architects outlined the specific problems facing League clubs under the new Act (see Safety) and the one which affected Newcastle most was that although the crush barriers themselves were strong enough, their foundations were not. When the terracing had been concreted over in the late 1940s, the barriers' original foundations were simply covered over, but had since become insecure. The base of each barrier was attached to the old timber 'stringer' which used to form the stepping of the terracing. So that whereas the Leazes End had once held a capacity of 17 000, under the new standards it had to be reduced to 7000. For this reason the club decided that since the cost of replacing every barrier was enormous, they might as well to continue the ground's redevelopment at that end rather than anywhere else.

Much to the regret of every Newcastle fan, the roof at the Leazes Park End was taken down in 1978, the same year as United went down to the Second Division – an ill omen for the future.

It cost Newcastle £500 000 just to remove the banking, build new foundations and take down two floodlight pylons. This was before any extension of the East Stand could occur. But now, as at Elland Road, the foundations are all there is to show for the work. The Leazes Park End terrace now holds only 5000 standing spectators, all without cover. One day it will form the paddock in front of the extended stand, which if built will put St James' Park well on its way to becoming one of the best grounds in Britain. Until then, it is like a ground in transit, too far along the journey to turn back, but not quite rich enough to reach the next stop.

The ground's present capacity is 38 000, of which 10 000 are seated. The extra seats are those on the terracing in front of the East Stand. After insisting that standing on that side should be preserved, the club had to install bench seats in an attempt to prevent crowd trouble, a blight which St James' Park has never quite shaken off since Good Friday, 1901.

There were serious pitch invasions in 1974, when United's Cup Quarter Final v. Nottingham Forest had to be replayed at Goodison Park, and again in 1977 during United's 4th Round Cup tie v. Manchester City. The latter came in spite of the most stringent efforts to prevent encroachment of the pitch by building special security barriers around the perimeter.

Happily there was no trouble for one of St James' Park most illustrious events – the staging of a Rolling Stones concert in June 1982. There were 25 000 in the stands and a further 10 000 on the pitch. Jackie Milburn, Malcolm MacDonald, Kevin Keegan, and now Mick Jagger – St James' Park has seen them all.

Ground Description

St James' Park sits on a rise above the city, perhaps not as splendid as the Parthenon, but in Newcastle at least as revered. It is even visible from the opposite bank of the Tyne, from Gateshead, where League football is now only a memory.

From the city centre we climb up to Strawberry Place, where a new Metro station is built, and St James' Park suddenly takes on a gargantuan scale; the West Stand facade like the side of a battleship. Along its dark grey corrugated walls written 50 feet high is, 'NEWCASTLE UNITED', filling the space from end to end – a masterly stroke and the idea of Harry Faulkner Brown, architect of the East Stand. And to add to the stand's battleship character, there are steel stairways up and down. To continue the metaphor we climb aboard and from inside, the stand is no longer a warship, but a paddle-steamer. The curved gable, with press box windows in the centre, makes an elegant sweep along the grey decks, un-rivalled since Liverpool demolished a similar shaped stand, although Middlesbrough have something similar on a lesser scale. But surely there are no stands so dark, so grey, so brooding as the West Stand. And now there is an ominous line of floodlight gantries flanking the gable, standing on the barrel roof like crows on a telegraph wire. On top of the gable is a flag-pole; a mast upon a great paddle-steamer.

A tall pylon towers over from behind, carrying yet more floodlights, but one wonders what it illuminates that the other lights cannot reach. The pylon stands in a large forecourt, where the offices are situated in a detached block, like the customs office on a quayside.

In front of the stand, another dark grey wall divides the seats from the open paddock. No frills, no executive boxes; concrete crush barriers like tank-traps.

From here, to the left is the now open Leazes Park End, another concrete mass of barriers. Newcastle was the first club to study segregation of rival fans, after the 1974 incidents, so they know all about fences and barriers here. They use not a tall security fence at the perimeter wall, but a couple of low walls divided by a shallow moat – a system borrowed by Crystal Palace and one which inhibits no-one's view of the pitch. Behind the terrace you can see the black, tall wall which once formed the rear of the original terrace. It is plain to see how the East Stand will eventually curl round the corner and fill this space.

Between here and the East Stand the row of houses called Leazes Terrace is visible. The East Stand has had to fit in as much as possible with its neighbours. Accordingly, the external facings have been textured and coloured to harmonize with the ageing stone of the terrace. St James' Terrace, also behind the East Stand, has had to change as well. Old houses have come down and a pedestrian courtyard created. You

cannot prevent a stand like this overpowering everything in sight, but at least care has been taken to preserve some of the street level's qualities.

The East Stand itself is a tall, exposed cantilever, without screen walls and therefore forming a dark silhouette of angled concrete standing out against the sky. Nowhere else is the wonder of cantilever technology more stunning than here. The roof has no right to defy gravity and stay up, but it does. It is composed of corrugated aluminium barrel vaults, tied along the front to seem flat. As on the West Stand there are floodlight gantries along the roof. There is a paddock in front, now covered with simple bench seats. The people's desire to stand has given way to the club's desire for peace.

To the right from the West Stand is the Gallowgate End, named after the main thoroughfare behind, leading to the city centre. As the name suggests, it is a dour terrace indeed, bordered by thick concrete walls like a huge open bunker, overlooking the town. From the top, the city lies behind to the south, falling down the valley into the Tyne. Directly behind the terracing is a neatly laid out slope covered in shrubs and trees.

At the top of the Gallowgate End is a new and dominant electric scoreboard. Directly behind it is Wellburgh House, home of the Newcastle Weather Centre. The building to the right of this block is the headquarters of Newcastle Breweries – a temple to so many – but also a source of some fairly acrid odours. The ground's other floodlight pylon stands on its original spot on the West Side of the Gallowgate End, sole survivor of the system installed in 1958.

Newcastle have conscientiously tried to solve the problem of hooliganism at St James' Park – it is hoped that shrub gardens might soothe many an angered brow and promote some pride in the place – and have gone some way to satisfying the demands of local conservationists, but they have not been able to solve that slope whereupon lies the 'eatage and her-bage'. Even when the East Stand was built the design had to slope with the land, otherwise all the sight lines of the West Stand would have been disrupted. As the stands' facings show, the drop is still 4 feet from north to south. But that is perhaps the least of the problems facing United. There are foundations to be built on, stands to be completed. The monument on the hill is far from finished.

• 8 •
SOUTH YORKSHIRE AND HUMBERSIDE

• SHEFFIELD • WEDNESDAY

Previous Grounds

Although Wednesday are the fifth oldest club in the League, having formed in 1867, a Wednesday cricket club had existed since 1816. It was so-called because its members played on their half-day holiday, Wednesday. The football club played their first games on a field now occupied by Highfields Library. In 1869 they moved to Myrtle Road, Heeley, and went on to use Sheaf House, Hunter's Bar and Endcliffe until 1887, when they moved to their first substantial enclosure, Olive Grove. Even then, some important games were staged at Bramall Lane until 1895.

Olive Grove was situated off Queen's Road, between Sheffield and Heeley railway stations, and like Bramall Lane was owned by the Duke of Norfolk. Wednesday secured a seven-year lease, but had to spend some £5000 to prepare the field, across which ran a brook. Olive Grove was proudly opened on 12 September 1887 with a 4-4 draw v. mighty Blackburn Rovers. A report of the occasion waxed lyrically:

'Upon entering the ground we were struck with the beauty and judicious disposal of the enclosure, an impression which was considerably augmented by the audible gratification of those assembled. The dimensions come within the minimum rules of the English Association viz. 110 yards × 70, and a massive iron railing has certainly the appearance of keeping the most excited or, perhaps, unruly audience from encroaching on forbidden ground. There is also a stand upon the north side to accommodate 1,000 persons, and a cinder path, six feet wide encircling the railing, which will be more comfortable than the grass, especially in damp weather.'

The most bizarre match at Olive Grove was in the 1898–99 season. Wednesday's November home game v. Aston Villa had been abandoned after 79 minutes because of bad light, with the score at 3-1. The infamous remaining 11 minutes were played at Olive Grove in March, Wednesday adding one more goal. The ground thereby staged the shortest encounter in League history.

The end of that season saw Wednesday relegated and also the last match at Olive Grove, which had been bought for development by the Midland Railway Company, owners of the adjoining line. The ground was then in a sorry state, only 4000 attended, and spirits were low indeed.

Olive Grove had been, in Richard Sparling's words, 'a most comfortable little ground. It was a place to foster friendships and it appeared to encourage that feeling in the spectators "The Wednesday are part of us." '

It was suggested that Wednesday share Bramall Lane with United and use Sheaf House for reserve games, but talks broke down – a pity in light of recent developments, which suggest that had one city decided on ground sharing others might have followed, but a blessing for the thousands who, like myself, consider a visit to Hillsborough as one of the joys of sport.

The supporters were asked to vote on their preferred new site: 4767 opted for one at Carbrook, 4115 for another at Owlerton, 124 were neutral in the matter, and only 16 fancied a return to Sheaf House. Meanwhile someone else bought the Carbrook land, and the Owlerton site proved to be impracticable, so with only a few weeks before the next season, another site was found at Owlerton. Perhaps only Arsenal's crossing of the Thames 14 years later was to be such a daring and speculative move.

Hillsborough

Owlerton in 1899 was not even in Sheffield, but in the unspoilt hills on the other side of the city to Olive Grove. The 10 acres Wednesday had bought were meadowland in need of at least £5000 worth of preparation. With only £2000 in the bank the club decided to form itself into a limited liability company.

Hillsborough in the 1930s (Aerofilms)

So began the task of building, 'out in the wilds'. The old stand at Olive Grove was re-erected at Owlerton, rubbish was tipped at either end to form banking. But even then, why should the fans come all that way to see Second Division Wednesday when First Division United were so close at hand? The Wednesday directors had made a shrewd prediction. The new electric trams ferried support from town at 1d a ride, and Owlerton was soon absorbed by Sheffield's expanding suburbs.

The ground was opened for Wednesday's first game in Division Two, v. Chesterfield on 2 September 1899, by the Lord Mayor, Alderman W. E. Clegg, one of two Clegg brothers who had dominated Sheffield football in its early days.

In 1914 Owlerton became part of the new parliamentary constituency of Hillsborough, and the ground changed its name accordingly, although Wednesday are still nicknamed the Owls.

The existing South Stand was opened in January of 1914, in place of the old Olive Grove Stand, for a cost of £10 000. Archibald Leitch was responsible, and it may be considered among his best designs, as I shall describe below.

The record crowd at the ground was 72 841 for Manchester City's visit in the FA Cup in February

1934. At that time there was, opposite the South Stand, a double-roofed stand with 2000 seats (which survived a bomb blast and was only replaced in 1961), next to which stood a funny little short cover over the terracing in the north west corner. The West End terrace was half covered by a low roof at the back. The Kop was much the same as today.

Hillsborough's first floodlit game was played between a Sheffield XI and an International XI in aid of Derek Dooley's trust fund on 9 March 1955. Dooley had tragically lost a leg after a playing accident. A crowd of 55 000 came to pay tribute to the man, and to see the new lights; the best in Britain.

The next development at Hillsborough really deserves a chapter of its own, but since space is limited, suffice to say here that the new North Stand was, at the time of its opening by Sir Stanley Rous on 23 August 1961, the most advanced football grandstand ever built at a British football ground. It not only raised spectators' expectations, but proved to architects and directors alike that football architecture need not be dull or merely utilitarian, a point Leitch and Ferrier (at Highbury) had tried to show before the War. (For a detailed appraisal of the North Stand, see *The Structural Engineer*, November 1962.) It took 11 months to build the stand, which cost

£150 000 and was the third cantilever stand in Britain, after Scunthorpe and Dundee United, but the first one to run the full length of a pitch. The roof is 45 000 square feet, weighs 17 tons and was made possible by the architect's (Husband and Company of Sheffield) use of aluminium sheets hung under a steel frame, supported at the back by three miles of pre-stressed, precast concrete units. The aluminium was of course lighter than the commonly used asbestos or corrugated iron sheeting. All 9882 seats are well protected from the weather.

The North Stand attracted more architectural interest than any other football stand since Wembley and even merits inclusion in Pevsner's mammoth work on the *Buildings of England*. No other League ground is mentioned.

We move on to the inevitable consequence of the North Stand's construction, the decision to stage four World Cup games at Hillsborough in 1966. For the occasion, the new West Stand was built in 1965 at a cost of £110 000, and extra seating put in the South Stand's paddock, lowering the ground capacity to 60 000, but giving Hillsborough more seats than any other ground at the time. A new tavern was also built behind the South Stand, on stilts, and a large sports hall erected behind the North Stand, for use during the World Cup as a press centre. Three Group Two matches were played here, plus a quarter-final between West Germany and Uruguay. With a grant from the Government, Wednesday had spent £200 000 on preparing Hillsborough for the event.

Apart from football, the ground has also staged world-class tennis, in 1938, boxing in the 1950s, a schools display for the Queen in 1954 and a Harlem Globetrotters basketball display in the 1960s. The present capacity of Hillsborough is 50 174, including 23 224 seats.

Ground Description

Hillsborough is a stadium, with all the grand connotations the term implies.

An unusually square set of six floodlight pylons rising above trees and factory roofs signal your approach to the stadium. Enter if you can at the South West End, across a bridge over the tree-lined River Don, which flows behind the South Stand from the Pennines to the Humber, via (of course) Doncaster. The West Stand proclaims Sheffield Wednesday along its back.

For an old stand, the South Stand is surprisingly roomy. Leitch obviously enjoyed the lack of restrictions, for inside there is a sense of spacious cleanliness and light, as is the case at Leitch's Main Stand at Ibrox. A better perspective however is to be had from opposite the stand.

Notice especially the Leitch trade-mark, the pointed central gable, with a clock and a copper ball on its pinnacle, reminiscent of White Hart Lane's West Stand, sadly no more. A television gantry on the front of the roof does its usual spoiling job.

Present-day Hillsborough (Aerofilms)

To the right is the huge Spion Kop, holding 16 850 in a wholly irregular shape that defies anyone to cover it. It is one of Hillsborough's strongest visual strengths, the juxtaposition of three, neat orderly stands with this wild hill.

To the left is the West Stand, with 4465 seats in an upper tier, and open terraces in front. Next to the other two stands it looks rather ordinary, but the view it provides is excellent, as are its facilities, and it does close off the ground effectively without cramping the style of either of its neighbours. The pitch slopes from this end down to the Kop by 2½ feet.

But the focus is all on the North Stand ahead. There is not a misplaced line in this remarkable stand. The roof is a clean sweep, from the concrete back to the ribbed blue roof fascia hanging 16 feet in front of the first row. A clock in the centre is flanked along the rooftop by a line of flagpoles, put up for the World Cup but now as much part of the stand as the central floodlight pylon protruding from the roof. Glass screen ends, like those of the South Stand, tie the flowing roof lines to the end walls, linked by a 362-foot long white perimeter wall.

From any angle the North Stand is quite breathtaking. It is like an architects' model of the dream stand of the future, a space age stand. Yet it still retains its fresh and modern appearance as if it had risen above the ravages of building fashion.

This bright spectacular stand, the vernacular charm of the South Stand and the rugged lines of the Kop make Hillsborough more than just a ground. They lend dignity to any game played there, give heart to Wednesday's followers who may just feel that 'the Wednesday fellows are part of us'. Hillsborough has proved that a club can provide all the facilities a supporter wants, without robbing the surroundings of their intrinsic character. It is surely no coincidence that Wednesday men are always ready to talk about the club and Hillsborough, and about the city of Sheffield that everyone seems to love. This is a place to buy boiled sweets at the corner shop, wear a rosette with pride but then go and sit in comfort.

◆ SHEFFIELD UNITED ◆

Bramall Lane

Sheffield United share with Chelsea and Plymouth Argyle the distinction of having been formed in order to make better use of an existing sports ground. A Sheffield Cricket Club was formed in 1854, and secured a 99-year lease for the Bramall Lane grounds from the Duke of Norfolk, who stipulated that matches 'be conducted in a respectable manner' and that there should be no 'pigeon shooting, rabbit coursing nor any race-running for money'. The first Yorkshire CC match was in August 1855, but no football took place until December 1862, when Sheffield FC (the oldest club in the world, formed in 1857) played Hallam. The Wednesday subsequently played a few games at Bramall Lane after 1867. Teams had to give the Bramall Lane Ground Company 25 per cent of their gross match receipts, 33 per cent after 1883. *Athletic News* described the ground in March 1877 thus:

> 'At the top or pavilion end there is a wooden stand that would seat . . . about 1500 spectators, whilst the side next to the lane is the place for the 6d 'pit,' safely and securely railed off and made in a succession of terraces so giving everybody an opportunity of seeing what is going on . . . the proprietors have been recently levelling one end of the ground, and I don't know how many thousand cartloads of earth have been put down to remove a dip which occurred at the bottom end of it.'

On 14 October 1878 Bramall Lane won a permanent place in the annals of football when it staged the first recorded floodlit match ever played (for a description, see Floodlights). The first football international at the ground was in March 1883, but it took

Bramall Lane football and cricket ground shortly after the Second World War (Aerofilms)

until 1889 for the cricket club to form their own resident football team. The decision was made soon after they hosted an FA Cup semi-final between Preston and West Bromwich on 16 March. Gate receipts amounted to a handsome £574, more than enough to persuade the club that football was big business. So in 1889 Sheffield United came into being, and three years later gained admission to the newly formed League Division Two (Wednesday were elected to Division One in the same year). They were promoted within a year, and in 1898 won their first and only League Championship. As a result, in March 1899 they formed a limited liability company, Sheffield United Cricket and Football Club, and bought Bramall Lane from the Duke of Norfolk for £10 134, announcing plans for concerts, dancing and other theatrical events, but still no 'pigeon shooting, rabbit coursing, nor any race-running for money'.

At exactly the same time Wednesday were being forced to leave Olive Grove, having been relegated, whereas United were FA Cup winners and full of confidence, a disparity which might well have prevented negotiations to share Bramall Lane with Wednesday from succeeding.

Before 1899 United's footballers had changed in the cricket pavilion, but now the John Street Side opposite was developed as the football club's headquarters. The Main Stand was built at the turn of the century, not dissimilar to Barnsley's Main Stand of the same era, but considerably distinguished by a tall, mock-Tudor gable in the centre of the roof. It had a gallery with five openings, like a small house, and later became the press box, but at the time it was undoubtedly also used by the growing number of cricket spectators. As well as hosting the occasional football international, Bramall Lane was also a venue for Test matches. There was even a cycle track round the perimeter. By the 1930s, the football pitch was covered on its three sides. The John Street Stand had an extra angled corner at its West End, which joined up with a lower roof covering the Bramall Lane End terraces as far as the corner flag. From this point round to the Pavilion, and round further to the high banking of the Kop opposite, the terraces were open. The Kop had a roof at the back. United's record crowd of 68 287 came in February 1936 for an FA Cup 5th Round tie v. Leeds, when many of the fans would have watched from the cricket side some distance away. For the 6th Round match v. Tottenham, the club built a temporary wooden stand along the open fourth touchline, actually over the sacred cricket wicket. This happened only once.

The War brought devastation to Bramall Lane. Ten bombs hit the ground in December 1940, destroying half the John Street Stand (and its marvellous gable), the Kop roof and badly cratering the pitch. By 1953 most of the Main Stand had been repaired, although the new gable was but a shadow of its predecessor. A new double-roof was erected over the restored Kop.

Bramall Lane's distinctive gable later destroyed in an air raid (BBC Hulton Picture Library)

Floodlights came back to Bramall Lane, permanently this time, in March 1955, a week before Hillsborough's. The opening game was v. neighbours Rotheram.

Although cricket was still played regularly, and the players certainly enjoyed the lively atmosphere at Bramall Lane, especially the noisy but witty comments they heard from the so-called Grinders Stand on the Bramall Lane Side, there was no denying that the football club wanted rid of the cricketers so they could build on that open side.

In a series called 'Homes of Sport', Norman Yardley and J. M. Kilburn wrote in 1952 that Bramall Lane, from a cricket lover's point of view, had 'scarcely anything to commend it'. Their further comments are ironic in light of the boast of the Duke of Norfolk's agent that Bramall Lane had 'the advantage of being free from smoke'.

'. . . there is not a tree to be seen, and both sight and sound reflect encircling industry. The clatter of tramcars and the scream of a saw-mill and factory hooters make a background of noise to the cricket, and a brewery chimney periodically pours smoke and soot into the air.'

They add the suggestion that the brewery would deliberately emit its foul fumes only when Yorkshire's opponents were at the crease! The cricket and football pitches actually overlapped only by about 20 yards, an area making a rough outfield, awkward for fielders and slow for batsmen expecting boundaries. Furthermore, the view was never quite right. The Pavilion was too far from the soccer pitch, the John Street Stand too far from the wicket. Since the perimeter was fenced off by a low wall and railings, fielders had to retrieve every boundary, whereas at other grounds they might leave the task to willing spectators. The spectators themselves had in many parts of the ground to sit on the concrete terraces, amid the crush barriers, and it was apparently quite common to see hundreds of people rise each time a wicket fell, to stretch their limbs and rub their aching buttocks! As cricket audiences declined, the football side developed further when a new 3000 seater stand, with room for 7000 standing below, was opened in 1967 on the Bramall Lane End.

But the sad financial truth had already become apparent. The club's 1962 accounts showed that revenue from football amounted to £127 802, but from cricket a mere £2927. In the club's own words, it was 'absurd' that they should 'have to suffer such a freak as a three sided ground'. That Northampton had managed, and even made a brief sortie into the First Division, mattered not one jot. Having visited Bramall Lane only a few times when it was three-sided, I can only say that the sensation was not so much freakish as different, like watching a drive-in movie or an open air concert. One soon became accustomed to the vast expanse of green beyond the opposite touchline. But no one can criticize United for wanting to be like the rest. Indeed it is likely that had they made their decision ten years earlier, the subsequent financial burden would have been considerably lighter.

The inevitable axe fell in 1971. United were punch drunk with the success of their first season back in Division One since 1968 and plucked up sufficient courage to give the cricket club two years' notice to quit Bramall Lane.

Some felt that this was akin to a son evicting his mother, to whom he owed both life and home, and that while United might gain a smart new grandstand, the city of Sheffield would lose for ever its ability to stage first-class cricket.

The final County match was on 7 August 1973, the end of 150 years of cricket at Bramall Lane.

I will leave the final judgement to the people of Sheffield, except to add that no sooner had the £750 000 new cantilever stand gone up over the old pitch than United began a six-year slide which eventually dumped them unceremoniously into the Fourth Division for the first time in their 90 years' membership of the League. Was this a judgement on the ungrateful child?

Ground Description

The new main entrance to the ground is in Cherry Street, where you see a large car-park in front of the imposing cantilever stand, with its striking facade. By the gates stood the Pavilion, finally demolished in 1982. The car-park covers what used to be the cricket pitch. How quickly, how comprehensively, the new obliterates all trace of the old. The new South Stand is a full length cantilever, designed by the same architects as Wednesday's North Stand, although inflated building costs and the need for extra facilities have dictated that this one is less pleasing to the eye from inside the ground. But the frontage is undoubtedly the most impressive of any post-war stand

in the country, helped because there is space to stand back and admire the red, black and white trimming.

It seats 7774 and was opened for a First Division match on 16 August 1975. Along the roof are 18 flag-poles, and suspended beneath it is a large television gantry with an electric winch to haul up the heavy cameras (most grounds need the crew to do this by hand).

The near touchline is some yards from the front row, to allow room should the club ever afford to redevelop the opposite side. You can see the four gothic pinnacles of St Mary's church tower, built in 1850, clearly above the John Street Stand roof straight ahead.

The John Street Stand is still well-used, although the dressing rooms and offices underneath are now redundant. It holds 4262 seats, with room for 5000 standing in front. In contrast with the hard metallic lines of the South Stand, its weathered sloping roof, convoluted steelwork and cramped schoolboys' pen at the Kop End look quite archaic. But it is not as dark and dingy as some stands of equal vintage.

To the right is the covered Kop, which used to hold 22 000 standing. Behind is open ground along Shoreham Street, where once were the cricketers' practice pitches.

To the left is the Bramall Lane Stand, a rather drab, tall construction in grey, brown concrete. The seats offer an excellent view, but the terraces immediately below are dark and cramped. On the roof fascia is a clock, donated by the supporters' club to replace the once familiar Pavilion clock – a nice gesture, but an unimposing clock.

The old clock had looked across a ground that was 8½ acres of grass, the size and shape of two football pitches side by side, with room for some 60 000 spectators. The capacity now is a still healthy 49 000, mostly under cover, with 15 000 seats.

In 1982 United escaped from the trauma of Fourth Division football, where they had certainly the best ground and facilities ever seen but found themselves in serious financial difficulty. This was mainly owing to falling gates, but the cost of the South Stand was a factor. Only time will tell whether the decision to dig up the cricket pitch will actually determine the club's future but I have absolutely no doubt that all over Yorkshire there are old cricketing stalwarts just waiting and watching, in anticipation of being able to say 'What did I tell you . . .' If Dame Fortune is forgiving towards a trier, they will not get that chance, but if the Almighty wears white flannels . . .

ROTHERHAM ·UNITED·

Previous Grounds

A club called Rotherham Town played from 1860 at Clifton Lane cricket ground (which still exists) and between 1895–96 was a member of the League. Meanwhile in 1884 another team called Thornhill United formed and played at the Red House Ground. The pitch was so small and uneven that United were prohibited from entering the FA Cup, so in 1907, having changed the name to Rotherham County in 1905, the club moved to Millmoor. In 1919 they joined League Division Two, and in 1925 amalgamated with Rotherham Town to form Rotherham United.

Millmoor

I shall deal quite concisely with the developments at Millmoor, because a description of the ground tells more than dates can. The first occurred not long after Town and County joined forces, with the building of the Main Stand, now considerably modified. About the same time a small cover was put up over the terracing opposite along Millmoor Lane.

It was during a run of success that Millmoor experienced its highest ever gate of 25 000, twice in 1955; first v. neighbours Sheffield Wednesday in January, then v. Sheffield United the following December, both in Division Two.

In 1957 the Railway End terracing was covered, and in November 1960 the floodlights were first used for a League Cup tie v. Bristol Rovers. In the mid-1960s an extended roof was erected over the Main Stand, and a gymnasium built adjacent to the stand. In 1968 a roof over the Tivoli End terrace was constructed.

Since then seating has been added to the Millmoor Lane Side, firstly under the old roof, then at the southern end over which a new roof was built in 1982, next to the old.

This brought the total seating to 3400, out of a capacity of 21 000.

Ground Description

However idyllic the name may sound, the reality at Rotherham is quite different. Millmoor stands in the three-sided grip of a collection of scrap yards, whose walls on two sides form the back of the stands. There is literally no room to manoeuvre, as cranes swing back and forward almost over the ground itself.

But we start on Masborough Street, the main access point to the ground. Entrance to the main stand is under the raised offices, along the side of a wall at an angle to the pitch, and from there into a cavernous underground corridor. Even the players must take this route to reach the changing rooms, and must

Millmoor, looking towards the Main Stand, with the inevitable crane in the background. The old Tivoli cinema is just visible above the far roof (right) (Sporting Pictures)

therefore be exposed to crowds on the terrace to the left of the Main Stand. A unique, but hardly satisfactory arrangement, though the reason is self-evident. Directly behind the wall and the back of the stand you can see the cranes and piled up debris of the scrapyard. As you pass along the wall, notice the press-box, a wooden hut perched above the terracing. Again, a unique arrangement.

The Main Stand itself is unusual. It starts just before the half-way line, and there is a wooden gate leading to the changing rooms and other facilities at the far end. Underneath it is like a dusty car-park. You can see the old, original roof peaking out above the newer roof, which as at Scunthorpe and Doncaster extends to the terracing in front but at Millmoor is actually cantilevered from the original pillars frontwards. It looks from one side as if the roof is balanced delicately on these old white uprights. The sloping roof fascia point down like a bird's beak. Its an all-red, dark wooden stand, denied any prominence by the adjacent drab, brick gymnasium and the scrapyard buildings beyond. From here you can see, ahead to the right, Boston Castle on a tree-lined rise in the distance.

The Millmoor Lane Side opposite is in three parts; on the left, open terrace, in the centre the old cover now seated, with four front pillars unusually rooted on the pitch-side of the perimeter wall, and on the right another seated section whose roof is on stilts, with no screens or a back wall behind the top row. Millmoor Lane behind here is a thin narrow alley leading down to the enormous yards of C. F. Booth.

You can see these yards quite clearly behind the Railway End, to your right from the Main Stand. The end itself is a good bank of terracing, but with a low roof and high security fences. Behind it are all manner of doomed items. When at Millmoor I could see quite clearly, beyond the entrances at the back of the end, two silvery London Underground trains ready to be chewed up. When United were up for sale in recent years C. F. Booth apparently wanted to make a bid for control, but having seen what his machines can do to rolling stock I would not have given frail Millmoor much of a chance.

To the left of the Main Stand is the Tivoli End, so called because behind on Masborough Street is the now delapidated Tivoli Cinema, a magnificent but now forlorn example of early cinema architecture. Built just before the First World War, you can just see the upper storeys over the stand roof. From here the pitch slopes nearly 3 feet down to the Railway End.

Altogether Millmoor is quite a mixture of oddities in odd surroundings, but as the result of good maintenance and lots of red paint, is actually a compact, cosy and cheerful island in the midst of a clanking and rather noisome sea of debris.

◆BARNSLEY◆

Oakwell

Oakwell has been the home of Barnsley since the Reverend Tiverton Preedy formed the club as Barnsley St Peter's in 1887, but as Grenville Firth noted in his club history, their first pitch was just behind the present Brewery Stand. The landowner, Arthur Senior, allowed the Reverend's boys to use the ground saying, 'You can have it so long as you behave yourselves'.

They turned professional a year later and moved to the present pitch by 1895 when the first stand, 20 yards long was built. Shortly afterwards it was blown onto the pitch in a gale.

In 1898 Barnsley joined Division Two and had to shift 3000 cubic feet of soil from one end to the other to level the pitch. The slope of several feet from side to side, apparent today, was obviously a lesser evil.

A Pontefract Road End Stand was opened in 1900, followed four years later by the central section of the present Main Stand. The Mayor, Alderman Bray, did the honours, and the stand cost £600, with 1200 seats. Since then wings have been added to give Oakwell a seating capacity of 2154, the lowest of any club in the top two divisions (in 1982–83). Modernization has been a considerable undertaking, for in anticipation of promotion in 1980 the club had to spend £250 000 on ground improvements alone. Present capacity is 35 554, although the record attendance was 40 255, in an FA Cup tie v. Stoke in 1936.

Andrew Ward and Ian Alister recalled much of Oakwell's life during the 1950s, when for example, the Main Stand had swing doors. It was one professional's jocular habit to enter them head first, until a mean joker reversed the hinges and the unfortunate player knocked himself out. In the same era, another Barnsley player tumbled over the perimeter wall and broke both collar and shoulder bones, but gallantly played on. The pitch was narrowed to its present width thereafter.

The first floodlit game was a friendly v. Bolton in February 1962.

Underdeveloped though Oakwell may be, it occupies a massive 25-acre site (contrast with Highbury's 10 acres) bought for a mere £1376 in 1911. Where there's muck in the surrounding car-parks there is also plenty of brass, and a valuable training ground to boot, with an artificial pitch well used by the club and local schools.

Ground Description

The Main Stand is set high behind the open paddock, and is remarkable for its lack of pretension, as is the Directors' entrance on Grove Road, a gate in a long red wall. But the stand's centre gable, which once announced the club's name, is now horribly obscured by an ugly television gantry.

Oakwell, from the Pontefract Road End (Simon Inglis)

Opposite, to the east, is the Brewery Stand, a cosy standing enclosure extended in 1954 when the wooden boards at the back were added for £6000. To the right, or south, is another covered standing area, the Pontefract Road End, whose cover dates back to the late 1940s. To the left is the Spion Kop, from whose blustery heights you can see the training ground and a bowling green behind, the huge brewery advertisements on the stand roofs below with the town centre ahead. To the north east is a sprawling landscape of scrubland and factories, and the coal mines and glass-works, Barnsley's industrial backbone, both represented on the club crest. A low white perimeter wall and bright terracotta track links all together; the red, grey and green of Oakwell knitting comfortably with terraces, chimneys and hills. To complete the scene simply add a Michael Parkinson football tale, narrated with brass band accompaniment. Oakwell says Pah! to your executive boxes. Barnsley fans like to stand and mingle, not sit and stew.

DONCASTER
·ROVERS·

Previous Grounds

Doncaster are the second oldest League club in Yorkshire. They formed in 1879 and played at the Intake Ground until 1916, in which time they managed to be elected then voted out of the League twice within four years! The pitch is still used, by pupils at the adjacent school for the deaf.

A new limited company was set up in 1920, and for two years Rovers played at Bennetthorpe, now submerged by the Great North Road, half a mile from their present ground, on Low Pasture, now called Belle Vue, where they have played since 1922.

Belle Vue

Just after moving to Belle Vue, Rovers were re-elected to the League for the third time. Their supporters completed most of the work of preparing the new ground, namely shifting large amounts of ash from nearby coal tips to form banking and a foundation for the pitch. They also jacked up the Main Stand at Bennetthorpe, wheeled it down the road and resited it on the northern terrace, where it remains today. A new Main Stand was built on the East Side, but has been extended since.

In 1938 the Popular Side was covered, and that is how Belle Vue has stayed, with the addition of concreted terraces.

The highest gate was 37 149, for a Third Division North derby v. Hull in October 1948. Capacity is now much reduced to 21 150, including 2010 seats.

Doncaster were the second club in the north of England to install floodlights, in February 1953, first used in a reserve game v. Lincoln. They were also credited with the largest pitch in the League, until manager Billy Bremner decided to cut off eight yards from the length. It now measures 112 × 77 yards. The surface has always been admired, and in the early 1970s Wembley Stadium's owners were so concerned about the perilous state of their pitch that, among other options, they offered Rovers between £10 000 and £20 000 for the Belle Vue turf. Rovers refused. They knew that the top surface was only good because of the drainage below, where the ash lay.

Belle Vue might soon be transformed. Next door is an old RAF station, known as Doncaster Airport. Its lease ran out in 1982, and the council wants to build a massive £12 million leisure complex on the site, including a new athletics stadium. Rovers suggest that it would be cheaper to convert Belle Vue than to start from scratch. A lengthy debate is certain.

Ground Description

The overwhelming sensation at Belle Vue is one of

spaciousness. On the east side is Bawtry Road, and the famous Doncaster Racecourse, and it is worth crossing the road to see one magnificent old grandstand which dates back to the late eighteenth century in parts, and an equally impressive 1960s' stand close by.

Rovers rent Belle Vue from the council for £1500 a year, which includes use of the vast car-park behind the Main Stand. If a race meeting clashes with a match, the former has priority use of the car-park. But except on St Leger day, the footballers usually attract a larger crowd than the horses. Traffic can be a problem however, especially as it must come to a complete halt to allow the horses to cross Bawtry Road from the stables to the racecourse.

The Main Stand is essentially in two parts; the back, tall thin section for seating being the original, the front terraces being covered by a later flat roof. Similar roof extensions have been put up at nearby Scunthorpe and Rotherham. Notice there are two players' tunnels, one for each team.

To the right is the tiny 700-seater wooden North Stand, looking almost as new as the day it was brought over from Bennetthorpe. Now called the Family Stand, ticket holders can move freely between the bench seats and the fenced-in terrace in front, a sensible arrangement for restless youngsters. The stand is quite lovely, decked in red, with white pillars and facings, nicely finished off with an advertisement hoarding on the roof and a clock in the centre.

Opposite is the Popular Stand, a covered terrace where the 'pigeon box' hangs from the roof. An owl used to nest in it, and fans would say that if the owl came out during a game, Rovers would win. A video camera now lives there.

To the left is the high, open south bank, from where one obtains the best appreciation of the open land surrounding Belle Vue, from the race-track to the right to the airfield behind. It is the perfect location for a leisure complex. While a new stadium would be welcomed, it is to be hoped that the football ground will form the basis, and that there may be someone willing to wheel the North Stand away to another home.

Belle Vue's North Stand, late of Bennetthorpe (Simon Inglis)

SCUNTHORPE ·UNITED·

The Old Show Ground

As the name suggests, Scunthorpe's home was once the venue for various popular events in the town, especially the Scunthorpe Show. One photograph taken at the turn of the century shows horse jumping at the ground. There was a club called Scunthorpe United who played there from their formation in 1899, then amalgamated with North Lindsey United in 1910. The new club chose the Old Show Ground as their headquarters and adopted the somewhat unwieldy title of Scunthorpe and Lindsey United Football Club. The date of formation was not, as is often quoted, 1904. Most dates are taken indeed from 1912, when the club turned professional and joined the Midland League. For this and much of the following information I thank the club historian John Staff.

United purchased the Old Show Ground from the Parkinson family for £2700 in 1924, a year which also saw the Main Stand destroyed by fire. In an effort to raise funds for rebuilding, the club organized a raffle for a pig, which then broke loose on the pitch as the draw was made. A new Main Stand was built in 1925, and survives in modified form.

During the Second World War the Old Show Ground played host to Grimsby Town, who were in 1939 a First Division Club. (Blundell Park was too exposed to enemy action to risk large crowds.)

Scunthorpe and Lindsey United were elected to the League in 1950 (they dropped Lindsey from the title in 1955) and for the next ten years the Old Show Ground changed considerably. The Doncaster Road End was covered in 1954, no doubt helped by the receipts from Scunthorpe's record gate of 23 935 for a Cup match v. Portsmouth in January. (Before then, as a non-League club their highest attendance had been 13 775.) The floodlights were first switched on for a game v. Rochdale in October 1957, but later that season the old wooden cover over the East Side burned down. It was replaced in 1958 with a stand that gives the Old Show Ground pride of place in the annals of football ground development. For here, on the East Side of the Old Show Ground, was built the very first cantilever stand at a British football ground.

You ask, quite naturally, why not at Old Trafford or Highbury or Villa Park? The answer is simple. The United Steel Structural Company Limited, with a base in Scunthorpe built the stand on generous terms, fully hoping that it would carve a place for them in the annals of football ground development. It did not, and thereafter everyone assumed the first cantilever stand was built at Hillsborough. But here the record has at last been set straight.

"They'll soon be playing soccer all the year round"
"I know. They only stop for about 3½ MONTHS as it is"
"Yes - just long enough for

UNITED STEEL STRUCTURAL CO.

to design, fabricate & erect this
GRANDSTAND FOR SCUNTHORPE UNITED F.C.
to seat 2,350 people"

Steel for Speed

UNITED STEEL STRUCTURAL COMPANY LIMITED *SCUNTHORPE LINCOLNSHIRE*

The cantilever stand at the Old Show Ground, the first in Britain (*FA News*)

The new East Stand was opened on 23 August 1958 by Lieutenant Commander G. W. Wells RN, having taken just the close season to erect; a fitting and proud way to begin the club's first season in Division Two. The transformation of the ground continued the following year, when the Fox Street cover, first put up in 1938, was replaced by the present more substantial roof. The capacity of the Old Show Ground is 25 000, of which 2850 are seated.

Ground Description

Despite the years of progress, from the outside, Scunthorpe's ground looks remarkably untouched by the glamour of League football.

Inside, the West Stand is a hodgepodge, a stand disunited. The original stand is evidently the seating section with its old sloping roof at the back, accommodating 650 in the vicinity of the half-way line. In front of this and to a few yards either side are portions of terracing, but only as far as each 18-yard line. These areas are covered by a flat extension roof from the seats to the terracing, a later addition and an awkward one at that. Strangely enough this use of the extended roof from an old Main Stand to cover terracing is also found at Scunthorpe's neighbours, Doncaster and Rotherham, although with rather less clumsiness. Then along the touchline to the left is a separate section of terracing and to the right more terracing, covered with its own lower and older roof up to the corner flag.

This convoluted West Side of the ground does not however spoil the ground's overall appearance. To the left is the Fox Street End covered terrace, to the right the Doncaster Road terrace. Both roofs are similar, box-like with supports along the front. Opposite the West Stand is that prized possession, the East Stand. It covers half the pitch on either side of the half-way line and is made prominent by having the letters SUFC picked out in the coloured seats. Although now somewhat weathered and scarred by vandals, the stand still has an air of self-importance. Its structure shows quite clearly how cantilever stands are built, because the base of the rear steel supports are open to view. The front wall where there is a narrow terrace, is in untreated brick, which does reduce the stand's overall impact, and the screen ends are glass. The designers and builders were obviously quite confident, for the roof is particularly deep and, for an original, the design in little apparent need of change. The curious thing is that copies did not spring up all over British football grounds. Without the East Stand the Old Show Ground would be ordinary and uninspiring, but its presence, far from casting aspersions on its neighbours, gives the ground added unity. It ties the rest together, and provides an attractive focus which, from outside, one would never have expected. Such surprise is surely one of the most alluring assets of our British football grounds.

◆ GRIMSBY TOWN ◆

Previous Grounds

The club was formed in 1878 as Grimsby Pelham FC, playing at Clee Park in Cleethorpes, except during the 1880–81 season when a ground on the site of Lovet Street was used. There, the players had to change in bathing huts brought up from the sea shore. One of the earliest signings came in 1883, while the club were having a 500-seater wooden stand erected at Clee Park. One of the joiners employed turned out to be a member of the Spilsby team, the best side in South Lincolnshire at the time, so Grimsby persuaded him to join them instead! Clee Park was the scene of two early floodlit games using Wells lights, v. Boston and Rotherham Town in April 1889. Shortly after Grimsby had to leave the ground, which belonged to the Earl of Yarborough, who wanted to develop the site more profitably. There had been plans to build a proper sports stadium there, but Clee Park now is the home of a pub of the same name. Appropriately, its sign depicts a Victorian footballer.

Grimsby's second ground was near the Top Town area of Grimsby at a field on the south side of Welholme Road. The club brought over the stand from Clee Park and spent £300 preparing a ground capable of holding 10 000 spectators, many of them on a large bank at one end. *The Eastern Daily Telegraph* even built its own exclusive press box by the pitch.

Abbey Park was opened in August 1889 with a match v. West Bromwich, the previous year's Cup holders. In 1892 Grimsby joined the newly formed League Division Two, and although they built another stand at the ground, always knew that Abbey Park would only be a temporary home. Initially the club had negotiated a seven-year lease with the landowner, Lord Heneage, who intended to build houses on the land. When the seven-year period expired, he did grant a further three years, but at the end of this Grimsby had to move. Abbey Park was between the park and Farebrother Street, on Welholme Road.

Blundell Park

Blundell Park was close to Grimsby's first ground at Clee Park, and formed part of the land which Lord Torrington had described in 1791 as 'three miles of boggy turf' on the coastal approach to Grimsby. Nowadays we call it Cleethorpes. Since the ground is not technically in Grimsby (just as the City ground is not technically in Nottingham) a favourite question at sport quizzes has been: 'which team plays all its home games away?'

The land had been part of the manor of Itterby, purchased by Sidney Sussex College, Cambridge in 1616, with money left to it by a Peter Blundell. There are also nearby recreation grounds called Sidney and Sussex Parks.

From research by Patrick Conway, Deputy Chief Librarian at Gateshead, we know that Grimsby took

Blundell Park showing the Findus Stand (*Grimsby Evening Telegraph*)

with them to Blundell Park the two stands from Abbey Park. One went on the south west side, where the new Findus Stand now is, the other, called the Hazel Grove Stand, was placed behind the goal where the Osmond Stand is now situated. Originally, the south west side was to be the ground's focal point and administrative centre. Grimsby's first game at Blundell Park was a Division Two match v. Luton in 1899, by which time a cover had also been erected over the Pontoon End banking. The players changed at the nearby Imperial Hotel, which still exists.

In 1901 a new wooden Main Stand was built on the sea-board side of the pitch, the central section of which is still the Main Stand. It is therefore one of the oldest surviving structures at a League ground. The sea air must have been kind to its ageing timbers.

Even at this stage, Grimsby were still unsure if Blundell Park would become their permanent home. Having lost their previous grounds to development, they had to have more security before the ground could be properly improved. *Athletic News* reported in 1909, 'the district is being rapidly built up and in the near future there is the probability that the site may be too valuable to be retained for purely athletic purposes'.

In 1925 a Ground Committee was formed at Blundell Park, resulting in considerable improvements all round. The old Abbey Park Stand was replaced by a cover on the half-way line named the Barrett Stand, after Alderman Frank Barrett, a patron of the club. Wooden terracing was laid on either side of the stand. In July 1927, thanks again to financial support from Barrett, Grimsby were able to purchase the ground.

During their spell in Division One, from 1929–32, Grimsby extended the Main Stand down to the east corner, then followed their most successful period in the years up to the Second World War. They reached the 5th Round in 1937, drawing Wolves at Blundell Park on 20 February. The ground's highest attendance of 31 657 saw Town held to a draw before losing the replay. The semi-final was reached in 1939, and with the revenue Grimsby replaced the old Hazel Grove Stand and built the Osmond Stand, a small 700-seater in the middle of the rear terracing. Like the Barrett Stand, it was named after one of a family of benefactors. Also during summer 1939 a cover over the corner terrace was built between the Main Stand and the Osmond Stand.

Floodlights were installed and first used on 9 March 1953, when the visitors were Lincolnshire neighbours, Gainsborough Trinity, for a Midland League fixture. Curiously, the lights were mounted not on conventional steel gantries or pylons, but on short concrete towers. They were, however, deemed inadequate for Football League games, so in 1960 new pylons were mounted on the concrete bases and with new lights Grimsby were able to stage their first floodlit League match in September of that year v. Newport. A year later the old Pontoon cover was replaced by the existing Pontoon Stand, paid for by

the supporters. There was even talk of moving the club to a new ground on Cambridge Road.

Promotion to Division Two in 1980 cost Grimsby £280 000 in ground improvements, of which £160 000 was a grant from the Football Grounds Improvement Trust (FGIT). But the club also decided to invest further money in building a dazzling new stand in place of the Barrett Stand, which was no longer safe.

One of the local frozen fish companies, Findus, provided £200 000 towards the total cost of £425 000, and the television companies chipped in to provide a camera gantry. The new so-called Findus Stand was intended to take all the offices and players' facilities away from the old stands opposite, and to provide Blundell Park at last with seating and executive accommodation which would reflect the team's ambitions of First Division football. But building took a long time. Every bore hole drilled for the foundations would fill up with water, the ground being only a few hundred yards from the sea. And the club had insufficient capital to put in the offices or to open up the executive boxes straight away. So the stand was not quite complete when it was first used on 28 August 1982 for a game v. Leeds United. Some of the Leeds fans were so overcome with excitement at seeing the Findus Stand that they kicked out the back of the Osmond Stand, tore out seats and, unable to contain themselves, urinated into the gardens behind.

In addition, the stand was so tall in comparison with surrounding buildings, that the club had to pay for installing cable television to nearby houses whose roof aerials had been rendered useless. But Grimsby being the generous club that it is went further, by giving out 65 free season tickets to the neighbours, by way of compensating them for all the disruption caused during building work, and throwing a Christmas party for local children and old age pensioners. There is a lesson to be learned here.

At the same time the Findus Stand was built, Grimsby put in seats where once had been a paddock at the front of the Main Stand. During these alterations it was discovered that the oldest section of the Main Stand, built in 1901, had simply been plonked onto the ground, without foundations. Its survival was even more remarkable for that. These extra seats, plus those in the Findus Stand, took the seating total to 6100 in an overall capacity of 22 500.

Ground Description

If you are travelling to the ground from the south, you need not enter Grimsby, which would be a shame. To fully appreciate the warmth of this club and its environs one really should wander round the town and docks beforehand.

Blundell Park is situated in a long, thin built-up area between the main road to Grimsby and the Humber Estuary. Beyond the Main Stand is open land leading down to the water, broken by the railway line from Cleethorpes to Doncaster and Lincoln.

In some ways, the situation is similar to that of the Victoria Ground, Hartlepool.

Rather than begin with the Main Stand, we will start in the new Findus Stand, destined to take over in the coming years. Behind is a small car-park hemmed in by the neighbouring houses. The facade is small when compared with new stands at bigger clubs, but cleanly faced and styled, like a small hotel. Grimsby have negotiated the establishment of a community centre in one half of the stand, with their own facilities in the other half.

From inside the Findus Stand is one of the finest views in football. Ahead, over the Main Stand roof, stretches the Humber Estuary, with the North Humberside peninsular (formerly North Yorkshire) visible in the distance. Over to the right is the furthest tip of the Estuary, Spurn Head, and to the left is Kingston-upon-Hull, across the water, but too far to be visible in any weather.

Turning to the land, to the right is the centre of Cleethorpes, and to the left Grimsby docks and the many warehouses of various frozen food companies. But most prominent of all is the Grimsby Dock Tower. Built in 1852, this landmark is the tallest brick building in Lincolnshire, and a replica of the Sienna Town Hall clock tower in Italy.

To concentrate on the ground itself, the Findus Stand does not run quite the length of the pitch, and is flanked by two sections of open terracing. In construction it is a propped cantilever, with angled uprights. There are 2400 seats, with the name Findus picked out among them in letters so high that on a clear day they can be seen by passengers on the ferry out in the Estuary.

Separating the upper tier from the paddock in front is provision for executive boxes. As the other stands are much lower, the Findus Stand towers over Blundell Park. But like Scunthorpe's cantilever stand or Wigan's Main Stand, it gives the ground that vital focal point which holds the rest together.

From here, to the left is the plain, flat roof of the Pontoon End, named after the fish docks in Grimsby. To the right is the Osmond Stand, an unusual arrangement comprising an ordinary terrace end, covered only from the near edge of the penalty area, but with a small island of seating directly behind the goal. The roof continues round the far corner to link up with the more recent section of the Main Stand.

In that covered corner the visiting fans are sectioned off, and in fairness, it is hardly surprising that there has been violence, because in some respects it resembles a cage. On either side of the corner are nets, from the floor to the roof. There are pillars and barriers in so many places that a clear view of the pitch is difficult, and to compound one's irritation, the roof is so low and the corner so dark that one feels almost trapped.

Next we come to the Main Stand, which is in two sections, the older, all-wooden half being that nearer the Pontoon End. On the right, the 1931 section is fairly typical of the period, with a light brown roof, steel uprights and wooden floors. But the older half is a miracle. Notice how the roof seems to waver unevenly along the gutter, and how the wooden roof supports branch out into different directions at the top, like a tree. Look closer at these uprights and you will find them worn thin and smooth by time, gnarled by repairs but still quite reassuringly solid. The roof overhangs to the touchline, and the glass panelled screen stops level with where the paddock used to begin. From the back rows of the Main Stand the roof is so low you can barely see a foot of turf beyond the far touchline, let alone the base of the Findus Stand. Even on a good day.

The Main Stand comes to a halt level with the penalty area, where open terracing begins towards the Pontoon End. Behind the stand is the old entrance way, where a series of gates and turnstiles, small out-buildings and offices lead onto Harrington Street. There is nothing on the other side of the street except scrubland, a railway line, and a few hundred yards away, the water.

The floodlights are unusually mounted on thick concrete frames, the remains of the first set of towers. Notice that the lamps are mounted on open-ended bars, not a boxed-in frame, as usually seen on pylons (Chester and Brighton's are similar). Note also the distinctive black and white striped goal-nets, a present to the club from a local fishing net company when Grimsby won the Fourth Division Championship in 1972. The netting, made from nylon and polythene, is very strong. Finally, all credit to Grimsby for keeping their wooden fence around the pitch, pointed stakes and all, like every ground used to have. Only Blundell Park and Bootham Crescent have retained them. They make the pitch seem more like a field with the spectators involved onlookers rather than fenced off intruders.

Apart from the awful visitors' corner, Blundell Park is a most appealing and likeable ground. So many grounds could be anywhere. They don't inspire you to explore, ask questions or care about the surrounds. Not so Blundell Park. You don't go there just for football, you go there for Grimsby; the town, the people, the smell of fish and the sea.

◆ HULL CITY ◆

Previous Grounds

When Hull City formed in 1904 the club began playing exhibition matches at the Boulevard Ground, the home of Hull Rugby FC. Hull was then, and still is a rugby stronghold, so the Football League was keen to encourage soccer in the area. In 1905 therefore, City turned professional, set up a limited company and joined Division Two. Hull's original plan was to share the Boulevard Ground, alternating home fixtures with the rugby team. But the Rugby League decided against the arrangement, fearing that soccer would become the more popular attraction, and promptly banned any member clubs from letting their grounds to a soccer club unless no admission was charged. Hull City were consequently members of the Football League, but homeless.

They found a new ground next to the cricket circle on Anlaby Road, by West Park, and stayed there until 1945. In 1934 Hull purchased the present site of Boothferry Park, in anticipation of a future move. The ground at Anlaby Road had never been developed substantially and was now needed for railway redevelopment. City's highest gate there was 21 000 for a quarter final Cup tie v. Preston in 1921. The adjacent cricket ground still exists and is sometimes used by Yorkshire.

Boothferry Park

Boothferry Park is the third youngest ground in use by a League Club, and was opened in 1946. City had to vacate Anlaby Road during the War, and although they bought the Boothferry site in 1934, little alteration was made to the ground until 1945.

Originally a cricket ground, Boothferry Park had the potential to become one of the top stadiums in the country. But Hull, with a population of about 280 000, is still the largest urban area in England never to have had a First Division soccer club.

City were in Division Three when their new ground was opened. The Main or West Stand was complete, with an entrance on North Road, and the North Stand, behind which was a large car-park by Boothferry Road, was one-third complete in the centre. By 1950, the North Stand was complete, giving the ground a total of 6000 seats, a respectable number for a club just promoted to Division Two, and more than many First Division clubs at the time. And the ground had already proved its overall capacity, when a record 55 019 attended City's 6th Round Cup tie v. Manchester United on 26 February 1949.

As war-time restrictions eased, more building was carried out. On 6 January 1951, the first British Railway's train pulled into Boothferry Park Halt, the ground's very own railway station behind the East Side, with 595 passengers aboard. They could enter the ground directly through turnstiles on the station platform, which backed onto the terracing; a unique

Boothferry Park (Adrian Gibson)

arrangement of which Hull was justifiably proud.

The following April, the cover on the East Side terracing was completed, so three sides were now sheltered. The first floodlit match took place on 19 January 1953 v. Dundee, with lights on gantries along each side roof.

As steady members of Division Three, Hull's prospects were made much healthier when in May 1963 Harold Needler, whose family had long been associated with the board of directors, made the club a substantial gift of £200 000. A large gymnasium took £50 000 of this. It was built south of the ground and opened on 21 January 1964. The existing floodlight system of six tall pylons was installed in 1965, and early in 1966, during Hull's promotion season, the South Stand seating 3000 was completed at a cost of £130 000. Boothferry Park was now a ground of First Division standard, with 9000 seats and a large car-park. Surely greater success on the field would soon follow.

Sadly for Hull it was a case of so near and yet so far. Everyone expected the team to rise to Division One and yet they slipped down into the Fourth Division, before a change of management reversed the decline.

Boothferry Park suffered with the team. In 1981–82 the average gate was just under 4000, in a ground that held 42 000. So in 1982 it was decided to demolish the North Stand to make way for a supermarket. It was a very similar deal to one completed by Crystal Palace, by which the club lease the land on a long-term basis, but keep a smaller section of open terracing in front of the supermarket.

And so the super-stadium was reduced in size just as the team began to fare better. If the public is no longer interested in their team, property developers will always find some use for a ground. But ironically, with this extra revenue, clubs can attempt to re-kindle support.

Boothferry Park's present capacity is 30 630, of which 6000 are seated.

Ground Description

Although a well-appointed ground in many ways, Boothferry Park is also rather soulless, like the sprawl of semi-detached houses lining Boothferry Road from the Humber Bridge to the town centre.

One of these semis houses the club offices. The secretary is in the front bedroom, the souvenir shop in the dining room, reception in the parlour.

Where the North Stand once stood is now the supermarket, with a large car-park in front. City's swish new ticket office block, built in 1966, was used as the builder's site office during construction, before being demolished also.

The West Stand, sometimes called the 'Best Stand' is the original construction, refurbished inside. It is fairly typical of early post-war stands, built on the same principle employed in the 1930s but with squarer lines and more use of brick and steel. A plain wall lines the back of a narrow paddock in front, the two screen ends are solid (as opposed to glass panelled) and the roof fascia is white and plain. In the centre is a television camera gantry and above the players' tunnel is the 'Hull City' sign donated to the club by British Railways, when the locomotive of that name was scrapped.

If the stand seems undistinguished from without, inside it is comfortable enough. The press-box is particularly well equipped, another improvement of the mid-1960s. Surprisingly, the dug-outs on either side of the tunnel are painted bright red.

From here, to the left is the now open, truncated North Terrace, in front of the new supermarket. This used to be the paddock in front of the North Stand, which had 3000 seats. City have done well to preserve this terrace, instead of closing it off altogether (as at Meadow Lane), but for those who knew Boothferry Park before 1982, the absence of a stand is sorely felt. A concrete shell is hoped to be built on the supermarket roof for the use of performing groups.

Opposite the West Stand is the East Side terracing, covered down to the touchline by a simple, low pitched roof. Behind here is the railway station platform, with its turnstiles on the right of the roof. The barriers are brightly decked in black and amber paint, and in the north east corner are especially unusual. At one stage of the ground's development these terraces were built up a couple of feet above the original banking. Instead of digging up the old barriers, the inverted V-shape supports were left intact, new supports built over them and the horizontal bar transferred from the original to the new vertical supports. The terracing is also unusual, having in parts beaded mouldings along the top of each step.

To the right is the more modern South Stand, beyond which you can just see the grey walls of the gymnasium. The stand sits behind a large paddock, and resembles in many ways the Sky Blue Stand at Highfield Road, built two years earlier at a similar cost. Hull's stand is extremely light, with glass screen ends, transparent panels in the roof, and a line of windows along the back, so that the roof almost seems to be suspended on glass.

In its day it was no doubt the height of fashion, with its clean lines, plain white fascia, polished wooden seats and boarding. Nowadays it enjoys a new lease of life, thanks to the addition of bright new yellow seats in 1983, one sign of the club's new-found optimism.

Boothferry Park does have another unique feature apart from the railway station. It is the only ground to have six, free-standing floodlight pylons, three, very tall, on each side. They, the South Stand, the gym and the press-box, were all part of the dream Boothferry Park in the mid-1960s. But they have survived the nightmare years, and the loss of one stand has by no means ruined the ground's potential. Boothferry Park still craves success and large crowds, and before long the dream might well revive even more strongly than before. The ground will be more than ready and able in that event.

NORTH AND WEST YORKSHIRE

• LEEDS UNITED •

Elland Road

Although Association football was well established in South Yorkshire by the turn of the century, West Yorkshire remained a solid rugby stronghold without one senior, professional soccer club until Bradford City was formed in 1903, by the members of a rugby club. Leeds City were born the following year, also with a strong rugby connection.

The club bought Elland Road from Holbeck Rugby League Club, and a year later joined Bradford in Division Two. The League was keen to challenge rugby's supremacy in the area, so Leeds were welcome. The ground then had a small main stand and three open sides of banking, but with acres of open space all around for expansion. Leeds did not look like winning anything until the arrival of Herbert Chapman as manager in 1912. When League football ceased in 1915, the ground was used for army drilling and shooting practice, Chapman became a manager at a munitions factory, and City's ailing affairs were put into the hands of a receiver, who tried to sell the club to Leeds Northern RFC at Headingley.

A syndicate rallied round to keep City at Elland Road, but after the War the League and FA ordered the club to present their accounts for inspection, suspecting there had been illegal payments made to players during the War. Leeds refused to hand over the accounts and were therefore expelled from the League. 'We will have no nonsense,' said the League President John McKenna, 'the football stable must be cleansed.' But it is doubtful whether Leeds were any more guilty than many other clubs.

For a short time Elland Road was used by Yorkshire Amateurs, a top northern club, until a new professional club, Leeds United, was formed. Within a few months they were voted into the League, no doubt aided by those clubs who had been so glad to escape punishment the previous year.

By 1939 United were a run of the mill First Division outfit and Elland Road a completely different ground to the one we know today. The Main or West Stand, built in the Leeds City era, had a double-barrel roof. The Elland Road terrace cover was a typical 'scratching shed' with a wooden barrel roof almost identical to one at Huddersfield, also built in the 1920s (and still in existence), and on the east side was the Lowfields Road Stand, built on a bank of terracing running the whole length of the ground. The North End was an enormous, open Spion Kop.

Immediately after the War Leeds were relegated, but though in danger of becoming Second Division also-rans, the club made a wise investment by buying the training pitches immediately behind the West Stand. They would have liked to buy all the land from the West Stand to the Leeds–London railway line, but did not have sufficient resources. With more land they could have developed the site profitably without losing any of the training areas.

On 9 November 1953 Elland Road's first floodlights were switched on for a friendly v. Hibernian.

Three years later disaster struck. Just as Leeds were fighting their way back to the top, the West Stand was destroyed by fire caused by an electrical fault. Leeds had to build temporary dressing rooms on the training pitch, until the replacement stand was ready in 1956.

Nowadays the West Stand seems almost quite ordinary but, in the context of stand design, it represented a bridge between the old and the new. It was a propped cantilever and although Birmingham City had built an early version of this type a few years previously, theirs did not extend so far. In addition the Leeds stand had a modern facade; a styled entrance way which gave the ground an added sense of importance. Such conceits are all too rare at football grounds, and before then only the facades of Villa Park, Highbury and, to a lesser extent Molineux and Craven Cottage, had any semblance of architectural dignity. Even in recent years only a few clubs have taken any pains to improve their frontages, the most notable being Sheffield United.

Elland Road's new stand cost the then astronomical sum of £150 000, but it has weathered well and remains a considerable asset. But United's fortunes rose most dramatically when Don Revie arrived at Elland Road in 1958, changed the team

Elland Road in the 1960s before redevelopment (Aerofilms)

colours, changed the staff, changed the whole outlook and eventually helped change the ground, all funded by a string of honours and near misses up to 1975. During this spell Elland Road's highest attendance was recorded, when 57 892 saw Sunderland hold Leeds to a 1-1 draw in a 5th Round FA Cup replay on 15 March 1967.

Huge profits poured in, and were spent largely on Elland Road. In 1967 the Spion Kop was removed, a process which took six weeks. The flattened area was then left unused and a new North Stand built behind it, right up to the extremity of United's land. When finished, the front terracing was therefore 60 feet from the nearest goal-line. The flat area where once the Kop had been, was then turfed and the pitch moved 30 feet towards the new Stand, so that now both end terraces were 30 feet from the goal-lines. The North Stand was standing only and cost £250 000.

The next development came in 1970, when the North Stand was joined to the West Stand with a covered corner section. As an indication of how building prices had escalated, this small section alone cost £200 000. It had seats at the back, standing in front.

A year later work began on the other side of the North Stand. Another corner section was to be built, needing the removal of yet more earth banking, and since the plan envisaged continuing the corner along the length of the east side, in place of the Lowfields Road Stand, a gap was left in order to build proper foundations. This cost Leeds another £250 000.

In 1974 the last major change began, at the Elland Road End, when down came the small scratching shed. Since there was already 60 feet of extra turf, the pitch was moved up to the North Stand, and on the space left the new South Stand was erected. This construction cost £400 000.

The next stage would have been to build a corner section linking the South Stand to the east side, and it was here that the Elland Road plan came unstuck. After losing the European Cup Final in Paris in May 1975 Leeds began to slip out of the limelight. Don Revie had taken the England manager's job in 1974, and inflation put paid to Elland Road.

It cost the club £1 million just to demolish half of the Lowfields Road Stand and build foundations for the new corner section. Leeds called it a day and pronounced themselves content with what they had. The foundations are still there should United ever wish to complete the scheme, but it is doubtful whether sufficient capital will be available for some time.

Apart from the building programme outlined

above however, there were other changes to the ground. For example, in the early 1970s the pitch was completely reconstructed with help from the Sports Turf Research Institute at Bingley, Yorkshire (see Pitches) and was generally held to be the best surface in the north. In the summer of 1982 Elland Road staged a rock concert by Queen and several thousand feet plus heavy equipment on the pitch compacted the top surface. Then in 1982–83 Hunslet Rugby League Club began using Elland Road, having lost their own ground, and although rugby does not in itself spoil the turf as much as soccer, the extra usage meant that greater care would be necessary to keep the pitch in order. But Leeds were crippled by debts and could afford only the minimum amount of maintenance, with the inevitable result that the pitch began to suffer.

Another development concerned the floodlights. When the new stands were built taller pylons had to be built outside the ground to provide adequate illumination. Three were erected in 1979, with temporary lighting in the south east corner. Now there are four 250-feet high pylons, the tallest in the Football League.

Finally, as attendances dropped, the club decided to put in extra seats in the west and south paddocks. This took the total number of seats to 19 626, in an overall capacity of 43 900.

Between 1956 and 1982 Leeds spent £2·5 million on Elland Road. To finish the development plan, by linking the north east corner with the South Stand, would cost a further £2 million at 1983 prices. With every season that goes by without success, the chances of it ever being completed diminish.

Ground Description

Not only has Elland Road changed beyond recognition in the past two decades, but its surroundings are also totally different, mostly due to the arrival of the motorway linking the M62 with the centre of Leeds. It passes within a hundred yards of the ground and makes Elland Road one of the easiest League venues to reach by road.

Elland Road itself, as the name suggests, takes you west to the town of Elland, near Huddersfield (where Leeds Road takes you back into Leeds).

The main entrance to Elland Road leads into a car-park between the West Stand and the training ground, where there are still the dressing rooms erected after the fire. Like so many 'ultra-modern' creations of that period – the same is true at St James' Park and the Victoria Ground – the 1956 facade looks tired and faded, but with an updated sign and new paintwork would soon regain its pride. The successful Leeds teams of the late 1960s and early 1970s would pose in front of the main entrance, their white kit standing out against the blue cladding and white lettering.

Inside the stand there is a problem. To illustrate this, the players' tunnel is now to the right of the half-way line, but when first built it was in the centre. Since the pitch was moved north, the south section of the stand has been rather out on a limb. Anyone sitting at this extremity has a better view of the traffic on Elland Road than of the pitch, and if they look straight ahead see the side of the South Stand. To compensate for this – obviously in 1956 they had not conceived the redevelopment plan – the club have added a curved section of seats linking the West Stand paddock with the South Stand paddock. But the upper tier of corner seats have a limited viewpoint.

From the West Stand, to the right is the South Stand, standing square behind the pitch. It is in the same style as all the new additions, a propped cantilever with deep overhanging roof, plain white fascia and all blue seating. Elland Road runs directly behind.

In the far corner the paddock curves round, the blue seats giving way to open terracing, at the back of which is a tall wooden fence. Behind are the foundations of the corner which was never built. It is claimed they will not suffer from continued exposure and could be built on at any time.

The Lowfields Road Stand is the oldest remnant at Elland Road, but fits in remarkably well. The southern half has been chopped off, but as a new glass screen end has been added one could never tell. Originally the stand was for standing only.

Behind is a large open space lying in the shadows of the elevated motorway. Leeds had hoped to buy this land and build a sports complex, linked to the ground by an overhead walkway above Lowfields Road.

Redeveloped Elland Road in 1975, with the Lowfields Road Stand still intact. Notice how the roof of the 1956 West Stand ends level with the goal-line of the old pitch (Aerofilms)

Apart from the lack of funds, the project was hindered by the local residents who were worried that if the nearby greyhound stadium site was used for light industry *and* United built a leisure centre, the area would lose what residential quality still survived. So many houses have been demolished in the area that those left on the estate behind Elland Road are in danger of being swamped in a sea of development.

To the left of the Lowfields Road Stand is another open space behind the paddock, where further development was also planned. Some 20 yards away begins the corner section of the North Stand.

Both corners of the North Stand have seating at the back and standing below, but the North Stand itself is all standing, still in the same style as the South Stand. At the back of the stand is an electric scoreboard, but for those in the North Stand who cannot see it, the club have installed smaller scoreboards facing inwards under the roof, a refreshing demonstration of concern for a section of fans sadly well known for their unruliness elsewhere.

Standing out on the skyline for miles around are United's four enormous floodlight pylons, distinguished not only by their height but by the diamond-shape lamp holders at the top.

Elland Road is so well equipped, with almost every modern convenience apart from executive boxes (in Yorkshire!), that it is surprising how little the ground has been used for major games. The capacity is reasonable, there are enough seats, and access is superb. But the ground lacks character. There are no features to hold one's attention and, the colouring is cold; blue seats, grey roofs, white fascia, grey concrete, almost as if all the faults of which Don Revie's team had been accused had been embodied in the bricks and mortar of Elland Road.

This is not quite the club's fault. No other ground has been so completely redeveloped at such a reasonable cost and in such a short time. Yet the fact that the scheme is unfinished is probably one of the most redeeming features of the ground. The presence of the Lowfields Road Stand at least provides a break from the uniform structures on the other three sides.

If the ground was completed, it would no doubt resemble a smaller version of Old Trafford, but even then there is a nagging suspicion that Elland Road would still lack character. Perhaps it changed too soon, founded on quick success and no long-term tradition. Once inside there is hardly any indication as to whom the ground belongs.

Throughout this book I have made a plea for clubs to put signs on their roof fascia, or flagpoles or clocks, or even to paint the club colours on a wall or two. Nowhere is this plea more heartfelt than at Elland Road. All white strips and functional architecture were all very well in the 1960s and 1970s, but now the club should put a bit of the gold and blue back into the ground to give Elland Road an unmistakable identity to match its excellent facilities.

·YORK CITY·

Previous Grounds
A team called York City played from the turn of the century until the First World War at a ground called Field View, Holgate, only a few hundred yards from the present ground. In 1922 York City were reborn, but on the other side of the city, near the university campus, at Fulfordgate. But Fulfordgate was too far from the railway station and the club's centre of support, so in 1932 the club asked its followers for their views on a move, and in the summer of that year York City took over Bootham Crescent. Fulfordgate was built over with a housing estate, and the ground stood where Eastward Avenue is now.

Bootham Crescent
Bootham Crescent belonged to York Cricket Club when York City purchased the land and set about converting it into a football ground. A Main Stand, a section of the existing structure, was built and a cover put up over the Popular Side. The ground was opened on 31 August 1932. Although the team hardly caused a ripple in the Third Division North, City did cause a few shocks in the FA Cup, and it was their 6th Round tie v. Huddersfield Town in March 1938 that attracted Bootham Crescent's highest gate of 28 123.

During the Second World War, the ground suffered damage when a bomb fell on the Shipton Street End. Soon after the War the terracing was laid properly with concrete. City's greatest achievement came in 1955, when they just failed to beat Newcastle in an FA Cup semi-final and then lost the replay. United won the Cup, but City spent their profits wisely, building an extension to the Main Stand.

Despite losing to Newcastle, good relations were maintained between the two clubs, and on 28 October 1959 United sent a team to Bootham Crescent to mark the switching on of York's new floodlights, which cost £14 500.

For two seasons, 1974–76, York played in the Second Division, and seats were installed under the Popular Side roof, increasing the seating total to 2762. The ground's capacity is reduced from 16 500 to 13 824.

Ground Description
The ground is a short walk from the old city walls, on the north west side of the centre. Bootham Bar is one of several medieval gates nearby, leading directly into the grounds of York Minster.

But as delightful as the city is, so Bootham Crescent is a disappointing ground, lacking any feature of note. The Main Stand sits along three-quarters of the pitch nearer to the northern end, a plain box-like construction with seats sandwiched between a line of advertisements along the roof facings, and a plain

Bootham Crescent Main Stand. A white wooden perimeter fence is a rare survivor of a once common feature (Sporting Pictures)

brick wall behind the narrow front paddock. The newer section can be distinguished only by the colour of the bricks and the fact that it has a glass screen end, whereas the other end is open. The tunnel is in the centre of the original Main Stand.

From here to the left is the uncovered Grosvenor Road End terrace. The rear of the bank has been fenced-off, a precaution taken by the club when cracks were found in the rear walls of the banking.

To the right is the Shipton Street terrace, also uncovered, but slightly higher than the opposite bank. At the rear is an old scoreboard, now used as an advertisement hoarding. Behind is the Shipton Street primary school, and if you look over the Main Stand from here you can see above the roof tops the fifteenth century central tower of York Minster. This view is one redeeming feature.

Opposite the Main Stand is the Popular Side, now all-seated except for the final section near the Shipton Street. Although installed only in 1974, the seats are in an advanced state of delapidation, but unusually they have armrests. Behind this stand are the Duncombe Barracks, used by the Territorial Army.

The area is sedately suburban, and Bootham Crescent must therefore retain a certain sense of decorum. Hardly surprisingly, one of its more endearing qualities is an original, white, wooden perimeter fence, although most of this is obscured by advertisements. The ground does not feel enclosed, nor does it, like Gresty Road or the Victoria Ground, Hartlepool, reflect in any way the city in which it stands. To borrow a phrase from Oliver Goldsmith, Bootham Crescent is 'dull without a single absurdity'.

HUDDERSFIELD ·TOWN·

Leeds Road

Huddersfield Town was one of those instant creations formed in a rugby stronghold, founded in 1908 as a professional club with a tailor made ground, laid out on the Leeds Road recreation ground by the country's leading ground designer, Archibald Leitch (see Design).

Leitch's design gave Huddersfield a main stand virtually identical to the one he had designed at Fulham three years earlier, based on a formula that was to survive well into the 1930s, with an upper tier of seating, paddock in front, sloping roof enhanced by a central pointed gable. The rest of the ground was simply open banking, with a wooden perimeter fence.

The record gate of 67 037 came for a FA Cup match v. Arsenal on 27 February 1932, by which time Arsenal had inherited not only Town's manager, Herbert Chapman, but also their almost overwhelming domination of English football.

During Huddersfield's run of success, Leeds Road changed little in overall appearance, but much in substance. The present roof was put up over the Leeds Road End terrace, but the most significant changes were to the terraces themselves. These were concreted over, and installed with barriers on solid bases all round the ground. At the time they were the strongest in the country, and even under the new safety regulations are well up to standard. This helps to explain why the present capacity is still relatively high. Close to the end of the 1949–50 season, a fire gutted most of Leitch's original stand. It took only 15 minutes for the entire stand to be engulfed in flames, but the cause was never established. The replacement stand, built the following summer, had a similar basic pattern, but was a squarer design and without the gable. Town's fortunes began to decline from then, but during a brief return to Division One, the club erected a vast cover over the Popular Side opposite the Main Stand, in the summer of 1955.

The first set of floodlights was switched on in January 1961 for a Cup replay v. Wolves and paid for from the proceeds of Denis Law's transfer to Manchester City, but in February 1962 one of them blew down onto the pitch in a gale. A new set were promptly installed for the start of the next season.

The present capacity of Leeds Road is 41 000. Additional seating was installed in the Main Stand paddock in 1970, before Town's last spell in the First Division, bringing the seating total to 6000.

Ground Description

The ground lies at the foot of a line of hills which an enthusiast would do well to ascend for a marvellous

Leeds road in the mid-1930s, the Popular Site in mid-construction (Aerofilms)

panoramic view of the football stadium and its sur-rounds. But down on street level we find the Main Stand, now quite open at the back because of exten-sive demolition in the vicinity. As is so often the case, local industry has declined even faster than the club's fortunes. But the club cannot be faulted for keeping a clean, well maintained house. Inside, the Main Stand is very orderly, but like other stands of the 1950s, rather characterless.

A new television camera gantry on the roof, how-ever odd, adds focus. From here you can see the Leeds Road End to the left. This has a wonderful wooden barrel roof, with a blue and white striped back wall. Between each upright is an arch filled with wooden lattice-work. It is predictably called the Cowshed – Elland Road had an almost identical one – but is much finer than the term usually implies. Opposite is the huge Popular Side bank of terracing, covered with a vast roof identical to one at Turf Moor. Notice how sturdy the barriers are, despite their age. To the right is the open Bradley Mill End, topped with an old fashioned half-time scoreboard. In the 1950s this end boasted the first electric scoreboard in the country, a

gift to the club from PSV Eindhoven. Unfortunately it burnt out and proved uneconomic to repair. Although the terracing is open here, the ground seems quite enclosed because, immediately behind, is the steep, grass-covered hillside, rising up to the Dalton Bank housing estate at the top. Bradley Mill, chimney and all, is also visible behind.

Huddersfield's pitch, which is the same size as Wembley's, is particularly fine, with lush turf and a perfect crown. The cinder track in front of the Main Stand was popular for sprint races held during the early years at the ground. The other three sides are fenced off by security barriers, the same type inciden-tally as those at Anfield and Old Trafford. On a summer's day Leeds Road shines with pride. The pitch seems to dazzle the stands and terraces with its glossiness. But in mid-winter it can be a gloomy place. Like the Den or Ninian Park – fairly large grounds of concrete and blue – without sunshine or a big crowd, Leeds Road looks as if it's sulking. But neither of those grounds has witnessed such glory as Huddersfield, which can make Leeds Road doubly poignant when the going is rough.

•BRADFORD CITY•

Valley Parade

Valley Parade was originally the home of Manningham Rugby Club, who after three years of struggle decided to adopt Association rules in the hope of increasing support and revenue. To everyone's surprise the new club was immediately voted into the Football League in Doncaster's place, because the League wanted to break rugby's hold on West Yorkshire. City's defunct neighbours, Bradford Park Avenue, evolved in a similar fashion four years later (see Lost but Not Forgotten).

On City's promotion to Division One, Valley Parade was transformed into one of the best grounds in the country, with a capacity of 40 000. The present Main Stand, built in 1909, was described then as 'a mammoth structure', seating 5300 with covered standing for 7000 more. Opposite, along Midland Road, was a smaller but elegant stand for 8000 standing. On its centre pointed gable was a clock, an unusual if not unique feature in those days. The Kop, large enough by any standards today, was then twice its present size.

In this golden era, City's was the first name to be engraved on the new FA Cup, coincidentally designed by a Bradford firm, in 1911. During that cup run, in March 1911, Bradford's largest crowd of 39 146 saw them play Burnley, and so the club can claim to have the longest standing attendance record of any League club.

But the glory soon faded, and after 1937 as Valley Parade became increasingly outdated, Bradford slipped into the lower divisions. In the early 1950s, Bradford Corporation ordered the Midland Road stand to be demolished, because the foundations were considered unsafe. (The frame of this stand went by rail to Berwick Rangers, who bought it for their new ground at Shielfield Park in 1952, for just £400. It cost Rangers a further £3000 to rebuild what is still today their main and only stand.) A new stand was built in its place in 1954, but this too proved unsafe and was pulled down six years later. The ground remained three-sided until 1966, when the pitch was moved closer to the Main Stand, and a very narrow, flat area along Midland Road covered for standing spectators.

City's first floodlights were on telegraph poles along each side, switched on for a friendly v. Hull City in December 1954. These lights are still in use at a nearby all-weather pitch.

The present pylons were bought second-hand from West Ham in 1960, and two years later the south east corner one was blown over in a gale (as happened at Leeds Road nearby). When Gateshead played here and lost in an FA Cup tie soon after, they complained unsuccessfully about the use of only three pylons.

In 1962 the club built new offices and dressing rooms in the south west corner of the Main Stand. Until then they had used an old house at the back of the Kop, at the north end of the Main Stand. The players changed in the cellars, which were often flooded and ridden with cockroaches, and entered the pitch along a tunnel under the Kop, through a gap still visible in that corner of the ground.

The Main Stand at Valley Parade, a lovable tangle of pillars and struts (Picture House)

For years the two Bradford clubs resisted amalgamation, to both their costs perhaps, since Park Avenue undoubtedly possessed the finer ground. For one poignant season, 1973–74, Park Avenue, then in the Northern Premier League, played their last games at Valley Parade before liquidation.

The present capacity of the ground is a much reduced 16 000, with 2000 seats.

Ground Description

Imagine watching football from the cockpit of a Sopwith Camel. That is the view from City's Main Stand. There are 22 thin verticals at the front, with cross struts in between each, plus more supports further back. The roof is black, with railway station-like, pointed boards lining the gutters. The seats and paintwork are red and amber, the perimeter fence white, and it really needs only a large roundel on the side to complete the biplane illusion. Underneath the seats are flaps which open to reveal piles of accumulated litter.

The stand is built into the side of a natural dip, so that the turnstiles at street level on Valley Parade bring you directly into the top of the stand. There, in the centre, is probably the most basic Director's Box in the League, the only route to which is past the turnstiles along a pathway used by everyone else queueing for refreshments and relief.

So many apparent disadvantages, yet this is one of my favourite stands; quaint, run-down and uncomfortable certainly, but homely, and I think fully deserving preservation.

To the right, past the players' entrance, is the Bradford End, a standing area covered in the late 1950s, with four, token twisted crush barriers. Opposite is the Midland Road cover, only 10 feet high and 12 feet deep running the length of the pitch over flat tarmac – the narrowest side at any League ground. If you look behind onto the sloping ground leading to the Midland Road below, you can see where the stand foundations were once sunk.

The Kop is quite magnificent, even in its diminished form today. The barriers, some rather bent, are red on one side of the central fence, yellow on the other. A white wall and an old half-time scoreboard cap off the mound splendidly against the sky. From the summit is one of the finest views of industrial England. The stands below, especially the barely discernible Midland Road roof, merge into a panorama of heavy stone buildings, mills and railway lines. Valley Parade is indeed an apposite name.

◆ HALIFAX TOWN ◆

Previous Grounds

Halifax began playing as a professional club in 1911 at Sandhall, where they remained until the First World War when the site was taken over for a munitions factory. For one season Town played at Exley until in 1921, the year they joined the League, the Shay Ground was finally made ready for use.

The Shay

The Shay, like many other football grounds, was originally a council refuse tip, and is still owned by the council. Town's first year's rent was £10, rising to £100 by their third season. No one is quite sure from where the name derives, except that the area was called Shay Syke.

The club spent £1000 on preparing the ground, much of it going towards buying a stand from Manchester City, who were then playing at Hyde Road. The stand still exists, but only just. Next to it is a hut which served as the players' dressing rooms, until moved to their present location on the opposite side of the ground. It is nevertheless still called the Main Stand, but has no extra facilities apart from a press box at the back.

The new administrative centre is behind what is now called the Patrons Stand, but was actually just a Scratching Shed to which seats were added in 1958.

The Shay's highest attendance was 36 885 for the visit of Tottenham Hotspur in the FA Cup 5th Round on 14 February 1953. The present capacity is 16 500, of which 2018 are seated.

Floodlights were first used in 1961 and cost £18 000 to install. Real Madrid were invited to provide the opposition for the first game, but Halifax had to be content with Red Star Belgrade from Yugoslavia instead.

Speedway was introduced to the Shay in 1948 until 1951, then brought back in 1965. The football club now share the Shay with the Halifax Dukes speedway team. There was also baseball at the ground just after the Second World War, and in the winter of 1962–63 when the pitch iced over the club opened it up as a skating ring and earned a welcome £100 during the cold spell. There was also an attempt to establish a golf driving range at one end, opened in 1966 by Jack Charlton, but this was short-lived as the stand roofs suffered from too many wild shots.

The biggest improvements at the Shay have been to the social amenities. Otherwise, the provision for spectators is probably the poorest in the League. A cantilever stand is said to be in the pipeline, but it will need higher gates before the stand is built.

Ground Description

It was once said that the Halifax manager liked to

The Shay (Martin Parr)

sign new players in the nearby railway station, before they had the chance to see the ground.

The approach up Shaw Hill is, however, pleasant rising through leafy surrounds with a modern and orderly high-rise estate opposite the ground. The car-park is spacious and smooth, decorated with old-fashioned lamp posts outside a new single storey night club, next to the club offices. So far all is favourable, tasteful and even apparently prosperous. Inside the ground is quite a contrast. The problem with speedway is that the track distances everyone from the pitch and seems to coat everything in a film of dust.

The Shay looks large, but is not; the pitch seems big, but is the smallest in the League, equal to those at Eastville and the Vetch Field. The players emerge from the Patrons Stand, which runs along the middle third of the east touchline. It is supposed to seat the executive element, but they will not need reminding that this is an old, simple cover for terracing with seats added. It is not the wood, or the fragility of the structure, or its distance from the pitch which makes the stand shabby, so much as the fact that some of the seats have been just plonked down on a cinder surface.

To the left is the Tramshed End, little used by spectators because the ash bank behind the high track wall is very shallow. There are bus sheds at the back, behind a line of tall trees.

To the right is the more popular, tall banking named after the Trinity Garage nearby. The centre section is terraced, the rest of the curved bank around the track being ash covered with patches of grass and weeds, punctuated here and there by a few crush barriers. At the very top is a tiny shelter, left over from the golf range. From here one has an excellent view to the left of the Pennines with Beacon Hill most prominent. The most noticeable building behind this end of the ground is the headquarters of the building society with which, rather than the football club, the town is now so readily associated. This end also provides the best view of the pitch – the side terraces are virtually flat – although at the front you are still 30 yards behind the goal, but higher because of the track's sloping angle.

Opposite the Patrons Stand is the forlorn old Main Stand, with bench seats in the centre and terraces on either side and in front. At one end is a poignant, faded remnant of an advertisement. Otherwise all is grey and drab.

Yet this could be a relatively smart and comfortable stand, far more so than the smaller structure opposite.

To the left of the Main Stand is a flat stretch of earth, the speedway pits, behind which is the very old dressing room hut, now used as offices by the speedway club.

The Shay is not gloomy. It is a wide, open ground, overlooked by hills. But it is inadequate for the average spectator, even by the standards of 20 years ago. Therefore it cannot even be called quaint in its decay.

·10·

EAST ANGLIA AND ESSEX

PETERBOROUGH ·UNITED·

London Road

The present club has played at London Road since their formation in 1934, although another team called Peterborough and Fletton United played there from 1923. For many years United drifted along in the Midland League, until in the mid-1950s the club began an almost miraculous run of success which eventually led them into the Football League. Not even Roy of the Rovers could have credibly concocted Peterborough's record between 1955–60, when in 103 games at London Road they lost just one game, scoring 428 goals in the process.

London Road improved with the team. Before 1955 there had been one small grandstand, seating 400 spectators, so during the 1956–57 season work began on building the present Main Stand, behind the old wooden one. Once completed, the original structure was taken down, and for a while the players entered the pitch across the site on wooden boards. Then the pitch was moved 20 yards towards the new stand, the club laying a new surface on soil bought from a sugar company's beet fields in the nearby Fenland. The space freed on the opposite touchline was banked up and terraced.

At the same time, two identical covers were erected at either terraced end of the ground. To complete the picture we have today, floodlights were installed during the autumn of 1957 and inaugurated with a friendly v. Arsenal. In just three years the ground had been transformed, gates were consistently

London Road, a 1950s' transformation (Sport & General)

above 10000, so it just remained to win sufficient support for election to the League, finally achieved in 1960.

London Road's highest gate of 30096, came during Peterborough's best Cup run to date, when they met Swansea Town in the 5th Round on 20 February 1965. The current capacity is 28000, with 3600 seats.

Ground Description

Born in the 1950s and untouched since, London Road is the spirit incarnate of British ground design during that unrewarding decade, even more so than Roots Hall. The basic tenet then was to copy everything that had been done in the 1930s, but replace curves with straight lines, wood with brick. Goodbye character, farewell warmth; welcome efficiency, insurability and long life.

The ground is approached from a private driveway off London Road, leading to a large council-owned car-park behind the Main Stand. A large market is held on this ground every Thursday evening. Beyond runs the River Nene.

The Main Stand is very plain, with a rather dark interior hardly relieved by a series of square windows along the back row of seats. Glass screen walls would have helped aesthetically, but no doubt detracted structurally, for the stand is solidly built in brick and steel with only two uprights supporting the roof along the front. Like its contemporaries at St Andrew's and Elland Road, the stand was an indication that the age of the cantilever was near. The roof is grey, with a steeply pitched front section, similar to that at Layer Road, though without any detail to alleviate the monotony. Similarly, the brick paddock rear wall is untouched by colour or embellishment.

From the Main Stand, to the left is the Moys Road End, to the right the London Road End, both covered terraces, each identical. But although the roofs are also dark, at least along the gutters are lines of advertisements. The roofs are quite low, supported by several uprights at the very front.

In the corner between the Main Stand and the London Road End is a small two storey block originally built by the club as a restaurant, but now rented out to a local branch of the Probation Service, perhaps a warning against potential recidivists on the terraces.

Opposite the Main Stand is the open Glebe Road terrace, built on the site of the old pitch and backed by a row of houses. Again it is a neat section, but lacking any focal point. London Road is one of only three League grounds to have both ends covered and one side terrace open. Sincil Bank and The Valley are similar.

London Road came a long way in such a short time, for which it was no doubt much admired at the time. Now that fashion and style have changed however, we must pronounce it dull. But it requires only a modern set of accessories and cosmetic change to give it renewed sparkle and a fresher face.

◆ CAMBRIDGE UNITED ◆

Previous Grounds

There can be few more idyllic places for a football team to play than the expanse of grass in the centre of Cambridge known as Parker's Piece, still used now as it was when the club was formed after the First World War, for public recreation. And there can be few more unusual and evocative names than that of the ground they moved to in August 1932, the Celery Trenches, so called because it was in an area of vegetable plots. The land was just off Newmarket Road on virtually the same site as the present ground, and belonged to the Marshalls, who ran a motor and aircraft firm, and gave most of the site to the club as a gift. The club's headquarters were in the Dog and Feathers nearby. Since the ground was in the Abbey district, actually some 300 yards beyond the Cambridge boundary, the club was called Abbey United. They became Cambridge United in 1949.

Abbey Stadium

If the city of Cambridge was destined to have a League club, the chances were that Cambridge City, not United, would be the likely candidates. It was the senior club, with once the better ground, and at one stage in their history they had a very rich and ambitious chairman. But United had determined supporters, and money cannot buy loyalty on a Saturday afternoon. Indicative of the United spirit were the club's first primitive floodlights in the early 1950s. They were paid for mostly by Len Sayward (brother of Pat), who contributed £400 from his own testimonial fund. Similarly, the Habbin Stand was built in 1960 by a group of supporters who called themselves the 'Auto Club', a pun on their tendency to spend many an evening telling each other 'they ought to do this, ought to do that . . .'

As the promise of League status grew stronger, a small Main Stand was built in 1969 (extended since then), and the present floodlights were inaugurated for a friendly v. Chelsea on 1 May 1970. This was also the occasion of United's highest crowd of 14000, which is nevertheless the lowest record gate of any League club, mainly because the Abbey Stadium is also the smallest ground in the League. (Although Eastville has the same 12500 capacity as Cambridge's, this is due only to safety restrictions.) The Abbey Stadium has 3500 seats however, which is more than many grounds of twice its size.

Ground Description

The name is perhaps misleading; there is no abbey any more, and this is not really a stadium. Nor is the area what a visitor might have expected in this fine old university city. The Newmarket Road is just like any arterial road on the edge of a town, lined with garages, factories and warehouses, such as the one

The Abbey Stadium Main Stand (Sporting Pictures)

belonging to the Corona soft drinks company, next door. Past this we enter the Abbey Stadium with the club offices in temporary buildings to the left, and the supporters' club straight ahead, in front of the standing cover known as the Corona End. The layout is similar to that of Oxford United's Manor Ground.

The Main Stand, though recent, is not especially modern in design, except in its facilities underneath. There are bench seats on either wing and at the front, where they are divided into several small sections which exit onto the perimeter track. At the Corona End of the stand, where a raised police viewing box occupies the last ten yards of the touchline, the screen wall is glass. At the far end it is brick, and thus you can see how the stand was built in two halves on either side of the half-way line. The paintwork is amber, yellow and white with trimmings of black, which helps unify both the Main Stand and the entire ground.

To the left is the Allotment End, home of the Celery Trenches, a narrow open terrace with a brick wall at the back and high-security fences at the front, divided into sections by yet more fences. Unless you stand at the very back you are likely to see as much metalwork as football. Not a place for claustrophobics. To the right is the aforementioned Corona End, covered along three-quarters of the goal-line

with a plain roof put up in the 1950s. Next to it is the supporters' club, overlooking the pitch, with a clock on the roof. In front is a token three wooden steps of terracing. Opposite the Main Stand is the Habbin Stand, named after Harry Habbin, a former president of the supporters' club whose name is commemorated on a plaque over the central entrance to the stand. To the left of the terraces are some backless seats, installed at an angle so that the spectators may see in spite of the standing people close-by – a system also used at The Dell. Underneath the stand ran a dyke, which the Auto Club had to fill in with scrap. The dyke ran into a water-filled claypit behind the stand, beyond the neatly clipped lawns and wooden fences that surround the turnstiles like a garden centre.

The view from the ground is of open land, the Ely to Cambridge railway line, a gasometer and a tall chimney. Hardly a spire or tower in sight. But small though it is, and unlovely compared with the nearby splendours of King's College Chapel, the Abbey Stadium is proof of what community effort combined with astute management can achieve. That is why the ground has hosted League Division Two football, while further into town only hundreds turn out to watch Cambridge City in the Midland Division of the Southern League.

◆ IPSWICH TOWN ◆

Portman Road

For the first 49 years of its existence, Ipswich was an amateur team playing on local sports grounds, about as far from the glamour of First Division football as it was possible to be. When they moved to Portman Road it was a field used for cricket, whippet racing, athletics, hockey and tennis, with a dressing room hut, stables and not much else. This was in the early 1930s, when Highbury was about to be redeveloped, when Goodison Park had double-decker stands on four sides, when Wembley was already the pride of the nation (although Ipswich had actually played at the Empire Stadium – see Wembley).

In 1936 Ipswich decided to turn professional and join the Southern League. It was about time, considering that neighbours Norwich were in Division Two, yet had roughly the same-size population as Ipswich. And if a city the size of Bradford could have two clubs in the League, surely Ipswich could manage to sustain one.

So the football club took over Portman Road and changed the pitch round so that instead of east to west, they were now playing north to south. The old dressing rooms in the south west corner were still used, and to divide what was once a large round cricket field, small temporary wooden terraces were laid along the west touchline. A wooden stand was built opposite on Portman Road.

Under the benevolent but stern patronage of the Cobbold family, Ipswich Town were an immediate success. Winning the Southern League in their first season and crowds of over 20 000 were both perfect credentials for League membership. This came in 1938 when Town replaced Gillingham. The South Stand was built by this time, with wooden terracing

and a steel-framed roof bought from Newmarket Racecourse. The terrace was then further back to accommodate a track around the pitch.

After only one season in Division Three South, War broke out and under Captain Cobbold's orders the ground was closed so that every man might do his duty. The enemy's response was to cause £13 000 worth of damage to Portman Road.

After the War and the rebuilding operations, the pitch was completely flooded in 1953 and 1956, when the nearby Gipping River, which flows into the River Orwell, burst its banks. As had happened at the City Ground, the groundsman had to learn how to use a rowing boat! In 1957 Ipswich were promoted to Division Two and the real development of Portman Road began.

One of the first tasks was to eliminate the 330 yards running track encircling the pitch. Then in 1958 a stand was built on the west side, thus cutting off the pitch from the open space on the west side, used by Ipswich as a training ground. This original West Stand had seats for 2000 and a paddock in front, but the dressing rooms remained in army huts in the south west corner.

Floodlights were installed and first used on 16 February 1960 in a friendly v. Arsenal, and the following season became Champions of Division Two. First Division football after only 18 seasons of professionalism! But if that was not enough Town then went on to win the League Championship in their first season in Division One.

Portman Road now developed apace. In 1961 the North Stand was built for standing spectators, and soon after the South Stand, originally just wooden terracing and banking, was extended. The bubble burst in 1964 when Ipswich went down to Division Two, but ever resourceful, optimistic, and above all organized, the Cobbolds made certain that the club would not feel sorry for itself. During the summer, new dressing rooms and offices were constructed in

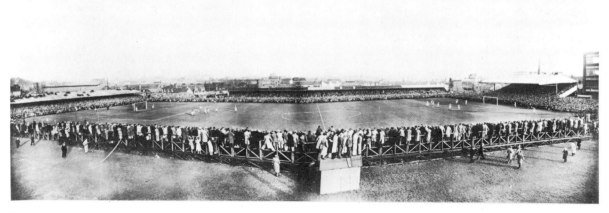

Portman Road in 1936, looking towards the Portman Road Stand. It seems hard to believe that until 1958 there were wooden terraces along the near touchline (ITFC)

the south west corner, with an indoor sports hall above.

The best however was yet to come. From 1972 Ipswich were hardly out of the limelight.

At the beginning of this period of success the old wooden stand on the east side was replaced with the new Portman Road Stand, built in three sections and finished in 1975, at a total cost of £1·5 million. Originally it had a paddock for standing, since seated, and 24 executive boxes were added at the back of this section, giving the Portman Stand a total of 7000 seats. The old wooden stand was resited at Ipswich's speedway stadium.

The South Stand was renovated, concrete terracing replacing the wooden steps and new barriers installed, and the floodlights were updated to a standard reckoned to be the best in the League, well above the minimum UEFA standard (see Floodlights).

The most recent development was to the West Stand, now named after the club's sponsors, the Pioneer Stand. This was a clever extension of a stand, in which the roof was taken off and an extra tier of seating added above the original stand, adding an extra 4000 seats. It took a year to complete, but did not prevent the existing seats being used during construction. The total cost of this work was £1·5 million.

Portman Road's record crowd was 38 010 for an FA Cup 6th Round match v. Leeds United in 1975, and despite the introduction of the Safety of Sports Grounds Act two years later, with the additional construction since then the ground has kept its capacity up to 37 000, of which 14 000 are seated.

Every move has been carefully calculated, every detail watched over, and now Ipswich have one of the finest stadiums in the League. Yet the club do not own the site. They have a 99-year lease from the local council.

Ground Description

The ground could not be closer to the town centre. Entrance to the Pioneer Stand is via the back of the South Stand (sometimes called the 'Churchman's End' after the tobacco factory behind) through a small car-park, past the old dressing room huts to the training ground behind the tall, new stand. On the other side of the practice pitches is a magnificent pre-war power station, like a municipal palace. It is hard to imagine that only half a century ago Ipswich played in its shadows on a large open sports ground.

The Pioneer Stand has much to commend it. Essentially an old base with a new top, the design is cleverly and neatly unified, with the only trace of awkwardness at the glass screen end, where the lines are somewhat disjointed. The roof, lined with black fascia and the sponsor's name in the centre, is a cantilever. There was a line of narrow wooden bleachers along this touchline until 1958.

From here, the North Bank is to the left, the oldest part of the ground. It has a low, pitched roof over terracing, with an electric scoreboard built into the roof, as at Carrow Road. The gates behind here are all electrically operated, to facilitate a speedy exit in case of emergencies. High walls and high fencing cater for more routine disturbances at this end.

Opposite is the Portman Stand, a dark, sleek stand with not a detail out of place. Grey and orange seats provide contrast, as does the Ipswich Town Football Club sign in white letters set against the matt black fascia. The orange steelwork supporting the cantilever, with rear props exposed at the back, adds a further element of high-tec stylishness. But as at St Andrew's and the Hawthorns, the executive boxes in the rear paddock with their sloping, black roofs, do stand out as late additions.

Although it does not appear to be large, the Portman Stand holds 7000 seated, 500 more than the new West Stand at White Hart Lane, an apparently much larger construction. But whereas the West Stand's roof predominates, at Ipswich the seating tier seems to almost disappear into the shadows.

To the right is the South Stand, another covered terrace, built up on supports behind a small bank. The pitch used to extend as far as the first few rows of terracing.

Here, as everywhere at Portman Road, the barriers, the steps, the paintwork is immaculate, as if Mr Cobbold has personally inspected every nook and cranny.

But the pride of Portman Road is the pitch, acknowledged by most players as one of the finest in the League, if not *the* best. It was reconstructed with the help of the Sports Turf Research Institute in Bingley (see Pitches) and has won awards for the best-kept pitch, despite the fact it was built on the site of a rubbish tip after the First World War. When it was relaid in the late 1970s Orient were having a similar pitch installed at Brisbane Road, and the two clubs had an unofficial race to finish. The winner is not recorded.

No doubt the temperate climate in East Anglia has been a major factor in the pitch's success, but still one has to salute the diligence of the groundsman. His ingenuity also. Stan Prendergast has developed a unique system for lifting up the goal nets so he can drive the mower between the posts. Every other club groundsman usually has to take down the goal-nets for tending the pitch, though since the introduction of hard-wearing nylon netting they can actually withstand all weathers and be left out. At Ipswich, the bottom sides and back of the net are attached to bars, which in turn are hinged to the foot of the post. The groundsman simply lifts up the bars to raise the net (see illustration on page 52).

That it was devised at Portman Road is no surprise. The ground and Ipswich Town may have arrived in the big league rather late, but in just a couple of decades they have certainly shown some of the old hands a trick or two.

◆NORWICH CITY◆

Previous Grounds

Norwich City are first recorded playing on a ground at Newmarket Road in June 1902. It was the base of Norfolk County FA and had been used by a team called Norwich FC since 1868. Photographs show wooden benches around the pitch, white boarded dressing rooms and one long, narrow stand. The ground is still used today, by the CEYMS. But it was not suitable for City once they turned professional in 1905, and on the initiative of chairman John Pyke the club found a new home on Rosary Road. It was to become probably the most unusual ground ever to stage League football.

Called The Nest – as might any home of 'the Canaries' – it was in a disused chalk-pit. A large work force had to level the crater with tons of earth and rubble. But the strangest aspect of The Nest was a 50-foot high concrete wall at the Thorpe End, barely a yard or so behind the touchline. This wall was at the side of a cliff, at the top of which was a row of houses. There were barriers at the top for spectators to look down on the pitch, making it the oddest Kop ever seen. If a shot went high over the goal, the ball would bounce back; while players might easily run into the wall, if not careful.

The other end was equally cramped. Immediately behind the touchline was a line of back gardens, and it was joked that the goalkeeper had to go into them so many times to retrieve the ball that one day he would marry one of the girls who lived there.

The Nest was opened with a friendly v. Fulham on 1 September 1908, in front of 3300 spectators. Two years later the pitch was relaid with proper drainage, extra terracing was laid on the St Leonards Road and Rosary Road sides and a cinder track squeezed in for training. It was never ideal, but it was certainly picturesque.

In March 1920 a new main stand was built opposite the so-called Chicken Run, but as crowds grew, The Nest's inadequacies became increasingly apparent. In April 1922 the barriers on top of the cliff broke and although there were no injuries, it was a lucky escape.

In March 1926, therefore, a plan for a 27 000 capacity ground was drawn up, to be built on a site on Highland Road, off Christchurch Road, at a cost of £20 000. But nothing materialized and Norwich stayed on. The Nest's highest attendance was 25 037 for the visit of Sheffield Wednesday in the 5th Round FA Cup in 1934–35, the last Cup match ever played at the ground. Ostensibly the concrete wall was the main problem, but as Russell Allison (whose son Russell later became groundsman at Carrow Road) recalled, the most important reason for City leaving the ground was the collapse of part of the pitch. Apparently the turf sank up to 30 feet in one corner

Carrow Road's River End Stand, of the same 'goalpost' design as Villa Park's North Stand (Colorsport)

when the old chalk workings gave way, and Allison had to shore up the chasm with soil and railway sleepers. He also had to warn players to be very careful when taking corners!

Finally, on 15 May 1935, the FA wrote to Norwich saying that The Nest was no longer suitable for large crowds and that measures must be taken. So City said farewell to their charming Nest, and moved about half-a-mile south along the banks of the River Wensum to their new home at Carrow Road.

The site of The Nest and the high wall can still be seen from Lollards Road or from Rosary Road although now built over by offices. It seems incredible that it was once a football ground filled with 25 000 people.

Carrow Road

As soon as it was realized City must move, the club received the offer of the Boulton Paul Sports Ground on Carrow Road. There were only three months before the start of the next season, a seemingly impossible time in which to build a Second Division ground.

But as Ted Bell in his history of Norwich City records, City put the job out to tender on 1 June 1935, the day they agreed a 20-year lease with Boulton Paul. On 11 June dumping began, with rubble for the River End bank coming from the old Chicken Run at The Nest. By 17 August most of the stands and terraces had been completed, and on 31 August, Carrow Road football ground was opened for the Second Division match v. West Ham United, in front of 29 779 wildly enthusiastic spectators. The miracle had been accomplished in just 82 days!

Carrow Road had a Main Stand, a covered end terrace, and two large open banks, with a potential capacity of about 40 000. It was totally different from The Nest, and so were the surroundings. There were no prim terraced villas and winding lanes here. Boulton Paul's factory surrounded Carrow Road on almost three sides, and on the fourth was the River Wensum and the Colman Mustard works.

Two years later, on 29 October 1938, Carrow Road was honoured by the visit of King George VI, for

City's game v. Millwall. He was thus the first ruling monarch to attend a Second Division match.

Carrow Road was an obvious target for German bombers because Boulton Paul was a major arms manufacturer, producing many of the gun turrets for RAF aircraft. To protect the area, two gun emplacements were built in the ground's car-park overlooking the Wensum, to be manned by the Home Guard. One of the pair still survives.

The club was in Division Three when floodlights were installed at Carrow Road at a cost of £9000, the first match being a friendly v. Sunderland on 17 October 1956. The ground's record attendance came during one of City's heroic Cup runs for the 6th Round FA Cup tie v. Leicester City, watched by 43 984 on 30 March 1963. Shortly afterwards, the open South Side was covered.

Owing to the introduction of the Safety of Sports Grounds Act, major changes were made at Carrow Road. The South Stand terrace was converted entirely to seating, and at the same time Norwich were told it would cost £400 000 to bring the River End bank up to safety requirements. City decided instead to replace the 15 000 capacity bank with a new River End Stand. It cost £1·7 million to complete and included the club's own public house – the only one built in a stand in the League – appropriately called The Nest. Seating 2350, with standing room for 6900, the new stand was opened in December 1979.

Carrow Road now holds 28 392 spectators, of which 12 675 are seated.

Ground Description

One definition of 'carrow' is a wandering Irish gambler, but the road itself takes its name from the twelfth century Carrow Abbey. Carrow Road now runs from the Wensum to the main railway line from Norwich, bending at a right angle to run along the north and west sides of the ground. On one side of the road is the Boulton Paul factory, on the other is the Main Stand, each building tall and plain, edging up against the pavement and reminding one more of an industrial dockland than a beautiful medieval city.

But as drab as Carrow Road may seem from the outside, inside the ground is bright and colourful. The Main Stand particularly appeals. It has yellow and green seats down to the touchline, and a sloping roof lined with advertising, with a mock gable-like board in the centre adding a touch of style. Both screen walls are solid, so it seems quite a busy, substantial construction.

From here to the left is the Barclay Stand, named after an ex-President of the club, Phyliss Barclay, a member of the Barclays Bank family which has strong connections in the area. The Stand is a dark, cavernous cover over terracing, tangled with a web of steelwork and security barriers. As at Portman Road, an electric scoreboard is mounted on the roof.

The Barclay Stand is linked to the South Stand by a covered corner section, similar to those at Old Traf-

ford, but with the floodlight pylon in front making the view from here rather awkward. The South Stand has a typical pitched roof, with advertisements lining the gutter. There is no perimeter wall, just a single railing. Unfortunately the yellow and green colour scheme is interrupted on this side by the new seats, coloured red and blue, but they are at least mounted on properly rebuilt steps to allow good sight lines down to the pitch.

On the right is the new River End Stand. This resembles the North Stand at Villa Park in design and construction, but the details are quite different. As at Villa, the roof is suspended by a huge goalpost construction, so that although not a cantilever, there are no pillars in the way. The two outside vertical posts are quite thin, and support a bare steel girder across the top, from which the roof hangs. Each vertical however continues upwards and holds a floodlight gantry, a very simple but effective arrangement. We are so used to seeing floodlights mounted on pylons, so the Norwich pair on steel poles look most unusual.

The upper tier has yellow seats, with green ones spelling out the word Canaries. Below these is a line of 20 boxes, and in front the paddock is covered entirely by the roof. Indeed, there is barely an uncovered section in the ground. The River End standing area is much larger than that at Villa Park, with bright yellow barriers standing out against the light grey concrete terraces. It is an attractively balanced piece of design.

Underneath the stand is the club's public house, The Nest, and behind lies the car-park, still belonging to Boulton Paul, leading to the River Wensum a hundred yards away. The Carrow Road pitch drains into the river, which flows into the North Sea, 12 miles east near Great Yarmouth. From the car-park the sprawling Carrow Works of Colmans, the mustard and pickle makers, is visible. Their silos are, appropriately for the club, coated in mustard-coloured dust. At the car-park entrance stands one of the surviving Second World War gun turrets, a round brick building which puzzles many visitors.

I have mentioned elsewhere in this book how important the choice of colours and care to detail are to the overall appearance of a football ground, whatever the style or state of its architecture. Carrow Road is a perfect example of a ground that could not possibly belong to any other club. It has yellow and green, canary colours, and reminders of Norwich all round, which lend Carrow Road a homely and cheerful identity.

COLCHESTER ·UNITED·

Layer Road

Although United are the youngest club in the League, having formed in 1937, strictly speaking, the club was the professional successor to an amateur team called Colchester Town, who had played at Layer Road since 1909. Before then the ground was used by the Army, whose barracks are very close.

The first known development at Layer Road was the building of the present Main Stand in 1933. United were elected to the League in 1950, having won much acclaim for being the only non-League side to have reached the FA Cup 5th Round, in 1948. During the following season's cup run, Colchester enjoyed its largest attendance of 19 072 for the visit of Reading in November 1948. Improvements to the ground followed, and during United's best spell in the League, floodlights were installed. Their first use was for a League match v. Grimsby in August 1959.

The present capacity is officially 16 000, including 1143 seats, but in practice the safety maximum would be nearer 10 000, for reasons outlined below.

Ground Description

Like the suburban sprawl of semi-detached houses all around, at first glance the ground is hardly inspiring. The sturdy floodlight pylons are painted green, while the Main Stand is a colourless affair. But it does have an unusual steep sloping roof on the pitch side, with what resembles a tiny airport controllers' tower in the centre but is actually a commentator's booth with room for cameras above. The stand is mostly wood, with basic wooden bench seats along the front. There are seats in the centre section only, the wings being for standing. The Layer Road End's wing roof is a later addition, built in the 1950s, while the other wing is under the same roof as the Main Stand but is separated from the seats by a brick wall topped by iron railings, like those at a primary school.

To the right is the Layer Road End covered terrace, which, it is said was constructed by prisoners of war during the 1940s, and moves one to suggest that they appear to have sawn up their beds to provide the materials. The roof is very low, and the terraces are formed out of rickety wooden planks, onto which are bolted wooden crush barriers. There is so little room that the back of the goal cuts into the stand.

It is also worth noting that the goal stanchions are like only those at Bloomfield Road, Blackpool, with two angles on each stanchion. In the right-hand corner of the Layer Road End are the club offices, overlooking the pitch, and in the other corner is the supporters' club.

Wooden terracing and barriers at Layer Road (Simon Inglis)

Opposite the Main Stand is a small cover over terracing, variously known as the Barn, the Shed or just the Popular Side. The old roof was once a source of complaint from those who stood under it and were showered with rust every time the ball thumped against it. To the left of this cover, along the touch-line, is an open section of terracing in such delapidated condition that it looks like the ascents of an Inca fortress; uneven, overgrown and in many places so collapsed inwardly that it is patently unsafe. Behind this side is a floodlit all-weather pitch.

To the left of the Main Stand is an open bank with no name. It was called the Spion Kop once, of course, then the Clock End, until the clock was removed in the 1970s. There are a few blue barriers haphazardly arranged, with a dividing fence down the middle of wood and chicken wire. At the back is a partly collapsing blue corrugated fence, almost horizontal in places, which provides an odd contrast with the large house and garden directly behind the small bank.

Layer Road badly needs attention, as the club well knows, if it is to maintain its League standing, but I fear that whatever improvements are made to the existing fixtures, the ground will never be anything more than ordinary. You can replace terracing and repaint fences, but it is a different matter to instil character. But appearances apart, a packed Layer Road is still dangerous ground for top visiting clubs in the Cup.

◆ SOUTHEND UNITED ◆

Previous Grounds

Southend United played their first game on 1 September 1906, on the same ground they now own, but with an important difference; the pitch was then approximately 50 feet higher than it is today! The ground was once the site of a house called Roots Hall, and had been used previously by a team called Southend Athletic. United used it until the First World War, but in 1919 moved to the Kursaal Ground where they began their League career a year later. The Roots Hall site was excavated, as the deposits of sand and gravel were needed for local housing developments. The club stayed at Kursaal, where the record attendance was 17 000, until 1934, when they moved to The Southend Stadium, Grainger Road. The highest gate there was in 1936; 22 862 watching Southend v. Spurs. But the club always wanted a ground of their own and in the mid-1950s began looking for a

suitable site. By coincidence the best land available was at Roots Hall, their first home. Kursaal is now the site of a housing estate on the other side of the town, but you can still visit The Stadium, now used only as a greyhound track. Southend have also played at Chelmsford City's ground, when The Stadium was used by the Army in 1939–41.

Roots Hall

If there is a monument to the British football supporter, it is Roots Hall, for here is a ground built almost entirely through the efforts of a small, but dedicated group of people.

When the directors chose the Roots Hall site, it was then a rubbish tip, partly owned by the local gas board, and recently levelled to provide extra car-parking space for the annual illuminations traffic. Negotiations began in 1950, the supporters' club provided the £10 000 needed to purchase the land, then financed the setting up of a Trust Fund, which comprised the Mayor, the Chairman of the Football Club and the Chairman of the Supporters' Club. This was

Roots Hall (Aerofilms)

almost a return to the pioneering days of football in the late Victorian period, when a football club was seen as vital a necessity for a municipality as a public bath or a statue of the Queen.

Work began at Roots Hall in 1953 and was carried out by just a handful of men, several of the players and even the club manager-cum-secretary Harry Warren. But one man in particular was responsible for building a stadium at Roots Hall, Sidney Broomfield. He was employed to oversee all the work, but inevitably had to do much of it himself. When the site had first been excavated in 1914, diggers had found neolithic and Anglo-Saxon remains, Roman and Viking coins. When Sidney Broomfield started his digging he found only tons of compressed rubbish.

Roots Hall was ready to stage its first match, a Third Division South fixture v. Norwich City, on 20 August 1955. Present on this proud occasion were Sir Stanley Rous, then Secretary of the FA, Arthur Oakley, President of the Football League, and to officiate over the actual opening ceremony, Arthur Drewry, Chairman of the FA. The Southend United Supporters' Club Band (probably the only such band in the country) accompanied community singing and the Mayor received a gift of £1000 for the Trust Fund from the club's President, E. J. Grant. Southend United were thus the last club in the Football League to have moved to their present ground.

However the ground was still incomplete. The Main East Stand did not run the length of the pitch until 1967. The North Bank cover ran only the width of the penalty area, so had to be extended. The West Side roof covered only the rear section of banking and was later doubled. But the greatest achievement was the terracing of the South Bank.

Because the site had been quarried for so long, the ground was a natural bowl shape on two sides, the highest point being at the top of the South Bank, at the original ground level. In 1955 only a narrow band of concrete terracing encircled the pitch, but in the course of five years, Sid and two other men laid every inch of concreting over the South Bank's 72 steps. 'Some days,' he recalled, 'we would arrive at the ground to discover that heavy overnight rain had swept mud from the top of the banking over the steps we had completed . . . it was a real slog.'

There were many teething problems with the pitch. As it had been laid on compressed rubbish, drainage was very poor. During the first winter, only days before a Cup tie v. Manchester City, the groundstaff had to dig a trench diagonally across the pitch and throw in tons of cockleshells in the hope of improving it. The following year it was decided to start all over again, so the pitch was dug up and replaced, and proper drainage and sub-soil installed, at a cost of £15000. Floodlights were erected during the summer of 1959.

Roots Hall was intended to hold 35000 spectators, but the highest attendance it has seen was 31033 in January 1979 when Liverpool were the visitors in the 3rd Round of the FA Cup. The present capacity is 27000 of which 2835 are seated.

Ground Description

If you did not know the history of Roots Hall, it would no doubt appear a most ordinary ground. No single part of it is remarkable, nor is the location especially appealing. But when you look at the slopes of the South Bank and think of how just a handful of men constructed the terracing, over the course of five years, then you can begin to appreciate that Roots Hall is rather special.

It is in the parish of Prittlewell, which existed long before the resort. Indeed the town's name derives from the fact that it was built at the south end of Prittlewell. The ground stands well back from Victoria Avenue, with a large car-park in between, used twice a week for large markets.

From here we enter the Main or East Stand, the archetypal 1950s' grandstand, as seen at so many other grounds in the country, its design hardly changed from stands built 30 years earlier, its character determined by grey, asbestos roofing, blue steel and wooden seats. Along the gutter a hoarding suggests you try the market at Roots Hall. The screen ends are glass, the narrow paddock's rear wall is blue, with stairs leading to the seats. You can just see where the two wings were added between 1955 and 1967.

From here the low North Bank is to your right, covered with a plain barrel roof, lined along the front with white hoarding. The pitch is surrounded by a track and low white perimeter wall, which has the effect of tying the ground together neatly. Underneath the roof hangs a sign commemorating the fact that the structure was donated by E. J. Grant.

Opposite the East Stand is the West Side, with a double-barrel roof running almost the whole length of the touchline. This type of construction, though long outdated, did have the advantage of being very economical. Incidentally, the stands were built by a firm called Boulton Paul, once makers of war-planes and guns, and neighbours of Norwich City, on Carrow Road.

To the left is the tall, open South Bank, once a rough mishapen slope with wooden barriers, now as neat as any Kop in the country. At the top are the floodlight pylons, large advertisement hoardings and a clock. From here the view is disappointing, mainly tower blocks and housing, with no sign of the sea. But the pitch is in excellent shape, thanks to the efforts of groundsman Sidney Broomfield and his long standing work-mate Joe Auger. Roots Hall was the house Sid and friends built for their club, and in 1974, United gave him a testimonial match to thank him for 21 years' service. But would the community spirit which created Roots Hall still be possible today? Football used to be about the supporters, and players lending a hand after training. Roots Hall is a monument to them.

·11·
SOUTH AND EAST MIDLANDS

·LEICESTER CITY·

Previous Grounds
City were originally called Leicester Fosse when formed in 1884, because they played on a field by Fosse Road South (a fosse is a ditch or moat in front of a fortified place). In 1885 the club moved to Victoria Park, where they were often competing with the more popular Victoria Park Rugby FC for spectators. On 5 November 1887 Fosse switched to their first enclosed ground, Belgrave Road Cycle Track, using the White Hart Hotel as changing rooms. But the rugby club followed their example a year later and made a bid for the stadium higher than Fosse could afford, so the soccer club moved back to Victoria Park. Soon after, however, Leicester turned professional and began playing on a ground at Mill Lane,

until the council evicted them and they were forced to make a temporary home at Ayleston Road County Cricket Ground. Finally, after seven years the club made its sixth and final move to the present site at Filbert Street.

Filbert Street
What is today known as Filbert Street or the City Stadium was in 1891 referred to as Walnut Street, then the nearest road actually touching the site. It is thought that the ground was first spotted by a Miss Westland, who considered the 3¾-acre site would make a very nice football ground, which indeed it did. Fosse played their first game there on 7 November 1891 v. Nottingham Forest.

In 1894 Leicester were elected to the League. From then until the First World War the pitch at Filbert Street ran from east to west.

In 1919 the club's name was changed to Leicester

Filbert Street, the pitch covered by a polythene balloon (Aerofilms)

City, and on 24 November 1921 the present Main Stand was opened.

In 1924–25 City reached the Cup quarter-finals, won the Second Division Championship and thereby began one of the most successful periods in their history. In the summer of 1927 the double-decker South Stand was built, an almost exact copy of West Ham's Main Stand built two years previously. Perhaps inspired by its grandeur the team went on to finish third in the Division in 1928 and on 18 February of that year Filbert Street enjoyed its highest attendance, 47 298, for the visit of Tottenham in the FA Cup 5th Round. In 1949, although low in Division Two, the club reached its first Cup Final, and with the profits built the cover on the East Side terracing on Burnmoor Street.

The first floodlit match at Filbert Street was on 23 October 1957 v. Borussia Dortmund, that year's West German League Champions. Then in 1961 Leicester made the first of five appearances in a Cup Final during the 1960s, but the only change to the ground during this period was the covering of the North Stand terrace. When the club bounced back to Division One in 1971, Filbert Street was extensively redeveloped. Seats were installed first at the North Stand, then along the East Side, and in 1975 a unique arrangement for shelter was provided for the newly seated terracing when the North Stand roof was replaced by a line of 20 private boxes directly above.

Being such a tightly enclosed ground, Filbert Street's pitch had always suffered from a lack of ventilation, and was notoriously muddy in winter. To alleviate this, in 1971, the club installed a huge plastic sheet which could be raised above the pitch with hot-air blowers, so high that players could even train underneath it (although in practice it made for a claustrophobic and uncomfortable environment in which to spend much time). But the cost of running such a system was high, the sheeting was prone to tearing, and since the club improved the drainage it only uses the cover now in the event of rain and frost before a match (see Pitches).

City now own Filbert Street, except for the car-park and roadway behind the Main Stand (both still belong to the council). The ground's capacity is just under 32 000, including 15 326 seats.

Ground Description

An observer once described Filbert Street as a 'shoe-box' ground, an impression certainly reinforced by television coverage. But the camera has been known to lie, and in reality the ground seems quite open, two of the stands being low. If there was a sense of confinement, this has been considerably diminished by the demolition of the neighbouring electricity generating station, whose enormous cooling towers used to form a shadow over the south east corner. But the ground is hemmed in quite tightly by the surrounding terraced streets, as for example in Burnmoor Street, where the entrance to the East Stand is,

and as in Kenilworth Road, actually part of the houses. There are bedrooms above the gateways.

The Main Stand is lower than the end South Stand but has a modest dignity all of its own. Most noticeable is the 'pigeon-loft' box on the roof which houses cameras. It has extra lamps perched along the roof. The most interesting feature is the mock-classical podium built behind the players' tunnel, presumably to act as a presentation area like that of Wembley. Otherwise the stand is unremarkable, with solid screen ends, a small front paddock and blue and white paintwork. The seats are a mixture of colours and therefore deny the stand any uniformity.

From here to the right is the South Stand, a copy of one at the Boleyn Ground but not so well preserved. At its rear is Brazil Street, a cul-de-sac leading to the site of the old power station. The back wall is plain, brown concrete.

The East Stand opposite the Main Stand is low with a shallow rising tier of seats from front to back, obviously a hurried conversion of the old terracing. Its roof is well lit by skylights, but as it reaches the northern corner it gets messily tangled in a web of steelwork which continues round the corner until meeting the North Stand's private boxes. Underneath this apparently impromptu roof is a section of bucket seats installed in front of a small section of terracing. This is the Filbert Street corner for the supporters' club, where the spectators pay the same and may choose whether to stand or sit.

The North Stand is most curious. The bottom section is covered in bright orange seats and is the usual converted terrace. But above this are the executive boxes, forming a roof over the seats. The glass fronts are virtually suspended over the goal-line, and have their own little canopy to keep off the rain. They look like an aquarium at the zoo. It is an unorthodox arrangement, but apparently most successful. Between here and the Main Stand you may notice that behind the odd, white floodlight pylon, is a figure at once familiar but highly unexpected in the depths of Leicester. It is a copy of the Statue of Liberty which dates back to 1920 when the directors of Lennards Shoes, whose premises were on Walnut Street, visited New York and decided they wanted a statue for the roof of their new building. Liberty Shoes, as the company became known, no longer exists but the large stone figure survives, minus her hundred-weight torch, which fell onto the pavement below during a frost attack! At the ground entrance in this corner is another quite classical feature, a gateway with a flag on top.

Filbert Street is cramped, with box-like aspects, and certainly there is little room within the stadium. Each goal is narrow, as is the running track. There was a plan to move out and rebuild at Beaumont Leys, on the outskirts of the town, but as so many other clubs have found, by adding seats Leicester have managed to convert their ground into one easily able to cope with the smaller crowds of today.

NORTHAMPTON ·TOWN·

The County Ground

Town share the County Ground with Northamptonshire County Cricket Club and it is therefore the only three-sided football ground in the League (Sheffield United built over the cricket pitch at Bramall Lane in 1974). The 8½-acre site was originally farmland, converted into a cricket field in the 1880s by Northamptonshire County Cricket and Recreation Grounds Limited. The football club formed there in 1897 and initially used the cricket pavilion. In 1901 Town joined the Southern League and turned professional.

The football side of the ground, to the north west, was first developed between 1907–12, the years when Herbert Chapman was at the County Ground, which helped to pay for some £2500 worth of ground improvements. In 1907 terraces were laid and a small main stand built.

Town joined the League in 1920 and a few years later the Main Stand was destroyed by fire. The present stand was built in 1924, but has since been modernized.

In the late 1940s the Hotel End was covered, and in the 1960s, the County Ground witnessed the most dramatic rise and fall in a club's fortunes football had ever known. The story begins in 1960. On 10 October Arsenal visited the ground to inaugurate the new floodlights, and the following May, Town were promoted to Division Three for the first time in their League career. In their second season in the Third Division, they were promoted to the Second and in their second season in the Second Division they were promoted to the First. But despite the rise in gates, the ground's owners would not permit stands to be built on the open side of the pitch, so the club had to be content with a series of small, portable wooden platforms which each held about 20 people.

Town never found life in the First Division easy, and it was for one of their final games at the end of only one season in the First Division that they recorded their highest attendance. A crowd of 24 523 saw them play fellow strugglers Fulham, on 23 April 1966, just before the World Cup. Four years later, at the end of the decade, Town were back in Division Four. (They even had to apply for re-election in 1972.) To cap it all, in 1970 the club reached the 5th Round of the FA Cup and were beaten 8-2 by Manchester United.

That game was the only occasion in the ground's history that a full length stand was put up along the open side of the pitch, which helps to explain why the game attracted Town's record receipts of over £17 000. However, the profits from those heady years of success from 1960–66 were not used to improve the County Ground.

The reason for Town's lack of investment in the ground is bound up in the administration of the County Ground. It is governed by The Cockell Trust, to which the football club pay rent. But because Town have a minority of members sitting on the Trust board, usually three compared with the cricket club's eight, they have great difficulty in changing the status quo. Their rent effectively goes straight to the cricket club. (The only other member of the Trust represents the bowling club, whose premises are also part of the ground, next to the Spion Kop.) Town also have to play their early and late season games away from home, so as not to clash with Northamptonshire's County cricket matches.

There have been a few improvements to the ground. In 1980 the Main Stand was reroofed, new seats put in and the facade refitted on the street side. None of the football club's stands or terraces are used for cricket matches, except as places for bored children to play, and indeed the two pitches overlap only by about 20 yards. The most unfortunate drawback is that during cricket matches the football pitch is used as a car-park and general picnic area; a nightmare for any groundsman trying to prepare a surface for the new season, but since Town also share him with the cricket club, he must be willing to put up with the inconvenience.

The cricket ground has about 7500 seats, and its highest crowd was for a match against the West Indies touring side in 1950, when 13 200 attended. The present capacity of the football ground is 17 000, including 1400 seats.

Ground Description

The main entrance to the football ground is on Abington Avenue, and is neatly faced in new maroon and white cladding. But this is a fairly busy thoroughfare and needs only a team coach to park outside for congestion to build up. From this entrance, the unknowing visitor would have no idea that the ground

Cars and cricket take over the County Ground, Northampton. The Kop is at the far end (Adrian Gibson)

was also a cricket field.

Inside the Main Stand he would find out immediately. But first, the Main Stand runs low along the length of the pitch, with a small paddock for standing in front of the seating section. The new roof is a propped cantilever design, and darkly overhangs the perimeter track. Predominant colours are red and white.

To the right is the Hotel End, so-called because in the corner between the two stands is a large public house. Its upper windows overlook the pitch, through the floodlight pylon. The terraces and low roof are sadly neglected, the gutters overgrown and the security fencing at the front rather primitive. Some of the crush barriers are wooden. At the end of the terrace one can walk directly onto the cricket pitch.

The cricket pitch stretches out in front of the Main Stand. Directly opposite is the pavilion, a building which won much admiration when erected in 1958 for its dainty concrete cantilever canopy.

To the left of the Main Stand is the Spion Kop, probably the most curious little appendage at any League ground. When football writers started flocking to the County Ground during that one hectic season in Division One, they all found something to say about the County Ground. John Moyniham wrote of his surprise at finding: 'no enormous, ominous overpowering Spion Kop but a small hummock'. Hummock it is, for it does not even extend to the far corner flag. Just as soon as it reaches its peak, behind the goal, it falls away rapidly to nothing, level with the edge of the penalty area. At the back is maroon wooden fencing.

From the summit of this prehistoric-looking mound, you can see the bowling club to the left, behind the cricket pitch. Notice also the lines along the edge of the pitch, where the football touchline cuts across the smooth arc of the cricket outfield. Northampton's pitch is the longest in the League, measuring 120×75 yards. It is the third largest in area.

Town feel the difficulties of playing on a three-sided pitch just as greatly as Sheffield United once did, but unlike United they can do nothing about it. Having achieved some success here, the club can hardly claim that it inhibits their progress, and as the only one of its kind in the League, the County Ground, I believe, makes a very welcome change.

•DERBY COUNTY•

Previous Grounds

Derby is the youngest of the 12 founder members of the Football League in 1888, having been formed four years earlier. The club played at the Racecourse Ground, the home then and now of Derbyshire County Cricket Club. It was chosen by the FA as the setting for the first Cup Final replay, in April 1886, between Blackburn and West Bromwich, attended by 12000, compared with 15000 for the first match at the Oval, and it was also the first time a Final had been settled outside London. In 1895 County moved to the Baseball Ground a mile and a half away where they have remained since. The County Cricket Ground can be found next to the Pentagon roundabout, near Eastgate.

The Baseball Ground

Even after Derby moved to their new home, the ground was still used for baseball. Indeed the football club ran their own baseball team and won the Championship in 1895. Several other football clubs used to play baseball, including Aston Villa and Orient.

The ground was little developed until 1926, when to celebrate Derby's return to Division One, the present Main Stand was built during the close season and opened on 4 September. Two years later, the double-decker Normanton Stand, named after the nearby district, was built behind the south goal and in the club's Jubilee Year in 1934, an almost exact copy of this stand was built behind the north goal. This was called the Osmaston Stand, also after a district in Derby. During this period of development, the fourth side opposite the Main Stand was also covered with a roof in two different sections, one higher than the other. So within the space of just ten years, the Baseball Ground was covered on all four sides. But the shape of the site had dictated that each stand be compressed – built tall at the ends, narrow at the sides. Understandably therefore, there were plans for a new ground built elsewhere.

In the late 1920s the council came up with a proposal for County to share a new municipal stadium, and in 1945, no less an architect than Maxwell Ayrton, who had worked on Wembley Stadium, drew up a futuristic scheme incorporating a football stadium with other sporting facilities and a health centre (see Design). It is unfortunate Ayrton's plan was never implemented, for Derby would have taken possession of probably the most advanced concept in stadium design in Europe. Instead, having suffered bomb damage to the Osmaston Stand during the War, and having won the FA Cup in 1946, the club stayed at the Baseball Ground.

The Baseball Ground was reckoned to have been built on the site of an old gypsy encampment, and

The Baseball Ground before the War. Notice the angle of stands and terracing (Aerofilms)

before that 1946 Final, a journalist visited some local gypsies and asked that they lift their curse – presuming one existed. It must have worked, for County beat Charlton easily. Birmingham City believed they suffered from a similar curse in 1982.

The first floodlights at Derby were mounted on gantries along each roof, and were switched on in March 1953 for a friendly v. Notts County.

Derby were again celebrating promotion back into Division One in 1969 when they built a new stand above the East Side terracing. It was a difficult space to fill, because the terrace is backed by the foundry works of Ley's Maleable Castings Company Limited which owns the land, and therefore to gain the maximum benefit it had to allow standing below, with a tall seating tier above. Access can be gained only from either end of the ground, necessitating gangways over the terracing to the seats. All these problems were solved, however, and the resultant Ley Stand was an attractive addition to an otherwise rather gloomy enclosure. It cost £250 000, and has since had private boxes added at the back.

Thus the Baseball Ground became one of only four League grounds to have seating and standing on all four sides, with White Hart Lane, Old Trafford and Goodison Park (Filbert Street, Highfield Road and Loftus Road have since developed seating on all four sides). In one of the club's first games back in Division One, the highest crowd at the ground, 41 826, saw Derby v. Tottenham on 20 September 1969. Soon after relegation in 1980, extra seats were installed in both the Osmaston and Normanton Stands, giving the Baseball Ground a healthy balance of 16 000 seats in a total capacity of 30 500.

Ground Description

This used to be one of the most cramped grounds in the League, but considerable slum clearance has created space at least on two sides so that you can now fully appreciate the mouldings around the entrance. The line of terraced houses opposite the entrance at the rear of the Main Stand was demolished to make way for a car-park, and the club has created a much improved facade.

The Main Stand is very similar to nearby Ches-

terfield's, built a decade later, and is typical of its period. The roof however has been replaced and sports a cheaper, modern alternative to a gable. County's 'Ram' logo is on a raised board in the centre, flanked by two boards bearing the name of the stand's sponsor. This detail alone gives the old stand an added sense of dignity, and might well be copied by other clubs having bare expanses of dull roof on view.

Notice at the Osmaston End how the Main Stand roof has been cut away to allow spectators in the top corner of the Osmaston Stand an unimpeded view of the pitch. In front of the seating tier is a narrow paddock, lined back and front with advertisements.

From here, to the right is the Normanton Stand, also sponsored. This is taller than the Main Stand and is a double-decker. Both decks are now seated, but as, for example, Everton's Bullens Road Stand, there is still a small terraced enclosure at the front. The Osmaston Stand opposite is identical in design but sits on a slightly higher section of terracing. Both stands are like upright boxes, the sloping roofs barely overhanging the front, and are lined with advertisements along each balcony wall. They touch each end of the Main Stand, so there are no gaps in the corners. The floodlight pylons are therefore behind the stands, peeping over the roofs.

Behind the Normanton End is the narrow Vulcan Street, which comes to an end as it meets the walls of the Ley foundry, running along the entire east side of the ground. Behind the Osmaston Stand the foundry continues and you can see the Ley company's 'Italianate' chimney in the north east corner. Colombo Street, behind the Stand, was also once a dark, narrow street lined with terraced houses, but these have also gone, and on the open ground behind the Baseball Ground is a new community sports centre.

Opposite the Main Stand is the Ley Stand, with its name on the white roof fascia. This is taller than either end stand, and is also a double-decker. The upper seating tier is by necessity fairly steep, covered by a plain, flat roof. Of all the stands of the 1960s, it probably has the most attractive lines, with strong emphasis on the horizontal white fascia. A steel gangway to the right links the seating with the Normanton End entrance; its presence suggesting that the foundry behind is beginning to spread into the ground like a steel Triffid.

The Baseball Ground will never be a sunny place, it is too boxed in by tall stands. The pitch is almost as small as it can be, with only a very narrow track round the perimeter, and there is no room to expand in any direction. But the club have developed their older stands well, and with an array of advertising and signs the ground appears much livelier than in previous years. When full there is nowhere for the noise to escape but upwards. Perhaps in the long run therefore, lack of space has been a blessing in disguise for Derby: they have a compact ground, easily converted with extra seats, but large enough for the likely size of audience attracted to top-class football.

Blackburn's fine, oak-panelled boardroom at Ewood Park in Leitch's Main Stand, built in 1906. On match days the huge table is laden with tea and cakes for admiring visitors

Leitch's South Stand at Ibrox Park, built in 1929 and the focal point of the ground's redevelopment. The castellated press box on the roof is nowadays less ornate. English football followers will recognise the Leitch style of balcony wall from his stands at Goodison, Roker and Fratton Parks

Hillsborough's cantilever stand retains its sleek appearance yet contrasts with the open, tree-lined Kop. Flags add to the sense of occasion

Nottingham Forest's Executive Stand illustrates the development of cantilever design and luxury boxes. Such stands allow for extension. The use of coloured seats to pick out the club's name is now very common

Chelsea's famous East Stand towers above the now-demolished North Stand, (which itself was twice the height of the original Main Stand). It is unlikely that such a large, expensive stand as this will be built again in Britain

Maine Road was designed to be the largest club ground in England, and the size of the exits shows how much space was available. The Main Stand roof has since been replaced with a most unusual structure (see Manchester City)

White Hart Lane before the new West Stand was built. Two generations of Leitch's stands face each other; they were built 25 years apart

The familiar television image of Wembley disguises the enclosed greenhouse effect seen from the terraces, while the perimeter track exaggerates the apparent size of the pitch

Gay Meadow has one of the most idyllic settings in League football, with the River Severn running behind the trees on the left. The castle tower is visible behind the far end. It would be possible to fit the entire population of Shrewsbury into Wembley Stadium (above)

In complete contrast to Chelsea's high-tec East Stand is their quaint office building at the entrance of Stamford Bridge

Highbury's main entrance reflects the prestige of the club and the orderliness of the stadium. Notice the symmetry, the use of emblems and colour, and the lamps flanking the doorway. The marble hall lies within

Capturing the spirit of the 1950s is Elland Road's entrance, now joined by a massive floodlight pylon

Wembley's pitch in mid-construction shows vividly how many layers it takes to build a good playing surface. The dark ash on the left is the bottom layer

Bramall Lane before the cantilever swamped the cricket pitch. Where the spectators once sat in the foreground is now a car-park behind an impressive main facade

Possibly the most unusual stand ever seen at a League ground, at the Racecourse Ground, Wrexham. This was a cinema steel frame perched on the Town End; the curved balcony still visible

West Bromwich Albion built their new cantilever Main Stand with the minimum of disruption to existing facilities, stage by stage, thereby reducing the loss of revenue and preserving the ground's atmosphere

Two aerial views show different methods of ground redevelopment. Old Trafford (above) has been modernised bit by bit, with the Stretford End (top) being five years younger only than the cantilever (right). Eventually the cantilever will continue around the ground. Rangers (below) redeveloped Ibrox within a few years, building three almost identical stands but preserving Leitch's South Stand. Before 1979 the ground was the same oval shape as Hampden. No other British ground has changed so dramatically as Ibrox

NOTTINGHAM ·FOREST·

Previous Grounds

As the third oldest club in the League, Forest have had more time to change grounds than most, and it is ironic that after so much wandering they should settle on the other side of the Trent from Nottingham, in West Bridgford. Thanks to Arthur Turner's centenary history of the club there is a detailed record of the club's first five homes, beginning at the ground which gave them their name, the Forest Racecourse. This was a large open space, 'the recreational lung of the town', where the club formed in 1865. Its members had first met to play not the newly formulated Association game, but a North Country variation of hockey known as shinny. The first use of a referee's whistle was recorded at this ground, in a game between Forest and Sheffield Norfolk in 1878. But if large crowds were expected, Forest sometimes played at an enclosed ground in Beeston, as for example when they played Notts County in 1878, in front of 500 people! Today the Forest hosts the annual Nottingham Goose Fair.

In 1879 the club moved to a ground called The Meadows which for several seasons had been the home of Notts County. Forest moved on after only a year, to the most famous sporting venue in the town, Trent Bridge Cricket Ground. They might have stayed here for longer than two years had not rivals County moved in. County's version of the 1883 move suggests that Forest were less desirable tenants of the cricket ground (see Notts County).

From 1882–85 the club played at Parkside, Lenton, at a ground which cost £300 to prepare. A further £500 was spent on the Gregory Ground, also in Lenton, where they played until 1890. Apparently, neither of these venues had any proper accommodation for members of the press. 'We hope a desk or table will be supplied as on most grounds in the country,' wrote one disgruntled reporter, adding pointedly, 'Notts have not finished laying out Trent Bridge but it is their intention to erect a covered desk.' But the major problem at Lenton was not the discomfiture of the press so much as the public's apathy, and having turned professional in 1889 the club needed all the support it could muster.

So in 1890 Forest returned to the Trent Bridge area, to a place called Woodward's Field. This new home, the Town Ground, cost £1000 and required considerable effort to level the pitch, build banking and erect a stand seating 1000 spectators. It was, wrote Turner, a great source of pride that this stand possessed a roof, and that the press had at last been properly accommodated.

The Town Ground was opened on 3 October 1890, in rather awkward circumstances. At Trent Bridge on the same afternoon, Notts County were staging a League match v. Bolton. Forest had invited another League club, Wolves, to play in the first game at their ground, and County naturally objected. So Forest played the Scottish club Queen's Park instead, winning 4-1 in front of around 3000 spectators, while about 6000 saw the League fixture. Since County's use of Trent Bridge was restricted at the beginning and end of each season, because cricket always took priority, the Town Ground was often used to stage County's home games, just as Forest had sometimes shared The Meadows with County in the late 1880s.

Continuing in their tradition of pioneering new developments, Forest staged the first official match using goalnets, between representative teams from the north and south, at the Town Ground in January 1891. In 1898, after winning the FA Cup at Crystal Palace, Forest made their final move, across the River Trent to their present ground. Thus they left the Town Ground, in the city of Nottingham, for the City Ground, in West Bridgford. Their old home became a tram depot and is still used by the local transport department.

The City Ground

The City Ground was only a couple of hundred yards across the river from Forest's previous home, and was almost next door to the cricket ground where Notts County had played since 1882. Despite their Cup triumph the club still needed to raise an extra £3000 to prepare the new ground and so they asked supporters and local businessmen to buy bonds worth £5 each. (The club was run by a committee, and did not become a limited company until 1982, the last League club to become one.) They were able to save some money, due to the efforts of a committee member, William Bardill, a landscape gardener and nurseryman. He must have been one of the first men (and there are so many 'firsts' in the Forest's history), to appreciate the value of a proper sub-soil for drainage. Accordingly he laid a 2-foot deep layer of clinker, on top of which he put high-quality turf from Radcliffe-on-Trent, brought to the site on river barges.

But if there were no complaints about the pitch, the rest of the ground left much to be desired, if compared for example with Villa Park, opened the year before, or Roker Park, opened in the same month, September 1898. This was partly because there was always a limit on how much money individual committee members could obtain guarantees for from the bank.

Forest spent most of the inter-war years in Division Two, but it must not be forgotten that they were again responsible for introducing a now commonplace feature; elliptical-shaped goalposts, first seen in 1921 at the City Ground. Apart from this innovation, the ground did not alter until the 1950s. The West Stand was identical to one built by the same contractors at Meadow Lane in 1910, with a barrel roof. At the Trent End was also a barrel roof, the rest

The two Nottingham grounds: Meadow Lane (above the River Trent) and the City Ground. Notice the old Trent Bridge Stand at the Meadow Lane End (Aerofilms)

of the ground being open banking.

There were two proposals in the 1930s; that Forest and County should amalgamate, and that the City Ground be used for greyhound racing. The former was scotched when the fans called a protest meeting. The latter, even though supported by the Corporation, Forest's landlords, was disallowed by the FA, which did not approve of gambling. So the City Ground and both Nottingham clubs continued to fight for survival.

The War left Forest relatively unscathed, bombs causing £75 worth of damage to the pitch in May 1941. Far worse, however, when during the winter of 1946–47 the Trent burst its banks and flooded the ground as high as the crossbars, and so brought about the unusual sight of swans slipping gracefully across the pitch. Forest beat a soggy retreat over the Bridge and sought refuge at Meadow Lane.

Forest began the 1950s by winning the Third Division South (a year after County had achieved the same distinction), and in an optimistic mood drew up plans for redeveloping the City Ground. The initial scheme proposed the erection of a stand at the Trent End, and when this was effected in 1954 with the building of the present standing enclosure, it was hoped to be able to build a new block between the Trent End and the West Stand, comprising offices and dressing rooms. In addition, the Trent End roof was to be lifted off and a seating tier added above, to make it into a double-decker. Quite why this over-elaborate plan was hatched is not clear, since it would

have been much simpler to install seating on either of the other two open sides. Perhaps the plan also included extra facilities overlooking the River Trent. Of course the Trent End roof has remained undisturbed ever since.

In 1958 a new stand was built on the East Side, providing an extra 2500 seats. Costing only £40000, it was not a very sophisticated construction – it even lacked toilets – situated at the back of the open terracing, but it at least improved the situation while Forest were back in Division One for the first time since 1925. The open Bridgford End was also improved and extended at this time.

Forest were the second but last First Division club to install floodlights, used first in September 1961 for a League Cup match v. Gillingham. Meanwhile, the old West Stand was reaching the point of collapse – although County's seemed solid enough (but had never been submerged in water) – so between 1962–65 it was reroofed, enlarged and refurbished and new offices were added. The City Ground's highest gate was on 28 October 1967. Forest had finished the previous season in second place, behind Manchester United, and when the two clubs met on that day 49945 attended. After the floods of 1947, came flames in 1968. On 24 August, during a game v. Leeds United the Main Stand caught fire, the match was abandoned and the spectators and players could only watch from the pitch as the whole building was gutted. It was back across the river to Meadow Lane. When the smoke subsided it was found that the columns and girders remained intact, so this time the stand was refitted entirely in concrete and steel, with seats in the paddock.

Forest slipped back into Division Two for a while, but in 1977 returned with a vengeance. A run of success made them League Champions in their first season after promotion, League Cup and European Cup winners twice each in successive seasons, plus runners-up in other years, when they picked up other sundry Cups around the world.

Inevitably, the East Stand was demolished, having proved unsafe under the 1975 Act, and in its place arose a mighty new structure, the new East or 'Executive' Stand costing £2·5 million. Opened in 1980, it closely resembled a stand erected at Molineux – a long angled cantilever with two tiers of seating divided by a line of executive boxes. The architects were Husband and Company of Sheffield, also responsible for the magnificent cantilever stand at Hillsborough, built 20 years earlier.

The new stand reduced the City Ground's capacity from over 40 000 to 35 000, but raised the number of seats from 6500 to 14 200. No doubt the rates have risen dramatically over the years, but the rent Forest pay to the council is still a peppercorn amount of £750 a year.

Ground Description

Of all the English Football League clubs, Forest and Notts County are closest together, just 400 yards apart with the River Trent between. (In Scotland, Dundee and Dundee United are even closer, and in non-League football, Witton Albion and Northwich Victoria are also near neighbours. Liverpool and Everton's grounds are 800 yards apart.) The City Ground is more prominent than Meadow Lane, by virtue of the height of the Executive Stand, which can be seen almost from the city centre.

The Main or West Stand itself is a simple but unusual construction. In design it is cranked very slightly inwards at each end, barely noticeable except when standing under the roof, which is supported by a prominent and exposed horizontal cross girder, housing the television camera platform and gangway. The stand's colouring is similar to that of Anfield; red seats, metallic grey steelwork, and a low white perimeter wall.

From here to the right is the open Bridgford End, terraced banking over which is a large electric scoreboard which has the irritating ability to spew out continuous advertisements throughout a game, so that one only has to look up from the action for a second to be told where to buy the best fish and chips in Nottingham or the cheapest engagement rings in Long Eaton. If spectators find it diverting during a tedious game, how much more distracting it must be for the players, if only because at night it flashes on and off repeatedly.

The Executive Stand is practically identical to those at Molineux and White Hart Lane, but with some important differences. At the City Ground the Stand is not cranked, and the cantilever roof girders are exposed beneath the roof panelling, which at the other two grounds is suspended, therefore hiding the steelwork. There is one line of boxes and 'Forest' is written in white seats amid the red seats. If any club can afford the enormous outlay, stands of this design are outstandingly efficient; they will mark the 1980s as effectively as Leitch's work did during the period before the Second World War (see Design).

The Executive Stand, all red and white, streamlined and tall, positively dominates the City Ground. Next to it, the Trent End cover looks quite preposterous, especially from the Bridgford End. It has a conventional sloping roof, pitched low over a fairly small bank of terracing, and on a crowded afternoon, clear vision from here can be quite a strain.

Behind this end, only a few yards away is the River Trent. From the Bridgford End you can see Meadow Lane's floodlight pylons above the Trent End roof, and Trent Bridge cricket ground behind to your left. From the very top of the Executive Stand is an unimpeded view of either, with the town centre clearly visible to the right. The tall, curved block behind the West Stand was once a hotel, and is now the Rushcliffe Civic Centre. Behind the new stand is the club car-park.

The pitch is no longer of bowling-green quality, as claimed during its early years, but has been considerably improved recently. Drainage is a serious problem, because the pitch and the land on which the ground is built is lower than the level of drains in nearby districts, so that water comes up through the drains after a heavy storm. Forest have tried protecting the turf with a plastic cover raised above the pitch with blowers. You can see the installations behind the Bridgford End goal, along the perimeter fence. As other clubs discovered, this was not the remedy once hoped for (see Pitches) and the cover is now used mainly as protection against rain in the hours before a match.

As the entrance way suggests, and the interior confirms, the City Ground is a Second Division ground in new clothes. Seated spectators can have no complaints, but if the club have any available capital they would be wise to concentrate on both ends of the ground and thus give the East and West Stands worthy neighbours. Perhaps then County and Forest might be persuaded to share these excellent facilities for football, while converting the outdated Meadow Lane Ground into a multi-sport complex convenient for either club's training purposes.

·NOTTS COUNTY·

Previous Grounds

Older than the FA itself, Notts County are the doyens of the Football League. They formed in 1862, and like all sporting clubs of the time were strictly for 'gentlemen only'. The name 'County' signified their genteel leanings. They first played at Park Hollow, part of the private park next to Nottingham Castle. For two years the members played games only among themselves, until in December 1864 County finally turned out against another club, in a 20-a-side game on The Meadows Cricket Ground. This open space became their regular pitch until 1877, although for important matches County hired the Trent Bridge Cricket Ground, then privately owned.

County moved in October 1877, in keeping with their image, to the home of the Gentlemen of Notts Cricket Club, Beeston. If necessary, they still used Trent Bridge, such as when they played Derbyshire on 30 November 1878 in one of the earliest floodlit games. November 1880 saw them at the Castle Cricket Ground, near the town centre, where they played until 1883. Until that time, Forest had been renting Trent Bridge from its new owners, Nottinghamshire County Cricket Club, but they left in 1883 for a new ground in Lenton. Keith Warsop, the Notts County historian, suggests that County's arrival in 1883 at Trent Bridge in place of Forest might have been engineered by the cricket club's secretary, Edwin Browne, who immediately assumed a similar post with Notts County. County's first game as permanent tenants of Trent Bridge was v. Walsall Swifts in September 1883.

At this ground County put aside their former inclinations and turned professional in 1885, becoming founder members of the Football League in 1888. But cricket still took priority at Trent Bridge and each September and April County had to find alternative venues for home fixtures. In the 1880s they used The Meadows and the Castle grounds again, and thereafter until 1908, used whatever ground Forest had at the time. For this reason alone, Trent Bridge was hardly a suitable venue for a League team, although unlike Bramall Lane and The County Ground, Northampton, the ground's owners did at least permit County to rest a portable wooden stand on the open touchline. The club had to move this stand occasionally to prevent wear and tear on the turf.

A more serious handicap was County's lack of support at Trent Bridge. An all-time low attendance for any normal scheduled League match was recorded at the ground when an estimated crowd of 300 saw County v. Crewe Alexandra in Division Two, on 17 February 1894. Such a pitiful turn-out is even more surprising in view of the fact that only a month later County won the FA Cup. No less baffling was one of the lowest attendances ever recorded for a First Division match at Trent Bridge, when 1500 were estimated to have watched County v. Preston North End on 27 March 1901. This was near the close of County's best season in Division One for a decade.

As early as 1905 the Football League had made it clear County should find a home they could use all through the season. Apparently certain clubs threatened by relegation had complained that while some teams had had to play County at 'home' on Forest's ground (when Trent Bridge was being used by the cricketers) they had had to play their fixtures v. County at Trent Bridge. The League agreed this was hardly fair and County began a half-hearted search for new premises.

It was not until 1910 that they moved, the final impetus coming from the cricket club who were anxious to see the footballers leave, even though the football pitch barely encroached on the cricket field – it was on the Fox Road Side of the ground, used mainly as a practice area by the cricketers. Perhaps feeling some pressure, County decided to sell their ground rights in the 1st Round of the FA Cup, when they were drawn to play Bradford City at Trent Bridge.

At last stirred into action, County found their future home across the River Trent, not far from where Forest's old Town Ground had been. Their final match at Trent Bridge was on 16 April 1910 v. Aston Villa.

Meadow Lane

Before County moved to the ground in 1910, as council tenants, Meadow Lane was open ground next to a cattle market. With admirable speed, the contractors managed to erect the steelwork and roof of the new Main Stand in just nine days (and some would say, 70 or more years later, 'it looks like it!') for £3000. Once fitted out, the total cost came to £10 000. The stand was identical to one at the City Ground, built by the same company a few years before.

At the south end of the ground nearest the Trent was placed a small wooden stand, seating 1400, which the club had literally floated across the river from Trent Bridge. It was probably the oldest stand in the League before being torn down in 1978, older even than the Gordon Road Stand at Priestfield Stadium. It may have been the portable stand mentioned earlier. The other two sides were open terracing, the County Road Side having an open stream, Tinkers Brook, running down to the Trent. A man with a long pole, cane basket on the end, would be stationed by the brook to fish out the ball during games. Naturally, Meadow Lane was opened with a friendly match against Forest, on 3 September 1910.

The Army took over Meadow Lane for much of the First World War, and this gap, together with some unlucky draws in the FA Cup, meant that County did not play a Cup tie at their new ground until January 1920, ten years after moving there. In 1923 the club built a new stand on the County Road Side, actually on top of the banking, over the Tinkers Brook. The terracing under the roof was wooden, and the stand sported a simple triangular gable, a lovable feature of Meadow Lane ever since.

In 1941, despite or because of a machine gun emplacement on the open Kop, bombs destroyed the northern wing of the Main Stand and cratered the pitch so badly County had to withdraw from the wartime League competition. Then during the winter of 1946–47, when prisoners of war were used to clear the pitch of snow, the Trent submerged Meadow Lane only marginally less than the City Ground. Being further from the river banks and slightly higher, Meadow Lane drained more quickly and suffered less than Forest's ground and for a time the clubs again shared their facilities. This happened once more in 1968, when Forest's Main Stand was gutted by fire.

Floodlights were installed at Meadow Lane in 1953, long before Forest's, and first switched on for a friendly v. Derby County on 23 March. How appropriate, for County's opponents in that first ever Nottingham floodlit game in 1878 had been Derbyshire. The lights were too basic for modern usage, however, and in 1962 they were updated.

The occasion of Meadow Lane's highest crowd was not a happy one because 47 310 watched Third Division York City beat Second Division County in the 6th Round of the FA Cup on 12 March 1955. In more recent years the capacity of the ground was reduced to 30 000, until in the late 1970s, both County's improved form and the introduction of the Safety of Sports Grounds Act dictated great changes. Sadly, the old wooden stand on the Meadow Lane End had to be demolished, although many supporters felt it might have gone in a more dignified way – it was after all probably the oldest stand in the League. In its place arose a huge, blank, brick wall, the back of an £800 000 sports complex, the Meadow Club. The complex was built because the club had won promotion to Division One in 1981 but knew that gates were unlikely to average more than 10 000 to 12 000; insufficient to keep County among the top few without extra income. With such low gates they also realized that extra accommodation behind the Meadow Lane goal would not be necessary and so left a void between the goal and the wall. The sports centre also had changing rooms installed, taking them out of the antiquated Main Stand. An uglier solution could not have been found, for now the ground is effectively three-sided, although there can be no doubt about the standard of sporting facilities housed beyond that blank wall.

A less dramatic change occurred in the County Road Stand, where a small section of seats have been bolted onto the wooden terrace in the centre. Meadow Lane therefore has 4000 seats, in a capacity of 23 680.

Ground Description

Despite its name, Meadow Lane is about as rural as the Boleyn Ground is Tudor. The ground is surrounded on all sides by light industry, Tinkers Brook has been concreted over, and the Trent is hidden from view by factory buildings.

The main entrance is in Meadow Lane, by the new sports centre and offices, behind which runs the Main Stand at a right angle. With the possible exception of Swansea's Main Stand, a less imposing stand, belonging to a top club would be hard to find, yet County's is not entirely without character. It has a barrel roof, angled slightly towards the centre. The metal work is black and white, like the rest of the ground, but the seats are for some reason blue, some of them being bench seats. In the centre of the roof a television camera gantry has been built. Notice at the Kop End of the stand, the roof panelling reveals where bomb damage was inflicted during the War. In front is an uncovered paddock. Outdated it most certainly is, but other clubs have proved how refurbishing can make even the most dilapidated look new.

From here, to the left is the uncovered Spion Kop, topped by a lovely half-time scoreboard with a clock, glass-panelled front, and loudspeaker hailers on each side. New black barriers against the light concrete give this bank a neat appearance. From the summit, Forest's ground is clearly visible straight ahead, but otherwise the view is dominated by industry. Behind are two five-a-side pitches, and beyond them is Iremonger Road, named after County's long serving goalkeeper, Albert Iremonger, who made a record total of 602 appearances between 1905–26.

Opposite the Main Stand is the County Road Stand, with the familiar pointed gable proudly announcing the club's name, 'established 1862'. Many visitors assume the stand must be as old, but it dates back only to the 1920s. It lies at the back of an uncovered terrace, built up on stilts above what used to be the open brook. All the terracing under the sloping roof is wooden, with an impromptu metal framework in the centre supporting a few hundred seats. Underneath this charming stand is a small prefab hut used by the supporters' club. From County Road itself, the stand looks remarkably like a chicken house, with wooden shutters along its rear wall. In the Meadow Lane corner, where the scoreboard used to stand, is a tall flagpole.

The County Road Stand, Meadow Lane (Adrian Gibson)

And so we come to the 'wall'; a brown and grey sheer cliff a few yards behind the Meadow Lane goal. Blue-clad dressing room extensions with slanting roofs abut against the wall; a sign of future intentions to cover them with a terrace? Unlike the supermarket developments at Selhurst and Boothferry Parks, there are not even a few token steps of terracing behind the goal. The only consolation is that when the Kop sings, the sound apparently bounces off the wall. County were used to playing on three-sided grounds in their early days, and now they have made Meadow Lane the same. Along the top of the wall is a line of executive boxes.

It would be unfair not to add that the Meadow Club has four squash courts, a multi-purpose sports hall and social facilities, and compared with many clubs is not expensive to use.

Finally, notice how odd are Meadow Lane's goals. The stanchions are L-shaped, so that the posts and net form a large rectangular box.

Overall, County's Ground has little beauty and is mostly under-developed, and in places even unkempt. The perimeter track, for example, is particularly untidy. Furthermore, it is hard to envisage the ground changing in future years, unless sufficient funds are found to smarten up both stands and construct some form of terracing in front of the sports centre.

There was a proposal in the 1970s to build a new sports stadium on Colwick Park Racecourse, nearer the City Ground across the River Trent, for use by both Nottingham clubs. Now that Meadow Lane has a new indoor centre of its own, plus five-a-side facilities behind the Kop, perhaps the best solution would be to play County's first team games at the City Ground and develop Meadow Lane as a training complex for both clubs, or as a community sports arena. No doubt the suggestion is abhorrent to both sets of fans, but in view of the Bradford experience can either Nottingham club afford to ignore the possibility of ground sharing much longer?

Notts County's new sports centre with private boxes above (Sporting Pictures)

♦ MANSFIELD TOWN ♦

Previous Grounds

Records indicate there was a Mansfield team playing on Parr's cricket field in 1870, and certainly there were several teams in early soccer history with the name Mansfield Town. But the present club's roots date back probably to 1894, to a team known as Mansfield Wesleyans. Their ground was off Newgate Lane, in the area now occupied by Pelham Street and Stanhope Street. This was bought by the local railway company, so the club moved to a ground in Broxtowe Drive, with the dubious title of 'The Prairie'. In 1905 as Mansfield Town they moved to Field Mill, which until then had been the home of Mansfield Mechanics, one of the town's former leading clubs.

Field Mill

Mansfield purchased Field Mill from the Duke of Portland, who issued a covenant stating that the ground must always be used for sporting activities. With the town expanding rapidly, and development swallowing up many open spaces this was a wise precaution. Field Mill was at least a lush patch of green in an increasingly drab town.

Mansfield Town became national news when in January 1929 they went to Molineux in the 3rd Round of the FA Cup and beat Wolves 1-0. Two years later Mansfield were elected to the League. At that time there was one stand at Field Mill, a very low wooden construction on the West Side. Before this the players had changed in the Bull's Head Inn on Portland Street and had to enter the ground along a footpath, which still exists, behind the North Stand. Field Mill was also used for greyhound racing during the 1930s.

Just before the Second World War the existing Bishop Street Stand was built, and this became the main stand, seating 1100. Next to it in the south east corner, were dressing room huts. There is still a gap in the perimeter fence through which the players used to enter the field.

The record crowd of 24479 was in January 1953, when neighbours Nottingham Forest visited in the FA Cup 3rd Round. Soon after the club built the cover over the North End. It had to be angled to fit the curved terracing which had been shaped round the greyhound track 20 years earlier. Their most important investment was the purchase of the training ground behind the West Stand, which was itself redeveloped completely from 1959. Mansfield bought a complete steel-framed stand from Hurst Park racecourse in South London for £30000, and erected it behind the original West Stand (a method copied by Swindon and Chester in later years). By the time the framework was filled in with new offices, dressing rooms and social facilities in 1961, the bill had come

The West Stand at Field Mill, the roof is similar in design to one seen at Highbury

to an enormous £200 000. In the same year Sheffield Wednesday opened their new cantilever stand at Hillsborough, and although it did not have any such facilities underneath, was much more sophisticated and £50 000 cheaper. For a Fourth Division club – a not very successful one at that – it was an extremely ambitious, and some might say foolhardy, investment. The wooden stand was demolished and a concrete paddock built in its place, in front of the new stand.

Also in 1961 Field Mill's floodlights were switched on for the first time, by Billy Wright, for Mansfield's League Cup tie v. Cardiff City on 5 October. Field Mill was thus one of the most modern and well-equipped grounds outside the Second Division. Total capacity is at present 23 500, including 3350 seats.

Ground Description

Similar to Elland Road, the main entrance brings you into a car-park lying between the stand and the training ground, where there is one full size and two five-a-side floodlit pitches, shared with the local community.

The West Stand facade is less grand than that at Leeds, but for a small club is quietly impressive; although like so many buildings of the 1950s and 1960s it is now quite dated. But the stand itself is a gem. It looks like a plastic kit, like an artist's impression from an old soccer annual of what a modern stand should resemble. In fact, the only stands which bear any similarity to it in design are the two at Highbury, albeit more luxurious by far. The date of its original construction at Hurst Park racecourse is not certain – it could have been the 1930s or, more

probably, a post-war model of streamlined efficiency.

The slightly pitched roof is concealed as at Highbury by a wide, overhanging awning, or 'marquise' with deep ribbed fascia, carrying round each side of the stand. The seating tier, with glass screen ends, protrudes beyond the line of the back wall like a modern cantilever, which indeed the roof would be but for one, very thin supporting pillar in the centre. There are 2250 seats. A high concrete paddock rear wall divides the stand from the uncovered terraces in front. Although the Stand has little colour, only steel and concrete, it has far more style and authority than many stands built since in more modern materials and designs. For the lover of football architecture therefore, it is a rare landmark.

From here, to the right is the open Quarry Lane End, slightly curved because of the old greyhound track, with the dilapidated supporters' club's headquarters behind. A half-time scoreboard is tucked into the far corner.

Opposite is the Bishop Street Stand, about 50 yards long, on the half-way line. The old dressing rooms were to the right. It is a fairly typical small stand of the lower divisions, with bench seats, a slightly uneven roof and murky glass screens at either end.

To the left is the covered North Stand, behind which lies an expanse of open scrubland with overgrown paths. The roof, covering half the terracing, is nicely capped by an advertisement hoarding with a clock in the centre.

Field Mill occupies 9½ acres of land, all owned by the club, full of potential, and the envy of many other clubs.

•LINCOLN CITY•

Previous Grounds

A Lincoln FC existed as far back as 1860, but the present club dates from 1883, on a ground off the High Street called John O'Gaunt's. It was also known as the 'Cow Pat' because cows were allowed to graze on the pitch. An early floodlit game was played here in 1888 and Lincoln began their League career at the ground in 1892, as founder members of Division Two. Space was limited, however, and so in 1894 City moved to Sincil Bank. John O'Gaunt's was situated where Abbott and Sibthorp Streets now stand.

Sincil Bank

Lincoln's ground takes its name from Sincil Drain, not an open sewer but a conduit serving as an overflow from the River Witham which flows through the centre of the city. The drain formed the west side of the ground. When Lincoln moved here in 1894 the supporters rallied round to build earth banks, prepare the pitch and erect a small wooden grandstand. A second wooden stand was built behind the south goal, known as the South Park Stand, but both stands were quite small and primitive.

Definitely the lowest attendance for a first-class match at Sincil Bank was during the First World War. Bradford City were to meet Norwich City in a 2nd Round replay in 1915, but the FA ordered that it be played behind closed doors, so as not to interfere with work at the nearby munitions factory. This was in response to a debate in the House of Commons about the apparent shortage of shells at the battle of Neuve Chapelle in March 1915 and the failure of some to explode. The Government blamed the munitions workers, who were said to be drawing high wages and idling around in public houses. Hence the official attendance of nil at Sincil Bank for that Cup replay – although 200 people were unofficially present. (Far more drastic was the Government's legislation which imposed afternoon closure on every public house, in an attempt to boost munitions' production. The law has remained with us ever since.) The South Park Stand was burnt down in 1924 and replaced with the existing wood and brick construction a year later. Until then all the club's offices and the dressing rooms had been under the South Park Stand, but these were now moved to the Main or St Andrew's Stand, built soon after the First World War.

During a spell in Division Two 1948–49 one observer wrote in the *FA Yearbook*: 'Spectators at Lincoln's Sincil Bank ground are well known to visiting sides for their hearty and sustained cheering . . . a Hampden Roar in miniature . . .' The pitch was also described as, 'one of the finest stretches of turf in the country'.

City's longest run in Division Two since the War was between 1952–61. At that time there was a very small wooden stand perched upon the top of Sincil Terrace, seating 200. In 1956 the supporters raised

View from the South Park Stand at Sincil Bank looking over the railway to the Cathedral (Adrian Gibson)

money to build a cover in the north east corner, linked to the simple pre-war cover at the North or Railway End.

Lincoln were on their way down to the Fourth Division when their first floodlights were installed. The president of the supporters' club officially switched them on for the Third Division game v. Barnsley on 31 January 1962. The lights have been updated since, and the original ones sold to Spalding United.

Lincoln's highest attendance came for a rare clash with a top team in the League Cup in 1967. A crowd of 23 196 saw City go down to Derby in a 4th Round replay on 25 November 1967. Since then the capacity has been reduced to 16 225, of which 2500 are seated. In the summer of 1982 the ground was sold to the local council for £225 000, and rented back for £11 000 a year on a 21-year lease, with the option to repurchase it within three years, should Lincoln's finances have improved by then.

Ground Description

The approach to the ground along Sincil Bank is like a winding country road, barely wide enough for a team coach, with open playing fields on one side and Sincil Drain on the other. There was a plan to transform the ground by building a supermarket and turning the pitch's axis to run from east to west, but because Sincil Bank is such a narrow lane and can scarcely be widened, the scheme had to be dropped. This is a relief in many ways. Sincil Bank is similar to St James' Park, Exeter; tree lined, coloured red and green, with a railway immediately next to the stands. It is a picturesque and unspoilt enclosure on lowland between Lincoln and the gently rising South Common.

The main St Andrew's Stand is rather a squashed affair, with an advertisement board along the roof almost as high as the small seating tier. Organized muddle is perhaps the best description, for there are steps everywhere, a little hut serving as the press-box in the tiny paddock, lines of hoardings along every available space and apparently only just enough space to fit in the small glass screens at either end.

The Stand does not quite fill the east touchline, and on the left is a separate low block housing the dressing rooms, so that the players enter the pitch in the south east corner. The building was originally an air-raid shelter, and has since been extended. Directly behind is a small fire-station.

From the Main Stand, you can see how wide the ground is. There are tracks along each touchline, with extra strips of grass between them and the perimeter walls. This allows more space for advertisement hoardings, but also means that the trainers' benches have had to be put several feet from the stand nearer the touchline. They are sheltered in two square boxes, like sedan chairs, both of course decorated with advertisements.

From here, to the right is the Railway End. A few feet behind the roof runs the by-pass line for goods and holiday traffic on the London to Lincoln route. As trains pass by it seems as if they are rolling along the roof of the stand. This end is standing only, and is in two parts, the older, lower half behind the goal and the more recent, higher section, covering the corner and ending a few yards from the St Andrew's Stand. Again, the stand is hidden with advertisements along the roof and perimeter fence.

Opposite is the open Sincil Terrace. The ground is one of three in the League having two covered ends but one uncovered side (The Valley and London Road are the same). The terrace is very attractive, with brown concrete steps, red streamlined barriers, and a clock in the centre, and it is framed by trees which run along the bank of Sincil Drain, behind the terrace. A detention centre is on the far side. Where once was a small wooden stand is now a wooden refreshment hut. Along the perimeter wall the foundations of the old dug-outs are visible, used before the sedan chairs were put on the opposite touchline.

Finally, to the left is the South Park Stand framed by the South Common. The Stand is in the same style as the Main Stand, like an advertising sandwich filled with a narrow layer of seats. But here the seats are plain benches worn smooth with time and the stanchions are of wood. Underneath is the social club, and in front, where there are as many as three levels of advertising on the paddock rear wall, is a narrow strip of terracing, barely deep enough for more than a handful of spectators. It has not been used since the perimeter wall collapsed during a League Cup tie v. Stoke in 1975.

From this stand you have a marvellous view of the city stretching out above the railway line opposite. Dominating the horizon in the centre is the main tower of Lincoln Cathedral, to the left of which is Lincoln Castle.

Sincil Bank's pitch is still a fine stretch of turf, largely due to its natural sand base. Even though Sincil Drain may flood two or three times a year, the pitch, which drains away in the opposite direction, to the east, is never affected.

With a fine medieval city in view and surrounded by trees and fields, not even the presence of so much advertising can mar the pleasant atmosphere of Sincil Bank. It is the sort of ground where it would be impossible not to talk to your neighbour, or to feel that your shouts of encouragement or disdain could not be heard by the players.

• CHESTERFIELD •

Previous Grounds

Chesterfield is the fourth oldest club in the League, dating back to 1866. For some years the club played on a site called Spital, near the town centre, until moving to the Recreation Ground on Saltergate in 1884, where football had been played since at least 1870.

The Recreation Ground

For many years the Recreation Ground was little more than an enclosed field, with a small cover on the half-way line along Compton Street. A photograph taken during Chesterfield's first spell of ten years in the League, when for a time the club was called Chesterfield Town, shows a clear view from one side of the ground to the famous crooked spire in the heart of Chesterfield. In 1921 the club bought the site from the corporation and rejoined the League.

On promotion to Division Two in 1936, Chesterfield built the existing Main Stand on the east side along St Margaret's Drive. It was opened for the home game v. Sheffield United.

The ground's record crowd of 30 968 came just before the War in April 1939, when Newcastle United were the visitors in an end of season Second Division match. After a good Cup run at the beginning of the 1950s the Compton Street cover was extended, the playing surface raised to improve drainage, and all the standing areas properly terraced.

When the law on fund-raising club pools was relaxed about ten years later, the Chesterfield and District Sportsman's Association helped erect the cover over the Kop on Saltergate, at a cost of £10 000 in 1961.

The Recreation Ground holds the unhappy distinction of being the last League ground to have floodlights installed. A £10 000 appeal fund was launched in 1964, in the hope of having a set in time for the club's centenary in 1966, but the ones bought from Sheffield United proved to be totally unsuitable.

After erecting only one pylon, which was too short, the bases were found to be insecure, so Chesterfield sold the unwanted set to Stafford Rangers and bought new ones. These were switched on in the presence of Sir Stanley Rous, for a friendly v. Sheffield Wednesday on 18 October 1967, more than 16 years after the start of the modern floodlit era. Ironically Chesterfield had been one of the first clubs to have a floodlit training pitch as far back as 1956.

The Recreation Ground's present capacity is 19 750, of which 3000 are seated.

Ground Description

The ground stands on a rise above the town centre and can be easily spotted from a distance. Saltergate itself is a main thoroughfare, but once in St Margaret's Drive all is tranquil suburbia, into which the football club must fit without disturbing the decorum. It succeeds in this assiduously, for the Recreation Ground is a neat, unfussy place.

The Main Stand is a perfect example of how little grandstand design changed between the Wars. There is a narrow standing terrace at the front, too narrow to necessitate a tunnel for the players (who emerge from a door) behind which is a low terrace rear wall with the seating tier above. An asbestos sheet roof parallels the rake of the seats. The formula is simple, and is executed with the minimum of additional detail.

To the right is the open Cross Street End, a low bank of terracing attractively backed by a castellated wall. Behind is a primary school. From here the famous crooked spire is to your left, now obscured by the Main Stand. In the far corner is a group of turnstiles built by supporters in 1939 after that record attendance.

To the left is the covered Kop, behind which is the social club and Saltergate. Again, the Kop roof demonstrates the timelessness of football ground architecture, for here, put up in the same year as Sheffield Wednesday built their famous cantilever stand, is a cover which might have been a contemporary of the 1936 Main Stand. But having said that, one should add that the design persisted because it was fairly successful, and is improved at Chesterfield by light-coloured paintwork, neat walls and some flag-poles. A plaque over the rear entrance reminds spectators who paid for it, which might account for its pristine condition. Not a barrier or step is out of place.

Opposite the Main Stand is the narrow and low Compton Street Stand, sometimes called the Popular Side. It is distinguished by a line of deep advertising hoardings across the roof, interrupted only in the centre by a wooden box protruding above the roof, as high as the stand itself. This is used by television cameras. The brightest feature of the ground is the orange running track. Otherwise all is quiet and orderly; the small town Third Division spirit perfectly encapsulated.

The Recreation Ground, Chesterfield (Sporting Pictures)

·12·
CENTRAL, SOUTH
AND SOUTH COAST

·OXFORD UNITED·

Manor Ground

Oxford may have had only a short League career but their history goes back to 1896. Originally called Headington United, they played on a ground next to the Brittania Inn. Shortly before the First World War United moved to Manor Park, a large sports ground used by several amateur organizations. In 1921 the Headington Sports Ground Company Limited formed and bought the ground, then sub-let to United, as well as to cricket, bowls and tennis clubs. There was a small pavilion on the south side, where the Main Stand is now, and sheep and horses used to graze on the pitch during the week. The slope was so severe (still noticeable) that whenever a batsman aimed towards the bottom corner he was sure of a rapid boundary.

The situation in Oxford was very similar to Cambridge in that there were two clubs – City and United – and either could have become the senior one. It was Headington who turned professional, leaving the Spartan League to join the Southern League in 1949.

At that point the other sporting clubs vacated the Manor Ground and left United as sole tenants. One of the first things the club did was to build a small stand in the south west corner, seating 180, with dressing rooms underneath. This was opened in October 1949.

A year later an event occurred at the Manor Ground which gives Headington a hallowed place in the annals of football ground history. Headington United were the first professional club in Britain to install floodlighting at their ground. They were only temporary lights, borrowed from those Oxford Colleges which lit up their facades at night, mounted on 36 wooden poles, but they were the first! (See Floodlights.) The first recorded match under lights at the Manor Ground took place on 18 December 1950, when Headington played a friendly v. Banbury Spencer (now Banbury United) in aid of local hospitals.

Then in 1953–54, Headington met Millwall in the FA Cup at the Den and managed a draw. They

approached the FA and asked to stage the replay under floodlights. Predictably, permission was refused (the first FA Cup match under lights was not until September 1955), but the story received national press coverage and Bill Shankly was quoted as saying, 'Good luck to little Headington for having the pluck to ask a very, very important question, and arouse interest which could be a portent for the future'.

In 1953 Headington won their first Southern League Championship and purchased the ground from the owners, who were close to liquidation, for the sum of £10 000. In 1957 the supporters' club presented United with £33 000 to pay for the new Main Stand built in place of the old pavilion, and the dressing rooms were transferred there from the corner stand. There were 1600 seats and the stand was opened on 24 August 1957 by Denis Follows of the FA. At the same time, the 36 wooden poles were taken down and four pylons erected for the floodlights. Headington were on their way up.

In 1960 the club changed their name to Oxford United and proceeded to win the Southern League in 1961 and 1962, before replacing Accrington Stanley (who resigned from the League in March 1962).

During the summer of 1962 the London Road Terrace was covered, again with money raised by the supporters' club. Also built that year was a tiny stand next to the corner stand, seating just 100 people but reserved for employees of the club, apprentice players, stewards and programme sellers. This Staff Stand was quite unique, and a symbol of the close relationship between the club and those who helped it attain League status.

Since then, little has changed at the Manor Ground, although a great deal has happened to the team. They rose to Division Two in 1968 and stayed there for eight seasons before relegation in 1976, but it was perhaps a timely demotion, for had United kept their Division Two status much longer the Manor Ground would have come under the jurisdiction of the Safety of Sports Grounds Act, inevitably forcing the club to lay out large sums in order to maintain a reasonable capacity.

The largest crowd to squeeze into the ground was

The Manor Ground's trio of stands (Adrian Gibson)

22 730, v. Preston on 29 February 1964 when United became the first Fourth Division club ever to reach the FA Cup quarter finals. The Manor Ground's capacity in 1983 was 17 350, including 1880 seats.

Oxford would very much like to leave the ground however, because it has very limited and awkward access points, and virtually no room for parking. There have been plans to redevelop elsewhere, but the local authority is reluctant to relocate the club even though they did not want them there in the first place and gave only temporary planning permission for the stands! But now the council believes it is best to have the nuisance where they can control it, rather than let it get out of hand somewhere else. What land is available for a new ground is mostly owned by the University. At the Manor Ground therefore, Oxford must remain. Ne sutor ultra crepidam.

Ground Description

Like the Abbey Stadium, Oxford's ground is far from the hallowed spires of the University, although it is in a pleasant, leafy suburb possessing much of the calm and stone-walled dignity of Oxford itself. One could imagine dons walking up Headington Road to visit the Manor Ground, but never up the Newmarket Road to Cambridge United.

Leafy suburbs do have their drawbacks when you are trying to run a professional football club, however. The main entrance to the ground is, for example, along a very narrow driveway from the London Road. From here the London Road Terrace is straight ahead, and to enter the Main Stand one must walk behind the south side of the ground. It is uncannily like the Abbey Stadium in lay-out.

The Main Stand is about 50 yards long on the half-way line and is a plain, 1950s' design with a plain brick front wall and a slightly pitched dark roof.

On the west side in the corner of the pitch at an angle, like Craven Cottage, is the Manor Club. This was the original stand, and is like a toy-town stand, neatly filling the corner.

Immediately next to it, on the west end goal-line is the even smaller Staff Stand, with some old fashioned wooden seats but an excellent view.

The rest of this end is taken up by the Cuckoo Lane Terrace, the tallest section of banking at the ground, rising up to a hump in the far corner. The crush barriers are blue and yellow, set against the brown steps, and with dense green foliage lining the back, it presents a rich and colourful background to the turf. Behind is the John Radcliffe Hospital, set in spacious grounds.

The opposite side is called the Osler Road Terrace, open on the western half, covered on the remainder by a rather ramshackle wood, steel and corrugated iron roof which it is thought was bought second-hand when Headington turned professional in 1949. The terracing here is very low, backed by a low fence, so that one hardly feels separated from the houses beyond.

The London Road End is the most modern section, having good, high-stepped terracing and a small moat in front. From here you can see just how the pitch slopes some 5 or 6 feet diagonally from the north west down to the south east corner.

In my opinion there is not a prettier ground in the League, with the exception only of Gay Meadow and St James' Park, Exeter. Of course, it is not perfect, but isn't Oxford full of attractive but unsuitable buildings? Nor is the Manor Ground everyone's idea of what a football ground should be. But then as George Bernard Shaw wrote in *Man and Superman*, 'Very nice sort of place, Oxford, I should think, for people that like that sort of place.'

✦ READING ✦

Previous Grounds

Reading formed in 1871 and is thus the oldest League club south of the Trent. They began at the Reading Recreation Ground, then played at Reading Cricket Ground until 1882. Seven years each at Coley Park and Caversham Cricket Ground followed, until their first game at Elm Park on 5 September 1896. All their previous grounds still exist as open spaces.

Elm Park

A photograph of Elm Park in 1906 shows a stand along the Norfolk Road Side, going round the ground to cover half the Town End. A gale blew this down in 1925, five years after Reading had joined the Football League. A year later the club celebrated promotion to Division Two and built the present Main Stand. The season it was opened also brought Elm Park's highest attendance, 33 042, for an FA Cup match v. Brentford on 19 February 1927.

During the War an enemy bomb destroyed the club offices, which were then in the town centre. After the War, a cover was erected over the centre section of the Tilehurst Road terraces, wings being added in the early 1950s. With the addition of floodlights, first used v. Carlisle on 27 February 1956 and updated three years later, Elm Park assumed the state it is today.

There was an attempt to move from the ground to Smallmead, a stadium only recently established on a council tip near the M4, where greyhound and speedway racing now take place. But even if the club could sell Elm Park, valued at about £700 000, it would cost at least twice that amount to prepare Smallmead.

A further complication is the existence of a community sports centre at Elm Park. The Sports Council gave Reading a £60 000 grant to install a floodlit, all-weather pitch with changing facilities, on the club's land. Reading also agreed to share with the Sports Council and Reading Borough Council, the salary of a Community Sports Officer, to be based at the club, but then withdrew their offer in 1981 for financial reasons. The local council would be further loath to see the club move, if that meant the community sports centre had to be sold for redevelopment.

Ground Description

Rather like Reading itself, Elm Park contains little of interest. Not that it is a bad ground – many clubs would covet its 27 200 capacity and 3500 seats. The very plain Main Stand on Norfolk Road has wooden floors, patchy seats and rusting blue corrugated iron sides, with noticeably low dug-outs on the touchline. The pitch is actually some 6 feet higher than Norfolk Road, as the ground is built into the side of a hill. Underneath the top surface is mainly blue-grey clay, poor for drainage, but in the far right-hand quarter of the pitch you might see a lighter patch of green. This is where there is a base of silver sand.

To the left is the Reading, or Town End, an open terrace next to the aforementioned sports centre. At the rear of the bank you can see remnants of the original stand, where the back is shored up with sleepers and supports.

Opposite is the sizeable Tilehurst Terrace, formed out of the hillside, its different roof levels showing clearly how it was constructed in two stages. A clock adorns the centre. To the right is another open terrace, the Tilehurst End.

Elm Park fulfils its role very well if but with little style and it is in too good a condition to arouse any feelings of pity or nostalgia, except for the lost crowds. With scarcely an arresting detail inside the ground and nothing of note visible beyond, Elm Park is probably the least interesting ground in the Football League. From an aesthetic point of view, I stress. Others will no doubt argue otherwise.

Elm Park *c.* 1905 (*Book of Football*)

·ALDERSHOT·

Recreation Ground

Aldershot are the third youngest club in the League, formed in December 1926. For months the club had no home, but the council-owned Recreation Ground was an obvious choice. As Jack Rollin relates in his club history, Aldershot Borough Council (now called Rushmoor) did not have statutory power to close the park for more than 12 times a year, so to circumvent this they invoked the 1925 Public Health Act which allowed local authorities to lease a ground for organized football, provided they bought land of equivalent value for public use. The council therefore purchased 40 acres of land at Aldershot Park and have leased the Recreation Ground to Aldershot FC ever since.

The first game was on 27 August 1927 attended by 3500.

There was a plan for a stand with winter gardens on the roof, but the South Stand was the first to be built in 1929. Three years later Aldershot entered the League in place of the East London club Thames. In the late 1930s the North Stand was built, followed after the War by the East Bank terrace roof.

The first floodlit game was a trial match between Scottish and English born players at the club, in May 1953. In 1954 the ground was host to an early BBC televised game when Aldershot played the Army, to celebrate a hundred years of the Aldershot garrison. The lights were renewed at a cost of £10 000 in 1962.

The ground's highest attendance of 19 138 saw a Cup-tie v. Carlisle in January 1970. Soon after, new offices and dressing rooms were built behind the North Stand, and with added seats this took over from the South Stand as the main stand. The capacity is now 16 000, with 1885 seats, and a very high proportion of this total, 14 000 approximately, is under cover.

Ground Description

This is the only League ground situated in a public park and access is almost unrestricted during the week. The park gates are shut on match days, when what appear to be ordinary municipal park shelters become turnstiles. From these you pass by clipped lawns and flower beds up to the High Street End, which is just a tarmac path behind the goal, the narrowest end of any League ground, with a high net to stop the ball going into the park or street (often unsuccessfully). A more pleasant approach is down through the eastern heights of the park along twisted, cobbled paths, through thickly wooded gardens past the tennis courts, from where the ground can be seen nestling cosily at the foot of the slope.

Behind the East Bank Terrace, which has a leaking barrel roof and a haphazard array of crush barriers, is a floodlit training area. The Main Stand, once all-standing, now has a central section with alternate rows of red and blue seats, with a new Directors' Box in the middle and a compact, well-designed new administrative block behind. Along the front of the stand is an unusual stone perimeter wall with curves and buttresses, dotted with ivy. Less picturesque is the tall British Telecom office block at the rear. The small South Stand, straddling the half-way line opposite, looks more modern than it is, with a substantial, almost cantilevered overhanging roof. Behind are the old wooden dressing rooms, now a multi-gym, backing onto the Guildford to Aldershot railway line. Because of the narrow, open West End the ground looks a shade incomplete, although there is at least 40 feet of spare turf beyond the goal-lines to develop it further.

The Recreation Ground is like part of an arboretum, with the nicely mildewed air of its surrounds. As the *Athletic News* put it in 1927, it is 'one of the prettiest football enclosures in the South'.

The Recreation Ground, Aldershot, looking towards the East Bank. Notice how far the South Stand roof overhangs without support (Simon Inglis)

·AFC BOURNEMOUTH·

Previous Grounds

In 1891 AFC Bournemouth were known as Boscombe St Johns and played on King's Park, next to the present ground. They moved east to Castlemain Road, Pokesdown in 1899 as Boscombe FC, paying £5 10s a season rent. When J. E. Cooper Dean became involved with the club they moved back to Boscombe, a suburb of Bournemouth.

Dean Court

Dean Court, like Fellows Park and Ninian Park, was named after the club's benefactor, who became Club President. When Cooper Dean let the wasteland to Boscombe FC at a peppercorn rent in 1910, voluntary labour prepared a pitch and built a stand for 300 spectators. Two years later the club turned professional, and in 1923 joined the League as Bournemouth and Boscombe Athletic.

The present Main Stand has a pedigree. Its framework came from the British Empire Exhibition at Wembley where it was built in 1923, as a restaurant. Athletic bought it for £12 000 and the League's Vice-President C. E. Sutcliffe declared it open on 27 August 1927 for a game v. Swindon.

The South End covered terrace was also opened before a Swindon match, in September 1936, by club director and Mayor, Alderman H. G. Harris. In 1957, following the club's most successful FA Cup run, in which they reached the 6th Round and recorded their highest gate of 28 799 v. Manchester United, the New Stand was built. It was refurbished in 1964. Floodlit football had a tenuous start at Dean Court in 1961 v. Northampton, when the new lights failed 15 minutes before kick-off and delayed the match nearly an hour.

The early 1970s promised great changes, as John Bond rescued the club from the Fourth and almost lifted them to the Second Division. To put them at least at the top of an alphabetical list, a new name, AFC Bournemouth, was sneakily adopted in 1971 but editors and compilers seem to have ignored the

Dean Court in the 1930s

hint. Meanwhile the club purchased about 20 acres of land from the Cooper Dean estate, ambitious plans for a new stand and sports centre behind the open end began. The foundations and superstructure went up quickly, like the cost, which rose from an estimated £250 000 to nearer £700 000. With the ground lying deep within suburbia, planning permission was an obstacle, and finally the project was abandoned. Bournemouth have been trying to sell the site ever since. Ground capacity is 19 175, including 4500 seats.

Ground Description

The Main Stand, despite its origins, is rather dull, although ironically it shares with Wembley Stadium clear sheeting along the roof front.

The New Stand opposite is a long, low and narrow cover over terracing, lined with advertisements. The South End is half-covered, but also half-boarded off where the back wooden terracing is deemed unsafe. The stands seem painted in a crust of moss, weather-worn but immovable, like park benches in autumn.

To the right is an open terrace, sarcastically called the Brighton Beach End because it used to be a stony bank! At the back stands the gaunt, grey wall of the abandoned sports centre.

All around are tall trees, with King's Park and a large car-park behind the Main Stand – no narrow streets here – and a line of prim semis pushing up against the New Stand. But the overgrown concrete structure remains a reminder of how Dean Court was forced to conform with its suburban surrounds, when it longed for just a touch of modernity.

·SOUTHAMPTON·

Previous Grounds

Southampton formed in November 1885 as St Mary's YMCA, playing at the Antelope Ground, now the site of Southampton's County Bowling Club. After turning professional and joining the Southern League in 1894, the club, now called Southampton St Mary's moved a few hundred yards to the County Cricket Ground on Northlands Road, and in their first season there won the Championship of 1896–97. They then became a limited company, thereby relinquishing their church origins, and were known thereafter as Southampton, although their nickname 'the Saints' has persisted to this day.

As crowds grew to 12 000 at the County Ground, Southampton decided to look for a new ground. They found a site nearby, although it was an unlikely spot for a football ground.

The Dell

A painting of The Dell in 1889 shows a tranquil pond in sunshine, surrounded by trees, with two small ducks gently gliding over the water. As Peter East in his history of the club points out, it was exactly on this quiet pond that less than a decade later a football ground would be built.

It cost one George Thomas £10 000 to develop the site, his first task being to reduce the pond to a series of underground streams. He then built two fairly sophisticated stands on either side, providing seats for 4000 spectators, with open terracing for a further 20 000. The 'charming' Dell was by no means a rustic enclosure, for its facilities were among the best in the country. In the Main or West Stand were 6-feet deep plunge baths for the players, two showers plus ordinary baths. Around the terracing were very solid iron railings, and there was even a special enclosure for supporters to store their bicycles during games, at a penny a time. The press were not content however, because they had no writing tables -- a common complaint at the time.

Thomas leased the ground to Southampton for £250 a year, and it was proudly opened on 3 September 1898, for a Southern League game v. Brighton United. Not only was The Dell the best non-League ground of the day – and a good deal better than many grounds in the League – the team was by far the most successful professional outfit south of Birmingham.

However, the club started to decline after 1904, and by 1906 had an overdraft of £3000. George Thomas raised the rent to £500, less £100 if certain repairs were carried out, and for a short time there was even the possibility of the club moving to another ground.

Eventually Southampton joined the League in 1920, as part of the mass exodus from the Southern League to the Football League, and it soon became

The house backing onto The Dell, now replaced by the West Stand (BBC Hulton Picture Library)

apparent that some of The Dell's facilities were not quite up to standard. For example, a house still stood at the north end of the West Stand, its rear wall almost bordering on the touchline. It was demolished in 1922 when Southampton won quick promotion to Division Two.

In 1925–26, with the team settling comfortably into the Second Division, the club purchased the ground, including some neighbouring property, but at the sacrifice of selling some of the star players. Money was raised through various schemes to improve The Dell, including a £20000 loan from an insurance company, and a newly-formed supporters' club began fund-raising. The existing West Stand double-decker was built with these extra funds, amid arguments that the team should be put before the ground.

Nevertheless the team did well, and finished the 1928–29 season in their best position yet of fourth in Division Two. Unfortunately only hours after the last home game, the East Stand burnt down, the flames spreading rapidly through the structure, fanned by a strong breeze.

Feverish work during the summer saw the new two-tiered East Stand ready for the start of the next season, and now The Dell had two almost identical stands providing a total of 6600 seats in a claimed overall capacity of 35000, although the figure was never tested.

The 1930s were less successful at The Dell, and when the Second World War broke out Southampton were among the bottom clubs of the Second Division. Being only a mile from the main Southampton docks, the ground's neighbourhood suffered heavily during the Blitz, and in November 1940 a bomb struck the pitch at Milton Road End, causing one of the underground water culverts to break and flood the pitch under a couple of feet of water.

To worsen matters, on 8 April 1941 a fire broke out in the centre of the West Stand, but was prevented from spreading to the wings and was, it is recorded, put out before black-out time.

While this went on, the team played their War League games at the Pirelli General Works sports ground in Eastleigh, and later at Fratton Park, before returning to The Dell.

After the War attendances rose all around the country, and at Southampton it was decided to raise the ground's capacity by erecting platforms of terracing above the Milton Road End terrace. At first two, then three of these odd-looking platforms were built, and they became affectionately known as the Chocolate Boxes. The existing extra level of terracing is really a modern version of the old boxes, which were quite unique at a football ground for being an upper tier of terracing, but without any cover.

The Dell hit the headlines in 1951 as the first English ground to stage a competitive floodlit match. Southampton had been one of the first clubs to install lights in the modern era, costing only £600 and intended primarily for training purposes. A few practice friendlies were held at first, then the club received permission from the Football Combination to stage a reserve match v. Spurs under the lights on 1 October 1951 (see Floodlights).

Since then, the ground seems to have changed little, but there have been substantial alterations, most of them since the introduction of the Safety of Sports Grounds Act. Viewing at The Dell has always been a major problem, one of which the club are acutely aware, but they were certainly unprepared for the large number of changes called for by the local authority safety inspectors. Since 1978 the club have spent up to £1 million on safety measures, using up their entire grant from the Football Grounds Improvement Trust (FGIT) (see Safety). Among the improvements was the complete renewal of barriers in the ground, which worked out cheaper than spending £2000 a year on just testing the old ones.

The Chocolate Boxes came down, but in their place was built a more solid upper tier of terracing, slightly overhanging the back wall on Milton Road. The club wanted to build a similar addition to the Archers Road End terrace, but this was denied planning permission, as the authorities felt that just the slight overhang would be enough to make drivers of high-sided vehicles move towards the middle of the narrow, busy road.

At one stage the club nearly decided to build a new cantilever West Stand estimated to cost £880 000, and there was another suggestion that they should sell up completely for £3 million and rebuild elsewhere, in less confined surroundings. But a new stadium would have cost at least £9 million to build, and the club are now relieved that they stayed at The Dell.

The Dell's highest ever attendance was 31 044, for a Division One match v. Manchester United on 8 October 1969. Since 1978 the ground's capacity has been reduced to 25 000, probably enough to satisfy current demands. Now bench seats have been installed in both stand paddocks, making a total of 9000 seats.

Ground Description

The Dell's real essence lies in its confinement, pressed between two roads which cut across the ground to form a parallelogram, so that each end terrace is like an elongated triangle. From the road to the goal-line is a matter of a few yards at either end. The two stands, facing each other like mirror images in a poor man's Highbury, increase the cloister-like feeling of the ground.

The West Stand is a double-decker, characterized by the lines of green floodlight gantries along the grey pitched roof. These are linked by a steel walkway along the front. There is simply no room to erect corner pylons, so these original gantries have never been replaced. In the centre of the roof is a white canopy housing the television camera platform, and to support it the two central pillars in the stand have

been doubled in thickness. This platform alone cost £36 000 to construct, divided between the club and the two television companies.

An unusual feature of The Dell, seen in both stands, is the arrangement of bench seats in the paddock. The supporters wanted some standing space in these sections, so the paddocks have been divided in half. But to avoid awkward sight lines, seats and terracing have been spliced together at an angle, with a diagonal gangway in between. This method allows the seated spectators to gain a view past the standing ones into the far corner.

There is no players' tunnel in this stand. The dressing rooms are up some stairs at the south end of the stand, so that losing teams have to suffer not only a long trudge to the end of the ground, but then a short climb up to the privacy of their quarters.

Inside the paddock of the West Stand can be seen the effects of some subsidence at The Dell, caused partly by the mass of streams culverted underneath. The rear wall of the stand shows signs of the problem at the southern end. Also in the paddock is a section for the disabled, directly behind the dug-outs.

The East Stand opposite is almost identical to the West, but has no space under the upper tier, and has aluminium rather than wooden bench seats.

To the left is the open Archers Road End, a narrow strip of terracing with St Mark's church and some student flats visible behind. The back of the goal is inches from the perimeter wall, so that fans can almost whisper to the goalkeeper. In fact the pitch is not the shortest length possible, measuring 72 yards, a yard longer than Highbury's, which seems huge in comparison.

To the right is the Milton Road End with two tiers of terracing. This section alone cost just under £500 000 to build in 1981. From the triangular-shaped top tier, which rises quite steeply, is gained a magnificent view of the ground, and to the left, Southampton docks and the distant New Forest.

From here it is evident how much attention has been paid to the ground's safety requirements, for although at first glance The Dell seems quite undeveloped for a First Division venue, every barrier and step is new, every piece of steelwork repainted. The club has made an enormous effort on a difficult site, not as limited as Kenilworth Road perhaps but nevertheless extremely expensive to modernize in proportion to its size.

It is unquestionably a Southern ground, in atmosphere and hue, yet however small and basic it may seem compared with its fellow stadiums in Division One, The Dell has one major asset – an administration which cares for its surroundings. Like Watford, Swansea, Luton, and Ipswich a decade ago, Southampton is a club with advanced ideas living in a small, old ground. In view of football's receding audiences, it is probably happy to stay that way.

·PORTSMOUTH·

Fratton Park

When the town's leading football club, Royal Artillery, was suspended by the FA for breaching amateur regulations, it was decided to form a professional club called Portsmouth. A limited company was set up in 1898, and for £4950 it purchased a market garden near Fratton railway station. The ground was made ready in time for the 1899–1900 season, and by 1902 Portsmouth had won their first Southern League Championship.

The club built a pavilion in the Frogmore Road corner of the ground, in which offices are now housed, and The Pompey public house behind the Main Stand, then a low, all-wooden construction. The buildings' mock-tudor style was extremely popular in vernacular architecture at the turn of the century.

Portsmouth joined the League in 1920 and while on their way up in Division Two they commissioned Archibald Leitch to design a new Main Stand on the south side of the ground next to the pavilion. A brass plate inside the stand shows that the first steel column went up on 17 June 1925, another indicates that J. McKenna, President of the Football League, officially opened the South Stand on 29 August 1925. The stand was one of the grandest in the country at the time.

Having lost the 1929 Cup Final, Portsmouth failed a second time at Wembley in 1934, but their Cup-run netted profits of over £10 000, as did the sale of Jimmy Allen to Villa. With this money in hand the club erected the existing North Stand during the 1934–35 season.

In February 1949 with Portsmouth going for the Double, Fratton Park saw its highest crowd of 51 385 for a 6th Round Cup tie v. Derby. The ground's lights were first switched on in 1953, but their most famous use was on 22 February 1956, the very first Football League match played under floodlights (see Floodlights).

The team was declining by 1957 when the club built the Fratton End Stand, providing covered standing accommodation for 10 000 spectators. It was an early example of prefabricated concrete design and merited a short study in the technical magazine, *Prefabrication* (April 1957, p. 254).

In 1962 the original floodlights were replaced by the existing pylons, a gift from the supporters' club in October of that year. The ground has changed little since, except that the capacity has been reduced to 38 000. There are 7000 seats.

Ground Description

Fratton Park is in the middle of Portsea Island, which is really a peninsular, and is a few hundred yards east of Fratton Station, on the line from Portsmouth to Waterloo. The best approach is along Frogmore Road,

Fratton Park entrance with The Pompey on the right (Simon Inglis)

from Goldsmith Avenue, to the ground's magnificent main entrance which occupies the end of the cul-de-sac. A small, mock-tudor cottage, half-timbered gable window in the centre, is placed over a large gate which leads straight onto the terraces. To the left are the club offices. Just in front is The Pompey, the club's public house, with a sign depicting a player who resembles the Scottish winger, John Robertson, after a gruelling 90 minutes.

Through the large blue gates we come into the south east corner of the ground, with the South Stand to our right. Underneath, it has a system of corridors and stairs like a small business warehouse, a little cramped but well lit from the roof. From inside the ground however, the South Stand is perfection: Leitch at his best. His trademark is especially prominent, the balcony wall criss-crossed with blue steel supports, apparently deeper than its younger sisters at Roker, Ibrox or Goodison, but actually the same dimensions, just lower down. Imagine the Bullens Road Stand at Goodison sunk a few feet into its foundations, moved nearer the pitch and you have Fratton Park's South Stand. (The Everton stand was 1926, Roker Park's 1929 and Ibrox's 1929, so perhaps in 1925 Leitch was just practising at Portsmouth!)

Notice how the skylights along the back of the roof help avoid the gloominess often found in older stands, even if they show up a rather unfortunate combination of blue and purple seats side by side. You will also see that instead of dug-outs, awkward wooden huts have been put onto the terracing on either side of the tunnel, which seems to disappear into the paddock. There is barely room for a television gantry in front of the balcony wall here, and in the past broadcasters have found this side to be too near the pitch. So the cameras were tried opposite, on the North Side, where they found the sun facing them. As they move from one side of the ground to the other, so must the advertisements! Hence the hoardings along the roof of the South Stand.

To the right of the South Stand is the uncovered Milton End. In the north east corner of this terrace where the floodlight pylon stands, is a section often referred to as the 'Boilermakers' Hump', apparently once a favourite spot for local shipyard workers.

To the left is the covered Fratton End; an unusual feature of this terrace is its division into two tiers, with a white wall between top from bottom. Anyone who has stood on the terraces will appreciate the benefit of grabbing a barrier just above such a wall, for the best possible view. Another detail is a clock, set in the centre of the roof fascia, common on side stands but rarely seen on an end roof. The Fratton End Stand itself is plain, but nicely boxed in against the elements. Behind are railway goods' yards. Commendably the club have opted to build a small moat and only a low security fence at this end, thus allowing unhampered vision.

Opposite the South Stand is a deep bank of terracing, on top of which sits a long, low blue stand, angled slightly inwards. The North Stand looks much older than its counterpart, although ten years younger, being mainly wooden. The terrace rear walls, all blue, are particularly high. From the South Side the pitch appears to slope quite badly, but on closer inspection it is the North Side terracing which slopes. The North Stand is built on stilts behind the banking and with much wasted space underneath. Milton Lane runs behind.

Fratton Park has a dowdy sort of appeal. Rather like Burnden Park, one senses that it has had great moments, yet never quite adjusted to the prevailing mediocrity of recent years. Because its surroundings are so dull, there is nothing to divert the eye from the stands which need to be filled with people. Fratton Park is possibly not what strangers might expect when they think of Portsmouth; it feels like a northern ground, inland and serious, unlike more airy coastal grounds such as The Dell or Home Park. Leitch's stand and the half-timbered pavilion entrance are very fine, but many more years collecting dust and they will become poignant relics. Fratton Park needs a dose of success, in the Second Division at the very least.

BRIGHTON & HOVE ·ALBION·

Previous Grounds

A team called Brighton United played on Sussex County Cricket Ground in 1898, but the ground lacked any cover, gates were poor, and the club was wound up two years later. In their place Brighton and Hove Rangers formed, at Home Farm, Withdean. Their players were so keen to establish the club that they would help collect the gate money before kick-off. From August 1901, as Brighton and Hove Albion, they were back at the cricket ground.

Meanwhile, another team, Hove FC had moved from Hove Park the previous April to a site known as Goldstone Bottom, paying rent of £100 a year. The town was clearly not big enough to sustain both clubs, so the following February Albion moved in with Hove, who soon after went back to Hove Park, having sold Albion the ground lease for £40.

Goldstone Ground

How Goldstone Bottom got its name is told in a history of the club by John Vinicombe. Apparently it is derived from a stone reputed to have belonged to Druids and which stood on a local farmer's land. He became so tired of visiting archaeologists that he buried it in 1834. The stone was recovered in 1900 and put up in Hove Park, just across the road from the ground.

When Albion first played at the Goldstone Ground in February 1902, the pitch was overlooked by Goldstone House, home of Alderman Clark, who owned the land on a lease from the Stanford Estate. On the north side was a large pond into which players were known to deliberately kick the ball to soften the leather. In the south east corner was a ladies' section. In 1904 a small, white stand with lattice-work decoration was put up on the West Side. In keeping with the town's genteel image, the stand had been bought from Preston Park where it was used for a horse show. Many years later it was hoisted up and plonked on a raised terrace. During the summer in those peaceful days, lambs would graze on the pitch, and ever since Brighton's reserve team has been nicknamed 'The Lambs'.

When the First World War broke out soldiers were drilled on the pitch, and they practised their marksmanship by potting at crows, but by 1918 the Goldstone was nearly derelict. Extensive redevelopment was necessary and the pond was drained to make way for the North Bank. In 1926 Brighton council bought the ground for £8000 – to Alderman Clark's annoyance since his lease was not expired – but with the important condition that in deference to the view and value of the houses along the rise, no structure

The Goldstone Ground, with the temporary West Stand extension on the right (Sporting Pictures)

higher than 50 feet above pitch level should be built.

The North and South Ends were covered, and then in 1957, to celebrate promotion after 37 years in Division Three, the old West Stand was replaced after over 50 years' service with the present structure, for a sum of around £30000. While in Division Two Brighton's highest crowd, 36747, watched a League match v. Fulham in December 1958.

The first floodlit game was v. Frem, a Danish team, on 10 April 1961. In the late 1970s, in compliance with the Safety of Sports Grounds Act, the North Stand roof came down, while next to it rose a temporary structure, built during the summer of 1979 on promotion to Division One, for £150000. It was not the first of its kind on the West Side, for in 1933 a similar sized extension was built for a cup tie v. West Ham. Even with the extension, the Goldstone was still about the worst in the top division, lacking parking facilities, restricted by the lease of 1926, and with insufficient seats and standing cover. The chairman wanted to move to a new site on the outskirts of town, but the money was simply not available. To improve matters a little, when a fire gutted the South Stand in May 1980, it was extremely well converted to a seated enclosure.

The present capacity is much reduced from 38000 to 28800, with 6050 seats.

Ground Description

Although it is next to a large park, the Goldstone Ground is actually hemmed in by narrow roads, small factories and the natural incline along the East Side. One notices the floodlights first, more in keeping with Brechin than Brighton, with their distinctly Scottish pylons, lamp holders angled down towards the pitch as if bowed in prayer. The system was called 'Drenchliting' by the Edinburgh manufacturers.

The three-quarter length West Stand is drab but spacious, and stands in contrast with its awkward neighbour, the 30-foot extension along the touchline. Tall, with six scaffolding pillars at the front, this Meccano-like structure seats 974, has rubber-covered wooden floors and is made darker inside by a solid blue screen wall at the northern end, perhaps a necessary shield against the wind. Brighton received planning permission for only an initial five years, but if treated well it could stay for years.

To the left is the now uncovered North Stand, really just a bank of terracing. Behind the enormous advertising hoarding which lines the back, is Old Shoreham Road and Hove Park.

The terraces curl round and rise up the open East Side, behind which stand the rows of houses overlooking the ground. All the crush barriers are painted, not in the usual gloss but in matt blue, which stands out most effectively against the light brown concrete.

As it nears the South Stand, the banking falls away rapidly to only a handful of steps by the corner flag. From here you can see how the pitch slopes 4 feet from the North to the South Stand, with its old roof and bright new seats in light and dark blue, which closes off the ground from the less attractive landscape beyond.

Altogether the Goldstone Ground may not be ideal for the car-driving, standing spectator on a wet day, but the club's attention to detail, including good facilities for the disabled in the south west corner and a neatly kept pitch with a fine reputation, all indicate willing, even if the budget is low and the site unpromising.

·13·
SOUTH WEST

·BRISTOL ROVERS·

Previous Grounds

Rovers first played at Purdown in 1883 under the evocative title of Black Arabs. A year later as Eastville Rovers they were at Ashley Hill, a mile west of the present ground, moving later to the Ridgeway, Upper Eastville. Eastville Stadium was the home of Harlequin Rugby Club, but in 1896 a syndicate of 'well-wishers' bought it for the football club. Rovers spent £1255 14s on laying out the ground for 20 000, with a small stand on the South Side. They also adopted professionalism and the name Bristol Eastville Rovers, dropping 'Eastville' a year later. The first game, a 5-0 defeat by Aston Villa, was on 3 April 1897. Rovers bought the 16-acre site later that year for just £150.

Eastville

No other League ground has been the subject of so much legal and emotional wrangling as Eastville, and the issue is still not fully resolved. It is a complicated story, well told by the club's secretary, Gordon Bennett, who might well exclaim after the club's recent history!

For two decades after 1897 the prospects seemed high. As crowds grew, Eastville's capacity was extended to 30 000, and cover provided on both sides. Three years after joining the League in 1921, a large South Stand was built, in conventional 1920s' style, with seats behind a standing paddock. The saga of Eastville really begins in 1931 when the ground's shape was altered to accommodate greyhound racing, operated by a separate company which became Rovers' tenant. By 1939, when the club had to seek re-election, a debt of nearly £16 000 had accumulated. Although his fellow directors refused to sanction the ideal, the chairman Fred Ashmead agreed to sell Eastville to the greyhound company for £12 000, in 1940.

Then in 1944 two members of the greyhound company bought a controlling interest in Rovers. They undoubtedly helped the team revive after the War,

Eastville with the greyhound results board and enclosed restaurant in the Main Stand. There were once flower beds behind each goal (Simon Inglis)

operating a tight policy of 'No Buy, No Sell' for some years, but they had to give up their majority shares in 1951 after investigations into the running of the club and the stadium company.

In 1958, as part of a general scheme of improvement, the present North Stand was built, paid for largely by the supporters, although three out of five projected bays were completed only. But the stand still automatically became part of the stadium company's property. The first floodlit game was in September 1959 v. Ipswich, after Rovers' best ever run in the Second Division. That year the club were granted a new 21-year lease, 'on favourable terms' and Eastville's record crowd of 38 472 watched a Cup match v. Preston the following January.

The Bristol Stadium Company tried to introduce speedway to Eastville in 1977, but the council stopped this after two seasons.

The 21-year lease was due to expire on 31 December 1979, and after repeated attempts to negotiate new terms, Rovers decided to exercise their right as tenants, under an Act of 1954, and take the dispute to the High Court. A hearing was set for 30 November 1981.

The club was determined to stay at Eastville, the

scene of so many happy years, not only for the supporters, but because they had invested so much capital in the ground, including £70000 on safety improvements since 1975.

The first blow fell on 16 August 1980. The South Stand was destroyed by fire, rendering the whole South Side unusable. Rovers were forced to play five 'home' games at Ashton Gate. Anxiously gauging average attendance Rovers noted that it was about 1000 lower than for the ensuing games against more attractive opposition at Eastville. Of course some die-hards would have died before watching Rovers at City's ground, but a permanent ground-sharing scheme at least showed signs of working, once regulars became used to the idea.

It was still a great shock when the axe did fall. If Rovers and the Stadium Company had left negotiations until the High Court hearing, their legal costs would have been a minimum of £50000 each and so instead they met a week earlier on 23 November. Rovers expected compromise, but instead were given until 15 May 1982 to leave Eastville.

Rovers agreed to accept £280000 compensation in return for giving up their rights under the Landlord and Tenant Act. They could also use Eastville rent free till the end of the season (they had been relegated to Division Three a few months earlier).

Negotiations with Bristol City began well. Rovers would pay £40000 annual rent and retain their autonomy. A public letter in December 1981 pronounced the end of Eastville ground, but the start of a brave new experiment that would be an example to every other city with two or more major clubs. Bristol were following the example set by cities all over Europe and South America. There was even talk of building a purpose-built multi-sports stadium. But as Rovers began to pack, City started to fold.

The Board of the new Bristol City (1982) company had different priorities and doubled the rent agreed with their predecessors. Rovers immediately reopened negotiations with the stadium company, and for good measure with Bath City FC, 13 miles from Eastville. The result was a further five-year licence to use Eastville, for a rent of £52000 a year. City meanwhile plummeted past Rovers into Division Four. For the time being, Bristol Rovers lead a tenuous existence, with no security of tenure at the end of five years, and no presence at Eastville except on match days. Administration is conducted from the club's 11-acre Hambrook training ground, which lies in a green belt and so cannot be developed further. The only Rovers' man at Eastville is the groundsman.

Ground Description

Eastville is closer to a motorway than any other ground in the country. Indeed it has been known for up to 200 people with cars to stop on the hard shoulder for a free view of the match, before getting moved on. The ground is ovoid, with large open spaces behind either end. It is littered with debris, like a building site, and has all the necessary trappings for greyhound racing.

In one corner of the Main Stand is a glass-fronted restaurant, for example, and an odd gantry suspended from the roof. It has never been a particularly distinguished stand – a typical brick and steel, post and beam design of the 1950s – but now it looks cluttered. To the right, on the same side, is a small primitive cover over the terracing, which curves round the track to the West End. The cover over this has a large results board across the roof, incomprehensible to all but race-goers, and a line of betting windows and a cafe at the back. Next to this is an older standing cover. Behind are some gas works. In the south west corner, opposite the Main Stand, are all the kennels and paraphernalia of greyhound traps, next to the now open South Side, where once stood a full length two-tier stand. A thin line of terracing is all that remains.

The elevated M32 Parkway, which links the city centre with the M4, touches the ground in the south east corner, where the uncovered East End banking is highest. One is constantly aware of traffic noise.

This end used to have a railway line running behind, and was known as 'the 13 arches end' till the Main Stand blocked the view. The North Side of this terrace is now an ill-concealed dumping ground for the stadium, and it is small wonder the ground's capacity has been cut from 38500 to 12500. Even the 1350 seats are reduced. It would cost Rovers, not their landlords, £50000 to add another 6000 places.

Finally the pitch, the only part of the ground still tended by Rovers. It used to flood frequently, until raised by 20 inches in 1950.

For many years, in the semi-circles behind each goal were decorative beds of flowers, a feature for which Eastville was justifiably renowned. The pitch seems large because of the surrounding track, but at 110×70 yards, is the smallest in the Football League, together with Halifax and Swansea. Eastville is host to a lucrative twice-weekly market, and has a contract with the Bookmakers' Afternoon Greyhound Service. There is still room for speedway and supermarket development. With a motorway exit just a few hundred yards away, Eastville represents something of a developer's dream.

The ideal solution, for Rovers and the community, would be to build a new multi-sports stadium on this very site. Failing such a bold initiative, ground sharing at Ashton Gate is inevitable.

·BRISTOL CITY·

Previous Grounds

Formed as Bristol South End in 1894, their first ground was at St John's Lane, Bedminster, still in use today as a sports ground. It was here that an early form of ground advertising was first used. South End became Bristol City in 1897 and simultaneously one of several professional teams in the city. Apart from Eastville Rovers, there was Warmley, whose ground held 9000, St George FC and a club called Bedminster, who played at Ashton Gate. As rationalization inevitably occurred, City amalgamated with but soon absorbed Bedminster, beginning in 1900. Both grounds were used alternately, but as Ashton Gate had an iron stand and a better pitch, it was the site chosen when Bedminster was absorbed completely and City settled permanently in 1904.

Ashton Gate

Ashton Gate's beginnings is well detailed in the club's history by Peter Godsiff. In the early years there were two stands on either side of the pitch, No. 1 and No. 2 Stands, but the first development as we know it today was at the Winterstoke Road End. This covered terrace was built in the late 1920s after the sale of two players, Keating and Bourton, for £3000. For a time it was called the Keating Stand. While in Division Three, City's record crowd of 43 335 assembled for a Cup match v. Preston in February, 1935. Yet such were the club's financial problems during this period that they offered to sell Ashton Gate to Bristol Corporation for £16 000, in return for a long lease with a rental of £640 a year. The Corporation declined.

In February 1941 half of the No. 1 Stand was destroyed by an unexploded bomb and the other half was bombed the following night. City received £16 500 from the War Damages Commission towards the rebuilding costs of £18 000, but by the time the existing Grand Stand was completed in the 1950s, the cost had escalated to £30 000. The supporters' club, who wanted accomodation underneath the stand, contributed £3000 for steelwork City could not afford.

At this time, the club chairman was Harry Dolman, who designed the club's first floodlights. Set on removable poles along each touchline, they had to be switched on individually. Their first use was in a friendly v. Wolves in January 1953. Floodlit rugby was also staged. The existing pylons cost £25 000 and were also switched on for a game v. Wolves in December 1965.

Opposite the Grand Stand, behind the old wooden cover, arose a new council block called Southbow House, from whose roof the view was so good that the caretaker would charge people to watch games, a practice which ended with the building of the new

Ashton Gate's Dolman Stand, built on the 'goalpost' principle later used at Ibrox (Sporting Pictures)

stand, named after Harry Dolman. As before costs rose faster than the structure. The first estimate was for £50 000, but by the time it was opened in 1970, and an indoor bowling green installed underneath, the cost was £235 000. The debt incurred was enormous for a Second Division club, and City had to sell all 16 of its club houses and obtain pledges of £3000 each from the FA, various companies and individuals. Yet one cannot blame the Dolman Stand for City's subsequent decline, because six years after its completion, the club won promotion to Division One, after a 54-year absence. City's record descent to the Fourth Division thereafter was due to other causes, although the drop in average gates from 19 000 to around 4000 made any repayments of debts impossible, and led to the winding up of the original 1897 Limited Company. Bristol City can at least claim to have had the best ground of any club ever to have occuped 92nd place in the League.

Ground Description

In 1982 no other ground had witnessed such a change in fortune in just 27 months of its existence. But the first-class facilities remain. The Grand Stand sits on a bank of terracing, not quite running the length of the pitch. The white terrace rear wall stands out, and unusually is castellated at the centre. From the seats you can see a famous Bristol landmark, Cabot Tower, which stands on a hill due north across the River Avon, to the left of the Dolman Stand opposite.

City's pride, or rather white elephant, is this modern, full-length stand whose roof is suspended from a cross girder mounted on two uprights outside the screen walls, as at Ibrox. Like a cantilever, the view from the stand is totally unimpaired by any uprights. In order to create sufficient height needed for the facilities beneath, the stand is fronted by a high, plain brick wall, which even with the very narrow terrace in front rather isolates it from the rest of the ground (as at Chester and Swindon). Large tobacco advertisements on this wall and elsewhere at Ashton Gate hardly enhance its appearance. The need, all too common, is for a club crest, or for their name, or flags, or something to liven up the stand.

But the view from all 5675 seats is superb, not only of the pitch but of Wills' Bonded warehouses to the left beyond the Winterstoke Road End, of the green expanse of Ashton Park straight ahead, and to the right of the hills beyond the Avon Bridge and Clifton Suspension Bridge. Behind the Dolman Stand is Southbow House, and the Bristol Bowling Club.

Harry Dolman was a keen bowler, hence the long, low hall underneath the stand, having two artificial flat greens, which alone cost £20 000 to lay. The bowling club pays City a £20 000 annual rent, and has a thousand members, who can play quite undisturbed even during a football match.

The Winterstoke Road End, or Covered End, but no longer the Keating Stand, is in fine condition for one so old, although it suffers in design from some awkward pillars at the front. The roof extends notably, and perhaps unnecessarily some 30 yards beyond the sidelines.

Opposite is the red-fenced Open End, backed by houses along Ashton Road. The floodlight pylons, which mark out the ground for miles around, are of the Scottish design.

Whenever there have been moves by either Bristol club towards ground sharing, Ashton Gate, with its superior facilities and 30 868 capacity (over twice that of Eastville's) is the natural choice. Rovers played here five times in 1980 when their own South Stand burned down, and were ready to move here permanently in 1981 before settling their dispute with the owners of Eastville. The economic sense of ground sharing is obvious but rivalry in Bristol is as fierce as in any other city, and it will need a severe jolt before Ashton Gate has to accommodate both teams, as surely it must.

◆ SWINDON TOWN ◆

Previous Grounds

Swindon did not stay long at their first ground in 1881. It was a field in the Old Town area, next to a quarry, now part of Bradford Road and Avenue Road. After a small boy fell into the quarry during a match the club moved to Globe Field, now Brunswick Street and Lansdowne Road, then in 1884 to the Croft, home of Swindon Rangers Rugby Club. Swindon switched to the County Ground in 1895 but began playing on where the cricket pitch is now.

County Ground

The club's early years at the County Ground were successful enough for them to move away from the cricket pitch and establish a separate enclosure beyond the boundary. The terraces were laid out and a full-length grandstand built by 1911. In 1920 Swindon joined the League.

The Shrivenham Road Side was first covered in 1932, and in August 1938 the Town End covered terrace, then called the Hotel End, was opened. The supporters' club met the cost of £4300. During the Second World War, the County Ground became a prisoner-of-war camp, with huts placed on the pitch.

The ground staged one of the first floodlit games in modern times, an exhibition match v. Bristol City in April 1951. There were just eight lamps behind each goal. In February 1956 Swindon were also one of the first clubs to host a League fixture under lights, by then improved from the originals. The present pylons date from 1960.

A new stand for the Shrivenham Road Side was bought in 1958 from the grounds of the Aldershot Tattoo, but there is no record of how long it had stood there. Thirty years would be a fair estimate. The stand was one of two at Aldershot's military grounds, the other went to Accrington Stanley. The original Main Stand made way for the present North Stand in 1971. Similar to one at Chester, it cost £264 000, and is the only stand in Britain to have a bookmaker's shop underneath, next to a squash club. Swindon Council, which owns the site, rent the space independently.

The highest gate at the County Ground was 32 000 for a Cup-tie v. double winners Arsenal in January 1972. Capacity is now 26 000, including 6423 seats, so the ground seems well suited for future footballing needs.

Ground Description

From certain approach roads, because the County Ground stands on such flat land and is surrounded by low buildings and open space, it is visible from a long way off. On arrival you will notice that only one end of the ground does not border on open land. Since the land belongs to the council, it has been suggested that

The ex-Aldershot tattoo stand on Shrivenham Road at Swindon's County Ground (Adrian Gibson)

the council should have built a leisure centre at the County Ground, at the same time as the North Stand was built, instead of at another site called 'The Oasis'. Certainly the ground's central location makes the surrounding land ripe for development.

The North Stand is not only similar in design to Chester's Main Stand, it also has a wide patch of ground between a high front wall and the touchline. The gaps exist because the new stands were constructed directly behind the old ones, in order to minimize disruption during building. The area desperately needs something better than the current assemblage of wooden shelters and temporary huts. The drab brick frontage could also be brightened up. Brightness is, however, not a problem inside the stand, where a sickly mix of blue, orange, lemon and green plastic seats makes one long for higher attendances! In contrast, behind the stand and across the cricket pitch where Wiltshire County Cricket team play, is a delightful wooden cricket pavilion, tastefully painted but probably extremely uncomfortable.

To the left is the open Stratton Bank, named after a nearby district, with a distinctive, if dated, clock at the back. To the right is the covered Town End for standing, with security fencing going right up behind the goal to the roof.

But the best feature of the County Ground is opposite the North Stand. Approached from Shrivenham Road, the South Stand, with its large green corrugated back, appears to have grown out of the parkland on which it rests. There are no fences or walls to separate it from the passing pedestrians. Entrance is from one of several snake-like stairways which rise from the banks below. It is a double-decker angled slightly inwards at each end, with a long line of pillars at the front, but the upper tier of seating is strangely shallow. You feel it ought to extend much more forward.

At the west end of the seats is a boxed-off section, apparently the old tea room. So much steel work for only 1423 seats. The paintwork is predominantly cream and green, a combination used to such good effect at Highbury, but closer inspection reveals much rust. Nevertheless the South Stand has a unique character, both outside and in, and it is to be hoped that with so much room in front of the North Stand no-one is tempted to move the pitch and redevelop this side of the ground. If they do, maybe another club will give it a third home, for there is no other stand like it in the League.

◆ PLYMOUTH ARGYLE ◆

Home Park

Plymouth formed in 1886 as the Argyle Athletic Club, a group of amateurs willing to play whatever sport they fancied, be it cricket, football, rugby or athletics. They had no settled home of their own, playing instead on their opponents' grounds, and then on various pitches in the Plymouth area. But in 1901 they were fortunate in securing a long and inexpensive lease on a ground called Home Park. The owners were only too happy to let Argyle move in, for it had originally been built for the Devonport Rugby Club, but since the club had departed after a rent dispute, the ground had lain deserted for three years.

Argyle took over on Whit Monday 1901, and immediately held a series of popular events. Even so, the leaseholder, Clarence Spooner decided that amateur sport did not yield sufficient revenue to maintain such a large ground. Since cities such as Bristol, Southampton and Portsmouth had their own senior football clubs, and the entire county of Devon had not one, it was decided that the successful amateur Argyle Athletic team should join the ranks of the professionals.

To test public reaction, Spooner invited some of the top clubs in the country to play Argyle in exhibition matches at Home Park. Aston Villa came first and beat Argyle 7-0 in front of an encouraging 16 000 crowd. Others followed, and on 24 April 1903 Home Park staged a game between The Wednesday and Notts County, both First Division clubs, to give the public a truer example of League standards.

The success of these matches persuaded Argyle to concentrate on professional football and take on a new lease of the ground. On 5 September 1903 Home Park staged its first senior competitive game, v. Northampton Town in the Southern League, watched by 4438.

Home Park then was surrounded by farms. One end of the ground is still known as Barn Park. The approaches to Home Park were along country paths, the main one leading from Pennycomequick between hedges and over a stile just before the ground. There was always considerable congestion at this point on match days. Inside, the ground had one small wooden grandstand, rough cinder banking on three sides, with no barriers, no cover and precious few facilities. But as we learn from W. S. Tonkin's history of the club (1963), there were two other structures built. One was known affectionately, or derisively, as the 'flower-pot', and held 100 spectators on the Popular Side. The other was a press-box, built on the halfway line high up on stilts, because carrier pigeons were then the reporters' fastest link with their offices.

Argyle won their first major honour in 1913, the Southern League Championship, then during the First World War the ground was placed at the dis-posal of Service teams.

In 1920 the club joined its fellow Southern Leaguers in a mass exodus to the Football League. To celebrate promotion to Division Two in 1930 an £11 000 grandstand was built in place of the old wooden one. At the same time the supporters' club paid £1511 for the erection of a roof, giving shelter for 6000 spectators at the Devonport or Milehouse End. Two years later this cover was extended towards the Grand Stand, for £400, and concrete terracing laid.

Home Park's record attendance of 43 596 came to see Plymouth play Aston Villa, in that club's first ever season out of Division One, on 10 October 1936. Also in 1936 the entrance to Home Park was rebuilt, again paid for by the supporters' club.

During the Second World War, as an important naval base, Plymouth became a natural target for the German bombers. Home Park was closed between 1940–45 but did not escape the air raids. The pitch was covered in bomb craters, but more distressing, the Grand Stand was completely destroyed by high explosives and fire, set off by incendiaries and made worse by piles of furniture people had stored in the stand during the raids.

For four years the ground lay in a heap of rubble and devastation, the grass became overgrown, twisted steelwork littered the craters, and nothing could be done until 1945. Fortunately for the club, a new board of directors under the chairmanship of Sir Clifford Tozer dedicated themselves to the enormous task of rebuilding both the club and its ground. Tons of rubble from the ruins of the town centre were dumped in the craters and on the banking around the pitch. Old tramcars were used as offices, army huts became dressing rooms, railway sleepers were laid on the terraces. The wrecked stand was cleared and temporary uncovered seating installed in its place. In the corner of the pitch a wooden pavilion was built for the directors. Home Park was back in use by the beginning of the 1946–47 season.

Two years later Argyle won the Third Division, and on their return to Division Two opened the present Grand Stand, an impressive double-decker in the pre-war style of Archibald Leitch, almost as if the club had simply followed the late architect's plans from the mid-1930s (see Design). It was certainly the last of this type ever built. On 26 October 1953 the club officially switched on their floodlights at Home Park for a friendly v. Exeter City. Unfortunately only 2000 attended the game, played in poor weather, whereas a total of 12 000 had seen two earlier reserve matches under the new lights.

In 1963–64 a large cover was erected over the Popular or Lyndhurst Side, so that Home Park was now open at only one end. In 1969 extra seats were installed in the Grand Stand, giving a total number of 4100 seats, in a capacity of 40 000.

The Devonport End roof was deemed to be unsafe in 1977. It would have cost £50 000 to repair, or £70 000 to dismantle and restore. For £100 000 Plymouth

Leitch's spirit lives on at Home Park. The old Directors' Stand in the far corner was built after the disruption caused by German bombs (Adrian Gibson)

could have replaced it completely. But they had neither £50 000 nor £100 000, so the roof came down and the end remains open. At least something was saved. The roof sheeting was used as fencing round the ground.

The effect on Home Park's capacity was not all that marked. It now stands at 38 000, and despite the loss of the Devonport End roof, that includes 20 000 under cover.

Home Park has two additional points of interest in its history. In 1960 the ground became the centre of a test case, between the club and the authorities. The Lands Tribunal assessed Home Park's rateable value at £2250 a year. Argyle appealed against this amount, arguing that a football club was the only possible tenant of such a site. They also invoked pleas of tradition and limited finances, with the result that the rates were lowered by a Court of Appeal.

Secondly, in 1977 Home Park staged a European Cup Winners Cup match (although Argyle had never progressed further than the 5th Round of the FA Cup). This was because Manchester United supporters had rioted in France and the club was ordered to play its tie v. St Etienne at least 200 miles from Old Trafford (Manchester is 280 miles from Plymouth).

Ground Description

It is apt that Plymouth Argyle should play in green, because the overwhelming impression of Home Park and the surrounding area is of greenery. There is not a prouder, more open location for a League ground than that enjoyed at Plymouth.

The main approach to Home Park leads into a vast car-park with room for 2000 vehicles. The ground stands on a slight, grass-covered rise, surrounded by trees and meandering pathways.

Behind the Grand Stand is an open plain, on which stands the Mayflower Sports Centre, a swimming pool and municipal football pitches. Argyle have two training pitches nearby, known as Harper's Field, named after a famous Scottish international who joined the club from Arsenal in the early 1930s and served thereafter as player, trainer and groundsman. On the other sides of the ground are Central Park and the ground of Plymouth Cricket Club.

We pass through the main entrance, above which is a plaque recording its construction in 1936 and the name of A. C. Ballard, president of the supporters' club at the time. The detached offices are on the right. But once inside the ground, a sense of openness is still prevalent.

The Main Stand, though substantial, manages to

seem quite light and airy, with a green and white balcony wall, in typical Leitch style (as for example on White Hart Lane's East Stand). A large uncovered paddock with silver crush barriers stands in front. Even the details seem delicate. There are flower boxes over the players' tunnel. The lower tier of seats behind the paddock is named the Mayflower Stand. There are glass panels along the rear wall, creating the impression of an enormous greenhouse – pleasantly light but solid.

From here to the right is a small pavilion in the corner, once for directors but now used by the announcer and the disabled. The only blot on the landscape is the security fencing at this end, a legacy of Chelsea's visit some years ago. The terrace is called Barn Park and is rather overgrown; at the top is another hut, used as a refreshment bar. Tree-lined steps on the far side lead down into the public park and have prominent signs above each section, as on end-of-the-line tube stations on the outskirts of London, except that this one is called '10 STEPS START HERE', and Ongar is over 200 miles away.

Opposite the Main Stand, backed by yet more trees and more greenery, is the Popular or Lyndhurst Side. This is another pleasant section, with wide terracing and silver barriers, covered by a well-lit roof. The steel-work is green and cream with black trimming, like a Southern Counties' bus station.

To the left is the now open Devonport End, curiously divided into two sections by a wide gap on one side of the goal. This is to facilitate the entrance of marching bands, tattoos and such like; Home Park is rented from the local council, and the club therefore have obligations to fulfil.

Plymouth is the second largest city in England never to have had a First Division club (Hull is the biggest), and it shows at Home Park. Rather like the city centre itself, there is plenty of space to breathe, and to cast a wide view over the surroundings. There is orderliness, not dull but reassuring.

But Home Park is obviously a ground untainted by glamour, unsullied by the constant demands of 'big matches'. It has the scale of the First Division, and the calm of the Third.

·EXETER CITY·

St James' Park

Though much less famous and imposing than its namesake in Newcastle, St James' Park, Exeter has a history as old and as colourful dating back to at least 1894. For some years a team called Exeter United used the ground, sharing it with a farmer who grazed his pigs there before slaughter. Such 'ground sharing' schemes were then quite common (see for example Brighton).

In 1904 Exeter City were formed at St James' Park from the successful St Sidwell's Old Boys team, and when in 1908 they turned professional and joined the Southern League, the first grandstand was built. Opposite, the terrace was nicknamed the 'flower-pot'.

In 1910–11 first Nelson, then Burnley refused to play City in the FA Cup unless another venue was chosen, because the St James' Park pitch was not long enough to meet FA requirements. This was a source of considerable annoyance to Exeter, badly in need of the revenue, but the owner of the land adjoining the far end of the pitch refused to sell them part of his land. City therefore began negotiating for the purchase of the St Thomas's County Rugby Ground on the other side of the city, until in 1911 the local MP, H. E. Duke, came to their rescue. He persuaded the landlord to part with some of his land, and Exeter were able to extend the pitch, first used on 14 October 1911. Before the game v. West Ham, H. E. Duke's daughter cut a red and white ribbon stretched across the new section of the pitch and then hoisted the new Exeter City flag. Among the attendance of 7000 people were the Archdeacon, several councillors, and the architect Archibald Lucas. In recognition of H. E. Duke's invaluable assistance, for some years that end of the ground was called the Duke Bank.

On 24 June 1921, at the end of their first season in the League, City purchased the 3.7-acre site for just over £5000, most of which came from the sale of goalkeeper Dick Pym to Bolton.

In 1925 the wooden cover now called the Cowshed was built, and a few months later on 17 November, fire destroyed the original Main Stand, together with all the players' kit, except for defender Bob Pollard's boots which were being repaired in Northampton. The present Main Stand was built during the following summer, after delays caused by the General Strike. The early 1930s were happy years at St James' Park. City enjoyed their best ever run in the FA Cup, which ended with the visit of Sunderland for a 6th Round replay on 4 March 1931. The game attracted City's highest gate, 20 984. The Cowshed was extended to its present length the following year, then in 1933 the club achieved their highest ever placing in the League, runners-up in Division Three South. St James' Park has changed little since. During the Second World War, US Army troops moved

St James' Park (Aerofilms)

into the ground, using the pitch for training and the stand for cooking and sleeping.

Floodlights were installed relatively early at Exeter, as at several smaller southern clubs. The first game was v. Plymouth in 1953. The lights were primitive indeed, but have been updated twice since, although they are still fairly basic.

St James' Park has a capacity of 17 500, including 1742 seats.

Ground Description

Like the town of Exeter itself, St James' Park is a rather sleepy, old-fashioned but appealing ground, caught in the midst of narrow, meandering streets. It was said that supporters would forecast match results by the relative positions of gulls which habitually settled on the crossbars at each end. The ground also has its own railway station, a few yards from the main entrance. The railway line, which links Exmouth with Exeter, runs directly behind the north east corner of the Main Stand, its grass-covered cutting providing a pedestal for the club's buildings above.

In the other corner of this side is the Grecian Gate (City are nicknamed The Grecians), which despite its romantic title, is hardly inspiring. It was paid for by the supporters' club after the War. The Main Stand runs three-quarters of the pitch's length and is the standard pre-war small club construction – sloping roof, dark wooden interior, glass screen walls – but with the players' tunnel, over which hangs the club crest, at the south end of the stand. Along the front of the roof and at either side are 13 floodlight poles, barely 2 yards higher than the gutters. They must be the lowest in the League, and make it hard to spot the ground from a distance.

From this side you can see the St James' Road open terrace to the right, just 13 steps deep, behind which the houses opposite command an uninterrupted view of the pitch. The turnstiles at this end of the ground are open, an unusual feature. Note that the two telegraph poles at either end of the ground, in the middle of the terraces, were part of the original floodlighting system.

To the left is the old Duke Bank, now known as the Big Bank. Between this rather irregular open mound and the Main Stand, where the railway cutting is within yards of the corner flag, there is no terracing, and the groundsman has planted a row of lime trees to help stop the ball going onto the line below.

Opposite is the 'Cowshed', a long low cover over some rather ramshackle wooden terracing. The darkness caused by the roof is worsened by some strangely placed advertisement hoardings hung along the gutters. A most unusual aspect of this side is the fact that the terracing starts about 4 feet above the pitch level, with a grass slope running from the touchline up to the front fence. This makes the Cowshed seem even more makeshift, and the name therefore that much more appropriate. In the centre of the grass slope is a cut-away section which the players used to use for shooting practice against the stand wall. Behind the stand, clearly visible because there is only a low back fence along one half, is the Bishop Blackhall School. On the roof are another 13 floodlight poles.

Much of the ground looks ready to fall down, as if a combination of nails, moss, wire and paint keeps St James' Park standing. But on a big match day the atmosphere is as vibrant as anywhere. Stepping through the Grecian Gate, you find a lovely football ground, quite unlike any other; a picture of warm red and green virtually untouched by the worst excesses of modernity, as quaintly southern as its namesake is so ruggedly northern.

·TORQUAY UNITED·

Previous Grounds

The club began in 1898 at Teignmouth Road, moving two years later to the Torquay Recreation Ground. In 1905 they were at Cricket Field Road, followed by the Torquay Cricket Ground in 1907. It is said that they should never have left this ground, now used by Torquay Athletic Rugby Club, because it is close to the station, on the sea front and situated in a natural bowl. But Plainmoor offered greater working class support, so as Torquay Town, they moved in 1910.

Plainmoor

Plainmoor is rented at a nominal rent from the council, which was bequeathed the land by the Cary Estate, on the condition that it would always be open for public recreation. In theory therefore, anyone can walk across the pitch at any time.

Torquay became United in 1921, after merging with Babbacombe FC, and joined the League six years later. The all-wooden Main Stand, which still occupies two-thirds of the South Side, was just finished in time for their first League fixture. It had come from Buckfastleigh racecourse, ten miles east.

In the early 1950s the Popular Side opposite was partly covered, as the team began a successful run. The visit of Huddersfield in the 4th Round of the FA Cup attracted Plainmoor's largest attendance, 21 908 in January 1955. A new end section was added to the Main Stand at this time, and floodlights on poles were installed for a friendly v. Birmingham in November 1954. They were not good enough for competitive games and had to be replaced late in the decade. The existing corner pylons date from the mid-1960s.

A few years later, the concrete cantilever 'Mini-Stand' went up on the Babbacombe End in place of the 'Cowshed' and would have covered the whole end had funds not run out.

Torbay Council has talked of resiting the club in a projected sports complex, but for the foreseeable future Plainmoor, with a 20 000 capacity and 1500 seats copes well enough.

Ground Description

Long before nearing Plainmoor you see signs pointing the way, almost pleading for your interest. The council obviously sees the value of a League club in its midst.

The ground is edged by neat avenues of daintily gabled guest houses and homes, all faced in light granite. Entering through the main gate you pass a white, detached chalet with porch, the club offices, and further along is the back of the Main Stand, wooden slatted with small windows. The stand is low, built entirely in dark wood, with blue and yellow pointed boards lining the gutters, like bunting. It is a showground stand, crafted and creaky, and is as much a reflection of its age as the 1950s' extension next to it; drab and metallic. The stanchions on the roof were for the old floodlights.

Left is the Ellacombe End, named after the district, in the centre of which stands the grey Mini-Stand, like an overgrown bus shelter. It is flanked by two open terraces with wooden sleepers, but without crush barriers. Lining the front is an unpopular, much regretted security fence, erected after a pitch invasion.

The Popular Side on Marnham Road has a flat section in front of a 40-yard covered terrace, and the open Babbacombe End on the right is another mound with sleepers but no barriers. Behind it are immaculate gardens with granite walls. Even the floodlights, squat and low, do not spoil the scale. They are like cartoon floodlights in a Roy of the Rovers comic.

I doubt if the neighbours would want to be troubled by enormous crowds too often and they are probably content that the ground is slightly old-fashioned, a threat to no-one. A real 'home' ground.

Plainmoor's Main Stand, formerly at a racecourse (Adrian Gibson)

·14·
SOUTH WALES AND BORDER

·HEREFORD UNITED·

Edgar Street

Edgar Street was originally the home of the town's senior club, Hereford City, who let United share the ground when they were formed in 1924. City were almost defunct by the time United joined the Southern League in 1939; and United went on to establish themselves as a consistent force in the early rounds of the FA Cup. They were one of the very first clubs in the country to have floodlights, given to them by a local firm which had constructed the Skylon for the

1951 Festival of Britain Exhibition. The first floodlit game was against Walsall in the Birmingham League in March 1953. Hereford's record crowd, 18114, came for one of their many Cup matches with League opposition, in January 1958 v. Sheffield Wednesday.

In 1968 the cantilevered Main Stand was built, no doubt a further factor in their successful application to join the League in 1972, in place of Barrow. A wave of optimism following quick progress to Division Two, led to the erection of another cantilever stand in 1974. The Len Weston Stand was named after the club president who had died just before seeing his dream of League football at Hereford come true.

The narrow, prefabricated Len Weston cantilever stand at Edgar Street (Simon Inglis)

Edgar Street thus became the only non-First Division ground to have two cantilevered stands, albeit comparatively small ones. There are 2300 seats altogether, in a capacity of 17500.

Ground Description

Edgar Street is on very flat land, with a light-industrial estate and a vast parking area on two sides.

The Main Stand is characterized by deep overhanging roof fascia, and at its front, at pitch level, by a box-like vice-president's club resembling a modern house extension overlooking a garden lawn. The large windows, which must give the players a clear view of the bar during games, are only 10 feet from the touchline. Further along, the secretary's office window also looks out onto the pitch.

Next to the Main Stand on the right, the terrace has been removed and foundations for a stand extension laid. From here the terrace curves round in a big semi-circle behind the right hand or northern goal at the Merton Meadow End. The whole site occupies what used to be Merton Meadow. There was once a thin running track all round the perimeter, but the stands on both sides now cover the straights, and the semi-circles at each end are walled in.

A simple rectangular cover sits on the rounded terracing, from where you can see the medieval tower of Hereford Cathedral straight ahead.

Both ends of the ground are the same shape, although the Blackfriars Street End opposite has a wider roof. In the main reception area is a plaque which records the names of those who donated 250 or more bricks to the Blackfriars Street Brick Wall Fund in 1976.

The Len Weston Stand, made out of pre-cast concrete for just £30000, is most unusual. Firstly, it covers a thin side of the ground hemmed in by Edgar Street, so by necessity is tall and narrow. The steep upper tier of 1200 seats, covered by the cantilever roof, is divided into only six rows, supported underneath by concrete pillars on a standing terrace. A double-decker stand in such a confined space is remarkable for such a small outlay.

Secondly, the stand follows not the line of the pitch but Edgar Street, and so the ends are further from the pitch than the centre, the exact opposite of many stands which are angled from the middle inwards.

Another visual curiosity is the floodlighting system. The four gantries are proportionately large and almost half the height of the pylons they rest on. The awkward proportions are accentuated by having only eight tiny lamps mounted on each gantry.

Most noticeable of all however is the pitch, the widest in the League. Measuring 80 yards across it is a full 30 feet wider than the smallest in England.

This width, despite two such modern stands, combined with the distance from each end terrace to the goal-lines and the lack of anything taller than a tree all round the ground, gives Edgar Street an exposed, even rather unspoilt appearance.

◆ SWANSEA CITY ◆

Vetch Field

Swansea Town was one of several teams in South Wales to begin their professional life just before the First World War, encouraged by the Southern League in its attempts to keep pace with the Football League. Town had actually formed at the turn of the century, and moved to Vetch Field in 1912 when they became a limited company. Before Town, an amateur team called Swansea Villa played at the ground, renting it from the local gas company. A tithe map of 1843 shows the site as 'cae vetches', a field for growing vetch or tare, a type of bean used for cattle fodder. David Farmer's history of the club (*Swansea City 1912–82*, Pelham Books, 1982) tells us that the first building at Vetch Field occurred in 1913, when the present Main Stand was built on Glamorgan Street, just after Town had won their first Welsh Cup Final. But for the first season the pitch was cinders only, and until turf was laid the players had to wear knee pads!

The 1920s were a period of excitement and success, resulting at Vetch Field in the erection of the present West Stand, a large double-decker, in the summer of 1927. Such large stands behind the goal were then a rarity.

Largely thanks to the supporters' money raising efforts, in 1959 the North Bank Side of open terracing was reshaped and covered at a cost of £16000, and in September 1960 Swansea's floodlights were first used, for a friendly v. Hibernian.

By 1967 the club had slipped into the Fourth Division, but still managed to record its highest attendance, 32796, for the visit of Arsenal in the FA Cup 4th Round in February 1968.

Exactly two years later Swansea became City instead of Town, but found the change of little help to their ailing fortunes. Desperate for money the club sold Vetch Field to the local council in December 1974, for £50000, plus an additional grant of £150000 to keep the club in business. A year later City reached their lowest point, having to seek re-election for the first time.

However, under John Toshack's management, Swansea rose from the Fourth to the First Division in just three seasons. For Vetch Field however, considerable changes to the ground's facilities and more importantly its safety had to take place to keep pace with this galloping success.

There has been one major piece of construction, the East Stand, completed in January 1981 at a cost of just under £800000. Seating 1841 the stand includes new offices and was intended to continue round the south east corner and replace the already antiquated Main Stand.

Although City received planning permission to continue the stand along the South Side, capital was

View from the West Stand at Vetch Field overlooking the original stand and its new neighbour (with the prison behind) (Simon Inglis)

simply not available. Apart from concentrating funds on building a team, City had also to spend a further £700 000 on safety improvements, almost stretching their grant from the Football Grounds Improvement Trust to the £360 000 limit. New terracing had to be laid, barriers replaced, access improved and steelwork in the West Stand strengthened. Little of this work is visible, but it was vital to ensure Vetch Field's capacity would be sufficient to cope with the demands of First Division Football – until, ironically, the drastic decline of attendances made such a concern almost superfluous, just as Swansea reached the top. For example, the club's average gate in 1979–80 was 14 391, but the following year when they were promoted only 13 143. It rose again to 18 225 in the First Division, but dropped to the earlier levels a year later in 1982–83. Swansea had risen with the recession, and paid the unforeseen cost. For the time being therefore, Vetch Field will remain as it is, with a capacity of 26 496, including 5300 seats.

Ground Description

It is hard to believe that the seafront is only 300 yards away, because there is not an inch to expand on any side. To illustrate this, two corners of the ground are actually cut across by the back gardens of neighbouring houses, divided from the crowds by just a brick wall.

There are two entrances on Glamorgan Street, one for players and officials – through a gate tucked in between two houses, if you do not look hard you will miss it – and a larger entrance leading to the new offices in the East Stand. The Centre or Main Stand is not visible from outside the ground, hiding behind a row of terraced houses. In design it resembles the County Road Stand at Meadow Lane, having a small, pointed gable in the centre of the roof.

Firstly, it is all seated only as far as the West End 18-yard line, after which there are terraces, but all under the same low, sloping roof, supported by a line of pillars along the touchline. The little white gable has a flagpole at each of its three points. One bay to the west, also mounted in the roof, is an odd, box-like gable several yards long, fronted by windows. Part of the corner terracing in this strange stand is now fenced off as a safety precaution.

Behind here are the taller buildings of a Territorial Army Drill Hall, with windows overlooking the pitch. The high walls of Swansea prison also overshadow the stand.

From the Main Stand you can see the tall West Stand to the left (sometimes called the Mumbles End after Mumbles Head, a point further down the South Wales coastline). Large enough to be a main stand, it is actually extremely basic, the top tier having long, worn bench seats only, the passageways and corridors being dark and cramped. The high screen ends are made of rusting, green-coloured corrugated iron. Underneath the balcony are terraces, flanked by space-consuming scaffold steps leading to the upper tier. Each corner of this end of the ground therefore resembles a builder's yard, and although the steps were installed for safety reasons, their presence is regrettable on aesthetic grounds, for they tend to detract from the scale and simplicity of the West Stand itself. The best view of the ground is from the upper tier and it is possible to see how cramped the ground is to the left, immediately below the West Stand. Here the terraces give way to an angled wall, behind which are the gardens of City's long-suffering neighbours.

Looking to the left side of the ground, the North Bank runs the length of the pitch, and is a large covered terrace built on earth banking at the front and steel supports at the back. There are some places along this rear section where you can actually see the ground through small gaps between the concrete steps. Before this was built there was a clear view of the Swansea suburbs rising up the distant hills.

Straight ahead is the new East Stand, painfully modern and efficient in comparison with its ageing neighbours. But again, this has an odd appearance, because it fills only three-quarters of the pitch's width. More gardens abut on the thin section of open terrace in the north corner. And rather than finish at right angles to the pitch, the East Stand begins to curve temptingly around the corner before coming to a dead halt next to the old stand.

However quaint the Main Stand may be, that it should stop this graceful sweep of the cantilever is visually most irritating. To confound matters, the new floodlight pylon in that corner is just about the oddest in existence, leaning over the back of the stand and hanging suspended above the roof at an angle completely at variance with the rest of the ground, like a crane waiting to lower its load onto a ship's deck.

Otherwise the stand is clean and simple, finished in white concrete – to blend with the predominantly white neighbouring houses – and open at either end to keep the view unhindered.

Hardly surprisingly, Vetch Field shares with East-ville and The Shay, the distinction of having the smallest pitch in the League, 110 × 70 yards. But if lack of space is a problem, lack of variety most certainly is not. The Vetch Field has four totally different stands, each with its own character, notably the two older constructions. These may not be wholly satisfactory, but they are unpredictable, and placed next to that odd pylon and the streamlined East Stand they make the Vetch Field seem an apparently disjointed venue, in which the only predictable feature is the pitch. For the traveller who thinks all football grounds are the same and cannot possibly divert one's attention from the field of play, this one is therefore an unexpected, but welcome curiosity.

⋆CARDIFF CITY⋆

Previous Grounds

Cardiff City's origins go back to 1899, when the Riverside Cricket Club formed a soccer team at their ground on the banks of the River Taff. No one is quite sure where the actual ground was, or when Riverside FC moved to Sophia Gardens, a large public park on the west bank of the Taff belonging to the Marquis of Bute. Riverside were still an amateur team when Cardiff Borough was granted the status of a city, and the South Wales and Monmouthshire FA decided, in 1908, that the club may change its name to Cardiff City on condition that the name would have to be transferred back to the first soccer team in the area to turn professional.

The comprehensive study, *Football in Cardiff* by Derrick Jenkins (1983), from which much of this information derives, relates how the club decided to gauge public opinion before risking professionalism, by staging a series of friendlies against first-class opposition. The first two such games were staged at Cardiff Arms Park, the national home of Welsh Rugby, City drawing with Southern League Crystal Palace and losing to Division One Bristol City in October and November 1909. In March 1910 Cardiff invited Middlesbrough, also of the First Division, for a friendly at the Harlequins RFC ground on Newport Road. Satisfied with the public's reaction the club decided to turn professional and find a permanent home.

Of their previous grounds, only Sophia Gardens exists as a sporting ground, now the home of Glamorgan County Cricket Club and also the site of the National Sports Centre, between Cathedral Road and the River Taff.

Ninian Park

In February 1910 Cardiff Corporation's Parks Committee agreed to grant the club a seven-year lease of a 5-acre site, the former rubbish tip on the fringes of Leckwith Common, between Sloper Road in Grangetown and the Taff Vale railway line. City had to guarantee their ability to pay annual rent of £90. All augured well until one of the guarantors withdrew his support, but after a short period of uncertainty, Lord Ninian Crichton Stuart, second son of the third Marquis of Bute, came to the rescue. Until then, the ground was going to be called Sloper Park, but since his intervention secured the lease, his name was adopted in appreciation.

Cardiff City turned professional and joined the Southern League Second Division, but they decided to open Ninian Park with an attractive friendly against Aston Villa, the current League Champions, on 1 September 1910. Among the new professional players' first tasks was clearing the pitch of broken glass and debris, left over from the rubbish tip, start-

Ninian Park in 1947 (Central Press)

ing at dawn on the opening day. The ground was prepared with a small wooden grandstand, low banks, and a dressing room built on the corner of the pitch on Sloper Road. A photograph taken on the first day shows the railway signal box clearly visible behind the then very low Bob Bank, opposite the stand.

A crowd of 7000 came to the match, which was scheduled at the unusual time of 5 o'clock on a Thursday afternoon (Villa presumably having League commitments at that time of the year). Lord Ninian kicked off for Cardiff, who did well to lose only 1-2. Lord Ninian thereafter became a firm supporter of the club and became an MP for Cardiff in December 1910 (he died only five years later in action during the First World War).

The first international match at Ninian Park was in March 1911 v. Scotland. City were elected to the Football League, Division Two in 1920 and won promotion in their first season, the beginning of a successful run.

Ninian Park advanced with the team. In 1920 the Canton Stand, named after the district, was built behind the north goal, a covered bank with bench seats. To have seats arranged like this was unusual at the time, if not unique, for it is only in recent years that clubs have started installing seats on their standing terraces. The Bob Bank was covered with a simple flat roof supported on columns, with an exposed girder along the front, as at the Racecourse Ground.

In the summer of 1928 a much larger roof was erected over the Grangetown End, also named after a district, for standing spectators only. But its presence did the players no good at all, for Cardiff were relegated the following season, and only two seasons later found themselves in Division Three South. During this miserable run, it was reported that for the game v. QPR on 14 November 1931, not a single person was standing on the Bob Bank, out of an attendance of only 2000. Cardiff were still in Division Three, struggling still, when on 18 January 1937 the wooden Main Stand burnt down, apparently the result of thieves trying to blast open the club's safe which they wrongly believed to contain the gate money from City's Cup tie two days before. In place of the old stand was built a brick and steel construction some 60 yards long on the half-way line.

The visit of League leaders and eventual Champions Arsenal, on 22 April 1953, attracted City's biggest home gate of 57 800. Cardiff were relegated in 1957, but in 1958 the Bob Bank was doubled in height and depth and a new roof built over the back section. Two years later the first floodlights were switched on for a League match v. Sheffield Wednesday at the opening of the 1960–61 season, when Cardiff were yet again back in Division One. Ninian Park's biggest ever crowd came for an international match v. England on 14 October 1961. The 61 566 attendance is the highest also for a Welsh international match played in Wales.

Since the Second World War, Ninian Park had become almost the permanent home of the Welsh team, with 51 games played here between 1946–77 compared with 16 at the Racecourse Ground and 7 at the Vetch Field. But the ground's facilities were still far behind those at Wembley or Hampden, although in 1973 the Main Stand or Grand Stand was extended on both sides to run the whole length of the pitch. But as an international venue, as well as the fact that City were then a Division Two club, when the Safety of Sports Grounds Act was brought into effect in 1977, Ninian Park was severely affected by the findings of the safety inspectors.

Despite the number of ambiguities and the implied need for reasonable interpretation when implementing the Act, it seemed that the South Glamorgan authorities chose to follow the book, and they reduced Ninian Park's capacity to just 10 000 until repairs were made. Such zeal cost Cardiff City £600 000, of which £200 000 came from the Football Grounds Improvement Trust, and in view of Ninian Park's national status, £27 000 was granted by the Welsh FA.

One of the most significant changes brought about by the Safety Act was the demolition of the Grangetown End roof in 1977, and the cutting back of the banking, reducing its capacity by half, and palpably affecting the whole ground's appearance and atmosphere. Identical measures were taken at Home Park and Bloomfield Road, with similar results. As already noted, Ninian Park staged two-thirds of all Wales' home fixtures between 1946–77. Having spent so much money on restoring the ground's capacity in order that it would be able to continue to host such matches, it was reasonable for Cardiff to believe that once the safety requirements were met the Welsh FA would return to the status quo existing before 1977.

Throughout 1977, Wales played at Wrexham, plus one 'home' game at Anfield v. Scotland in the World Cup. With much of the repairs effected, the national team returned to Cardiff in 1978. Between then and Wales' final unsuccessful World Cup qualifying match v. USSR in May 1981, Swansea staged two games, Wrexham six but Cardiff only five.

The club felt cheated. They had a large capacity ground which they were unlikely to fill for League matches, but which was now liable only for one or two internationals a year. Since the host club can only keep 15 per cent of the takings (the Welsh FA entirely depend on such matches for its revenue) the prospects of recouping their outlay were small indeed. In addition, the city of Cardiff, home of the Welsh national rugby team, felt slighted that the Welsh football team should be shunted around the country apparently at whim. The fact that the FA's headquarters remained at Wrexham was equally resented. Cardiff City's capacity is 43 000 (average gate 1981–82: 5573). There are 7040 seats.

Ground Description

Although very close to the centre of Cardiff and the main railway station, Ninian Park stands on the edge of a large expanse of flat, open ground, with playing fields, Ely River, woods and the large Trelai Park to the west, and a huge web of railway shunting yards to the east. Beyond lies the district of Riverside, where the club originally formed (Cardiff Arms Park, three-quarters of a mile to the east, is in contrast completely submerged in a built-up area on the banks of the Taff).

From certain approaches therefore, one can see Ninian Park from a considerable distance, and it is an imposing sight with the city skyline in the background. Close to, however, Ninian Park holds no surprises. The Grand Stand is a very plain unembellished design, with a slight, pitched roof, white terrace rear wall and an open paddock in front. The roof fascia bears the club crest and name, and one can see quite clearly from the roof where the new wings were added in 1973. It is a neat stand, but colourless also. It holds 5000 seats.

From here, to the left is the Canton Stand, its low pitched roof so brightly covered with a large advertisement that it almost overpowers the ground. At the back of the stand, under the original roof, the club has built a restaurant, the best alternative Cardiff could find when the safety inspectors determined that the rear section was unsafe. This has reduced the number of seats to 2000, while the view from the very front is poor anyway, being too low for seated spectators. The stand is also much closer to the Grand Stand than to the opposite side, giving the impression that the pitch was either shifted or widened when the Bob Bank was redeveloped.

The extremely large Bob Bank, so called because it cost a shilling to stand there, is opposite the Main Stand. There are taller sides in the League, at St Andrew's or The Valley, but none are quite so deep as this one. From the very back in the centre, it is about 50 yards to the nearest touchline. The terracing is only half-covered, and rises in shallow steps, divided by wide gangways. It has been said the safety inspectors ordered so many crush barriers to be built here in 1977 that there's hardly any room left to stand!

From the back of the bank, looking behind the cover, one can see the signal box, the shunting yards, the docks and all of Cardiff city centre stretching ahead, including Cardiff Arms Park.

Finally, to the right is the now open Grangetown End. Its roof is missed no less than those taken down at Plymouth and Blackpool, for it was the largest cover at the ground, dark and low, and without it the ground seems far more exposed. There is naturally a tendency for spectators to seek cover under the Bob Bank roof in wet weather, leaving just a handful of individuals on the Grangetown End. Ninian Park's atmosphere has suffered accordingly.

Behind the terrace a wide gangway has been built, floodlit by pylons at the top of the terrace, providing access from Sloper Road to the Bob Bank. Each of the main floodlight pylons is wrapped in barbed wire. Notice the extra lines on the pitch. Ninian Park has dared in recent years to stage Rugby League on a similar basis to that at Fulham, Carlisle and Leeds.

Ninian Park has had to undergo more modifications than most grounds in order to maintain its capacity, at some cost to the appearance and atmosphere. Since there is little grandeur, colour or sense of enclosure, the present size seems more of an encumbrance than a blessing. It falls uneasily between the possible demands of staging major international fixtures, and the smaller audiences at club level. It is doubly ironic therefore that nearby lies Cardiff Arms Park, so cleverly and neatly built, side by side to the smaller, but very adequate ground of Cardiff RFC. If only the soccer authorities could have been so clever.

◆NEWPORT COUNTY◆

Somerton Park

Newport have played at Somerton Park since their formation in 1912, but it is only in recent years that they have enjoyed any security of tenure. County were formed by workers of the Lysaght's iron and steelworks, and rented Somerton Park from a private concern. During the First World War the property was sold, but the new owners demanded a higher rent from County. Not wishing to waste what progress had already been made the Lysaght company decided to buy Somerton Park in 1919, at a cost of £2200, and handed it over to a committee of employees to use as they thought fit. They were naturally determined that County should remain at the ground.

During the 1931–32 season when the club were out of League action, after years of depression, significant changes occurred at Somerton Park. In order to save the club from extinction the workers' committee which leased the ground to County, sold it to a bookmaker. They gave Lysaght back the £2200 invested in 1919, settled the rest of the club's debts, and then discovered the bookmaker had sold it to the Cardiff Arms Park Greyhound Racing Company, at a vast profit. The company set about transforming Somerton Park, which had only a small main stand, opposite where the Main Stand is now, and a cover over the Cromwell Road End dating from 1922. To accommodate the dog track, the pitch was moved, the banking reshaped, and the present Main Stand built. County's original Main Stand was converted into a social and viewing area and a gable on the roof added to house the starter and timing devices needed for greyhound racing. So although County were again tenants of an outside company, at least they had a better equipped ground for their return to the League.

For a Third Division derby v. Cardiff City on 16 October 1937, Somerton Park's highest gate of 24 268 was recorded. The team won the Third Division

Somerton Park, showing the 'Social Side' (Adrian Gibson)

South Championship in 1939 and were just beginning the following season when War broke out. Black-out was imposed and the greyhound company was forbidden to hold Saturday evening meetings at Somerton Park, so they switched to Saturday afternoons and forced County to play elsewhere. For a time the club played at the ground of a works' team on the other side of Newport, Lovell's Athletic. Somerton Park was then taken over by the Civil Defence, and County played on at the Rodney Parade Rugby Ground.

Floodlights were installed in 1957, and first used on 21 October for an exhibition game v. an All Star FA XI.

In 1963, after years of fading interest, the Cardiff Arms Park Greyhound Racing Company decided to leave Newport (it vacated the rugby stadium in the 1970s) and sold Somerton Park to the local council for £30 000. Now down in the Fourth Division, County found themselves sharing the ground with a speedway team. Then in 1978 the team began to improve culminating in 1980 with their winning promotion to Division Three and the Welsh Cup. At last they had the resources to buy Somerton Park, and in April 1980, for a sum of at least £100 000, negotiations were concluded with the council.

The ground they bought has a capacity of 18 000, including 1200 seats.

Ground Description

This is another ground which is difficult to find, with low stands and floodlights hidden amid railway lines, pylons and gantries. Once spotted there can be no mistake about whose ground it is; Somerton Park is a splash of amber and black on the landscape.

Passing through the courtyard, lined by sundry offices and social facilities, the Main Stand is seen on the Somerton Road Side of the ground, some 50 yards long. It has a gently pitched black roof supported at the front, with plain white fascia and amber paintwork. Now all seated, the original paddock is divided by the tunnel, distinctively covered in red and black sheeting, with the warning that the paint is of the variety that stays wet.

From here, to the right but on the same touchline, is an awkward standing cover in the top corner. It is close to the Main Stand, but set several yards back, so that the view from underneath is rather impeded. Perhaps it was built before the Main Stand.

To the far right is the Railway End, a shallow earth and cinder bank curving round the old track, which is fenced off by a wall topped by meshed fencing. It is a miserable end indeed, with no concrete terraces, no crush barriers, made grimmer by the railway line from Cardiff to London and the West Country running directly behind.

To the left is the Cromwell Road End. (Newport are known as The Ironsides because the link with Lysaght's ironworks and the proximity of Cromwell Road made this the most popular submission when the local newspaper held a competition to find a nickname.) This end of the ground is oddly square next to the curved ends of the pitch and old track, because it predated the arrival of the greyhound company. There is a flat roof at the back of some extremely shallow terracing, with an open set of flat concrete in front, bounded by a curved wall around the track. To make viewing worse, the front level is a couple of feet below the pitch level, and in the middle of the covered section is a large gateway where there is no terracing, and a toilet block jutting out, taking up valuable covered standing space. Almost in recognition of this, between the toilets and the gate is a section of concrete terracing just 1 foot wide!

The roof continues round the far corner at a right-angle, and because of the track's curvature, the corner is some way from the pitch. It meets up on the far side with the 'Social Side'. This is a stand covering thick wooden terraces, backed by a social club whose windows look out on the pitch. On the roof is a little covered platform for cameras. Another stretch of flat concrete divides the stand from the perimeter track. To the right of the Social Side, meeting up with the Railway End is a 20-yard length of open terracing.

For standing spectators, Somerton Park is most unsatisfactory. One is either too low down, too far back, blocked by fences and pillars, or just out in the open on a rough bank. Of all the grounds once used or still used by greyhounds or speedway, Newport's is the most awkwardly adapted. However County do at last now own the ground and although none of the stands are less than 50 years old, and very little has been spent by the ground's previous owners, a few coats of amber and black have managed to stamp some identity on the surroundings. It is an encouraging start to their period of ownership, but if the team were to win promotion to Division Two, a great deal would have to be done to satisfy the Safety Act's requirements.

·15·

WEST MIDLANDS, SALOP AND STAFFORDSHIRE

·COVENTRY CITY·

Previous Grounds

Coventry City began life as Singers FC, a work's team attached to a bicycle factory. From 1883 the club played on a ground almost next to the present site, where King Richard Street and Lansdowne Street are now situated. In 1896 they moved a few hundred yards south to where Britannia Street meets Wren Street, until making their final move to Highfield Road in 1905.

Highfield Road

In recent years Coventry City have been something of a trendsetter, whose innovations have been studied and copied by clubs all over the country. Some of Coventry's ideas have been sound and some controversial, but they have succeeded in transforming the ground from an ordinary, small town's enclosure to one of the best in the League.

In 1905 the club, having changed its name to Coventry City, secured a lease for what was then called the Athletic Ground (Highfield Road is one of several small streets near the ground).

To celebrate their first very promising run of form, in 1935 a new Main Stand was built on the South Side. It was a plain but clean looking construction with a steeply pitched roof, white paddock wall and large, glass screen ends. On the West End was a simple roof over the terracing. Opposite the Main Stand was the smaller Thackhall Street Stand, barrel-roofed behind a large, open paddock.

The first floodlit match at Highfield Road was on 21 October 1955 v. Queen of the South, attended by 17 000. The city was then in the awesome process of recovering from the destruction of the War, and appeared to be an important symbol of Britain's future prosperity. But the team still had to hit the bottom before it could reach the top. In 1958 City went down to the newly constituted Division Four, escaped at the first attempt and then welcomed James W. T. Hill as their new manager, recently retired from playing. From that moment on, High-field Road was never the same.

Hill did not just build a team, he created an image; one which was to mould the corporate development of the club on the Sky Blue theme. Without a decent team this might have seemed like empty gimmickry but Hill took City out of the Third Division and into the First within six years.

The crowds loved it. Hill's image building coincided with exciting developments in the city, for example, the building of a new shopping precinct.

To begin Highfield Road's development the Thackhall Street Stand was replaced, section by section with a revolutionary type of prefabricated construction. There had been one such stand built before, at Fratton Park, but City's Sky Blue Stand – as it was inevitably dubbed – was larger and more sophisticated. Built by a firm called Banbury Grandstands it was claimed to be 'a future concept' in stand design, could be made to fit any size, and at Highfield Road was built at a cost of £120 000 between 1963–64. Suddenly Coventry became the focus of other clubs' attention.

The next improvement came in September 1964, when the *Coventry Evening Telegraph* gave City a £3000 electric scoreboard. Compared with today's computer-operated data boards it was a primitive collection of bulbs and wires, but again, in 1964 it was yet another demonstration of Sky Blue razzmatazz. In the same year the League's first real executive club was set up in the Main Stand (costing members 100 guineas a year) while the Kent and England cricketer Godfrey Evans introduced Radio Sky Blue to keep fans entertained before matches. There were netball matches, dog handling displays, even pop groups on the pitch.

Other clubs' officials were now visiting Highfield Road to pick up ideas and advice on pepping up their own outdated images. In 1965 came another innovation, which although it proved to be just a novelty was nevertheless a bold scheme. Coventry filmed their away match at Cardiff on closed circuit television, and screened it live at Highfield Road, on four huge boards placed on the pitch, on 6 October 1965. For a while it seemed as if fog might ruin the whole event. But fortunately the weather cleared and a crowd of

Newly-seated Highfield Road, with the distinctive, vaulted Main Stand roof (Sporting Pictures)

10 295 at Highfield Road watched in wonderment as their team won 2-1 at Ninian Park, where the live attendance was 12 600. Such a system was made even more potentially viable by the fact that Coventry were then staging their reserve games in mid-week – another innovation – and gates were sometimes as high as 12 000.

There was only one more closed-circuit broadcast at the ground; Coventry's match at The Valley later in the season. The attendance was a healthy 11 321 at Highfield Road, but the experiment was dropped thereafter. The two Liverpool clubs tried it with great success in March 1967, but by then televised football was becoming established and the idea was never revived. Naturally, the 'away' clubs objected because closed-circuit television reduced their potential gates.

Coventry were certain of promotion on 29 April 1967 when Wolves were the visitors for a match which would help decide which of the two would win the Second Division Championship, attracting Highfield Road's largest ever attendance, 51 455.

City became Champions and looked forward almost incredulously to life in Division One. During the close season a double-decker West Stand was built at the relatively low cost of £85 000, with seats for 3200. A new idea for match programmes was launched; the Sky Blue match day magazine, a fore-runner of many of today's more successful publications, and all boded well, until at the beginning of the new season, Jimmy Hill resigned as manager.

Suddenly the dream was shattered and with relegation looking increasingly likely, disaster struck on 6 March 1968. The Main Stand was destroyed by fire and with it the Second Division Championship Trophy.

City rebuilt the stand immediately, a larger version of the Sky Blue Stand, with a restaurant on the first floor – a rare feature then – thereby raising the seating capacity to 12 000. If the team did not always seem of First Division standard, Highfield Road certainly was.

In 1970 the original roof of the Sky Blue Stand, which like the new Main Stand was a series of light-weight aluminium vaulted sections, was found to have structural defects and was replaced with a plain, flat roof. (Even this new roof was to have problems, when a gale blew part of it down in 1983.)

But the greatest transformation came during the summer of 1981. City took the momentous decision to turn Highfield Road into the first all-seater stadium in England (Scotland had two: Aberdeen and Clydebank). Again the ground became the centre of widespread attention. The conversion required an extra 8000 seats and cost £400 000 to complete, reducing the overall capacity from 38 500 to 20 616. City's main motive was to reduce hooliganism, which they felt had deprived the ground of its 'family' atmosphere. After almost annual destruction of certain sections of the ground, especially the toilets, vandal-proof fixtures were installed wherever possible. Every game was made all-ticket, with only a small number of tickets available on match days, at £5 each, again in an attempt to dissuade the casual away fan.

It did not succeed entirely, for hooligans still managed to destroy seating. But the all-seating arrangement did at least allow outbursts of violence to be quelled from the outset. Attendances flopped disastrously however. In 1979–80 they were, on average, over 19000, with the team struggling as usual. By 1981–82 the average was down to 13000 and dropping further, despite the team's improved form the following year. Gates were falling all over the country but the recession hit Coventry harder than most cities in England and so the concept of all-seated stadiums did not enjoy a fair trial, and it is impossible to judge whether City's declining support can be attributed to the seats. Certainly fewer people could afford to go to a football match, whether it was £2 for standing up or £2 for sitting down.

Ground Description

For anyone unused to watching football in an all-seated stadium, Highfield Road can be an unsettling place to visit. Every seat is light blue, of course, and unless a large crowd is in attendance, this colour, combined with a bright terracotta track and an excellent playing surface, makes the ground seem almost synthetic, almost too bright.

The Main Stand is the most interesting construction, largely because of its vaulted roof, like a huge section of corrugated iron. The wavy lines protrude far beyond the slanting pillars and from below resemble the underbelly of a fantasy spaceship. There are two lines of private boxes, 12 at the front uncomfortably close to the touchline, and 17 at the very back, and in addition several other small boxes dotted about the stand. Even the dug-outs are covered huts moulded into the stand above the tunnel. All the facings are in dark, polished wood. Further evidence of the club's ambition and foresight is the existence of a high-quality restaurant in the stand. Many clubs have now built restaurants but none which carry the approval of Egon Ronay, as at Coventry.

To the left from here is the West Stand, a simple but efficient double-decker, similar to its contemporary at the Baseball Ground. It is the same height as the Main Stand, but has a flat roof and vertical pillars. The balcony wall also has polished wood panelling, much of it obscured by advertising.

Opposite is the Sky Blue Stand, on Thackhall Street. Now looking rather faded from the road, it has had a new lease of life inside since seats have been added to the large paddock. When this also had a vaulted aluminium roof the two side stands were in perfect harmony. Now the Main Stand steals the show.

To the right is the uncovered East Terrace, divided in half by a black fence. Behind the fence are the old concrete terraces, with the crush barriers still visible around the old electric scoreboard – still in use and surmounted by two flagpoles. This terracing was reinstated in 1983 for the controlled usage of up to 2000 spectators, for those who continued to express desire for standing. In the corner above the concrete steps is a small section of wooden terracing, now fenced off.

None of the new seats have simply been attached to the old terracing. Experience at grounds like Villa Park and St Andrew's made Coventry realize that for the best view, new concrete steps would have to be laid with higher risers. But since the pitch level had once been so distorted the original terracing sloped at all the wrong angles. Indeed between 1963–81 the pitch had been surrounded by a concrete white wall, which to compensate for the varying heights rose from nearly 8 feet high in one corner to just a few inches in the opposite corner. All this had to be corrected to create acceptable sight-lines for the new seats.

Both the club and the players insist that the seating has not affected the atmosphere. On the contrary, with Coventry's smaller crowds, the acoustics are said to be much improved. The West Terrace fans still sing on regardless. It would be dishonest to say nothing has changed. Highfield Road is very different from the other 91 grounds where there are still standing spectators. One club had to initiate the experiment, just as QPR did with artificial turf, and if Coventry have made mistakes these will serve as a valuable lesson to other clubs.

However, one may be convinced that this is the stadium of the future, but to be seated on a cold afternoon without protection in a sullen crowd of 9000, during the home team's best season in the League, having paid as much as £5 for the privilege, one is filled with doubt. Highfield Road is an admirable ground, but it might have been much better suited to another city.

·BIRMINGHAM CITY·

Previous Grounds

City's first ground in 1875 was on a piece of waste ground in Arthur Street, near St Andrew's, as Small Heath Alliance. To gain some revenue they rented an enclosed pitch on Ladypool Road, Sparkbrook for a short time, but as interest grew they moved back to Small Heath in 1877 to Muntz Street. Although it had a fine, ornate, white wooden stand at one end, with a pointed gable and flagpoles, the pitch was notoriously full of pot-holes. To avoid playing there, Wednesbury Old Athletic offered Small Heath £5 to reverse the venue of a cup-tie, which Small Heath then won. By 1891 the asking price was £200, paid by The Wednesday to play their cup-tie at Olive Grove. To the annoyance of their fans, Small Heath lost.

The rent at Muntz Street began as £5 a year, but in 1905 with the club established in the League it rose to £300, for a ground already too small for Small Heath's growing support. The largest gate was for a First Division derby v. Villa in 1902–03 when 29 000 attended. While at Muntz Street the club became Small Heath FC Limited, the first limited liability company in football, and in 1905, just before moving to St Andrew's they adopted the title Birmingham.

St Andrew's

St Andrew's was typical industrial wasteland, a desolate valley with a railway line along one bank, but director Harry Morris convinced the board that the site had potential and a 21-year lease was secured. A year of hard work followed, in which the Kop was raised to a height of 47 feet on rubbish dumped by anyone who cared to pay for the privilege. The ground plans were drawn up by a young carpenter, Harry Pumfrey, whose only credentials were that he had once studied at the School of Art, and that he gave his services cheaply. A huge main stand was built, reputedly the second largest in the land, and St Andrew's was opened on a snowy Boxing Day in 1906 by Sir John Holder, with a goalless draw v. Middlesbrough.

By 1939 there was a small roof at the back of the Tilton Road End and a low cover at the Railway End with two angled wings, one of which survives in part. Often this end would be obscured by smoke as passing engine drivers let off steam during matches. In this year the highest attendance at St Andrew's, 66 844, watched an FA Cup-tie v. Everton.

If Old Trafford suffered the costliest damage in the Second World War, St Andrew's had the worst luck. Weeks after the War began the local Chief Constable closed the ground in fear of air-raids. MPs raised the matter in Parliament, and although the Home Secretary refused to overrule the decision, because St Andrew's was the only ground in the country to be shut the ban was lifted by March 1940. The Chief Constable did have a point, however, for the ground was subsequently hit by no less than 20 bombs during the Blitz.

More was to follow, for in January 1942 the Main Stand was destroyed by fire, not from bombs but by a member of the National Fire Service! The stand had become an auxiliary fire station, and one of the men tried to put out a brazier with what he thought was water but turned out to be petrol.

With St Andrew's now a sorry wreck of twisted steelwork and cratered terraces, Birmingham sought refuge at Leamington and at unscathed Villa Park, until 1943. After the War, now called Birmingham City, the process of rebuilding began once funds and materials were available. The new Main Stand was begun in the early 1950s, with a rather advanced propped cantilever roof. In October 1956 the floodlights were switched on for a game v. Borussia Dort-

Muntz Street at the turn of the century. It is hard to believe how all trace of this apparently substantial ground has disappeared. Notice how crooked some of the wooden barriers were (*Book of Football*)

St Andrew's. Notice the remnant of the old Railway End cover in the bottom corner (Aerofilms)

mund. Although each pylon is 114 feet high, the Tilton Road End pair is sited appreciably higher.

As the club prospered after successful runs in the early years of the European Fairs Cup, the Tilton Road End and the Kop were both covered and in the mid-1960s the Railway End gave way to the City Stand, a carbon copy of the Main Stand. There are now 9000 seats in a capacity of 44 500. Percy Young was perhaps right in 1958 when he wrote of St Andrew's, 'Here was the quintessential Second Division atmosphere', and although much improved since, there is no noisier ground than Birmingham's when the team are in the throes of yet another promotion or relegation battle. A more partisan Kop I have yet to visit.

Ground Description

There is a utilitarian 1950s' drabness about both the stands, which cry out for some uplifting feature – a crest on the roof fascia perhaps, or a clock. Flagpoles along both roofs help slightly. Now the paddocks in front of each stand are seated, with 26 boxes added rather awkwardly to the Main Stand, similar to the Hawthorns and Portman Road. In the corner between the stands, where once the players used to leave the pitch through a gate, there is a token remnant of the old Railway End cover, a funny little enclosure barely sufficient for a hundred spectators. It is sometimes used by fans who have paid for a seat in the paddock

but prefer to stand.

On the other corner of the City Stand is the 90-minute Longine clock, brought back by a club chairman after a Swiss tour. Next to it is the Jeff Hall Memorial half-time scoreboard. Hall was only 30 when he died of polio in 1959, after 227 appearances as a right-back for City. (He played a record 17 successive games for England in partnership with Manchester United's left-back, Roger Byrne, who also died tragically in the Munich air crash.)

The Kop, with its vast roof, has for some years been the centre of a political wrangle in Birmingham. Asda Supermarket wanted to develop the large open space behind it, sharing the cost of a new stand with the club – as has happened at Selhurst Park and Boothferry park. But one of the councillors approving the plan was a City director, and the Co-op also had a plan for a superstore nearby. Accusations flew as councillors and planners battled over the rival schemes.

Opposite the City Stand is the Tilton Road End, formed by a natural rise which is surmounted by the works of T. Williams, drop forgers. St Andrew's stands on a hill overlooking Birmingham, the most panoramic view being from the railway bridge behind the City Stand. For neighbours, the ground has small factories, a bus garage, and some council flats – maybe not as grand as Aston Hall, but then practicality rather than pomp is St Andrew's stamp.

WEST BROMWICH ·ALBION·

Previous Grounds

Albion began life as the West Bromwich Strollers in 1879, the last of Birmingham's three League clubs to form. Thanks to research by Peter Morris and Tony Matthews, there is a detailed account of the club's grounds, beginning with a field on Cooper's Hill in September 1879, where a bowling green is now situated next to The Expressway.

In order to save wear and tear on the pitch, West Bromwich played some games at the newly opened Dartmouth Park. The players carried a pair of portable goalposts with them, since they were never quite sure if they would be playing at Dartmouth Park or Cooper's Hill. Hence the name Strollers. Dartmouth Park still exists, also next to The Expressway.

In 1881 the club moved to Bunn's Field, on the corner of Walsall and Alfred Streets, and adopted the title Albion. Although it was their first properly enclosed ground, it was very primitive and the players had to change at the nearby Roebuck Inn.

At this time Albion's main local rivals were West Bromwich Dartmouth FC, who played at a well known sporting arena called Four Acres. As Albion began to dominate the local football scene, Dartmouth decided to concentrate on cricket, so in September 1882 Albion took a lease on Four Acres, on condition they played there on Saturdays and Mondays only. The ground had been dedicated to the citizens of West Bromwich by William, fourth Earl of Dartmouth. Albion's first game there was v. Stourbridge Standard on 7 October.

In July 1883 Dartmouth agreed to let Four Acres to Albion for a further two years at £15 a year, and to pay a third of the cost towards a new ticket office and pavilion.

The biggest crowd at this ground came in February 1885, when Albion played Blackburn Rovers in the quarter finals of the FA Cup. A crowd of 16393 packed into Four Acres, according to a report in *The Athlete*, filling all the stands, both temporary and permanent, as well as 'the walls and house-tops, everywhere, in fact where a footing could be obtained . . .'.

Aware of the ground's limitations, Albion were even then looking for a new ground, and on 6 April 1885 played their last game there v. Wednesbury Old Athletic. Four Acres is to be found today off Seagar Street.

The next move took the club to a field at the back of the Sandwell Brewery in Stoney Lane, conveniently close to the club's headquarters at the Plough and Harrow public house. The site belonged to an undertaker, Mr Webb, who gave Albion a seven-year lease

at an annual rent of £28.

The pitch had to be returfed and a wooden grandstand was built on the Sandwell Road Side. Holding 600 people on bench seats, the stand became known affectionately as 'Noah's Ark'. The cost of preparing Stoney Lane amounted to £370, and the first game was a friendly v. Third Lanark Rifle Volunteers on 5 September 1885.

Despite the improvements, viewing was still a problem, and Albion allowed vehicles to park behind the banking to allow extra vantage points. During one match, v. Blackburn, the iron railings broke and sent 20 fans hurtling into the next field. Furthermore, the pitch suffered from a pronounced slope. As one reporter wrote: 'What a terrible set the Albion forwards were when they came sweeping over the brow of that hill and down the incline, carrying everything before them.' An interesting feature at Stoney Lane was that admission was by ticket only. Having found the pay boxes unsuitable, the club sold tickets from small openings around the walls, and in the Plough and Harrow.

By 1899 the club faced a financial crisis, and although some £2500 had been spent on the ground, the directors were loath to spend more on a rented property. By the end of the century therefore Stoney Lane had deteriorated quite badly, and was probably the worst in Division One. Another move was planned in the hope of finding a ground closer to the expanding populated areas, nearer Birmingham, and with a cheaper annual rent. Albion's average gate at Stoney Lane had been around 6000, reaching a peak of about 12000. These figures, and the state of the ground, despite Albion's Cup successes, made the club very much the poor neighbours of Aston Villa and Wolves, each boasting large new grounds and growing support.

The site of Stoney Lane is now covered by the aptly named Albion Field Drive, off Sandwell Road and Stoney Lane itself.

The Hawthorns

The Hawthorns site was an attractive proposition because rent was lower than Stoney Lane, and it was situated on the border between three boroughs, West Bromwich, Smethwick and Handsworth. The tram fare from the densely populated suburb of Handsworth had just been reduced to one penny, and although the new ground was over a mile south east of West Bromwich town centre, the directors felt that the Birmingham side offered greater potential support, even though the ground was close to Aston Villa's patch.

The land belonged to Sandwell Park Colliery, and on 14 May 1900 Albion signed a lease giving them the option to buy within 14 years. There were two farms and two large public houses adjacent to the field. On the Handsworth Side stood the Woodman Inn, and on the Halford's Lane corner was the Hawthorns Hotel, from which the ground's name was derived. On the

The original Main Stand at The Hawthorns. Oxo advertisements were prominent at almost every League ground (*Book of Football*)

Smethwick End of the field stood a large private house, Oaklands.

The field itself presented enormous difficulties. It measured 10½ acres, sloped quite badly and worst of all had a brook running diagonally across. It took 120 men to build a culvert, lay 1600 yards of drains and shift tons of soil to level the surface. Once this was done, 300 loads of ashes, new top soil and 12000 square yards of turf were laid. The original pitch was a massive 127 × 87 yards with a 9 feet wide cinder track around.

The Handsworth Side was covered by Noah's Ark, from Stoney Lane, while opposite was built the 5000-seater Halford's Lane Stand, designed by Enoch Wood. A month before the big kick-off, the Hawthorns had been just an open meadow. Now it was ready, Albion having spent some £6000 on preparations, twice as much as their first estimate. The Hawthorns had to be a quick success, or the club would fold.

The grand opening took place on 3 September 1900, Albion playing Derby in front of 20000 people. Present were William McGregor, an official of Aston Villa and founder of the Football League, and the League president, John Bentley. The following week 35000 came to the ground to see Albion v. Villa. Receipts were high, much to the directors' relief, but the team were in such terrible form that the season ended with a crowd of just 1050 to see Albion play Sheffield United, one of the lowest attendances ever recorded at a First Division match. Albion were relegated for the first time in their League career.

On Guy Fawkes night 1904 Noah's Ark burnt down. Two years later the first part of the Smethwick End roof was put up, in a style known as a 'Belfast' roof, with lattice work wooden planks curved over in a barrel shape. An identical construction was used for Preston North End's West Stand, also built in 1906. Judging by the current state of both roofs, however expensive the method may be to maintain, the result is highly durable.

In 1911 Albion managed to win promotion back to Division One, and during the close season the Main Stand on Halford's Lane was overhauled and the opposite embankment increased in size. A year later they reached their sixth FA Cup Final, and their share of the receipts enabled them to purchase the ground's freehold in 1913, at a price of £5350. The Main Stand was extended at a cost of £2860.

After the War, West Bromwich won their first League Championship, made a dazzling profit of £7432 and during the summer of 1920 a concrete wall was built around the pitch and the first concrete terracing laid.

Despite the team's decline, The Hawthorns continued to develop. The Handsworth Side embankment was extended still further and the roof heightened, and the club's offices were improved in the Main Stand, at a total cost of £25000.

The ground staged its first full international in October 1922 and on 8 December 1924 staged England v. Belgium, only the second time a foreign international team had played against England on English soil (see Big Match Venues).

The ground at this time had a capacity of 70000, which was never to be tested. In 1931 Albion became the first club to win both the FA Cup and be promoted to Division One, and again the profits were put back into the ground, with the concrete terracing being completed and tip-up seats (as opposed to the then almost universal bench seats) installed in the Main Stand wings. The Hawthorns was visited by the Prince of Wales that year, and on Christmas Day the Great Western Railway officially opened the Hawthorns Halt, Albion's very own railway station. In 1934 a corner stand, seating 750, was added to the Main Stand, at the Smethwick End corner. The club reached their eighth FA Cup Final in 1935, and in the 6th Round v. Arsenal on 6 March 1937 recorded the highest attendance at The Hawthorns, 64815. Yet two years later, after Albion had slipped into Division Two, only 3109 watched Albion's last home game v. Norwich in 1938–39.

The summer before the outbreak of war was taken

up with the replacement of the original wooden roof of the Main Stand with a new steel and asbestos sheeting cover.

In the late 1940s the original wooden terracing in front of the Main Stand was replaced by seating, for an additional 750 people, and The Hawthorns became the first British ground to have electronic turnstile counters installed.

The first floodlights cost £18 000 and were switched on for a Division One game v. Chelsea on 18 September 1957, but officially inaugurated in a game v. CDSA, the Russian Red Army Club, on 29 October in front of 52 800 people. (The lights have been updated twice since.)

In 1958 the Birmingham Road End corner stand was added to the Main Stand, and in 1964 a new 4300-seater stand replaced the Handsworth Side embankment. The cover that had stood on this side was re-erected over the Birmingham Road End Terrace. Albion had spent a total of £250 000 on ground improvements between 1945–65, including laying out car-parks. So convenient had the ground become for parking and road access that in April 1968, a few weeks before Albion's fifth FA Cup triumph, the Hawthorns Halt station closed. The ground was now a few hundred yards from the M5 and only three miles from the M6.

Since then executive boxes have been added to the Handsworth Side Stand, now called the Rainbow Stand because of its multi-coloured seats, and in November 1980 the first stage of rebuilding the Main Stand began. When completed in August 1981 it had a full length cantilever roof with 4000 seats and 27 private boxes. The contractors were Norwest Holst, builders of new stands at Molineux and the City Ground.

Finally, due to the introduction of Safety of Sports Grounds Act, the end terraces have been completely reconstructed, and the Birmingham Road End has a new cover. The Hawthorns now holds 38 600, of which 12 500 are seated.

Ground Description

West Bromwich is to Birmingham what Watford is to London, yet The Hawthorns is situated on the border of Sandwell Borough, in which West Bromwich lies, and Birmingham. Furthermore, between the ground and West Bromwich is the M5 motorway. So Albion live in a sort of no-man's land between two centres of population, and it could be argued that the adjacent suburbs of Handsworth and Smethwick are as much Aston Villa's territory as Albion's.

Since its reconstruction, the main entrance on Halford's Lane is much improved, with a long, clean white facade along the pavement. Inside, the new stand is as impressive, but on a quite modest scale. It has one tier of blue seats, from the boxes at the back down to the touchline. Unusually, the television camera position is in a gap between the centre boxes, rather than on a special gantry. Called variously the Halford's Lane, the West or the Main Stand, it is a remarkably compact construction, imposing its character on the ground not through its size so much as its glossy brightness.

At both ends are the old corner stands, still in the original pitched roof style, each holding about 550 seats. In front of the north corner is an excellent section for the disabled.

From the new stand, to the right, is the Smethwick End terrace. The wooden Belfast roof is quite distinctive, still with pointed boards along the white wooden fascia, where there is now an electric scoreboard in the centre. The roof curves at each end, to join in the west corner with the old corner section of the Main Stand.

Since 1977 the terrace has been divided into three sections, totalling 14 400. To aid the flow of spectators the central section has at the back a tall corrugated fence, a favourite noise-maker for visiting supporters. In 1982 Leeds' fans managed, after 20 minutes of rocking back and forth, to tear down the perimeter security fence which cost Albion £10 000 to £20 000 to rebuild.

Opposite the Main Stand is the Rainbow, or East Stand, on the Handsworth Side, behind which runs the border of Sandwell and Birmingham. The stand is typical of the mid-1960s, being rather plain in style but has been considerably smartened by the addition of new seats, executive boxes at the back of the paddock (as at St Andrew's and Portman Road, with sloping roofs), and additional seats now in the paddock.

To the left of this in the north east corner is the uncovered Woodman Paddock, named after the Woodman Inn directly behind. A half-time scoreboard stands at the back of the terrace, topped by the Golden Throstle, an emblem which derives from the days when the club's headquarters were at the Plough and Harrow. The landlady kept a small thrush, or throstle in a cage, and this was adopted by the team as its mascot. For some years there was a bird in a cage inside the Main Stand. It was claimed that when the bird was 'on song' so was the team.

The Birmingham Road covered terrace fills the North End, and holds 10 000 standing. It is still possible to see sections of the old-style timber and ashes terracing on parts of the banking behind the stand.

Albion have never quite managed to level The Hawthorns pitch. It slopes about 3 feet from the Main Stand down to the Rainbow Stand, and about 6 feet from north to south, clearly visible along the walls of the new stand.

Although now just over half its original capacity, the ground seems perfectly proportioned for the current demands of first-class football. It is one of several middle-range grounds – very neat but not quite imposing, yet better equipped than the average ground in the Second Division: as Woody Allen might have put it, a good ground but not a great ground.

• ASTON VILLA •

Previous Grounds

The site on which Villa Park is built was the mid-Victorian Aston Lower Grounds amusement park, with facilities almost as varied as those at Crystal Palace in London. It was thus the natural venue for the newly-formed Aston Villa to play in 1874, although their first pitch was actually across the road in what is now Aston Park. The Lower Grounds park was the scene of much illustrious sport, as Gibson and Pickford's 1906 *Book of Football* describes:

'There George and Snook, the great pedestrians, put up their records; there H. L. Cortis rode his 60 inch "ordinary" bicycle in a way which (relatively) no living wheelman could parallel; there Iroquois Indians played lacrosse, the national game of Canada; there the Australian cricketers won their match v. an England XI in 4½ hours; there W. G. Grace drew the Midland multitude which was privileged to watch him when he was at the zenith of his powers, and there was founded the Birmingham Cricket and Football Club, the first club of importance which played the Association game in Birmingham.'

With so much competition in the district, and because the club needed a properly enclosed ground, Villa moved in 1876 to a field in Wellington Road in the adjacent suburb of Perry Barr. There was a hayrick in the middle of the pitch which had to be shifted before each game, a hump near one goal and a line of trees along one touchline. The land was sub-let to Villa by a butcher, for £5 a year. Just behind the pitch was Birmingham's first steam tram depot, now a bus garage. The players changed in a blacksmith's hut.

Despite the poor facilities the club enjoyed great success at Perry Barr, which also hosted several important games, including an amateur international v. Ireland in February 1893. It was at Perry Barr that one of the most serious incidents in early football occurred, when part of a 27 000 crowd twice invaded the pitch during a Cup game v. Preston. Although the cause was overcrowding rather than violence, Hussars had to be called in to restore order, and Villa, the Cup-holders, were subsequently disqualified from the competition for failing to maintain order at their ground.

By the mid-1890s less successful First Division clubs like Blackburn, Wolves and Everton had moved to fine new grounds, and with Villa's annual rent raised to £200 the club looked elsewhere. The choice fell, not surprisingly, on the Lower Grounds, which had in the meantime staged various big matches,

such as Cup semi-finals in 1884 and 1890. Work began on preparing part of the amusement park for a stadium in 1895, and on Good Friday 1897 Villa played their last game at Perry Barr, a reserve game v. Shrewsbury. The old ground was soon swallowed up by houses, on what are now Willmore and Leslie Roads. There was talk in the 1970s of the club returning to Perry Barr, to the athletics stadium of Birchfield Harriers, near the old ground, but the plan thankfully stayed on the drawing board. Otherwise football would have lost one of its prized possessions.

Villa Park

The return of Villa to Aston signalled the end of the amusement park as an open leisure centre. The surrounding land was already being bought up for redevelopment into housing and the park's popularity had been waning. Football was the new mass spectator sport, and Villa were the most powerful team in the country. Just one week before their first match at the new ground, a friendly v. Blackburn on 17 April 1897, the club equalled Preston's feat of winning both the League Championship and the FA Cup.

The transformation of Aston Lower Grounds, not called Villa Park until later, was swift, total and in view of the club's success, fully justifiable. The land belonged at the time to Flowers and Company, brewers in Stratford upon Avon, who charged Villa £250 a year rent, with the option to buy the land at 5 shillings a square yard within 21 years.

For a while the ground was unfinished – most spectators were soaked at that first match – but gradually, under the astute direction of Frederick Rinder, a committee member and surveyor, all trace of the amusement facilities were removed or adapted. The old aquarium, skating ring and restaurant became Villa's new offices and gymnasium. The ground's maintenance man took charge of the rifle range. At the rear, a practice pitch and car-park was laid on the site of a theatre and concert-hall, and on the far side of Witton Lane, housing was built where once had been a boating lake with ornamental island. The Witton Lane Stand covered what had been a sub-tropical garden. Another lake became, as at Crystal Palace, the site of the new pitch. Until 1914 a 24-foot wide concrete cycle track encircled the pitch which was used for major events.

However grand Villa Park appeared, it was in fact a cramped ground for the 40 000 spectators who would often attend, so before the First World War Rinder and an architect E. B. Holmes made bold plans for a redeveloped stadium holding 130 000. The first stage was in 1911, when Villa purchased the land for £8250 and the office buildings and car-park area for £1500. The carriage drive and a bowling green, which remained a unique feature of the ground until 1966, were also bought for £2000.

In the summer of 1914 the cycle track was removed, the Witton Lane Stand extended, and the banking at both ends built higher. An observer wel-

Villa Park in 1907. Notice the use of the cycle track for extra spectators and the boards on Trinity Road (top right) to deter people from watching on the slopes of Aston Park (Colorsport)

comed the fact that there was now 'no track to terrorize visiting players', and that the crowds were now closer, but not close enough 'to whisper to the players'.

Had not the War interrupted development, Rinder and Holmes might have gone further to create the largest stadium in England, although with post-war average gates of 30000 it was probably just as well.

The most important post-war development was the building of the Trinity Road Stand in 1922. Its use was delayed by a series of disputes among the builders until 26 August, for a match v. their old rivals Blackburn Rovers. The stand, which was and still is unique, was officially opened two years later by the Duke of York, later King George VI. The players' facilities were moved here from the Witton Lane Stand.

Much later than planned, because the 1930s saw Villa's fortunes flag for the first time since their formation, the Holte End banking was built up just as the Second World War broke out. The work was finished in February 1940, the only example of any ground development being effected during hostilities. By that time the Trinity Road Stand had been refitted as an air-raid shelter and the home team's dressing room occupied by a rifle company of the 9th Battalion of the Royal Warwickshire Regiment.

Soon after the War, the extended Villa Park had its highest attendance of 76588 for a Cup match v. Derby County, in March 1946.

Floodlights were installed relatively late at the ground, and first used in a friendly v. Hearts in November 1958. In 1962 the Holte End was covered at a cost of £40000, and two years later, down came the wonderful Witton Lane roof, one of the landmarks of English football. It was replaced with a plain sloping roof.

The decision to stage World Cup matches at Villa Park brought further changes. The Witton Lane Stand became all seated, the players' tunnel covered by a grill, the pitch widened 3 yards, 6250 temporary seats were put on the then uncovered Witton End banking and most drastic of all, the bowling green in front of the Trinity Road Stand was built over with a new social club. Thus was lost yet another link with the Aston Lower Grounds.

Altogether Villa spent £99000 on improvements for the competition of which £45000 was a government grant. From 1966 the club went into decline, but once safely re-established back in the top ranks, prepared for another major development; one which was not only to change the appearance of the stadium but also shake the entire club to its Edwardian foundations.

The eruption was caused by the new North Stand, which replaced the Witton End in the late 1970s. Its design or facilities can hardly be faulted, but payment for its construction was so badly managed as to prompt a police investigation into the club's affairs. Never had the erection of a stand caused such a

The Trinity Road Stand, Villa Park. The curved balcony wall is unique, as is the gable design (Sport & General)

scandal. A report commissioned by the club's directors, two of whom sold out their shares as a result of the inquiries, revealed that around £700 000 of work had been unaccounted for, yet the report was ignored for five months. Sports Ground Consultants, the company whose representative had been employed as clerk of works at the stadium, went into liquidation, and the building company which had installed new offices under the stand were unable to justify how 'grossly inflated' amounts were charged for the work.

The effects of these major lapses of control were incalculable. Despite Villa's success in winning the League Championship and the European Cup, the club remained heavily in debt because of the North Stand, a situation which further damaged the relationship between the club and its fans, who felt they had been ill-informed. They especially resented the apparent squandering of money which might otherwise have been spent on new players.

The lessons for other club directors were clear. Over-ambitious design and inflationary costs have always been obstacles to ground developments, but Villa had demonstrated the possibilities of outside parties exploiting the ill-guarded riches of a successful club.

Unfortunate though the scandal was, Villa Park has been considerably improved by the North Stand.

The current capacity is 48 000, of which 19 900 are seated.

Ground Description

In true Parliamentary tradition, I should first 'declare an interest' for it was at Villa Park that I saw my first football match at the age of seven, sitting in the Trinity Road Stand. My description of Villa Park is therefore coloured by long familiarity.

Approaching the ground from the city centre or from nearby Spaghetti Junction, you pass under the Aston Expressway and see the floodlights ahead. On the right is the tall spire of the Victorian Aston church, and on the left, high on a hill in Aston Park is the red-brick Jacobean mansion, Aston Hall, built in 1618 by Sir Thomas Holte, from whom the name Holte End is derived. The Holte public house stands directly ahead, where Witton Lane and Trinity Road fork apart, gripping Villa Park like a pair of open tweezers.

Would anyone argue against the assertion that the Trinity Road entrance of Villa Park has more pomp and style than that of any other ground? In the 1930s, Arsenal came close but does not enjoy the benefit of an open space in front of the entrance, and recently Bramall Lane has created equal scale and effect but significantly less grace with its new South Stand.

In wider context, the Trinity Road facade is only as grand as any good municipal building of the period, a library or town hall perhaps. The twin towers are relatively simple, topped by pediments, the balcony balustrade not too ornate, and the circular windows along the front are of a type which might easily be found at public swimming baths. The imposing features are the sweeping central steps, leading up to the upper seating tier, like those of a Palladian villa, and the central, also Italianate, pediment. A flagpole and some gold flourishes, with the words Aston Villa marked out on the towers, enlivens the red-brick walls. Football grounds, as stated earlier, are hardly resplendent with examples of worthwhile architecture, but here at Villa Park is one example that merits some critical attention. Yet Pevsner did not give it even a cursory glance. From here, we pass along Trinity Road to the main drive, where the social club covers the old bowling green, and enter the grounds by the car-park. Apart from a wall or two, any trace of the former Aston Lower Grounds buildings has disappeared.

Inside the Trinity Road Stand is a typical 1920s' construction, with a sloping roof supported by a maze of steelwork and several pillars. There are now seats in the paddock, with a line of private boxes at the back. Above is the distinctive balcony wall which is gracefully curved to accommodate the steelwork underneath (compare with the balcony walls at Ibrox, Goodison or Roker Parks, where the steelwork is exposed), and painted in light blue with claret stripes. The reflective glass of the boxes rather detracts from the balcony feature.

At either end of the stand, angled screen ends, at the Holte End flush with Trinity Road, are lit by round windows with patterned glass, a detail typical of this stand. Crowning the roof is a wide, flat-topped gable, with the club's motto 'Prepared' and the lion crest featured in the centre, flanked by vertical bordering. The gable used to have short iron railings, but even without these it is quite splendid, and unmatched by any other gable.

At the Holte End screen wall of the Trinity Road Stand, where once was a familiar half-time scoreboard, is now a long and narrow electronic data board. There is another one in the opposite corner.

To the right is the tall Holte End, able to hold 22 600 and therefore, marginally the largest Kop in the country (although Molineux's South Bank could hold up to 30 000 until the introduction of safety laws). Notice that the barriers on the Holte End run the width of each section, to comply with the 1975 Act's guidelines. The roof is plain and covers half the terracing.

Opposite is the Witton Lane Stand, also plain and simple, badly in need of a more compelling focal point than the present square clock. Along the front perimeter wall, behind the advertising hoardings, is a rolled up plastic pitch cover, which unfurls under mechanical power.

After the North Stand was built, the pitch suffered badly from lack of ventilation. A new pitch was laid, but this too had problems. The new cover has improved matters very little and is now used mainly during heavy rain. (For the failure of such covers in general, see Pitches.)

To the left is the North Stand, as tall as the Holte End, with 4000 seats, two lines of private boxes and standing room for 5500 in front. It is built with a roof suspended from a huge crossbar, whose posts stand outside the screen walls, as at Ibrox and Carrow Road.

The outside walls and facings are in rippled concrete, the support beams are dark brown. The only claret and blue is the seats, which pick out the initials A.V. in huge letters, visible even from the motorway.

The floodlights are also arranged in the shape of A.V., the outside walls have the name painted everywhere, and even the two clocks inside the ground have the letters of Aston Villa arranged around the face instead of numerals.

These details apart, Villa Park has actually very little unity. Each stand is a separate entity, totally different from its neighbour in size, shape and design. It will never therefore achieve the enclosed atmosphere found at Anfield or Old Trafford. But it shares with Hillsborough, Highbury and Goodison Park that aura of tradition and class, which regardless of executive facilities, makes Villa Park a sporting institution and a perfect stage for football. More people go there than to Aston Hall, which makes Pevsner's omission all the more surprising, since both structures represent the wealth and prestige of their respective owners.

WOLVERHAMPTON ·WANDERERS·

Previous Grounds

Wolverhampton Wanderers were formed by the amalgamation of two clubs, St Luke's, Blakenhall, and The Wanderers (not the famous team of the 1870s). Their early grounds were at Goldthorn Hill, from 1877–84, then a nearby field on Dudley Road, south of the town centre. But accompanying the town's growth were the property developers, and during the summer of 1889 Wolves moved a mile north to the Molineux Grounds. Dudley Road was rapidly built over with terraced villas, but when the club won their first Cup Final in 1893, the developer decided to name a street on the new estate Wanderers Avenue, and some of the houses Fallowfield Terrace, after the Cup Final venue. In addition, small stone replicas of the trophy were placed in front of each house. Some remain to this day, somewhat weatherworn and masked with paint.

Molineux

The Molineux Grounds were a famous sporting venue long before Wolves arrived. Like the Aston Lower Grounds, on which Villa Park was built, the site accommodated pleasure gardens, a boating lake, and most important of all, a cycle and athletics track, where many major events had been staged. Indeed Molineux was the home of a professional cycle racing team. Above the grounds stood the Molineux Hotel, once the home of the Molineux family who owned the land.

In common with many clubs of that period, Wolves were helped in their attempts to settle by brewers, the Northampton Brewery Company, which built dressing rooms, an office, a stand seating 300 people and shelter for an additional 4000 on cinder banking, for only £50 a year rental. At roughly the same time Villa were paying up to £200 for their much less developed ground in Perry Barr. The first game at Molineux was v. Villa on 2 September 1889.

In 1923 disaster struck, as Wolves crept down into the Third Division. But out of failure came renewed hope, for a new limited company was formed which immediately bought Molineux from the brewery for £5607, a very reasonable price for such a large site.

Promotion to Division Two came a year later, and in 1925 the first major stand was built at the ground, on the Waterloo Road Side. This was the present Main Stand, with seats for 2600 and standing room for 4000. Around the same time a 'cowshed' cover was put over the North End.

To celebrate the club's return to Division One in 1932, the Molineux Street Stand was built, in place of an old cover blown down in a gale. This distinctive structure held 3400 seated and 4500 standing, under a multi-span roof, with a clock mounted in the centre

Molineux in the 1970s. Notice the multi-span roof, now demolished together with the houses behind, to make room for the extended pitch and new stand. The Molineux Hotel is top right (Aerofilms)

gable. (The only other stands of a similar design and size were at Highbury, built in 1913 but demolished in 1936, and at Clapton's Homerton ground. The Valley had a shorter version in the same style.)

During the 1930s Wolves were dominated by the autocratic figure of their manager, Major Frank Buckley. One of his most controversial ploys was to water the Molineux pitch just before home games, because he knew the team preferred playing on heavy pitches and wished to gain maximum advantage. The League soon ruled there should be no artificial irrigation carried out between the months of November and February.

During the successful years up to the Second World War the present North and South Bank roofs were built, and Molineux housed its highest attendance. A crowd of 61 315 saw Wolves v. Liverpool in the FA Cup 4th Round on 11 February 1939.

The team reached their pinnacle during the 1950s, and Molineux saw one major development, the installation of floodlights. Between 1953 and 1956 Molineux was almost synonymous with floodlighting, as top European clubs visited Wolves to play friendlies and later European Cup ties. Indeed it was games like the Wolves v. Honved match in December 1954 which gave the European Cup much of its impetus, as all Europe considered the possibilities created by both air travel and floodlit mid-week matches (see Floodlights).

The first game under lights at Molineux was on 30 September 1953 against a South African XI (a fixture not allowable today under FIFA rules). Other visitors included Moscow Spartak and Moscow Dynamo. The present pylons were installed only a few years after the original set, which were sold to a non-League team in the area.

Molineux changed little until the introduction of the Safety of Sports Grounds Act, when in 1978, it was felt the Molineux Street Stand – by then all-seated – would not pass the required standards. At the same time a plan was drawn up involving re-development of that side of the ground but allowing room for expansion on the cramped Waterloo Road Side. So the Molineux Street Stand was demolished – farewell the gold-gabled-roof – and the club purchased 71 terraced houses on Molineux Street and demolished them also. Where the stand once stood the pitch was extended; where the houses once stood the new stand was built. The architects were Mather and Nutter, who had designed the cantilever stands at Old Trafford.

It was quite a revolutionary design, the first of a new generation later to be copied at the City Ground and improved on by Mather and Nutter at White Hart Lane; a sweeping, curved cantilever stand with two tiers of seating divided by a single row of private boxes. The new stand had 9500 seats, with 42 boxes, and cost Wolves £2 million. But in real terms it cost a great deal more, because after the team were relegated in 1982 Wolves were closer to closing down

than any other League club had been for years. They were heavily in debt and apparently unable to find a solution, until at the last moment Derek Dougan and friends stepped in to form a new company.

The new regime began to adopt more progressive policies for Molineux. For example, the Molineux Hotel, a listed mid-eighteenth century building overlooking the ground, and once the home of the old pleasure garden's owner, had become sadly derelict. Now there are plans to restore it. With sufficient funds there would also be a chance of redeveloping the Main Stand. There is potential at the ground and now it may be realized.

Molineux's capacity is 41 074, including 12 200 seats.

Ground Description

You have to be very sharp to spot Molineux from Wolverhampton town centre. The roads take you endlessly around the town, giving you teasing glimpses of the solid floodlights, yet you always seem to be higher than the stadium.

The Molineux Hotel is on the heights of the main ring road. In 1982 it was almost derelict. The old signs on the wrought iron gates were broken and not a window was intact. It was like a memorial to the old regime at Wolves. Passing to the left of this building, is a narrow alleyway which runs adjacent to the South Bank. Both its length and slope give an indication of the massive size of the South Terrace. Molineux Alley is a public right of way, but part of the 15-acre site owned by Wolves. Eventually you emerge into Waterloo Road, a gentler slope now, with the main entrance right up against the pavement of this narrow, busy road.

This entrance is another indication of how the ground has been neglected. The design tried hard to emulate Villa Park's impressive facade, but on a smaller and cheaper scale. Two 'Italianate' towers flank the central stairs, but where Villa Park has decorated brickwork, Molineux has fading yellow corrugated sheeting. The foyer is even gloomier with low ceilings, uneven floors and glass-fronted cupboards packed with silverware.

Inside the ground, the Waterloo Road Stand continues to show its ageing character, but rather than seeming forlorn actually looks quite cosy and appealing. In plan the stand is cranked (see Glossary) with the wings nearest the pitch. Every bit of wood is yellow or ochre, even the television camera gantry on the roof. At one end of the paddock is a half-time scoreboard, at the other a section for the disabled, complete with its own little roof. Close to, the stand is obviously patched and ailing, but from a distance it appears quite charming.

From here, you can see how changed the Molineux plan has become. The near touchline, for example, is about 15 yards from the perimeter wall, and the pitch is 174 yards wide, so football could be played the other way, from east to west, and a game of cricket or baseball would be quite acceptable. But for viewing football, the distance can be irritating. To add to the visual imbalance, the two end terraces finish well within the new touchlines. If you look hard, you can see the crown of each of the original goalmouths, some 12 yards wide of the present posts.

From the Main Stand, to the left is the North Bank, with a light brown, weathered pitched roof with solid screen ends. The rear terracing is constructed in wood, providing excellent acoustics. A tiny camera gantry sits on the roof in curious isolation.

Where the pitch continues but the North Bank ceases, a tall yellow fence carries round towards the new stand, behind a rather awkwardly isolated scoreboard which barely fills the void in the corner.

Dominating Molineux, yet somehow distant from its heart, is the new stand, named after the club president, John Ireland. It does not have streamlined glass screen ends as at Forest or Spurs, nor are there any words spelt out in coloured seats. But the effect is no less impressive. The red seats contrast richly with gold fascia, and a line of flags along the roof adds a touch of glamour. But its chief value, which lessens its financial burden on the club, is the office complex incorporated in the rear section, rented by the nearby Polytechnic's Faculty of Art and Design.

If Molineux derives new found confidence from the John Ireland Stand, it gains a sense of scale from the South Bank. As tall, if not taller than the Holte End at Villa Park, the sheer enormity of the concrete terracing, climbing up the natural slope towards the hotel, makes Molineux seem quite massive. The South Bank is actually a fraction smaller than the Holte End, holding 22000, but before 1977 it held 30000. The roof sits back from the rest of the stands, and from its sheltered terraces one can see, far beyond the North Bank, a panoramic view of South Staffordshire.

One can also see the roof construction of the new stand. At Molineux the roof is suspended from the top girders (as at White Hart Lane), whereas at the City Ground the girders support the roof and are therefore visible from below. Behind the South Bank some old air-raid shelters are buried. The signs pointing to them are still visible.

But from here the most notable feature is the distended nature of the ground, for between the terrace and the new stand is a bare slope of earth, fenced off but quite destroying the sense of enclosure which is so important to football grounds.

It is however too easy to criticize Molineux for being in a state of flux. It must be remembered that the building of the new stand, accompanied by lax control, very nearly put an end to Wolverhampton Wanderers completely. The new company cannot forget the expensive building work. Still less can it finance the plan to extend the new stand, or rebuild the old. But it can ensure that football remains at Molineux, and no matter how odd the ground may seem, for that at least we should be grateful.

·WALSALL·

Previous Grounds
Two teams, Walsall Swifts and Walsall Town amalgamated in 1888 to form Walsall Town Swifts, a convenient merger since they used adjacent pitches on a sports ground at Chuckery (a district near the famous Walsall Arboretum). It was here that the club played their first League match, in September 1892, but residents in Sutton Road complained about the noise. The club found a new ground on West Bromwich Road for the following season, although it was not ready in time for the first two games, played instead at the Wednesbury Oval. The first game at the new ground was on 23 September 1893. In 1895, Town Swifts failed to be re-elected to the League, and the club's name was changed to plain Walsall. The following year their return to the League was marked by the opening of the present ground in Hillary Street.

Fellows Park
The future of Fellows Park has always been uncertain. There have been plans to share Molineux with Wolves (they could almost play side by side, so wide is the Molineux turf), and most recently, a scheme was put forward to build a supermarket on the present site and give Walsall a new home on nearby Broadway West.

Walsall played their first game at the ground in September 1896, a friendly v. Glossop North End, but within a few years were in financial trouble. On 8 December 1900 the club had to return to West Bromwich Road for a short spell, unable to pay the rent at Hillary Street, even though the owner was also the club president. Agreement on leasing Hillary Street was finally reached in September 1903.

After rejoining the League in 1921, it was decided around 1930 to rename the ground Fellows Park. The suggestion came from the *Walsall Observer*'s correspondent Bill Rowlinson, pen-name 'Philistine', who thought the club should honour the chairman H. L. Fellows, the key man to Walsall's survival. Fellows Park is one of only three grounds to be named after an individual, the others being Bournemouth's Dean Court and Cardiff's Ninian Park.

The first section of the Main Stand was built on the south east side and a roof was provided over the Popular Side opposite, in time to witness Walsall's finest hour, the famous 2-0 victory over Arsenal on 14 January 1933.

During the next two decades, Walsall flitted between the Northern and Southern Sections of Division Three; their location made it easy for the League to swap them about to balance numbers. In December 1955, Fellows Park held its first floodlit game, a friendly v. Falkirk. In 1961 Walsall won promotion back to Division Two, after a 60-year absence, and

The Main Stand at Fellows Park, with a small roof extension covering the paddock

built a new dressing room block next to the Main Stand. A record crowd of 25 453 attended their opening home fixture v. Newcastle United, just relegated from Division One, in August 1961. In the same period the northern end of the ground, until then almost wholly occupied by laundry buildings, was cleared for spectators' use, although it remained a very narrow terrace.

In 1965 the Hillary Street End was covered. Ten years later, with funds raised by a Cup run, an extension was added to the Main Stand, and the dressing rooms moved back into this section of the ground. The extra stand accommodation gave Fellows Park a total of 1500 seats, in an overall capacity of 24 100.

Ground Description

With respect, if Fellows Park is lost to developers one could hardly lament its disappearance on aesthetic grounds. It is one of the least attractive enclosures in League football.

The Main Stand runs the length of the touchline between each penalty area, with open terracing on each wing. Nearer Hillary Street is the original section, mainly wooden, with a black, gently sloping roof. Built onto this is the more recent addition, constructed to the same pattern but with a plainer, glass-panelled screen end and a brick paddock rear wall. The join is clearly visible on the roof. A narrow roof extension gives shelter to those in the small paddock. Red walls and white facings give the stand a

modicum of unity. From here, the terracing on the left is entirely wooden, even the crush barriers, and because it rises adjacent to the screen wall, commands a poor view from the back. Just behind are the old dressing rooms.

To the far left you can see the covered Hillary Street End, which continues round the corner terracing until level with the penalty area. Its roof steps up to form three levels, like Kenilworth Road's Oak Road End, and is most modern nearer the Main Stand. Underneath, the barriers are like those once built at bus-stops, and about as distantly spread.

Opposite the Main Stand is the Popular Side, its roof covering only the rear half of the terracing. A large advertisement for the local commercial radio station tries hard to brighten the dark roof, and at the end of the terrace, stands a scoreboard.

Finally, the Railway End to the right is just a few steps of terracing with a brick wall behind. Behind this is a patch of unused land once occupied by the laundry, backing onto the Walsall to Birmingham railway line. In the corner nearest the Main Stand is an enclosure for the disabled.

An open ground can often seem quite pretty, with a pleasant surrounding landscape diverting the eye from the enclosure, as is the case for example at Spotland and The Shay. Lacking any of these external qualities, and enjoying no stands or terraces of any note, Fellows Park is unappealing. A move to another site would therefore be no loss, and could give Walsall a new lease of life.

SHREWSBURY ·TOWN·

Previous Grounds

Shrewsbury's origins date back to 1886. The club used two grounds, at Sutton Lake and Copthorne, before moving to the Old Racecourse Ground on the Mount. The site is now covered over by a council housing estate. Town made their final move to Gay Meadow in 1910.

Gay Meadow

In a town so steeped in history, it is inevitable that Gay Meadow had a story of its own long before the football club arrived. The field acquired its name because it was a favourite spot for fun and games. Adjacent to the Abbey Church it is pleasantly situated on the banks of the River Severn, overlooked by the town and castle.

One of the first recorded events on Gay Meadow took place in 1581 when Sir Henry Sidney (whose son Philip was studying at the grammar school in Shrewsbury) paid a visit to the town. A group of 360 schoolboys gathered on the meadow and several addressed speeches to Sir Henry, who was President of Wales and Lord Deputy of Ireland. He arrived at the field by barge to a wooden jetty just behind where the present Riverside Terrace is situated.

One of the most spectacular but tragic events to take place at the field was in 1739. A young steeple-jack, Thomas Cadman, made a bold attempt to walk along a tightrope stretched from the spire of St Mary's Church, over the ice-bound River Severn down to Gay Meadow. The memorial plaque on the wall of St Mary's tells the tale:

Let this small Monument record the name
Of CADMAN and to future times proclaim
How by'n attempt to fly from this high spire
Across the Sabrine stream he did acquire
His fatal end. 'Twas not for want of skill
Or courage to perform the task he fell:
No, no, a faulty Cord being drawn too tight
Hurried his Soul on high to take her flight
Which bid the Body here beneath good
  Night.
Feb. 2nd 1739 aged 28

One of the last public events at the ground took place in 1903, when to celebrate the 500th anniversary of the Battle of Shrewsbury a grand fête was held. Miss Kathleen Penn, who lived in Merevale House, on the site of the Wakeman School, recalled how the Meadow was used to stage a series of Shakespeare plays performed by the well respected company of Sir Frank Benson. The proceeds were spent on the repair of the Abbey church roof. Miss Penn also remembers how her family used Gay Meadow as their own playground and for haymaking parties.

When Shrewsbury Town moved to Gay Meadow, they therefore found a well-used, much loved venue,

The riverside enclosure at Gay Meadow. Notice there is no running track (Adrian Gibson)

barely changed over the centuries except for a railway embankment along the eastern side of the field, carrying the line from mid-Wales and Hereford into Shrewsbury station. Railways and football clubs were close associates during that period, before motorways developed. Shrewsbury built a small wooden grandstand on this east side, with some huts under the embankment for dressing rooms. In 1921 new dressing rooms took their place next to the stand, and it is recorded how a year later the club trainer, a jack of all trades, installed electric lights. On 28 October 1922 the new Centre Stand, built, around these dressing rooms, was officially opened by the Lord Mayor.

The 1930s brought many improvements to Gay Meadow. The Station End cover was built in stages between 1932–37, followed by the centre section of the Riverside cover between 1936–39. Also during this decade the terracing was concreted over, and in 1938–39, just after Shrewsbury had joined the Midland League, a new wing was added to the Centre Stand at the Station End, at a cost of only £1500.

All these improvements were paid for by the supporters' club, formed in 1922, and were a sign of the club's growing stature in a part of the country remote from the hustle and bustle of League football.

A development outside the ground between 1936–38 was the building of the Wakeman Technical School, on the site of the old Merevale House. The southern terrace, which backs onto the school, was named thereafter the Wakeman End. Shrewsbury were renting the ground from the council at this time, for £125 a year (they have since bought the site).

After the War Shrewsbury's success continued to make them firm candidates for League membership. They won their second Midland League Championship and staged an amateur international between Wales and England, both in 1948, and finally achieved League status two years later when the Third Divisions were extended by four clubs.

Gay Meadow in those years was a remarkably open ground. It was quite possible to view matches from high vantage points on the other side of the river. Apart from the Castle Tower, the infirmary opposite had a splendid view, at least before the Riverside cover was completed and tall trees planted. It was apparently quite common to see invalids being wheeled out onto the balconies and grass slopes for a glimpse of the action.

The first floodlights at Gay Meadow were switched on for a Third Division match v. QPR on 21 November 1959, although their official inauguration took place four days later for a friendly v. Second Division Stoke City.

It was a Third Division match which attracted Gay Meadow's highest attendance, 18 917, on 26 April 1961, the crowd no doubt boosted by travelling Walsall supporters anxious to see their team win promotion to Division Two (Walsall's next match, on the opening day of the following season, also attracted the record crowd at Fellows Park).

Cast-iron Victorian turnstile at Gay Meadow's Station End (Adrian Gibson)

In 1965–66 Town enjoyed their best ever run to date in the FA Cup, reaching the 5th Round before succumbing to Chelsea. With the profits gained, the club built new offices behind the Centre Stand and at the same time extended the roof over the open terracing at the Wakeman End on the east side. Previously this terrace had had a 'pigeon-loft' press-box perched at the back. The whole development was officially opened at the start of the 1966–67 season by the Minister of Sport, Denis Howell.

Since then the Stand has been converted into one full-length stand with the adaptation of the paddock and the Wakeman End section to seating, giving Gay Meadow a total of 4000 seats in an overall capacity of 18 000.

One of the ground's appealing qualities has also been one of its major drawbacks in past years; the closeness of the river. There is no other League ground that is a matter of a few yards from touchline to water, and not surprisingly Gay Meadow has suffered from serious flooding over the years. The worst in modern times occurred in 1948 and 1967, when the water level reached as high as the top of the Abbey doors and Town's playing gear had to be stored at the top of the stand. The problem has been alleviated by the building of dams, but excess water may still seep up through the drains.

But of course the most famous consequence of this proximity to the river has been the antics of Fred Davies, the official ball retriever. His job is to jump into his coracle, tied up behind the Riverside terrace, and fetch the balls as they are kicked over, once a game on average, at 25p a ball. It could be a hazardous job, for 500 yards down river is a treacherous weir. Once, by mistake, Fred picked out a swan from the river!

The dangers of the water, however, are small compared to the most recent threat to Gay Meadow. The council plans to build a road between the club offices and the railway embankment – it could only be a narrow single carriageway – to carry traffic behind the ground and over a new bridge to a projected multi-storey park, built next to the station. Shrewsbury town centre suffers such horrendous traffic congestion that any relief would be welcome, but not unnaturally the club are reluctant to lose their tarmac training pitch, which is rented to Wakeman School for part of the week and is a useful car-park on match days. The traffic would be at its heaviest for Saturday shopping when the ground is also busiest. This matter became so controversial that the authority's attempt to get a compulsory purchase order for Shrewsbury's land was debated in Parliament, and Town wrote to the MP of every constituency with a League club to ask for a vote in their favour.

Ground Description

Grounds like those at Chester and Cambridge do not reflect at all the towns they are in. Gay Meadow not only reflects the town of Shrewsbury but is an inescapable part of it. It has no special architectural merit. Rather, it derives its appeal from the riverside setting.

From the climbing, winding streets of the town centre (the old medieval stronghold is almost encircled by the river as it doubles back on itself) you approach Gay Meadow across the English Bridge, built in 1774 and reconstructed in 1927. At the far end there used to be a portcullis and drawbridge. Ahead is the Benedictine Abbey Church. An unlikely location for a football ground.

A private road between the Wakeman School and the railway embankment leads to the ground. The Main Stand, theoretically three stands joined into one, is by no means outstanding but is a neat modernization. It has become less interesting from inside the ground since the central gable was removed in the mid-1960s. One unusual feature, however, is that the aisles between the seats run down to the pitch, where a gap in the perimeter wall leads onto the turf, as a safety measure. There is no track around the pitch, which adds to the field-like appearance of the ground.

From here, to the left is the uncovered and fairly narrow terrace named after the Wakeman School. The school's windows look down onto the ground and

are used as a vantage point for the club's video camera. Behind this terrace is the Abbey Garden into which many a ball is kicked (and often lost). From the ground one can see the white stone head of a statue only feet away from the terrace rear wall. This is Viscount Hill (1800–75), a local dignitary whose devoted tenants and friends erected the statue after his death.

On the far side of the terrace is a lovely old half-time scoreboard, built in 1936 and adorned with a disproportionately large loudspeaker. The club will never be able to cover this end because of the school's proximity.

Opposite the Main Stand is the Riverside, an equally narrow stretch of terracing covered by a quaint, slightly curving low cover. It is a simple corrugated roof over the rear section, supported by a closely spaced line of pillars. To compare it with a bicycle shed would not be unkind, yet this is one of the most charming sides of any football ground. Above it is a thick range of trees along the river bank, hiding most of the view of the far bank. Running behind the back of the stand is a narrow and overgrown pathway by the river, leading from the car-park to the Abbey Gardens, but there's hardly a crack or a hole in the wall for any potential peeping toms. Finally, to the right is the Station End, also covered with a simple roof. This is the visitors' end, and Shrewsbury, perhaps because of the narrowness of their terraces, were one of the first clubs to segregate properly rival supporters. Behind this end you can see Laura's Tower on the hill, a small red, sandstone tower, standing out above the trees, which was built in the Castle grounds in 1790 by Thomas Telford.

Immediately behind the Station End is the club's floodlit practice pitch and car-park, both threatened by the road scheme. The station is a few hundred yards from here, spanning the river. The other large building, just visible, is HM Prison.

There is one feature at the Station End of particular note. One of the turnstiles dates back to 1885 and was made by Stevens and Sons, Southwark (London). It is suggested that this superbly intricate piece of metalwork may have arrived at Gay Meadow via the old Crystal Palace ground, where the Cup Final was staged between 1895–1914.

There are certainly grounds with more intrinsic merit and certainly more old-fashioned charm than Gay Meadow. Far from seeming outdated or run down, everything at this compact ground is quite fresh and neat. Gay Meadow's appeal lies in its location, which like Sincil Bank or Valley Parade lends it a firm identity. All around are definitive sights that could only be Shrewsbury. As at Blundell Park, a visit to Gay Meadow is itself a visit to the town, tempting one to venture back across the bridge for a stroll.

·STOKE CITY·

Victoria Ground

Stoke is not only the second oldest club in the League, but has been in continuous occupation of its present ground longer than any other English League club. In Scotland, Dumbarton have been at Boghead Park since their formation in 1872, but in England, Stoke have kept the same address since 1878.

The club was formed by clerks of the North Staffordshire Railway Company in 1863, but did not settle until 1875 at a ground called Sweeting's Field. This was opposite the present site, and is now covered by the Victoria Inn. In 1878 Stoke moved to the New Athletic Club Ground across the road, where they were forbidden by the ecclesiastical owners to play on Sundays or Good Friday. A covenant to this effect still exists. The ground owes its name to the Victoria Inn opposite.

As an athletics venue, the ground was originally an oval shape to accommodate a track. Both ends were open banking, with one small wooden stand on the East Side, on Boothen Road. Although Stoke were founder members of the Football League, their early years were fraught with difficulties. They dropped out of the League in 1890, to be replaced by Sunder-

land, rejoined it in 1891 with Darwen, thanks to an expansion of the competition, then after being relegated to the Second Division resigned their place on 17 June 1908. The board, perhaps for financial reasons, sponsored Tottenham's application to join the League in Stoke's place, then realized their folly in resigning and tried to rejoin. But it was too late. Spurs were in and Stoke were doomed to play non-League football until 1919. By strange coincidence, neighbours Port Vale were also out of the League, from 1907–19, so Stoke at least did not lose its seniority in the area.

When Stoke returned to Division Two in 1919, followed in October by Port Vale (in place of Leeds City), the Victoria Ground had two stands, another small wooden stand seating 1000 having been built opposite the Main Stand. In the south west corner, between where the Boothen Stand and Boothen End are now, was a small hut for the players' dressing rooms, remembered especially for an old stove in the centre, around which players would huddle after winter games. Above the hut was the directors' box, rather like a primitive version of the Craven Cottage.

During the 1920s, a new but still mainly wooden main stand was built alongside this hut, with seating for 2000 spectators, and in 1925, with the joining together of the towns of the Potteries to form the new corporation of Stoke-on-Trent, the club added 'City'

The Victoria Ground looking towards the Stoke End. The Trent is on the right (Chris Doorbar)

to their title.

In 1930 the Boothen End of the ground was ter-raced and later covered, and thus the original oval shape of the ground was lost. In 1935, with Stoke now back in Division One and a young winger called Stanley Matthews beginning to make news, the But-ler Street Stand was built. This had 5000 seats with a small paddock in front, and at each end the barrel roof curled slightly round the corners. The stand was no doubt full when the Victoria Ground's highest crowd, 51 380, saw Stoke v. Arsenal in March 1937, in the First Division. During the Second World War, the Butler Street Stand was used as an army camp.

The Victoria Ground's first floodlights were switched on in October 1956 for a match v. Port Vale, when both clubs were in Division Two. The Main Stand and dressing room facilities had long been outdated, and in 1960 the club at last began the process of modernizing that side of the ground. The new stand was built in three stages, the last one coinciding with Stoke's return to Division One in 1963. During the summer months, the players were offered one shilling an hour to help lay the concrete terracing in the paddock!

The 1970s were bright years for Stoke, seeing them reach two FA Cup semi-finals and winning their first major honour, the League Cup, in 1972, in their 109th year of existence. They had even begun to compete in Europe, and almost as a reminder not to get too carried away with success, a gale carried away the roof of the Butler Street Stand. The club had to play one home game at Vale Park, but soon replaced the roof with a smart, new white cover. The south east corner section survived, and has not been mod-ernized for the simple reason that its foundations are sunk deep into the bed of the River Trent, which almost runs underneath that corner. It would be very expensive to make alterations.

Finally, in October 1979 the Stoke End Stand was opened. A simple two-tiered stand, with 4000 seats behind a paddock, its erection dictated a change of the floodlighting system, since the original pylons had stood on the open banking. In their place were installed two smaller, more compact pylons, and so the Victoria Ground now has two different pairs of lights, as at Carrow Road. This new stand completed all-round cover at The Victoria Ground, pleasant for the fans, but difficult for drying the pitch. It had always been a muddy surface, because of the proxi-mity of the River Trent, and had been returfed in 1965. Now it had to be sand-injected, and at the same time a proper track was laid around the perimeter.

The Victoria Ground holds 35 000, of which 12 338 are seated.

Ground Description

Once found, there are no parking problems at the Victoria Ground, for behind the Butler Street Stand between the Trent and the motorway link road is space for about 2000 cars, next to Stoke's training ground. This facility alone makes the ground a plea-sure to visit.

The main entrance is on Boothen Road, in a narrow street dominated by the back of the Boothen Stand. No doubt when it was first built this was an exciting, modern piece of architecture. Britain abounds with such buildings; 1960s' blocks dressed in coloured panelling. But they faded quickly and already look dated.

Inside the Boothen Stand – I recommend you have a peep at an enormous and grotesquely executed oil painting in the foyer – the 'modern' design continues throughout like an exhibit from the 1951 Festival of Britain, although of course once into the ground all is forgiven. The stand appears quite ordinary, faced in red with a plain sloping roof, a paddock in front of the seating tier. To the right is the Boothen End, named after a nearby district. In the corner between here and the Boothen Stand, on the site of the old dressing rooms, is a block comprising various social facilities, and a unique feature – a place for players' wives to view the match. The Boothen End itself is a sloping bank, covered at the back and joined at either side to the adjacent stands. It holds 11 000 standing.

In the corner between here and the Butler Street Stand is the surviving section of the original stand, which managed to hold onto its roof during the gale in 1976. Because it is in such contrast to the modern sections it appears even older than it is, like an antiquated bird cage sat next to a steel box. All that is new about the Butler Street Stand, however, is the roof and the fencing. Otherwise the seats, floors and walls are all original. What a difference a modern white, flat roof can make to an old stand! Almost like a hairpiece, you cannot see the join.

The River Trent flows past this corner somewhat narrower here than it was when it passed by Notting-ham Forest because its source is just a few miles north, east of Vale Park, three miles away.

The new roof links up in the north east corner with the Stoke End Stand, a plain construction again but brightened by red seats and a white roof. The roof fascia of both these two new sides of the ground are left plain, and might well suit a crest or clock.

The Victoria Ground has never been highly praised; always classified as one of those 'quintessentially Second Division grounds'. Since the addition of the Stoke End Stand, I consider it to be one of the best in the League, small but with good seating providing clear vision all round. The new stand also adds a more enclosed atmosphere, so that taking into account the splendid access and parking, the Victoria Ground would seem perfectly equipped to face soccer in the late twentieth century. All that it lacks now is a tradition. The least altered part of the ground is the trophy cupboard, and of course great football grounds depend not only on their outward appearance but also on their atmosphere. As yet the Victoria Ground does not have one. It is not yet a place to fear.

· PORT VALE ·

Previous Grounds

Port Vale were formed in a house of that name in Longport, Burslem, one of the six towns of the Potteries, in 1876. Their first ground on Limekiln Lane, near Alexandra Road, has since been built over. From 1881–84, Vale played on a pitch by Westport Lake, then for two years used some waste ground on Moorland Road, Burslem, adjacent to the present ground. Here they adopted the title Burslem Port Vale, but had to move in 1886 when the ground was bought by the corporation. It now forms part of Burslem Park. Vale moved south, to the Cobridge Athletic Ground on Waterloo Road. When the Cobridge Ground began to subside, and their support decline, Vale moved to Hanley.

The club's new home, the Old Recreation Ground, was in the centre of Hanley, so Vale dropped the prefix Burslem from their name. A crowd of 13 000 came to their opening Central League match v. Blackburn Rovers in September 1913.

The players at Hanley had to change in a room over some stables and walk between the houses to enter the pitch, until a new stand was built for £12 000 along what was called Swan Passage, part of which still remains near Market Square. In their first season back in the League, Vale had their highest attendance at the ground when 22 993 saw them play neighbours Stoke in Division Two on 6 March 1920. This match had particular significance because both clubs had been out of the League for some time. After limited success in the Division until 1927, the club bought the Old Recreation Ground from the corporation.

In 1943, despite advice to the contrary and much protest, the board decided to ease their financial burdens by selling the ground back to the corporation for £13 000, and play there on a short lease. They then bought another site in November 1944, next to Burslem Park, although Vale's final game at the Old Recreation Ground was not until the end of the 1949 –50 season, when the lease ran out. The site is now a car-park on Bryan Street, where you can just make out the slopes of the old banking. Part of the pitch covered what is now Quadrant Road.

Vale Park

Two other clubs have moved to new grounds since the Second World War, Hull City in 1946 and Southend United in 1955, but neither had such ambitions as Port Vale in 1950. The club had no money after the War, was living in the shadows of First Division Stoke City, and yet it planned to build a super-stadium holding 70 000 spectators! This was to be the 'Wembley of the North', the envy of every League club and the pride of the Potteries.

An artist's impression of Vale Park as planned in 1950, the Wembley of the North (PVFC)

The prime-mover behind this ambitious, and even foolhardy scheme was Vale's chairman, Alderman Holdcroft. In 1944 when work began, the 14-acre site (later expanded to 18½ acres) was an old marl pit, a common feature in the Potteries, excavated for deposits of lime clay. Levelling the surface required the shifting of 30 000 cubic yards of earth, but finding building materials during those austere, post-war years of rationing was far more difficult. Somehow, however, Holdcroft managed to obtain the necessary steel, timber and concrete.

When Vale's lease at Hanley ran out, the new ground was just about ready for football. The turf was large enough for a huge pitch measuring 115×83 yards, and a running track around the perimeter. At the North End was placed the steel-framed stand taken from Hanley, and on either side of the ground were to be two identical stands each seating 4000, with large paddocks in front. Behind the East Stand ran the loop line from Stoke to Kidsgrove, and it was intended to build a station there, just like Wembley.

That Vale Park did not become a super-stadium was largely due to the state of both the club and the country. Holdcroft could not make Vale a wealthy club, nor could he divert sufficient materials from post-war rebuilding efforts. Despite initial expenditure of £50 000, the ground on its opening day was almost entirely open. A crowd of 28 000 saw Vale play Newport County, and heard it announced that the ground was to be called Vale Park. Temporary dressing rooms had been built at the rear of the Lorne Street Side, and around them laid the foundations of the planned Main Stand. The opposite Railway Stand was begun, but not completed until 1953. Not that despondency had set in. Dreams take time to come true, and the team was at least helping to raise the extra funds needed to complete the stadium. In 1954, they enjoyed their best season to date, winning promotion to Division Two and becoming only the second Third Division team to reach the FA Cup semi-final. The average gate at Vale Park in that memorable season was 20 801.

Vale Park. The Main Stand (right) was never built, but the tunnel indicates its intended scale. Notice how open the ground is on all four sides (Aerofilms)

Floodlights were installed at a cost of £15 000 and first used for a friendly v. WBA on 24 September 1958, and two years later Vale Park witnessed its highest gate of 50 000, for the visit of Villa in the FA Cup Fifth Round on 20 February 1960. But by then, Vale were back in the lower Divisions and the dream for a super-stadium was no longer in cold storage, it was over.

Inevitably, the ground has declined. The Railway Stand has begun to rot, the old Hanley Stand on the Bycars Lane End had to be replaced after a fire, and the covered corner between the two roofs was fenced off as a safety measure. Now the capacity is 35 000, half the figure projected in 1950, and there are 4200 seats.

Ground Description

If you were not aware of Vale Park's short history, it would seem at first sight an odd sort of ground, built the wrong way round. The offices, changing rooms and directors' box are housed in a tiny structure, opposite a much larger stand, rather like The Shay.

The administrative centre looks like a sea-side promenade restaurant. It is a low but quietly dignified building, the now permanent 'temporary structure' erected when the ground was opened. Some 50 yards long, it has a small covered enclosure for the directors and their guests, seating 200, and lies above an open terrace, divided down the middle by a grand player's entrance, lined in white concrete. This was intended to be the centre piece of the Main Stand, and you can see some of the original foundations behind the terracing. Placed over this tunnel is a large clock. If completed, it would have been quite a stand.

From here, to the left is the Hamil Road open terrace, behind which is the market place, a vital source of revenue. To the right is the Bycars Lane End, covered at the back.

The Bycars Lane End roof continues round the corner to meet up with the Railway Stand, the largest structure. To imagine the stadium as it should have been: each end was to have been covered, joining up with the side stands in each corner to create an all enclosed stadium.

If the Railway Stand looks impressive from a distance, at close quarters it is sad indeed. The seating tier is dark and gloomy, the seats are dilapidated, and the railway line behind is now disused. No station was ever built.

Vale Park thus has a strange lop-sided feeling; terraces exposed to winds which whip across the open surrounds, dark little corners, rickety fences, all overlooked by a cosy little directors' box.

The site still has possibilities. For example, the playing surface is still large, with plenty of turf to spare beyond the touchlines. And since the ground is a perfect bowl with space behind all four sides, the scope for expansion and modernization is enormous. There are car-parks on either side of the ground, a thriving market place and two social clubs, so that if Port Vale did achieve success – and local support has been forthcoming whenever this was promised – they could, with help, transform Vale Park into something approaching Holdcroft's dream. Not Wembley of course, but certainly a multi-sport stadium, perhaps all-seated. Holdcroft and his fellow board members might have bitten off more than they could chew in 1944, but for comparatively little outlay they did endow the club with a ground of enviable potential.

· 16 ·
MERSEYSIDE, CHESHIRE AND NORTH WALES

· LIVERPOOL ·

Anfield

Liverpool's birth as a football club is quite unique in the history of the English game. There were to be cases where a club utilized an already existing ground, as at Chelsea and Plymouth, but none where that ground had previously been the home of an established First Division side. If Everton had not rowed with their landlord and most ardent sponsor, John Houlding, Anfield today would be decked in blue, Goodison Park would never have existed, and perhaps a club like Bootle might have become the second most important team in the city.

Everton made the decision to move to Mere Green in January 1892, half-way through the season. On 15 March Houlding established his own club, Liverpool FC. He had wanted to keep the name Everton, but the Football League ruled against this. The title Liverpool FC was then challenged by a local rugby union team of the same name, so the soccer team adopted Liverpool AFC as their name. Houlding's investment was £500. By the end of the season Everton had gone, and the Reds moved in. Their first year's rent at Anfield was £100; one of the reasons for Everton's argument with Houlding was that he had raised their annual rent to £250. There is a tiny road named after Houlding very near Anfield, off Walton Breck Road.

Liverpool were an instant creation; professional players, a limited company and a ground all at the same time. Just one season later they were elected to Division Two, and one season after that, in 1894, had their first taste of First Division football. But Anfield was still much less advanced than its new neighbour across the park. Liverpool's first League game attracted 5000, far fewer than Everton were used to. By the turn of the century however, the two clubs were at least on a par in footballing terms, Liverpool winning their first Championship in 1901.

The first change at the ground had come in 1895, after Liverpool won the Second Division for the second time in three seasons. A Main Stand seating 3000 was built on the site of the present Main Stand

and for the next 75 years was something of a landmark in English football. It resembled Newcastle's West Stand (built in 1906), with a semi-circular gable in the centre of a barrelled roof. The gable was red and white mock-tudor style with the club's name displayed in the centre, topped by ornate ironwork.

In 1903 the first stand on Anfield Road was constructed, mainly from timber and corrugated iron, also with a barrel roof, and in 1906 when Liverpool won their second Championship the first 'Kop' was built. It was by no means the first tall section of banking at a football ground, but almost certainly the first to be christened Spion Kop, on the suggestion of a journalist, Ernest Edwards, sports editor of the local *Post and Echo* (see Appendix). On Kemlyn Road was built a third barrel-roofed stand, with an uncovered paddock in front.

During the 1920s Anfield was a busy place. In 1921 George V and Queen Mary attended the ground. Having watched the Grand National at Aintree the day before (the race used to be held on Fridays) they saw a Cup semi-final replay between Wolves and Cardiff. The 1920s began for Liverpool with two Championship wins in a row, there was a fire in the Main Stand during a game in 1922, and a few years later the ground became the finishing point for the annual Liverpool Civic Marathon. Apparently the runners would enter the stadium during the closing stages of a game and had to complete one lap of the pitch before finishing. The race was held until the outbreak of the Second World War. World Championship boxing matches were another regular attraction, as was exhibition tennis, played on boards in the middle of the pitch during the 1930s.

A major ground development occurred in 1928, with the extension and covering of the Kop in its present form. Designed at the time to hold 30 000, it was without question the largest covered Kop in the country. On the Kemlyn Road corner of this new structure was installed another landmark, a tall white flagpole with a history of its own. Originally it had been the top mast of the *Great Eastern*, one of the first iron ships in the world, whose maiden voyage was in 1860. By 1888 she lay broken up in the Mersey docks, having served in latter years as a floating

Just in case the players forget . . . the tunnel (Colorsport)

advertisement for Lewis's, the department store, and as a fun-fair in the Liverpool Exhibition of 1887. When the Kop was completed, the surviving top mast was floated across the Mersey and hauled up to Anfield by a team of horses.

The ground's biggest crowd came after the Second World War, for Liverpool's 4th Round FA Cup tie v. Wolves, in February 1952. The attendance was 61905. Liverpool's first floodlights, which cost £12000 and were on four quite small pylons in each corner, were installed in 1957. To celebrate the 75th anniversary of the Liverpool County FA, the first floodlit game at Goodison Park had taken place on 9 October, Everton beating Liverpool 2-0. The Anfield lights were switched on three weeks later, this time Liverpool beating Everton, 3-2.

At that time Liverpool were in the Second Division, but once they were promoted in 1962 life at Anfield changed dramatically. The old Kemlyn Road Stand came down in 1963 and the present cantilevered stand was erected at the then enormous cost of £350000 (Hillsborough had paid about £100000 a few years earlier). The new stand was an all-seater with room for 6700 spectators, and has remained one of the most unusual constructions at any British

ground. It was given a national airing on 22 August 1964 when Anfield was the venue of the very first broadcast of BBC's *Match of the Day*, then on BBC 2. A television audience of only 75000 saw Champions Liverpool beat Arsenal 3-2.

The following season Liverpool won the FA Cup for the first time and with the profits the club built a new stand on the Anfield Road End, a covered standing enclosure.

Another television event at the ground came in March 1967, when a crowd of 40149 saw Liverpool's FA Cup 5th Round match v. Everton on closed circuit television, beamed onto huge screens direct from Goodison Park, where a further 64851 watched 'live' as Everton won 1-0. That game would have been seen in black and white, but on 15 November 1969 the first colour transmission of *Match of the Day* took place from Anfield, for a game v. West Ham.

Liverpool's most consistent run of success began in 1971, after losing their fourth FA Cup Final. Between then and 1982 the club won the Championship six times, the FA Cup once, the UEFA Cup twice, the European Cup three times and the League or Milk Cup twice. There were really only two aspects of the ground that they could improve with the revenue left after buying players, namely the old Main Stand and the floodlights.

The new Main Stand was opened officially by HRH the Duke of Kent on 10 March 1973, during Liverpool's eighth Championship winning season. At the same time the present floodlighting system, along the roofs of both side stands (as at Goodison Park) was installed at a cost of £100000. Anfield's present capacity is 45000, including 21700 seats, and it is hard to imagine how the ground might develop without committing the unthinkable – putting seats into the Kop. The only remaining space to expand has come recently with the demolition of a row of houses immediately behind the Kemlyn Road Stand, but with Liverpool's gates unlikely to rise significantly, Anfield will remain as it is for some years to come.

Ground Description

Anfield has the reputation of an opera house, dental surgery and casino all rolled into one. You visit the ground expecting to see finesse and hear fine tunes, but if an away fan you go in fear of pain, and never expect to come away with a win. What makes Anfield most daunting of all is the team, and although the stadium is enclosed and cavernous, and the atmosphere can at times be electric, for partisanship, vehemence and noise level I consider Old Trafford or Celtic Park to be more oppressive for visiting teams and supporters. The people of Liverpool are too friendly and far too confident of winning to make Anfield anything but hospitable and welcoming.

The Anfield experience begins, perhaps more than at most grounds, in the approach roads. Gradually all the houses and shops seem to be decked in red and white, or red and yellow. There are road signs directing you to Anfield and Liverpool FC (yet very few pointing to Goodison Park), though you barely see the ground until you reach the doors. Particularly disorienting is the approach along Walton Breck Road, from where you can see the hump-back shape of the Kop and the odd floodlight gantries on the Kemlyn Road Stand roof. It is hard to work out what the back of the Kop is, so strange are the angles of its roof.

The entrance to the Main Stand on Anfield Road should be seen by every visiting spectator, whatever section of the ground he is bound for, because it has a magnificent set of wrought iron gates dedicated to the memory of Liverpool's late manager, Bill Shankly. Above the gates is the inscription, 'You'll never walk alone'.

The Main Stand is very plain at the back and has an unimaginative entrance hall. Considering the unparalleled success of the club in recent years, it is a shame that it did not try to emulate those grand entrances found at Highbury or Ibrox, or at least build a small facade on the impressive lines of Elland Road or Bramall Lane. Nevertheless, Liverpool's success does tend to speak for itself.

The Main Stand seats 8600 in the upper section, 2150 in the paddock. The roof is enormous, supported by two thin central uprights, with a large suspended television camera gantry. Otherwise this is a very plain structure; clean, modern and better to sit in than to look at. As the players emerge from the tunnel in this stand, they see a sign above, proclaiming: 'This is Anfield'.

To the left is the smallest section of the ground, the Anfield Road Stand. Constructed mainly in plain brick and concrete, it has a slight roof, pointing upwards and supported by columns near the back. It used to be all standing, until seats were installed over all but the Kemlyn Road corner section in the summer of 1982. The rest of Anfield has a pleasant sort of dignity created by the colour combinations of red, grey and white, so the new seats in this stand come as a particularly glaring shock. They are from left to right, orange, ochre, violet, red, emerald green and cream. These colours were partly chosen because when the Main Stand paddock was seated in the summer of 1980, the Liverpool manager Bob Paisley watched a reserve match at Anfield and was irritated that the red shirts of his team seemed to get lost against the new red background of seats. There is no danger whatsoever of this happening with the new Anfield Road seats.

Opposite the Main Stand on Kemlyn Road is one of the most unusual constructions at any League ground. It is an early example of a cantilever roof, but one never copied since, because it has not been a success. The space was confined by a row of houses directly behind the stand, and the roof therefore had to be angled in such a way as not to cut out what little light the houses enjoyed. Massive wedges of steel necessary to support the ungainly roof meant that fewer seats could be installed at the back, with the result that more had to be crammed in at the front. The result was an expensive stand which did not fulfil its potential. It cost more than the United Road cantilever stand built at Old Trafford, yet held over 3000 fewer people. Visually however it is quite remarkable. From the top of the back wall the roof leans forward at an angle of 45 degrees, reaching a peak about half way over the seating tier. It then dips down at a sharp angle, ending above the perimeter track. This front section, unsupported at the edge

The old Main Stand, demolished in the early 1970s (*Liverpool Daily Post & Echo*)

almost looks precarious enough to fall onto the pitch. And to confuse the design further, the floodlight gantries protrude high above the back of the roof while the front slopes down.

Mather and Nutter, the architects who designed the new stands at Molineux and White Hart Lane, as well as the cantilever stands at Old Trafford, have drawn up plans for a redeveloped Kemlyn Road Stand which would alleviate its current problems. Making use of the space created by the demolition of houses in Kemlyn Road, the plan is to take off the existing roof and add a rear section of seats, built into a new stand with 36 private boxes and an impressive frontage. The roof would be the same as the Main Stand, and would cover all 10 000 seats. But until Liverpool's finances improve, redevelopment is out of the question.

Finally, we come to the Kop, the southern end of the ground whose patrons have made Anfield famous with their passion, wit and sportsmanship. The capacity of this enclosure is now reduced to 21 500, and although it seems physically much smaller than for example, Villa Park's Holte End (capacity 22 600), because the terracing is covered right up to the front, it has a darker, more ominous presence. It is the Kop, more than any other part of the ground, which makes a visit to Anfield such a potentially daunting experience. As mentioned earlier, the roof looks rather odd from the outside. It is predominantly grey topping a high, well fenestrated wall of cream concrete and red brick. The famous flag-pole is situated on the corner with Kemlyn Road.

Inside, the Kop appears surprisingly bright because of the windows and sky-lights. The barriers are all white. Apart from the corners, where there are dividing fences, the view is very good, despite security fencing at the front. Since the other three sides are now all seated they have low perimeter walls only, which has the effect of bringing one closer to the players. It is said that Liverpool's men always seem that much taller as they emerge from the tunnel, and this lack of barriers is one of the reasons. In addition the pitch is the minimum length, none of the stands is very tall and their roofs pitch relatively low on each side; factors which combine to create an almost claustrophic atmosphere. Even the players stand out more clearly against the shadowy backgrounds. It is hard to say whether this effect was intentional, but the psychological advantage it has given Liverpool either through fact, illusion or merely by suggestion is indisputable.

Anfield on a big match day is probably the most exhilarating, and at the same time, unnerving experience one could sample in English football. The design of the ground helps this, as does the temper of the crowd. But the club, and especially the late Bill Shankly, have deliberately created a fearsome reputation for the place. Anfield would not seem half so imposing if it were not for the formidable team who call it home.

◆ EVERTON ◆

Previous Grounds

It is seldom remembered outside Merseyside, but never forgotten in Liverpool, that Everton played at Anfield for eight years between 1884–92, and it was only their departure from the ground that prompted the formation of rivals Liverpool. Furthermore, Everton even won the First Division Championship at Anfield in 1891. For a fuller account of Everton's early years see John Roberts' excellent centenary history of the club.

The club began life as St Domingo's FC in 1878 and found a pitch in Stanley Park, which had just been laid out for the public and still stands between Anfield and Goodison Park. They played opposite the house of local Alderman and Conservative MP, John Houlding, who was soon to become known as 'King John' of Everton. (Everton is the name of the district just west of the park.) By 1882 unofficial attendances for Everton's matches had risen to 2000 and so it was decided that a properly enclosed ground where the club could charge admission would be advisable.

At a meeting in the Sandon Hotel, owned by Houlding's brewery, in March 1882, a Mr Cruitt of Coney Green offered Everton a fenced and gated field in Priory Road, opposite the park. Enough funds were found to move in the following year and changing rooms and a small stand were built. The first match, a representative game between Liverpool and Walsall raised gate receipts of only 13 shillings. The ground was inconvenient for public transport and the noise from Everton's growing number of followers: 'disturbed the pastoral serenity of Mr Cruitt's environment'.

Instead, in 1884, Houlding secured them a field which he partly owned in Anfield Road. He also acted as agent on behalf of the landlord of the other part, a Mr Orell. The Sandon Hotel became the club's headquarters, and fences and hoardings were erected by members. Match receipts rose immediately from £45 at Priory Road to £200 at Anfield by 1885. In Everton's last season before joining the new Football League in 1888, they paid Houlding a rent of £100, but after finishing as runners-up in their second League season their rent increased to £250 a year. Houlding also had the sole right to sell refreshments at Anfield.

Unhappy with this situation, the committee met in May 1889 and decided to look for another ground. Some of them objected to having the club's affairs run from a licensed hotel, while others were reluctant to lose the money invested in fixtures and fittings at Anfield. The ground was quite suitable after all, and in March of that year had been host to an international match between England and Ireland. They offered Houlding a compromise rent of £180 for the next season, but received no reply. In fact Houlding was incensed. He had already tried to buy out Orell, who planned to make alterations to his part of the field, and offered to sell Everton the entire plot for £6000. When the club refused, Houlding served them notice to quit, and attempted to form his own Everton FC and Athletic Grounds Limited at Anfield. (He succeeded, but the new club became known as Liverpool, since the League ruled that Everton should take their name with them.)

In response to Houlding's wrath, Everton held a special meeting in January 1892, by which time they had consolidated their position by winning the Championship in 1891, making a profit of £1700. A committee member, George Mahon, the organist at St Domingo's church, revealed that he had an option on a field on the north side of Stanley Park, called Mere Green. Gibson and Pickford's *Book of Football* in 1906 described the field as having: 'degenerated from a nursery into a howling desert,' rather similar to the site on which White Hart Lane was built. Everton formed a limited company and with considerable help from another committee member, Dr

James Baxter, bought the 30 000 square yard site for £8090, a high price even in those days. At last they had a home of their own, and were free of Houlding's tyranny! Houlding even tried to stop Everton officials as they attempted to take away the turnstiles and fittings from Anfield.

Goodison Park

Goodison Park was the first major football stadium in England. Molineux had been opened three years earlier but was still relatively undeveloped. St James' Park, Newcastle, opened in 1892, was little more than a field. Only Scotland had more advanced grounds. Rangers opened Ibrox in 1887, while Celtic Park was officially inaugurated at the same time as Goodison Park. Everton performed a miraculous transformation at Mere Green, spending up to £3000 on laying out the ground and erecting stands on three sides. For £552 Mr Barton prepared the land at 4½d a square yard. Kelly Brothers of Walton built two uncovered stands each for 4000 people, and a covered stand seating 3000, at a total cost of £1640. Outside,

Goodison Park in the late 1930s. Notice how the church cuts into the terracing (Aerofilms)

hoardings cost a further £150, gates and sheds cost £132 10s and 12 turnstiles added another £7 15s to the bill.

The ground was immediately renamed Goodison Park and proudly opened on 24 August 1892, by Lord Kinnaird and Frederick Wall of the FA. But instead of a match the 12 000 crowd saw a short athletics meeting followed by a selection of music and a fireworks display. Everton's first game there was on 2 September when they beat Bolton 4-2.

The following description comes from *Out of Doors*, October 1892:

> Behold Goodison Park! . . . no single picture could take in the entire scene the ground presents, it is so magnificently large, for it rivals the greater American baseball pitches. On three sides of the field of play there are tall covered stands, and on the fourth side the ground has been so well banked up with thousands of loads of cinders that a complete view of the game can be had from any portion.
>
> The spectators are divided from the playing piece by a neat, low hoarding, and the touch-line is far enough from it to prevent those accidents which used to be predicted at Anfield Road, but never happened . . . Taking it altogether, it appears to be one of the finest and most complete grounds in the kingdom, and it is to be hoped that the public will liberally support the promoters.

A year after moving, Everton were FA Cup finalists in 1893, then runners-up again in the First Division in 1895. The ground was honoured in 1894 when Notts County beat Bolton in the FA Cup Final, watched by a disappointing crowd of 37 000, but Everton were still the richest club in the country, and League gates such as the 30 000 which attended in February 1893 were still regarded as enormous.

Despite the initial developments, it was not long before Goodison Park was improved even further. A new Bullens Road Stand was built in 1895 at a cost of £3407 (although the original construction seems to have been more than adequate, unless the work involved only spectator facilities) and the open Goodison Road Side was covered for £403.

Meanwhile competition in the city was reaching peak levels. Everton were yet again runners-up in both the League and FA Cup, while across Stanley Park, Liverpool won their first Championship in 1901.

The Goodison of today really began to take shape after the turn of the century, beginning in 1907 with the building of the Park End double-decker stand, at a cost of £13 000. In 1909 the large Main Stand on Goodison Road was built. Costing £28 000 it housed all the offices and players' facilities, and survived until 1971.

At the same time another £12 000 was spent on concreting over the terracing and replacing the cinder running track. The *Athletic News'* correspondent wrote in the summer of 1909, 'Visitors to Goodison Park will be astonished at the immensity of the new double-decker stand'. The architect was Archibald Leitch, and the front balcony wall bore his criss-cross trademark, which can still be seen on the Bullens Road Stand opposite and on the Main Stands at Ibrox and Roker Parks.

In recognition of the fact that the ground was by far the best equipped in England, Everton hosted the 1910 Cup Final reply between Newcastle and Barnsley. On this occasion 69 000 attended. Then on 13 July 1913 Goodison Park became the first League venue to be visited by a ruling monarch, when George V and Queen Mary came to inspect local schoolchildren at the ground.

During the First World War Goodison was used by the Territorial Army for drill practice. Soon after, the US baseball teams Chicago Giants and New York Whitesocks played an exhibition match at the ground. One player managed to hit the ball right over the Main Stand.

The next major development followed in 1926, when at a cost of £30 000 another double-decker, similar to the Main Stand, was built on the Bullens Road Side opposite. Again, Leitch was the architect.

In the 1930s, Everton borrowed an idea from Aberdeen FC, who they had visited for a friendly. At Pittodrie in 1931, trainer Donald Colman had built the first ever dug-outs in the country, and probably the world. Not only did Colman want shelter on the touchline, but also a worm's eye view of his players' footwork. From Pittodrie and Goodison Park the idea soon spread, and now the covered dug-out is a feature of almost every ground. (Quite how managers and coaches can command a decent view of the game from this level is beyond the average fan, and in recent years several managers have taken up vantage points higher in the stands, with telephones linking them to the bench. This seems much more sensible, but does rather isolate them from the centre of the action.)

Another Royal visit occurred in 1938. George VI and Queen Elizabeth, the present Queen Mother, came to Everton and saw the new Gwladys Street Stand, just completed for £50 000. Notice how costs had escalated over the years. Goodison Park thereby became the only ground in Britain to have four double-decker stands and was newly affirmed as the most advanced stadium in Britain. Some writers referred to it as 'Toffeeopolis', after the club's nickname.

Goodison Park suffered quite badly during the Second World War, because it lies so near the Liverpool docks, and the club received £5000 for repair work from the War Damage Commission. Shortly after the work was completed Everton enjoyed their highest ever attendance, 78 299, for the visit of Liverpool in Division One, on 18 September 1948.

Floodlights came to both Liverpool clubs in October 1957. The Goodison Park set, which were originally mounted on four extremely tall pylons, were switched on for an Everton v. Liverpool friendly on 9 October.

A year later the club spent £16 000 on installing 20 miles of electric wire underneath the pitch. The system melted ice and frost most effectively, but the drains could not handle the extra load, so in 1960 the pitch was dug up yet again and new drainage pipes laid.

The 1960s, like the 1930s, saw Everton win the Championship twice and the FA Cup once, and in 1966 Goodison Park staged five games in the World Cup, including that memorable quarter-final between Portugal and North Korea. No other English venue apart from Wembley staged so many World Cup games. In preparation for the World Cup, the club had bought and demolished some of the Victorian terraced houses which stood behind the Park End Stand, in order to make the present entrance way from Stanley Park. The houses had originally been built by the club for players, and Dixie Dean lived in one of them.

The final and perhaps most spectacular development was in 1971, when the 1909 double-decker Main Stand on Goodison Road was demolished to make way for a massive new three-tiered Main Stand. The old stand had cost £28 000 and was then considered immense. The new stand cost £1 million, was nearly twice the size, and was the largest in Britain until 1974, when Chelsea opened their mammoth East Stand, which cost twice as much.

Because the Goodison Road Stand is so tall, the floodlight pylons were taken down and lamps put on gantries along the roof. The Bullens Road roof was replaced by a modern roof and similar gantries installed there also. Anfield's lights followed the same pattern a year later.

When the Safety of Sports Grounds Act came into effect in 1977, Goodison Park's capacity was greatly reduced from 56 000 to 35 000, mainly due to outdated entrances and exits. So Everton had to spend £250 000, in order to reach a capacity of 52 800. The 1982 figure stood at 53 091, of which 24 900 were seated.

Ground Description

Anfield, at the top of Stanley Park, is a solid mass on the skyline while Goodison Park, at the foot of the gentle slope, is a gaunt cathedral among low terraced houses. Two such important clubs, so close, yet seemingly turning their backs on each other across the green expanse.

Goodison Park is difficult to see from street level, not merely because it has no floodlight pylons. The tall Main Stand does not at first look like a football stand, but part of a factory or brewery perhaps. The main entrance is on Goodison Road, where on one

Main Stand number three at Goodison Park, the first triple-decker in Britain, built in 1971 (Simon Inglis)

side is an unbroken line of terraced houses, on the other the high wall of the stand. There is no room for a gate or a courtyard. Above the doors and windows are a succession of signs, pointing here and there, telling you where you are or how you can get to where you should be; one of those admirable grounds that likes to keep its public informed and does not assume that everyone is a regular.

Inside, the stand seems titanic. The front section is for standing, and in part is backed by a line of executive boxes, later and clumsy additions similar to those at St Andrews or Portman Road. When the stand was built, the club either saw no demand for this kind of accommodation or were unable to afford them – Manchester United had built boxes years earlier – so they have had to add boxes in a way which detracts from the original design. The middle tier houses, among others, the directors, sponsors and their like, above which is the upper tier.

Unfortunately, because of the angle of Goodison Road, at the end closest to the Park End, the back wall angles in towards the pitch, and creates the illusion that the stand is somehow falling down, because the top tier of seats falls away, row by row, into the corner in a most alarming way. At this corner, between the Main Stand and the Park End Stand, is a tall rectangular block, clad in blue. It houses stairways vital for safety in such a large stand, but has the additional and detrimental effect of closing off that corner in darkness. The opposite end is much more impressive. A large expanse of glass panelling is dramatically cut in half by the sloping rake of the upper seating tier, apparently suspended in air. Notice at the front the very compact dug-outs, and the barely visible players' tunnel in between.

This dominating, but scarcely attractive structure holds a total of 15 065, more than the total capacity of several grounds in the lower divisions. It has 10 045 seats, standing room for 4900, plus 12 private boxes.

From here, look down to the left where there is a clock in front of Goodison Park's most famous landmark, the church of St Luke the Evangelist. The church presses into the corner of the ground so far that its walls are just feet from the stands. Everton once tried to pay for its removal in order to gain extra space, but had they succeeded a familiar landmark would surely have been sorely missed. As it is, this corner is the most open of all. On the left is the Gwladys Street End, similar to the two ends at White Hart Lane, with a balcony wall distinguished by thin blue vertical lines along white facings. There is standing room for 14 200 in the lower section, which at one stage had the front terracing nearest the goal cut away to prevent missile throwing incidents . The terracing is now happily back to normal. The stand's sloping, deep blue roof continues round the corner to link up with the Bullens Road Stand.

The Bullens Road Side, opposite the Main Stand, is now in three tiers, the terracing having had its rear section converted to seating, as at Highbury. There are 8067 seats on two levels, with space for 5900 standing. Notice particularly the distinctive balcony wall, criss-crossed with blue steelwork on a facing of white wooden boards. The seating in the upper tier, now much less gloomy with the new upturned roof, has the name Everton picked out in white seats among the blue. Notice also that there are two positions for television cameras, under the roof and in front of the balcony wall. Between this stand and the Park End Stand, to the right, is another clock, with another blue wall closing in the corner.

The Park End Stand, the oldest surviving part of the ground, is lower than its fellows, and has been considerably modernized. The front standing section, for example, which holds 4000, now stops at the wall which runs directly under the seating balcony wall. There are 2340 seats above. Along this back wall is an electronic scoreboard, which must frustrate the people sitting above who cannot see it. Sadly, because of the high security fencing, the view from these terraces is rather obstructed, and demands much straining from the visiting supporters who stand there.

Goodison Park still has the hallmarks of a fine stadium, and although it can no longer claim to be the most advanced in the country, it does offer seating and standing on every side of the pitch, a feature much appreciated by spectators and found elsewhere only at Old Trafford. It has none of the grandeur or impression of space experienced at Hillsborough or Highbury, neither do any of the stands have the individual appeal of those at Villa Park or White Hart Lane. The site also suffers from being hemmed in. Nevertheless, perhaps because of its crucial place in the history of football grounds, and the atmosphere which prevails here on special occasions, Goodison Park is still one of the best grounds, despite the success of that other club across the park.

TRANMERE
·ROVERS·

Previous Grounds

Tranmere's roots go back to a club called Belmont FC, formed in 1881 by the members of two Birkenhead cricket clubs. The name Tranmere Rovers was adopted in 1882. Their first home was Steele's Field, from where they moved in 1883 to a ground in South Road, Devonshire Park, not a hundred yards from the present ground but now built over with houses. Rovers played on Ravenshaw Field, also close, from 1886–96, when they opened a new ground called Prenton Park. This ground was on the site of a school which now stands on Prenton Park Road, opposite the main entrace to the present ground, also called Prenton Park.

Prenton Park

When Rovers finally settled at Prenton Park (the second), Prenton had lost most of its identity as a village in Birkenhead. The area derived its strength from the nearby docks and shipyards of Cammell Lairds, and Goodison Park and Anfield were then just too far to draw away all the local support. Nevertheless, Prenton Park has been developed on a shoestring, since the first game there in March 1912. The club joined the League in 1921 and brought over an old wooden stand from the nearby Oval sports ground (referred to below). Known as the Weekend Stand, it was basically a showground building with a few seats and no dressing rooms. Opposite this stand, on Borough Road, was a cover similar to the existing one.

During the War, Birkenhead suffered considerably from bombing raids because of the important shipping in the dock areas, and the Prenton Park carpark was used as a base for sending up black smoke screens to confuse German aircraft. There were huge tank traps in Borough Road and the cover on this side was destroyed during a raid.

After the War Rovers struck a bargain with the local council. In return for giving up 6 feet of land behind the Borough Road Side, which the authorities wanted for bus loading bays and pavement widening, Rovers would have the tank traps lifted over to the Kop End in order to provide a base on which to raise the banking. Since each one weighed 10 hundredweight, they needed the council's help.

The cover on Borough Road was replaced, and in 1956 the Cowshed on Prenton Road West built. Floodlights were first switched on at Prenton Park in September 1958 before a game v. Rochdale. The supporters' association raised the £15 000 cost of the new lights.

On promotion to Division Three, Rovers began

building a new Main Stand in place of the old wooden structure. The Sports Minister and ex-football referee, Denis Howell, opened it in December 1968. Although the club had insufficient capital to build dressing rooms under the stand for a while, it was still at the time one of the best new stands outside the First Division, and had cost only £80 000.

In February 1972, Prenton Park's highest crowd, 24 424, attended an FA Cup tie v. Stoke City, a match which also brought Rovers record receipts of nearly £9000. The present capacity is 18 000, of which 4000 are seated, all in the Main Stand.

Developments since then have centred largely beyond the stands. With aid from the Sports Council, Tranmere built a sports centre at the back of the Kop, including squash courts and one of the first indoor crown bowling greens in the world. But the club's own costs escalated during construction, they were unable to run it properly, and so in November 1981 the centre was sold to private interests.

Rovers also had their own social club, now sold, and have since parted company with three-quarters of their large car-park behind the Main Stand. This used to be the site of a brick-works, but will now have a new public house and restaurant. Prenton Park has thus contracted rapidly, and with it the club's assets.

One side effect of this financial hardship is that Rovers can afford only a part-time groundsman, assisted by a youth on the YOP scheme. To save wear and tear of the pitch, the club plays all its home reserve games and also trains at the Oval, in Bebington. (Just south of Prenton Park, the Oval, part of a large sports complex now owned by Wirral Council, was built in 1888 for the workers at the Port Sunlight Soap Works. The Lever family once offered to buy up Rovers, move the whole club to the Oval and change its name to Port Sunlight.) The Oval retains a splendid grandstand which was used on location in the film *Chariots of Fire*.

In 1983 Rovers applied for permission to install an artificial pitch, but sadly the other League clubs voted against the idea.

Ground Description

Despite the club's recent financial plight and its long-standing struggle for support on Merseyside, Prenton Park does not externally bear many scars. It stands in a post-war housing area, on ground so flat and in air so fresh that although you cannot see it, you know the sea must be close. In fact it is five miles north, and five miles west. A short distance east takes you to the River Mersey.

From Borough Road the back of the stands are entirely green. Even the floodlight pylons are green. A couple of flags fluttering in the wind add some style and already Prenton Park looks orderly and respectable.

The main entrance on Prenton Park West takes you into the car-park, behind the large Main Stand frontage. With more money this could have been

Prenton Park (Adrian Gibson)

made quite grand, but it is still impressive for a small club.

The flat roof pitches upwards, and has just two central supports. The seating tier stops at a brick wall which forms the rear of the terracing in front, and although slightly drab is compensated by the liberal use of blue paint all over the stand. Underneath it is quite spartan, but dressing rooms must come before refreshment rooms in order of priority. Even so, it was said that Rovers had the best toilets and turnstiles in the Fourth Division, but one of the worst teams. From the back rows of the Main Stand one has a panoramic view of the land between Devonshire Park and the Mersey.

To the left of the stand is the much lower, multi-span cover called the Cowshed, with Prenton Road West behind. Since being reroofed after a gale in the 1970s, and more recently repainted with advertising, this stand looks quite dapper. The terracing underneath is shallow, without barriers, and has at the back a section marked out with a court for training.

Opposite the Main Stand is the Borough Road Side, its roof in somewhat poorer condition. Be careful where you stand on wet days! This covered side also has no barriers, since the terracing is not deep enough, and comes close to the touchline. The flagpoles brighten it up considerably.

To the right is the open Kop End, the banking built up on the old tank traps. For some reason the crush barriers here are very low. Behind this bank you can see the Shaftsbury Boy's Club's headquarters and the old social club, and nearer the Main Stand the sports centre.

So much potential and now it is all but lost to pay the bills. It is a great pity that the sports centre and car-park could not have been developed under the club's control, and thus given Rovers a sounder base, but nevertheless they have a tidy ground with facilities deserving of League football. That gift (if such it is), however, is not God-given and it could be that Rovers should have put those tank traps in the Mersey tunnel and thereby stopped the weekly exodus towards Stanley Park.

◆ CHESTER ◆

Previous Grounds

Chester were formed in 1884 and first played at Faulkner Street, in the district of Hoole, just east of their present ground. Soon after, they switched to Chester's Old Show Ground on Lightfoot Street also in Hoole, then in 1904 used a ground on Whipcord Lane, near Sealand Road. All three of their previous grounds have been built over, although the roads still exist. Chester moved to Sealand Road in 1906.

Sealand Road

When Chester were elected to the Football League in place of Nelson in 1931, Sealand Road and its environs were very different from the ground we know today. There were fields all around which are now covered by light industry and the ground was covered on two sides only. The Main Stand, which survived until 1979 was a small, wooden construction, made distinctive by vertical blue and white stripes on the paddock rear wall, and along Sealand Road was the standing cover known as The Barn, still in existence.

It has been claimed that Sealand Road was one of the first League grounds to have a public address system installed, at least as far back as August 1931 when the club began their League programme. For many years the announcer would begin with the words 'Hello Spion Kop, hello Albert!' apparently addressing a long-standing supporter in the crowd.

Like Brunton Park, one of Sealand Road's major problems in those early years was flooding from the nearby River Dee, which flows through the town centre, at every high spring tide. This was solved in 1936 when the club installed proper drainage at a cost of £400.

One of the most unusual events at the ground came on 5 January 1935, when the FA organized an experimental game using two referees for a match between two amateur international trial teams. A similar experiment was tried at The Hawthorns in March of that year, before the idea was dropped completely.

Sealand Road's highest attendance, 20500, came in January 1952 for Chester's replay 3rd Round Cup tie v. Chelsea, won by the visitors. The club's first floodlit game at the ground was on 12 October 1960; a League Cup match v. Leyton Orient. The lights were later updated in 1974.

In 1968 the Popular Side opposite the Main Stand was covered, then in December 1979 the old wooden stand was replaced by the present Main Stand at a cost of £556000. Like Swindon's new stand, it had been built directly behind the old one, and in consequence there is now an awkward flat space between the front wall and the touchline. This development raised the number of seats at Sealand Road to 2874, in a total capacity of 20000.

Ground Description

I have described Reading's ground as the least interesting in the League, even though it has satisfactory facilities. Chester's ground does not lack interesting details, but the overall effect is very dismal, largely owing to its drab surroundings. Sealand Road is like any road leading out of a beautiful town, where

Sealand Road has interesting details but is spoilt by the plain, high facing of the Main Stand (Sporting Pictures)

all the grey, industrial buildings and warehouses have been congregated to keep out of sight of visitors.

The entrance leads you behind the Main Stand, which despite its youth, looks remarkably tired. It is of the same design as one at the Racecourse Ground, Wrexham, with a flat roof pitched slightly upwards, supported by pillars along the front. The most prominent feature is the high, breeze-block wall at the front, broken only by staircases leading up to the seats. If there was a terrace in front, as at Wrexham, even a token terrace, as at Ashton Gate, or a few large advertisements to cover up the grey wall, the stand might look quite smart. As it is the wall is bare, and in front is a 30-foot gap before reaching the touchline. And where Swindon have at least turf, Chester have only a flat expanse of compacted earth. To make matters worse, instead of a perimeter wall or a few low advertisement hoardings, there is a chicken-wire fence with concrete posts dividing the pitch from the patch of earth. Miserable enough to look at, this arrangement has an inevitably detrimental effect on the atmosphere at the ground.

Apparently the regulars had complained for years about the old wooden Main Stand, but when this new concrete and steel structure was finished they pined for the warmth and friendliness of the old one.

To the left from the Main Stand, which at least provides a reasonable view, is the open Spion Kop. Although overgrown at the top, it has good terracing, formed unusually out of paving stones. The barriers are extremely thin. To the right is The Barn, a decaying barrel-roofed cover over the Sealand Road End terrace, with 16 uprights along the front. At the back are some very worn, uneven, but quite solid wooden terraces, with an ancient sign above from the Liverpool, London and Globe Insurance Company Limited warning that dropping lighted matches is dangerous. Between here and the Main Stand is a modern block overlooking the pitch housing social facilities.

Opposite the Main Stand is the all covered Popular Side, a simple cover over terracing. Behind is an overgrown pathway along the side of some scrubland and beyond is the impressively titled Stadium Way, another drab road which leads to Chester's old ground in Whipcord Lane. But the floodlights are interesting; on the Scottish pattern, having lamp holders leaning down towards the pitch. Unlike most systems, the lamps are mounted on open-ended bars, rather than on a box frame, as at Grimsby and Brighton.

Chester do have the option of moving the pitch nearer the Main Stand and redeveloping the Popular Side, but with the club in such a parlous financial state in the early 1980s (they were losing £3500 a week in the summer of 1982) this is a remote possibility. Failing the application of some bright paint and a bit of imagination, The Stadium might be more accurately renamed The Tedium.

· CREWE · ALEXANDRA

Previous Grounds

Crewe's first home in 1877 was Earl Street Cricket Ground, which they soon vacated in favour of Nantwich Road, a comparatively well developed ground. It was chosen as the venue for a Wales v. England international in 1880, and for an FA Cup semi-final between Aston Villa and Glasgow Rangers in 1887, the last year Scottish teams entered the English competition. Perhaps inspired by the occasion, Crewe went on to the semi-finals themselves the following year, their greatest achievement. Nantwich Road was also witness to one of the very earliest floodlit games in November 1878 but was finally swallowed up by the rapidly expanding railway industry. In 1896 the club moved to Edleston Road, then to Old Sheds Field, now the Royal Hotel car-park. Crewe returned to Earl Street, used nowadays for stock-car racing, and from there to Gresty Road. All five grounds were within a stone's throw of each other.

Gresty Road

Although Crewe Alexandra is a romantic name for a football club, Gresty Road sounds anything but mysterious. The first point of reference is during the early 1930s, when the original Main Stand burned down. The present structure was opened by Sir Francis Josephs, ironically on Guy Fawkes Day, 1932. The ground was first floodlit in October 1958, by lights on telegraph poles bought second-hand from Coventry City, for a game v. an All Star XI. The club were in the new Fourth Division in January 1960 when all-conquering Tottenham came to Gresty Road for an FA Cup 4th Round tie, and were held to a draw in front of Crewe's record gate of 20 000. In the early 1970s Crewe came second in the Ford Sporting League for good behaviour. Their £30 000 prize money was spent on rebuilding the Popular Side.

Gresty Road, which the club owns, has a capacity of 17 000, with 2300 seats.

Ground Description

It is easy, when approaching the ground for the first time, to mistake the proliferation of lighting gantries around Crewe station for the club's floodlights. In fact they are still mounted on the original telegraph poles, linked by a web of smaller poles, gantries and wires, so that Gresty Road appears to be held up like a marionette. The frontage is marked by a long, uneven, red corrugated iron fence. The old dressing rooms stood where the main entrance is now. Further down the road on the corner of South Street stood the club offices in a terraced house, until in 1981 a runaway car inflicted sufficient damage to necessitate the building's demolition.

The Main Stand, plain but neat in its scarlet coat, with an ordinary house door in the centre marking the players' tunnel, looks rather impromptu from the narrow alleyway behind, where more poles and wires perform a delicate balancing act.

To the left, or south, is the Gresty Road enclosure; concrete paving at the front, a slight cinder bank, then four wooden steps along the graffiti-covered back fence. The roof, put up in the 1930s, actually stands at an angle away from the pitch, preferring to hug the line of Gresty Road. In the far corner of this end is what at first appears to be a reconstruction of a First World War trench, open to the gaze of all and sundry behind a low fence, a mere yard in width and shored up with sleepers. In a Urinal Design League this would be my candidate for re-election.

But the Popular Side deserves no such scorn. The roof is rainproof, the terraces firm. Looming behind is the office block of the town's raison d'être, British Rail. At such an open ground as Crewe's, a tall building so near has a barrier effect on the wind, causing swirling currents to whip up the ball.

Behind the open small Railway End to the right – five steps below a cinder bank – is the main goods line to Chester and the north.

Comparison with a railway sidings yard is tempting, but not fair. The yards all around Crewe are none so appealing as Gresty Road's unpretentious red and green enclosure. The club may never have reached the First Division, but has survived commendably well in the guard's van of the League. And in common with fellow strugglers Rochdale and Halifax, it is what goes on in the adjacent social club which has often more significance than events on the field of play.

Wooden steps behind the covered banking at Gresty Road (Adrian Gibson)

⬥ WREXHAM ⬥

Previous Grounds

Although most sources give the date of Wrexham's formation as 1873, as Anthony Jones reports in his history, the present club dates from 1875. But the first ground, Acton Park, had certainly been used by a Wrexham team of sorts since 1873. Nevertheless, Wrexham is the oldest Association football club in Wales. Acton Park is now part of a council estate, but there was once a Hall there, standing in substantial grounds, of which the lake still survives. The present day Acton Park is not the same location of Wrexham's first ground.

The town was also the birthplace of the Welsh FA, so Acton Park had the honour of staging Wales' first home international, v. Scotland in March 1877.

Racecourse Ground

Wrexham had used the Racecourse Ground on a few occasions before moving there permanently in 1905. But many years before the site had been typical of nineteenth century sporting venues, described in 1850 as 'a place where drunkardness and vice were encouraged to a terrible extent'. Later the Racecourse became more respectably occupied by fêtes and charity shows.

On the Mold Road Side of the ground was and still is the Turf Hotel, which Wrexham used initially as a dressing room. The players stepped down a wooden staircase and across the paddock to the pitch. The Turf Hotel belongs to Border Breweries, which owns the Racecourse Ground.

Perhaps soon after moving, Wrexham built the first stand in the corner of the pitch along the touchline from the Turf. Called the Plas Coch Stand (Red Hall), the stand had bench seats for a few hundred, and new dressing rooms below. The only entrance to the ground was between this and the Turf, where the club installed a turnstile on wheels.

Wrexham joined the League in 1921, and were helped considerably by the formation of a supporters' club in 1926. This immediately raised £300 to pay for the erection of a cover behind the Plas Coch goal, which was extended round the far side at a cost of £2000 in the late 1930s. Also during the inter-war period, a stand was built between the Turf and the original stand, parallel with Mold Road. In front of the stands, supporters laid terracing. The standing covers were low, and characterized by large girders along the front, parts of them lined with advertisements. They made the Racecourse seem small and cramped on two sides, whereas the rest of the ground was fairly well set back from the pitch. Advertising in the club's programme in 1937 the builders of these covers, W. H. Smith of Whitchurch, described themselves as 'specialists in cowsheds' and other farm buildings.

The Racecourse in the mid-1970s with the new Yale Stand on the far side and the old "pigeon loft" stand on the right (Aerofilms)

After the Second World War the supporters layed down concrete terracing over the Kop. In January 1957 the Racecourse Ground had its highest crowd, when 34 445 came to see a Cup tie v. Manchester United, the eventual losing finalists, and two years later in September 1959 the floodlights were switched on for the first time, in a game v. Swindon Town.

Wrexham won promotion, also for the first time, in 1962, and in order to increase the seating capacity at the Racecourse, then only just 1000, the club erected one of the oddest stands ever to grace a football ground. Its steel frame and seats came from the Majestic Cinema in Wrexham, and when covered it provided accommodation for 1000 spectators. The stand was dubbed 'The Pigeon Loft' and stood on top of the Kop. Its origins were obvious since it had a curved balcony wall such as one would see at any cinema. Underneath the seating tier was a little refreshment stall amid the open steel supports. Incredibly the stand lasted until 1978, when it was deemed unsafe (as an international ground The Racecourse came under the jurisdiction of the 1975 Safety

of Sports Grounds Act, even though Wrexham were not in Division Two until 1978–79), but it won a third chance when sold to Wrexham Rugby Club.

European football was staged at Wrexham in the early 1970s, as the club was a regular winner of the Welsh Cup and thus eligible for the European Cup Winners Cup. The revenue from these games helped finance a substantial building programme which changed the ground completely. First, a new stand was built along the Popular Side. Called the Yale Stand, because Yale Further Education College is behind, this became the Main Stand and was completed in 1972. Three years later the dressing rooms were transferred here from the Plas Coch Stand. In December 1978 another new stand, the Border Stand, was opened behind the Plas Coch goal. The two new structures cost nearly £900 000 to complete and provided a further 6000 seats. Finally in 1980, in place of the Pigeon Loft, a new cover was erected at the top of the Kop.

One of the most important effects of this rebuilding was the return of regular Welsh international football to the Racecourse. Before and after the Second World War, Cardiff had taken over from Wrexham as the established home of Wales, acting as host for 51 international matches between 1946–77, compared with a total of only 16 at the Racecourse, and 7 at Vetch Field. Since 1977 Wrexham has enjoyed the greater share of Welsh international fixtures, undoubtedly due to the better facilities, but also partly because with smaller crowds attending games, the Racecourse can provide a better atmosphere than a half-empty Ninian Park.

Townspeople also claim that they are the more passionate patriots, and that as the birthplace of the Welsh FA as well as the location of its headquarters, Wrexham is the natural choice. So where were they all when Wales played Northern Ireland on 27 May 1982 at the Racecourse Ground? The attendance of 2315 was the lowest for any international match in Great Britain since 1892.

The ground's total capacity is now 28 500, including 7000 seats.

Ground Description

The ground is conveniently situated north west of the town centre, a two-minute walk from the main railway station. From Mold Road one sees only the older stands next to the Turf Hotel, where the official entrance used to be. It looks an unlikely international venue. Yale College and its playing fields provide a pleasant, green background to the modern Main Stand, which although very similar to the one I have been so unkind about at Chester, is a busy looking construction brightened by liberal amounts of red paint.

Inside, it is dominated by cross beam girders supporting the roof, just as the old covers on this side were. The seating tier seems quite small, sandwiched between girders and the high brick terrace rear wall. But far from seeming bare and exposed, as at Swindon or Chester, this wall is relatively hidden by its stairways and by the spectators in the front paddock. Both this and the similar Border Stand, to its right, are very simple, plain and economically constructed. Wrexham have opted, rather like QPR, for cheap stands providing seats and standing accommodation, and have maintained them well. But if once they start to fade they would be miserable indeed, as only modern buildings can be.

From the Yale Stand to the left you can see the tall Kop, known as the Town End, behind which lies Crispin Lane and the railway station. Again, the application of red and white paint to the barriers smartens up the banking, as does the new roof over the rear half. This section of the ground holds 13 000 standing spectators.

But the most interesting part of the Racecourse Ground is opposite the Yale Stand, along Mold Road. From the Town End corner we see first the Turf Hotel, standing behind the paddock. Built in the nineteenth century, it is not a particularly distin-

guished piece of architecture, but with its balcony overlooking the pitch the hotel forms an apposite link between the ground when used as a racecourse in Victorian times and its sporting activities now.

Between here and the Mold Road Stand is an awkward gap, forming an entrance to the paddock and backyard to the hotel. The Mold Road Stand runs along a third of the length of the touchline, but still is set some way back with the paddock in between. From here the pitch looks wide enough to kick the other way, or stage cricket. In fact the width is not more than 78 yards. Touching the end of the Mold Road Stand is the corner Plas Coch Stand, but since they seem like one long stand together they are referred to by either name. On the roof of what I shall term the Mold Road Stand, the younger of the pair, is a small viewing box.

However old and quaint, the Plas Coch Stand is in good condition, with rows of bench seats visibly smoothed with age. Each bench has curious little handgrips for every spectator. The view from here across the pitch, wooden pillars and all, is like that from an old pavilion. Underneath, nearest the corner, the paddock stops and there is a flat section by the pitch. The players used to enter from here, from the old dressing rooms under the stand.

Notice how many lights the floodlight pylon holds, over 40 on each, in differing sizes. New lamps were installed in 1978, but the very smallest ones are used only for European and international games.

If the Mold Road Side is a little disjointed, this is only a reflection of the ground's previous life as a racecourse, and it by no means detracts from the modernity of the other three sides. The Racecourse Ground has a comforting scale, cluttered in places yet apparently wide open in others. No doubt visiting international players and officials, accustomed to vast concrete stadiums, look at the old Plas Coch Stand and have a quiet scoff, without realizing how much the ground had advanced in recent years, or indeed that when it comes to building football grounds the British are quite different from the rest of the world. The Racecourse Ground is a perfect illustration of haphazard development compensated by restrained modernization.

·17·
WEST, NORTH AND EAST LONDON

·LUTON TOWN·

Previous Grounds

All three grounds used by Luton have been within a few hundred yards of each other. The club formed in 1885 at the Excelsior Ground in Dallow Lane, where in 1890 Luton became a pioneer of professional football in the south, and later joined the Southern League. Just before being elected to the Football League in 1897 they moved a short distance to a ground on Dunstable Road, opened by the Duke of Bedford on 3 April for a game v. Loughborough Town. In 1900 Luton failed to be re-elected, ironically dropping out with Loughborough (Stockport County and Blackpool took their places). Dunstable Road was never large enough however, so in 1905 Luton moved to their present ground, also just off Dunstable Road. The old stand at Dallow Lane, now called Dallow Road, lay rotting in a timber yard built on the site until the 1950s. The Dunstable Road site is covered by the Odeon cinema.

Kenilworth Road

When Luton took over their new ground on Kenilworth Road there was little to indicate how cramped the site would become in future years. A picture taken soon after 1905 shows an open field surrounded by white railings, with a picturesque house on one of the low banks. There was one small stand on the West Side while the other three sides were open cinder banks.

In 1920 Luton joined the mass exodus from the Southern to the Football League but at the same time suffered the misfortune of having their stand burnt down. In its place was built the centre section of the existing Main Stand, the structure having been brought from Kempton Racetrack.

By the beginning of the 1930s the team began to look more promising, and in 1933–34 a club was formed for the regulars on the Bobbers Side – so called because it cost a shilling to stand there. This club raised sufficient funds to build the narrow stand along the ground's East Side, and their faith was

rewarded in 1936 when Town won promotion to Division Two. To cater for the larger crowds the Kenilworth Road terrace was raised to its present height and the opposite Oak Road terrace covered. At the same time the Main Stand was extended to join up with the Oak Road roof in the north west corner. By 1937 therefore, the ground had assumed the size and shape it has today.

Floodlights were installed in 1953, and first used on 7 October for a friendly v. Fenerbahce, the top club in Turkey. The lights were individually mounted on short poles on each stand roof, but even when the system was updated several years later there was insufficient room to erect four corner pylons, hence the present system of four narrow pylons along the front of each stand.

The late 1950s brought great excitement to Kenilworth Road after Luton had reached Division One in 1955. As crowds grew there was only one way to expand the ground – apart from building extremely narrow double-decker stands, for which planning permission would certainly have been denied even if the capital had been available – and that was to steal a few yards from the houses behind the Oak Road terrace and build a few extra steps. Luton were able to do this because they owned the houses until 1974.

The record attendance for the ground occurred on 4 March 1959, for an FA Cup 6th Round replay v. Blackpool. A crowd of 30 069 saw Town win 1-0, who then went on to their only Cup Final appearance.

Between then and 1974 the club slipped down to the Fourth Division, then rose back up to Division One, and it was as a Second Division club in 1977 that their ground came under the jurisdiction of the Safety of Sports Grounds Act. Until then the club had done little to improve the ground, simply because the site was so inadequate that they always hoped to resite further away. There were plans for a 50 000 capacity stadium, dropped when the team went into the lower divisions, but in 1977 they had no choice. To bring the ground into line with the safety recommendations £350 000 had to be spent, mainly on improved access points and barriers, and the capacity dropped from 30 000 to its present level of 22 601. This includes 4506 seats, of which 1539 were instal-

Kenilworth Road; the controversial railway line, to the left, cuts across the ground. There is not even room for corner floodlight pylons (Aerofilms)

led in the Bobbers Stand on the original terracing.

But the story does not end there, for Luton have been engaged in a 25-year-long struggle with Bedfordshire County Council over plans to build a new road on the site of the railway line, directly behind the Main Stand, a plan which would force Luton to move. (The railway line is from Dunstable to Luton but is used only for the transport of concrete. The projected road was to be a relief road for the main route, also from Dunstable to Luton.)

Of course the club wanted to move, but unless the local authorities were able to grant hefty compensation and co-operate in the building of a new stadium, they simply could not afford to. Three years' negotiation cost Luton £200 000 in legal fees alone.

The problem is exacerbated by the fact that it is very difficult to find a new site acceptable to local residents. As at Watford it is a case of, 'better the devil you know . . .'

Meanwhile, Kenilworth Road cannot develop, the club will not spend more than absolutely necessary on the ground, and there is the danger that support will dwindle because facilities, especially parking, are increasingly inadequate.

Ground Description

Whenever the state of modern British football grounds is discussed, one of the most popular points to be raised invariably concerns how cramped many grounds are by their surroundings. Until you have been to Kenilworth Road you cannot appreciate how cramped is 'cramped'. Compared with Luton's ground Filbert Street is spacious, the Baseball Ground well

situated, even Millwall might just feel a little less aggrieved (but only a very little) with their lot.

You can approach Kenilworth Road along several small streets from Dunstable Road, but Kenilworth Road itself leads to the club's offices in converted terrace houses. There was no room for them in the Main Stand. Past the offices you enter the small car-park behind the prominent dark blue and light blue barriers of the Kenilworth Road terrace with its large electric scoreboard at the back. A grey corrugated iron fence wraps round the bank, effectively closing it off from the surrounding houses. This is the largest section of the ground, holding 8646 spectators.

From here the Main Stand is to the left, pressed against the pitch by the railway line behind. At the back of the stand is a roadway just wide enough for a coach, and a line of assorted clubs and executive areas, a champagne cork's pop from the fenced-off railway. Further down the roadway is the club's training ground, beyond a rare patch of open ground next to the line.

The Main Stand appears quite tall, but this is an optical illusion, enhanced by the ground's narrowness and by the four floodlight pylons poking up through the front of the roof. As if these were not enough of a viewing obstacle, one also has to contend with another 11 vertical supports from the seats, plus a suspended television camera gantry.

Inside, the stand is mainly wooden, with creaky floors and very wide gangways. It runs only three-quarters of the length of the touchline, with a full length paddock in front. The most unusual feature is an extremely long players' tunnel.

To the left of the Main Stand is the Oak Road terrace, covered by an unusual roof built in three sections, climbing from the Bobbers to the Main Stand roof, with advertisements hung below the gutters which make the terracing underneath very dark. Perhaps here more than in any other part of the ground one is reminded of how little space Luton possess.

To enter this terrace supporters pass through gateways underneath the first floors of the terraced houses on Oak Road, under their bedrooms and bathrooms, then through a small pathway and up some stairs where they can look down on the gardens below. Here they can throw things at people's washing, urinate onto someone's vegetable patch, and generally cause a great deal of upset and disturbance.

Finally we come to the Bobber's Stand, a low, narrow enclosure with room for just eight rows of seating on a wooden frame. The perimeter fence and the roof are lined with advertisements, two deep on the roof, and above these are the original floodlight poles which now support netting – to stop the ball going over. It's as bad as that! There are another four thin floodlight pylons on this side, also lining the front. Behind here is the Beech Hill Path, an alleyway between the houses and the stand, just wide enough for two people walking side by side.

The Kenilworth Road pitch is usually in excellent condition, neatly edged with a bright orange track. It slopes 6 feet from the south west corner (between Kenilworth Road and the Main Stand) down to the opposite corner, and about 4 feet from the south east corner to the opposite corner. But this is the least of the problems. It is not that Kenilworth Road is too small; the present capacity is just about right for current demands. But it lacks sufficient seating, access to parking facilities is limited, and worst of all there is precious little space to build on what they already have. There would be no point in having a new double-decker stand if access to it was so limited that half the space could not be used because of safety regulations.

The road plan is due to go ahead in 1985 and will rob Luton of their executive and social facilities behind the Main Stand. If the council cannot help with an alternative site in Luton, the club may have to relocate to Milton Keynes.

Luton are in almost the same predicament as their nearest neighbours Watford; anxious to leave, thwarted by the authorities, unwanted elsewhere, yet driven by their own success to improve their facilities. If only they had stayed in the Fourth Division, probably none of this fuss would have arisen.

⬩WATFORD⬩

Previous Grounds

Two clubs joined forces in 1898 to form Watford FC: Watford St Mary's, who played at Wiggenhall Road, near Vicarage Road and West Herts, who played at the West Herts Sports Ground on Cassio Road, in the centre of Watford. This latter club had originally been called Watford Rovers and played until 1891 on a field behind the Rose and Crown, on the parish church side of Market Street. It became apparent that the town was not large enough for two professional clubs, and as the ground in Cassio Road was better suited, this became the newly-formed club's permanent headquarters.

In 1909 a limited company was formed and Watford became tenants of West Herts Sports Club, at an annual rent of £50. The ground was an enormous circular bowl, large enough for two football pitches, and other attractions at Cassio Road were athletics, fêtes and concerts, as well as cricket during the summer. The only covered accommodation was on either side of the pavilion, the opposite touchline being open.

The team struggled in the Southern League, and were continually in need of financial aid from benefactors, whose faith was rewarded in 1915 when Watford won their first honour, the Southern League Championship. Unfortunately, war-time football was hardly a major attraction and despite their success, Watford's gates were so low that West Herts decided to end the club's lease of Cassio Road. In 1916 therefore Watford had no ground, no players, £3 in the bank and assets of £30 only, consisting of a stand and some turnstiles.

The board of directors began looking elsewhere, and settled on the Recreation Ground, Vicarage Road as the likeliest venue. Watford Urban District Council was happy to give its approval for the move, but the Local Government Board refused permission. It was the first of many tangles with the local authorities.

Benskins Breweries offered to buy Cassio Road for them from its owner, the Dowager Lady Essex. She turned out to be an opponent of professional sport, and had actually told West Herts Sports Club that they were not to continue sub-letting the ground to Watford, although this had not been revealed when the lease ended in 1916. Benskins' persuasion worked however, and the 1919 season began with renewed confidence.

Several makeshift stands were made from brewery drays and hay wagons and even a press-box built. Attendances in the immediate post-war era rose to unprecedented levels at Watford, and as the team became more successful it became apparent that Cassio Road would not, after all, be such a suitable home. Apart from the lack of facilities for spectators, the

Watford's new stand at Vicarage Road in 1924. Newcastle (in the stripes) are visitors in the FA Cup Third Round (BBC Hulton Picture Library)

players' baths had to be heated in two large copper containers and carried up six steps to the pavilion in buckets. Then in 1920 Watford were one of the leading Southern League clubs absorbed into the Football League's newly formed Division Three. A new ground was therefore a priority, although further improvements were made to Cassio Road.

Cassio Road's highest gate was 13 000, recorded for the League derby match v. rivals Luton Town.

Shortly after this, as we learn from Oliver Phillips' comprehensive history of the club, to which I am indebted for much of this section, a local character called Joey Goodchild performed his usual trick of climbing onto the stand roof to perform a tap dance for the delight of the crowd. But on this occasion someone asked him to stop, he fell off the roof and landed on a gentleman, whose glasses were broken, and an unfortunate lady. She received £25 compensation from the club, and Joey's dancing had to come to an end. The last Watford match at Cassio Road was v. Gillingham, attended by 5000 spectators. The ground is still open land today, used by West Herts Rugby Club.

Vicarage Road

Vicarage Road was an obvious choice for Watford's new ground. It was large enough in 1919 to have two junior pitches running side by side and was a natural bowl shape; perfect for redevelopment and expansion. On one side of the recreation ground was a cart track, on the other stood the old Union Work House on the site of what is now Shrodells Hospital.

On the South Side were the old buildings of the Rookery silk mill, in 1922 occupied by the Watford Steam Laundry. The present terrace end of Vicarage Road is still known as the Rookery.

Watford had wanted to move to Vicarage Road as early as 1916 but were prevented by the Local Government Board. When negotiations reopened in 1921, the authorities were still not wholly in favour. Benskins offered to buy the Recreation Ground for £2300, but Watford Urban Development Council wanted compensation for the three remaining years which the site still had to run on its lease. The problem even became an issue in the local elections of that year. Eventually Benskins agreed to pay £450 compensation, and Vicarage Road was handed over to Watford on a 21-year lease.

The club had little money to invest in the new ground so Benskins loaned Watford a further £12 000 for improvements, in return for 10 per cent of the club's gate receipts. Half of this was to pay interest on the loan, the other half to pay off the capital sum. The brewery also insisted on having three directors on the seven-man board, all of whom had to be in agreement before any Watford player could be sold. But in the end, Benskins managed to have not just three, but five of their men on the board, and as Oliver Phillips writes, 'Not surprisingly Watford became known as the Brewers'.

The main work to prepare the ground was carried out under the direction of architect S. E. Gomme, his most notable contribution being the design of the 3500-seater East Stand, built by the firm of Harbrow Limited. Costing £8000 it was considered at the time to be among the best and most modern in the country.

Vicarage Road was opened on 30 August 1922, by Charles Healey of Benskins; a crowd of 8000 then saw Watford and Millwall Athletic play out a goalless draw. Money was very limited for a long time after this, with Watford having to hand over a tenth of their receipts and attendances affected by rival attractions, such as the rugby at Cassio Road. To raise more cash the club staged a horse show, coaches and carriages included, during the summer of 1923, with inevitable consequences to the turf.

The club's financial problems reached crisis point in 1926, with Benskins considering putting in an official receiver, the Football League issuing an ultimatum that Watford must pay its way and Harbrow Limited about to sue for non-payment of £5800 worth of building work to the rest of the ground, plus £1000 interest charges.

In despair, Watford sought help from the people of the town. Harbrow had settled behind the scenes for a sum of only £3500, and at the public meeting other creditors were asked to take a similarly indulgent line. Again Benskins came to the rescue, and again Watford lived to fight another day.

During the 1930s Vicarage Road developed gradually while the club remained in the Third Division South. Towards the Second World War, they finished just behind the promotion contenders three seasons running. During this period concrete terraces were laid by the players during the close seasons, and the present West Stand was built on the Shrodells Side, to replace an old wooden stand brought over from Cassio Road in 1922.

In 1934, Vicarage Road was first used for the then extremely popular dog-racing, organized by the Dutch family twice a week. The track was not the right shape for top-class greyhound events, and was used for 'flapper' racing instead, that is, one class above whippets.

Vicarage Road's first floodlights were switched on in October 1953 for a friendly v. Luton Town. They were then on poles along the touchlines, until being updated on the present pylons in 1960. Shortly before then one of the more unusual features of the ground was removed, the trees which stood on top of the Vicarage Road Terrace. Also in 1959 the supporters' club raised the money to build a roof over the Rookery End terrace.

In 1967 Watford were granted security at Vicarage Road when Benskins gave the club a 150-year lease, due to expire in March 2118. But for the time being, Watford were more concerned about the immediate future. Having slipped into Division Four for two seasons, the club was promoted the following year, and in 1968–69 at last escaped Division Three by winning the Championship. During that eventful season Vicarage Road's highest ever crowd, 34 099, watched Watford's 4th Round Cup tie v. Manchester United on 3 February 1969. Though they failed to surmount this hurdle, to celebrate promotion the club spent £45 000 on an extension to the Main Stand, adding a further 1700 seats. It was intended to replace completely the old stand, but sufficient funds have not yet become available. Also in 1969 the Dutch family stopped holding dog-racing at Vicarage Road. For three years the track was unused, until in 1972 the Greyhound Racing Association began staging meetings. They installed modern equipment and built new kennels and outbuildings behind the Rookery.

If Watford thought promotion in 1969 was to signal the start of a new era, they were mistaken. Only six seasons later the club was back in Division Four. A new era did not begin until 1977, when the partnership of Graham Taylor as manager and Elton John, the rock singer, as chairman began. As the team started to rise up the Divisions, so Vicarage Road began to change, almost imperceptibly.

In 1978, after winning Division Four Watford installed one of the first American-style electric scoreboards, at a cost of £40 000. In December 1979, by which time Watford were in the Second Division, the greyhound company's lease ran out and the track was removed.

Meanwhile, unseen but vital improvements were being made in line with the recommendations of the Safety of Sports Grounds Act, under whose jurisdiction Vicarage Road fell once Watford were promoted. Every metal fitting in the ground had to be replaced, the cinder banking in the south west corner was terraced for the first time and access points were redesigned at a total cost of £750 000. Watford therefore used up almost their entire allotted grant available from the Football Grounds Improvement Trust. But the money was well spent, for in 1982 Watford realized their dream of First Division football.

Vicarage Road now had a capacity of 30 000, perfectly adequate for future demands, although the total number of seats, 6000, was still too few for first-class fixtures. The West Stand paddock had 2200 seats added in 1979, and a small section of open terracing next to the Main Stand was converted with an extra 250 seats in 1982 (all sold immediately). But the club would like to install more, if money was available.

Ideally they would like to have moved away from Vicarage Road. It is now badly situated for parking and the crowds can enter the ground only via the busy Vicarage Road. Furthermore, the local council has refused Watford planning permission to cover the open Vicarage Road Terrace or redevelop the West Side, on the grounds that the area is residential – a claim open to dispute since there is a hospital on one side and allotments, an industrial estate and a power station on the south side.

Watford cannot effect the changes they want at this ground and the council is also denying them permission to develop a new stadium elsewhere, even though it is clear the authorities would be happy to get the club out of an already congested locality. Caught in such a trap, Watford have resigned themselves to carry on at Vicarage Road for the foreseeable future.

Ground Description

Access to the ground is not easy. The West Side is hemmed in by Shrodells Hospital, the South Side has no road, so the only route from Vicarage Road to the other side of the ground is via an old cart track, now called Occupation Road, running behind the East Stand. At the bottom of this track, which leads to allotments, are the club's offices, now housed in the old greyhound buildings and kennels behind the Rookery!

The immediate impression is one of bittiness, yet Vicarage Road does have some sense of unity, largely due to colour coding and graphics. Every sign and every building is marked in some way with the red, yellow and black of Watford. If the actual structures are nothing special, one must award the club full marks for effort. The East Stand is an example of this. No doubt it was quite modern in 1922, but in design it is now quite ordinary, especially since the original striped paddock rear wall has been painted over (as it has at most grounds). But nevertheless it looks as smart as possible, with all the woodwork yellow and all steelwork and the roof black. The upper tier seats are orange, the paddock seats are red.

Next to this central stand is the more recent extension, a rather uncomfortable neighbour, but then even in 1969 £45 000 bought very little. Here the roof slopes upwards, at variance with the pitched roof of the older stand, and has a solid screen wall at the Rookery End. The old stand has a glass screen wall. No unity but everything is quite spruce.

On the Vicarage Road Side of the East Stand, where the terracing curves round to the North End, is the small section of red backless seats. Uncovered seating is always a risk, but here they are very popular.

From there the terracing continues round to the Vicarage Road End. The old elliptical shape of the ground from the greyhound days is still in evidence behind each goal, where there is a semi-circle of extra turf. The open terrace is dominated by the large scoreboard at the back, behind which you can see the row of houses on the opposite side of the road.

Opposite the East Stand, but not filling the whole length of the pitch, is the very odd West Stand. Essentially wooden, with bright yellow bench seats and a slightly pitched roof, it has a tent-like television camera gantry perched on the centre. But the buildings of Shrodells Hospital immediately behind are actually taller than the stand, and it seems as if the old stand is somehow bolted onto them. Further-

more, it is so compact and basic that it seems quite out of place alongside the technological wizardry of the scoreboard. It is a Fourth Division stand in a ground coloured by First Division thinking. In front of the West Stand is another uncovered section of red, backless seats.

From here the terracing curves round once more to the covered Rookery. In the uncovered south west corner, behind the terracing, are two full size advertisement hoardings. Such hoardings are often to be seen outside League grounds, but Vicarage Road is the only one to have them inside, and they form a neat backdrop.

The Rookery is another oddity. The cover itself is satisfactory, like an open fronted box, with a clock in the fascia. But the terracing it shelters is surprisingly shallow, rising only 8 feet in about 60 feet of steps from front to back. If these were close to the pitch it would be acceptable, but because of the old greyhound track there is a flat section in front of the terrace with a high wall dividing it from the pitch. Therefore the view from the back of the Rookery is not ideal in a packed crowd. It also seems curious that the back wall of the stand should be so high when the back steps are so low.

Altogether the ground is far from perfect. But as a football manager would say, attitude is what counts, and Watford have assembled a dedicated administration who have not only taken the club to the top but made the best of their ground. While Coventry were able to teach a lesson to some of the wealthier clubs, Watford are an example to smaller outfits with less suitable stadiums.

Vicarage Road, whether it is staging a football match or a fireworks display for the community, is proof of what careful planning and imagination can achieve.

TOTTENHAM ·HOTSPUR·

Previous Grounds

In common with so many football clubs, Tottenham's origins go back to a group of cricketers. They formed Hotspur FC in 1882 and played on public pitches at Tottenham Marshes until 1887. (The club's name was chosen because of the fiery reputation of Shakespeare's Harry Hotspur, who was based on a fourteenth century ancestor of the Northumberland family, landowners in the Tottenham area in the 1880s.) It is widely recorded that the early Hotspur team had no headquarters of their own until 1886 and so the committee had to meet under a gas-light lamp-post on Tottenham High Road, very close to the present ground. It is also suggested that they built their own goalposts and touchline posts (in the days before pitch markings at public parks) and 'bitterly regretted not being able to make their own footballs'.

During the week the blue and white striped Hotspur goalposts were stored at Northumberland Park railway station, and the players had to cross the Great Eastern railway line to reach the Marshes. In 1885 'Tottenham' was added to their title, and a year later they set up headquarters at the Red House, 748 High Road, in the building later to become the offices of White Hart Lane. As the team improved it became apparent that they would need a ground of their own. Crowds of up to 4000 had been assembling on the Marshes to watch them, but of course no gate money could ever be collected.

In 1888 Tottenham moved to their first enclosed ground at Northumberland Park. This was a playing field behind the Northumberland Arms public house on Trulock Road, on the other side of the railway line from the Marshes and only a hundred yards from the present ground. Rent was fixed at £17 a year and Tottenham's first game there was in September 1888, a reserve match v. Stratford St Johns. Yet even then, as Phil Soar writes in his history of the club, *And the Spurs go marching on . . .*, there were still some people who thought the club was overreaching itself by hiring a ground. But the club was cautious, for the first stand was not built until 1894 and it was not until 1895 that professionalism was adopted. The stand cannot have been terribly substantial because it blew down in a gale soon after.

The crowds soon began to outgrow even this ground, as southern professional football became more and more competitive. Northumberland Park was closed down once, in 1898, when Spurs' fans invaded the pitch and assaulted three Luton Town players. The ground's highest recorded attendance was 14 000, for a match v. Woolwich Arsenal in April 1899. During that game the roof of a refreshment stall, on which many spectators were perched, collapsed causing several minor injuries.

It was clear that Tottenham would have to move again if their ambitions were to be realized. The surrounding districts were expanding so rapidly that they were sure to attract even larger gates in the future. The answer to their problems was almost on their doorstep.

White Hart Lane

Tottenham may have been comparatively late in developing as a top professional club, but once moved into their present ground their ambition was given full rein. The site of their new home could not have been better placed; close to White Hart Lane railway station, on the main thoroughfare in Tottenham, and in the midst of an expanding North London suburb with no professional club for miles around. Nevertheless, the beginnings were still relatively cautious. White Hart Lane was not developed as rapidly as The Dell, or Hillsborough and Roker Park, opened in the same period.

The site was a neglected nursery which the brewers Charrington had bought from a firm called Beckwiths. There were still greenhouses and sheds on the land, but the brewery intended to build houses there. Charringtons also owned the nearby White Hart Inn. The landlord, however, was quite keen on having a football club on his doorstep, for his previous hostelry had been close to Millwall Athletic's ground and he knew the profits large crowds could bring. The Tottenham directors came to hear of his preference and approached Charrington. Agreement was reached whereby Spurs could rent the ground on condition they guaranteed attendances of 1000 for first team matches and 500 for reserve games.

An added convenience of the ground was that the club's headquarters were already at 748 High Road, next to the public house. The only stands to begin with were those brought from Northumberland Park, providing cover for 2500 spectators.

Tottenham's first game there was a friendly v. First Division Notts County. A crowd of 5000 saw the Southern Leaguers win 4-1. By the end of that season Tottenham were Southern League Champions. As a result of their success, Tottenham were able to purchase the freehold of the ground for £8900 and with the help of Charringtons were able to find another £2600 to buy land and houses behind the northern end, then known as the Edmonton goal, now Paxton Road.

Photographs taken in the early years of the twentieth century show the pitch surrounded by a white wooden fence. Until 1904 there had been extra seats inside the perimeter fence, such as there were at many other grounds, given to people on a first come, first served basis for the same price as entry to the terracing. But on 20 February 1904 the ground was packed to overflowing, and those on the touchlines led a pitch invasion at half-time, when visitors Aston

The West Stand at White Hart Lane, the most expensive ever built in Britain, largely due to the two tiers of executive boxes. Notice the awkward link with the old roof (right) (Sporting Pictures)

Villa were one goal up in an FA Cup match. Spurs were heavily fined.

The East Side was partially covered by a simple cover, lined with advertisements, and on the West was a small wooden stand from their previous ground.

In 1908 Tottenham were elected to the Second Division of the Football League, thanks mainly to the resignation of Stoke; Spurs had resigned from the Southern League in a fit of frustration because of the organization's over-conservative approach. It took Tottenham only one season to gain promotion to Division One and to celebrate this momentous event they officially opened their new West Stand in September 1909. The designer was Archibald Leitch. It was a larger version of his stands at Craven Cottage and Stamford Bridge, both 1905, seating 5000 with room for 4000 in the covered paddock in front. A large, mock-tudor gable displayed the words 'Tottenham Hotspur F. & A. Co Ltd' in ornate lettering, and there were flag poles at both points on the pitched roof.

In 1910, the famous ball and cockerel symbol was added to the top of the gable which became synonymous with Tottenham thereafter. As Phil Soar suggests, its origins are obscure but probably have a connection with Harry Hotspur, so-called 'for his often pricking' his horse with his spurs. Spurs were attached to the legs of fighting cocks, so perhaps the two symbols were linked – the cockerel on a ball – to signify the football club.

At the same time both open end banks were doubled in size and soon after the East Side cover taken down so that the terraces there could also be expanded. The ground now had a capacity of 40 000, and appeared to be the archetypal Leitch ground – one grandstand and three large open sides, almost identical to his other designs in London, at Leeds Road and later at Selhurst Park.

When the First World War broke out the ground was taken over for use as a rifle range, opened by the founder of the Scout movement, Baden-Powell.

Until then, Tottenham's home had usually been called the High Road Ground. Several other names had been suggested but eventually White Hart Lane was popularly adopted, even though the lane itself is a few hundred yards from the ground. The fact that the nearest station was called White Hart Lane was probably the most important factor, because it meant Tottenham were on the map.

The first season after the War found Tottenham in Division Two, in completely new circumstances. Before the War they had been the senior club in North London, their nearest neighbours being Clapton Orient, five miles to the south east. But now they had The Arsenal only three miles to the south west. Their position was considerably worsened by the scandalous events in 1919 which saw the new arrivals take Tottenham's place in Division One. Briefly, Spurs finished bottom of Division One in 1915, just behind Chelsea. In 1919 it was decided to expand Division One to 22 clubs, but instead of keeping both Chelsea and Spurs in the division, Chelsea were retained, the two promoted Division Two clubs admitted, and instead of Spurs, The Arsenal were voted to move up, despite the fact that in 1915 they had finished only fifth in Division Two. In addition to this insult, there was the scandal of a fixed match involving Manchester United, whose win v. Liverpool in 1915 kept them above Spurs at the foot of the table. Players were suspended, but United were not penalized. So Tottenham were justifiably bitter when peace-time football resumed in 1919 (see Arsenal).

It took Spurs only one season to get back to Division One, and they soon overtook their new neighbours. During the first few years after the War they also effected major changes at White Hart Lane. The Paxton Road End was covered with a two-tier stand, paid for by the profits of Tottenham's victorious Cup run in 1921, and then in 1923 an almost identical stand was built at the Park Lane End. Together these two new structures raised the ground's covered accommodation to 30 000 spectators, a figure exceeded only by Goodison Park. Each stand had seats for 3000 with paddocks in front. They were both designed by Leitch, who was again commissioned when Spurs decided to build a stand on the uncovered East Side in 1936.

This project was in many ways a terrible risk. Spurs had spent the years 1928–33 in Division Two, at exactly the time Arsenal were beginning to impose their almost total dominance over English football, and had also started to redevelop Highbury into the most modern and fashionable ground in the League. Tottenham were in danger of being totally eclipsed.

Leitch's huge new East Stand cost £60 000; potentially crippling for a club just relegated. Fortunately Barclays Bank was willing to finance the deal. In addition, a row of houses had to be demolished and the tenants rehoused.

In design it appeared to be one of the largest stands in the country, although it was essentially a standard Leitch design placed on an extra pedestal of terracing. The gable housed the press-box and was similar to one Leitch had designed for Ibrox in 1929. There were 5100 seats and covered standing for 10 000, with extra uncovered terracing in the front paddock. It was probably Leitch's last major work before he died in 1939 (see Design).

But even at the proud moment of opening the new stand, Spurs were again eclipsed by events at Highbury, for only a month later in October 1936 Arsenal's new East Stand was opened. It had cost more than twice the one at White Hart Lane. The architectural press gave coverage to Highbury's and none to Tottenham's.

It was in this otherwise gloomy spell that Tottenham's highest attendance was recorded at White Hart Lane, when 75 038 saw Spurs lose 0-1 to Sunderland in the FA Cup 6th Round on 5 March 1938. Spurs were still in Division Two when the Second World War broke out, and in 1941 the club gave Arsenal use of White Hart Lane while bomb damage at Highbury was repaired. Tottenham's ground was untouched by the Blitz, unlike the surrounding areas and for a time the top part of the East Stand was used as a mortuary for victims of the raids. Another section of the ground was used as a gas-mask factory.

For many years the White Hart Lane pitch had drained poorly and was consequently very muddy in winter. During the summer of 1952 it was completely reconstructed; 3500 tons of soil were dug up and dumped on nearby Hackney Marshes. Underneath the pitch the old foundations of the Beckwith Nursery greenhouses were found. These were removed and a new filter bed system installed, with one and a half miles of drains and a 9-inch layer of ash, covered over by 2000 tons of specially imported topsoil and 25 000 squares of turf. It had been claimed that the heavier pitches had been a factor preventing Tottenham's famous 'push and run' side winning their second Championship in 1952 (they finished runners-up), but it can also be said that there have been many other Champions with pitches as poor. The system Tottenham installed was one of the most advanced ever laid.

Floodlights came to the ground in September 1953 and were switched on for a friendly v. Racing Club de Paris. The system was mounted on four corner poles (not pylons) each a few feet lower than the East Stand, with additional gantries on the two stand gables. It was because of these extra lamps that the ball and cockerel was moved to the East Stand gable, where it remains today, flanked by the lights. About the same time, the West Stand gable was repainted with a new motif in which the letters T.H.F.C. were intermingled in dark blue on a light background.

Spurs won the Double in 1961, the FA Cup in 1962 and 1967, the League Cup in 1971 and 1973, the European Cup Winners Cup in 1963 and the UEFA Cup in 1972. Throughout these decades of success, very little changed at White Hart Lane. The ground held 60 000, including 16 000 seats, had two-tier stands on all four sides, an excellent pitch and adequate floodlights (updated in the late 1950s). What else could be done?

The answer came in 1979, when it was decided to rebuild completely the West Stand. The stand was getting old and also had been designed at a time when a football ground was used only for football. Tottenham could no longer afford this luxury, so they decided to invest in a new structure which would give White Hart Lane the potential for every day usage. The architects chosen were Mather and Nutter, the designers of Old Trafford's and Molineux's cantilever stands, and consultant architects at Anfield.

In the autumn of 1980 demolition of the old stand began, and slowly in its place arose the most spectacular modern stand built in England.

Officially opened for a game v. Wolves on 6 February 1982 by Sir Stanley Rous, the new West Stand has seats for 6500, 72 executive boxes in two tiers, costing £10 000 each for a three-year lease, and two very large reception areas called the Bill Nicholson Suite and the Centenary Club. There are four main office areas and of course facilities for the players. Furthermore, this was to be just the first stage in a complete redevelopment of the ground on all four sides.

The controversial decision to go ahead with the project was made even though the chairman knew that the projected expenditure of £3·5 million could either make or break the club, which had an annual turnover in 1980–81 of £2·8 million. It was hoped the new stand would bring in two to three times more revenue per seat than the old one. It was an enormous gamble.

On paper, all seemed well, Tottenham's average gate in 1981–82 was 35 099 (compared with Arsenal's 25 493), the club won the FA Cup two years running again in 1981 and 1982, and were losing finalists in the European Cup Winners Cup also in 1982.

But the cost of finishing the stand in 13 months had taken the total expenditure to over £4·2 million (the stand at Molineux had cost £2·8 million), and inevitably, there were repercussions. During the autumn of 1982 there were major changes at board level, forced to a certain extent by the fact that the stand was not financing itself as planned. Only two-thirds of the executive boxes had been sold and no sponsors agreed on. After the changes prospects looked better, and plans have been discussed to continue White Hart Lane's development by replacing the East Stand with a similar design to the West Stand, incorporating a leisure complex.

In addition, there were at long last moves to put the club's covered ball-courts, built in the Double years behind the West Stand, to greater public use. This was especially important because since training had moved to a private ground in Cheshunt, the ballcourts had been badly underused. Neglect such as this showed that Tottenham still had much to learn from the younger generation of top clubs like Watford and Ipswich.

Ground Description

White Hart Lane is not just a football ground, it is part of a small kingdom. The block in which Tottenham are based is owned almost entirely by the club; the houses, the majority of the shops, and the Chanticlear night-club. In rents alone Spurs receive at least £50 000 a year.

On the High Road between Paxton Road and Park Lane is the Spurs souvenir shop, supporters' club headquarters and even a Spurs travel agent. Gate-

way to the kingdom is the Red House, with its large clock on the wall surmounted by a proud cockerel. On the other side of the house is the White Hart Inn, now part of the Bass Charrington group.

Entrance from here to the main courtyard is through tall, wrought iron gates, threatened with removal when the new stand was built but happily since preserved. Through these we come to a small open space, on the left of which are the drab ball-courts which consist of two indoor courts, large and small. To the right of the courtyard is an engineering factory.

And so into the plush new East Stand, a wall of tinted glass forming the facade. The stand itself is typical of the new generation of cantilever stands, curving slightly round the touchline, with textured concrete facings, a vast roof supported from above so that no steelwork is visible, and sleek, glass screens at each end. It is the logical successor to the Hillsborough cantilever, built 20 years before, but with greatly more sophisticated facilities underneath. The architects described it as 'a hotel with seats on top'.

The Tottenham stand differs from Molineux's with its double line of executive boxes. The club obviously felt the income from these would go a long way to help financing the project. Eventually they may be proved right, but other clubs have decided against installing boxes. Both upper and lower tiers are filled with royal blue seats.

Overall it seems enormous, both tall and deep, and indeed there are stands with larger seating capacities that still have less visual impact. Nevertheless, there is still somehow a lack of focus; nothing has replaced the old gable in drawing one's attention to the stand. It is a large mass, bereft of detail.

One effect of the West Stand, hardly the architects' fault, is that the two corners of the end roofs which used to link up with the old stand, now appear to jut out in awkward suspense. In addition, many of the seats under these corners have been rendered useless because the larger dimensions of the new stand obscure the view. Had the club not ordered two tiers of boxes but one, the upper tier of seating could have been less steep and the roof lower.

These end stands are in comparison homely little structures. Each has a grey, pitched roof supported by white pillars, with a seating tier tucked away behind the standing paddock in front. Barely perceptible is the fact that both of them are built at an angle to the pitch, moving slightly away from the touchlines towards the East Side. This is because they follow the lines of Paxton Road and Park Lane respectively, rather than the right-angle of the terracing. This is most pronounced at the Park Lane End, to the right of the West Stand. The broken line of roofing just above the goal shows where the stand begins to bend away from the pitch.

Both stands have a familiar Leitch balcony facing, painted with light-blue steelwork and white walls. The barriers are coloured silver.

If the West Stand represents the mood of the new era, the East Stand represents a pinnacle of the old. It is built in three tiers: an ordinary open paddock at the front, with a double-decker placed above, each section a little further back than the one below, and there is a quite magnificent gable in the centre. Along the front of this is a line of windows, of what used to be the press-box before the new stand was built. Above appears the club crest, and surmounting this, standing against the sky is the ball and cockerel.

This single gable alone has everything that the West Stand lacks. It proves that scale and uniformity are not enough, that there has to be a touch of grandeur, however self-conscious or unnecessarily pompous, to give a grandstand any sort of visual merit. On the East Stand the gable not only provides this, it also makes the stand appear deceptively larger.

Looking more closely one sees the Leitch trademark along the balcony wall, not as intricate as those at Roker or Goodison Parks, but the steel supports fulfil the same function of tying the construction together. The standing area below is called 'the shelf' and is most popular with Spurs supporters. It is fenced off from the lower paddock by a white, wooden wall.

It is a wedding cake stand, shining with whiteness; the light-blue trimmings like icing, the gable like the top tier and the floodlights and cockerel like candles. It is a joy to behold, at once perfectly proportioned yet apparently extraordinary. But sadly, as dramatic as the stand is from the inside, from the street it appears massively drab and ugly. As Alan Ross wrote in 1950, 'Huge grey walls surround the ground, a barrier to revolution. They might have enclosed a prison or a mental home'. In both corners of the East Stand are short rows of terraced houses. On Paxton Road next to the night-club is a Salvation Army building. Every palace has a back yard and every empire its uglier face. But inside, the heart of the kingdom is vast and empty, until homage time on Saturdays.

·ARSENAL·

Previous Grounds

Between 1886 and 1913, Arsenal was just another small club playing without much success in South London. They were like Newton Heath before the coming of J. H. Davies, like Watford before Elton John. In 1913 the club was transported far from its roots, transformed into a new organization, until in the 1930s it transcended all opposition. Highbury Stadium stands as monument to this achievement, and as such has crucial significance to the study of football grounds.

The beginnings were humble. The workers of the Royal Arsenal put together a scratch team and played impromptu games behind the workshops where they were based, as Dial Square FC. In 1886, reorganized under the name of Royal Arsenal, the team began playing on Plumstead Common, which still exists, before moving a year later to the Sportsman Ground, in Plumstead Village. When this pitch became waterlogged one afternoon the club were forced to play at the nearby Manor Field, where they moved in 1888 for two seasons. The players changed in the nearby Railway Tavern.

Royal Arsenal's first substantial ground was a few hundred yards away at the Invicta Ground, also in Plumstead. It belonged to George Weaver, of the Weaver Mineral Water Company, and stood at the rear of Plumstead High Street, where Mineral Street is now. There are still traces of the old terracing in some of the gardens in Hector Street. Royal Arsenal played there between 1890–93, crucial years in which they turned professional – the first London club to do so – and changed their name to Woolwich Arsenal. At first Weaver charged a rent of £200 a year, extremely high in view of the club's status, but in 1893 when he heard they had been elected to League Division Two this amount rose extortionately to £350 plus tax. Only a few years earlier Everton had thought their rent increase to £250 sufficiently extreme to look for a ground elsewhere.

Woolwich Arsenal also decided to seek alternative accommodation, having unsuccessfully offered the landlord a compromise of £300 including tax. Immediately the supporters rallied round and decided to try and buy the Manor Field, where the club had played before moving to the Invicta Ground. A limited company was formed and £4000 raised to purchase the site. At first conditions were fairly basic. There was one iron stand, and until banking could be raised, military wagons were brought in as viewing platforms.

When Arsenal began their League career at the Manor Ground they were the only members south of Birmingham. All the other Southern professional clubs were in the Southern League. So for northern teams travelling down to play Arsenal, the visit was something of a novelty, and soon became linked with exhibition games and friendlies played at other London and southern grounds.

Woolwich's first success came in 1904 with promotion to Division One, but by then the club's whole complexion had changed. Until the turn of the century it had been run essentially by working men, still closely connected with the Woolwich Arsenal. But the outbreak of the Boer War in 1899 meant more overtime for the men, and less time spent on the football club, which soon ran into debt. The organizers had never wanted it to become 'a proprietory or capitalist club' but now they were helpless to prevent capitalists moving in. The team was not the problem, solid middle of the road performers, but the ground was a non-starter. The mortgage payments were too high, and gates were too low, mainly because it was in an awkward location for public transport. By 1910, when the team just escaped relegation, Woolwich Arsenal were £3000 in debt and went into liquidation.

But for the intervention of Henry Norris, Arsenal may have remained yet another struggling club. Norris was a director of Fulham, Mayor of Fulham, a wealthy estate agent and property developer, responsible for building over 2000 houses in the Fulham and Wimbledon areas. And yet for some reason he felt that Fulham FC were not champion material. They had just developed Craven Cottage into one of the best grounds in the country and joined the Football League, but still Norris was not happy. He wanted to mastermind the best. And he chose Arsenal, at the point when they were most vulnerable, and therefore most malleable.

At first Norris proposed a merger between Arsenal and Fulham, but the FA and League refused permission, saying that two clubs could not play on the same ground (Norris had suggested Craven Cottage) with the same name. So Arsenal stayed at Plumstead, and Norris started to plan a move.

The Plumstead area was simply unable to or uninterested in supporting League football, even though a few miles west Millwall Athletic had recently opened their new ground, The Den, and an amateur team Charlton Athletic were just becoming successful almost on Arsenal's doorstep.

The club's last season at the Manor Ground, 1912–13 was an unmitigated disaster from every point of view. The team were relegated while off the pitch financial matters went from bad to worse. The last game played at the Manor Ground was on 28 April 1913, and of this unloved little enclosure there is now no trace.

Highbury

Highbury Stadium as it is known today is not the ground that Norris built. He was responsible for the move to North London, for the purchase of the site and for the establishment of Arsenal's potential as a leading club. But Highbury itself did not become a major stadium until the 1930s, by which time Norris's involvement with football had come to an end. Nevertheless, as Bob Wall wrote, Norris's action in taking Arsenal to Highbury 'was the most astute single decision ever taken by the club', but it caused a barrage of reaction.

Firstly, Tottenham and Clapton Orient did not want a third professional club in North London. Survival was hard enough without more competition. Furthermore, the whole concept of physically transporting a football club from one place to another seemed quite preposterous. Until then about the most adventurous move any club had taken had been Newton Heath's relocation to the other side of Manchester, but if clubs were going to be allowed to resettle on someone else's patch the moment life started to get tough, the whole fabric of professional football would be damaged irreparably.

Secondly, Islington Borough Council did not want Arsenal. So much so they gathered a petition to protest against the granting of the lease at Highbury, claiming that football clubs exploited footballers for dividend purposes and that a popular football ground in the area would decrease property values (that was more honest at least). In short, they mounted a campaign described variously as one of: 'calumny, misrepresentation and jealousy' and 'unscrupulous agitation'.

Thirdly, the local residents around the proposed ground did not want Arsenal, fearing the 'undesirable elements of professional football'. Arsenal were taking a huge gamble and had no way of knowing if there would be sufficient surplus spectators.

The new ground was to be situated on playing fields belonging to the St John's College of Divinity. It cost Arsenal £20 000 for only a 21-year lease, negotiated with the Ecclesiastical Commissioners on condition that the club were not to play home games on Good Friday or Christmas Day.

The site had two main advantages. It was in the centre of a densely populated area which although only four miles from White Hart Lane and even less from Clapton's Millfields Road Ground, was closer to the inner city areas of London. But most importantly, next to the site was Gillespie Road underground station, opened in 1906. No other ground in London had such an advantage.

Archibald Leitch was asked to design the new stadium, which was to have one main stand on the East Side and three large banks of open terracing – the usual Leitch format (see Design). But Highbury's stand was to be quite different from any of his previous designs, and became the largest in London. It was a two-tier stand, with 9000 seats. The roof was also unusual. It was a multi-span roof, with the individual letters of the word Arsenal painted on each gable front. Another stand of a similar construction was built at Molineux, ironically just a few years before this East Stand was demolished to make way for the present one. The banking was raised using excavations from the underground railway, and the West Bank called the Spion Kop.

On the opening day, 6 September 1913, the ground was not nearly complete and the stand least of all. The pitch was not up to standard, having been raised 11 feet at the North End and lowered 5 feet at the South, and the players had to wash in bowls of cold water. When a player was injured in the first game, v. Leicester Fosse, he had to be carried away on a milk cart. According to one observer, the match was played in the atmosphere of a builder's yard.

However The Arsenal, as the club was now called, did win the game, and by December the seats were completed and conditions improved. The team finished in a creditable third place in Division Two.

The First World War was a disaster for Norris. He had invested the then enormous sum of £125 000 in the club, but especially the ground, and there was no way of recouping it during hostilities. By 1919 The Arsenal were £60 000 in debt, paying 10 per cent interest on their overdraft, and perhaps even more ominously, support was no more than lukewarm. The problems that had beset the club in Plumstead had not only persisted but had become magnified. Sir Henry (he had been knighted in 1917 and elected as Member of Parliament for Fulham in 1918) desperately needed a miracle. But rather than wait for one, he made his own.

The Arsenal had finished in fifth position in 1915. In 1919 it was decided to expand Division One by two clubs. The bottom two clubs in Division One in 1915 had been Chelsea and Tottenham, the top two clubs in Division Two were Derby and Preston. Norris bargained behind the scenes and when Chelsea, Derby and Preston joined the new-sized First Division, The Arsenal went in place of Tottenham.

This was quite scandalous. The whole affair had obviously been a complete fix, leaving Spurs quite understandably fuming at their new neighbours. But for Arsenal, and especially Norris, the vote to promote them was a lifeline. They have not left the First Division since, the only club in continuous membership since 1919, and they are the only League club not to have been promoted on playing merit to their present status.

Highbury soon became a focal point in the capital, if only because it was so large. In March 1920 the ground staged its first international (before White Hart Lane, even though Tottenham's ground had more cover and better facilities) and in 1923 Highbury became the first English ground ever to play host to the national team of a foreign country, when Belgium played England on 19 March.

The Arsenal however failed to make much of an impression in Division One, and finished the 1924–25 season in twentieth place. Norris needed another miracle to save his plan from financial ruin, and yet again, he found one. Herbert Chapman was appointed manager in May 1925. A new chapter began. The 10-acre ground was purchased outright

Highbury's original East Stand in 1925. The last bay (under 'C') was all standing. Such roofs were very heavy and costly to maintain (BBC Hulton Picture Library)

for £64 000 and Norris even persuaded the Ecclesiastical Commissioners to drop their prohibition of games on Good Friday or Christmas Day. It was to be one of Norris's last acts for the club, because in 1925 he was suspended by the FA for illegal use of funds, for among other things, hiring a chauffeur. But having lured Chapman away from Leeds Road he had most certainly assured the realization of his dream.

Although the team's success enabled the club to rebuild completely the stadium, without Chapman's progressive thinking and the support of the board, those changes might have been quite different.

In the 1930s Arsenal ruled almost supremely. It was during their third Championship winning season in a row in 1934–35 that Highbury witnessed its largest crowd, 73 295, v. fellow title challengers Sunderland, on 9 March 1935.

The redevelopment of Highbury began in 1931. In order to increase the banking, Arsenal (they dropped the 'The' from their title in 1927) asked local inhabitants to bring in their rubbish. One coal merchant duly responded to the call, backed up too near the hole dug for the North Bank, and in fell both his horse and cart. The animal sustained so many injuries it had to be put down. The body was buried there and then, and remains under the North Bank to this day.

The following summer work began on the new West Stand. Until then this side had been uncovered banking, but in its place arose the most advanced, the most architecturally dazzling grandstand ever seen in Britain. The difference between this and Leitch's work of the same era was that whereas Leitch was a fine structural engineer, the West Stand at Highbury was designed by an acclaimed architect, Claude Waterlow Ferrier.

Ferrier worked in partnership with Major W. B. Binnie, and had already designed important works such as Trafalgar House, in London's Waterloo Place, the Army and Navy Club in Pall Mall, the National Institute for the Blind and the Western Synagogue, off Edgware Road. Ferrier's acceptance says a great deal for the importance of Highbury and for the club's prestige and taste, not to mention resources. The

West Stand was completed six weeks before schedule in December 1932, and cost £50 000, making it the most expensive stand of its time. It needed 700 tons of steel for the frame, had three flats built into the facade on Highbury Hill, and most unusual of all had an electric lift. There were seats for 4000, plus standing room for 17 000, in a simple double-decker arrangement but in a totally new style.

The team's success had already earmarked Arsenal. Now Highbury too had to be special, and the inspiration came not from well-tried ideas dating from the beginning of the century, as did most of Leitch's work, but from bold statements of modern style. The West Stand was unquestionably a child of the 1930s.

There were other changes at Highbury at the same time and in the same spirit. Most important was Chapman's success in persuading London Transport to rename Gillespie Road underground station after the club. The authorities took several weeks to agree to the suggestion, feeling that a station named Arsenal would be tantamount to subliminal advertising, which of course was exactly what Chapman intended. The official change of title occurred on 5 November 1932, just in time for the opening of the West Stand. Another change of name was the ground's, from Highbury to 'Arsenal Stadium'. This change has not survived the test of popular usage.

Still Chapman did not relent. His next innovation was to place a 12 feet diameter 45-minute clock on top of the North Bank. The FA objected on the grounds that it would impinge on the referee's authority. That it might be of value to spectators, only Chapman had the foresight to realize.

His other ideas included numbering players' shirts, a cause taken up by many progressive people in the game, the use of a white ball – the dark leather ball was often hard for the crowd to follow (although after a trial he gave up the idea) – and the adoption in 1933 of red shirts with white sleeves as Arsenal's new strip, because so many teams played in all-red shirts.

Finally, the Arsenal manager was an early exponent of floodlit football. He put on a public demonstration of floodlights at Highbury in November 1932, on the eve of a London conference at the Great Eastern Hotel on the future of floodlit football, but despite the game's success, the FA heartily disapproved and Arsenal had to wait until 1951 to use lights (see Floodlights).

It was Chapman who suggested in 1929 that the 10-yard penalty area be introduced to this country, as used abroad. Again the FA refused, and the marking was not introduced until 1937. He was the first manager to try out rubber studs, to suggest 'all-weather' pitches, and even the idea of roofed sports' stadiums. He was not in search of gimmicks, but of new methods to maintain professional football as a popular spectator sport. Highbury was in many ways only the first ground to benefit from his foresight, and long after his death in January 1934 Chapman's spirit lived on.

In 1935 the North Bank was covered by a roof identical to the one seen today, while the clock was moved to the opposite end, called thereafter the Clock End.

In 1936 work began on a new East Stand on Avenell Road. This one was to be almost identical to the West Stand, but would house all the offices, players' and executive facilities, and unlike its counterpart would actually have a façade visible to the road. It therefore became the grand entrance to the new Highbury.

Claude Waterlow Ferrier had died in 1935 but his partner Binnie carried on their work, so that apart from a few structural changes the two stands are virtually indistinguishable. The East Stand had five floors, held 4000 seated on the top tier and 4000 on a lower tier, with a narrower paddock in front. Without question it was the finest grandstand of the era, but then it cost £130 000 to build, more than twice as much as Leitch's East Stand at White Hart Lane, also completed in 1936.

The East Stand at Highbury was opened before a match v. Grimsby Town in October 1936, and apart from a few alterations the stadium has remained the same ever since.

There was one other major occurrence at Highbury during the Chapman era, the arrival of broadcasting. This was not merely Chapman's influence; the proximity of Arsenal to the BBC's unit at Alexandra Palace was decisive. Highbury was the scene of the first radio broadcast of a football match on 22 January 1927, H. B. T. Wakelam providing the commentary of Arsenal's game v. Sheffield United. The ground also featured in the first television transmission of a game, a practice match at Highbury between Arsenal and Arsenal Reserves on 16 September 1937.

When the Second World War began the ground became a first aid post and an air raid patrol centre, with a barrage balloon flown from the practice pitch by the college. The dressing rooms became clearing stations for casualties, all windows were boarded over, and a blast wall was built inside the main entrance, in that famed marble hall. A 1000-pound bomb fell on the training pitch, while five incendiary bombs destroyed the North Bank roof and burnt the set of goalposts to the ground. Arsenal had no choice but to vacate Highbury and accept refuge at White Hart Lane. Then just as hostilities were ending, in 1945 the college behind the Clock End was also destroyed by fire, and so the last remaining link was lost with the ground's previous owners. A housing estate now occupies the site.

Although post-war developments at Highbury have hardly changed the ground's outward appearance, they have had a substantial effect. In September 1951 the first official game was played under floodlights, v. Hapoel Tel Aviv of Israel, in front of 40 000 spectators. The lights were mounted on gantries along the stand roofs, so that unlike lights on four corner pylons there were no awkward shadows

Typical of 1930s' design, Highbury's East Stand, already blackened by London smog. Notice the mouldings on the balcony wall below the streamlined glass screen end (Sport & General)

on the pitch. Unfortunately these gantries replaced the original roof fascia, although these have now been restored with the updating of the lamps.

Also in the early 1950s the Highbury pitch was relaid, with turf specially brought from Sussex. In 1954 the North Bank roof was rebuilt, an exact copy of the pre-war construction, with money granted by the War Damages Commission.

Arsenal were one of the first clubs in Britain to try undersoil heating, when in 1964 an electric wiring system costing £15 000 was installed. Five years later an extra 5500 seats were put into the West Stand paddock, at a cost of £80 000. Had the club done this when it had first considered the idea in 1960 the bill would have been £42 000. At the same time Arsenal also reconsidered Chapman's idea of erecting a roof over the pitch, to slide over from either stand. The estimated cost was £750 000 (when the country's most expensive player, Allan Clarke, had cost a mere £150 000), but if contemplated nowadays the price would be, at very least, twice the amount. In 1970 the present undersoil heating system was installed, for £30 000.

If a fan of the late 1930s was to return to Highbury today he would see little difference. More barriers perhaps, since the Safety of Sports Grounds Act, a better pitch certainly, advertising even, but essentially Highbury as it stood before the War. The stadium's present capacity is smaller, but is still one of the largest, at 60 000, with 17 200 seats.

Ground Description

If you were to leave the underground station without knowing the stadium's location you might easily fail to spot it between the houses. The lack of floodlight pylons is one reason, the other being that the ground is tucked into the side of Highbury Hill, surrounded on three sides by tall houses.

The main entrance is in the East Stand on Avenell Road and it immediately sets the tone. There are few really impressive facades at football grounds, the most notable being at Villa and Ibrox Parks, Bramall Lane and here at Arsenal, where despite the narrowness of the road one can still appreciate the clean, unfussy, frontage dependent on understated detail rather than intricate mouldings.

Like the rest of the stadium, the walls are cream, the metalwork is grey or green. Above the main doors is the AFC motif, and above that the Gunners' emblem, framed in a moulded recess flanked by tall windows. The words Arsenal Stadium adorn the top, where there are two flagpoles.

When writers refer to the marble halls of Highbury, they mean the main foyer of the East Stand; a tall, almost spartan hall, rightly focusing on a bust of Herbert Chapman by Jacob Epstein, lit reverently in a niche.

We make no excuses for making a brief description of the stand's interior, for more than any in England (though Ibrox is similar in Scotland) this stand is in itself full of history. From the foyer, the offices are on the left, with the club's very own red post box in the corridor. On the right are the dressing rooms. Up the curving stairway we enter the board room and guest rooms. On view is Herbert Chapman's carved chapel seat, presented by his Yorkshire church in Easter 1931. Glass cases bulge with silverware and memorabilia, such as many clubs have, but these are presented in quite a different atmosphere. At Anfield or Old Trafford the cups and trophies are all stored behind glass in the rooms used for entertaining. At Highbury it is like being at an exhibition.

Inside the boardroom are two small cannons. One of them was reputed to have been fired before each game in the Woolwich Arsenal days. There is also a most unusual five-legged chair, once specially designed for a gout-suffering director who had the habit of suddenly rising from his seat and knocking it backwards.

On the opposite side of the stairway are the reception rooms, including one specially for the directors' wives and lady friends, with flowers laid out for each game in red and white, and the colours of the opposition. The press room beyond is equally impressive, equipped by the sponsors with a video playback of the game for journalists to watch at half-time and after the match. Highbury has the capacity for 300 outgoing telephone lines at any one time.

But now we must enter the stand side, and emerging into the daylight the first impression is of the ground's symmetry, for directly opposite is a mirror image of the East Stand. Red seats in the directors' box face red seats in the executive box. Crest faces crest.

One should think of these two stands as belonging to the same era as bakelite encased wireless sets, early airliners at Croydon airport, Odeon cinemas and Ovaltine. In architecture it was an age of rationality, of linear designs and metal frame windows. Highbury embodies the spirit of this age.

Each stand is in three tiers: an upper tier, each with 4000 light green seats. The lower tier is divided in two, a rear section of seats, a front section for standing. The West Stand lower tier holds more,

being further back from the pitch and having no offices or other ground floor rooms.

Along the roof, wrapped round the sides, is an awning, or 'marquise' hiding the very slightly pitched grey roof. The awnings were originally intended to shield spectators from bad weather, but it was found that installing glass screen ends was more effective. Only at Mansfield's ground can a design remotely similar to this be found.

The roof or awning fascias are covered in an ornamental frieze, embellished with the club's crest and name at intervals. On each side of the stand is the Gunners' emblem in red on cream backgrounds. The balcony walls are also cream, apparently plain until close up one sees scrolled stonework lining the ledge. Again the understated detail allows the overall form to dominate.

There are, however, some differences between East and West. The East for example has side towers at each end, and houses all the touchline facilities. The tunnel is flanked by two sections of bench seating, reserved for the club reserves and juniors, and the managers' shelters (they are not dug-outs), encased in glass, like small greenhouses. In winter the home team's shelter is very warm – it has a plug for an electric heater. The away team's does not!

To the left of the tunnel in the paddock is a square section of green covers, beneath which is found the undersoil heating mechanism. The system can either blow steam or suck in water, according to conditions, but on one occasion it got mixed up and blew water everywhere in thousands of fountains. To the left of this is the area for invalids, next to the band's section, the only such facility in the League. Arsenal even had opera singers providing pre-match entertainment.

Across to the West Stand we find a television camera gantry in front of the balcony wall, and entrances on each wing that go under the houses on Highbury Hill. From this road, apart from the flats built into the centre of the rear stand, the ground is again almost invisible.

Arsenal have made the conscious decision not to build private boxes at Highbury, much to the relief of those who would wish to preserve the structural integrity of the stands, but they have provided excellent catering facilities on the top floors of the West Stand. In one of these areas is another bust, this one of Claude Waterlow Ferrier, the main architect of the stand. Some stands, as at West Ham, have a plaque commemorating the architect, but only Arsenal have a bust.

Back in the ground, the Clock End forms the South or what used to be the College End. The clock itself is large, round and white, with black markings, and is unchanged since its installation in the 1930s. It would seem the perfect spot for an electronic scoreboard. As important as the clock is the high grey corrugated fence lining the back of the terrace, sealing it off from the buildings behind. These are the flats of Aubert Park Estate, and the Arsenal indoor training hall, built on their old practice pitch in 1964. In past years the indoor surface was shale and acted as a car-park on match days. Now there is an artificial surface, well used by the club during the day and the local community at night.

The North Bank is covered by a simple, pitched black roof, but far from seeming plain it has a white rippled fascia all round, with red and white corners and two Arsenal crests at the front. Here, exemplified, is the attention to detail which I have cried out for at so many other grounds.

Indeed the entire stadium is enhanced by such detail: by four flag poles along the front of each stand roof, by the Gunners' emblem on the side of the stands, by the careful balance of cream and green.

Despite the scale of the ground, the pitch is actually the smallest in London, measuring 110 × 71 yards, even smaller than West Ham's apparently tiny playing surface. There is a slight slope of 2 feet, from the Clock End penalty area down to the East Stand, and that end's set of goalposts is a trifle warped. The groundsman has tried hanging buckets of sand from the crossbar to straighten it, but with little success.

Adding to the sense of openness is the lack of tall perimeter fencing. Arsenal have built shallow moats at each end, thus enabling them to retain the old iron railings.

This apparent obsession with preserving the ground's visual integrity has been scoffed at by many, who see Highbury as a cold, outdated, dusty mausoleum of long-lost glory. Others would perhaps rightly point out how few improvements standing spectators have been given in recent years, how although the club had sufficient funds, the Clock End remained uncovered, and the dark North Bank roof was not updated.

Now of course the money is not available and Highbury is a very expensive stadium to maintain. But the critics have a point. Highbury does seem lost in the past, caught in a time trap. I believe, however, that Arsenal have a responsibility to preserve Highbury, as a symbol of a bygone age and as an example of fine architecture. Pevsner ignored the stadium on his perambulation around Islington, perhaps he did not notice it. I cannot believe that if he had ever set foot inside the stadium he would have failed to give it a mention, for quite simply it is the most balanced and orderly ground in the country. There is not a line out of place; all is in total harmony. Perhaps the ground is best summed up by the fact that in his obituary, the architect Claude Waterlow Ferrier was described as a man to whom 'untidiness was anathema'. May his vision and that of Arsenal be preserved.

QUEEN'S PARK ·RANGERS·

Previous Grounds

If any club is worthy of the name Wanderers, it is this one. QPR have had more home grounds than any other League club – 12 altogether – and have played individual home matches at two further venues. They were formed when two West London teams merged into one, St Jude's and Christchurch Rangers. Queen's Park was the district most of the players inhabited, and there is still a park of that name today.

The marathon succession of grounds began on a piece of waste ground near Kensal Rise Athletic Ground, before moving to nearby Welford's Fields for a rent of £8 a year. Both these grounds were in the vicinity of present day Harvist Road, Queen's Park. Next came the London Scottish ground in Brondesbury, rented between 1887–89 for £20 a year. Here the club began to collect gate money for the first time, although at times they might not have bothered, so few were the spectators. Eventually the pitch became so waterlogged QPR had to move again.

Between 1890–92 the club used four grounds: Home Park; back to Kensal Rise Green; across the Grand Union Canal to the ground of the Gun Club, on Wormwood Scrubs, then back to their roots at the Kilburn Cricket Ground on Harvist Road. Here they settled until 1896. This was the club's first properly enclosed ground, and their reasons for leaving in 1896 were most encouraging. Gates were rising, so they moved to the Kensal Rise Athletic Ground, with a ten-year lease at £100 a year. It was here that Rangers turned professional in December 1898 and joined the Southern League the following summer.

The first years of professional football did not bring prosperity, and the club was forced to give up the ground and move to one at the rear of St Quintin's Avenue, on Latimer Road in North Kensington. The players had to change in the Latimer Arms and run down the road to reach the pitch, hardly ideal for professional sportsmen, and apparently not for the local residents either. They felt QPR's presence lowered the tone of the area and in 1902 took the matter to court, which ruled against the club. It was time to pack their bags once more, this time back to the Kensal Rise Athletic Ground, where their old landlord gave them a two-year lease, but at £240 a year, more than twice their previous rent.

Even worse was to come however, for at the end of the lease in 1904 the landlord offered them a five-year lease for £2000 (£400 a year), expensive even for a top club, and though QPR tried to bring down the annual rent to £300, they failed. This time they moved further west to Park Royal, two miles south of

Loftus Road showing the artificial turf. In this game the home fans are about to celebrate by running onto the pitch, not that the turf will suffer (Sporting Pictures)

the site of Watkin's Tower, later to become Wembley Stadium.

They played at the Royal Agricultural Society's ground in Park Royal, reputed to hold up to 40 000 spectators, between 1904–07, before moving a few hundred yards to a new ground which had been built by the Great Western Railway Company. This stadium held 60 000, including 9000 under cover and 4000 seated, and was opened on 2 November 1907. With time and prosperity it may well have become one of the leading grounds in London.

Certainly QPR enjoyed their most successful spell at Park Royal, winning the Southern League Championship in 1908 and in anticipation of election to the Football League they even resigned from the Southern League. When their application failed they found that their former competition would only readmit the club if it played all its games in mid-week, since the fixtures had already been arranged. Undaunted, the team continued to improve. During the 1912 season they played a few games at White City (opened in 1908) when a coal strike prevented any trains from reaching Park Royal.

After the outbreak of the First World War, the Army took over Park Royal in February 1915. Rangers were homeless yet again, and finished off their home fixtures at Stamford Bridge and their previous ground on Harvist Road, Kensal Rise. And just in case the club seemed to be establishing roots, the

Kensal Rise site was taken over in 1917 for use as allotments, and QPR were home hunting once more! This time they found Loftus Road, but as subsequent events showed, even this was never a totally permanent base for the apparently restless wanderers, until very recently.

It is almost impossible to trace the location of the club's previous grounds, because although almost most of the roads still exist, the open ground has long been built over by housing, or as at Park Royal, by industrial units.

Loftus Road

QPR's move in 1917 took them to within a few hundred yards south west of White City. Their new home had belonged to Shepherd's Bush FC, an amateur club disbanded during the War, and although it became known as Loftus Road, that was only one of four roads bordering the ground. It was however the nearest to Shepherd's Bush underground station.

QPR took one stand with them, originally built at Park Royal, and this became the Main Stand, housing the offices and dressing rooms on Ellerslie Road. The other three sides were open, and an almost unobstructed view could be had from blocks of flats built all around the ground between the wars.

Loftus Road was closed in 1930 after crowd disturbances, so Rangers yet again played a home fixture at another ground, this time, Highbury. By then their playing fortunes had improved, crowds had risen, and in 1931 the board decided to play first team matches at White City, at that time one of the major greyhound racing circuits in London. They may have thought a bigger stadium would increase public interest or inspire the team. But although White City was only a minute's walk from their ground, once inside it was another world – an ex-Olympic stadium designed to hold 60000 spectators. Their first game there was v. Bournemouth on 5 September 1931, a crowd of 18000 seeing Rangers lose 3-0. The team continued to lose, yet by the end of the season even though the team finished in only thirteenth place, gates averaged a respectable 17000.

On 4 January 1933 two London representative teams met at White City for a floodlit game, played with the FA's approval. Also at White City Queen's Park enjoyed their highest ever attendance recorded at any of their many grounds, when 41097 saw them beat Leeds United in the FA Cup 3rd Round on 9 January 1932. But the following season White City started to turn sour for Rangers. Gates fell, and crowds of under 10000 in a huge stadium seemed completely lost. They struggled on at White City until the end of the season, which saw them finish even lower than before, and they returned to Loftus Road with a huge loss of £7000.

Once home, life began to improve almost immediately. The team achieved fourth place in the division in 1933–34, and in 1938 the supporters' club collected £1500 to build a cover over the Loftus Road End terrace, providing shelter for 6000 spectators.

The club's commitment to Loftus Road increased when they won promotion to Division Two for the first time, in 1948, and bought the ground's freehold plus 39 houses adjoining Ellerslie Road and Loftus Road for the sum of £26250. At the same time the terraces were concreted and plans discussed for a double-decker stand on the Popular Side, along South Africa Road, although these were not realized for many years.

A further improvement came in 1953 when floodlights costing £5000 were first switched on for a friendly v. Arsenal on 5 October. By then Rangers were back in Division Three, where they stayed until 1967. During that time Loftus Road hardly changed.

For just a few months of the 1962–63 season the club tried out White City once again, on the suggestion of the manager Alec Stock. He felt that although some £300000 had been spent on Loftus Road in ten years, the effect seemed negligible. It remained an underdeveloped, even somewhat ramshackle ground. If Rangers used White City, argued Stock, they might perhaps share it with another League club, perhaps Fulham. But as in the 1930s, small attendances in the large stadium were too distant from the players, whose form was affected by the huge surroundings.

In 1966 Rangers won promotion again, and this time they decided to improve Loftus Road. An architect, Michael Newberry, drew up a plan for the complete redevelopment of the ground, to cost £340000 and to provide a circle of stands in two phases, due for completion in 1969. In fact the plan was used by Rangers only to get planning permission from the local authorities for their subsequent intention, which was to build a new stand on the Popular Side. This was the South Africa Road Stand, a two-tier construction, built quickly and at low cost, £162000, to celebrate Rangers' promotion to Division One. The new stand and the new status made Loftus Road a proud ground, and even though the team was relegated in its first season at the top, the plans for the ground continued.

In 1972 the old Main Stand came down and in its place was built another very cheap, but remarkably cost-effective 5000 seater single-tier stand, also designed by Newberry. Quoted in *Design*, Newberry described the QPR board as 'very hard-headed, very successful businessmen who know the value of money very well'.

The importance of their attitude may easily be seen when contrasted with that of their neighbours at Stamford Bridge, who at the same time opted for a much larger, more prestigious rebuilding programme which was to cost over £1 million and plunge Chelsea into deep financial trouble. Loftus Road was being developed bit by bit, with simple, almost spartan stands which could be improved in time. Certainly, the shock to both players and spectators was minimal. Loftus Road seemed to grow, rather than sprout up suddenly. It was intended to be used, not to be admired.

Rangers reached a peak in the mid-1970s. On 28 April 1974 Loftus Road's highest attendance was recorded for a match v. Leeds United, that season's League Champions. The crowd of 35353 was nevertheless smaller than their best gate at White City, coincidentally also for a game v. Leeds. Two years later Rangers achieved their highest ever placing in the League, runners-up to Liverpool, then in 1979 found themselves back in Division Two.

At that time the School End sported a very impressive new-style electric scoreboard, and the opposite Loftus Road End cover was taken down to make way in 1980 for a double-decker stand. Again, nothing grand, but cheap and utilitarian, although as described below by no means unattractive.

It was joined by an almost identical stand opposite, at the School End, a year later, and executive boxes were installed in the South Africa Stand, which had now taken over as the club's administrative centre.

Loftus Road is now covered on all four sides, with a capacity of 27000 of which 17500 are seated.

In the summer of 1981 QPR became the first British League club to install artificial turf at their ground. The system they chose was called Omniturf and cost £350000 to lay, in place of a pitch which for years had been notoriously compacted and threadbare. (For a full account see Pitches.) Rangers' decision was one of the most controversial ever taken in the entire history of British football. Not only was the whole future of natural grass questioned, but the essence of what a football ground should be: an expensive enclosure in use for perhaps two or three hours a week, or a community centre for leisure and spectator events.

Rangers opted for the latter, and inevitably there were many who criticized the new pitch. It is by no means proven that the new surface does answer the problem of modern football grounds, but at least Rangers were brave enough to make the decision while many others hesitated.

Outsiders might do well to learn from Loftus Road. It is probably the least costly yet most rapidly completed, and also one of the most capable grounds in Britain of catering for current spectator demands. It was significant that in the summer of 1982, the club actually took out seating from the main stand paddock, because supporters had expressed a preference for standing in that part of the ground.

Loftus Road does suffer from its location. It is so hemmed in by housing that even if the ground were booked six or seven days a week for sporting events, it would be very difficult to get permission to stage them all, because of residents' objections. After Rangers' experience with the residents of Latimer Road back in 1902 they would not wish to cause antagonism again.

Whatever surface Loftus Road has, plans suggest that the ground will continue to pioneer new ideas. The next plan is for a permanent roof over the ground, perhaps even air-conditioning.

Rangers have undoubtedly made mistakes, as argued in the chapter on pitches, but one could also argue that someone had to make them. We may not all like artificial turf, but it is not going to go away.

Ground Description

Officially of course it should be called South Africa Road, or at least the Rangers' Stadium, but old habits die hard. Loftus Road is a short walk from Shepherd's Bush underground station, in an area made famous not only by White City but by the BBC television centre on Wood Lane, just behind the ground.

The main entrance is on South Africa Road, where the stand is fronted by a three-storey section of offices leased out to the BBC.

Inside, the ground is quite unlike any other. There are grounds such as the Baseball Ground which are as enclosed, but none quite as boxed in as this. It appears that every stand has been built in kit form, not because they are primitive, but because they are each so simple. That is their virtue.

The Main Stand is the tallest, with blue fascia, and blue steelwork standing in marked contrast with the bright shiny green of the turf, which reflects and enhances all the colours around. There are private boxes under the top tier, with dark reflective glass making it impossible to see from the outside how luxurious they are within. The stand is not a canti-

lever, but simply a modern, plain post and beam construction, with a paddock in front.

Pressed up on either side are the two double-decker end stands, Loftus Road to the left, the School End to the right (the road behind this stand is Bloemfontein Road – far too long for the average supporter to fit into a chant: 'We are the Bloemfontein Road End'). Each stand is like a shoe box cut-out, again with all blue facings and steelwork, and with a standing terrace under the seating tier.

The Ellerslie Road Stand is different, being one tier of seats and with less bright blue appeal. Along its deep, plain roof fascia is the club crest. But it too is of simple design, post and beam.

Loftus Road always had a reputation for being a cramped ground where players and fans could exchange banter, and even though the ground has been rebuilt entirely within the space of 14 years, that atmosphere still prevails. The pitch comes right up to the perimeter, and even the rear sections of seating are comparatively close to the touchlines. Economy of space is emphasized by the new floodlight system, four thin poles with small gantries at the top. Very continental and why don't other grounds have such attractive installations.

Loftus Road is a theatre, an arena to perform in, in which you expect fans to clap rather than chant obscenities; eat choc-ices rather than chips, drink coffee, not bovril.

Loftus Road is quite unique among British grounds, and one can pay no higher tribute to the ground's planners than to say it should serve as a model to any club of the size or status of QPR. They may have moved around more than any other club, but at least they have got it right so far.

◆ FULHAM ◆

Previous Grounds

When formed in 1879 Fulham St Andrew's Cricket and Football Club was one newcomer in an already established soccer scene in a part of West London thriving with sporting activity; while what open spaces there were available were being steadily bought up and developed. Fulham's early grounds were all within a mile of their present home. They began at Star Road, near where Earl's Court is now, then moved to the Ranelagh Club, changing in rooms above the Eight Bells on Fulham High Street. The Ranelagh Club had to move in 1884 so Fulham St Andrew's moved to a ground on Lillie Road at Fulham Cross. This was close to the Queen's Club and also to Lillie Bridge, West Brompton, where the 1873 FA Cup Final was staged.

In 1886 Fulham moved across the River Thames to the new home of the Ranelagh Club, at Barn Elms, Barnes. This is still a sporting ground and is exactly opposite Craven Cottage on the west bank of the Thames. Here they dropped St Andrew's from their title in 1888. The club moved back to the Fulham side, to a ground by Purser's Cross, on Fulham Road, near the present Parsons Green underground station. From here it moved to Eelbrook Common, which still exists on the junction of Kings Road and Wandsworth Bridge Road, very near Stamford Bridge.

But Fulham's first properly enclosed ground was back across the river, off Putney High Street, behind the Half Moon. They shared this with Wasps Rugby FC until the ground was closed in 1894. The club was by this stage anxious to have a home of its own, and so it was the present ground was purchased in 1894. We learn this and more from club histories written by Dennis Turner and Morgan D. Phillips.

Craven Cottage

The site Fulham bought was a wilderness, overgrown and neglected, and the original Craven Cottage no longer existed, having burnt down in May 1888. Built in 1780 by the sixth Baron Craven, the Cottage stood on land once part of Anne Boleyn's hunting grounds. George IV used it as a hunting lodge after which it became the home of a money lender, Charles King, Sir Ralph Howard, and an author, Edward Bulwer-Lytton. The latter wrote *The Last Days of Pompeii* during his sojourn at the Cottage, and therefore provided later writers with a useful tit-bit to pad out reports of less scintillating matches. Of course the present Cottage is an entirely different structure.

The land partly belonged to the Church and partly to the Dean family, who have been closely involved with Fulham since 1894, and it was prepared for play by the building firm of Mears, which was to build Stamford Bridge and found Chelsea FC a decade later. The original Cottage stood in the centre of what

is now the pitch, which had to be levelled with excavations from the nearby Shepherds Bush underground railway. The workers found a secret underground tunnel linking the old cottage site to a wharf on the Thames. Banking was raised on three sides with road sweepings, courtesy of the Borough Council, while on the Stevenage Road side a most distinctive stand was erected nick-named the 'Rabbit Hutch'. Seating 300 in four distinct blocks, it was about 40 yards in length, very tall and narrow, covered by four separate gabled roofs with two canopies added to cover the standing area in front. But trade disputes and problems with the site meant that Fulham were unable to play at the new Craven Cottage ground until 10 October 1896, having spent the two previous seasons wandering around West London from ground to ground.

Now at last the club was able to progress. In 1898 they turned professional and joined the Southern League, and in 1905 hired Archibald Leitch to re-model the ground. It is possible that Craven Cottage was Leitch's first major commission at a football ground south of the border. His work at Fulham certainly coincided with other work at Ewood Park and Stamford Bridge, and only just predated his efforts at White Hart Lane (see Design).

Leitch designed banks of terracing on three sides, with an impressive new full-length stand on Stevenage Road, costing £15 000. The format was one he used at virtually every other ground he worked on, up to the mid-1920s at Selhurst Park. But Fulham's ground was to have one significant difference. In the south east corner on Stevenage Road, Leitch built the present day Craven Cottage, in the same red brick of all his stands but in a more familiar residential style. Indeed the Cottage did have a small apartment for a player to occupy, as well as a boardroom, offices and a dressing room. It is reputed, however, that there was no electricity connected to the building until 1933!

The new stand was opened on 2 September 1905, and no doubt inspired the team to win the Southern League Championship in the next two seasons. During the club's last season before joining the League, Craven Cottage was chosen as the venue for England v. Wales in March 1907. This was the first time the ground of a professional London club had been used for an international, apart from the stadium at Crystal Palace.

Fulham's chairman at this time was Henry Norris, who three years later decided to leave Fulham and sponsor Arsenal. He was convinced that Fulham did not have the potential to match the great clubs of the day, and indeed between 1907 and the Second World War Fulham were an almost permanent resident at the middle of Division Two, broken only by a four-season spell in Division Three. Not that the club lacked ambition; in 1935 there was a proposal to build a stand on the river side of the ground and Leitch was again called in.

Craven Cottage showing the Cottage in the top left-hand corner; the Eric Miller stand is to the right (Colorsport)

It is not clear whether the proposed stand's designer was Leitch or his son Archibald Kent Leitch, who followed in his father's footsteps and continued to liaise with Fulham until after the Second World War. Whoever it was, Fulham could not afford the projected cost of £11 000, and though the idea was revived in 1950, when Fulham were in Division One for the first time, that estimate had risen to £40 000. It was another 20 years before the matter was raised again.

When Craven Cottage's record attendance of 49 335 came for Fulham's derby game v. Millwall in Division Two, on 8 October 1938, they found therefore a ground unchanged since 1907. From the top of the Riverside banking one had a clear view of the river, and especially of the annual Oxford and Cambridge Boat Race. Often the ground was opened early, to let the crowd see the boats negotiate the stretch between Hammersmith and Putney Bridges. At the top of the Riverside terrace was a line of advertisement hoardings in the centre of which was a clock. The central gable of the Main Stand announced the words: 'Fulham Football and Athletic Co. Ltd. Craven Cottage'.

Fulham were back in Division One in the 1960s and the first major changes were made to the ground. Firstly, a cover was erected over the Hammersmith End, the tallest bank of terracing at Craven Cottage. Then in September 1962, Fulham became the last Division One club to install floodlights, first used in a League match v. Sheffield Wednesday. One reason given for this tardiness was the club's worry that being so close to the river, the pylon's foundations would not be sufficiently firm, which would explain why the City Ground was also late in having its lights installed. But Fulham really wanted to use their available capital to buy back Bobby Robson (later to become the England manager) in August 1962. As at so many clubs, it was the supporters who rallied together to pay for the floodlights.

Other changes at the ground during that summer included the construction of an electric scoreboard on the terracing, which according to one observer no-one could understand, and the replacement of the familiar advertisement hoardings with a smart set of flagpoles, each carrying the flag of a First Division club. But at the cost of £1500 a set, when Fulham found themselves relegated twice in successive years, there was hardly time or money to buy replacement flags from all the different clubs they had to face, and sadly the idea was allowed to drop. After returning to Division Two the Riverside terracing was built over with a fine new stand, opened in February 1972 with a friendly v. Benefica. The Riverside Stand cost £334 000 to complete, of which £250 000 was still claimed by the builders five years later. It was named the Eric Miller Stand to commemorate the Fulham director who committed suicide in the aftermath of a financial and political scandal, revealed in 1977.

Fulham have been particularly hard-hit by the

requirements of the Safety of Sports Grounds Act, because all the entrances to the ground are on Stevenage Road. To reach the Eric Miller Stand you must walk behind the two end terraces. This, rather than any deficiencies in the actual terracing, has forced a reduction of the capacity from 39 518 before the Act, to a present figure of 19 830. Within that number, many seats have had to be taken out of use. The previous total of 8048 is now reduced to 6610.

Ground Description

The first sight on entering the ground is Leitch's red-brick facade, nicely understated with a faint trace of decorative mouldings along the top. Notice the line of windows, shaped like classical thermal openings; a semi-circle divided by two vertical mullions, one of Leitch's favourite early features. But before entering the Main Stand, remember this is not the power house of Fulham. That is in the Cottage. Entering the Cottage up a flight of stairs, there is a reception office like that of a run down insurance broker's. But through the offices, onto the balcony overlooking the pitch, and all is forgiven.

The Cottage is a landmark of football; there is no other building quite like it. Underneath the balcony is a high white wall, behind which is the entrance to the dressing rooms, so that the players enter the field at the corner. Just like a cricket pavilion, the Cottage has benches overlooking the pitch and that homely atmosphere which lends itself to tea and cucumber sandwiches. But it is also the vantage point for chairman and manager, who can look out upon their domain. And it is, from here, a pleasant view indeed.

To the right is the Main Stand, with its familiar gable in the centre, now bearing the title 'Fulham Football and Rugby League Club'. The stand is almost the same design as Tottenham's old West Stand, but on a slightly smaller scale, as it does not house any dressing rooms or offices. From the pitch it seems to be all roof, dark and sloping, but closer to, the plain brick facings are also distinctive. You can see where Leitch's thermal windows have been bricked in at the back of the paddock, though the top ones at the back of the stand are still prominent. Each section of seating is divided by wooden slatted fencing, giving the stand the look of a well-tended railway station. Notice also how at each end of the stand, the sides of the roof above the paddock curve in a slight arch. This was typical of Leitch's work.

The far covered terracing is the Hammersmith End, named after the district nearby. An example of how drastically the Safety Act cut Fulham's capacity is that this end once held 14 750. Now, because of limited exits, it can hold only 6600. Under the roof are sections of the old electric scoreboard, barely discernible in the shadows, and still hard to fathom.

Opposite the Main Stand is the Eric Miller Stand, tall and efficient, its hard lines and metallic and concrete finish in stark contrast with the stand opposite. But the new stand does have its problems. Inside,

the seats and gangways are liberally bespattered with droppings from birds who frequent the river banks.

The stand seats 4216, although not all these can be used, because access is so limited. The river bank is a few yards behind and you can see clearly over the water, to the trees and green spaces of Barnes. How nice it would be to look over the river from the top of this stand, like spectators used to do when there was an open terrace here. But the builders have installed frosted glass along the top corridor behind the seats, unlike Chelsea's West Stand which has clear glass at the top giving a superb view.

At the back of the Eric Miller Stand is a line of private boxes. They look like waiting rooms at a DHSS office. But in the stand's favour: it has a clean grey roof fascia, bearing the crest of the Borough of Fulham and Hammersmith, and so looks modestly dignified.

Finally, the south open terrace is called the Putney End, and is attractively lined at the back with tall trees in Bishop's Park. At the top is an advanced type of electric scoreboard which has 8500 fluorescent discs. Underneath the terracing you can see old Anderson air raid shelters half buried in the earth. The pitch was cratered by bombs during the War.

In recent years the pitch has suffered increasingly from disease and wear and tear, though the proximity of the river is not a problem, as any excess water tends to drain away when the tide goes down. Nor especially is the presence of a Rugby League club detrimental. Fulham were the first club to experiment with ground sharing of this nature, and have been able to offer their findings to clubs like Cardiff, Carlisle and Leeds. For example, they developed a green vegetable dye to cover over the markings of the game not being played, and if you look closely, you can see faint green lines across the pitch. The halfway line and touchlines are the same for both codes. But the rugby players do not cut up the pitch as badly as footballers, and as the groundsman has found there is no concentrated wear, such as soccer causes, in the centre circle and penalty areas. Nevertheless extra usage has demanded a tougher pitch, and in 1983 Fulham was the first club to install a Cell System pitch, a revolutionary system described fully in the chapter on pitches.

The proximity of the water and of Bishop's Park makes the environment particularly pleasant at Craven Cottage, while the ground itself has an intriguing balance of styles, old and new, large and small. Quite how pleasant it would remain without the Cottage is hard to say, but we may soon find out. Plans are afoot for a 4000-seater stand at the Putney End, incorporating self-contained flats overlooking the park, executive boxes, an underground car-park and a sports hall. An admirable plan except that it entails demolishing Craven Cottage. All football winces at the thought in helplessness. There is no preservation order. Only progress.

· BRENTFORD ·

Previous Grounds

There is a popular belief that the game of football began when Julius Caesar crossed the Brent, kicking the skull of a defeated Briton. It was some 1800 years later that the sport caught on in the area, when Brentford FC were formed in 1889. They began playing on a field behind the Wesleyan Chapel in Clifden Road, just by Braemar Road. Two years later they moved north to Benns Field, Little Ealing, then in 1895 to Shotters Field in Windmill Road, now a main road. From 1898–1900 Brentford played at the Cross Roads, South Ealing, followed by four years in Boston Park, a mile west of Griffin Park, their new home in 1904.

Griffin Park

After an unsure start in the Football League, by 1935 Brentford were in Division One, having built the Main Stand on Braemar Road in 1927. They had won every League match at Griffin Park in 1929–30, and risen from the Third to the First in three seasons. The other two stands were completed in this period of prosperity, which included their best ever Cup run in 1938, when a record crowd of 39 626 saw Brentford fall to Preston in the quarter-finals. The ground has hardly changed since the 1930s.

Back in Division Three by October 1954, they met Chelsea in a friendly to inaugurate the new floodlights.

In 1967 QPR, dissatisfied with their ground at Shepherd's Bush, tried to take over Brentford and Griffin Park, but were thwarted and sent back to redevelop Loftus Road. Only a year later, Brentford announced that they would be leaving anyway, to Hillingdon Borough's ground several miles west. But they are still at Griffin Park, in spite of an incident during a game v. Millwall, when one malefactor threw a grenade onto the pitch. Had it not been a dud, the next section might have been rather different.

Ground Description

The ground lies in the centre of a triangle formed by Gunnersby Park, Syon Park and Kew Gardens, the last two across the river. From Braemar Road the Main Stand appears as a splash of red, white and black, with a tangle of gangways, fences and huts hemmed in behind by a row of the small, terraced cottages that encircle Griffin Park. It is a typical wooden stand, whose well-worn, darkened steps gently smell of many years of creosote. 'Commit no nuisance', say the signs, as if one would in such congenial surroundings.

Inside, Griffin Park is unexpectedly spacious. Red and white stripes greet you from the New Road roof opposite, reflected on the Main Stand's terrace rear fencing. Here is a club with either pride in a once

Brentford's players help to build a corner addition to the Main Stand in 1935. It was quite common for clubs to employ players for ground work during the summer break (BBC Hulton Picture Library)

fashionable mode of decor, or just not enough money for repainting. Whatever, too many clubs have erased their stripes in favour of monotones. At the ends of the Main Stand are angled wings with rickety fences. In the stand's centre, the press are honoured with their own white suspended ceiling above their seats. To the left is the Brook Road Terrace, whose roof has sections in glass, lending it a feeling of spaciousness. Clubs with dark, constricting enclosures might follow suit. Red and white barriers add a further sense of identity.

The New Road covered terrace is less tidy, much of it fenced off, with weeds abounding in the north west corner.

To the right are the equally forlorn terraces of the open Ealing Road or Clock End, behind whose wayward barriers is at last some clear space for the ground to breathe.

With capacity at a surprising 37 000, of which 30 000 are under cover, there is scope, as QPR no doubt sensed, to develop Griffin Park from a quaint relic of pre-war design into a modern stadium with extra seating and improved terracing, without disturbing too much of its present tranquillity. Perhaps its greatest asset however, as far as some fans are concerned, is that Griffin Park is the only League ground with a public house on each of its four corners.

·CHELSEA·

Stamford Bridge

Stamford Bridge is unique in the history of English football grounds as the only ground to have been built before the creation of the team whose home it became. Stamford Bridge was bought and developed even when it was not clear if it would be used by an existing club, a new club or for Cup Finals and internationals.

The story begins in 1896, when two brothers, H. A. and J. T. Mears tried to buy the leasehold of Stamford Bridge, then the headquarters of the London Athletic Club who had taken the site over in 1876, when it had been a market garden. H. A. or 'Gus' Mears intended to turn the ground into the biggest and best football stadium in London – hardly a difficult task considering that of the leading London clubs at the time, only nearby Fulham had moved into their present ground and all the other club grounds were highly primitive compared with some northern stadiums or the great Scottish grounds. That London should have only one large venue at Crystal Palace, and that hardly adequate, seemed ridiculous to the Mears, who foresaw how the game would capture the metropolitan imagination.

But they were unable to take over Stamford Bridge until the owner, a Mr Stunt, relinquished control. Even when he died in 1902, the Mears had to wait because a clause in the lease gave the London Athletic Club tenure of the ground for two years after the owner's death. Finally they took possession on 29 September 1904, eight years after their original idea.

Several options were available to them. Should they develop Stamford Bridge and then rent it out to another club, perhaps nearby Fulham, or should they start their own club? Or even more sensibly, should they accept an attractive offer made to them by the Great Western Railway, which wanted to turn the site into a coal dumping yard?

Gus Mears was very tempted by the railway offer and the prospect of a quick profit, and it was only the influence of his friend, Frederick Parker, that saved Stamford Bridge from the railway company. Parker tried to persuade Mears that the ground would be viable for football and that it could be rented out for Cup Finals (Crystal Palace was already almost obsolete) for a potential profit of £3000 a game. But Mears was unconvinced. At that point, Mear's dog bit Parker's leg! The story goes that as Parker reacted in such a cool manner, Mears decided that maybe Parker's judgement was to be trusted! On such a small incident rested the fate of Chelsea FC.

Parker and Mears' first step was to visit Glasgow, home of three of the biggest football grounds in the world, and the man who had been responsible for their design, Archibald Leitch.

Suitably impressed, the pair returned to London

and by early 1905 the work at Stamford Bridge was well under way. Like Leitch's Glasgow designs, the London ground was to be a large bowl with one main stand, on the East Side. That stand was to hold 5000 seated, with a covered paddock in front, and was virtually identical to those Leitch built for Fulham and Tottenham at the same time (and Huddersfield a few years later) with that distinctive central gable.

The other three sides were open banking, built up with thousands of tons of soil and clay excavated during the construction of the nearby underground line. Gradually, the earth was raised up to form the now familiar bowl shape, and extra cinders were brought in from a local sewer.

Stamford Bridge, it was claimed, 'will stagger humanity', alleging to have a capacity of 95 000, a figure tested only once. It was the second largest stadium in England, behind Crystal Palace, which had its own professional club installed.

Mears offered Fulham the chance to rent the ground for £1500 a year, but they chose to develop their own home at Craven Cottage in 1905, so he had no alternative but to form his own team. The story is well told elsewhere, so suffice to say here that Chelsea was born in April 1905, without players but with a very determined board of directors.

Stamford Bridge was closer to the centre of London than any other ground and in the midst of one of the most fashionable and wealthiest parts of the city. It was little wonder therefore that one of the names considered for the new club was London FC. But in the end Chelsea was the preferred choice, although even this was something of a pose, for Stamford Bridge actually stood almost opposite Fulham Town Hall and close to Fulham Broadway. (In fact many of Fulham FC's previous grounds had been within a very short distance of the Stamford Bridge site.) Chelsea were charged £2000 for the use of Stamford Bridge by Mears, who also ran the ground's catering facilities.

The new club began to make some impressive signings, but incredibly were refused admittance to the Southern League. Chelsea therefore applied to the Football League, whose membership included only two clubs south of Birmingham; Bristol City and Woolwich Arsenal. They had a strong case, for not only was their ground superb but they had £3000 in the bank. It needed only one ballot for them to be elected, and after a friendly v. Liverpool, Stamford Bridge staged its first League competitive match when Chelsea beat Hull City in Division Two 5-1, on 11 September 1905.

One of the new team was the famous 6 feet 3 inches tall, 20-stone plus goalkeeper Willie Foulke; the club's first captain. It is said that Stamford Bridge was the first ground ever to employ ball-boys, because manager John Tait Robertson thought that if two small boys stood behind Foulke's goal it would emphasize his enormous frame. It seems more likely that the boys were there because there was so much

Chelsea built a special platform in order that Charles Cundall could paint this picture of a match v. Arsenal in the 1930s (*Football and the Fine Arts*)

room behind the goal that Foulke did not want to have to keep retrieving loose balls.

A bright start in the League saw Chelsea enjoy healthy gates, including one over 60 000, and win promotion in only their second League season. In 1911 a record Cup tie crowd of 77 952 packed into Stamford Bridge for a 4th Round match v. Swindon Town. Parker had been right, the ground was a success.

A weather-vane became one of the landmarks of the new stadium at about this time and it has a history of its own. Originally placed on the apex of the Main Stand gable, the vane had a silhouette of a footballer on one side, a ball on the other. The figure was said to have been modelled on one of Chelsea's greatest players, George 'Gatling-Gun' Hilsdon, an England international who played for the club before the First World War but who was sadly crippled by mustard gas in 1918.

The weather-vane and Hilsdon became legendary at Stamford Bridge. It was reckoned that if ever the vane came down, so would Chelsea's luck. Such a prediction was to prove correct.

Meanwhile the ground continued to improve. Chelsea became popular very quickly, and their arrival on the local scene may even have had some bearing on Henry Norris's decision to quit Fulham and take over ailing Arsenal (see Fulham and Arsenal). In 1909 extra banking was raised behind the goals, adding room for a further 10 000 spectators, and in 1913 Stamford Bridge staged its first international fixture, England v. Scotland. Stamford Bridge did not become a regular home for England games (it

has staged only four in total), but it did take over from Crystal Palace as home of the FA Cup Final in 1920. There had been one Final between the takeover, played at Old Trafford.

Stamford Bridge did not really develop sufficiently to maintain its status. It had a marvellous chance in 1920, when it staged the Cup Final, but the crowd of 50 018 was a great disappointment and well below pre-war gates at Crystal Palace. The following year was better, but the 1922 Final down to only 53 000. But by then another venue had been decided on. Wembley took away the Cup Final from 1923 onwards, while Highbury became the favourite choice for internationals in London. Quite simply, the Chelsea ground had too few seats, too little cover and suffered from limited access from Fulham Road (the other two sides were hemmed in by railways).

The 1930s began with Chelsea in debt – some £12 000 by 1933. Stamford Bridge therefore became a centre for the new craze, greyhound racing, so popular at nearby Wembley and White City. The ground also had a speedway team between the wars.

The first major piece of construction at Stamford Bridge since 1905 was the building of the so-called Shed, at the South End, although it did not acquire the nickname until after the War, and its unwholesome reputation not until the 1960s. It was a plain cover at the back of the terracing, at an angle which suggested it was only half finished and had been intended to continue round towards the Main Stand. In 1935 Stamford Bridge's official record attendance, 82 905, came for the First Division game against Champions Arsenal on 12 October. This is the second highest club attendance record after Manchester City's 84 569, recorded in March 1934. There is an oil painting of this match, painted by Charles Cundall, from a platform specially erected by the club in the north west corner. The club has always had a good relationship with local artists, and it was significant that of 130 works exhibited in 1953 to show Football through Fine Art, ten depicted Stamford Bridge.

The odd looking North Stand was built in the summer of 1939, a double-decker stand seating about 1000, built on stilts above the terracing, immediately next to the Main Stand. It sat rather awkwardly in the corner, slightly angled but giving the impression that the roof was sagging. It had a large pitched roof, with two large glass screen walls at either end, one of which, because the stand was taller than the Main Stand, looked down on its roof. The two buildings looked quite uneasy next to each other.

Although the Arsenal fixture in 1935 was the official attendance record, this was broken when immediately after the Second World War Moscow Dynamo visited Stamford Bridge for the first in a series of friendlies against British clubs, in November 1945. A total of 74 496 people actually went through the turnstiles, but so vast was the crowd that gates and fences were torn down and the final total numbered anything from 90 000 to 100 000, with several thousand spilling onto the greyhound track and the touchlines.

Floodlights were first used on 19 March 1957 for a friendly v. Sparta of Prague. There might have been more improvements had the club not adopted such a high and mighty attitude towards the supporters, who had attempted to form a supporters' club in the late 1940s but were rebuffed by the parent club. When one sees how many grounds all over Britain were transformed by the fund-raising efforts of supporters' clubs, Chelsea's attitude at that time seems quite foolhardy, let alone heartless, and it was fortunate it changed in later years.

The Bridge was shaken up during the 1960s, and especially by the efforts of manager Tommy Docherty, and at last in 1965 a new stand was built on the West Side of the ground. Costing £150 000, with seats for 6300, it was a relatively plain construction, essentially a roof over the reshaped banking. Incorporated at the back were some of the country's first, though not luxurious private boxes – a significant sign of future developments. (Old Trafford had the first boxes in 1964.)

The stand was designed by an architect called Skeels, who had great visions of 'the stand of the future'. Among his plans was the provision for cars to drive onto the roof and for their occupants to watch the game from there! Another revolutionary idea, which was carried out, was to build gangways between the seats at diagonals, so that the spectator would not have to watch over the head of the person in front – a fine idea had play been static, but with the action moving from end to end the idea proved rather self-defeating.

But the important fact from the club's point of view was that the stand was soon paid for, by runs in the FA Cup and European Fairs Cup, and by continuing good form in Division One. 'Chelsea' during the 1960s did not merely suggest football but was associated with the swinging image of the surrounding areas and the Kings Road.

Sadly, Chelsea were the first club to erect security fences at their ground, 8-foot high barriers being put up behind each goal in October 1972.

Between 1963–72, the club finished lower than the top seven only once and the directors decided to give Stamford Bridge a face lift. There are many cases of a club building a new stand and suffering the consequences – Wolves are the best known victims of their own ambition in recent years. But Chelsea were probably the first to have almost planned their own extinction, even though they had no reason to suspect, that their winning streak would come to an end so abruptly. But they must have forgotten that warning about the weather-vane. Once it came down, nothing seemed to go right.

The club planned a new look stadium that would not only cater for football, but would include a swimming pool, gymnasiums, squash courts, and an open piazza for the public's enjoyment. The ground was to become a huge leisure centre.

The decision to commission a new stand came in 1970, and resulted in March 1971 with preliminary discussions with a firm of architects called Darbourne and Darke. Although this firm had no previous experience of stadium design the plans drawn up seemed most impressive. Their clients were keen to portray image and status in the designs.

Furthermore, an attempt by another design company to urge restraint on Chelsea failed miserably. A consortium of companies put together a strategy which argued that Chelsea had to take into account falling gates and the comparative value of their land. Stamford Bridge, they said, was worth about £7 million in land value, yet was hopelessly under-used. To make a profit the club would have to attract at least 30 000 people each home game. The consortium argued that Chelsea should diversify their activities before building a new stand. Their proposals included the staging of pop concerts, exhibitions, markets, restaurants, night clubs, and so on, allied to an intensive marketing of Chelsea FC as a package like any other.

Either the club could build bit by bit, or they could do it all at once, but with artificial turf and a community sports centre. Alternatively they could sell the site and build a new ground on the profits at their training ground in Tooting.

Chelsea opted for Darbourne and Darke's much more prestigious plan for a £1·6 million stand, to be built as part of an overall £5·5 million scheme to enclose Stamford Bridge completely and create a 60 000 all-seater stadium. (As reported in *Design*, March 1975, the unsuccessful consortium went on to advise Leeds and Arsenal, again without joy.)

Work began in June 1972. Down came Leitch's stand, and the weather-vane was stored in a shed. Chelsea had finished that season in seventh place, but by the time the new stand was ready in August 1974, they were down among the bottom clubs.

For two years the East Side of the ground had been taken up by the building work, and it was surely more than coincidence that in such an unsettling atmosphere for both players and supporters, Chelsea's fortunes plummeted. By the end of the stand's first season in use, they were relegated.

Of course the building work was not the sole factor – problems with the players and the break up of the successful team caused much of the decline – but the stand stood almost as a symbol of the reversal.

Ominously, gates began to drop alarmingly. Who would pay for the stand now? Chelsea spent two seasons in Division Two, and by May 1976 their debt stood at £3·4 million, most of it caused by the East Stand – tall, massive, imposing, but ruinous.

Danny Blanchflower, manager of the club for a short spell, wrote in his *Sunday Express* column, shortly after the resignation of the chairman Brian Mears: 'They had to do something about the old stand. It would fall down if they did not. So they spent a lot of time planning a new one to match their winning desires and ambitions. They spent too long thinking about it. And the stand they planned was too grand.'

John Moynihan, in whose book Blanchflower's words were quoted, wrote that 'the giant construction of steel and concrete was already bleeding one of the country's great clubs to death'. The disaster had occurred at Chelsea primarily because for two years the club had no income from seats on the East Side and because the stand was designed for a top, successful club, not an ailing one with small gates.

After the East Stand came the Safety of Sports Grounds Act. By now any intention of carrying on the Darbourne and Darke plan had been frozen (probably for a very long time), and the ground's capacity of 52 000 was reduced to 41 500. The North Stand had to come down, after less than 30 years of use, and benches were put in on the West Stand paddock. After various improvements the capacity is now fixed at 45 000, including just under 21 000 seats.

Chelsea has a new chairman, who rents Stamford Bridge on a seven-year lease from the holding company, now mortgaged to the hilt in order to pay the debts. But although the club had been saved, the struggle was going to be long and hard. In 1982–83 the average gate at Stamford Bridge was 12 728. The East Stand alone holds 11 058.

Ground Description

The ground is on Fulham Road, and has three gates only. The main one leads onto a courtyard next to a line of tall houses behind the South Terrace. The East Stand appears before you like a space rocket on the launching pad, quite isolated. Such high-tec, and yet the club offices are in an unsophisticated little block next to the main entrance, almost like a converted stable.

Walking past the offices we reach the south east corner of the ground, and may turn either left, onto the open terracing, or go straight ahead into the concourse under the new stand. To the right, behind the stand, is a goods railway line in a cutting, with the large Brompton Cemetery behind.

The East Stand is quite the largest single free-standing construction at any League ground, or at least seems so in its isolation. It has three tiers, each quite visibly separated by distinctive balcony walls. The top tier has 5250 blue seats, the middle tier 2061 brown seats and the lower tier, much of it uncovered, has 3747 khaki-coloured seats. This colour scheme is designed to blend gradually with the yellow railings, the pitch and surroundings, although actually the lower tier seats just look weathered and dirty.

Surrounding all this is a gigantic frame, completely exposed to view, and finished in brown cor-ten steel with sides of semi-transparent plastic, hung several feet from the ends of the tiers. The cantilever roof, suspended from yet more exposed steel frames, is 140 feet long, and at the front can sway up to 18 inches in high winds.

If you look through the clear glass windows at the back you can see right across London as far as St Paul's Cathedral and the Houses of Parliament. Straight ahead, Craven Cottage's floodlights are visible.

Some credit is due to the designers, because even at the very back one is still relatively close to the touchline, although the ground seems a long way below. There are only 22 seats in the stand with an impaired view, these being the ones next to the rear cantilever supports at the very back of the stand.

Beneath each seat is a 10-centimetre hole, or at least a litter-filled 10-centimetre hole. These were originally intended to convey warm air which when mixed with cold air would provide a mean temperature of 70 degrees Fahrenheit around the ankles. The system was never installed.

One of the main problems of this stand, apart from its horrendous cost, is the lack of protection it offers against the elements in certain sections. In addition, despite the claim that the stand can be completely evacuated within the statutory seven-minute period (see Safety), the corridors and gangways have proved awkward for a smooth flow of spectators. When Sir Matt Busby visited the stand his reaction was, it was all very well but 'you canna get out at half-time for a pee'.

From a purely aesthetic point of view there is no doubt that the stand is quite startling. Above all, it is quite disproportionately massive. Everton have a three-tier stand of the same scale, but because it has two double-decker neighbours it is not overwhelming. Chelsea's East Stand hovers over Stamford

Bridge, making the surrounding terraces appear like neolithic ruins next to a twenty-first century intruder. It is over twice as high as Leitch's old stand.

The East Stand has been built over the length of the greyhound track which used to surround the pitch, but now is visible only on the three other sides. The last races took place in August 1968, and the surviving track is now overgrown and very untidy. The elliptical shape of the ground has been kept however, so each end terrace is curved around a semi-circle of turf behind each goal.

To the left is the South End, covered by the Shed. In the near corner are the remains of a concrete base for an old floodlight pylon, taken down because the East Stand has lights mounted in the roof. There is a fenced-off section of terracing in front of it, found to be unsafe. The actual Shed cover sits at a strange angle, far back from the pitch, as if it does not want to be part of the action.

Despite the many changes in the ground, it is quite remarkable how similar the view over this side of the ground is to that in 1905. Many of the buildings in the vicinity have survived, with the Lots Road gas works and a power station's chimneys still visible, as in Cundall's painting of 1935.

The West Stand is dull in contrast with its new partner; a typically dour 1960s' construction which like most of them has not weathered well. It has a plain, flat roof, with six square boxes at the back, and is generally in need of large amounts of paint. Even the white perimeter wall is cracked. To the right of the stand is another fenced-off portion of terracing, another sign of how the ground has decayed through lack of funds. Along this side are the three remaining floodlights, each as tall as Nelson's Column.

To the right is the open North Terrace, behind which, in a cutting runs an open section of the District Line, between West Brompton and Fulham Broadway stations. The massive building visible behind is Earl's Court Exhibition Hall. The foundations of the old North Stand, which stood in the eastern corner, are partly visible beyond the embankment, where there is an expanse of flat ground used for parking, behind the disabled viewers' section. There was for a short time an electric scoreboard at this end of the ground, but it was too expensive to rent. Now there are just a few advertisement hoardings, and stuck up on a pole alone, a weather-vane. Not the original, but a fair copy. Somehow its return in 1982 seems a forlorn gesture.

Stamford Bridge in the 1980s is in a state of confusion. Trees and bushes at the back of crumbling terracing; concrete and steel walkways and glass-fronted bars and restaurants; plush new executive boxes; decaying wooden steps leading to archaic offices, all in acres of space leaving plenty of room for doubt. If the Darbourne and Darke scheme were ever finished it would be the best stadium in London, without question, but if it stays as it is, Stamford Bridge will be lost in limbo.

◆WEST HAM UNITED◆

Previous Grounds

Contrary to common belief, West Ham are not called 'The Hammers' because they come from West Ham. Rather, the hammers symbolize the tools of a shipyard worker, for it was in London's East End docks that the club originated. The idea for a football team came from Arnold F. Hills, the owner of the largest surviving shipyard, the Thames Ironworks. In order to stimulate interest among his workers he organized a floodlit match between Woolwich Arsenal and WBA on a ground in Hermit Road, Canning Town.

The team formed in 1895 and played at Browning Road, East Ham, a mile north east of the present ground. But Hills was an ardent sponsor, a Victorian capitalist who appreciated the efficacy of physical recreation for the welfare of his men, and in March 1897 he announced in the *Thames Ironwork Gazette* that he had found a suitable site for a new and magnificent stadium. It would be opened on the sixtieth anniversary of Queen Victoria's accession, and have facilities for football, cricket, tennis and 'a cycle track equal to any in London'. The ground became known as the Memorial Recreation Ground and was reputed to have a capacity of 120 000, 'good enough to hold the English Cup Final'.

Fine though the setting no doubt was, the football club was anxious to improve and since professionalism was abhorrent to Hills, he asked the team to leave so his amateurs could use the ground. So four years after adopting the name West Ham United and forming a limited company, the new professional team looked elsewhere and found the site of their present ground in 1904. The rift between Hills and West Ham widened when United's directors heard that the then amateur Clapton Orient were hoping to play at the Memorial Ground; they threatened to publish Hills' letter to them which stated that he had reserved the stadium for his Thames Ironworks' team and no other. And to incense their former patron ever further, West Ham sought help to establish their new ground from local breweries. Professional sport and alcohol was more than a Christian philanthropist could bear.

The most recent owners of the Memorial Recreation Ground, East London Rugby Football Club, planned to build a new sports complex at the stadium, and you can check its progress by looking to your right from the train as you emerge from West Ham underground station on the way to Plaistow.

Upton Park

Although most people refer to West Ham's home as Upton Park, it is strictly speaking only the name of the district. The ground's exact title is the Boleyn Ground. The name derives from a house which stood until the 1950s, next to the ground, on Green Street.

The Boleyn Ground looking towards the original West Stand and the directors' pavilion *c.*1905 (*Book of Football*)

It was built in 1544, but had two prominent turrets added soon after and thenceforward was traditionally known as Boleyn Castle after Anne Boleyn. The house served many purposes over the centuries, including a reformatory, a Priory and a bowling club's headquarters.

When United left the Memorial Grounds in Canning Town in May 1904, the site they chose was just a cabbage patch next to Boleyn Castle, then being used as a Catholic School. The club rented the land from the Catholic ecclesiastical authorities and at the same time merged with a local side called Boleyn Castle FC. It took two months to prepare the ground, in time for United's Southern League games the following season.

The Boleyn Ground, as it was inevitably called, then had a small grandstand on the West Side, a covered bank opposite; on the south west corner stood a directors' box with press facilities (rather like the Cottage at Fulham's ground), and on the north west corner a hut for changing rooms. A more substantial West Stand with dressing rooms was erected in 1913 as part of a general improvement scheme which cost United £4000.

In 1919 West Ham were admitted to League Division Two, played in the first Wembley Cup Final and gained promotion, both in 1923. This quick success enabled them to build a large new West Stand with a terraced enclosure in front in 1925. The stand, which has since been enlarged, was designed by Sir E. O. Williams and D. J. Moss. At the same time the old West Stand roofing was transferred to the South Bank.

Opposite the West Stand was the cover known for years as the Chicken Run, a primitive construction of corrugated iron and timber. The terraces were simply wooden bleachers, under which accumulated vast amounts of litter. Miraculously it did not burn down.

The Boleyn Ground's record gate probably came for United's Division Two match v. Charlton Athletic on 18 April 1936; 43 528 were reported to have attended, but this cannot be officially confirmed because during the Second World War the ground suffered considerably during the Blitz and records were lost. The West Stand had to be evacuated, so the club set up offices in Green Street House, the so-called Boleyn Castle. The worst destruction befell the South Bank.

It needed until the 1950s to repair the bomb damage, during which time the ground's floodlights had been installed. They were used first for a friendly v. Tottenham on 16 April 1953.

When United returned to the First Division in 1958, after a 26-year absence, a new main entrance on Green Street was built. Sadly this necessitated the demolition of the last remaining turret of the Boleyn Castle. The house had been in an advanced state of dilapidation, but one cannot help feeling it would have been appropriate to preserve just one feature. The site of the house is now occupied by the school behind the South Bank, on Castle Street.

The 1960s brought considerable changes to the Boleyn Ground, beginning in 1961 with the covering of the North Bank. In 1965 an extra block was built onto the West Stand, which had always been a bit lop-sided, then in May 1968 to the consternation, if not surprise, of the club's followers, the Chicken Run was demolished. In place of this venerable shack was built, at a cost of £170 000, the East Stand, opened in January 1969 with a standing enclosure in front.

West Ham's official record attendance, 42 322, was in October 1970 for a Division One game v. Tottenham. Since the introduction of the Safety of Sports Grounds Act, the capacity of the Boleyn Ground has been reduced to 35 500. There are now seats on the West Stand's front terracing, but a corner of the North Bank has had to be fenced off as a safety precaution. The total number of seats is 11 600.

Ground Description

As I have mentioned, the ground is in Upton Park, not West Ham. The underground station nearest the district of West Ham is called Plaistow. Visitors to West Ham United must alight at Upton Park, a couple of miles east of West Ham station, which is actually on the doorstep of United's first ground in Canning Town. Students of early football history should not confuse West Ham with the famous London amateur club, Upton Park, who apparently played in Epping. Nor should one think that the short-lived East End club Thames FC, who played at somewhere called the West Ham Stadium, had anything to do with West Ham United. There!

The main entrance to the Boleyn Ground is on Green Street, but before you enter it is worthwhile making a quick perambulation. Just past the entrance is the narrow Castle Street, with a small, nicely proportioned chapel on the corner, the sole reminder that this was once all church land. On the next corner, on Barking Road, is the large Boleyn Tavern. Down Castle Street next to the West Stand is the Roman Catholic primary school which occupies the site of the old house. Notice that the surrounding streets are all named with the Tudor connection in mind.

Back at the main entrance, you pass through a pair of wrought iron gates and along a short driveway, which opens out on the right where there is a five-a-side pitch. The back of the West Stand is less imposing than it might be, having several bare concrete uprights forming open bays, cluttered with outbuildings and stairways. How much it needs a sign boldly announcing the club's name, especially since the facade is so clearly visible from Green Street. Inside, the stand is spacious without being particularly attractive, but has some awkwardly arranged offices squeezed into the southern end. This is behind the A block, seating 750, added in 1965. Previously the stand ended at right angles to the pitch. Because the rest of the ground is much lower, the West Stand dominates the pitch quite considerably. Notice the prominent ventilation grilles built into the apex of the roof, and how far the roof extends beyond the seating tier (an almost identical stand, but in shorter form, exists at Filbert Street).

To the right is the South Bank, a covered terrace with room for about 9000. It is a simple, low construction, backing directly onto Castle Street. To the left is the North Bank, a larger terrace not quite fully covered, but still cavernous, dark and ominous at the back. In the north western corner is an awkward section of terracing which actually runs parallel to the west touchline and thus almost faces the North Bank. This is the fenced off portion. Facing it on the east corner of the terracing is another section, raised above the corner flag, which has steps leading up to a refreshment bar. It may be suitable for children, since the viewpoint is higher, but prolonged patronage might lead to a stiff neck, as the terracing here also faces the North Bank. The eastern corner of the South Bank is at a similarly awkward angle.

At the back of the north terracing are signs warning fans to 'Remember Ibrox, please leave slowly'. Above them is a white line. The paint above this line is of the non-drying variety, put there to deter enthusiasts climbing the roof girders. I have some sympathy for such people, having stood at this end and developed all kinds of muscular strain trying to see goal-mouth incidents. Security fencing adds to this difficulty, mainly due to the fact that the goal line is only two yards from the front terrace. The fans there can almost breathe down the goalkeeper's neck, but from the back, clear vision is the prerogative of the fittest.

Opposite the West Stand is of course the East Stand, quite clearly the most modern part of the Boleyn Ground. The light grey roof is cantilevered and extends over the touchline. There are seats for 3500, and although the enclosure has room for 3300 standing there are no crush barriers, because the steps have an 8-inch rise and the section is apparently narrow enough not to suffer from crushing. I have felt differently when standing there. Behind the East Stand are a range of tower blocks, part of a large new estate set in parkland. The back of the East Stand is covered in graffiti making it look distinctly seedy despite its young age. From within the ground however it is clean, obviously efficient, but looks narrower than it is.

Other odd visual details are the floodlights; notice that the pylons just sit on the terrace roofs, with no strengthening support underneath, and the pitch, which looks deceptively small because the ground is so enclosed, the touchlines so close to the spectators. Standing on the corner one feels eminently capable of knocking over a far-post cross. In fact, although the pitch is the minimum length, in width it is a fraction wider than Highbury's, such is the optical effect of the surrounds.

West Ham are fortunate to attract sufficient support to create a daunting atmosphere even when the ground is two-thirds full. Players cannot fail to see, hear, even smell the crowd and sense their delight or their derision. This is surely in keeping with the cramped nature of London, echoed most strongly at Loftus Road, but rarely encountered at top grounds in the north. The dimensions make the greatest player seem human but his greatest acts that much more breathtaking. Unlike Highbury or White Hart Lane, pride and glory do not exude from every stand. Instead the Boleyn Ground is a hideaway, a place to jostle and cheer and not worry too much about the final score.

The Boleyn Ground is considerably less hemmed in today owing to slum clearance (Jack Helliar)

·ORIENT·

Previous Grounds

Orient are relative late-comers to their present ground on Brisbane Road. The club was formed by members of the Glyn Cricket Club, for the usual reason of keeping together during the winter months, and first played football on waste ground near Glyn Road in 1884. The road still exists, in Homerton. In 1888, on the suggestion of a player who worked for the Orient Shipping Line, the club adopted the current name, apt indeed since it plays in East London.

Four years later the club moved a short way up the road to the Whittles Athletic Ground, Pond Lane Bridge. Next door was the Whittles Whippet Ground, so spectators could watch either sport over the fence. When the borough took over Orient's pitch to build a power station, the club simply moved next door. Meanwhile, in 1898 they added the prefix Clapton to their name in the hope that since Clapton was a desirable suburb they would gain some respectability.

Orient moved once again in 1900, also not far away to Millfields Road, Homerton, a ground which had belonged to the Bailey Fireworks Company. It was at the time one of the best venues in the south, holding 12 000 spectators, with terracing built on top of slag from the nearby power station. The players had to change in horse-drawn tram cars.

Admission to the Football League came in 1905, but the expense of running a professional club proved hard for the club to bear. A new company was formed in 1906 to replace the one set up a year earlier, and among various fund-raising activities at Millfields were boxing matches, and baseball. A crowd of 3500 saw Orient beat Fulham in 1908 to win the 'British Baseball Cup Final'. There were even plans to increase the ground's capacity to 40 000.

During the First World War, when Orient players formed the largest single contingent of the Footballers' Battalion, Millfields Road was taken over by the Army. In recognition of the club's patriotism, the Prince of Wales visited the club soon after the War, and a year later was followed by the Duke of York. A new multi-span stand (similar to Highbury's) costing the enormous sum of £30 000 was opened at the ground in 1923, and in the late 1920s crowds of up to 30 000 flocked to see Orient's FA Cup exploits against First Division opposition. But the record gate was for the visit of Second Division Tottenham in 1928–29: 38 219 attended, the highest at any of Orient's three League grounds.

During the Easter of 1927, the syndicate which owned the Millfields Road Ground spent £80 000 on installing greyhound racing facilities and inevitably a few years later Clapton Orient were asked to move. To exacerbate matters, the club had just been relegated to Division Three South. The Clapton dog track

no longer exists, it was built over with homes for the aged in the mid-1970s.

Orient's new ground was only half a mile away, at the large but rather bleak Lea Bridge Speedway Stadium. They managed to take with them a few fittings from Millfields Road, but soon encountered problems. After beating Torquay United at Lea Bridge in one of their first games there in 1930–31, complaints were made that the perimeter fences were too close to the touchlines. The League ordered Orient to lay extra turf within a fortnight, since the lines could not be moved inwards as the pitch was already the minimum width. The speedway company refused to sanction this alteration, so Orient had to make hurried arrangements to find another venue for their home games. Neighbours Leyton FC and Walthamstow Avenue were approached unsuccessfully, then incredibly, Wembley Stadium agreed to host Orient's next fixture v. Brentford. Wembley's officials had already been considering leasing the stadium to a League club in order to increase its usage, and were therefore pleasantly surprised when a crowd of 10 300 watched Orient's 3-0 win on 22 November 1930. (Although Wembley is a long way from Clapton, it is very near Brentford.) The *Daily Herald* correspondent 'Syrian' noted, 'I question if Brentford will ever play at Wembley again' and also reported that the sacred turf had been a quagmire and might need relaying.

At this point the speedway company agreed to add the turf at Lea Bridge, but Orient, flushed with victory in nobler surroundings went to Highbury for their next home fixture, a Cup replay v. Luton on 4 December. But after their second game at Wembley two days later against Southend – the attendance was only 2500 and receipts of £100 were insufficient to cover Wembley Stadium's guarantee – so they returned to Lea Bridge, poorer but wiser. Wembley also decided to drop the idea of staging League football.

The 1930s continued to be difficult years for Clapton. There was talk of a merger with Thames FC, another East London club in the Third Division, and of moving to Hackney Wick Stadium where the rent would be less. Nevertheless, Lea Bridge gates averaged 7000, and in 1936–37 Orient's match v. Millwall attracted the ground's highest attendance, 20 400. But the club was never happy at the Speedway Stadium, and in 1937 made their final move to Brisbane Road, a mile away in Leyton. The Stadium has gone since, the site having been taken up for industrial use.

Brisbane Road

Orient's present ground was the home of Leyton Amateurs in 1937, who were having some difficulty paying their rent to the council. Wasting no time, Orient stepped in and took over the ground during the summer. There was one stand seating 475 people, scathingly referred to as 'the orange box', and a cover on the West Side for standing spectators. All the

The East Stand, Brisbane Road in 1962 (Sport & General)

banking was cinder. The club's first game there was on 28 August 1937 v. Cardiff City, watched by 14 598.

At last it looked as if Clapton Orient had a permanent home, but the club's financial problems had not disappeared. After the Second World War, when the club changed its name yet again, to Leyton Orient, a fighting fund was needed to save the club. This, and the appointment of a new chairman and manager, paved the way for a successful period ahead.

In 1951 a new perimeter wall was built in place of the rather quaint white wooden fence left over from the pre-war years, and in the summer of 1956 after celebrating promotion, a new Main Stand was erected on the East Side. The stand was bought from Mitcham Greyhound Stadium in South London, but initially Orient rebuilt only two-thirds of the structure, storing the remainder elsewhere.

The East Stand was opened for a game v. Nottingham Forest in October 1956, and very nearly ruined the same day by a fire, thankfully spotted in time. The late chairman, Harry Zussman, quoted in Neil Kaufman's and Harry Ravenhills' history of the club, said afterwards, 'For years we hoped the old stand would catch fire to collect the insurance, and now the new one nearly goes up on its first day of use!'

Brisbane Road's floodlights were first used for a game v. Brighton in August 1960, and cost £15 000.

The club reached its zenith in 1962, winning promotion to Division One for the first time. To accommodate extra seats, the remaining section of the East Stand, at the southern end, was completed, and the west terracing opposite improved. But their joy was shortlived, for one season later Orient were back in Division Two, their financial struggles returning as gates dropped. By 1966 Orient (they dropped the prefix Leyton that year since the area had been absorbed into the new Borough of Waltham Forest) had to pass a bucket around to help raise cash needed to keep the club afloat. More mergers were mooted, with Romford FC and with Basildon.

By 1970 Orient were back in Division Two, and so in 1977 came under the jurisdiction of the Safety of Sports Grounds Act. It is interesting that the club found it cheaper to put seats onto the West Terrace,

rather than pay for new crush barriers, even though this reduced the capacity of that section from 11 000 to 3700.

Brisbane Road's highest gate had been in January 1964 for the Cup visit of neighbours West Ham: 34 345 attended. The capacity is now 26 500, including 7171 seats.

Ground Description

Brisbane Road, Osborne Road, Leyton Stadium, call it what you will, lies between Leyton High Road and Hackney Marshes. The main entrance, now much improved and faced in red and white, is on Brisbane Road, although some of the club offices are above the souvenir shop on the corner of Osborne Road.

The East Stand runs the length of the pitch, with the common arrangement of a paddock in front of the seating tier. The asbestos roof is noticeably clean and light, with a plain central gable, believed once to have housed the photo-finish equipment used at the greyhound stadium.

To the left is the open South Terrace, behind which are the neat, municipal Coronation Gardens on Buckingham Road. The terrace is slightly smaller than the open North Terrace to the right of the East Stand. Behind this is a typical suburban London street of small terraced villas. In the north east corner of the ground is the Bowater Scott enclosure for disabled spectators, sponsored by that company since it discovered that one of its disabled staff was an Orient fanatic. This is an excellent feature, with room for 20 people.

Opposite the East Stand, is the West Stand, which dates back to the 1930s but has been modernized since. It incorporates throughout the new type of backless plastic seats which many other clubs have also begun using. Underneath the roof is the television camera platform.

The pitch, once troublesome and muddy, is now much improved since being resewn in 1978 (see Ipswich Town). Notice how it slopes a couple of feet from north to south. Since the ground is still rented from the council, but on favourable terms, the pitch is often used for important schoolboy and junior matches.

Overlooking Brisbane Road are tall blocks of flats behind the North Terrace, and the disused chimney of the sewage works behind the West Stand. Behind these works stretch the vast open fields of Hackney Marshes, the site of reputedly the largest number of municipal pitches in Britain.

Brisbane Road is such a bright and uncluttered ground, and Orient such an hospitable club, that visiting it is always a pleasure. But this is also partly owing to the fact that small gates, in an area torn between Upton Park and White Hart Lane, make access and parking almost trouble-free. Small wonder the club have struggled, but full credit for their maintenance of such a friendly enclosure.

·18·
SOUTH LONDON AND KENT

·MILLWALL·

Previous Grounds

Formed in 1885 as Millwall Rovers, the club began life in the docklands of Millwall, which form the southern district of the Isle of Dogs. The club's first home was on Glengall Road, now built over. In 1886 they switched to a ground at the back of the Lord Nelson public house on East Ferry Road, now a park. Four years later, having changed their name to Millwall Athletic, the team moved to another ground in East Ferry Road, opposite Millwall Docks. This ground, which was to become one of the better ones in London, was known for its unseemly surroundings and the unpleasant nature of its surface. A visiting Corinthian player remarked that he did not mind playing there, but objected to falling down on the pitch because 'the smell wouldn't come off for weeks'. Despite the conditions, Millwall became one of the best professional teams in the south. They left the Isle of Dogs in 1901 to go south of the river, where they have stayed ever since. The East Ferry Road Ground became a timber yard, and is now built over. Millwall played in North Greenwich until 1910 when they found their present ground.

The Den

The new ground in Cold Blow Lane was immediately named The Den, since it was home of 'The Lions', and although hemmed in considerably by railways and narrow lanes, had the advantage of being within walking distance of three railway stations and in the midst of a rapidly growing residential area.

Although the Football League was gradually taking the place of the Southern League as the major competition in London and the south, Millwall Athletic was considered an important enough club for the FA President, Lord Kinnaird, to open The Den officially in 1910. Only the Main Stand had been built, a smaller section of the existing one, and there was open banking on the other three sides. But again, it was sufficient to stage an England v. Wales match on 13 March 1911.

Millwall joined the League in 1920 and in 1925 dropped the title Athletic. The ground developed in the next decade along lines similar to today's appearance and saw its highest ever crowd of 48 672 for the club's 5th Round tie v. Derby County on 20 February 1937. Like most of south east London and the dock areas, New Cross suffered badly during the Blitz. The Den's Main Stand was damaged, as were sections of the terracing. Millwall sent their first team to play at the Valley, while Charlton's reserves used the bomb scarred Den. But even when the seniors returned, they found the directors sitting on two wooden benches by the track and the press similarly accommodated behind one of the goals.

Millwall were in Division Two when League Football resumed in 1946, and with compensation from the War Damages Commission, set about restoring the ground. In addition, in 1947, they began covering the Ilderton Road End terrace, and by the mid-1950s there were covers on the remaining two sides of terracing. Also at this time floodlights were installed, first used for a friendly v. Manchester United on 5 October 1953.

Little has changed within the ground since, apart from the addition of a wing to the Main Stand, bringing it up to the Ilderton Road End, and the installation of seats in the paddock.

Outside the ground much has changed. Formerly, one of the railway lines close to The Den used to run within yards of the back of the Main Stand, as at Bloomfield Road. Once the line became disused the club were able to buy the land, make a narrow carpark and improve access to the seats and terraces. Also, the New Cross Speedway and Greyhound Stadium was once behind the Ilderton Road End. This too became disused, in the late 1970s, and is now open parkland. The only railway line still in use runs across Cold Blow Lane, from London Bridge to Croydon. Drivers would stop to watch from their cabins.

The Den's major problem has always been access, as described below, and since British Rail owns much of the surrounding land but has proved unwilling to sell, Millwall have no room to expand. There would be little point in developing the ground further

The Den in 1939. Although bombs destroyed many of the roofs, it was rebuilt after the War on a similar pattern. Notice the intricate ironwork on the gable – a common feature before the War

unless access, especially by car, was also improved. One supermarket chain offered to help the club rebuild the site into a sports complex, perhaps using part of the land occupied by the old stadium, but then withdrew its offer.

The Den holds two distinctions it would prefer not to have. It has been closed by the FA following crowd disturbances more frequently than any other ground, in 1920 (their first League season), 1934, 1947, 1950 and 1978. It is also the only League venue in London, excluding recent arrivals Wimbledon, never to have staged First Division football. But it was certainly the first League ground to host a League match on a Sunday, when Millwall played Fulham on 20 January 1974. The Den's present capacity is 32 000 which includes 3200 seats.

Ground Description

Many factors make The Den probably the hardest ground of all for strangers to find. Firstly, you must not make the mistake of going to Millwall. Millwall FC play in New Cross, south of the river. Secondly, if approaching the ground by car, only one road actually touches the ground, Cold Blow Lane, which meanders away from the ground and disappears under railway tunnels before emerging in a sprawling new housing estate.

But worst of all, The Den is barely visible from any of the main roads, being shielded behind New Cross Hospital and various railway embankments. Its floodlights are so low and inconsequential against the skyline as to be almost worthless homing guides, and even if you can spot them, can you get through the maze of roads to find the ground? Cold Blow Lane on a dark, wet night might be a perfect setting for a *Jack the Ripper* horror film; dry ice wafting about the cobbled streets and under the low tunnels. There are mysterious yards full of scrap, malodorous goings-on behind high fences, tower blocks looming in the distance, even old tram lines still embedded in the roads.

They knew what they were dealing with when they called it Cold Blow Lane.

The main entrance is unexpected as the narrow lane bends, only just wide enough for a coach, with just enough space for a crowd to gather in the forecourt before the banking rises up sharply to the Cold Blow Lane terrace. Stairs half way up the bank lead to the offices, squeezed in behind the stand. Underneath are all the players' facilities, the Den being one of only four grounds to have its tunnel behind one of the goals. The Main Stand runs up the left, and you can see where one railway bridge across Cold Blow Lane has been taken away, leaving the embankment to form the new car-park. Still, there is little room.

Behind the bank are more embankments, yards, tunnels, dark brick houses, the hum of traffic and tall tower blocks in the distance.

The Main Stand is dark with a low roof lightened only by the retention of the white paddock rear wall and the addition of orange seats. Unusually, those seats have been put on metal frames placed on top of the terrace, to provide a better view than is normal from such conversions. On the top of the roof in the centre is a sign with the club's name, in place of the original gable.

To the left is the Ilderton Road End, whose roof joins the Main Stand in the corner, where netting protects the seats from the terracing. Everywhere are signs warning spectators not to throw missiles. In the front section of this terrace, some of which is quite uneven, a large cut-away section gives groundstaff access to the pitch from behind the stand. The old greyhound stadium was just a few yards beyond this end.

Notice that the two end roofs are identical, supported by attractively splayed pillars. Also, each floodlight pylon is on a white concrete base on the terracing, with a blue lion painted on each facing side. A nice touch.

Opposite the Main Stand is the large open North Side banking, with a cover at the back, in the same style as the other roofs, grey with blue steelwork. To its right a high wall cuts across the terracing at an angle towards Cold Blow Lane. On top of this grey concrete wall is a clock and a police observation hut.

To the right is the Cold Blow Lane End terrace, into which is buried the well-protected tunnel, on the right of the goal. All three terraced sides are fronted by security fences built on a light blue perimeter wall, and the goals have especially close-mesh nets. All are reminders of The Den's past.

The Den is a tight enclosure, dominated by the drab, weathered tones of its uniform roofs and terracing. Because the approaches are so twisted and awkward, one feels it is an island of order in a sea of confusion. But the walls, the police hut, the dark stand and the low roofs also make it resemble a huge trap. It is no surprise that Millwall established a record of 59 successive League matches here without defeat.

CHARLTON ·ATHLETIC·

Previous Grounds

When Charlton Athletic formed in 1905, they were just one of many amateur teams in South London, but in an area dominated by rugby enthusiasts. A mile or two east was Plumstead, home of First Division Woolwich Arsenal. To the east, also a mile or so away, was North Greenwich, where another professional club, Millwall Athletic, played in the Southern League. Being sandwiched between two senior clubs was reason enough for Charlton to remain amateurs, as they did until 1920.

Their first ground was Siemens Meadow, almost on the banks of the River Thames next to the Royal Dockyard, Woolwich. Siemens Road still exists a few hundred yards from The Valley across Woolwich Road. In 1907 Charlton moved south to Woolwich Common, which is still on Shooters Hill Road, a mile south east of The Valley. Two years later found them playing in Pound Park, almost next door to the present ground by Maryon Wilson Park, and in 1913 Charlton moved east to Horn Lane. Their ground was next to Greenwich Marshes, also on the banks of the Thames, and the land can still be seen next to the approaches to the Blackwall Tunnel.

Charlton decided in 1919 to find a permanent home, no doubt prompted by the fact that the club had only 2s 3d in the kitty and needed an enclosed ground to raise revenue. With the help of Colin Cameron, the club's historian, I shall relate how Charlton have been plagued either by big ideas but limited resources, or limited ideas and no lack of capital.

The Valley

Charlton were playing in the Kent, London and South Suburban Leagues when they chose to set up home in the centre of Charlton Village. The site was then a derelict chalk pit with a well; a natural bowl but one hardly big enough to accommodate a mini-mum-size pitch. An army of volunteers helped dig the pit into shape, forming the vast banking which was to dominate the ground on three sides. Some of the extra gravel and earth brought onto the site came from a nearby hospital excavation, and was said to have been full of old bones! A boost came from the MP, Sir Ion Hamilton Benn, who promised to act as guarantor on behalf of the club for a sum of £700. But in the event, such was the enthusiasm of all concerned that the money was raised independently.

Charlton called their new home, aptly enough, The Valley, and first played there in a match v. Summerstown on 13 September 1919. There were no stands and no fences, so a collecting box was sent around the crowd. The players had to change in a house in Ransom Road, just behind the present offices. This was at the time when Highbury was getting ready to host its first international, Goodison Park was fully developed as the finest ground in England and, just a few miles down the road, the country's most illustrious venue, Crystal Palace, still lay unused after war-time use as a munitions dump. Yet within a few years The Valley had become the biggest ground in England, and even a possible successor to Crystal Palace as a Cup Final venue. But if you expect a fairy tale story of rags to riches, remember also why Arsenal had left the area only a few years before.

Charlton turned professional in 1920 and joined the Southern League. The first professional match at The Valley was on 4 September 1920, v. Brighton and Hove Albion (whose first team had just started playing in the League's Third Division).

The Valley was still without a stand when Charlton were elected into the Football League in 1921, to join the Third Division South in its first season. The engineering firm of Humphreys Limited was contracted to build a grandstand on the flat, West Side of the ground, and add dressing rooms, terracing and all the necessary turnstiles and fittings. For a club so new to senior football the £14000 estimated cost of this work seemed enormous, particularly when the final bill came to £21314, nearly £20000 of which was for the Grand Stand alone. Although only some 60 yards long, the Grand Stand was tall and distinguished, with a multi-span roof that was for years to become the endearing trademark of The Valley. It was in fact an almost exact copy of the main East Stand erected at Highbury (replaced in 1936), but only four spans long. Charlton however had to begin their League career without it, since the work was delayed and not fully completed until 1922.

Nevertheless, The Valley was taking the shape of a magnificent new stadium, prompting the *Athletic News'* correspondent to state that here was a: 'prospective Venue for future FA Cup Finals', and representative matches. The Valley, it was claimed, would make a suitable site for the FA to construct 'a national home' (work was soon to begin on Wembley Stadium). Yet despite this apparent promise, in 1923 Charlton's directors made a quite startling decision to leave The Valley, after only four seasons in residence! Support, they said, was not sufficiently forthcoming in the area. The summer of 1923 was spent preparing a new ground called 'The Mount', on Ringstead Road, home of Catford FC, four miles south west of The Valley and slightly south of The Den. A further, enormous sum of £17330 was spent preparing the new ground, which was not ready until 22 December 1923, for Charlton's game v. Northampton. Even then, Charlton had to seek special permission to stage an FA Cup match v. Wolves in February 1924, because the Catford ground lacked adequate seating accommodation.

The move was an unmitigated disaster, both financially and in terms of attracting extra support.

The Valley in 1939. The distinctive roof has gone but the base of the stand remains (BBC Hulton Picture Library)

Although some games had attracted capacity crowds of 10 000, by the last match of the 1923–24 season only 1000 people attended. So poorer but wiser Charlton Athletic returned to The Valley after only half a season away. There can have been fewer decisions more unwise than that taken by the Charlton board to leave in the first place, but as subsequent years were to prove, no administration at the club was ever able to really develop the ground to its full potential, until very recently.

In his autobiography, the ex-Sunderland, Tottenham and Sheffield Wednesday player, Jimmy Seed, who managed Charlton during their finest years in the 1930s, wrote of the possibilities which never materialized:

'. . . if Charlton had built a second stand and had improved the accommodation, not only for fans but also for visiting directors and officials, they may well have staged international games which would have put the club on the map, like Arsenal and Tottenham. Members of the FA visited the ground on international selection duty, but quite clearly the club could never cope with an important international occasion.'

That The Valley was inadequate is borne out by the fact that although so close to the old Crystal Palace stadium, no major games were staged here, and that although Highbury, Stamford Bridge, White Hart Lane, even The Den and Craven Cottage had been or were being used for England matches more than Wembley up until the Second World War, The Valley was never chosen. Even Selhurst Park staged one international in 1926.

The only development seen at The Valley was the construction, in 1934, of a cover for standing spectators at the northern end. Costing about £3000 it was officially opened on Good Friday, March 1934. In the following years, under Jimmy Seed's beguiling con-

trol, the team's fortunes began to rise. They were higher than mighty Arsenal and they had the largest club ground in Britain, proved when on 12 February 1938, 75 031 attended Charlton's 5th Round Cup tie v. Aston Villa. Although six clubs have recorded higher attendances at their grounds, the important fact was that at The Valley there had still been more room! It is probable that its capacity was around 80 000 at this time, but it was never filled. However the money collected by Charlton during this incredible spell of success was not used to improve facilities at The Valley.

During the Second World War there was slight damage caused to the North Stand, but not as much as their neighbours at The Den suffered, so for the 1943–1944 season Charlton shared The Valley with Millwall.

After the War, Charlton ceased to be such a force in the First Division but The Valley became the first venue ever to have an FA Cup match other than the Final itself broadcast live on television, when Charlton met Blackburn Rovers in the 5th Round on 8 February 1947. But still, incredibly, the money from these successes was still not used to develop the ground. Charlton's First Division career came to an end in 1957, and with it, apparently, any chance of The Valley realizing its potential. Since then the club has been back to the Third Division twice, and only recently has begun the painful process of adapting the ground to modern demands.

Floodlights, for example, were installed relatively late at The Valley, on 20 September 1961 v. Rotherham United.

Charlton raised very little capital when The Who played at The Valley in 1974. Official estimates put the attendance at 80 000, but others reckon the total was nearer 90 000 to 100 000. A repeat concert two years later was more controlled, but still some 65 000 were thought to have bought tickets. Charlton were paid only a rental fee by the promoters of each concert.

Finally, in 1979 the club began a series of developments at The Valley which were to radically alter the ground's character and capacity. When the Safety of Sports Grounds Act came into effect in 1977, The Valley's capacity dropped more than any other League ground, from 66 000 to 20 000, and then in January 1981 to only 13 000. Vast open stretches of decaying terracing were half the problem, as were the lack of entrances and exits to handle any larger crowds. So the directors rightly opted for a smaller stadium with more cover and seats, just as their predecessors might have done 30 years earlier.

Between 1979–81, three major alterations were effected with the eventual aim of making the ground all-seated. The total cost of £350 000 was raised by an extremely successful lottery. The charming but by then infirm roof of the West Stand was replaced with a square, modern cover. Seats were installed on the covered North Stand, and on the South Bank a completely new stand was erected, all-seated and appropriately named 'The Jimmy Seed Stand', when officially opened on 18 August 1981.

The extra seats gave The Valley a total of 10 000 seats, in an overall capacity of 20 000. At last, the ground had caught up with time and Charlton harnessed its capabilities to their best advantage.

Ground Description

The main entrance on Floyd Road takes you past the small detached block of offices into a large car-park behind the West Stand, large enough to accommodate a floodlit pitch with plenty of room to spare. The open ground is surrounded on three sides by houses and lawns around Valiant House, and a tower block which stands on Sam Bartram Close, named after Charlton's most famous goalkeeper who played a record 583 games for the club but was never capped for his country.

The West Stand is the old original construction, with red, corrugated sides, wooden floors and a mixture of seats, sitting in isolation on the half-way line. At the very back is a discreet row of private boxes. A white roof covers the whole stand, overlapping a few feet on either side, and is supported at the front by pillars at each end. Because the stand is so short, no glass screen walls have been erected, so that although the seats might not be too well protected from the elements, the view is excellent. If the dear old roof had to go, it was as well that such a tidy and bright construction should be its successor.

Along the roof fascia in large letters is the message: 'Marman Ltd welcomes you to Charlton Athletic'. For nearly 50 years, Charlton was run by members of the Gliksten family. The previous chairman, Michael Gliksten, owned all but one of the company's 20 000 shares, and that one belonged to his son. Gliksten owns The Valley and the club's recently purchased training ground at New Eltham. In 1982, Mark Hulyer, about whom little was known, bought Gliksten's shares on behalf of Marman Limited. So now Marman owns Charlton Athletic, but has to rent the ground from Gliksten. Hence the sign. But The Valley has long been accustomed to strange goings-on in the boardroom, ever since that time the directors abandoned their greatest asset for Catford, and however odd some of the recent events, few will deny that New Eltham and The Valley are at least proof of a new lease of life for the club. (Eltham also has a well used, all-purpose pitch shared with the community.

On either side of the West Stand are low banks of open terracing, behind which is flat ground, thus accentuating the stand's height and sense of importance. From here, to the left is the North Stand, apparently older than the rest of the ground because of its conventional, dark sloping roof. The old terracing has been properly replaced with new concrete steps on which seats are now placed, and although the front row has been sensibly raised 4 feet above the touchline, to give the optimum view, the security fencing is still much in evidence.

From the West Stand, the new Jimmy Seed Stand is to the right; a clean, white roofed structure built on the sloping bank. Once this was complete, almost all sense of The Valley's bowl shape disappeared. The stand has two sections of red seats, divided across the middle by a higher step. Close to, you can see how cheaply and effectively the stand has been built, literally covering over a frame built onto the bank.

Notice how close to the corners of the pitch are the floodlight pylons, which are therefore very tall. With so much space on the terracing it seems strange that shorter pylons further up the slopes were not used.

Opposite the Main Stand is the vast East Terrace; a massive, tall bank of open terracing topped by an unruly crop of trees and bushes, with houses beyond. Without cover it appears quite the largest side at any football ground in England, and indeed from the top, one is much higher than the three stand roofs, with an unimpeded view over Greenwich and South London. The terrace is a blanket of greyish concrete, enmeshed with silver coloured barriers, of different heights and some rather bent. No doubt their condition, and the fact that the very top section is fenced off, has determined that The Valley's capacity is now so low. Without safety restrictions this terrace might easily accommodate 35 000 spectators.

In the top northern corner are the foundations of old turnstiles and buildings, and because of the Jimmy Seed Stand, the view of the pitch from this corner is now restricted, although the pylon was already an obstacle. In the north west corner is a large, electric scoreboard. Behind towers Valiant House, undoubtedly offering the best view of the ground from its top floor.

The Valley is still an impressive stadium, which if fully developed as planned will undoubtedly be one of the best in the country. The inaction of several decades, when the ground threatened to become a huge white elephant and nothing but a burden to an average club side has at last been ended, and whoever controls the club, at least The Valley now has a future. It will never stage a Cup Final, nor an international match, but it wears a slightly more optimistic face nowadays, one which Jimmy Seed might appreciate if he were alive to sit in the stand named after him.

· GILLINGHAM ·

Priestfield Stadium

The Medway towns were home to one of the most formidable of early teams, a team of officers, the Royal Engineers. But the best local side was Excelsior, who played on a ground called the Great Lines (still used today), known for its downward slope and proximity to a manure heap. This team was so successful that it was decided to put their activities on a more formal basis and look for a properly enclosed ground of their own.

Thanks to the excellent research of the club's historian, Tony Conway, this is one of the few surviving accounts of how such choices were made in those early years. No doubt the process was similar at many other clubs. From the *Chatham and Rochester News*, 13 May 1893, came this report of a meeting at the Napier Arms:

Probably the oldest stand still in use; Gillingham's Gordon Road Stand still in pristine condition (Simon Inglis)

'Is it possible and practicable that the New Brompton football enthusiasts shall have a ground of their own, to centralise and encourage local players and to run the club on democratic lines as well as make it pay? That question – not a slight one by the way – is at present occupying intense attention at New Brompton, and has been the object of many meetings. Time will show . . .'

One of the committee reported to the assembled he had been unable to agree terms with a Mr Webb for his land. Another member produced a plan of ground on the Beacon Court estate, 6½ acres in all, and informed the meeting of its cost. A third committee member came with another plan of land which had the advantage of being almost flat, 'the fall being only one foot in 190'. He thought the land might be had at a reasonable price, but thought it would be wiser to buy it outright. Again costs were mentioned, prompting Mr Croneen to remind the meeting that if it were made public that they were keen on a particular plot, they would 'have to pay through the nose for it'. From then on, it was agreed, no figures were to be mentioned. The reporter notes, however, that sums of between £600 and £1200 were discussed.

Mr Croneen now stood up with his plan, of land near the level crossing, on Gillingham Road. It was large enough for football and even a cycle track, and was hedged on two sides, so that less fencing would have to be erected. The chairman, Dr Warren, then asked the assembled if the club intended entering for the All England Cup, meaning the FA Cup. 'This drew forth a unanimous "yes"' from all concerned, and Dr Warren had to remind them therefore that hedges would not be sufficient to satisfy the Association. The FA 'would insist on having the ground properly enclosed,' he said.

The discussion then turned to the matter of using a future ground for cricket as well as football, but it was concluded that after the rough wear of winter, the pitch would not be suitable for cricket but might make a splendid tennis ground. It was also asked how long a pitch would need to be prepared, followed by an inconclusive exchange on 'the properties of lucerne, grass-seed, etcetera'.

Mr Winch spoke next, in a clear and practical speech on how to go about obtaining the ground; whether to secure 'a site on a lease' with 'a number of gentlemen to guarantee a sum of money to defray initial expenses,' or perhaps to 'float a company to secure the ground and then let it to the Football Club.' He made the following calculation; the population of Gillingham was 30 000, of whom one-fifth were adult men. Only about half of them could be expected to attend regularly, giving a potential gate of 3000. Mr Winch 'did not wish to throw cold water on the idea' but wanted to raise the 'question of preliminary costs, future expenses and probable returns (cheers).'

The first plan brought to the meeting had not been properly explained, said one. Some favoured another plan. Dr Warren said they must get a ground, or where would all these famous clubs they wanted to invite play? Another speaker hoped that if a company was formed, some of the 'bunce' would go to the players. Finally, Mr Thompson proposed: 'a limited liability company be formed with £1 shares.' The motion was seconded, and after a lengthy discussion, carried. A provisional committee to investigate setting up a company was formed and the meeting adjourned.

A week later the company was formed, then a name decided on – New Brompton Football Club Company Limited – and finally Mr Croneen's suggestion of adopting 'a section of land in Gillingham Road close to the level crossing' was agreed on. This was the present ground, and the land cost £600. £10 was paid for a turnstile, and then an argument ensued. The committee argued over what type of goalposts to buy with their Brodies Patented Goal Nets, and whether a 16- or 24-inch lawnmower be purchased. Also from Mr Conway's history we learn that a flagstaff was presented to the new company to add some dignity to the ground.

This is a report of the opening day:

'Here everything was of the newest, even the grass, in fact there had not been time to indulge in the luxury of paint; but a little powder there may have been, as ladies mustered a strong force, and they do sometimes use "just a little" you know [so much for Mr Winch's calculation at that opening meeting!]. Finishing touches were being put here and there and "Mein Host" of the "Napier Arms" was making ready for his share in the day's proceedings – not inconsiderably as events turned out, and Mr Chairman H. G. Croneen, at last triumphantly exclaimed, "Now we are ready for them." Spectators dropped in by twos and threes until some 500 were present to witness the first match.'

New Brompton soon discovered the financial burdens of running a football team, so the Priestfield Ground was used for all manner of fund raising events, including smoking concerts, fêtes, athletics meetings, and even a ladies' football match. In common with many other grounds, sheep were allowed to graze on the pitch during the week. But still the club struggled and had to sell part of the land for £2500, where Gordon Road is now. They even had to rent out their turnstiles for other events. But the aforementioned hedges around the ground remained for some time.

It is hard to say what stands and terraces were built in those early years, though photographs taken at the turn of the century show a stand identical to one which still exists on the Gordon Road Side of the ground. Hence we may suppose that this is the oldest surviving structure at any League ground, dating back to the middle or late 1890s. Certainly the stand has been virtually unaltered since, and looks as neat as ever thanks to careful maintenance. Dockyard workers were responsible for its erection.

In 1913 New Brompton changed their name to Gillingham and in 1920 joined the newly formed Division Three. By 1938, the Main Stand on Redfern Avenue had been built, and pictures show it to have been characterized by a slatted wooden wall at the rear of the paddock. A white wooden fence surrounded the pitch, but even in the 1920s the hedge around the ground survived.

As Gillingham struggled to get back their League status after the War, huge gates in the Cup and Southern League allowed the club to level the pitch, concrete the terracing and build proper turnstiles. A record gate of 23 002 saw Gillingham's 3rd Round Cup tie v. QPR on 10 January 1948, when the club was still in the Southern League, and such success

(though they lost that particular match) no doubt helped them in their return to the Third Division, when the League was expanded in 1950.

Developments since have been the erection of a roof over the Gillingham End terracing and floodlights in 1963. Priestfield was one of the very last League grounds to be lit up, and the club's highest gate for years, 17 500, came to see the first game v. Bury in August of that year. On promotion from Division Four in 1964, in a series of further improvements, the Main Stand was completely refurbished and reroofed and a floodlit pitch built behind the Gillingham End. In more recent years this area behind the ground has been enhanced by a £50 000 sports centre.

Priestfield Stadium's present capacity is 16 000, of which 1500 are seated.

Ground Description

Priestfield Stadium is a bitty ground, in five sections. The Main Stand is some 60 yards long astride the half-way line, flanked by open terracing to the right, and a smaller patch of newer terracing to the left, behind which are the modern club offices. The original Main Stand is enveloped by a more recent roof, covering the paddock, now seated. Inside, you can see the original slatted wall, in white and blue, and the back of the old rear wall of the stand, now within the newer structure. The roof slopes upwards from the road, then pitches sharply down to the gutter, and has awkward cross struts at either end to increase its strength. In effect, Gillingham have done what Charlton were to do many years later, giving an otherwise obsolete stand a new lease of life. Notice that the front row of seats is open to the touchline, with no perimeter wall.

To the right is the uncovered Rainham End terracing, named after the nearby district. Behind here, at right angles to the ground, is Priestfield Road, a cul-de-sac. An interesting feature of this end is the way the terracing was obviously laid in line with the old slope of the pitch. Now that this has been levelled, the steps themselves slope down about 3 feet from Gordon Road towards Redfern Avenue. Adding to the weird sightlines is the fact that the front terraces are a couple of feet above the perimeter track.

The open terracing continues around the pitch until 25 yards down the touchline we come to the Gordon Road Stand, the oldest in the League. The lines of this are also rather odd. From the side it seems tiny, but the rear wall is angled back and runs parallel with the road. About 30 yards long, the stand sits above a narrow line of open terracing, holds 300 spectators on long thin bench seat. Despite the primitive construction – there are nine uprights supporting its small roof – it looks remarkably neat. This is because the club have employed here, as elsewhere in the ground, an effective combination of blue and white woodwork, and yellow steel and ironwork. If the design hints at its age, its condition most certainly does not.

Almost touching the Gordon Road Stand is a slightly taller cover over the terracing which extends to the corner flag, and rather awkwardly turns a few yards into the Gillingham End. Next to this simple, sloping roof, along the rest of the Gillingham End, and in turn going round the corner to where it meets up with the terracing next to the Main Stand, is a clean, light-grey, barrel roof cover, curling slightly upwards at the gutter. Behind this end is the sports centre and floodlit pitch, which doubles as a car-park on match days.

There is no room to expand on either side, while both ends have plenty of space behind. Extra seating will be the club's main priority in the coming years, if it can be afforded, no doubt meaning the end of the Gordon Road Stand, unless a way can be found to move it to another part of the ground. In the meantime, however much it may affect the symmetry of the Priestfield Stadium, the club should be proud of possessing such a handsome Victorian curiosity.

· CRYSTAL PALACE ·

Previous Grounds

As the name suggests, Crystal Palace's early history is bound up with the famous glass and iron palace built by Joseph Paxton in 1851 for the Great Exhibition of Hyde Park, but soon after moved to Upper Sydenham heights in South London (see Big Match Venues). A football club called Crystal Palace was formed as early as 1861 by members of the exhibition groundstaff, and played in the park grounds. It entered the very first FA Cup in 1871 and reached the semi-final. Roy Peskett's club history tells us much about those early years.

The idea for a professional club at Crystal Palace first came in 1904, when the ground's owners tried to form a team to enter the Southern League, only to find the FA thought it unwise for the Final's hosts to have their own team in the FA Cup. So the following year a separate company was formed, and became tenants of Crystal Palace. If ever there was a big match at the ground, such as a rugby international, Palace had to switch to other venues, but in 1915 they had to vacate the ground altogether when it was taken over by the Army.

Keeping the same name (for they were not to know that they would never return to Crystal Palace) the football club moved to Herne Hill, a few miles north to where the athletics ground is now, a short distance from The Den.

In 1919, Palace moved again, further south to the district of Selhurst, to a ground called The Nest. This had been the home of an old Southern League team, Croydon Common, and it was here in 1920 Palace began their League career.

But the ground was not entirely suitable for a club with ambition, and was about to be submerged by railway developments, so Palace rented it out to Tramway FC, for 10 per cent of their gate receipts, and secured the freehold of a site nearby.

Selhurst Park

Selhurst Park cost the club only £2570 in January 1922, but needed considerable preparation. The site was a brickfield belonging to the London Brighton and South Coast Railway Company. Two chimney stacks stood where the pitch is now. But the advantages were apparent, for it covered 15 acres and was within walking distance of three suburban railway stations, Thornton Heath, Selhurst and Norwood Junction.

Palace commissioned Archibald Leitch to design their new ground. He predicted that Selhurst Park would be the largest ground in London, the most modern in the country, but could do little to prevent industrial disputes holding up the work. The official opening by the Lord Mayor of London, on 30 August 1924, took place in a still unfinished stand. The contractors at Selhurst Park were Humphreys of Knightsbridge, a firm which built, among other grounds, The Valley. Leitch's Main Stand was virtually identical to his designs of 20 years before at Fulham, Huddersfield and Stamford Bridge, but without the triangular roof gable. The rest of the ground was open banking, although terracing only covered the lower reaches of each bank, the tops being covered in grass.

At the end of the first season Palace were relegated. But the club was honoured on 1 March 1926 when Selhurst staged England v. Wales.

In those early years at Selhurst there was a ditch running in front of the Main Stand along the touchline. To save players having to retrieve the ball from its murky waters, Palace covered it over in 1935 and relaid the pitch. They also installed a tap by the trainer's bench, for wetting the magic sponge. The ground was used for Army internationals and like most London grounds, by Millwall, when their own ground had been closed because of crowd disturbances. But it remained completely unchanged during the club's long sojourn in Divisions Three and Four; a large, but increasingly unkempt ground with cover only on one side, holding 55 000 spectators.

Floodlights were first installed in September 1953, when Palace played a friendly v. Chelsea, and were updated in December 1955. Also in that year a new entrance hall and boardroom were opened by Sir Stanley Rous. The floodlights were still rather too primitive however, being mounted on four poles on the open side, four gantries on the stand roof, all apparently linked by wires draped around the ground, so in 1962 Palace spent £18 000 erecting a new set on four corner pylons. They then effected a major footballing scoop by persuading Real Madrid to visit Selhurst Park to play in the first game under the new lights, watched by 25 000.

Palace's fortunes in the League began to improve during the 1960s, and in 1966 work began on a new stand on the uncovered side. It was named after the club's long serving chairman, Arthur Wait, who was a builder by trade and was occasionally to be seen working on the construction himself. Seating 5000, the stand was fully finished in 1969 when Palace won promotion to Division One.

The last major development at the ground took place in the early 1980s when the Whitehorse Lane End, an open bank of terracing, and the large car-park behind, were leased to a supermarket chain in a £2 million deal. The supermarket built their store on the car-park, but also had to refit the terraces along its back wall. There is now a more modern, but truncated bank holding 5000 standing spectators, but designed in such a way as to make possible the provision of a roof, or even a stand above the shop behind the terracing. It is identical to the project undertaken at Boothferry Park.

The Main Stand has also been adapted, into an all-seated stand holding 5000. There are therefore

Selhurst Park in the 1970s. Notice the two floodlight systems (Colorsport)

10 000 seats in a total capacity of 38 266. So Leitch was wrong in predicting that Selhurst Park would be the biggest ground in London, although before the Whitehorse Lane End was cut down, the ground did at least come close to that distinction. When Palace were again chasing promotion to Division One in May 1979, a record attendance of 51 482 saw them win the Second Division Championship after a game v. Burnley.

Ground Description

Selhurst and its neighbouring districts all seem to lie at the foot of the hill on which the Crystal Palace stood until destroyed by fire in 1936. The ground merges into its surrounds, tucked in between the rising slopes of South Norwood and the flatter land of Selhurst. Entrance is from Whitehorse Lane, a thoroughfare made busier by the arrival of the new supermarket. The Main Stand is entered via a private road between the ground and Lady Edridge School, but instead of finding the normal foyer, one finds the entrance to a rather seedy-looking night-club, its presence under the stand seeming rather incongruous.

Otherwise, the stand looks very sombre indeed. All the steelwork and seats are black, and the once so familiar and homely claret and light blue striped paddock rear wall disappeared when the terracing was seated. The stand facings are now dark blue with touches of white and red along the centre and exits. In the left-hand corner remains just a short section of the old striped wall. Quite why Palace opted for such a dark colour scheme is difficult to understand, for although Leitch's stand was never so distinctive as its forebears at Craven Cottage or Leeds Road, it was bright.

One unusual feature of the stand is the lack of any front perimeter wall. As the stand is old and mainly wooden, the club considered the best fire escape to be straight onto the pitch. Hence anyone in the stand can simply walk down to the front, and enter the pitch past a few low advertisement hoardings on the touchline. If anyone does, he might notice that the dug-outs have polished pine benches inside. Very fashionable. As a further precaution in the event of fire, two extra staircases have been built behind the stand, like twin towers.

At the back of the stand is a line of executive boxes, which on closer inspection resemble slightly outdated small hotel rooms with intricate light fittings. The directors are less fussy: their seats are just like those in the rest of the stand. Very egalitarian.

From here, to the left is the Whitehorse Lane End with the supermarket directly behind. It used to be twice as high and hold 12 000 standing. The terrace stops within a few yards of each corner, allowing room for the floodlight pylons which face the pitch square on, staring at their opposites on the other side like totem poles guarding Selhurst Park from evil spirits. Each pylon has 48 large lamps.

The new terracing is sturdy, with thickset steel barriers. Opposite here is the taller and original banking, the Holmesdale Road End, or the Kop. Palace tried to persuade the home fans to move over to the new terracing, but they held firm on these exposed slopes. Here the barriers are red and blue, rising up to a grass-topped bank, which then subsides towards the road. At the front, Palace have borrowed an idea from Newcastle, using not tall security fencing but a low angled fence divided from the pitch by a slight moat. I cannot understand why this excellent device is not used more often, for it not only works as an anti-hooligan measure but also prevents that caged-in effect. Most important, the view from the lower terraces is not in any way impeded. This end holds 17 000.

Opposite the Main Stand is the Arthur Wait Stand. It follows the traditional pattern, combining seats and a paddock, with a large, propped flat roof, whose fascia is marked with fading claret and light blue stripes. It should sparkle, it should sport the club's name in big letters, it should have a flagpole or two to lessen the monotonous lines, but all it has is a small square clock in the centre. Behind the white concrete paddock rear wall are 5000 seats, but unfortunately placed on very shallow raked steps. Altogether it is rather a dull stand, like a loading bay of a warehouse. Finally, notice how many different colours are used at Selhurst Park, from the garish tones inside the foyer to the blue stanchions and orange nets on each set of goals. Consequently, there is no unity, no indication of who plays here and in what colours. Selhurst Park was underdeveloped for so many years, and now it has been improved it still does not look modern.

Now to be really provocative, further along the road, on the very site this club was born, is one of the finest stadiums in Britain, the new Crystal Palace athletics stadium, with two superb cantilever stands. If only a way could be found for Palace to share the ground once again, for it is a home surely more befitting their grand title.

· WIMBLEDON ·

Plough Lane

Wimbledon were for 75 years among the top amateur clubs in London. They formed in 1889 and under the name Wimbledon Old Centrals played on Wimbledon Common until moving to Plough Lane in 1912. As a successful South London club, they were able to attract gates of up to 10 000 during the 1930s.

At that time the ground had two stands. The Main Stand was a small, all-wooden affair with separate dressing rooms. Opposite, the club installed the South Stand in 1923, purchased from Clapton Orient who were then playing at Millfields Road. The South Stand is still on the Plough Lane Side. A particularly unusual feature of the ground was a privet hedge which grew between the Main Stand and the touchline. The ground's highest attendance, 18 000, was at an Amateur Cup match v. HMS Victory in 1935.

Plough Lane really developed in the late 1950s and early 1960s, under the chairmanship of the late Sidney Black, a generous, forward-thinking man to whom in many ways the club owe their present status. The Sportsman public house was built at the ground on Durnsford Road in 1958. In 1959 Wimbledon bought the site from the council for a sum of £9000, but only on the condition that if the ground were to be sold, it would have to go back to the authorities at the same price. As a result, the club have never been able to borrow much money using the ground as security, although they are trying to establish a more realistic valuation nearer £100 000. Until this is achieved, Plough Lane will not be developed too extensively.

Also in 1959, the rear section of the present Main Stand was built, and instead of the privet hedge, shrubs were grown along the front railings. The following year saw the construction of the slight cantilevered cover at the West Terrace end, and all the concrete terracing. In October 1960 Arsenal visited Plough Lane, to play in the first floodlit game at the ground. The existing lights are more recent installations.

This transformation of the ground would have been impossible without Black's financial help. In their third Final and their only appearance at Wembley Stadium, Wimbledon beat Sutton United to win the Amateur Cup in 1963. They were then in the Isthmian League. A year later they turned semi-professional, formed a limited company, and within a comparatively short time became candidates for League membership. This they achieved in 1977.

Extra facilities have been added since then; an extension over the small paddock in front of the Main Stand in 1979 and the building of bars, a lounge and a multi-gym behind the stand.

Plough Lane's current capacity is 15 000 including 2300 seats.

The Main Stand at Plough Lane

Ground Description

Anyone expecting tranquillity such as one might expect to find in the neighbourhood of the All England Tennis Club will be very disappointed by Plough Lane. Because Plough Lane's stands and terraces are so low, the constant sound and smell of traffic is never far away.

To find the ground simply follow a line of electricity pylons. One such pylon towers over the ground, making the floodlight pylons look distinctly insignificant. Although called Plough Lane, the main entrance is on Durnsford Road, along which you could go almost directly four miles north, across the river, to Craven Cottage. A little further to the south east will take you to Selhurst Park. (If this seems rather too many League clubs in such a small area look how close to each other are the four West London or the three Birmingham clubs.)

The Main Stand is about 60 yards long on the half-way line, a miniature version of Doncaster's at Belle Vue, with an older rear section and a newer extended roof over the paddock, which has now been fully seated. It is too small and unevenly built to have any impact on its surroundings, especially as the pylon behind is over twice its height. To the left of the stand, on the same touchline, stands a now derelict prefabricated building once intended as a youth club and day nursery, but now an eye-sore; a relic from the era of Ron Noades, a controversial ex-chairman.

From the Main Stand: to the left is the open East Terrace, with the river behind, and to the right, the West Terrace with its cover at the back, behind which is Durnsford Road, forever shaking under lorries and buses.

Opposite the Main Stand, also sitting on the half-way line, is the very narrow South Stand. It presumably dates back to the turn of the century, and has just a few rows of narrow bench seating behind a wooden terrace rear wall. After the Second World War the stand was thought to be unsafe as the result of a nearby bomb explosion, but it survives nevertheless. Plough Lane is directly behind.

Though lacking sophistication or aesthetic value, Plough Lane does have the neat and homely atmosphere which is more often the mark of non-League grounds. The perimeter fence is, for example, the old curled iron railing type, once found at better grounds but now replaced by ugly concrete and steel security fencing. The colour scheme is tastefully uniform; yellow railings, yellow, royal blue and white steelwork and barriers, black seats.

Wimbledon have crammed a respectable array of facilities into their ground and if it still looks slightly unprofessional from the terraces, you should not decry their efforts. Something of the spirit of their amateur days still lives on. The ground's major drawback is that in its underdeveloped state it is unable to shut out from view the overwhelmingly uninteresting bits of South London in which it finds itself absorbed.

·19·
SCOTLAND

The game of football is indebted to Scotland for many reasons. The Scottish invented the passing game and the two-handed throw-in; Scotsmen were the first professional footballers in the world, and a Scotsman set up the Football League. When it came to building football grounds, the Scottish were again at the forefront. At the turn of the twentieth century Celtic, then Ibrox, then Hampden were the three largest football grounds in the world, with only Goodison Park, Villa Park and a few other English grounds surpassing them in terms of facilities. Until the Maracana Stadium was built for the 1950 World Cup in Brazil, Hampden Park was the largest ground in the world.

The most influential designer in the history of British grounds was Scottish, Archibald Leitch (see Design), who had a hand in all three Glasgow grounds, as well as almost every other major English ground between 1905–36.

In Scotland were found the first all-ticket matches, the first ever lock-out game, the first managers' dug-outs, and in recent years the first all-seater stadium in Britain. Ibrox is one of the most modern football grounds in Europe.

Celtic Park

Celtic's ground is south east of the city centre, and is often called Parkhead, after the district. The club was formed by Catholic Irish inhabitants of Glasgow's East End in November 1887 and secured its first proper ground a few hundred yards from the present Celtic Park, on land rented for £50 a year. The official opening match was on 29 May 1888, a friendly v. Rangers. Having become founder members of the Scottish League in 1890, Celtic were, as W. Maley writes in his history of the club, forced to leave their ground 'in true Irish fashion', as victims of rack-renting when the landlord raised Celtic's rent to £500. The site of this first ground is now covered by the works of Barr and Coy, Parkhead.

From here Celtic moved across the Janefield Cemetery to a quarry hole, purchased from Lord Newlands for the very high sum of £10 000. During the summer of 1892, while Everton were building the finest ground in England at Goodison Park, Celtic constructed an even more dramatic ground in Parkhead. Celtic Park had a running and a cycling track, and was intended to be the venue not only for Celtic but also for Scotland's home fixtures. As the Irish patriot, Michael Davitt, laid the first turf he recited a poem: 'On alien soil like yourself I am here, I'll take root and flourish, of that never fear.' For many years Celtic Park was called 'Paradise', after someone had described Celtic's move as 'like leaving the graveyard to enter Paradise'.

Celtic Park was considerably improved by the erection of wooden terracing and the concreting of the cycle track in preparation for the staging of the World Cycling Championship in 1898, the first and only time Scotland has been the host of this event. The ground at this time had a pavilion – as was the practice in Scotland, rather than a main stand incorporating the players' and directors' facilities – and a long, low covered stand with seating opposite (destroyed by fire in 1904, possibly by an arsonist).

Also in 1898 an Irish director of the club, James Grant, decided to build his own small stand opposite the pavilion, agreeing with the club that he should take a share of the profits. It was a pavilion-style, two-storey building, lavishly equipped with padded tip-up seats and large, sliding windows which could be shut when it rained. Unfortunately Grant had not allowed for condensation and the windows had to be removed to allow clear sight of the pitch. In addition the stand was set away from the pavilion and had four flights of stairs leading up to the seats. Grant lost all his investment, sold the stand to the club at a loss, and in 1927 fire destroyed it.

After the cycling, Celtic Park staged a number of other exciting events, including motor-cycle racing, a Coronation parade in 1911, and during the First World War soldiers took over the pitch and demonstrated the art of trench warfare to a huge crowd with the aid of mock bombs and explosions.

Although Celtic Park had promised to be Scotland's premier football venue, by 1903 Hampden Park had joined the Glasgow limelight and from then until Parkhead's last full international match in 1933, the ground was mainly used for Scotland v.

Celtic's new South Stand roof with suspended press box. Compare with the far East End and the floodlight pylon with that of Hampden (Adrian Gibson)

Ireland fixtures.

Celtic Park's first major new development – the opening of the South Stand – took place in 1929. It was almost identical to Rangers' new Main Stand, also opened in 1929 and designed by Archibald Leitch. It cost £35000 to build.

The ground was by this time smaller than both Ibrox and Hampden Parks, though still larger than any English club's ground. Its record attendance is 92000 for the traditional New Year's derby match v. Rangers, on 1 January 1938. Floodlights were first used at Parkhead on 10 December 1959, for a friendly v. English Champions Wolves.

After Celtic's triumph in the European Cup in 1967, the club borrowed the design of Hampden Park's newly-covered West End and built a cover over Parkhead's East End. But the most startling development occurred when the club removed the roof of the South Stand and replaced it with a most unusual, angular white roof between April and August 1971. Costing £250000, the work was done in such a way as not to disturb the facilities below (as also happened at Maine Road in 1982).

A huge girder, measuring 97·5 metres long and 5·3 metres deep, was transported to Parkhead all the way from Chichester, and hoisted up on two supporting posts on either side of the stand, to create a goalpost-like frame on which to rest the roof. It was a quite revolutionary way of redeveloping a stand, although not very economical, and it transformed Leitch's base, which was converted to an all-seater stand with room for 8686 spectators. But has it been a success?

In purely aesthetic terms there is no doubt it enhances the dramatic quality of Parkhead, especially at evening matches when the lights underneath the roof give it an awesome appearance, exaggerated by the suspended 100-seater press box hung from the roof girder. But as a means of protecting people from the elements it fails somewhat, especially in the front.

Since the Safety of Sports Grounds Act, Parkhead's capacity has been reduced to 67500, which makes it the second largest club ground in Britain. But despite the new roof, it still appears to be rather an old-fashioned place and an incongruous neighbour to the notorious Barrowfield housing estate, and the Eastern Necropolis, a wild, sprawling graveyard directly behind the North Enclosure. This side of the ground is covered terracing, otherwise referred to as 'The Jungle'.

The large, curved West End terrace is also called the Celtic End. It has a roof over the rear section, and strange crush barriers – concrete uprights with wooden bars wedged in! Even more surprising, especially in view of the reputation of a minority of Scottish fans, is the total lack of security fencing around the elliptical perimeter wall. This welcome omission helps to make an apparently distant pitch seem slightly nearer.

Behind the west goal is a semi-circle of grass, big enough for the players to use as a five-a-side pitch. Behind the east goal there is no grass, thus providing another training area when the turf is unplayable. This end of the ground is often called the Rangers' End, since this is where visiting fans stand for local derbies. The large roof makes the end look like Wembley, except that the floodlights here are the typical Scottish variety with slanting lamp holders. The pylons rise through the roof from the terraces.

Finally, the Parkhead pitch is still surrounded by a track which once measured a perfect 440 yards. Celtic were the first club to install undersoil heating in Scotland.

Parkhead is, with Hampden, the last of the really enormous grounds, and without people can seem quite soulless. Now that crowds are dwindling – 50000 is about the maximum for a meeting of the Old Firm – the club will no doubt install more seating and improved facilities. But the people of Glasgow do not want private luxury boxes, they want football; so compared with the likes of Hillsborough, Old Trafford or Villa Park, Celtic Park is underdeveloped. But once the action gets started and the supporters reach full voice, if anything this becomes an asset rather than a failing.

Hampden Park

Hampden Park has the same time-worn appeal as Parkhead, only more pronounced. Recent years have seen the beginning of a long period of redevelopment of the ground, so at present allowance must be made for its state of transition. But it must also be said that the present work is long overdue, and that as the home of one of soccer's oldest footballing nations, Hampden Park lags way behind almost every national stadium in Europe, and indeed many in the developing countries. This is a great drawback for Scotland, for the ground has almost unlimited potential.

Hampden Park belongs to Queen's Park, Scotland's oldest League club and one which has faithfully retained its amateur status.

Queen's Park formed in July 1867 (five years after England's oldest League club, Notts County) and for six years played on the Queen's Park Recreation Ground, which still exists. During this time the team pioneered the passing game and for a while made up the bulk of, and sometimes the whole, Scottish representative team. In 1873 the club moved a few hundred yards to a ground overlooked by a row of houses called Hampden Terrace, named after John Hampden, an English Parliamentarian during the Civil War. Queen's Park decided to call the ground Hampden Park, and seemed to like the name so much they used it for two of their subsequent grounds.

Funds were not a problem as Queen's Park were forever winning. The ground cost only £20 a year to rent, and at the same time a club house was bought for £21, although there was no water laid on for a year, and there was no lease. In 1876, the first grandstand was built, at a cost of £306, and two years later the club bought a pavilion from the Caledonian Cricket Club.

In 1883 work began on the railway line between Mount Florida and Crosshill, so Queen's Park had to move. For one season they used Titwood Park, on the western side of Queen's Park, before moving back to the east side in 1884 to the second Hampden Park, a few hundred yards from the first.

The new ground had proper terraces built, a large brick pavilion with its own gymnasium, and a stand on the South Side. Although Queen's Park were already beginning to lose their complete dominance of Scottish football by 1883, and the club did not join the Scottish League until 1900, the second Hampden Park was always the preferred venue for Scottish Cup Finals. It was also the venue for the first all-ticket match ever staged, when 10 000 tickets were sold for the Scotland v. England match on 15 March 1884, the first international to be played at the ground.

But Queen's Park did not want to stay there long, because they had only a five-year lease and wanted to develop their facilities with greater security.

In 1903 therefore they found another site, also a short distance away, overlooked by the houses on Somerville Drive. The 12½-acre area was for sale at £850 an acre, but as well as purchasing the land the buyer would have to lay down streets and sewers, and culvert the Mall's Myre Burn which ran across the land. In view of these conditions, Queen's Park offered £750 an acre, and finally settled for £800. This was expensive even for a professional outfit, and it gives some idea of the status enjoyed by the club.

They left the second Hampden Park at the end of 1902–03 season, after which the site was renamed Cathkin Park and became the home of Third Lanark, until that club disbanded in 1967.

The third Hampden Park was developed during the summer of 1903, with Archibald Leitch playing a major role in the design and lay-out.

The ground was to be very similar in shape to those at Parkhead and Ibrox, that is, an elongated oval with large, uncovered ends and one main stand. But at Hampden the centrepiece of the stand was a tall pavilion, with what appeared to be two separate stands on either side. The terraces were lined with barriers made with 1-inch thick wire rope hung between uprights. Hampden Park number three held 40 000 standing, 4000 seated, and 530 in the pavilion.

Opening day was 31 October 1903, when the honours were performed by a man closely connected with Rangers, the Lord Provost of Glasgow, Sir John Ure Primrose. Queen's Park played Celtic in a Division One match and won by a single goal.

Celtic were back at the new ground in April 1904 to participate in the first Cup Final at Hampden, which they won v. Rangers in front of 65 000, the largest crowd ever for such a game.

In 1905 the original, proud pavilion was burnt down, and for a while the two stands stood apart, until in 1914 the existing four-storey centre section was built at a cost of £4700, and the whole stand made to look as one. It now included all modern facilities, with a swimming pool for the players, and room for 1000 people seated. Its twin-tower entrance was quite the most ambitious piece of building yet seen at a football ground, as was the enormous press box on the roof, with room for 110 journalists. And it is no coincidence surely that the twin-tower image was to reappear a decade later.

In 1923 additional surrounding land was purchased, new roads laid down and Lesser Hampden, a practice pitch behind the ground, built for the Queen's Park junior teams. In 1927 extra terracing added a further 25 000 places, and in 1928 new rigid crush barriers replaced the 'wire-rope' variety, so strongly recommended by the club only four years earlier at the meetings of the 1924 committee on ground safety (see Safety). Hampden reached its peak in 1937, the year when the North Stand was built at the back of the enormous terracing opposite the Main Stand. This added a further 4500 seats, in a total capacity of 150 000.

From this year onwards, Hampden began accumulating almost every attendance record possible.

The Scotland v. England match on 17 April 1937 was watched by the highest official attendance ever recorded in Britain – 149 415 (sometimes given as 149 547), but at least another 10 000 gained free entry after smashing down the gates.

The Aberdeen v. Celtic Cup Final a week later on 24 April attracted the highest ever attendance recorded for a match between two club sides, given as either 144 303 or 147 365.

Hampden also has the record attendance for a club game other than a final – the semi-final Rangers v. Hibernian, 27 March 1948, watched by 143 570, and for a European club game, when Celtic played Leeds

Hampden Park before redevelopment. The North Stand (right) has gone. Note the precariousness of the press box (Popperfoto)

United on 15 April 1970, in the European Cup semi-final in front of 136 505. This figure is higher than for any European Cup tie – including finals – and the game was played mid-week!

Finally, the Glasgow public turned out again in force to see a friendly match between Rangers and Eintracht Frankfurt on 17 October 1961. The crowd of 104 493 was the highest for a friendly ever played in Britain, but it was also the first time Hampden's floodlights had been used. Queen's Park sometimes attracted large gates. Their highest was 97 000 for the visit of Rangers in the Scottish Cup on 18 February 1933 – bigger than any English club and no small achievement for amateurs.

In 1949 Hampden's capacity had to be reduced for safety reasons to 135 000, and when the Maracana Stadium in Brazil was built Hampden lost its title as the biggest ground in the world. It was also beginning to get slightly shoddy. The terracing was in poor condition and there was no cover for 90 per cent of the spectators. This was greatly alleviated in 1967, when to celebrate Queen's Park's Centenary a large cover was built over the West Terrace. The architects were Thompson, McCrae and Sanders, who were later responsible for planning the complete redevelopment of Hampden Park.

This has come not a moment too soon. Walking round the ground in the late 1970s it was obvious how neglected the place had become. The North Stand in particular resembled a disused warehouse. All this was confirmed by the findings of the safety inspectors, who after the Safety of Sports Grounds Act, determined that Hampden's capacity be reduced to 81 000.

The development plan is to be in two phases. Phase One, which began in October 1981, involved demolishing the North Stand, removing the top of the East Terrace, and most important of all, concreting all the terracing. Incredibly, Hampden's terracing up to 1983 was all ash and timber, with the crush barriers bolted onto the wooden risers. There is hardly a ground in England with such dilapidated terracing, although Hampden's may have survived so long because of the strengthening effect of millions of beer can ring-pulls being trodden into the ash!

Once completed, Phase One meant that Hampden had seats only in the Main Stand, but at least had the foundations on which to revamp the stadium along modern lines. After the first phase, it is planned to built a cantilever roof on all three sides around the Main Stand, and add seats onto the terracing.

For the time being Hampden is therefore very exposed, and about as advanced as a ground built in the 1930s. But it does have an unmatchable aura still; a sense that this is an historic place which craves reverence rather than recrimination.

Part of its appeal is its sheer vastness; a huge, elongated bowl on the slopes of Mount Florida. It is like the mouth of a volcano, the pitch being 35 feet below street level. This shape has undoubtedly helped to create the acoustic effect known as the Hampden Roar – a term first coined in 1929, apparently when the Scottish forward Alec Cheyne scored a last gasp winner against England direct from a corner and the ecstatic crowd roared continuously until the final whistle.

Apart from its shape, Hampden retains much of its old world charm. The Main Stand has a grand red-brick entrance like a Highland castle, and its most distinguished feature inside is the press box, which resembles a tumble-down house, balanced on the pitch of the roof at such an angle that it seems likely to fall off at any moment.

To the west is Lesser Hampden, an undeveloped ground with grass slopes and a few wooden patches of terracing. There is a small, dilapidated pavilion which was originally a farmworker's cottage. But a good, large pitch (larger than Hampden's) and floodlighting make it a fine little ground. Queen's Park's reserves, 'the Strollers' and the third team, 'the Victoria Eleven' play here, as do occasionally the first team. Residents in the tenement blocks on two sides have an excellent view of the pitch.

Comparing the situation with Cardiff Arms Park it is a wonder that Queen's Park have not developed Lesser Hampden into a reasonable ground with some seats and cover for the first team games, which never attract more than a few thousand at most. Lesser Hampden would make a perfect 2000 to 3000 all-seat ground, and could be well-used by the community.

Had an appeal fund not been launched by the SPA to redevelop the stadium, the best alternative would have been for Queen's Park to sell the main site, and build themselves a super mini-stadium at Lesser Hampden, perhaps to share with Clyde.

But the ever faithful fans of Scotland deserve a great stadium. Hampden Park should be staging European Championship Finals, perhaps even the World Cup Finals, not struggling to maintain Third Division standards. So the recent work is welcome, but very late indeed.

Ibrox Park

Ibrox Park is in complete contrast to Hampden Park. Rangers have spent £10 million transforming it from a large, oval-shaped ground with few seats, to a rectangular stadium with 36 000 seats. It is now totally unrecognizable from the old Ibrox, apart from the sensible and sensitive retention of Archibald Leitch's excellent South Stand.

Rangers formed in 1873, playing first at Glasgow Green, then Kinning Park, a ground which has gone down in footballing history as the first to have its gates locked before a match. A crowd of 10 000 squeezed in to watch Queen's Park play Dumbarton in the 1881 Scottish Cup Final (the game could not be played at the first Hampden Park because of Queen's Park's involvement). Dumbarton lost 2-1 and protested that too many spectators had obstructed the touchlines. In the replay, also at Kinning Park, the gates were locked with only 7000 in the ground, and this time Dumbarton lost 3-1.

Rangers had to leave Kinning Park in 1887 but found Ibrox Park a mile only to the west, in the district of Govan.

The opening was on 20 August 1887 with a friendly v. Preston North End, but it became less friendly when the Old Invincibles led 8-0 and the crowd invaded the pitch.

For the next 15 years Ibrox was relatively undeveloped, with low, wooden terracing around the elliptical track and a small pavilion in the corner. The ground staged its first international in March 1889 v. Ireland, and in February 1890 its first Scottish Cup Final, when 11 000 saw Queen's Park (who else?) draw with Vale of Leven. A crowd of 14 000 saw the Glaswegians win the replay a week later.

The ground's capacity stayed around that figure until the turn of the century, when in 1902 massive wooden terracing was erected at either end, giving Ibrox room for up to 70 000 spectators. But the first time the stands were open, for Scotland's match v. England, disaster struck (see Safety), and Ibrox suffered the first of two major accidents before being rebuilt.

It became clear from that incident, in which 26 people died, that solid earth banking was the only sensible solution for large numbers, and rebuilding began accordingly. By 1905 the capacity had risen to a safe 25 000, and by 1910 to 63 000. Ibrox was then very similar to Parkhead or Hampden, and staged athletics, cycle meetings, and in September 1917 even a Royal Investiture attended by George V.

In 1928 Rangers achieved their first League and Cup Double and began building a dazzling new stand on the South Side of the ground, designed by Archibald Leitch. Rangers had the money and space to give Leitch the chance to surpass himself, and the end result probably represented the pinnacle of his career. It was superficially similar to previous designs at Goodison Park and Fratton Park, and was

built at the same time as the South Stand at Parkhead, but inside Rangers fitted it out like an exclusive country residence (described below).

Still Ibrox grew, until on 2 January 1939 it proved able to hold 118 567 spectators for the annual New Year duel with Celtic. Thus Ibrox had outgrown Parkhead by some 26 000, and became second only to Hampden Park in Britain. It was also the first Glasgow ground to have floodlights, switched on for the annual friendly v. Arsenal on 8 December 1953.

In 1961 two more people died when a barrier collapsed, followed by the second Ibrox disaster in 1969 (see Safety). This obviously forced Rangers to consider seriously the design and facilities of the ground. In 1975 the capacity was cut by almost a half to 65 000, as a result of the Safety of Sports Grounds Act, and so Rangers made the momentous decision to rebuild Ibrox completely. Again, Scotland was to place itself at the forefront of stadium design. The redevelopment plan was probably the most ambitious undertaken by any club, certainly the most expensive, and yet it was executed with remarkable efficiency and the minimum disruption to spectator facilities.

Rangers were meticulous in their preparation. This was to be no piecemeal development such as had plagued so many other grounds, nor was it to be a compromise. Quite simply, the club aimed for three new all-seated stands, to include office and showroom space for rental, and instead of spending extra money on luxury accommodation for the minority, opted for maximum comfort and an unimpeded view for everyone. It was to cost £10 million in total.

Apart from Leitch's fine stand, lovingly preserved, there is absolutely no trace of the ground's former shape. Every piece of banking was taken away and dumped in a railway cutting the club bought especially for the purpose. The notorious Stairway 13 became a memory overnight.

Phase One of the plan began in August 1978, with the removal of the east and west terracing and the erection of two, identical stands each seating 7500

Ibrox Park before redevelopment. The notorious stairway 13 is bottom right. Compare this with the picture in the colour section (Aerofilms)

spectators. The method of construction was similar to that used at Villa Park and Carrow Road, with a goalpost frame 78 metres wide supporting the roof. Each stand is a separate unit, with closed screen ends, and is within yards of the goal-line, so that for the first time at Ibrox the fans are close to the pitch. The space once taken up by the massive banking was flattened and became a concourse area for parking and pedestrians.

Phase Two began in August 1980 and involved the demolition of the Centenary Stand and its replacement by a new North Stand, simply a longer version of the East and West Stands, except that the main cross girder being 110 metres long had to be double the depth for strength. This girder alone cost more than the entire roof built on Tottenham's new West Stand two years later. But this was Rangers' choice, and was partly due to the fact that British Steel was the main supplier of the material and quite rightly saw Ibrox as a prestige development. But the main reason for the club's lavishness was the fact that they are an extremely rich club, with a massive income from weekly pools.

The North Stand holds 10 300, giving Ibrox a total capacity of 45 000, of which only 9500 are standing, all in the paddock of the South Stand. Since each unit is free standing, there are gaps in all four corners, but these have also been carefully considered. It was decided that the cost of building rounded corner segments would have added unreasonable cost, and that the free movement of air would be of benefit to the turf, newly installed with undersoil heating.

In addition, the design of the three new stands meant that every spectator, apart from a few hundred in the back corners of the old stand were within the 90-metres optimum viewing distance (see Design).

Rather than being left flat, the corners have been landscaped with earth-banks, shrubs and attractive stairways. Every part of the lower walls and stairs are in red brick, to echo the materials used by Leitch.

So Ibrox is not an unsatisfactory mix of old and new. Indeed, the old is enhanced and brightened by its vast, white-roofed neighbours. The admirable Ibrox wrought-iron gates have been preserved as well, on each side of the South Stand.

Without the retention of the older features, Ibrox may have become a soulless modern nightmare, certainly less acceptable to the club's supporters, whose patience and understanding have been tested to the full by the transformation of the ground. The wholesale change of one's favourite football venue is not easy to accept, so the continued presence of the South Stand acts as a vital link with the past. Not that Rangers would have kept it standing for just tradition's sake. It does have several features which would have been expensive to rebuild today. The red-brick frontage, for example, exudes power and importance. It is in mock neo-classical style with arched windows on lower and upper floors, square windows in-between, and pedimented windows at either end. On each corner is the club crest, in blue and gold mosaic, with the motto 'Ready'.

Inside, the foyer is one of the great marble halls of football, decorated with potted plants, art-deco lamps, trophies and a huge oil painting of the *Wee Blue Devil*, Alan Morton (a Rangers' hero of the 1920s). A uniformed commissionaire is on regular duty during the week, the staircase is cleaned twice a day, and on the first floor are dark wood-panelled corridors leading to a stately boardroom, vast offices and a bulging trophy room. Like Highbury, it is not just a football stand, it is a museum and a symbol of prestige.

Each dressing room is the size of a small gym, with polished wooden benches and clothes' hooks which had to be lowered a few inches because the club disliked so many players standing on the benches and spoiling the wood!

The referee and linesmen have a changing room as large as most other clubs allow each set of players. The route to the pitch is some distance, passing by a long shale practice area under the stand, where players can train in bad weather and warm up before kick-off; a unique feature.

From the hallowed halls of Leitch's stand, the new stands appear at the end of the tunnel in stark contrast. The South Stand is typical Leitch, with criss-crossed balcony wall, pitched roof with prominent press-box high up in the centre, and paddock in front of an upper tier of 10 000 seats (the largest stand Leitch designed).

The new stands are light, sleek and colourful. Each has two tiers, although they are not double-deckers, with sections of different coloured seats; a rather ugly combination of red, yellow, orange, brown and blue.

Rangers insist that both players and fans are happy with their new home. It has brought the two closer together, reduced crowd trouble to a minimum (because police find it very easy to spot potential problems) and although the fans tend to sing less than before, there is still as good an atmosphere as one could expect from today's smaller attendances.

Understandably the older supporters still prefer the Main Stand, and younger spectators find it difficult to remain seated at each end. It will take time for them to adjust to the new Ibrox, and time for them to appreciate how this ground will radically change the entire thinking behind what a football ground should be.

But Rangers have done the right thing. They have two stands containing large rented-out offices, thereby providing a steady income (occupants include the IBA, a firm of architects and a travel organization); sufficient accommodation to cope with the likely demand; viewing standards and playing facilities which could not be improved, and perhaps most important of all, the memory of Stairway 13 has been cast aside forever. Ibrox is undoubtedly the best club ground of its size in Britain, and perhaps even in Europe. Once again, the Scots have set the trend.

·20·
BIG MATCH VENUES

Early Cup Final Venues

Before Wembley the FA Cup Final (known originally as the English Cup Final), was held at seven different venues, with three additional grounds being used for Final replays.

1872–94

The Kennington Oval in south east London was the ground of Surrey County Cricket Club. It was chosen as the first venue simply because the FA secretary at the time, Charles Alcock, was also Secretary of Surrey CCC. Wanderers played the Royal Engineers in that first final on 16 March 1872, watched by 2000 spectators, who paid a minimum entrance fee of one shilling. This was at least double the amount usually charged, which helps to explain why the attendance was so disappointing.

The Cup rules stated that the holders would be exempt until the next final, and could choose the venue. The Wanderers, having no home at the time, chose to meet their challengers at Lillie Bridge, a ground near the present Stamford Bridge. A crowd of 3000 saw them win again. But this time the rules were changed and the Wanderers had to play in the early rounds of the next competition. Also, the Oval was settled as the venue.

Twenty finals were played at Surrey's ground, but as attendances grew for both finals and internationals, the cricket club became increasingly worried about their ability to hold so many people, some of them described in London as: 'a Northern horde of uncouth garb and strange oaths'.

By 1892 the Final's attendance had reached 25 000, squeezed into temporary wooden stands and seats inside the ropes. Surrey also worried that their pitch was suffering from rough usage, so in 1892 they asked the FA to look elsewhere.

Of the finals played at the Oval, three needed replays, of which only one was played elsewhere, in 1886. The venue chosen for Blackburn Rovers' replay v. WBA was the Racecourse Ground, Derby, but if the northern venue was expected to yield a higher gate the reality was otherwise, because 15 000 saw the first game in London, and only 12 000 the replay.

Nevertheless, stuck for anywhere else to play the 1893 Final, the FA decided to go north again, at the suggestion of the northern representative J. J. Bentley. He thought the Manchester Athletic Club's ground in Fallowfield would make a very suitable venue, even though it had never been previously used for football.

But the result was chaos. Some 45 000 people paid to get in, but thousands more gained free admittance, preventing ticket holders from reaching their seats and making it hard for even the officials to enter the ground.

Chaotic though the 1893 Final was, the attendance was almost twice that of the previous year and was not matched until 1896. Indeed the large numbers probably took the authorities quite by surprise, as did the record receipts of £2559. But the ground was not chosen again, although it did stage one more major game in 1899, the third semi-final replay between Sheffield United and Liverpool. This time it was a Monday afternoon and only 30 000 attended, but the referee had to abandon the game at half-time, 1 hour and 50 minutes after kick-off, when the crowd yet again spilled onto the pitch. (The ground still exists as an athletics track in a tranquil lane off Moseley Road.)

After the fiasco in 1893, the FA turned its attention to the best League ground in the country, Goodison Park. But only 37 000 watched the 1894 Final there, and the FA decided to take the Final back to London.

1895–1914

The FA thought that London could handle crowds better than any other city. The capital could also give the Final greater national importance. Northerners and Midlanders were far more likely to enjoy a day out in London than in Liverpool or Manchester; it would be a proper occasion. And, the FA's headquarters were in London.

Crystal Palace in 1895 was a natural focal point for recreation, with Paxton's iron and glass palace on a rise overlooking the park. The football pitch was laid on the bed of a bowl, originally created for an artificial lake in the amusement park.

Once inside the grounds, spectators could wander

Crystal Palace during the 1911 Cup Final. Notice the ornate multi-span roofs. The crowd on the bottom right and those on the grass between the front and middle slopes at the far end could not see properly (BBC Hulton Picture Library)

about quite freely, and as William Pickford wrote in *A Few Recollections of Sport*, Crystal Palace: 'was more than a venue for a football match; it took on the character of a pic-nic. Long before the game happy parties sat in groups under the trees, munching sandwiches, and generations of football folk met there to renew acquaintances.' If this sounds idyllic, once the match started the reality was very different.

There were three stands at Crystal Palace, all on the North Side. Two multi-span stands with decorated gables crowned with flags stood on either side of a smaller, pitched roof construction. But the vast majority of spectators were crammed onto sloping grass banks, without any terracing or crush barriers, many of them 50 yards or more from the nearest touchline. Moreover, none of these slopes was particularly high, so that it is probable that when the first six-figure attendance was recorded for the Spurs v. Sheffield United final in 1901, up to a third had little or no view of the proceedings.

When it was wet, the slopes turned into 'slippery banks of mud', according to the angry *Athletics News*' correspondent, writing after the largest crowd ever to assemble for a football match in the world, 120 081, had struggled to see Villa v. Sunderland. 'It is not pleasant to think,' he wrote, 'that Glasgow has a far better arena for a great match than England, and that arena owned by an amateur club.'

The pitch also came in for criticism. Its rich turf suffered considerable drainage problems, not helped, suggested that same newspaper, 'by galloping horses over the turf'. This was a reference to the other events staged at the ground, among which were rugby internationals.

There is no doubt that the ground had a wonderful setting, especially with the Crystal Palace in the background, and a railway station only a hundred yards from the pitch. And attendances were consistently high – averaging 73 000 in 20 Finals.

Had the First World War not intervened it is possible the FA might have invested some money in the ground and turned it into a stadium approaching the standards of several League clubs. Otherwise we can only assume that the FA opted to use the ground because of its scale, because compared with the relative merits of Goodison and Villa Park, Crystal Palace was undoubtedly third rate.

When hostilities broke out, the ground was quickly taken over as a War Service Depot, and consequently the 1914 Final between Burnley and Liverpool, which was the first to be watched by the King, George V, was also the last at the ground.

After the War it was used by the amateur Corinthians until the Crystal Palace itself was destroyed by a fire in 1936 and the land went into decline.

For a while it was used to stage motor-racing, but in recent years it has become the National Recreation Centre. On the exact site of the football pitch is the magnificent Crystal Palace athletics stadium, with two superb cantilever stands plus additional facilities such as football on artificial turf and indoor sports.

All that is left of the Palace are crumbling foundations, but the rest of the site has new life, with enough of the old park retained to gain an impression of what it must have been like in those early days. It is well worth a visit.

Of the 20 Finals at Crystal Palace, five needed replays. The first, in 1901, was staged at Burnden Park – a disastrous decision which led to only 20 740 officially attending (see Bolton); the second, a year later was replayed at Crystal Palace. The 1910 replay took place at Goodison Park, the 1911 replay at Old Trafford and the 1912 replay at Bramall Lane. After these three in a row, the FA belatedly decided to introduce extra-time into the Final (incredibly extra-time for semi-finals was not allowed until 1981).

1915–22

The only official war-time Cup Final ever played was at Old Trafford in 1915, known as the Khaki Final. After the War, when it became known that Crystal Palace was still not available, the FA switched the game to Stamford Bridge, the obvious choice in London (though Arsenal would not have agreed).

Chelsea, or rather the Mears brothers, had always hoped their ground would become a Final venue, and for three years their dream came true. But in 1921 the FA decided to sign a contract committing them to the new stadium at Wembley.

Had Wembley not been built, might Chelsea have kept the Final? It is impossible to say. Charlton had a much bigger stadium which with proper investment might also have been a contender. Highbury and White Hart Lane were also improving rapidly. But the FA had never been keen on using the ground of one of the Cup entrants, and having suffered the inadequacies of Crystal Palace for 20 years, Wembley was too tempting a prospect.

Wembley

Compared with other modern stadiums around the world, Wembley Stadium is uncomfortable, unsuitable and outdated, yet it remains the mecca of English soccer and the envy of the world. Wembley is an English institution. But it is not, as is sometimes believed, the property of the nation nor even of the FA.

Wembley Stadium Limited owns the stadium and the surrounding complex, and soccer is just one of several sporting activities played there, under contract. If the stadium had to depend on football, rugby or hockey, it would go bankrupt tomorrow. Its most regular income is from twice weekly greyhound meetings, attended on average by 1200 to 1500 people. A further 100000 pass through its doors every year for the guided tours.

The neighbouring indoor 8000-seater Wembley Arena, or Empire Pool was opened in 1934, and is in more frequent use for tennis, table-tennis, skating, horse-shows, five-a-side soccer, ice-hockey, badminton, boxing, basketball, rock concerts and so on. There is also a large new conference centre, with a 2700-seater auditorium, opened in 1977, a hotel and a squash centre. Cup Finals therefore play only a small part in the annual events at Wembley. But they are still the most cherished tradition.

The site of the stadium was parkland, in an outer reach of London only connected by the Metropolitan Railway in 1901, when the area's population was recorded as 4519. Where the pitch now lies stood a monument to failure, known as 'Watkin's Folly'. This was the base of a tower which Sir Edward Watkin had intended to reach a height of 1150 feet and therefore dominate the skyline as dramatically as its model, the Eiffel Tower in Paris. But the tower reached a height of only 200 feet before being abandoned, the foundations having proved unstable, despite an infilling of molten lead and concrete.

After several years of inaction, the tower was finally removed in 1908, leaving four large craters where its legs had stood.

Otherwise Wembley Park remained blissfully rural and unspoilt until 1920, when it was chosen as the site for the British Empire Exhibition, a project which promised to enhance the country's reputation and provide much needed jobs for returning soldiers. Although Lloyd George, King George V and the Prince of Wales each gave the project their support, there was little progress until 1921, when it was announced that the Exhibition's centre-piece would be a national sports stadium, a possible venue for the FA Cup Final itself. Mention of football changed everything. Suddenly the appeal fund was oversubscribed! Among many contributors to Wembley were the people of Glasgow, who sent £105000. From then until opening day, Wembley Park became the scene of a minor miracle. Certainly in engineering terms the stadium was the most advanced in Britain,

and the architects, John Simpson and Maxwell Ayrton claimed it to be the largest monumental building of reinforced concrete in the world.

The use of ferro-concrete was responsible for Wembley's swift construction in just 300 working days, from January 1922 to April 1923, at a cost of £750000. Each section was constructed on site (rather than prefabricated), and by placing V-shaped strips of wood inside the concrete the outer walls were given the effect of monumental masonry. This was quick and cheap, and very convincing from a distance. Even now it only begins to look impromptu close-up. A more dramatic effect was created by painting the exterior in brilliant white – whereas it is now a fading cream colour and shows all too many signs of cracking.

The focal point was the entrance, the now famous twin towers, 126 feet high. The twin-tower motif as a symbol of power and grandeur was nothing new; Leitch had used it at Hampden, borrowed in turn from countless castles and medieval cathedrals all over Europe. But the sheer bulk of each white tower, topped by domes and reinforced concrete flagpoles pronounced a new style, echoed throughout the Empire from London to New Delhi. Wembley was an expression of British confidence in a decade otherwise fraught with problems.

It was a very different stadium to the one we know today. Both ends were open, and the two stands covered only the seated sections, that is 25000 spectators. The terraces were timber steps with cinder infill on the lower tier, concrete on the upper, providing room for 91500 standing. In addition, there was provision for 10000 on bench seats in five rows around the perimeter – giving a total capacity of 126500.

The pitch was laid with turf cut the same day from the surrounding exhibition grounds (where work was carrying on at a much slower rate).

A last minute addition to the stadium was a 220-yard long sprint track, a common feature at US stadiums. In order to provide one at Wembley, and the only one in Britain, a 150-foot section of the terracing had to be cut away to allow the extra length for the straight track, in front of the North Stand. This cut-away, where the sprint would begin, still exists but is now used for access of maintenance vehicles.

Also at the western end of the stadium was the players' tunnel, directly opposite where it is now situated. It was just wide enough for the players to enter the pitch side by side.

The FA's president, Sir Charles Clegg, signed a 21-year contract with Wembley's owners, and it was no coincidence that the first event to be held at the stadium, and indeed at the exhibition grounds as a whole, was the fixture which had stirred so many people to invest in the stadium – the FA Cup Final.

It had been quite a risk for the FA, which signed the contract long before the stadium was completed and with no guarantee that attendances would justify the costs. At the three preceding Cup Finals at Stamford Bridge attendances had been 50 018, 72 805 (when a London team was involved) and 53 000. So no-one knew quite what to expect.

The stadium was completed only four days before the opening Final, and the most rigorous safety test the construction underwent was a battalion of infantrymen stamping in unison on the terraces, while workmen marked time!

But the stadium withstood a much sterner test on 28 April when Wembley was beseiged with over 200 000 people, eager to see not only West Ham v. Bolton, but also the King and this new wonder of the Empire. A few important lessons are worth noting. Firstly, the event proved that the Cup Final had the pulling-power to justify the use of Wembley, and that Wembley itself was a popular venue. Secondly, it was realized that from then on Finals should be all-ticket affairs. Although the official gate had been 126 047, an estimated 200 000 actually squeezed into the arena, with thousands more outside (two of whom tried to dig their way under a barrier). The FA had to return nearly £3000 to ticket holders who had not managed to gain admission (out of total receipts of £27 776) while many who had bought seat tickets were forced to stand.

It was a miracle no-one was hurt and that there was no violence despite the crush and the rival supporters who were thrown together. As one observer, Professor A. M. Low commented afterwards, 'It could only have happened in Britain'. (In fact he was not entirely right. Soccer violence was known in Britain, especially in the north east and Scotland, but the occasion, and the presence of the monarch has meant that Wembley has had an almost trouble-free reputation over the years.) Nevertheless as a result of that chaotic day a government inquiry was set up to investigate the phenomenon of large crowds (see Safety).

The Bolton v. West Ham match took place a year before the Empire Exhibition was opened on 23 April 1924. Eleven days earlier England played their first international at the stadium, before a very disappointing crowd of 37 250 (the previous year's game at Hampden attracted nearly twice that number). Three days after the Exhibition's opening, the second Wembley Cup Final took place, this time an all-ticket crowd of 91 965 watching Aston Villa v. Newcastle. The next six-figure crowd to watch a Cup Final was in 1950, when Arsenal played Liverpool. Since then every game except mid-week replays has drawn 100 000 crowds (Wembley has a capacity limit of 92 000 mid-week).

Once the Exhibition closed in October 1925, after 30 million people had visited it, the organizers wound up their company and the site was put up for auction, but no-one was interested. One reporter described Wembley as: 'A vast white elephant, a rotting sepulchre of hopes and the grave of fortunes.' Not even the

The site at Wembley in May 1922 when work began; the craters were the foundations of Watkin's Folly. Within a decade the surrounding area was built up (Aerofilms)

lowest price of £350 000 for the entire site was taken.

In the introduction to his history of Wembley, Neil Wilson describes the events which saved the stadium from a premature end. Jimmy White, a renowned speculator who was then close to bankruptcy, bought the site for £300 000 with a £30 000 down payment.

At the same time Arthur Elvin, who had returned from the War penniless and had bought eight kiosks at the Exhibition realized the potential scrap value of the decaying buildings and was appointed by White to sell them off.

The Palestine building became a Glasgow laundry, the West African building a furniture factory, and some cafes were rebuilt as Bournemouth's new grand-stand. After nine months Elvin had made enough to offer White £122 500 for the Stadium: £12 500 initially and the rest in annual instalments.

No-one else was interested in the investment and the Stadium was even in danger of demolition, when White committed suicide with his creditors pressing, leaving Elvin to face the Official Receiver alone. White's debt on the Stadium was still £270 000.

Wilson writes: 'Elvin was presented with an alternative – find the balance of the £122 500 he had offered White within a fortnight or lose his deposit. Quickly, he persuaded friends and friends of friends to back him, and at 6.30 on the evening of 17 August, 1927, he phoned the Receiver to clinch the deal. A minute later he was on the telephone again, to sell the Stadium to the syndicate he had gathered together for £150 000, a one-minute profit of £27 500.'

Elvin then made himself Managing Director of this new company, called the Wembley Stadium and Greyhound Racecourse Company Limited, and set about rejuvenating the stadium, while most of the surrounding buildings were cleared. The choice of greyhound racing proved to be the life-saver, for Wembley could not possibly survive on one Cup Final a year and one international every two years. It cost £100 000 to install the necessary facilities, but this was soon earned as 50 000 attended the first race meeting in December 1927. From then on, there were

View of Wembley Stadium, in its original form, uncovered at both ends (Sport & General)

always greyhound meetings after every Cup Final, starting at 8 o'clock.

The dogs were soon joined in 1929 by Rugby League, which although a northern preserve staged its annual Cup Final at Wembley thereafter (apart from 1932). Weekly speedway was also a great success, attracting crowds of up to 70 000 for some meetings, and in 1931 an average of over 19 000. It eventually died out in 1956, and after a failed comeback in the 1970s was dropped completely, although Wembley continued to host the World Championships every year until 1981.

The original pitch was replaced in the 1960s by turf from Solway Firth, Cumberland, but this soon deteriorated badly, mainly owing to poor drainage. The final straw was the use of the pitch for two Royal International Horse Shows, culminating in one manager describing it as 'a cabbage patch'. The present pitch was installed under the supervision of the Sports Turf Research Institute, Bingley, at a cost of £30 000 (see Pitches) and the turf comes from Ganton Golf Course, near Scarborough in Yorkshire. At one stage, however, it is suggested that Wembley offered to buy Doncaster Rovers' pitch, which was both large and in good trim. Rovers sensibly turned down the offer (see Doncaster).

There have been many structural changes to Wembley since 1923, beginning with the building of a 250-seater restaurant behind the Royal Box in 1938, designed by Sir Owen Williams, who was also the architect of the Empire Pool. This steel and glass construction was designed to be dismantled for Cup Finals, when extra seating space would be needed, and to have front windows on pulleys, to open up the restaurant in good weather. In fact once built it was never dismantled and the windows are now permanently in place.

After the War the stadium had a major facelift in order to stage the 1948 Olympics, for which the Stadium Company gave its services free and paid for such improvements as the building of the Olympic Way (now with a ramp), linking the stadium with Wembley Park Station. The present players' tunnel and dressing rooms were built. Above the tunnel was placed the Olympic torch. Bench seats were temporarily installed at both ends.

The entire operation, although a tremendous prestige boost for Wembley, ended in a loss of £200 000, and thereafter the Stadium Company's profits began to fall steadily, as greyhound racing and speedway lost popularity and entertainment tax milked off more each year.

In 1955 the now Sir Arthur Elvin sold a million shares in the company, mostly to Sir Bracewell Smith, then Chairman of Arsenal, and on 4 February 1957 at the age of 57, Elvin died aboard a cruise ship.

The 1950s saw one long-awaited advance at Wembley, the installation of floodlights in 1955 at a cost of £22 000. The first game was a representative game between London and Frankfurt in the European Fairs Cup in 1955, but the first time lights were used for a major match was at the end of England's match v. Spain on 30 November 1955. That England's national stadium should have waited so long was quite scandalous, but predictable in view of the FA's opinion (see Floodlights).

After Elvin's death the new regime restored the stadium's finances and in 1960 the firm which ran London's weekend commercial television, Associated Rediffusion Limited, bought up most of the stadium company's share capital. The stadium became part of the British Electric Traction Company group, and has therefore always been in private hands. Most other countries have state- or municipal-owned national stadiums.

The new owners were responsible for Wembley's most significant facelift, in 1963, when £500 000 was spent completely reroofing the stands and covering both ends for the first time. A major innovation was the use of translucent fibre-glass panels on the inner 36 feet of roofing, giving Wembley that greenhouse feel so familiar now. This gave cover for all 100 000 spectators, of which 44 000 were now seated.

Also at this time the 300-feet long suspended press box and television gantries were built, and Wembley staged its first ever all-floodlit international, England beating Northern Ireland 8-3 on 20 November 1963. Since then the floodlights have been replaced, in 1973, by metal halide lamps with seven times more power than the original ones, at a further cost of £53 000.

Wembley was by this time known not only for its Cup Finals, both FA and Amateur (since 1949) but also for European Competition Finals. It staged the European Cup in 1963, 1968 (when Manchester United won) and 1971, and the European Cup Winners Cup Final in 1965 (when West Ham won). The height of its international renown came in 1966 with the staging of the World Cup. Wembley is obviously a favourite home for English teams, since none have lost important finals here.

Apart from these important matches, unlike most

national stadiums Wembley is not used regularly for football. In the early years there was a plan to base an amateur team at the stadium, called the Argonauts, to play in the League as the Queen's Park of England. But the experience of League matches played at Wembley in 1930 suggested it would not be a suitable venue. Clapton Orient played two Third Division games here when their own ground was out of commission, but the low gates and lack of atmosphere did not augur well (see Orient). One amateur game that did take place at Wembley in those days was between Ipswich Town and the Ealing Association, on 13 October 1928. The Southern Amateur League fixture was scheduled for the nearby ground at Corfton Road, but when the pitch was passed unfit the game was switched to Wembley.

The last 21-year contract between Wembley Stadium and the FA expired in 1982. This stated that for every FA match – internationals, FA Cup Finals, Charity Shield, FA Challenge Trophy and FA Challenge Vase – the gate money was divided into 25 per cent to Wembley and 75 per cent to the FA. The Football League has a separate contract for the Milk Cup Finals, which expires in 1988.

Until recently neither body has contributed towards the upkeep of the stadium (apart from the gate money), but a £5 million redevelopment scheme for Wembley's facilities is planned, with help from the FA. In this way the two organizations' interests will be more closely bound, and it is increasingly unlikely therefore, as suggested in the section on International Venues, that more representative games will thereafter be played at alternative venues. For better or worse, Wembley will remain the national home of soccer.

Ground Description

The traditional approach to Wembley Stadium is along the famous Olympic Way from Wembley Park underground station, through the grounds of what was the Exhibition site in 1924. Where the car-park is now situated were massive pavilions – Australia's to the right, Canada's to the left. The rest of the site is now an apparently random collection of buildings: hotels, the Empire Pool, the Conference Centre, squash centre, light industrial units and disused structures.

At the end of the Olympic Way, appropriately, are two plaques commemorating the Olympic Champions of 1948, on either side of the enormous arched blue doorway which serves as the Royal entrance. It looks more like the entrance to one of Her Majesty's Prisons.

Above the door is another plaque, to commemorate the 1966 World Cup, or as the memorial puts it, The World Football Championship. Above this, on the parapet, is a bust of Sir Arthur Elvin. It is said that the ghost of Sir Arthur still haunts the stadium. On the balcony behind the parapet stands the original Olympic torch from 1948. From here one can see how time has ravaged the concrete facings of Wembley, where the surface is cracked and the twin towers beset by mildew. Restoration work is thankfully in progress. The balcony also offers an excellent view of north and west London.

For those who have seen Wembley previously only on television, inside the stadium seems curiously different – smaller, more enclosed, and yet the pitch further away than one might imagine.

Now that the company operates tours one can see Wembley in all its intimate details, from the graffiti-ridden balcony in the Royal Box (covered for matches), where the VIP seats are aged wicker armchairs which you would hesitate to buy from a second-hand shop, to the players' enormous baths and toilets. Yet the dressing rooms are tiny by First Division standards.

Like every large building, Wembley revels in statistics: 40 miles of terracing, 14 miles of concrete beams, half a million rivets and so on, but a few facts are worth noting. Somewhere under the pitch, for example, is a train, buried during the construction of the stadium. The lift shaft of Watkin's Folly is believed to be 60 feet under the Royal entrance.

Under the box, above where the managers sit, side by side during games, is a leaded gable window, behind which is the Royal retiring room. From the Royal Box, the tunnel is to the left, below the electric scoreboard. Directly opposite this, to the right, is the much smaller, original tunnel. Offices now occupy the area where the dressing rooms once stood. Also on the right is the cut-away section built for the 220-yard sprint.

Underneath the stands, in the corridors and gangways, one really appreciates how old and outdated is Wembley Stadium; yet the stadium still retains an irresistible aura which hopefully will only be enhanced by a £5 million redevelopment scheme.

Although it is hard to imagine a Cup Final being played anywhere else, the FA might easily have built its own tailor-made stadium not far away at, for example, outside Watford at Ricketts Wood. A 100-acre site was offered to them in the 1970s for possible sharing with Watford FC, where a soccer school and England's training facilities could have been added. Many administrators within football believe that the decision to stay at Wembley was a great mistake, and that English football suffers as a result. The idea of a new Stadium was turned down, mainly for financial reasons – projected running costs were estimated at £200 000 annually – yet the FA pays high rates at Lancaster Gate and has invested higher sums at Lilleshall and in the building of better rail links with Wembley. Having paid the Chancellor something in the order of £230 000 in taxes after the World Cup in 1966, it might seem that a golden opportunity had been lost. The owners of Wembley Stadium would doubtless disagree, as would thousands of other football lovers, to whom Wembley is still mecca; the ultimate goal.

International Venues

England

Nowadays, we are so accustomed to Wembley as the home of English international football that it is hard to imagine England playing anywhere else. Yet Wembley assumed this monopoly only in 1951, and in the years between the stadium's completion and the Second World War, of 33 full England home games, 7 only were staged at Wembley. Even the much humbler homes of clubs like Burnley, Middlesbrough and West Bromwich were chosen in preference to Wembley during this period.

English international football officially started in London at the Kennington Oval, a year after the ground had staged the first final of the English Cup (see preceding section). The first game was of course v. Scotland, on 8 March 1873.

The Oval hosted England's first five home games, until in February 1881 the FA decided to broaden its horizons by playing its second game v. Wales at the home of Blackburn Rovers, at Alexandra Meadows, then headquarters also of the East Lancashire Cricket Club. This was partly because Blackburn was closer to the borders, but mainly because in those early days a match v. Wales was very much regarded as a trial, a second-class affair designed to help choose the side to play in the real battle, against Scotland.

Slower travel also meant that games against Ireland, similarly treated as trials, had to be at grounds nearer the west coast. The first game was played at Aigburth Park Cricket Ground, Liverpool, in February 1883. Three weeks later England played at another cricket ground, Bramall Lane, when they met Scotland on 10 March 1883.

For the next home fixture v. Ireland another venue was tried, Whalley Range, South Manchester, close to where Maine Road now stands and a mile from Fallowfield, scene of the 1893 Cup Final.

Bramall Lane staged the next home match v. Ireland in 1887, and two years later the fixture moved to Anfield, then home of Everton. This was the only time Anfield staged a full England international.

Six weeks after this, the Oval saw its last England game, a home defeat by Scotland on 13 April 1889, and London had to wait another four years before seeing another soccer international.

In March 1891, England travelled to Sunderland's Newcastle Road ground and to Wolverhampton's new ground, Molineux, for internationals v. Wales and Ireland, and as had happened once before (on 15 March 1890) two England teams turned out on the same day, beating the Welsh 4-1 at Sunderland and the Irish 6-1 at Wolverhampton on 7 March. A month later at newly-opened Ewood Park, England beat Scotland 2-1. The opening of a new ground was often celebrated by the staging there of an international.

The problem of finding a London venue was not solved until 1897. Having been told only a short time before that Surrey CCC did not want soccer played at the Oval, England played their next home match in April 1893 v. Scotland at Richmond Park, the home of a rugby club and the only ground they could find at short notice. But the Scots, despite the relative scale of the First Hampden and the newly-opened Ibrox Park, thought that other than Richmond: 'they had never played in such spacious and handsome surroundings'. Richmond also staged the 1894 Amateur Cup Final, but never hosted England again, despite the Scots' recommendation.

The next home game in London was at the Queen's Club, Kensington, then used by the famous amateur club, Corinthians. England met Wales there on 18 March 1895 (Corinthians were asked to select the team), but it was obvious that the best available grounds still existed beyond the metropolis, and a month later the game v. Scotland was held at Everton's new ground, Goodison Park.

For the return to London two years later, England found a new and proud home for internationals, Crystal Palace, the Cup Final venue (see previous section) and the largest stadium outside Glasgow.

But promising though the new venue seemed, in fact it only staged four internationals (the Oval held ten), all against Scotland, between 1897 and 1909. The 1899 Scotland match was held at the recently-opened Villa Park, as was the 1902 match, and Bramall Lane and St James' Park took the 1903 and 1907 matches respectively. Large though Crystal Palace was, it was pitifully short of proper spectator facilities, and hardly surprisingly the FA switched its London internationals elsewhere.

Its choice of venue for the Wales match in 1911 must have been controversial however, for it was The Den, the new home of Southern League Millwall Athletic. Stamford Bridge was the next London venue, in April 1913 v. Scotland. Indeed Chelsea's ground seemed the natural successor to Crystal Palace for both Cup Finals and internationals, because not only was it large, it was also convenient for the West End and the FA's headquarters in Russell Square.

Until the First World War, England played at several other venues around the country, not mentioned above; v. Ireland at Roker Park in 1899, six months after the ground was opened, Aston Villa's Perry Barr Ground (February 1893); Derby's Racecourse Ground (February 1895); Trent Bridge (February 1897); The Dell (March 1901), while Southampton were still in the Southern League but had the best ground south of Birmingham; Ayresome Park (February 1905, soon after the opening and again in February 1914); the Baseball Ground, Derby (February 1911); and perhaps most surprising of all to the present generation, Bradford City's Valley Parade, one of the finest grounds in the north, where England beat Ireland 4-0 on 13 February 1909.

Venues for matches against Wales, apart from those already mentioned, were Stoke's Victoria

Ground, used in 1889 and 1893; Ashton Gate, home of Bedminster (March 1899); Bristol City (March 1913); Fratton Park (March 1899); Craven Cottage (March 1907); and the City Ground (March 1909). Crewe is often referred to as staging an England v. Wales match in February 1888, but this was in fact a home fixture for the Welsh.

Altogether therefore, between 1872–1914, England played 56 home games, at a total of 31 venues in 17 different cities and towns. Only 19 of these games (34 per cent of the total) were held in London, and only 19 of the grounds are surviving League venues. In addition, none of these home games was against foreign opponents. All England's matches with continental teams had been abroad.

Between 1920–51 London started to attract a much higher proportion of England's games. Wembley was built in 1923, and substantial redevelopment at Highbury and White Hart Lane provided two more possible venues to rival the provincial grounds. Of 55 England home games played between the First World War and April 1951, a total of 21 different venues were used, and 26 games were played in London (47 per cent). Gradually the provinces were losing their hold.

The first post-war international in England was played at London's newest ground, Highbury, which was even closer to the FA headquarters and had excellent travel links with the rest of the city (although the FA chose Stamford Bridge as the successor to Crystal Palace as venue for Cup Finals).

In the 1920–51 period Highbury staged ten England games, more than any other ground, including Wembley which staged nine. The first was v. Wales on 15 March 1920, but one of the most significant was on 19 March 1923, when England played Belgium, the first continental national team to play a full international on English soil. From then on, Highbury staged internationals against foreign opposition only, and indeed it was rare for any provincial ground to hold such matches at all.

The Hawthorns staged England v. Belgium in December 1924; St James' Park staged England v. Norway in November 1938 (because Newcastle is much nearer to Norway than London); and Leeds Road staged England v. Holland in November 1946. All other games against continental teams were played in London; at Highbury (nine matches, including one v. FIFA in 1938); at White Hart Lane (four matches) and at Stamford Bridge (one match). Wembley's nine matches in this period were all v. Scotland.

Home Internationals were staged at several new venues. Hillsborough was first used in March 1920 v. Scotland, The Hawthorns v. Northern Ireland in October 1922, and to celebrate its opening, Selhurst Park, v. Wales in March 1926. Burnley and Blackpool were awarded matches v. Northern Ireland in 1927 and 1932 respectively. Old Trafford entered the scene in April 1926 with a match v. Scotland (the last time a ground other than Wembley was used for this fixture). Neighbouring Maine Road was used twice after the War while repairs were being effected at Old Trafford, at a time when Manchester City's ground was the largest club ground in England, for matches v. Wales in 1946 and Northern Ireland in 1949.

After Wembley's match v. Scotland in April 1951 however, the Empire Stadium began its tenacious hold on the England team. It already had the FA Cup Final firmly under its belt (since 1923), the Scotland match (since 1928) and had recently become the venue of the Amateur Cup Finals (in 1949), so with attendances at a peak level it was inevitable that Wembley should now assume the role of England's home ground.

Of the 58 home games played between April 1951 and May 1966 (just before the World Cup) only nine were staged at grounds other than Wembley (15·5 per cent). These have been at Goodison Park v. Portugal (1951), v. Northern Ireland (1953) and Poland (January 1966); at Highbury v. France (1951) and Luxembourg (1961); at Villa Park v. Northern Ireland (1951) and Wales (1958); at Molineux v. Denmark (a World Cup qualifier in 1956) and Hillsborough v. France (1962). Curiously Wembley did not stage an England game v. foreign opposition until the May 1951 match v. Argentina.

Since the World Cup, England have only played one full international on an English ground other than Wembley, and that was at Goodison Park in May 1973 when the away game v. Northern Ireland was switched because of the unstable situation in Belfast. England is therefore now synonymous with Wembley.

Before 1966 the England team had played at a total of 40 different venues apart from Wembley, in 20 different cities and towns. Every League ground's pitch conforms with the minimum international requirements (see Pitches) and many have sufficient facilities to play host to foreign opposition in terms of spectator, media and executive requirements.

Furthermore, in recent years attendances for several Wembley internationals have not justified the use of such a large stadium. Indeed it could be argued very strongly that a capacity crowd at Villa Park or Old Trafford would provide a better atmosphere for the England team than a half-filled Wembley. It would be wrong to suggest that other grounds could or should host a large proportion of the games, because the organizational problems would be immense. But occasionally the FA should go elsewhere, for the mutual benefit of the team, the clubs and also the spectators, most of whom can never afford to see an England game in person. Provincial grounds should be given back their right to play host to the national team, but as long as London dominates and the FA invests in Wembley, there is little hope.

Scotland

Glasgow's hold on the Scottish international scene is of longer standing than London's is on England, for the simple reason that it has always had the biggest stadiums and crowd potential. Furthermore, since Scotland is a much smaller country, with the bulk of League clubs dotted around Glasgow within a 60-mile radius, Glasgow is a natural focus for international games.

The first international, Scotland v. England on 30 November 1872, was also the first recorded international in the world, and like the follow-on game in England 14 weeks later was played on a cricket ground. This was and still is the home of the West of Scotland Cricket Club on Hamilton Crescent, in the Partick district of Glasgow. It can be seen on Fortrose and Peel Streets. The attendance was 3500 compared with 2500 at the Oval game.

After four games at Hamilton Crescent, Scotland switched to Queen's Park ground, since known as the First Hampden Park, for their next six home games. The first was v. England on 2 March 1878. For a short period Queen's Park were based at Titwood Park, so Scotland played their two games v. England and Wales in 1884 at Third Lanark's First Cathkin Park, before following Queen's Park to their new ground, Second Hampden for the match v. England on 15 March 1884. (The ground is often referred to as New Cathkin Park, the name it assumed when Third Lanark took it over from Queen's Park.)

In March 1888 Scotland played Wales in their first home game outside Glasgow, at Hibernian's first Easter Road ground, the only time the club's ground has been used. Almost exactly a year later on 9 March 1889 Scotland met Ireland at the new home of Rangers, Ibrox Park. The game v. Wales a year later was played at Underwood Park, the home of Abercorn in Paisley.

Second Hampden's last international was v. England on 5 April 1890 watched by a record crowd for a Scotland home game of 26 379, and between then and the opening of the Third Hampden in 1903 Scotland shared its favours among several different venues.

First came Celtic's ground (not the present Parkhead), v. Ireland on 28 March 1891. The following year's game v. Wales went to Tynecastle Park, the home of Hearts, while Ibrox staged the England game a week later on 2 April 1892.

Celtic's new ground, opened in 1892, then became a regular venue, beginning in March 1893 with the game v. Ireland.

Other grounds used as venues for games v. Wales were Rugby Park, Kilmarnock (1894 and 1910); Carolina Port, Dundee (1896); Fir Park, Motherwell, shortly after its opening (1896); Pittodrie, Aberdeen, also soon after its opening (1900); Cappielow Park, Morton (1902); and Dens Park, the new home of Dundee (1904).

Between 1872 and March 1906 therefore, Scotland played 43 games (excluding the April 1902 fixture v. England at Ibrox, declared unofficial after the disaster (see Safety)) of which ten were held outside Glasgow (23 per cent of the total). Altogether 16 different

venues were used, 9 of which survive as League grounds today.

The Third Hampden was opened in 1903, but did not stage its first international until 7 April 1906, v. England, in front of the highest crowd ever recorded for an international, 102 741. Therefore the new Hampden's potential was proven immediately. Although Hampden Park has staged every Scotland and England match since 1906, it was not until after the Second World War that it established an almost total monopoly on all Scottish internationals.

Between 1906–39 Scotland played 46 home games. Of these 17 were at Hampden, of which all but two were against England. Surprisingly Scotland did not play against any continental opposition at home until Austria's visit to Hampden in November 1933. Of the 46 home games, 12 were played at grounds outside Glasgow (26 per cent of the total). The grounds used apart from Hampden were Parkhead: eight times; Ibrox: eight times; Tynecastle: five times; Dens Park and Pittodrie twice. Rugby Park (1910), St Mirren Park (1923) and Firhill Park (1928), each staged one international during the period 1906–39.

After the Second World War Hampden took over. Indeed since 1946 only two Scottish international home games have been played elsewhere – an unofficial game v. South Africa at Ibrox in 1956, and a European Championship match v. Belgium at Pittodrie on 10 November 1971.

Attendances had boomed so considerably that Hampden became the natural choice. For example, before 1946 the highest crowd ever to have watched a Scotland v. Wales match was 55 000 at Ibrox in 1928. The first post-war match at Hampden attracted 86 582. Similarly the highest for a Scotland v. Northern Ireland match before 1946 had been 54 728 at Firhill Park, also in 1928. The first post-war match Hampden drew 97 326.

Since then attendances have dropped steadily, even for games v. England, and there is now a case for using other grounds, such as Ibrox or Pittodrie, for games against Wales, Ireland and lesser continental sides. This however is unlikely to happen, because too much money has gone into rejuvenating Hampden in recent years and the income from international matches is crucial to their rebuilding programme (see Hampden Park).

Wales

The situation in Wales has greater parity than either Scotland or England, with Welsh international matches being spread regularly between the two main centres, Cardiff and Wrexham, with occasional games held at Swansea.

The first Welsh home game was at Acton Park, Wrexham on 5 March 1877 v. Scotland, attended by 4000 spectators. As the headquarters of the Welsh FA, Wrexham was the main venue until Cardiff began to enter the scene in 1896. The only home games not played at Wrexham before this date were those in February 1888; at Nantwich Road, Crewe, in February 1890, at the Old Racecourse Ground, Shrewsbury; in February 1892, at Penrhyn Park, Bangor; and in February 1894, at the St Helen's Rugby Ground, Swansea.

The first games in Cardiff were also staged at a rugby ground, at Cardiff Arms Park, where Wales played six soccer internationals until Ninian Park was opened in 1910.

While Cardiff Arms Park and Wrexham shared the England and Scotland games, between 1896 and 1910, the Ireland fixture was still moved about. In 1898 and 1900 it was played at Llandudno, in 1904 at Bangor, and in 1908 at the Athletic Ground, Ynis, home then of Aberdare Athletic.

Also at this time the Wrexham venue was changed, from Acton Park to the present Racecourse Ground, from about 1905 onwards (see Wrexham).

The first international at Ninian Park was on 6 March 1911 v. Scotland, attended by 14000. The Vetch Field staged its first international on 9 April 1921 v. Ireland, and since then with only one exception, Cardiff, Wrexham and Swansea have been the venues of all Welsh international home games. Between 1911 and October 1981 the approximate proportion of games at each venue has been: Cardiff 60 per cent, Wrexham 32 per cent and Swansea 8 per cent.

But within that period there were variations. For example, between 1911 and 1950 the proportion was respectively 48:46:6.

Between 1951–81 the ratio was 67:24:9, showing the tendency to concentrate more games in Cardiff. There is still tremendous rivalry between Wrexham, as the Welsh FA headquarters, and Cardiff, as the capital. Between 1956–72 Wrexham staged only four internationals and seemed beyond contention, but once the Safety of Sports Grounds Act temporarily ruled out Ninian Park, while the Racecourse Ground was almost completely transformed, Wrexham began to re-establish its claim to international games.

The one match not played at any of these grounds was on 12 October 1977 when Cardiff's ground was limited to only 10000 capacity, so the Welsh FA switched the World Cup qualifying game v. Scotland to Anfield.

· 21 ·
LOST BUT NOT FORGOTTEN

All who frequent local football clubs can imagine how chilling it must be to see the ground they love reduced to nothing. This chapter records a few such grounds.

We start this unhappy tour at the site of Peel Park, once home of Accrington Stanley. Accrington FC were founder members of the Football League in 1888 and played at the Accrington Cricket Club grounds, which still exist. But the Old Reds dropped out of the League in 1893, unable to pay their bills, and finally disbanded in 1896. At about the same time an amateur side named Stanley Villa (whose players lived around Stanley Street) achieved prominence, and in 1919 bought the site of Peel Park for £2500. Stanley joined the League in August 1921, and that year a crowd of over 20000 was said to have watched a Lancashire Junior Cup Final at the ground.

Peel Park's official record gate was 17634 v. Blackburn Rovers in a friendly (Blackburn is only five miles away). But undoubtedly one of the proudest moments was on 13 October 1955 when BBC cameras, Kenneth Wolstenholme and all, televised a Third Division North v. South match under Stanley's new floodlights. Peel Park had floodlights and was on television before most current First Division grounds.

The ground was notorious for its sloping, narrow pitch, and also had cramped dressing rooms with only a thin partition between so that team talks were often overheard.

The last League match at Peel Park was on 24 February 1962 v. Rochdale, after which Stanley dropped out, £60000 in debt. Low gates were one reason, but the club's refusal to accept the setting up of a

Peel Park, Accrington. Nothing remains except a hump and a wall (Aerofilms)

The Dolls House crumbles at Park Avenue. Only the terracing remains (Martin Parr)

supporters' club was more ruinous.

Peel Park soon declined, and despite efforts to restore the ground it eventually reverted to a bare field. Hardly a trace remains today. There is a wall, the hump of the old terracing, now covered with grass, but otherwise no sign at all that the place was once alive with crowds of up to 20 000. One might easily walk past without realizing.

Next is Gateshead, just south of the River Tyne, in the shadows of St James' Park. The club originated in 1899 as South Shields Adelaide, played at Horsley Hill and joined the League in 1919. Their record attendance at this ground was 21 000 v. Luton, 29 January 1921. In 1930 the club moved about ten miles west to Gateshead. (Horsley Hill Road is now a housing estate.) Their new ground was Redheugh Park, an elliptically-shaped ground also used for greyhound racing. It had cover on three sides and a record gate of 20 752 v. Lincoln, 25 September 1937. When the team finished third from bottom in 1960, they had to apply for re-election for the first time since 1937 but surprisingly were not re-elected, and Peterborough United took their place. Theirs was probably the most unjustified dismissal in League history.

Redheugh Park went down with the team, and now all that remains is a flat expanse of grass overlooked by some tower blocks. You would be hard pressed to make out any signs of the former ground, apart from a slight bump or two. (Gateshead FC, reformed in 1977, now play at one of the best grounds in the north east, the Gateshead International Athletics Stadium, which has a superb 7300-seat cantilever stand – a situation similar to that of Meadowbank in Edinburgh.)

Third on this doleful survey is perhaps the most depressing relic of all, Park Avenue, Bradford. By rights, Bradford should never have had two senior football clubs at all, being only half the size of Leeds and a rugby stronghold. But the success of Bradford City, formed in 1903, encouraged Bradford Rugby FC to form a soccer team on the pitch next to Park

Avenue, Bradford's major cricket ground, in 1907. The new club was so keen it spent its first season in the Southern League, before joining the Football League in 1908. In 1913 Park Avenue reached the First Division for a three-season spell, before slipping into Division Three in 1922. Their best spell came in the early 1930s, when as a very solid Second Division club they recorded their highest gate of 34 429 for a match v. Leeds. Even in the 1950s they were often higher placed than Bradford City, and there can be little doubt that Park Avenue was a better ground than Valley Parade. It had cover for 14 000.

But in 1970 Park Avenue failed in their fifth bid for re-election and dropped down into the Northern Premier League (Cambridge took their place). Amalgamation with City would have been the logical outcome, with the new club moving to Park Avenue, but instead beleaguered Park Avenue spent one last dying season sharing Valley Parade with City, before calling it a day in 1974.

Nowadays Park Avenue is as poignant a sight as football can offer. It is in the Little Horton suburb of Bradford, next to Horton Park and a run-down post-war housing estate. The Bradford CC cricket ground still exists and is in reasonable condition (Yorkshire play there occasionally), but Park Avenue's ground is a ruin. The three stands have all gone. One of them, the main stand, was a quite remarkable structure with three pedimented gables and a small corner pavilion at the end, known as the Doll's House. At the back of the stand was a small balcony overlooking the cricket pitch. There was a clock in the centre which adventurous batsmen used to aim for, often overpowering their shots and sending the ball onto the football pitch.

Still visible are the perimeter walls, a very bumpy and neglected pitch, and three sides of crumbling, overgrown terraces. The floodlight pylon bases also survive, as do a few old turnstiles, overwhelmed by trees, bushes and scrap.

Standing on the forlorn concrete steps one can easily reconstruct the picture of Park Avenue at its best, for unlike Peel Park and Redheugh Park the basic shape and form still exists. But there is a ghostly presence, almost as if the departed stands still cast a cold shadow over the pitch and warn one not to tread on too many memories. No doubt it will be soon built over or landscaped.

These three grounds had the longest history of all the defunct grounds once host to League football. The following are, in alphabetical order, the clubs who have also played in the Football League, with whatever details of their grounds are available. Notice that of the 26 individual clubs who have dropped out of the League (this list does not include clubs whose grounds were taken over by later League clubs, such as Wigan Borough and Leeds City), all but one were either northern or Welsh.

Aberdare Athletic played at the Athletic Ground, Ynis. Record attendance 16 350 v. Bristol City, 2

April 1923. League members 1921–27 (replaced by Torquay).

Ashington played at Portland Park, still used by present club of same name. Record attendance 11 837 v. Aston Villa, 12 January 1924. League members 1912–29 (replaced by York).

Barrow played and still play at Holker Street. Record attendance 16 874 v. Swansea Town, 9 January 1954. League members 1921–74 (replaced by Hereford).

Bootle played at Hawthorne Road, Liverpool and were the first League club to resign membership, after only one season – 1892–93.

Burton Swifts played at Peel Croft. League members 1892–1901.

Burton Wanderers played at Derby Turn. League members 1894–97. In 1901 **Swifts** and Wanderers amalgamated to form **Burton United**, playing at Peel Croft, now the home of Burton RFC. League members 1901–07. (The present Burton Albion are no relation.)

Darwen played at Barley Bank, League members 1891–99. Soon after dropping out, the ground was built over. The Club now play at the Anchor Ground.

Durham City played at Holiday Park near Frankland Lane, also used as a greyhound stadium, until 1949. It is now built over. League members 1921–28. (Replaced by Carlisle.)

Gainsborough Trinity played and still play at The Northolme. Record attendance 9760 v. Scunthorpe 1948. League members 1892–1912.

Glossop North End (Glossop after 1903) played at North Road. League members 1898–1919. Glossop is the smallest town (25 000 inhabitants) ever to have supported First Division team, for one season 1899–1900.

Loughborough Town played at the Athletic Grounds (were called Loughborough Athletic, but did not change ground name). League members 1895–1900.

Merthyr Town played and still play at Penydarren Park (now as Merthyr Tydfil). Record attendance 21 686 v. Millwall, 27 December 1921. League members 1920–30.

Middlesbrough Ironopolis played at the Paradise Ground. League members 1893–94 (see Middlesbrough).

Nelson played at the Seedhill Ground, now covered by a motorway. Record attendance 15 000 v. Bradford PA, 10 April 1926. League members 1921–31 (replaced by Chester).

New Brighton Tower played at the Tower Athletic Grounds, still visible as park. League members 1898–1901.

New Brighton played at Sandheys Park, off Rake Lane and the above named ground after the Second World War. Record attendance 15 173 v. Tranmere, 26 December 1924. League members 1923–51 (replaced by Workington).

Northwich Victoria played and still play at The Drillfield. League members 1892–94.

Southport played and still play at Haig Avenue. Record attendance 20 010 v. Newcastle, 26 January 1932. League members 1921–78 (replaced by Wigan Athletic).

Stalybridge Celtic played and still play at Bower Fold. Record attendance 9753 v. WBA, 17 January 1923. League members 1921–23.

Thames played at the West Ham Greyhound Stadium, which stood on Prince Regent Lane before being built over. Their record low attendance of 469 v. Luton in 1930 is believed to be the lowest for any scheduled Saturday afternoon League fixture. League members 1930–32 (replaced by Newport).

Workington played and still play at Borough Park. Record attendance 21 000 v. Manchester United, 4 January 1958. League members 1950–77 (replaced by Wimbledon).

Finally, there is one other ground used for League football which deserves a mention: **White City**.

White City was built for the 1908 London Olympic Games, and earned its name because it was the centrepiece of the massive Franco-British exhibition, housed in predominantly white buildings. It was in design a forerunner of Wembley, holding 70 000 spectators, and even had the Olympic swimming pool in the centre.

After the Games it lay unused, until the arrival of greyhound racing in 1927, the sport which has kept it in business ever since.

It was used twice by QPR, whose Loftus Road ground is a few hundred yards away, in 1931–33 and 1962–63 (see QPR), by Pegasus for one season and for sundry representative games and a few fixtures of Corinthians.

It has been used also for speedway, cycling, athletics, rugby, boxing, show-jumping, rodeos, prayer meetings and baseball. Up to 1958, a total of 44 world records had been broken at White City. In 1937 it had the world's biggest Tote.

The most important football match to be held there was in July 1966, when because Wembley was holding a greyhound meeting, France played Uruguay in a World Cup Finals match. Ironically, it could have once staged a World Club Championship, in 1930, but the FA vetoed the plan which Brigadier-General Critchley MP had drawn up.

The stadium is now used regularly only for greyhounds, and has hardly changed since the late 1920s. It resembles a smaller version of Wembley as it was before 1963, and must surely be the largest, yet least attended and most old fashioned stadium in the country. The present safety limit is 35 000, but top gates are now around 20 000 for the annual greyhound derbies.

It could have remained London's top stadium, but since losing its athletics track in the 1960s has led a precarious life, and despite an incredible survival bid in the mid-1970s still does not have an assured future. So visit while you can.

APPENDICES

APPENDIX A

The 1946 Bolton Disaster

A brief summary of the events of 9 March 1946 at Burnden Park, as recorded in the report of R. Moelwyn Hughes KC, appointed by the Home Secretary, Chuter Ede. (Command Paper 6846.)

The disaster was unique in that no structure collapsed and was the first inflicted by a crowd on itself. The use of the East (Burnden) Stand by the Ministry of Food for storage had no bearing on the accident. The accident occurred in the Railway Enclosure, so called because it was formed on the embankment supporting the LMS main Yorkshire to Bolton line. There were 14 turnstiles, all on the West Side of the enclosure (including two for schoolboys and servicemen). The gaps between the barriers on the higher terraces in the north west corner were wider, because of the curvature, than on the lower terraces, and there was a barrier-less gangway leading from the fatal corner up to the top of the terrace, where the bottleneck occurred. Sufficient police were used. Railway policing prevented anyone from crossing the railway line to gain unlawful entry over fence at rear of enclosure.

The events were detailed as follows:

2.20 p.m. pressure builds up outside turnstiles.

2.30 p.m. some people in crush already trying to escape by moving away from turnstiles.

2.35 p.m. already impossible for those coming through the turnstiles to pass along the terraces. PC Lowe calls for turnstiles to be closed but cannot find Head Checker (who supervised the turnstiles). Some people want to leave ground because they cannot reach terraces.

2.40 p.m. Head Checker looks at the situation. Outside the Chief Inspector of Police cannot get through crowd and has to shout instructions. Inside the police are helping people out of north west corner onto the perimeter track. One man is seen trampled on the ground. Invasion begins over railway line fence and at eastern end of enclosure. Police reluctant to release extra men from East Stand, where they are guarding stockpiles of food. Turnstiles eventually shut, but more clamber over walls and force doors

open. These sealed again at 2.50 p.m.

A father and small son want to escape crush inside the ground near turnstiles. Father picks padlock of exit gate next to boys' entrance and they slip out. But open gate lets rush of people into ground.

More spectators pulled out at front, more seen trampled underfoot. Sergeant orders section of crowd to tear down wooden perimeter fence in order to relieve crush. Inspector and sergeant agree that exit doors should be opened to allow more to leave but cannot find keys or officials with keys.

2.50 p.m. most gates closed. Crowd outside begins to disperse, except around boys' entrance, where fence is torn down and approximately 1000 climb over.

The Railway Police cannot cope either. About 2000 to 3000 people on railway line but few can actually see over fence into ground, except when they perch on wagons of a goods train which pauses there for a short time, so most disperse.

A further 200 to 300 rush through gate by boys' entrance, most of them servicemen. Mounted police and two constables manage to seal this gate.

Still pressure increases in north west corner, despite more people passing onto perimeter track.

2.55 p.m. teams come out, crowd swaying. People at top of terrace find themselves forced down into bottom corner. By boys' entrance two barriers are bent. The weight carries down through the bottleneck where there is barrier-less gap. The two barriers nearest the corner flag collapse. Crowd seems to sink, but crush so great that nothing clearly visible. Two, three then four people pile up and are trodden underfoot. A large number are asphyxiated.

3.00 p.m. match begins as hundreds spill out onto track.

3.12 p.m. bodies brought out and referee informed that there have been fatalities. Players leave pitch, 33 bodies found and laid out on pitch before being taken to mortuaries. First aid given to 500. Hardly anyone not in the north west vicinity realizes seriousness of accident. Chief Constable and referee decide it would be advisable to restart match. East Stand opened for 1000 spectators. A further 1000 remain on track.

Seven of the 33 dead were from Bolton. The *Man-*

chester Evening News commented two days later that this kind of disaster was always likely to happen at one of the older grounds. On the fact that so many broke into the ground, many of them servicemen, it says, 'Possibly the war has left some people with less respect for law than they used to have'. Bolton's semi-final at Villa Park was all-ticket, with a capacity reduction from 80 000 to 70 000.

APPENDIX B

Admissions

Going to a football match is marginally less expensive, on average, that it was 25 years ago.

For example, the receipts for Stockport v. Liverpool (att. 27 833) in February 1950 were £4312, an average of 15½p per person. The receipts for Stockport v. Arsenal in 1980 (att. 11 635) were £19 382, an average of £1.56 per person.

In relation to the average weekly wage of a manual worker in 1950, admission costs were about 1 per cent of his gross income. The same applied in 1980. But if we take the average admission cost (15½p in 1950 and £1·56 in 1980), we can see that although the cost is ten times higher, average weekly wages during the same period increased approximately by a factor of 12·5. At the same time average retail prices rose eightfold. So average football admission prices fall exactly between the rise in prices and the rise in wages. In 1950 the average admission fee at Stockport represented 1·8 per cent of the average manual worker's wage. In 1980 it represented 1·6 per cent.

The gap between the cost of sitting and standing has been reduced quite dramatically. For example, in 1910 Manchester United charged 6d to stand and 5s for the best seat. In 1982 they charged £1·80 to stand and £3·80 for the best seat. In 1910 therefore the price ratio of standing/seating was 1:10. In 1982 it was 1:2.1. Comparatively it is now more expensive to stand, but much cheaper to sit (although one can argue that the best seats are now in the private boxes, which do not form part of this calculation).

Collecting gate money was, in the early days of football, a difficult business. Before turnstiles and properly enclosed grounds, the most common method was for clubs to pass a hat around. At Perry Barr, when turnstiles were introduced match takings rose from an average of £75 to £200. The gatemen were, of course, incensed when this became known, since it implied a measure of dishonesty. In June 1895 the Everton chairman and four directors resigned, 'owing to acute administrative difficulties', despite having announced a £6000 profit in the previous three years. The mystery, it is suggested, may well have been connected with a scandal involving gatemen. But the problem did stop when new turnstiles were installed.

Clubs also had a problem when announcing receipts, because no accurate attendance figures were known, the most publicised figures being a guess by a newspaper reporter, which, clubs often complained was far too high.

The League has always set a minimum price for admission, but there have been some attempts by clubs to reduce admission for the unemployed. An extreme example of this occurred in 1932 when up to 75 per cent of Merthyr's adult male population was unemployed, and gates were down to 500. In August 1932 the football club, who had lost League status in 1930, largely as a result of the Depression, reduced admission for the unemployed from 9d to 2d. Immediately gates rose to 4000. But the club were forced to stop the reduction when neighbouring clubs and the Welsh FA objected.

Entrance was free at half-time or during the second half at most grounds. Another way of gaining free admission was to help clear the pitch of snow.

In the early days free viewing was possible at several grounds. When Darwen played Blackburn Rovers, the hills surrounding the Barley Bank Ground were said to be 'black' with people watching. Similarly for Bolton's Cup Replay v. Notts County in 1884, 4000 to 5000 watched from the surrounding hills. One farmer charged spectators half the normal admission cost!

Women were allowed in free at most grounds until the mid-1880s. *The Daily Telegraph* noted in 1873 that: 'ladies always turned up in some numbers for matches at Bramall Lane'. At Deepdale on Easter Monday 1885, some 2000 women attended the game without paying, so the club dropped the concession thereafter. But this did not discourage them. In the reserve stand at Aston Villa it was said that there were 'almost as many ladies as men'. Even when free admission was dropped, women could still buy season tickets at half-price.

But as crowds grew and conditions became more cramped, fewer women attended. Aberdeen allowed women in free up till 1908, and in 1982 Meadowbank revived the practice, with great success.

The most remarkable example of free admission was in 1982 when the Kuwait FA allowed 40 000 spectators to watch a World Cup qualifying match, in gratitude for the fans' support at previous games.

APPENDIX C

Players' Views

This book has been written almost entirely from a spectator's point of view, so the following results of a questionnaire sent out to professionals in all four divisions convey some idea of players' views.

The questionnaire asked quite simply, what were players' favourite and least favourite grounds. In each case the players had to indicate which of six factors governed their decision and in what order of importance.

Of the 35 players who replied, most were playing in the Third and Fourth Divisions at the time of the survey, but the majority had some experience of the upper Divisions. In every case, the main interest lies not in the grounds they chose, but in their reasons for choosing them.

Favourite Grounds

This does not necessarily mean the best grounds.

The three categories given as the most important reason for their choice were:

(1) quality of the playing surface (16 players)
(2) a good atmosphere (11)
(3) dressing room and other players' facilities (5)

Three players based their choice on past experiences at particular grounds. The least important factors were the friendliness of 'away' fans and the design of the ground.

Anfield won eight players' votes as their favourite ground, mainly because of the atmosphere, the playing surface and the facilities. Five players chose Old Trafford because of its atmosphere. Highbury, White Hart Lane and Villa Park were also popular, but more for their pitches and facilities.

Least Favourite Grounds

The results of this part of the survey were most revealing, for although design played little part in the choice of favourite grounds, it was obviously quite important when players selected their least favourite ground. The most important factors were: poor facilities (13) and poor playing surface (12). Design was almost always the second or third reason given for disliking a ground, and the larger, more open grounds were all disliked.

Several players chose their least favourite ground because of bad experiences there, and nine considered a long journey to the ground an important factor.

Hartlepool was the least popular because of its facilities, while Northampton was disliked because of its pitch and the three-sided nature of the ground.

If any conclusions can be drawn from these comments it is that players like grounds for their atmosphere and good pitches, but dislike them for lack of facilities, poor playing surfaces and their design.

APPENDIX D

The 92 Club

This dedicated group of enthusiasts was set up in 1978 to recognize the achievements of those who have attended every Football League ground for a first team match. By 1982 it had approximately 180 full members, and 50 or so associate members (those who have visited 70 grounds but pledge to see the rest within two seasons).

The club's first Honorary Member was Alan Durban, who as a player for Cardiff, Derby and Swansea played at his 92nd ground in 1976. Alec Stock also visited them all, as manager of Orient, QPR, Luton, Fulham and Bournemouth.

Details of this elite group can be obtained from G. Pearce, 104 Gilda Crescent, Whitchurch, Bristol, BS14 9LD.

APPENDIX E

Names

I have endeavoured throughout this book to trace any links between names of grounds with their beginnings. Of the 92 Football League grounds 24 only are commonly referred to by the street or road name (16 roads, 2 streets, 5 lanes and 1 crescent).

There are also 24 grounds commonly using the suffix 'Park'. In Scotland all but four League grounds have names other than with this suffix. Of the 24 Parks in England, only two suggest the name of the club – Villa Park and Vale Park.

Three grounds have been named directly after an individual (in each case a benefactor): Dean Court, Ninian Park and Fellows Park. Thirty-one grounds without the suffix Park give no direct clue to their location or identity – such as The Dell, Hawthorns, Vetch Field, Gay Meadow or Molineux.

Seven grounds indicate their former use, three of them called the County Ground (Northampton, Swindon and Notts County, the latter known more familiarly as Meadow Lane). There are also two Recreation Grounds (Aldershot and Chesterfield). Other duplications are St James' Park (Newcastle and Exeter) and The Victoria Ground (Stoke and Hartlepool).

Eight grounds have tried to adopt the title 'Stadium' but with only two successes; Abbey Stadium (Cambridge) and Priestfield Stadium (Gillingham). Otherwise, Arsenal Stadium is more commonly referred to as Highbury, Leyton Stadium as Brisbane Road, Rangers' Stadium as Loftus Road (although officially South Africa Road), Bristol Stadium as Eastville, and the City Stadium as Filbert Street.

But the name most commonly found at British football grounds is 'The Spion Kop'. Spion Kop was a hill in South Africa, which British Army officers tried to capture in January 1900 during the Boer War. The bloody action cost 322 British lives and 563 wounded, plus 300 casualties on the victorious Boer side.

Reporters, among them Winston Churchill, described the 'astounding inefficiency' of the British artillery, calling Spion Kop that 'acre of massacre, that complete shambles'. Leading this futile assault on the hill were the 2nd Royal Lancaster Regiment and the 2nd Royal Lancashire Fusiliers.

Afterwards the mounds on which Lancashire men stood at their football grounds became known as Spion Kops in memory of the tragedy. The first recorded use of the name was at Anfield, in 1906, apparently on the suggestion of a journalist, Ernest Edwards.

GLOSSARY

There is no formal glossary of terms used for describing
football ground architecture, but the following simplified
terms refer to the main structures.

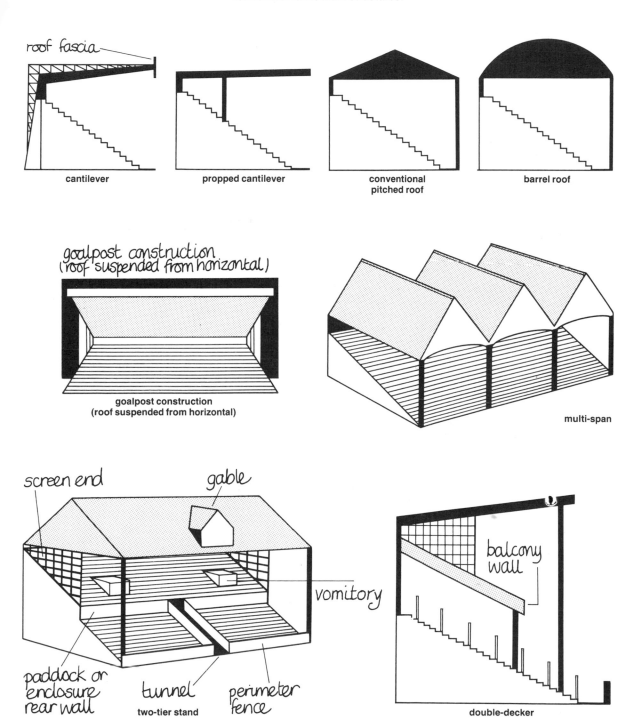

roof fascia

cantilever

propped cantilever

conventional
pitched roof

barrel roof

goalpost construction
(roof suspended from horizontal)

goalpost construction
(roof suspended from horizontal)

multi-span

screen end

gable

vomitory

balcony wall

paddock or
enclosure
rear wall

tunnel

perimeter
fence

two-tier stand

double-decker

BIBLIOGRAPHY

GENERAL BACKGROUND

Alcock, A. W., (ed.) **The Book of Football**. London: Carmelite House, 1906.

Appleton, Arthur, **Hotbed of Soccer**.

Douglas, P., **The Football Industry**. London: Allen and Unwin, 1973.

Fabian, A. H., and Green, G. (eds), **Association Football**. London: Caxton, 1960.

Gibson, A., and Pickford, W., **Association Football and the Men Who Made It**. 1906.

Golesworthy, Maurice, **Encyclopedia of Association Football**. London: Robert Hale, 1956–76.

Green, G., **The Official History of the FA Cup**. 1949.

Hutchinson, John, **The Football Industry**. 1982

Keeton, George W., **Football Revolution: A Study of the Changing Pattern of Association Football**. David & Co., 1972.

MacDonald, Roger, **Soccer: A Pictorial History**. London: Collins, 1977.

Marples, Morris, **A History of Football**. London: Secker & Warburg, 1954.

Mason, Tony, **Association Football and English Society 1863–1915**. Eastbourne: Harvester, 1980.

Morris, Desmond, **The Soccer Tribe**. London: Cape, 1981.

Moynihan, J., **The Soccer Syndrome**. St Albans: Macgibbon & K., 1966.

Richards, Harold, **How to Get There**.

Strutt, Joseph, **The Sports and Pastimes of the People of England**. 1903

Studd, Stephen, **Herbert Chapman, Football Emperor: A Study in the Origins of Modern Soccer**. London: Peter Owen, 1981.

Sutcliffe, C. E., **Story of the Football League 1888–1938**. 1938.

Wall, F., Sir., **Fifty Years in Football**. 1935.

Walvin, J., **People's Game: A Social History of British Football**. London: Allen Lane, 1975.

Young, P. M., **History of British Football**. London: Stanley Paul, 1968.

Young, P. M., **Football Year**.

REFERENCE AND STATISTICS

Robertson, Forrest, **Mackinlay's A–Z of Scottish Football**.

Rollin, Jack (ed.), **Rothmans Football Yearbook**. London: Queen Anne Press, 1970–83.

Soar, Tyler and Widdows, **Encyclopedia of World Football**. 1980.

Soar, Phil, **Hamlyn A–Z of British Football Records**. London: Hamlyn, 1981.

Williams, Tony (ed.), **Rothmans Non-League Football Yearbook**. London: Queen Anne Press, 1983.

OFFICIAL PAPERS AND GOVERNMENT PUBLICATIONS

Report on Crowd Behaviour at Football Matches, Command Paper 2088, 1924.

Inquiry into Bolton Disaster, Command Paper 6846, 1946.

Wheatley Report, Command Paper 4952, 1975.

Safety of Sports Ground Act, 1975.

Guide to Safety at Sports Grounds, 1976.

Chester, N., **Report of Committee on Football**, 1968.

Laing., **Report on Crowd Behaviour at Football Matches**, 1969.

Economic Trends, CSO, 1982.

CLUBS AND GROUNDS

Wherever possible I have made reference to club histories in the text. The following authors (clubs) have also provided information: Brown, Deryk; Finn, Ralph; Joy, B., and Wall, B. (Arsenal); Morris, P. (Aston Villa); Garrad, John (Birmingham); Francis, Charles (Blackburn); Daniels, Robin (Blackpool); Jackson, Peter (Cardiff); Lawson, Martin and Cowing, Ronald (Carlisle); Sewell, Albert (Chelsea, 1955); Finn, Ralph and Moynihan, John (Chelsea); Foulger, Neville and Henderson, Derek (Coventry); Peskitt, Roy (Crystal Palace); Edwards, George (Derby); Keates, Thomas (Everton); Ekberg, Charles (Grimsby); Conway, Tony (Gillingham); Folliard, Robert (Leicester), Liversege, Stan (Liverpool); Lawson, John (Notts Forest); Kaufmann, Neil and Ravenhill, Alan, (Orient); Signy, Dennis (QPR); Brown, Dennis, Finn, Ralph Holland, John and Soar, Phil (Spurs); Korr, Charles P. and Helliar, Jack (West Ham), Young, P. M., (Wolves); Crampsey, Bob (Queen's Park); Fairgrieve, John (Rangers).

NEWSPAPERS AND PERIODICALS:

Athletic News;

Daily Mirror;

Daily Sketch;

F.A. News;

F.L. Review;

Manchester Guardian;

Pall Mall Gazette;

The Times;

American Architect (7 May 1924);

The Architects' Journal (24 Feb 1926; Nov 1932; Apr 1936; Aug 1973; Jan 1979);

Architect and Building News (25 Feb 1938);

Architectural Psychology Newsletter (Aug 1972);

Architectural Review (Nov 1932; May 1968; Jan 1973);

Art and Industry (Aug 1945);

British Builder (Jan 1923);

The Builder (Oct 1922; July 1935; Mar 1957; Jan 1962; Apr 1963; Nov 1963);

Building Design (May 1972; Nov 1974; Oct 1976);

Building Materials (Nov 1961);

Design (Feb, Mar 1975; Sept 1978);

Design Methods and Theories (Vol. 2., No. 2);

Journal of Architectural Research (Aug 1979);

Prefabrication (Apr 1957);

Progressive Architecture (Mar 1973);

R.I.B.A. Journal (Vol. 43 No. 9, Vol. 88 No. 4);

Structural Engineer (Feb 1933, Nov 1962, Nov 1974);

Tubular Structures (Nov 1972).